Floating Poverty

Floating Poverty:

The Poor in Eighteenth-Century Massachusetts

Nian-Sheng Huang

2012

Copyright @ 2012 by Nian-Sheng Huang
All rights reserved.
Printed in the United States of America.

Published by Nian-Sheng Huang
July 31, 2012
ISBN-13: 978-0615651330
ISBN-10: 061565133X

To

the Common Soldiers in the American Revolution

Contents

Illustrations	vi
Acknowledgements	x
Introduction: "This Is Want. This Is Poverty!"	xiii
Chapter 1 Coalescence	1
Chapter 2 Financing Relief	49
Chapter 3 Local Exodus	84
Chapter 4 Meiosis	134
Chapter 5 Soldiering	173
Chapter 6 "As Much Sorrow As Joy"	236
Conclusion	289
Biographies	295
Chronology	346
Bibliography	392
Name Index	425
Place Index	442
Subject Index	449

Illustrations

Book Cover: Color reprint of William Hogarth's engraving "The Idle 'Prentice Executed at Tyburn," plate 11 in the series of his *Industry and Idleness* originally designed and engraved in 1747. Author's collection.

p. 22
Paul Farmer, master of the Almshouse, bill to Boston, March 2, 1772.

p. 25
Title page of the *Work-House Act of 1743*.

p. 26
Management of the Boston Work-House (ca. 1735).

p. 27
A page from the Boston Work-House payroll, 1794.

p. 32
Title page of *Acts and Laws of 1692*.

p. 50
Design of Massachusetts paper currency: a bill of six pence, 1737.

p. 53
Dispensation of charity to the poor, November 3, 1701 to February 28, 1701/2, The First Church (Old North) in Boston.

p. 58
Boston overseers of the poor inspected the wards on Wednesday, September 26, 1711.

p. 62
Title page of John Colman's *Distressed State of the Town of Boston* [1720].

p. 65
Report of the Committee to the Society for Encouraging Industry and Employing the Poor, February 1752, Boston.

p. 70
The Manufactory House (1754-1808).

p. 76
A page from the "anonymous account book" (1755-1759).

p. 94
Map of Chesterfield, Hampshire County (1762-1962).

p. 115
Removal warrant by Elijah Danforth, Justice of the Peace for Suffolk County, Dorchester, October 25, 1726.

p. 140
Health certificate in a smallpox outbreak, Boston, August 13, 1776.

p. 145
Subscription for the manufacture of duck and sail cloth, March 15, 1768.

p. 185
John McCleary pleaded for wood, March 11, 1771.

p. 194
Signatures by veterans of the Revolutionary War and their widows who applied for federal pensions.

p. 196
Property schedule of veteran Caleb Church, August 20, 1823.

p. 219
Signatures by veterans of the Revolutionary War and their widows who applied for federal pensions

p. 229
Veteran Ephraim Barker's pension card, 1818.

p. 231
Property schedule of veteran Peter Cary of Shrewsbury, Worcester County, July 10, 1820.

p. 233
Property schedule of veteran Thaddeus Gibson, July 11, 1818.

p. 246
Return of 11 prisoners in the Northampton County jail after the failure of Shays's Rebellion, April 9, 1787.

p. 250
Warning-out warrant, Bridgewater, July 7, 1777.

p. 260
Middleborough public vendue, April 5, 1791.

p. 263
Reverend Abiel Holmes's discourse at the opening of a new almshouse at Cambridge, September 17, 1818.

p. 274
Title page of Samuel Parker's discourse *Charity to Children Enforced*, 1803.

p. 279
Lancaster's bill to the commonwealth, 1791.

p. 280
Seth Copeland's charge to selectmen of Chelsea, January 24, 1792.

p. 282
Certificate by selectmen and overseers of the poor of Washington in Berkshire County to the commonwealth. January 20, 1800.

Back end paper: Map of Massachusetts.
For sources and scalable digital maps go to
http://www.sec.state.ma.us/cis/cispdf/City_Town_Map.pdf
http://www.sec.state.ma.us/cis/cispdf/County_Map.pdf

Acknowledgements

My mentor Michael Kammen, professor emeritus at Cornell University, warmly supported this project more than a decade ago when it was only a two-page concept. He has always been a source of inspiration, and his kindness to me and my family over the last thirty years is most appreciated.

Professors David Waldstreicher at Temple University, Seth Rockman at Brown University, and Barry Levy at the University of Massachusetts Amherst took time from their busy schedules to read and comment on early drafts of the book manuscript. Their critical suggestions sharpened my ideas and helped me significantly improve the manuscript, from its title and organization to many details of the contents. Although deeply indebted to their insights and generosity, I am solely responsible for any error in the work.

I would like to thank the Massachusetts Historical Society and its Editor and Director of Research Conrad E. Wright for permission to use my essay "Financing Poor Relief in Colonial Boston" from the *Massachusetts Historical Review* 8 (2006): 73-103, in a slightly modified form, as chapter two of this book.

Several faculty development grants awarded by California State University Channel Island greatly facilitated this project. Financial aids also came at various stages of my research from these institutions, including a Benjamin Franklin

Stevens Fellowship at the Massachusetts Historical Society in 2003, a Peterson Fellowship at the American Antiquarian Society in 2005, and a New England Regional Consortium Fellowship in 2006. An MHS-NEH long-term fellowship for 2007-08 allowed me to complete much of the research and writing. I express my sincere appreciation to them all.

Working on eighteenth-century poverty and the poor has been a special personal experience, and my journey of searching for the lives of real people in the past has given me an invaluable opportunity to get to know them. The final product of this journey is therefore dedicated to those who taught me a great deal about the true meanings of history and how it was made.

Introduction:

"This Is Want. This Is Poverty!"

This book probes into how the poor were treated in eighteenth-century Massachusetts. Any attempt to investigate marginalized members in society, particularly of early times, can be a challenge as their lives tend to be scantily recorded and elusive to recapture. Scholars have made significant progress in studying history from the "bottom up" since the 1960s.[1] Thanks

---

[1] Robert W. Kelso, *The History of Public Poor Relief in Massachusetts, 1620-1920* (Boston: Houghton Mifflin Company, 1922); Carl Bridenbaugh, *Cities in the Wilderness: The First Century of Urban Life in America, 1625-1742* (New York: Ronald Press, 1938); James A. Henretta, "Economic Development and Social Structure in Colonial Boston," *William and Mary Quarterly*, 3d ser., 22 (1965): 75-92; Jesse Lemisch, "Jack Tar in the Street: Merchant Seaman in the Politics of Revolutionary America," *William and Mary Quarterly*, 3d ser., 25 (1968): 371-407; Stephen Foster, *Their Solitary Way: The Puritan Social Ethic in the First Century of Settlement in New England* (New Haven, Conn.: Yale University Press, 1971); Allan Kulikoff, "The Progress of Inequality in Revolutionary Boston," *William and Mary Quarterly*, 3d ser., 28 (1971): 375-412; Douglas Lamar Jones, "The Strolling Poor: Transiency in Eighteenth-Century Massachusetts," *Journal of Social History* 8 (1975): 28-54; Jones, "Poverty and Vagabondage: The Progress of Survival in Eighteenth-Century Massachusetts," *New England Historical and Genealogical Register* 133 (1979): 243-54; Jones, "The Transformation of the Law of Poverty in Eighteenth-Century Massachusetts," in *Law in Colonial Massachusetts, 1630-1800*, ed. Daniel R. Coquillette (Boston: Colonial Society of Massachusetts, 1984), 153-90; Jones, *Village and Seaport: Migration and Society in Eighteenth-Century Massachusetts* (Hanover, N.H.: University Press of New England, 1981); and Alfred F. Young, "George Robert Twelves Hewes (1742-1840): A Boston Shoemaker and the Memory of the American Revolution," *William and Mary*

to their efforts, the public now has considerable knowledge about the ordinary people, women, slaves, and other lower classes in eighteenth-century North America.[2] Yet more can be done to inform today's readers about the distress and misery many experienced in the past, including the poor, the needy, the transient, the deprived, and the propertyless. The fact that their lives have yet to become a central focus of an extensive and up-to-date search has led to this investigation, which examines early Massachusetts life from the prism of the least fortunate people.

Few contemporaries of that era failed to witness poverty firsthand. As a newly elected local selectman, John Adams visited his neighbor Robert Peacock and his wife Elizabeth (Crane) in Braintree. While writing down what he had seen in his diary on a Saturday in March 1767, Adams

---

Quarterly, 3d ser., 38 (1981): 561-623, which was later incorporated into *The Shoemaker and the Tea Party: Memory and the American Revolution* (Boston: Beacon Press, 1999).

[2] Based on a large collection of statistical data, Gary B. Nash demonstrated the declining fortunes of those lower and middle classes in Boston, New York, and Philadelphia. His *Urban Crucible: Social Change, Political Consciousness, and the Origins of the American Revolution* (Cambridge, Mass.: Harvard University Press, 1979), remains a comprehensive study of colonial politics and poverty. For recent studies see Billy G. Smith, ed., *Down and Out in Early America* (University Park, Penn.: Pennsylvania State University Press, 2004); Simon P. Newman, *Embodied History: The Lives of the Poor in Early Philadelphia* (Philadelphia: University of Pennsylvania Press, 2003); Carla Gardina Pestana and Sharon V. Salinger, eds., *Inequality in Early America* (Hanover, N.H.: University of New England Press, 1999); Sharon V. Salinger, *"To Serve Well and Faithfully": Labor and Indentured Servants in Pennsylvania, 1682-1800* (New York: Cambridge University Press, 1987); Woody Holton, *Forced Founders: Indians, Debtors, Slaves, and the Making of the American Revolution in Virginia* (Chapel Hill: University of North Carolina Press, 1999); and Billy G. Smith, *The "Lower Sort": Philadelphia's Laboring People, 1750-1800* (Ithaca, N.Y.: Cornell University Press, 1990). Ruth Wallis Herndon's *Unwelcome Americans* (Philadelphia: University of Pennsylvania Press, 2001) is a detailed and moving account of those people living in the shadows of the warning out system, under which strangers must pay sufficient security or receive legal notices demanding their departure, in Rhode Island in the 1780s and 90s. Jacqueline Barbara Carr's *After the Siege: A Social History of Boston, 1775-1800* (Boston: Northeastern University Press, 2005) gives good recounts of poverty in the context of urban growth and cultural renewal in the last quarter of the eighteenth century. Eric Nellis and Anne Decker Cecere, eds., *The Eighteenth-Century Records of the Boston Overseers of the Poor* (Boston: Colonial Society of Massachusetts, 2006) is a highly valuable documentation for the study of urban poverty and relief in colonial Boston. Although advertised for several years, Cornelia H. Dayton and Sharon V. Salinger's *Warning Out: Robert Love's Search for Strangers in Pre-Revolutionary Boston* remained unavailable when this book went to print.

could hardly contain his emotions. Peacock had been bedridden for seven weeks and unable to move. His distressful family gathered in one room that—although "excessive[ly] cold and dirty"—served as their "kitchen, cellar, dining room, Parlour, and Bedchamber." Poor Peacock held a baby in his arms while three small children—all aged under ten—huddled in another bed across from his. The mother was the only one standing by a fire and making a few chips no larger than Adams's palm. Apparently disturbed to realize what a selectman now had to cope with, Adams recorded that "[T]hese are the Conveniences and ornaments of a Life of Poverty. These the Comforts of the Poor. This is Want. This is Poverty! These the Comforts of the needy. The Bliss of the Necessitous."[3]

Although Adams's diary reminds subsequent generations of the harsh realities and wretched miseries he was facing, modern scholars and readers may still encounter difficulties assessing the extent and nature of poverty, which the current book explores. Thus the term "floating poverty" stresses the heterogeneous configurations of the poor as well as the fluid, transitory, precarious, and ever-shifting characteristics of eighteenth-century poverty.[4] The book shows that the poor in early Massachusetts were not a single class of similar people, but rather a great variety of dissimilar individuals in diverse situations, including the disabled, the aged, the sick, the lame, the blind, and the homeless as well as orphans, laborers, servants, drifters, and transients. Just as no sole condition caused poverty, no exclusive conflict between the rich and the poor or a singular dichotomy of the haves vs. the have-nots could fully explain the mixed natures of eighteenth-century poverty. Many fell into poverty for a wide range of reasons and

---

[3] L. H. Butterfield et al. eds., *Diary and Autobiography of John Adams* (Cambridge, Mass.: Harvard University Press, 1961), 1: 332-33.
[4] "The Mediterranean is not even a *single* [original italic] sea," as Fernand Braudel advised, "it is a complex of seas." *The Mediterranean and the Mediterranean World in the Age of Philip II* (New York: Harper & Row, 1972), 1: 17.

circumstances, such as old age, disability, unemployment, war, diseases, natural disasters, financial crisis, indebtedness, fatalities or sudden deaths in the family (resulting in orphans, widows, widowers, or single parents), divorces and abandonments, injuries and accidents, a decline of available land, or a significant jump in the number of new births and family sizes. As dissimilar as these sources are, the treatment of the poor varied significantly. Idleness was a sin as well as a crime according to the law. Local communities were primarily responsible for supporting legal residents of low circumstances, just as churches and benevolent societies extended charity to the needy members of their organizations. Distressed resident civilians and veteran soldiers had the option of petitioning the provincial government for relief. In the century-old policy of warning out, prejudice against incoming migrants and strangers did exist, but the practice had never held outsiders and newcomers down as permanently as racial and gender discriminations did. Equally important, people moved out of poverty in a step-by-step manner, as evidenced by servants who finished their terms, bound-out orphans who grew up to become independent, and migrants who finally established their legal settlement.

The nature and extent of poverty in early American history have long intrigued two groups of modern scholars who hold opposite views. Believing that the number of the poor is insignificant in a predominantly middle-class society, one group has stressed America's great promise, abundance, opportunity, and mobility. Meanwhile, the other group—convinced of having found so severe a conflict between the haves and have-nots as close to the brink of a class war—has underscored America's glaring inadequacies, limits, inequalities, and inconsistencies.[5] New details in this book suggest a mixed dual process moving back and forth between poverty and mobility, neither one of which excludes the other to the previously assumed degree. Thus, the study of the drifting qualities of poverty recognizes both the strengths and weaknesses of these two principal interpretations in American historiography while providing a different lens through which to observe the intertwined cross-influences and intense flowing dynamics between poverty and mobility—something polarized views have not yet taken into consideration.[6]

In recent years, a growing number of scholars have conducted valuable studies of poverty. Nonetheless, several noticeable omissions, simplifications, and broad generalizations require further examination and careful reconsideration. For example, few historians have explored the rich literature of the large debate on poverty since the Protestant Reformation, which provided the critical transatlantic context of how the New World would deal with poverty and relief.[7] Equally

---

[5] Representative of the first group of affirmative views are Louis Hartz's *Liberal Tradition in America: An Interpretation of American Political Thought Since the Revolution* (New York: Harcourt, Bruce and Company, 1955), Robert E. Brown, *Middle-Class Democracy and the Revolution in Massachusetts* (Ithaca, N.Y.: Cornell University Press, 1955), and David M. Potter's *People of Plenty: Economic Abundance and the American Character* (Chicago: University Chicago Press, 1958). Many writings by progressive historians Charles A. Beard and Carl L. Becker and by recent scholars Gary B. Nash and Alfred F. Young represent the second group of revisionist views. See also the controversies over Gordon S. Wood's *The Radicalism of the American Revolution* (New York: Vintage Books, 1993), *William and Mary Quarterly*, 3d ser., 51 (1994): 679-716.

[6] The contention is likely to continue. Stephen Innes's review of *Inequality in Early America*, eds. Carla Gardina Pestana and Sharon V. Salinger (Hanover, N.H.: University Press of New England, 1999), *Journal of Interdisciplinary History* 31 (2001): 468-69. John L. Brooke's review of Gordon S. Wood's *Empire of Liberty: A History of the Early Republic, 1789-1815* (New York: Oxford University Press, 2009), *William and Mary Quarterly*, 3rd ser., 67 (2010): 549-57. "In North America, moreover," Steve Hindle and Ruth Wallis Herndon wrote, "social inequality was less marked." Herndon and John E. Murray, eds., *Children Bound to Labor: The Pauper Apprentice System in Early American* (Ithaca, N.Y.: Cornell University Press, 2009), 23-26.

[7] Whereas specialists in American history rarely pay attention to this dimension, many in European and English histories do. Preserved Smith, *The Age of Reformation* (New York: Henry Holt and Co., 1920); Brian S. Pullan, *Rich and Poor in Renaissance Venice: The Social Institutions of a Catholic State, to 1620* (Oxford, UK: Blackwell Publishers, 1971); Robert M. Kingdon, "Social Welfare in Calvin's Geneva," *American Historical Review*, 76 (1971), 50-69; Olwen H. Hufton, *The Poor of Eighteenth-Century France* (Oxford, UK:

Introduction

surprising, even fewer historians have deemed it necessary to investigate the long history of the English laws, institutions, and practices related to the poor, which were central to any continuity or departure for the treatment of the poor in the British North American colonies.[8]

Although historians have frequently used the interpretive frameworks of race, ethnicity, and gender when analyzing social disparity and economic degradation in several colonies, the composition of Massachusetts's population in the eighteenth century defied these convenient paradigms. Investigations into slavery in the South have long been an important part of understanding colonial poverty, and Virginia

---

Oxford University Press, 1974); Natalie Zemon Davis, *Society and Culture in Early Modern Europe* (Stanford, Calif.: Stanford University Press, 1975); William C. Innes, *Social Concern in Calvin's Geneva* (Allison Park, Penn.: Pickwick Publications, 1983); Margo Todd, *Christian Humanism and the Puritan Social Order* (Cambridge, UK: Cambridge University Press, 1987); Jeannine E. Olson, *Calvin and Social Welfare: Deacons and the Bourse francaise* (Selinsgrove: Susquehanna University Press, 1989); John Walter and Roger Schofield, eds., *Famine, Diseases and the Social Order in Early Modern Society* (New York: Cambridge University Press, 1989); Carter Lindberg, *Beyond Charity: Reformation Initiatives for the Poor* (Minneapolis, Minn.: Fortress Press, 1993); Bronislaw Geremek, *Poverty: A History* (Oxford, UK: Basil Blackwell Ltd., 1994); Robert Jütte, *Poverty and Deviance in Early Modern Europe* (Cambridge, UK: Cambridge University Press, 1994); Beat A. Kümin, ed., *Reformations Old and New: Essays on the Socio-Economic Impact of Religious Change, c. 1470-1630* (Aldershot, England: Scolar Press, 1996); and Thomas Max Safley, ed., *The Reformation of Charity: The Secular and the Religious in Early Modern Poor Relief* (Boston: Brill Academic Publishers, 2003).

[8] Even though this body of literature has been impressive, few pieces were produced by American historians and even fewer were connected to the studies of the colonies except for the introduction in Ruth Wallis Herndon and John E. Murray, eds., *Children Bound to Labor: The Pauper Apprentice System in Early America* (Ithaca, New York: Cornell University Press, 2009). See Gertrude Himmelfarb, *The Idea of Poverty: England in the Early Industrial Age* (New York: Alfred A. Knopf, 1984); E. P. Thompson, *Customs in Common* (New York: The New Press, 1993); Margaret Spufford, ed., *The World of Rural Dissenters, 1520-1725* (Cambridge, UK: Cambridge University Press, 1995); Beat A. Kümin, *The Shaping of a Community: The Rise and Reformation of the English Parish, c. 1400-1560* (Hants, UK: Scolar Press, 1996); Norma Landau, *The Justices of the Peace, 1679-1760* (Berkeley, Calif.: University of California Press, 1984); Landau, ed., *Law, Crime and English Society, 1660-1830* (Cambridge, UK: Cambridge University Press, 2002); Tim Hitchcock, *Down and Out in Eighteen-Century London* (London: Hambledon and London, 2004); Paul Slack, *Poverty and Policy in Tudor and Stuart England* (London: Longman, 1988); Slack, *The English Poor Law, 1531-1782* (Cambridge, UK: Cambridge University Press, 1995); and Slack, ed. *Rebellion, Popular Protest and the Social Order of Early Modern England* (Cambridge, UK: Cambridge University Press, 2008).

was often used as a primary example.[9] However, according to the first federal census of 1790, the African population in Massachusetts numbered fewer than 5,500, which could not constitute a key factor in the labor market despite the fact that slavery existed until the state constitution of 1780 abolished it. Similarly, Massachusetts did not attract a great number of European emigrants in the eighteenth century, when no fewer than 70,000 Scottish, Scotch-Irish, and Germans poured into Pennsylvania, making them both an easy target for and a major source of cheap labor. Such a reality perhaps explains a corresponding scholarly focus on the poor in Pennsylvania and several mid-Atlantic colonies,[10] while providing no substitute for a viable model of research into what Massachusetts experienced. Furthermore, despite an increasing output of gender studies that shed light on female poverty, no conclusive investigation has demonstrated that Massachusetts had either a significant gender imbalance with an unusually large number of poor females or worse bigotry against women than other regions. In fact, a stable family structure, a balanced gender ratio between adult males and females, a high percentage of women and girls who were able to read, and ample evidence of female business activity, as David Hackett Fischer and

---

[9] Edmund S. Morgan, *American Slavery, American Freedom* (New York: W.W. Norton, 1975); Woody Holton, *Forced Founders: Indians, Debtors, Slaves, and the Making of the American Revolution in Virginia* (Chapel Hill: University of North Carolina Press, 1999).

[10] A G. Roeber, "'The Origin of Whatever Is Not English among US': The Dutch-speaking and the German-speaking Peoples of Colonial British America," and Maldwyn A. Jones, "The Scotch-Irish in British America," in Bernard Bailyn and Philip D. Morgan, eds., *Strangers within the Realm: Cultural Margins of the First British Empire* (Chapel Hill, N.C.: University of North Carolina Press, 1991), 220-83, 284-313. Sharon V. Salinger, *"To Serve Well and Faithfully": Labor and Indentured Servants in Pennsylvania, 1682-1800* (Cambridge, UK: Cambridge University Press, 1987), 52-57. Billy G. Smith, *The "Lower Sort": Philadelphia's Laboring People, 1750-1800* (Ithaca, N.Y.: Cornell University Press, 1990); Smith, ed., *Down and Out in Early America* (University Park, Penn.: Pennsylvania State University Press, 2004); Carla Gardina Pestana and Sharon V. Salinger, eds., *Inequality in Early America* (Hanover, N.H.: University of New England Press, 1999); Simon P. Newman, *Embodied History: The Lives of the Poor in Early Philadelphia* (Philadelphia: University of Pennsylvania Press, 2003).

numerous historians have pointed out, distinguished Massachusetts from many other colonies since its early days.[11]

Not to minimize Gary B. Nash's enormous and pioneering contributions to the studies of colonial women and other underprivileged groups, his article "The Failure of Female Factory Labor in Colonial Boston," which was later incorporated into his book *Urban Crucible* (1979), provides a case in point regarding how the conundrum of eighteenth-century poverty has confounded some modern scholars who sought to fit the multi-faceted past into a dichotomous prototype of gender conflict.[12] As the article's title suggests, Nash detected a struggle between "Boston's most successful merchants and entrepreneurs" and the town's lower classes and laboring population. According to the article, organized as the Society of Encouraging Industry and Employing the Poor, the well-to-do Boston elite founded a linen manufactory, attempting to drive poor women and children into this new labor system, thereby reducing tax burdens and public relief. Nevertheless, the linen manufactory—a design to control the lower classes, according to Nash's characterization—ultimately failed. Nash stressed that "much of the answer to the Manufactory's failure lies in the resistance of the supposed recipients of the Society's efforts," although he acknowledged that his method of authenticating the resistance was "mostly

---

[11] David Hackett Fischer, *Albion's Seed: Four British Folkways in America* (New York: Oxford University Press, 1989); Laurel Thatcher Ulrich, *Good Wives: Image and Reality in the Lives of Women in Northern New England, 1650-1750* (New York: Vintage Books, 1991), *A Midwife's Tale: The Life of Martha Ballard, Based on Her Diary, 1785-1812* (New York: Vintage Books, 1991); Elain Forman Crane, *Ebb Tide in New England: Women, Seaports, and Social Change, 1630-1800* (Boston: Northeastern University Press, 1998); James E. McWilliams, *Building the Bay Colony: Local Economy and Culture in Early Massachusetts*. Charlottesville, Va.: University of Virginia Press, 2007); and Barry Levy, *Town Born: The Political Economy of New England from Its Founding to the Revolution* (Philadelphia: University of Pennsylvania Press, 2009).

[12] Gary B. Nash, "The Failure of Female Factory Labor in Colonial Boston," *Labor History* 20 (1970): 165-88; *The Urban Crucible: Social Change, Political Consciousness, and the Origins of the American Revolution* (Cambridge, Mass.: Harvard University Press, 1979), 189-97.

indirect" (see his article "Failure of Female Factory Labor," pp. 180, 184, 189). Providing neither independent nor collaborating proof, Alfred F. Yong repeated Nash's conclusion in *Liberty Tree: Ordinary People and the American Revolution* (New York, 2006, pp. 106-107), as did Nash's student J. Richard Olivas in his article "God Helps Those Who Help Themselves," in Billy G. Smith, ed., *Down and Out in Early America* (University Park, Penn., 2004, pp. 280, 281, 288n). In 2004, without offering up-to-date research or new evidence, Nash reiterated his own conclusion that women's resistance "scotched" the first "workfare" experiment (see his "Poverty and Politics," in *Down and Out*, pp. 15, 20). The extent to which the Boston linen manufactory was a failure or success will be addressed in chapter two of this book. However, suffice it to say here that Nash seriously exaggerated the element of gender conflict in that episode while significantly underestimating how much the linen manufactory helped not only many urban poor women and children, but also hundreds of needy families, both inside and outside of Boston.

At a deeper level, this confusion further indicates a similar but larger problem of casting eighteenth-century poverty into the unmitigated mold of rich against poor—a frequently adopted approach that has left at least two essential questions unanswered. First, Nash's *Urban Crucible*, one of the most widely quoted authorities on these topics, used such terms as "the working poor," "the lower orders," "the laboring classes," and "the bottom of the urban hierarchy" to describe the deprived peoples of the colonial era. However, except for a few cursory words (say, on page 196 about Henry Neal), not a single poor person's career in Massachusetts was sufficiently presented, explained, or analyzed. Second—but no less problematic—based on the vast amount of information collected largely from tax rolls, mortgage books, and inventories of estates, Nash's aggregated data spoke for those taxpayers of low brackets, householders of limited means, and property owners of small fortunes, most of whom would be considered lower to middle classes, but not exactly "poor" in those days. Perhaps Nash's findings actually revealed less about the destitute people *per se* than about the specter and capricious nature of eighteenth-century poverty. That is to say, his extensive studies have depicted the middle and lower-middle classes' worst nightmares of falling down into poverty, but stopped short of the real-life experiences of those hundreds of impoverished families and individuals who were already in destitution and misery. The chief concerns for the poor (as distinct from those for small to modest property owners) were perhaps more about day-to-day subsistence than about declining estates or rising taxation according to Nash's delineation because, as non-taxpayers and individuals of few possessions, their deplorable circumstances had long deprived them of the opportunity to show up on most tax rolls, land deeds, mortgage books, business transactions, registered wills, or estate inventories.

More recently, younger scholars and their works, such as Ruth Wallis Herndon's *Unwelcome Americans* (2001), Jacqueline Barbara Carr's *After the Siege* (2005), and Seth Rockman's *Scraping By* (2009), have filled some of the gaps and addressed some of the weaknesses of the earlier generation of researchers. Nevertheless, in such writings that pursued the evil versus good paradigm of rich against poor, many readers still cannot find straightforward answers to another set of seemingly minor but basic questions—namely, how much wealth would ultimately put an individual into the category of the rich in those days, who those well-to-do people really were, or how rich was "too" rich or "too" corrupt to deserve the hatred of the poor. Without sufficiently addressing these essential questions while instead using broad terms of "the rich," "the powerful," and "the affluent members of the community"

Introduction

(*Urban Crucible*, pp. 133, 186), Nash moved on to discuss class antagonism and class consciousness, although he was unable to draw any unambiguous conclusions.

Others have been bolder. Accepting Nash's promise, Howard Zinn proceeded to declare that indeed another conflict existed at home between the rich and the poor in the era of the American Revolution, just as the progressive historian Carl Becker had suggested.[13] In his chronicle *Boston Riots: Three Centuries of Violence* (2001), Jack Tager's narrative phrases (all appearing on the first fifty pages) included the "lower and upper classes," "thousands of common people in Boston," "all classes," "the upper classes," "the ruling classes," "the increasing and pronounced inequality, poverty, and general economic depression from the 1730s," "[that] violence became the plebeians' means of political expression," "the working poor," "the powerless lower classes," "the poor," "the laboring poor," "the unworthy poor," "the plebeians," "the common people," "the poorer sort," "hungry Bostonians," "middling and poor Bostonians," "the poorer classes," and "the dispossessed"—few of which were adequately explained, although nearly all of them were more asserted than proven.

As the interest in studying poverty has grown, it seems that some historians have sometimes confused the poor with declining families of the lower and middle classes (whose definitions will be given in chapter one), whereas others have inadvertently blended the rich with the middle classes (whose unmistaken divide will be highlighted in chapter five), who had a distinction of no less significance. Although the focus of this book is the poor, it is useful to keep in mind that for much of the eighteenth century the majority of the ratepayers and property owners were not rich, but rather people and families of

---

[13] Howard Zinn, *A People's History of the United States* (New York: Harper & Row, 1980), 60-68. The book has maintained the same position through numerous printings for the next 30 years.

modest means. Thus, a necessary dimension of this book involves exploring how the middle classes responded to poverty, which can hardly be transfixed to the straight terms of rich against poor. As manifested in the roles played by participants in town meetings, local selectmen/overseers of the poor, charitable organizations, learned ministers, newspaper commentators, trained professionals, and various levels of governmental agencies, the middle class's attitudes were far more complex than what a black-and-white class antagonism could explain; although often expedient, theirs were perhaps as ambivalent, disunited, and ever shifting as the floating qualities of poverty itself. Caught in an inescapable web of dilemmas that many still feel today, the middle-class taxpayers in particular had the responsibility of supporting the poor on the one hand, but had no unlimited resources to keep up with the rising burdens of public relief on the other. They were taught to have charity and compassion to care for their neighbors, but they were also taught to loathe indolence and punish vagabonds. The Holy Scriptures (Matthew 26:11) told them that the poor shall always be with them, which was a message unlikely to persuade them to alter the existing social hierarchy. Yet the middle class could spring into action for the rescue if rising poverty threatened to destroy their interests and ransack their community. In this sense, the study of poverty also reflects a large picture of society, including the uncertainties and mixed successes and failures of the Massachusetts middle class, whose varied efforts to deal with the poor left a permanent imprint on the serrated history of eighteenth-century poverty. In other words, a close examination of floating poverty questions the inflexibility inherent in several dichotomous patterns of interpretations, replacing it with a more realistic approach not only to the poor, but also to the troubled and yet more elastic cross-relationships between the poor and their better-off neighbors in society.

Diametrically divided interests and uncompromising conflicts in race, ethnicity, gender, and class not only exist, but have also played vital roles in history. Yet lacking careful assessment, a dichotomous mode of interpretation based exclusively on binary tensions can exaggerate the degree and functions of extreme forces, thereby simplifying reality. The notion of floating poverty intends to break that rigidity and study a great variety of overlapping and indeed oftentimes competing interests and motives of the poor and the middle class, whose mutual misgivings, ugly squabbles, painful clashes, and palpable confrontations as well as their frequent alliance, interdependence, and continuous realignment shaped their lives and communities.

Compared with existing studies, the findings detailed in this book add several new aspects to the previous understanding of poverty in early Massachusetts. First of all, the scope here broadens the awareness of poverty, which has often been presented as a predominantly urban or sometimes exclusive Boston phenomenon. Eighteenth-century poverty affected people from all communities at the local, county, and provincial levels. Thus, urban poverty cannot be fully understood without these closely associated regional contexts.[14] Second, this broadened scope extends investigations beyond an examination of tax rolls or probate records, which contained information primarily about lawful residents and taxpayers of the middle and lower middle classes.[15] Nevertheless, more than any other economic or social precondition, community membership was a

---

[14] Due to paucity of documentation, the study of the poor in early Massachusetts has not attracted the same degree of attention accorded to that in Pennsylvania, New York, New Jersey, Rhode Island, South Carolina, and Maryland. See Smith, *Down and Out*; Newman, *Embodied History*; Pestana and Salinger, *Inequality*; Salinger, *"To Serve Well and Faithfully"*; and Seth Rockman, *Scraping By: Wage Labor, Slavery, and Survival in Early Baltimore* (Baltimore: Johns Hopkins University Press, 2009).

[15] As in convention, "the poor" in this book refers to those who could neither earn enough income nor hold adequate estate to be rated and pay taxes, while "the lower and middles classes" were those who could. Smith, *Down and Out*, xviii-xix. More details in chapter one.

must to public relief, and many of the poor in this period had yet to fight for the chance to gain legal residence and rise into the category of lawful inhabitants of a local community. Third, the broadened scope allows modern readers to realize not only how key English poor law concepts influenced Massachusetts, but also how that influence was far from adequate for solving the problems in the Bay Colony. Fourth, the broadened scope demonstrates that the existence of poverty was never as static or irreversibly bad as previously thought. Except for the incompetent poor who were on long-term relief, the minimum cost of living was such that the competent and strolling poor were able to survive; indeed, many did gradually improve their lives. Finally, the broadened scope helps understand the important contributions and great sacrifices the poor made during the American Revolution, as particularly evident in their extensive and long-term military service in the fight for independence.

By definition, floating poverty requires both a broad perspective and a long time span to observe. Arranged in a chronological order, this book's six chapters try to unveil and capture several particular aspects of that floating quality. The first chapter (Coalescence) traces the major influences from England that impacted the ways in which the poor would be treated in the colony—a critical connection that has not received adequate attention in past scholarship. However troubled they had been with poverty since the Reformation, few European countries passed more laws to regulate the poor than Tudor and Stuart England. Armed with the reformed concepts of work, charity, and relief, the Massachusetts Bay Colony set out to regulate the poor based on familiar models inherited from the mother country. Yet, in addition to conventional indoor and outdoor relief, the General Court also served as a unique form of relief agency by granting pensions, permits, land, and even townships to distressed petitioners. Not found in the English experience, this broad range of relief activities from the community to the provincial level helped alleviate the pains of those in hardship.

Although many previous studies have tended to view poverty as an economic or social problem, Chapter 2 (Financing Relief) investigates some serious financial constraints in poor relief, examines private and public charity, and reassesses the successes and failures of the Linen Manufactory—an undertaking with which Bostonians experimented in the 1750s. Dramatic events and changes after the Seven Years' War had a profound impact on the poor: the volatility presented as much anguish as opportunity. Chapter 3 (Local Exodus) shows that an unprecedented number of people took to the road, moving from place to place in hopes of starting a new life in a new community. Local authorities often warned those in low and poor circumstances to depart—a standard practice according to provincial law. However, neither a township nor any settlement law was ever able to halt the massive internal migration, which ultimately allowed considerable mobility for many disadvantaged but aspiring individuals and families. Chapter 4 (Meiosis) discusses the tumultuous decade after the end of the Seven Years' War in 1763 by analyzing a series of catastrophic disasters (e.g., fires and diseases) as well as the rising external pressures on a contracting domestic economy. Coupled with all the political controversies that emerged after the Stamp Act crisis, these calamities and hardships converged to make this period one of the most volatile in history, with the fear of poverty and the cry for relief putting unprecedented burdens on the colony.

The American Revolution would never have succeeded without the strong support of the poor, who actively participated in both pre-Revolutionary activities and the War for Independence. Chapter 5 (Soldiering) delineates the roles that people in low circumstances played during the

Introduction

Revolutionary War. Many who joined the Continental Army and the Massachusetts Militia came from the poor, whose spirit to fight for independence was perhaps as strong as anyone else's. Records show that those with few material possessions were as ready to join military actions as those who had more despite the fact that many of the former were not yet legal residents of the community, that had in fact served official warning-out warrants to exclude them. Yet these individuals responded to the Lexington and Concord alarm on April 19, 1775—and many subsequent patriotic alarms—as swiftly as any legal residents. In numerous cases, young apprentices, servants, and laborers were more willing to join the revolutionary cause than their employers, whose superior wealth and material possessions had not necessarily made them more ardent patriots. Although all soldiers faced suffering and death, the poor served longer terms than the average enlisted men. Even more of them remained poor after the revolution. Never serving as colonels or generals or even captains or ensigns, the poor assumed humble roles as foot soldiers, privates, corporals, gunners, drummers, and fifers. Yet their humble roles should not obscure their enormous contributions to the American Revolution, which succeeded only because of the great sacrifices made by those thousands of unsung heroes among the poor.

The last chapter ("As Much Sorrow As Joy") discusses how and to what extent the thorny issue of poverty continued after the revolution. Shays's Rebellion—albeit a failed rebellion in western Massachusetts—revealed the danger of ignoring the just claims of those in grief. After the turmoil, most demands the "Regulators" raised were eventually met by state legislations. Although the new conditions of the post-war era necessitated modifications in poor relief, most communities continued pre-war relief practices. Several new laws were passed in the 1780s to ease the pains of debtors. Theoretically speaking, the states' poor laws of 1794 ended the warning-out system, but the practice continued in some places until the early 1800s. Yet for the most part, the poor were left alone to move and fend for themselves, although the state government still required a legal settlement for public relief. Justices went back to enforcing the doctrine of property rights. Public relief was once again given to local authorities, which adopted policies and regulations not drastically different from those in the prewar years. In the new era of progress and prosperity, poverty spread while the number of the poor at both local and state levels rose. Although many charity and relief organizations were set up around the turn of the century, they remained instruments of assistance, not of change.

The study of the fluid qualities of poverty does not deny its severity, which could—as many heart-wrenching cases in this volume show—devastate a person or family at any moment. Nor does the suggestion that the diverse and mobile population of the eighteenth-century poor was not a unified mass in a perpetually angry mood minimize the sufferings and frustrations of the poor. Poverty in early Massachusetts was neither a fast-moving conveyer sending the poor directly to hell nor a necessary purgatory ultimately leading to heaven. As the teenage fifer John Greenwood described it years later while recalling the alternate rain, snow, sleet, and nasty wind on the march toward Trenton, "owing to the impossibility of being a worse condition than their present one, the men always liked to be kept moving in the expectation of bettering themselves."[16]

---

[16] Quoted in David Hackett Fischer, *Washington's Crossing* (New York: Oxford University Press, 2004), 208. Isaac J. Greenwood, ed., *The Revolutionary Service of John Greenwood of Boston and New York, 1775-1783* (New York: De Vinne Press, 1922), 40. The son of Boston dentist Isaac (1730-1803) and grandson of Isaac Greenwood (1702-1745, the first Hollis Professor at Harvard College), John Greenwood (1760-1819) was enchanted by the fife from childhood and joined the American forces at fifteen against his parents' wishes—both were members of King's Chapel and both knew Governor Thomas Gage. After the war he became a successful dentist in New York City and sometimes cared for George Washington's dental need. Isaac J. Greenwood, ed., *The Wartime Services of John*

Introduction

Thus, the emphasis on floating poverty aims to draw attention to the sinuous movements in various directions that its powerful impact could produce. Even in the darkest days of shattering poverty the survival instinct of the poor endured as their desire and struggle for mobility persisted—perhaps similar to the kind of strength that sustained Greenwood and many of his fellow soldiers during the arduous fight for independence.

If John Adams knew the poor all too well from his personal encounters, the revolving phases and shifting experiences of the underprivileged could be difficult for later generations to comprehend. The vicissitudes of poor people's lives were never monolithic, static, or one dimensional. Given their daily misery, anguish, and hardship, nor is it easy to see them as lively, active, and aspiring as others. Admittedly, many cases of the poor are no longer traceable as they were not as extensively documented as the rich or well-educated. Yet no fewer than 40,000 names have survived in selectmen minutes, charity books, warning-out notices, and almshouse records, providing tangible clues for studying the poor. Sensitive to their distinctive circumstances and appropriate perspectives, the following chapters bring together the life experiences of more than 8,000 ordinary people (about a thousand of them indexed) under a great variety of individual hardships at different times and locations without treating them as sheer numbers in a statistical tabulation. Based on evidence collected from town records, local histories, overseers of the poor papers, court documents, legislative journals, family genealogies, vital statistics, muster rolls, pension files, and official collections in state archives, this book approaches poverty at a close personal range and across an extended time period. Readers therefore can visualize the collective plight of the poor as intimately they

---

Greenwood: A Young Patriot in the American Revolution, 1775-1783 ([New York] Westvaco Corp., 1981), 31-32, 79-82, 149-51.

Introduction

should while observing the ever-changing movements of eighteenth-century poverty as fully as possible.[17]

---

[17] Jackson Turner Main's sensitive assessment in *The Social Structure of Revolutionary America* (Princeton, N. J.: Princeton University Press, 1965) has served as a model for my inquiries into the present topic, so have the following works—Charles A. Beard, *An Economic Interpretation of the Constitution of the United States* (New York: Macmillan Publishing Co., 1913), Perry Miller, *The New England Mind: The Seventeenth Century* (Cambridge, Mass.: Harvard University Press, 1982), Richard Hofstadter, *The Age of Reform* (New York: Vintage Books, 1955), William Hinton, *Fanshen: A Documentary of Revolution in a Chinese Village* (New York: Vintage Books, 1966), E. P. Thompson, *The Making of the English Working Class* (New York: Vintage Books, 1966), David McCullough, *The Johnstown Flood* (New York: Simon & Schuster, 1968) and *John Adams* (New York: Simon & Schuster, 2001), Michael Kammen, *People of Paradox: An Inquiry Concerning the Origins of American Civilization* (New York: Vintage Books, 1973) and *A Machine that Would Go of Itself: The Constitution in American Culture* (New York: Vintage Books, 1987), David Hackett Fischer, *Historians' Fallacies: Toward a Logic of Historical Thought* (New York: Harper & Row, 1970) and *Albion's Seed: Four British Folkways in America* (New York: Oxford University Press, 1991), Edmund S. Morgan, *American Slavery, American Freedom: The Ordeal of Colonial Virginia* (New York: W. W. Norton, 1975), Daniel T. Rodgers, *The Work Ethic in Industrial America, 1850-1920* (Chicago: University of Chicago Press, 1978), Nick Salvatore, *Eugene V. Debs: Citizen and Socialist* (Urbana, Ill.: University of Illinois Press, 1982), Warren I. Susman, *Culture as History: The Transformation of American Society in the Twentieth Century* (New York: Pantheon Books, 1984), Sean Wilentz, *Chants Democratic: New York City and the Rise of the American Working Class, 1788-1858* (New York: Oxford University Press, 1984), Bernard Bailyn, *The Peopling of British North America: An Introduction* (New York: Vintage Books, 1986) and *Voyagers to the West: A Passage in the Peopling of America on the Eve of the Revolution* (New York: Alfred A. Knopf, 1986), Joyce Malcolm, *To Keep and Bear Arms: The Origins of an Anglo-American Right* (Cambridge, Mass.: Harvard University Press, 1994) and *Peter's War: A New England Slave Boy and the American Revolution* (New Haven, Conn.: Yale University Press, 2009), Kenneth Cmiel, *Democratic Eloquence: The Fight over Popular Speech in Nineteenth-Century America* (Berkeley, Calif.: University of California Press, 1990), Laurel Thatcher Ulrich, *A Midwife's Tale: The Life of Martha Ballard, Based on Her Diary, 1785-1812* (New York: Vintage Books, 1991), Gordon S. Wood, *The Radicalism of the American Revolution* (New York: Vintage Books, 1991), Richard White, *The Middle Ground: Indians, Empires, and Republics in the Great Lakes Region, 1650-1815* (New York: Cambridge University Press, 1991), Jane Kamensky, *Governing the Tongue: The Politics of Speech in Early New England* (New York: Oxford University Press, 1997), Kai Bird and Martin Sherwin, *American Prometheus: The Triumph and Tragedy of J. Robert Oppenheimer* (New York: Vintage Books, 2005), and J. A. Leo Lemay, *The Life of Benjamin Franklin*, 3 vols. (Philadelphia: University of Pennsylvania Press, 2006-2009).

Chapter One

Coalescence

Other than Native American Indians and African slaves, the most critical students of American history have not been able to identify a single class of local population that lived in perpetual poverty throughout the eighteenth century. Thus, comparatively speaking, the first clue to the floating nature of colonial poverty was the lack of those visible characteristics of uniformity, homogeneity, and permanency that could be associated with the industrial classes of subsequent periods. Instead, the poor in early Massachusetts were hardly a single class locked in an irrevocable situation, but rather a mixture of countless groups of diverse people who had fallen into poverty due to widespread reasons and circumstances ranging from economic exigencies, financial crises, trade fluctuation, market shifting, and natural disasters to human tragedies and foibles. Yet even if poverty was more circumstantial than structural and overwhelming, the pain of poverty and the presence of varying crowds in a multiplicity of miseries, frequently transcending race, ethnicity, gender, class, and age, were no less troubling to the commonwealth than to the individual. Hence, from churches and charitable organizations to big towns, small villages, local officials, county magistrates, and the provincial government, institutions of diverse capacities seriously engaged in discussions about responses and policies concerning both governance and treatment of the poor. None of the institutions intended to eradicate poverty, nor did they harbor a venomous conspiracy that the poor should either be subject to total control and brutal oppression or be completely alienated and ostracized. Instead, many of them tried different means of mitigating poverty and alleviating the pain of the poor, especially during the early decades of the eighteenth century, when the number of the poor remained low and the pressure for public support was sustainable. If none of these efforts was a complete success, few would deny their energetic, imaginative, and at times frustrating fight against intermittent and yet permeable and convoluted poverty.

For example, at a town meeting on January 3, 1708/9, Watertown selectmen "considered the need condition of the aged widow Sanger, and agreed with George Robinson to take her into his house and to provide for her sufficient meat, drink, washing, and lodging convenient for one in her old age for the term of one year next ensuing the date hereof." "The sd Robinson," they further decided, "to be paid by the town for his so providing: the sum of 5 pounds & sd money to be paid quarterly."[1] Within five years, Watertown selectmen made a series of additional arrangements with townsfolk for the care of the aged Nathaniel Holland, the impoverished Nathaniel Green, the needy Mrs. Shearmen, the impotent Sippeo Timson (an African), the measles-stricken Apphia Freeman (despite being a stranger of African descent from Cambridge), and several other families, including Nicolas Wyeth and his wife, Ephraim Smith (blind), and George Dill (seriously sick). The town paid for the

---

[1] *Watertown Records* (Watertown, Mass.: Fred G. Barker, 1894-1904), 1: 185.

expenses associated with lodging, food, bedding, clothing, shoes, and firewood for these people's maintenance. In addition to the nursing and doctors' visits that several of them required, the town paid for the cost of a coffin, the digging of a grave, and drinks at the funeral of George Dill, who was still under public charge at the time of his death.[2] In 1727 alone, the town spent £22—half its tax income—on expenditures for poor relief.[3]

Dealing with the poor had seemingly all but become a routine business of that township, which only reflected the growing pains of many communities in the colony. Yet who were the poor? Why and how did they become poor? How or according to what criteria should they be categorized and treated? What offices may be involved? Who could decide what aid they should receive, including how much and for how long? On what principle and authority should any local community decide its policies on the poor or when, where, and to what extent should the county or provincial government intervene in relief? No easy answers existed. Only when a variety of attempts to address these questions and the corresponding trials, failures, and progressions along the uncertain path coalesced would the volatile contours of early eighteenth-century poverty reemerge.

Who Were the Poor?

At first glance, the question seems simple enough because common sense suggests that a poor person is an individual whose income cannot support him- or herself. As such, according to colonial convention, all of those who were not rated to pay property taxes would be considered poor.[4] However, for any serious discussions on poverty among later generations, this rule of thumb can be a problem for little was

---

[2] *Watertown Records* (Watertown, Mass.: Fred G. Barker, 1894-1904), 1: 188, 189, 190, 191, 196, 197, 198; 2: 73, 74, 82, 83, 207, 208, 219, 220, 221, 222, 223, 225, 237, 276, 304, 346.
[3] *Watertown Records*, 2: 346.
[4] Billy Smith, ed., *Down and Out in Early America* (University Park, Penn.: Pennsylvania State University Press, 2004), xviii-xix.

done to calculate (1) what kind of income may have been necessary in Massachusetts at the time to sustain the livelihood of an individual and (2) how that living standard could have been measured against taxation. Therefore, a realistic assessment of the basic cost of living in eighteenth-century Massachusetts has to be established before a sensible discussion of the poor and poverty of that particular region and era can proceed.[5]

Extant evidence suggests that the minimum cost of living was about six shillings per week (about £15 12s. per year) for a single adult person in Massachusetts for much of the eighteenth century.[6] This benchmark, initially hypothesized and subsequently confirmed by contemporary data,[7] indicates a highly consistent demand of what a single adult had to earn to

---

[5] Paul Slack has wisely suggested both the usefulness and difficulties to establish a minimum cost for subsistence, *Poverty and Policy in Tudor and Stuart England* (London: Longman, 1988), 2-5, 38-40. But few historians have seriously studied the living standard in colonial Massachusetts. For related references see Karen J. Friedmann, "Victualling Colonial Boston," *Agricultural History* 47 (1973): 189-205. Gloria L. Main, "Inequality in Early America: The Evidence from Probate Records of Massachusetts and Maryland," *Journal of Interdisciplinary History* 7 (1977): 559-81. Gloria L. Main, "The Standard of Living in Colonial Massachusetts," *Journal of Economic History* 43 (1983): 101-108. Carl Bridenbaugh, "The High Cost of Living in Boston, 1728," *New England Quarterly*, 5 (1932): 800-811. Jackson Turner Main, "Standards of Living and the Life Cycle in Colonial Connecticut," *Journal of Economic History* 43 (1983):159-65. Richard B. Morris, *Government and Labor in Early America* (1946; Boston: Northeastern University Press, 1981), 1-84, 156-66. Billy G. Smith, "The Material Lives of Laboring Philadelphia, 1750 to 1800," *William and Mary Quarterly*, 3rd Ser., 38 (1981): 163-202, which later became "Material Conditions" in *The "Lower Sort": Philadelphia's Laboring People, 1750-1800* (Ithaca, N.Y.: Cornell University Press, 1990), *92-125*. Sharon V. Salinger and Charles Wetherell, "Wealth and Renting in Prerevolutionary Philadelphia," *Journal of American History*, 71 (1985): 826-40. Gloria L. Main and Jackson T. Main, "Economic Growth and the Standard of Living in Southern New England, 1640-1774," *Journal of Economic History*, 48 (1988), 27-46. Lois Green Carr and Lorena S. Walsh, "The Standard of Living in the Colonial Chesapeake," *William and Mary Quarterly*, 3rd ser., 45 (1988): 135-59.

[6] During the Seven Years' War a provincial soldier received, in additional to bounties, a wage of 4s. 4d. to 6s. (Lawful Money) a day, which British officers considered as "overpaid." Fred Anderson, *A People's Army: Massachusetts Soldiers and Society in the Seven Years' War* (Chapel Hill: University of North Carolina Press, 1984), 167, 225. At the other end of the spectrum 38 female inmates at the Boston Workhouse earned from 4 to 20 cents (1s. 2 1/3d.) a day by picking oakum in the 1790s, averaging 10 cents (7 1/6d.) a day per capita. Eric Nellis and Anne Decker Cecere, eds., *The Eighteenth-Century Records of the Boston Overseers of the Poor* (Boston: Colonial Society of Massachusetts, 2007), 73.

[7] Assuming the cost of living and the purchase of provisions were usually higher in the urban than rural areas, this segment of study on the minimum cost of living drew the extensive records of the assize in Boston from 1716 to 1798 to avoid underestimation. See

buy enough daily provisions for survival.[8] In other words, no matter how the prices of grain, produce, dairy, clothing, and other goods might varied throughout the colonial era, six shillings would always purchase no less than nineteen pounds of white bread, twenty-nine pounds of wheaten bread, or thirty-nine pounds of household bread, even in the most commercialized urban areas.[9] Thus, half the sum (three shillings) could buy enough wheaten or household bread for one adult to survive for a week, enabling the person to use the other half to purchase additional necessities, such as drinks, meat, milk, shoes, and clothing.[10]

---

the section of "Vicissitudes" in Chapter 5 for what kind of nutrition and diet 6s. per week could buy during the Revolutionary War.

[8] The grain shortage and riotous action against Andrew Belcher, the commissioner general who dominated the provisioning business during the Queen Anne's War in the early 1710s, perhaps prompted a highly consistent assize of the grain and foodstuffs in Boston beginning in 1716. See Michael C. Batinski, *Jonathan Belcher, Colonial Governor* (Lexington, Ken.: University Press of Kentucky, 1996), 19-22. Gary Nash's brief comment on the grain and bread prices during the 1730s and 40s is inadequate for a sound understanding of the long history of Boston assize, *The Urban Crucible: Social Change, Political Consciousness, and the Origins of the American Revolution* (Cambridge, Mass.: Harvard University Press, 1979), 174-75. So is Jack Tager's narrative of foot riots, *Boston Riots: Three Centuries of Social Violence* (Boston: Northeastern University Press, 2001), 26-38. For comparison see E. P. Thompson, "The Moral Economy of the English Crowd in the Eighteenth Century" in his *Customs in Common* (New York: The New Press, 1993), 185-258; Sidney Webb and Beatrice Webb, "The Assize of Bread," *Economic Journal* 14 (1904), 196-218.

[9] Boston selectmen used this formula to regulate the assize of bread—A = B x (C+D), or, the total weight of bread produced from a bushel of wheat (A) equals a unit weight of bread (B) times the total of the price of wheat per bushel (C) plus the baker's charge (D). Anyone who wants to test this benchmark can find data in the Boston assize on these (or any other) days: 15 May1716 (the first recorded case but information incomplete); 3 December 1720; 13 June 1726; 27 September 1726; 6 August 1729; 26 June 1731; 26 July 1736; 31 January 1742; 30 March 1743; 25 April 1748; 30 May 1748; 25 July 1748; 5 October 1748; 3 May 1749; 16 April 1750; 15 August 1750; 27 May 1751; 31 October 1763; 29 October 1764; 2 September 1767; 30 August 1769; 16 December 1772; 14 August 1782; 29 May 1786; 29 October 1787; 2 September 1796; 27 June 1798 (the last recorded assize in the selectmen's minutes). Details can be found in corresponding volumes of the Boston selectmen minutes as in *Reports of the Record Commissioners* (Boston, 1885-1896), 13 (1716-1736), 17 (1742/3-1753), 19 (1754-1763), 20 (1764-1768), 23 (1769-1775), 25 (1776-1786), and 27 (1787-1798). For severe bread shortage and precipitous price inflation during the French Revolution see Alan Forrest, "The Condition of the Poor in Revolutionary Bordeaux," *Past and Present* 59 (1973), 163-74.

[10] Rent is not included here on the assumption that average Bostonians lived in a one-room house, which served as the kitchen and bedroom for everyone in the household, including the husband and wife, their children and servants. Even if paying the rent was financially feasible, any poor individual would be less likely to feel the need for renting a room all for him or herself. Lodging, therefore, cost far less than boarding, and the two were often counted together. Little evidence indicates that there was a homeless population in colonial Massachusetts, where hundreds of transient poor people came and went. As far as those warning out notices show, they always seemed to be able to find a place to stay. This

If anyone's total income hovered around six shillings per week (£15 a year),[11] the person was highly unlikely to accumulate any assessable property to pay taxes, much less to meet the franchise requirement of £20 for a man above the age of twenty-one.[12] Thus, it seems that the amount between an annual income of £15 (the level of bare survival) and an assessable estate of £20 (the level of some basic security and comfort) may serve as a reasonable threshold of separating the

---

suggests that lodging was not too hard even for those uprooted and distressful newcomers, many of whom had no connections with the local population. For housing conditions in colonial Boston, see Nian-Sheng Huang, *Franklin's Father Josiah: Life of a Colonial Boston Tallow Chandler* (Philadelphia: American Philosophical Society, 2000), 12-14, 64-70. During the crisis of receiving the "French Neutrals" a government committee suggested, in 1759, that "the Rent of a house for each Family not exceeding Three pounds per annum." *Acts and Resolves, Public and Private, of the Province of the Massachusetts Bay* (Boston: Wright & Potter, 1881), 4: 101. The problem of overcrowding per household Gary Nash has found in Boston was more a reflection of the general living arrangement in that city for a very long time than one of a sudden degradation, *Urban Crucible*, 195-96. In Philadelphia where houses were generally larger than those in Boston, renting could cost considerably more. Sharon V. Salinger and Charles Wetherell, "Wealth and Renting in Prerevolutionary Philadelphia," *Journal of American History* 71 (1985): 826-40. Billy G. Smith, *The "Lower Sort": Philadelphia's Laboring People, 1750-1800* (Ithaca, N.Y.: Cornell University Press, 1990), 103-04.

[11] Like any statistical indicator, this benchmark was not absolute and carried with it at least three important variables. First, colonial currency changed a great deal; thus, the six shillings must be considered in the value of Lawful Money or an equivalent. Second, early in the century until the late 1720s, the benchmark dropped by as much as 2 shillings, making the minimum cost of living close to 4 shillings a week (or £10 8s. a year for 52 weeks). Third, from the mid 1770s until the end of the century, the benchmark rose higher by as much as 2 shillings, making the minimum cost of living 8 shillings a week (or £20 16s. a year). The fluctuation of currency impacted the cost to support civilians and the military personnel. William Douglass stated that, in 1725, a guard at "Castle William in Boston harbour was victualled at 7s. per man, per week; anno 1748, victualling was 38s. per week, because of depreciations." The sharp increase of cost was consistent with currency change in Old Tenor and the rising price of grain during that period. Also in the land service, the standard allowance of provisions to each soldier included—(1) for garrison allowances, 1*l*. bread per day, half pint of peas per day, 2 *l*. pork for three days, 1 gallon molasses for 42 days; and (2) for marching allowances, 1*l*. bread, 1*l*. pork, and 1 gill rum per day. *A Summary, Historical and Political, of the First Planting, Progressive Improvements, and Present State of the British Settlements in North-America* (London: Reprinted for R. Baldwin, 1755), 1: 535-36. In a 1792 proposal of a nationwide plan for the support of the poor in England, Thomas Paine suggested to pay £6 per annum for a person at fifty, and £10 for one at sixty. *Rights of Man* (Garden City, New York: Anchor Books, 1973), 480.

[12] Robert E. Brown, *Middle-Class Democracy and the Revolution in Massachusetts, 1691-1780* (Ithaca, N. Y.: Cornell University Press, 1955), 38-60, 78-99. At Concord town elections, a resident property owner whose estate could rent for £3 6s. 8d. a year shall be eligible to vote. Robert A. Gross, *The Minutemen and Their World* (New York: Hill and Wang, 1976), 11. See also Richard C. Simmons, *Studies in the Massachusetts Franchise, 1631-1691* (New York: Garland Publishing, 1989).

poor from the rest of the population. Namely, the colonial convention was on the whole accurate in the sense that a man who did not hold enough wealth or income to be rated to pay property taxes would likely face a far more serious problem of survival than those who did.

Yet in addition to the loose assumption based on convention, this benchmark can further separate three groups of poor people at the very bottom of society, whose distinctions have all but become blurred to those who would not pay adequate attention to the varied meanings of being poor in the past.[13] First, the dejected poor, who could not earn 6s. per week, would indeed face starvation and despair. They were perhaps the poorest of the poor, who were commonly called sturdy beggars in the Old World. Some of them were idlers, but most belonged to the incompetent, the aged, and the lame who badly needed relief. Second, healthy adults who could earn 6s. a week would manage to survive, although their lives were little better than bare subsistence. Often categorized as the competent poor, they caused concerns in a community where the better sorts lamented their presence and intermittent need for public aid.[14] Finally, those people who could earn significantly more than 6s. per week had the opportunity to save and climb into the higher economic ranks. According to colonial wage scales, most healthy men, women, and children could earn 6s. a week so long as they found employment,[15] even though they did have to

---

[13] Stephen Edward Wiberley, Jr. discussed how the lack of such a benchmark may lead to inaccurate assessment of the poor and other classes. Four Cities: Public Poor Relief in Urban America, 1700-1775, Ph.D. diss., Yale University, 1975, pp. 56-57, 141.

[14] Elain Forman Crane has discussed women's earning power, their various roles as producers, vendors, and distributors, and a continuous threat of poverty to their well-being and survival, *Ebb Tide in New England: Women, Seaports, and Social Change, 1630-1800* (Boston: Northeastern University Press, 1998), 98-138. Also see Olwen Hufton, "Women and the Family Economy in Eighteenth-Century France," *French Historical Studies* 9 (1975), 1-22.

[15] A common laborer could earn 2 to 3s. a day if not more since settlement, and so could a hired-out boy as early as the late 1600s. Spinning allowed a woman to earn 1s. a day in mid-1700s and more specialized piece work could pay more (see chapter 2). James E. McWilliams, *Building the Bay Colony: Local Economy and Culture in Early Massachusetts* (Charlottesville, Va.: University of Virginia Press, 2007), 110, 117-18. G. B. Waren, "The Distribution of Property in Boston, 1692-1775," *Perspectives in American History* 10 (1976), 86-7. Richard B. Morris, ed., *Government and Labor in Early America* (1946; Boston: Northeastern University Press, 1981), 55-84. William B. Weeden, *Economic and Social History of New England, 1620-1789* (1800; Williamstown, Mass.: Corner House

deal with many additional costs during unemployment, underemployment, and seasonal employment—not to mention accidents, injuries, sickness, disabilities, deaths, and marriages as well as raising a large family. Thus, the majority of the colonial poor were not the first group, who were facing imminent starvation,[16] but rather the second and third groups, who—still hovering near the poverty lines—had to struggle long and hard to escape poverty permanently and move into a more secured economic and financial condition.

Lacking clarity, some vague notions of and broad commentaries on the poor may be useful in general discussions on poverty, but they tend to blend several groups of categorically different people into the same domain. For example, although the fear may be terribly true, the lower and middle classes' frequent outcry of "oppression," "want," "deprivation," "misery," and "poverty" should not be equated with destitution or penury itself. By the same token, whereas approaching the status of non-taxpayers did suggest poverty, falling into the non-tax-paying category (below £20/year) still did not mean either immediate low subsistence or looming starvation (below £15/year), although the threat and fear of both could be real. However archaic, elusive, minuscule, and insignificant they may seem to a modern person, these subtle differences could be crucial and even highly personal to eighteenth-century people. A case in point is that for all the lower class's vulnerabilities and insecurities, modern researchers cannot readily assume an inevitable connection between the lower trades and poverty, which is an important

---

Publishers, 1978), 1: 83; 2: 879-81, 883-85, 887, 896, 898-904. Between 1718 and 1723 the young Benjamin Franklin was an apprentice to his older brother James in Boston. Reflecting on his life and income, he boasted that he had not only survived on half of his regular weekly pay by a vegetarian diet of "Boiling Potatoes, or Rice, making Hasty Pudding, & a few others," but also managed to save half of that money to buy books. The "light Repast," said he, had nonetheless produced "greater Clearness of Head & quicker Apprehension which usually attend Temperance in Eating & Drinking." J. A. Leo Lemay, ed., *Benjamin Franklin: Writings* (New York: The Library of America, 1987), 1320-321.

[16] See G. B. Warden, "Inequality and Instability in Eighteenth-Century Boston: A Reappraisal," *Journal of Interdisciplinary History* 6 (1976): 585-620; William Pencak, "The Social Structure of Revolutionary Boston: Evidence from the Great Fire of 1760," *Journal of Interdisciplinary History* 10 (1979): 267-78. Stephen Edward Wiberley, Jr., Four Cities: Public Poor Relief in Urban America, 1700-1775, Ph.D. diss., Yale University, 1975, pp. 64-65, 196-97, 203-04.

but separate topic beyond the scope of this book. Only at the risk of overlooking many special circumstances can they characterize some humble colonial craftsmen, such as shoemakers, butchers, and soap boilers, as the "working class" and "plebeians." Such a slight shift of descriptive phrases gives the impression that the distinction between the lower class and the poor then was little more than semantic, and that a host of narrative terms to describe them—such as the poor, the lower sort, the laboring people, the proletarian, and even the commoners—were all but interchangeable. Yet the fact that any colonial could formally title himself a shoemaker or a candle maker already suggests the person's honorable status accepted by his peers. Being as well as being called a shoemaker or tallow chandler carried a marked personal pride and social distinction—an unmistaken symbol of not belonging to one of those hovering close to the poverty lines. His business may go up or down and he may indeed protest against taxation and complain about his burdens of debt, sufferings, or misfortunes from time to time. Yet for anyone else to label him "poor" in those days would be tantamount to a serious personal insult, i.e., the malicious insinuation of his lost independence along with the humiliating reliance on alms and charity. The historic lines separating the poor from members of the lower class could no doubt be thin, unsteady, and shifting, but they certainly existed in the past nevertheless.[17]

---

[17] However narrow and elusive those lines may be, a historian's job is not to dismiss or exaggerate but to illuminate those subtle distinctions and to investigate those special circumstances under which they have fluctuated. The characterization of a "working class" or "plebeians" in the eighteenth century, as what some revisionist historians have done, is a tricky proposition. Most urban craftsmen of that era did labor and sweat to make a living. However, once they (after finishing apprenticeship and working as journeymen) could title themselves and be called by their neighbors, as a blacksmith, a shoemaker, a cooper, a soap boiler, and a roper, they were already a member of the lower to middle class. As owners and proprietors of their own businesses, they provided as much labor as supervision, working alongside any number of servants, apprentices, journeymen, and helps they may hire, including even some slaves they may own. However "low" their profession and livelihood may seem to others, these tradesmen, craftsmen, and mechanics were categorically different from the later industrial working classes who, even though they sometimes did call themselves mechanics or craftsmen, were rarely proprietors of their own business establishment and much less likely employers of others. The connection between the "lower trades" and the poor is not a settled subject but a topic for further research, compare Alfred F. Young, *The Shoemaker and the Tea Party: Memory and the American Revolution* (Boston: Beacon Press, 1999) with Nian-Sheng Huang, *Franklin's Father*

A set of clearly defined parameters for the colonial poor helps clarify these easily confused areas, yet the emphasis here is more on the importance of finding such a benchmark than a set of fixed numbers (i.e., the £15 to £20 range may shift up or down, varying over time as any historic circumstances would). Still, determining this range now may encourage observers to read other political discourse, social commentaries, and economic data more carefully than without it when assessing poverty, as its fluctuation was often a matter of a few dollars and pounds. In other words, a reasonable comparison between the minimum cost of living and any Massachusetts census, tax rolls, wage scales, estate inventories, almshouse records, and poor books indicates several tendencies: (1) Massachusetts was never completely free from poverty, even though the number of poor people may have only constituted a small segment of society, especially at the beginning of the eighteenth century. (2) No matter how limited they might be, public relief, mutual help, and private charity did play important roles in reducing the pain of the poor. (3) Poverty was never static or inescapable, and few were born poor by birth and remained so for life except for some orphans and the disabled. (4) Depending on different steps and strategies that poor individuals and families were taking, their potential of climbing out of poverty could be as real as the dreadful prospect of falling back into poverty that many members and families of the lower and middle classes would face.

Finally—and also for the sake of clarity—this book mentions three additional categories of people, whose distinctions in wealth and material possessions are as follows:

Josiah: Life of a Colonial Boston Tallow Chandler, 1653-1745 (Philadelphia: American Philosophical Society, 2000). As the Franklins (soap boilers, candle makers, dyers, printers, and cutlers) owned several slaves, so did the Hewes, according to at least one source. The shoemaker George Robert Twelve Hewes' father George Hewes (tanner) and uncle Robert Hewes (butcher) owned, among other possessions, four male slaves—Cato, Nero, Quaquo, and Scipio. Annie Haven Thwing, *Inhabitants and Estates of the Town of Boston, 1630-1800* (Boston, 2001), CD-ROM. Also for comparative purposes, it may be useful to recall that at least two people in Massachusetts later became quite well-known during the same period—John Glover of Marblehead and Roger Sherman of Newton—both coming from a shoemaking family background.

	For rural inhabitants *annual grain production per household*	For urban dwellers *yearly rated estate & other income per household*
The lower class	below 40 bushels	below £20
The middle class	from 40 to 300 bushels	from £20 to £1,000
The rich/upper class	above 300 bushels	above £1,000

"There are degrees of *Poverty*"

Although poverty did mean paucity and scarcity, people in Massachusetts knew all too well that the composition of the poor was never as simple, uncomplicated, and undivided as someone might assume. As Benjamin Wadsworth, pastor of the First Church in Boston and later president of Harvard College, emphasized in 1719, "There are degrees of *Poverty*."

First on Wadsworth's mind about the deprived world was perhaps the old-fashioned distinction between the sinful and the noble poor. The Gospel held that poverty embodied certain nobility, for it was the poor—not the rich—who had received Jesus Christ in biblical times. Thus, church fathers in the Middle Ages placed the poor close to God. "The poor are favored in God's sight," as Carter Lindberg pointed out, "for God has specially chosen the poor for his own people."[18] Under a cloud of covetousness, greed, or usury, wealthy members in society had a hard time saving the soul.[19] Did not the Scriptures say, in Matthew 19: 16-24, that "it is easier for a camel to go through the eye of a needle than for a Rich man to enter the kingdom of God"? However, when the Reformation stormed the world, it turned this assumption upside down.

Denying the covenant of works, Protestants redefined the path to heaven. Stressing faith and grace, Calvinists in particular effectually eliminated the role of a person's economic status in salvation. Because salvation was achieved by grace alone, not by good works, no material distinction would make

---

[18] Carter Lindberg, *Beyond Charity: Reformation Initiatives for the Poor* (Minneapolis, Minn.: Fortress Press, 1993), 22-33.
[19] Lee Palmer Wandel, "The Poverty of Christ," in Thomas Max Safley, ed., *The Reformation of Charity: The Secular and the Religious in Early Modern Poor Relief* (Boston: Brill Academic Publishers, 2003), 15-29.

any difference in that spiritual journey.[20] The salvation of both the rich and the poor depended on God's grace, which was believed to be an absolute and free gift. As such, poverty "no longer possess[ed] any special sanctity,"[21] nor would it position the poor any closer to God than how wealth may separate the rich from Him. The poor now had the same fate of becoming condemned sinners as their rich neighbors in the eye of divinity.

As the insistence on the holiness of poverty waned, neither Protestants nor Catholics would continue to view the poor as a monolithic body of the same impoverished creatures in a strict biblical sense.[22] In fact, abject poverty and widespread vagrancy aroused a heightened sense of social instability in many European countries. Both Catholic and Protestant institutions began to distinguish the deserving poor from the undeserving poor. They separated the native and resident poor from the traveling, non-resident, and foreign poor. They carefully differentiated the noble and honest poor from the able-bodied poor. They further classified the latter into idlers, beggars, wanderers, vagabonds, rogues, thieves, cheats, Gypsies, pickpockets, lepers, and so on and so forth. They began to scrutinize those who would be entitled to relief and who would not. They registered those who would receive the dole and those who were to be sent to work. They ultimately determined who would go to almshouses, hospitals, and

---

[20] It was believed that prayers by the poor for the charity they received would aid the souls of their benefactors in Purgatory. Charitable activity, therefore, was part of the good works with merit for salvation. Joke Spanns, "Welfare Reform in Frisian Towns: Between Humanist Theory, Pious Imperatives, and Government Policy," in Thomas Max Safley, ed., *The Reformation of Charity: The Secular and the Religious in Early Modern Poor Relief* (Boston: Brill Academic Publishers, 2003), 123-24.

[21] Carter Lindberg, *Beyond Charity: Reformation Initiatives for the Poor* (Minneapolis, Minn.: Fortress Press, 1993), 165.

[22] Claiming that "we should not show our liberty indifferently to all who come to us," Canon Law indicated the church's attempt to distinguish the deserving and undeserving poor by establishing an "order of charity" as early as the twelfth century. Carter Lindberg, *Beyond Charity*, 173-74. For the fact that a beggar would need a special license in a Middle Age town such as Venice, see Bronislaw Geremek, *Poverty: A History* (Oxford, UK: Basil Blackwell Ltd., 1994), 133. Medieval laws in East-Frisian also distinguished the "shameless and greedy poor" from the rest of the poor, see Timothy Fehler, "The Burden of Benevolence: Poor relief and Parish Finance in Early Modern Emden," in Beat A. Kumin, ed., *Reformations Old and New: Essays on the Socio-Economic Impact of Religious Change, c. 1470-1630* (Aldershot, England: Scolar Press, 1996), 222.

sanctuaries and who would be sentenced to imprisonment, stocks, a house of correction, or a whipping post.[23]

Albeit similar, Wadsworth's focus was narrower. Less concerned with an overwhelming number of beggars, rogues, and vagabonds roaming the streets, he and his Calvinist contemporaries were more worried about certain sinful behavior that could lead to "pinching poverty." He thus warned:

> We should avoid *Idleness, Intemperance, Uncleanness, bad company, oppressing, cheating, promise-breaking*; We should cast off *pride* and *extravagancy*, not live above our abilities and so make a prey of our neighbours, while we really spend and sink their Substance. We should be diligent in lawful business: children and servants also should be well Instructed in Religion, well govern'd, well and diligently Imploy'd in business proper for them. We should be true to our word and promise, Just, upright and honest in all our dealings; readily and seasonably pay every one his due; do our part honestly to support both church and State, to maintain God's worship, to relieve the poor and needy; and we should pray to God for his blessing on us.[24]

---

[23] The large literature on European welfare reform in the Reformation is a rich source for this segment, see Preserved Smith, *The Age of Reformation* (New York: Henry Holt and Co., 1920), Brian S. Pullan, *Rich and Poor in Renaissance Venice: The Social Institutions of a Catholic State, to 1620* (Oxford, UK: Blackwell Publishers, 1971), Robert M. Kingdon, "Social Welfare in Calvin's Geneva," *American Historical Review* 76 (1971): 50-69, Natalie Zemon Davis, *Society and Culture in Early Modern Europe* (Stanford, Calif.: Stanford University Press, 1975), William C. Innes, *Social Concern in Calvin's Geneva* (Allison Park, Penn.: Pickwick Publications, 1983), Jeannine E. Olson, *Calvin and Social Welfare: Deacons and the* Bourse francaise (Selinsgrove, Penn.: Susquehanna University Press, 1989), Carter Lindberg, *Beyond Charity: Reformation Initiatives for the Poor* (Minneapolis, Minn.: Fortress Press, 1993), Bronislaw Geremek, *Poverty: A History* (Oxford, UK: Basil Blackwell, 1994), Robert Jütte, *Poverty and Deviance in Early Modern Europe* (Cambridge, UK: Cambridge University Press, 1994), Beat A. Kumin, ed., *Reformations Old and New: Essays on the Socio-Economic Impact of Religious Change, c. 1470-1630* (Aldershot, UK: Scolar Press, 1996), and Thomas Max Safley, ed., *The Reformation of Charity: The Secular and the Religious in Early Modern Poor Relief* (Boston: Brill Academic Publishers, 2003).
[24] Benjamin Wadsworth, *Vicious Courses, Procuring Poverty. Describ'd and Condemn'd* (Boston, 1719), 31.

Clearly, Wadsworth promoted the doctrine of calling and saw the Protestant work ethic as the best defense against poverty. He did not see a pressing need to send hundreds of the dejected poor to the almshouse or the workhouse. However, he did consider pride, ignorance, sloth, laziness, lying, stealing, drunkenness, fornication, prostitution, and various sorts of wickedness as "vicious courses procuring poverty." According to him, the best approach for fighting against poverty was a strict practice of honesty, prudence, diligence, frugality, business, and good husbandry. Above all, he envisioned a world in which—although poverty may not disappear—the poor must behave.

Conflation

The governance of the poor was as important in Massachusetts as in anyplace and those governing ideas and principles, shared by Wadsworth and most of his contemporaries, came from the confluence of two important sources—the English poor law practices combining with colonial realities. This conflation of experiences produced a mixture of institutions and policies to regulate the poor in Massachusetts throughout the eighteenth century, which were functionally similar to and yet characteristically different from their English counterparts. For the sake of discussion, the principal continuities and influences will be explained first in this and next segments while the rest of the chapter will elaborate the differences.

For more than a century after the Reformation, the Tudor and Stuart monarchs built a nationwide system to cope with poverty. Their standard practices strongly influenced the colony, which adopted three most important policies after the English model—(1) that authorities divided the poor into two groups of the incompetent (or deserving) and competent (or undeserving and able-bodied) poor, (2) that local communities took the primary responsibility of supporting the incompetent poor, while local rate payers were obligated to pay for the cost, and (3) that the competent, undeserving, and able-bodied poor shall be compelled to work if found idle.

Massachusetts thus inherited several major consequences from a two-hundred year tradition which spared the Bay Colony an enormous amount of trouble had it had to develop its own model. After the Tudors revived state policies to deal with the poor in 1495 and 1531, the national government continued to pass new poor laws almost every decade for more than half a century,[25] culminating in two Elizabethan laws of 1598: the Act for the Relief of the Poor and the Act for the Punishment of Rogues, Vagabonds and Sturdy Beggars. These poor law regulations crystallized five key principles that, although not duplicated to the letter, strongly influenced the ways in which the Bay Colony would treat its poor.

First of all, an active government involvement and a strong paternalism the state held toward the poor. The succession of English sovereigns since Henry VIII created an all-encompassing and uniformed poor relief system under the ubiquitous guidance of national statutes. In 1598, the government allowed an estimated £4,000 to be collected for nationwide poor relief.[26] A century later, in 1696, annual expenditures for the poor reached £400,000, which once again increased tenfold to four million pounds by the end of the next century.[27] Clearly, over the years the English government consistently mandated, carefully built, and greatly expanded a nationwide system of relief.

Second, unlike many European countries, in which little unison existed between the central and local authorities in their

---

[25] According to Paul Slack, modern scholars have found three reasons for the Tudor (and later Stuart) rulers to take serious actions: (1) high pressure from population increases, (2) public attitudes toward what should be done about the poor, (3) government ambition of what it could accomplish in controlling destitution, see his *English Poor Law, 1531-1782* (Cambridge, UK: Cambridge University Press, 1995), 3-13, 51-2.

[26] 39 Eliz. I c.3, *Statutes of the Realm* (Buffalo, New York: William S. Hein & Co., 1993), IV, Pt. II: 898. The act allowed a poor rate of two pence (averaging) per parish. In estimating the total levy of £4,000, a conservative number of 9,000 parishes was used, instead of the "15,635 parishes or places" given in Sidney and Beatrice Webb, *The Parish and the County* (1906; London: Frank Cass and Co., 1963), 3n., or the number of 15,535 given in Thomas Mackay, *A History of the English Poor Law* (New York: G. P. Putnam, 1900), 3: 345, 346.

[27] Paul Slack, *The English Poor Law*, 22.

dealings with the poor, the English system of relief depended on a fusion of two strengths: one led by the central government and the other by local administrations. Setting the local government as the primary authority for dealing with the poor, the system possessed both the awesome might of the central government on the one hand and an omnipresent network of local institutions, particularly the parish organization and the justices of the peace, on the other.[28] Whenever Parliament passed statutes to set directions, a host of government employees and community officials went on to enforce the laws. They included not only county magistrates, commissioned justices, and every civil office from high constables to bailiffs and jailers, but also churchwardens, overseers of the poor, municipal aldermen, and local selectmen, wardens, searchers, tithing men, governors, guardians, almshouse keepers, and directors and masters of Bridewell. The suffering and the miserable could hardly escape this state-dictated and locally executed system, which controlled the fate of their survival in big cities, small towns and villages, and even remote hamlets.

Third, the system insisted that the two categories of the poor be dealt with separately as legal or illegal, deserving or undeserving, able-bodied or incompetent poor.[29] English authorities always acknowledged the need to relieve the deserving poor, such as the aged, the impotent, the lame, the sick, the orphaned, the wounded, and the widowed; however, they unequivocally discriminated against any undeserving ones, such as the able-bodied poor, idlers, sturdy beggars, rogues, vagabonds, cheats, Gypsies, thieves, and all other lewd persons and petty criminals. A strong desire and a persistent effort to distinguish the deserving from the undeserving poor permeated throughout the history of poor law legislations. Controlling the size of the deserving poor would certainly limit the scope of relief, yet controlling the eligibility of relief was only the

---

[28] The parish organization and the office of the justices of the peace, of course, became a target of strong criticism by late nineteenth-century social reformers, see Sidney and Beatrice Webb, *The Parish and the County* (1906; London: Frank Cass and Co., 1963).

[29] Contemporary Europeans also had the "shamefaced poor" (unemployed craftsmen), or some modern scholar would name them the "respectable poor." Paul Slack, *Poverty and Policy in Tudor and Stuart England* (London: Longman, 1988), 61-90.

beginning of the English system, which also aimed to restrain the behavior and movement of the undeserving poor. More aggressive than many other European countries, the English government applied a great variety of punitive devices to control the behavior and whereabouts of the undeserving poor, such as bans, restrictive licensing, fines, forfeitures, flogging, cutting of the earlobes, burns through the ear, public humiliation (such as putting one in the stocks or burning a hot-iron sign of "V" on a vagabond's chest), imprisonment, settlement regulations, removal procedures, indemnities, recognizances, bound services, hard labor, and criminal prosecution. At times, even the threat of banishment and enslavement was incorporated as legal punishment for those who had stubbornly resisted vagrancy laws.[30]

Fourth, the English system introduced several powerful institutions to deal with the deserving and undeserving poor. In addition to traditional facilities of charitable hospitals and almshouses (later poor houses), new institutions were set up, ranging from stocks and Bridewell or houses of correction (beginning in the sixteenth century) to workhouses and charity schools (in the seventeenth and eighteenth centuries). Based on a method adopted in Norwich during the early 1570s, a "stock" was a large sum of money raised—through voluntary contributions or compulsory rates—to procure materials and implements for setting the poor to work. The stock, therefore, was the fund specifically raised to provide work for the unemployed. The stocks could also mean the stores of those materials and implements acquired for the same purpose.[31] Bridewell was a special program to put the able-bodied poor to work, named after the royal palace that Henry VIII gave to the City of London during the relief crisis of the 1550s. Although the name later became synonymous with the many houses of correction set up across the nation, Bridewell—officially

---

[30] For allowing enslavement of those who violated the poor law, see 1 Edw. VII c. 3 (1547), *Statutes of the Realm* (Buffalo, New York: William S. Hein & Co., 1993), IV, Pt. I: 5, 7, 8. This law was repealed three years later in 3 & 4 Edw. VI c. 16. For banishment of dangerous rogues and incorrigible vagabonds out of the realm, see 39 Eliz. I, c. 4 (1598), *Statutes of the Realm*, IV, Pt. II: 900.

[31] E. M. Leonard, *The Early History of English Poor Relief* (1900; New York: Barnes & Noble, Inc., 1965), 222-23.

opened in 1557—represented only the central building in a network of facilities for the training and employment of the poor. Separated by the type of work and employment each provided, the facilities were scattered across town and included wool houses, yarn houses, spinning houses, nail houses, bake houses, and a number of other mills and manufactories. Therefore, as many as sixty-six governors had to be appointed to supervise the operations of Bridewell, which also ran three hospitals in London.[32] A local or county house of correction was never near such a scale and usually required no more than one master, his wife, and several wardens for maintenance and supervision.

Finally, whereas most European countries still relied on voluntary contributions for relief throughout the 1500s, attempts to establish a compulsory poor rate began in England in the mid century and continued for decades.[33] The 1598 Act for the Relief of the Poor required the poor rate to be collected weekly, ranging from a half penny to six pence per parish and averaging two pence for each parish.[34] This seemingly small levy, which grew significantly in subsequent years, gave the national government a powerful new leverage to conduct poor relief. Exacting money from a subject's pocket was no simple task, and this governmental victory in taxing the local population for poor relief did not come easily. The first attempt to break away from the ancient tradition of voluntary contributions appeared in the harmless form of a "request." An Act for the Provision and Relief of the Poor (1552) allowed local officials to "gentellie aske and demaunde everie man and woman what they of their charitie wilbe contented to give wekelie towards the relief of the Poore."[35] Yet the "gentle request" failed to work, ultimately leading to a second form of "persuasion" ten years later. Local pastors, vicars, and church

---

[32] E. M. Leonard, *The Early History of English Poor Relief* (1900; New York: Barnes & Noble, Inc., 1965), 31-7.

[33] In 1572 justices of the peace were authorized to estimate the weekly charge for maintaining the poor under their jurisdiction, and the local population shall be assessed to pay for that cost. 14 Eliz. I c. 5, *Statutes of the Realm* (Buffalo, New York: William S. Hein & Co., 1993), IV, Pt. I: 593.

[34] 39 Eliz. I c. 3, *Statutes of the Realm*, IV, Pt. II: 898.

[35] 5 & 6 Edw. VI c. 2, *Statutes of the Realm*, IV, Pt. I: 131.

wardens were to "gently exhort" residents "toward the relief of the Poore" according to a new law enacted in 1562. If they were not persuaded, reports were to be made to bishops and ordinary chancellors, who would "induce and persuade" them "by charitable means." Justices of the peace would put those who still declined under recognizance of ten pounds until they changed their minds. Two justices also had the power to send them to jail should they continue to be obstinate.[36] Clearly, the national authority was determined to press the rate-payers into submission by applying alternate strategies from "charitable means" and the dreadful recognizance proceedings to jail time. As these tactics finally began to work, the government was able to strip the cover of "persuasion"—gentle or otherwise—and directly impose the compulsory poor tax, a dramatic turnaround that few European governments were able to achieve.[37]

Thus, the mother country had clearly established a highly elaborate system to regulate the poor by 1629 when the first group of Puritans prepared to set sails for New England. A succession of English poor law legislation ended the medieval practice of indiscriminate almsgiving. English authorities not only decidedly broke the ecclesiastical monopoly over charity, but also built an elaborate bureaucratic machine of control which enabled the central government to extend its grip to those at the very bottom of society. Poverty generated both pity and fear in the country, which became increasingly concerned with how to maintain law and order down to the lowest social strata, including a growing population of the humble but perhaps malcontent poor.[38] Far beyond the sporadic remedies to poverty, the English poor laws created an extensive system of relief institutions to distribute charity and simultaneously manage the

---

[36] 5 Eliz. I c. 3, *Statutes of the Realm* (Buffalo, New York: William S. Hein & Co., 1993), IV, Pt. I: 413.
[37] The 1572 law said nothing more about those who refused to pay the poor rate, but it did say that anyone who refused to be an overseer of the poor, an office which frequently dealt with the poor and the poor rate, shall forfeit 10s. for each default. 14 Eliz. I c. 5, *Statutes of the Realm*, IV, Pt. I: 593.
[38] It is no coincident that the emphasis on the welfare of commonwealth gained increasing currency, and that stressing the necessity of a coherent body politic was widely used by Protestant, Catholic, and humanistic thinkers alike. Abel Athouguia Alves, "The Christian Social Organism and Social Welfare: The Case of Vives, Calvin and Loyola," *Sixteenth Century Journal* 20 (1989): 3-22.

poor. A vast administrative network to impose power and authority, the English poor law commanded local officials to join the national government to exact poor rates, regulate relief, and control the poor people's behavior, work, residence, and movement.[39] Under these circumstances, the question seems not to be whether or not the Bay Colony would follow suit, but when, where, how, and to what degree.

Filtering

As the English relief system grew, the massive scope and powerful force of its bureaucratic machine shall never be underestimated.[40] Still within this grand orbit the Bay Colony, however, quietly embarked on a filtering process which embraced some traditional concepts when they suited its purpose while downplaying others when they did not. The small size of the colony and the low number of the poor, while negating the need for a comprehensive network of poor law administration, did necessitate a modest start of several institutions.

Of all the English poor laws affecting Massachusetts, one cardinal rule was that local communities ought to take the primary responsibility for the care of their poor. Based on this long-held principle, the colony adopted two traditional methods of "indoor" and "outdoor" relief to fulfill that goal. Responding to the dual classifications in the mother country, population centers in the Bay Colony went on to emulate the English models by building two kinds of institutions: almshouses for the impotent poor and workhouses and houses of correction for the able-bodied poor. Both institutions conducted "indoor relief"

---

[39] For various sorts of revolts against that controlling system see Christopher Hill, *The World Turned Upside Down: Radical Ideas during the English Revolution* (1972; New York: Penguin Books, 1991) and *Society and Puritanism in Pre-Revolutionary England* (New York: St. Martin's Press, 1997), Arthur F. Kinney, ed., *Rogues, Vagabonds, & Sturdy Beggars: A New Gallery of Tudor and Early Stuart Rogue Literature Exposing the Lives, Times, and Cozening Tricks of the Elizabethan Underworld* (1973; Amherst, Mass.: University of Massachusetts Press, 1990), and Douglas Hay et al., *Albion's Fatal Tree: Crime and Society in Eighteenth-Century England* (London: Penguin Books, 1975).

[40] As the 1700s dawned, debates over poor law reforms were in the air and would continue for more than a hundred years until the first reform act in 1834.

because they dispensed aid or provided work inside a public facility.

Few public institutions in the past have become all but synonymous with poverty as the almshouse. Overseers of the poor, in collaboration with local selectmen, were responsible for supervising the institution, which included the power to appoint or dismiss its keeper. Early records indicate that about 1 percent of the urban population were thus institutionalized. In 1742, the Boston Almshouse had 111 inmates and the workhouse 36.[41] A 1756 census shows that more than 130 adults and 40 children were living in 33 rooms of the almshouse in Boston,[42] the oldest and largest almshouse in the province, which had been established in 1686 and expanded from 1741 to 1742.[43] Typically, the overseers or selectmen would only commit the unfortunate to the institution under certain conditions—namely, (1) they had to be legal residents of the community, (2) they had to be the deserving poor who had lost their ability to work, and (3) they had to have no family member or relative to whom to turn for support.[44] Therefore, indoor relief was strictly a local welfare extended only to those qualified community members who were feeble, infirm, aged, widowed, or orphaned. This communal nature (and the limited resources of the time) not only set the almshouse as the main poorhouse in the community, but also turned it simultaneously into a shelter for the homeless, a hospital for the sick, an orphanage for abandoned children, and a retirement home for the helpless elderlies. Few clues better illustrated the multiple functions the almshouse played than the fact that not all its inmates were destitute. Records show that a number of its

---

[41] William Douglass, *A Summary, Historical and Political, of the First Planting, Progressive Improvements, and Present State of the British Settlements in North-America* (London: Reprinted for R. Baldwin, 1755), 1: 531.

[42] The Almshouse Census and Inventory, 1756, in *The Eighteenth-Century Records of the Boston Overseers of the Poor*, eds. Eric Nellis and Anne Decker Cecere (Boston: Colonial Society of Massachusetts, 2007), 113-18.

[43] In 1662 a small Almshouse opened in Boston. It had only a few inmates and was burned down in a year or so. The town later voted to rebuild the Almshouse and a brick one was constructed in 1684. Nellis and Cecere, *The Eighteenth-Century Records of the Boston Overseers of the Poor*, 13, 95n.

[44] "An Act for Regulating of Townships, Choice of Town Officers and Setting Forth their Power," *Acts and Resolves*, 1692, 1: 67-8.

inmates could be the relatives and kinsfolks to several well-known middle-class families in town, such as the Bulfinches, the Dolbeares, the Greenleafs, the Hubbards, the Palfreys, the Proctors, and the Scollays. At least four of those inmates—George Skinner, Mary Pilsberry, Mary Crawford, and Thomas Eastwick—were admitted into the almshouse with their personal belongings, including such valuable items as two feather beds, some pillows, chairs, rugs, wearing apparel, clothing, and even books.[45]

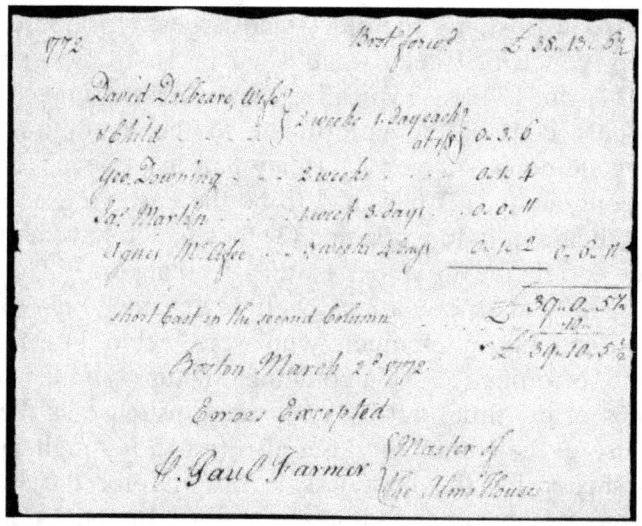

Bill by Paul Farmer, Master of the Almshouse, for the maintenance of David Dolbeare, his wife and child, George Downing, James Martin, and Aguis McAfee, on province account. Boston, March 2, 1772. (Boston Public Library)

The almshouse provided beds, blankets, sheets, shirts, and shifts. Medical care and nursing could be available as needed. The inmates' diet included corn, wheat and rye flours,

---

[45] Eric Nellis and Anne Decker Cecere, eds., *The Eighteenth-Century Records of the Boston Overseers of the Poor* (Boston: Colonial Society of Massachusetts, 2007), 79-80. The editors considered these cases as a "vivid example of the diverse social composition of the Almshouse."

milk, beans, fish, and pork.[46] Because they were committed for miserable conditions in the first place, a considerable number of the sick and elderly passed away at the almshouse. Some summoned their last energy and chose to run away from the institution, while still others were discharged or sent to a workhouse if deemed strong enough to return to work. Fragments of data also suggest that a feminization of poverty could have been taking shape given the disproportionately large numbers of females among those in need of relief,[47] particularly single women and aged widows,[48] although the same trend may also suggest the paternalistic and even chauvinist idea of communal responsibilities for maintaining the fair sex in distress. Poor pregnant women, sometimes unmarried, gave birth at the almshouse. If these mothers could not raise their infants, they and other orphans in town became public charge. Observing a long-time tradition in the English poor law practice, selectmen and overseers of poor were authorized to join justices of the peace in binding out those poor children as maids, servants, or apprentices to families that needed them. This institutionalized binding out practice lasted throughout the century when Boston bound out some 560 orphans to more than 180 towns across the province (and several towns in Maine, New Hampshire, and Connecticut).[49]

According to custom, boys were bound to serve until they reached the majority age of twenty-one while girls were bound until the age of eighteen or until they married. Under terms similar to indentured servants, both bound-out boys and girls served and obeyed the orders and instructions of their foster parents while these new parents or masters provided them with food and lodging and taught them reading, writing, and other skills. At the end of the term, the children could

---

[46] Eric Nellis and Anne Decker Cecere, eds., *The Eighteenth-Century Records of the Boston Overseers of the Poor* (Boston: Colonial Society of Massachusetts, 2007), 119. Stephen Edward Wiberley, Jr., Four Cities: Public Poor Relief in Urban America, 1700-1775, Ph.D. diss., Yale University, 1975, pp. 37, 149, 151-52, 157.
[47] Stephen Edward Wiberley, Jr., Four Cities, pp. 25, 26, 29, 31, 33, 40.
[48] Elain Forman Crane, *Ebb Tide in New England: Women, Seaports, and Social Change, 1630-1800* (Boston: Northeastern University Press, 1998), 109-15.
[49] Nellis and Cecere, *The Eighteenth-Century Records of the Boston Overseers of the Poor*, 645-67.

receive a small reward, such as clothing, shoes, or tools, as freedom dues to enable them to start a new life. The binding out system diffused the cost of maintaining poor children and orphans by shifting the burden from town authorities to foster families. The former avoided a permanent expense to care for the poor children/orphans while the latter gained several years of stable help and service. Although separating children from their biological parents was a harsh practice, those poor children and orphans who did survive the process had a better future than to abandonment at an almshouse or on the streets.[50]

Both the workhouse and house of correction (Bridewell) were set up for the undeserving poor, whose idleness, indolence, and other non-productive habits were regarded more as a crime than as a misfortune. Therefore, the consent of a justice of the peace, the lawful enforcement officer at the county and local levels, was required to commit anyone to the house of correction, which really was a prison, forcing idle and non-productive persons to reform under severe discipline. One Boston newspaper had no trouble announcing that

> Last Tuesday a Woman of a scandalous Character, who had gone thro' the Discipline at Bridewell, not being an Inhabitant of this Town, was conducted over the Neck by an Officer, and a number of merrily-disposed Persons, attended with Instruments of Musick to delight her Ear, and was delivered up according to Law, to the next Town, and from hence she is to be carried from Town to Town, till she comes to the Place of her proper Residence.[51]

---

[50] Isaiah Thomas, who had been a bound out as a boy when he was six years old, became a successful printer and publisher in Worcester. He took in a bound-out boy from the Boston Almshouse as an apprentice thirty years later in 1774, see his *History of Printing in America* (1810; New York, 1970), x, 154-55. For the important roles orphans played in the town-directed local economy, see Barry Levy, who analyzed 11,832 cases in 13 Massachusetts communities between 1630 and 1799, *Town Born: The Political Economy of New England from Its Founding to the Revolution* (Philadelphia: University of Pennsylvania Press, 2009), 237-62.

[51] *Boston Weekly News-Letter*, November 3, 1741. Commitments to and escapes from Bridewell were reported in *Boston Weekly News-Letter*, November 26, 1741; *Boston Evening-Post*, May 31, 1742; *Boston Weekly News-Letter*, September 2, 1742.

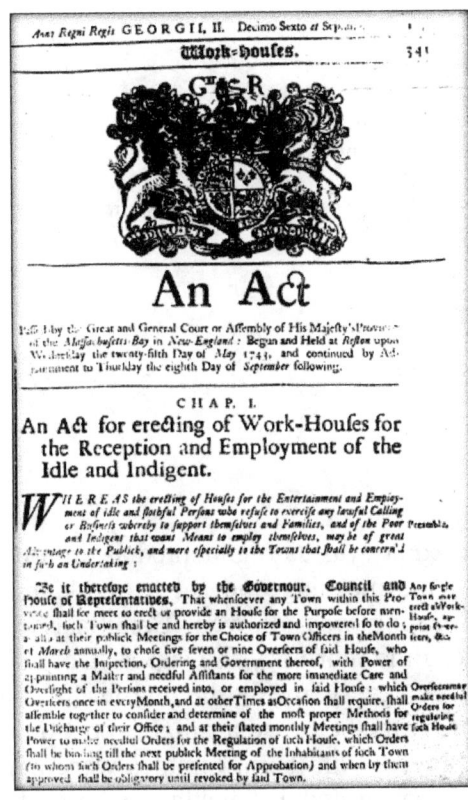

Title page of the *Work-House Act of 1743*. Insistence from the provincial government notwithstanding, the workhouses never became as numerous in the local communities of Massachusetts as they did in England. (American Antiquarian Society)

The workhouse in Boston, constructed after a provincial law of 1735, followed a new trend in England, where numerous workhouses mushroomed after the Workhouse Act was passed in 1723. The colonial legislature followed the mother country's footsteps with little hesitation, indicating a similar determination to reform the poor's behavior and to turn idlers into a productive force for the colony. The law clearly stated that a regular whipping could apply to those incurables who had ostensibly refused to work. Overseers of the poor were authorized to make rules to regulate the workhouse, hold monthly meetings to examine accounts, and supervise the master of the workhouse.

Book Cover of Boston Overseers' Management of the Work-House, ca. 1735. (Massachusetts Historical Society)

The workhouse schedule was as regimented as an army camp.[52] Inmates got up in the morning and set to work until noon, when one hour of dining was allowed. Breakfast was from eight to nine o'clock in the morning, and supper from six to seven in the evening. At every meal, the master of the workhouse called all inmates together, read a suitable portion of the Holy Scriptures, and prayed with them. Inmates were paid for the menial labor they performed in picking oakum, for example. As long as conditions allowed, inmates could engage in feasible trades, such as tailoring, shoemaking, mop-making, and nail-making. Female inmates could find suitable assignments in carding, spinning, knitting, and needlework. Some inmates were allowed to contract work outside the institution, but they were not allowed to leave before eight o'clock in the morning and had to return no later than ten o'clock in the evening.[53] In 1741 the Workhouse had 55 inmates, 38 of whom were women.[54] Although the institution did allow inmates "at play," "out on liberty," and attendance at

---

[52] Stephen Edward Wiberley, Jr., *Four Cities: Public Poor Relief in Urban America, 1700-1775*, Ph.D. diss., Yale University, 1975, pp. 88-98.
[53] Eric Nellis and Anne Decker Cecere, eds., *The Eighteenth-Century Records of the Boston Overseers of the Poor* (Boston: Colonial Society of Massachusetts, 2007), 975-80.
[54] This large presence of females also seems to be the pattern in the 1790s. Ibid., 72.

lectures as well as Thanksgiving holidays, the incarcerated life was a humiliation and disgrace for many. Indeed, after Rebecca Hill visited a girl at the workhouse in Boston, she met the overseer Samuel Abbot and sent him a letter the next day, pleading for the overseer to intervene: "[I] would beg of you to save her from the workhouse," she wrote, "that you be so kind as to endeavour to get a place in the Country and bind her—she said if she goes there, she never shall care for herself any more." She ended the letter by insisting that the overseer "take her into your hands and govern her."[55]

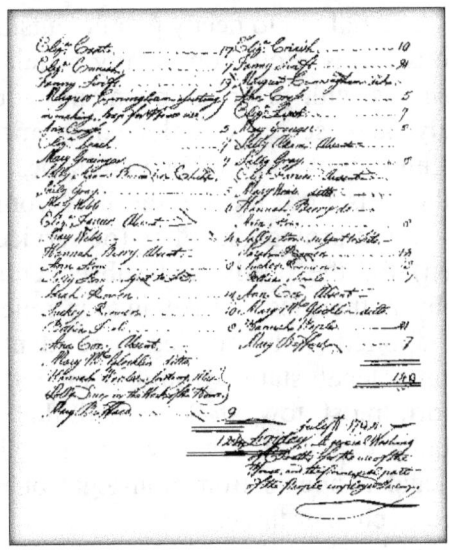

A page from the Boston Work-House payroll, July 12, 1794. (Massachusetts Historical Society)

Amplification

In spite of the above-mentioned emulations in the urban areas, small towns and villages in Massachusetts did not have any poor law institution. In fact, most of them did not set up an office of the overseers of the poor until the end of the century, even though the provincial statute as early as 1692 explicitly

---

[55] Overseers of the Poor Accounts, 1750-1775, Samuel Abbot Collections, box 71, folder 17, Baker Library, Harvard University.

allowed them to do so. A widespread control and institutionalization of the poor did not happen in the colony as it did in the mother country. Instead, because of the lack of a powerful central government and of a systemic network of bureaucratic machines which could enforce the wills of the central government down to every parish, small towns and villages in Massachusetts had much freedom and liberty to handle the local poor in the ways of what Watertown had practiced for a long time, namely, through numerous combined methods of outdoor relief.

More flexible than the institutions for indoor relief, "outdoor relief" (direct and material aid to needy people outside public facilities) took various forms. Both community officials and individuals and households with prior arrangements with local government routinely and severely doled out small amounts of cash, food, clothing, firewood, and pairs of shoes to poor families. Thus, with the consent of local authorities, some individuals and households could provide supplies (or services like teaching poor children) for the needy and subsequently apply for reimbursement by authorities.[56] Like indoor relief, however, outdoor relief applied only to legal residents. Precisely because a person's legal status would decide the eligibility of public support, most townsfolk agreed that a critical step of keeping public expenses down was to remain vigilant in distinguishing legal residents from non-legal ones, whose fate will be discussed in chapter three.

Within the confines of legal inhabitants, needy families could expect relief financed by local taxes and few residents protested this policy largely due to the long settled experience in England. As historian Stephen Foster has indicated, Salem, Boston, Watertown, Charlestown, Dorchester, and Springfield all paid relief, beginning in the 1600s.[57] Watertown paid poor charges as early as 1642 and in the ensuing years often spent ten, twenty, thirty, and sometimes forty to fifty percent of the town budget for the poor. The town began to maintain Nicolas

---

[56] Eric Nellis and Anne Decker Cecere, eds., *The Eighteenth-Century Records of the Boston Overseers of the Poor* (Boston: Colonial Society of Massachusetts, 2007), 889-901.
[57] Stephen Foster, *Their Solitary Way: The Puritan Social Ethic in the First Century of Settlement in New England* (New Haven, Conn.: Yale University Press, 1971), 137.

Wyeth and his wife Deborah Parker Wyeth in 1714 when they lost their abilities to support themselves, even though the couple just became legal inhabitants a year earlier and the husband had twice openly opposed town policies in the 1690s. After his died in 1720, the town continued to support his widow until her death in 1727.[58] As protected by law, residents had the right to apply for aid. When Hannah Topkin's husband left her without support, she wrote to selectman Samuel Abbot,

> Honored Sir it is ten month Now that I have ben able to support my self & Child & now the wether grows severe & I have little or No work to do & not in good health my Child being sick some time past I have not received nothing from my Husband all the while he has ben gone wich obliged me to beg that you woud be so kind as to let me have a little Wood for I have not got one farding by aney, with in my desires pray Sir consider me & Let me have a little & you will releave your Humble Servant   Hannah Topkin[59]

How much a community could spend on outdoor relief was rather uneven, ranging from a few pounds a year to several dozen. Although a single official might disburse small and temporary aid on an individual basis, long-term care and more costly relief must have either an approval by the selectmen or the community's consent at a town meeting. Like most communities in the Bay Colony, the treasury of Watertown depended on levies collected from proprietors. The fact that substantial land owners were the main source of revenues for the community left members with lesser fortunes little choice but to accept their dependent status, especially in times of need and distress. A 1642 town meeting set a rate of £100 to discharge public debts (mostly for building a house and for the back pays of two ministers' salaries), including some small

---

[58] *Watertown Records* (Boston: 1894-1904), 1: 9; 2: 4, 73-4, 82-3, 191, 186, 197, 198, 208, 220, 223, 276, 346.
[59] Overseers of the Poor Accounts, 1750-1775, Samuel Abbot Collections, box 71, folder 17, Baker Library, Harvard University.

obligations (less than 5% of the rate) incurred by selectman Thomas Haftings for charges to the poor.[60] Similar disbursements of money for relief steadily rose as the eighteenth century dawned. On June 20, 1709, selectmen at Watertown met to discuss the case of Nathaniel Green, a local resident who was too poor to have "a fixed place of a bode & not capable to provide for himself." The selectmen requested that Jabez Beers take Green into his family until some other means could be found to support him. Beers would be able to profit from Green's labor, who was allowed to work with Samuel Speer, a shoemaker. However, the selectmen instructed Beers to keep an account of all of Green's activities and work and submit a report to the town's authority.[61]

Several points must be stressed here to provide better understanding of the nature and scope of outdoor relief. First, the design was to help the incompetent poor. Many if not most of them were not born poor but became so because of old age, sickness, injuries, disabilities, and other tragedies. Second, many of them were not only long-time legal residents but also members of the middle or lower middle class families, especially in the cases of widowhood. That is to say, a large (or sometimes an increasing) number of widows who lost their husbands because of war, ship wreckage, diseases, or abandonment was not necessarily synonymous to a worsening condition of the existing poor; it may also suggest a vulnerable and declining state of many middle class families, the housewives of which used to depend heavily on their husbands' income and support. Third, outdoor relief held no gender or race bias against females and minorities, at least not to the degree of excluding them completely. As much as what extant evidence can show, widows, African Americans, and Native American Indians frequently received a significant share of local aid so long as they were legal residents of the community, while white Anglo-Saxon males could not receive any aid as long as they remained strangers. Not to suggest a total equalitarianism among all genders and races in those days by

---

[60] *Watertown Records* (Watertown, Mass.: Fred G. Barker, 1894-1904), 1: 8, 9.
[61] *Watertown Records*, 2: 189-90.

any means, the key factor in separating those who were entitled to public relief from those who were not was clearly based on residence and membership of the community, not gender, ethnicity, or race. Finally, outdoor relief could include public payment for the education (or any special) expenses of the children from needy families which,[62] contrary to some modern interpretation, strongly suggested an attempt to help restore the status of the declining families instead of keeping the poor in perpetual poverty.

Provincial Aid

For all the similarities and continuities between England and Massachusetts in regulating the poor, poverty never moved along a straight line, just as relief practices were by no means identical in both places. The few almshouses and workhouses in Boston, Salem, and elsewhere did not expand into a large network of poor law institutions in the colony, as they had in the mother country. Nor did the colony develop a powerful poor law administration running from the top levels of provincial government down to every settlement. Most communities dealt with the poor without any formal poor law institution or office, while the numbers of parish structures and the justices of the peace were never as large as they were in England. Although most relief took place locally, provincial aid was also available. As a creation of the Massachusetts Bay Company and without any counterpart in the home government, the General Court, which consisted of the governor, the

---

[62] A Boston town meeting decided to pay for the schooling of poor children as early as 1744. Stephen Edward Wiberley, Jr., *Four Cities: Public Poor Relief in Urban America, 1700-1775*, Ph.D. diss., Yale University, 1975, pp. 18, 187. In 1749 Topsfield selectmen warned out Benjamin Rogers, wife Alice (Perly) Rogers, and their children (perhaps as many as ten). On March 6, 1750, however, they voted and "allowed to Mr Benjamin Rogers for house room for children at school" for 5s. Sidney Perley, *The Dwellings of Boxford, Essex County, Mass.* (Salem, Mass.: The Essex Institute, 1893), 109-111. In addition to the common items of necessity (such as food, petty cash, and firewood), one less expected item overseers paid was the educational expenses for children of poor families in the Boston Almshouse. For example, as an instructor to poor children, Mary Snell was paid quarterly between 13s. and 17s. from 1769 to 1770. Eric Nellis and Anne Decker Cecere, eds., *The Eighteenth-century Records of the Boston Overseers of the Poor* (Boston: Colonial Society of Massachusetts, 2007), 889, 890, 894, 897.

governor's Council, and the House of Representatives, served as a multi-functional relief agency through much of the colonial period—a unique development perhaps least visible to later generations.[63]

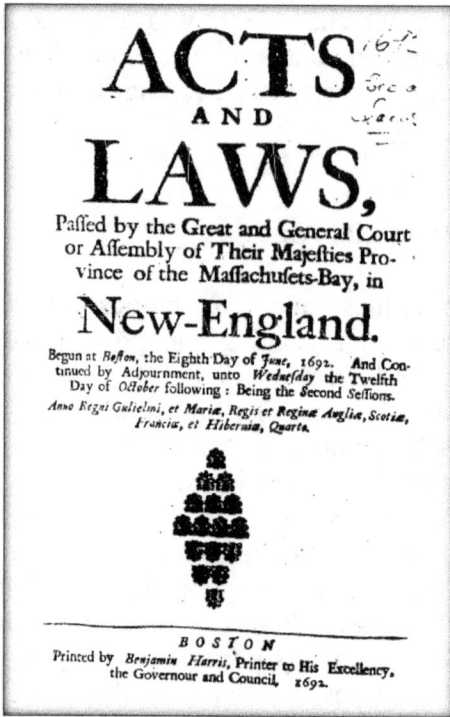

Title page of *Acts and Laws of 1692*, a significant legal step to formalize the local governmental structure and to regulate the poor in the province. (American Antiquarian Society)

Unlike local authorities that concerned mostly with the native and impotent poor, two large groups of people fell into the colony's domain. First, the provincial treasury often reimbursed local communities' expenses related to caring for the homeless, war refugees, and wanderers who had no legal residence in the colony. Second, the General Court routinely reviewed and accepted individual petitions for relief. Most of those petitioners were not the poor people, but members of the lower and middle class families. The General Court was willing

---

[63] Stephen Edward Wiberley, Jr. is one of the few modern scholars who noted this unique characteristic of Massachusetts relief. Four Cities: Public Poor Relief in Urban America, 1700-1775, Ph.D. diss., Yale University, 1975, p. 32.

to do so largely because those petitioners had involved in provincial service in some capacity (such as public employees, soldiers, physicians, and nurses), or suffered losses in that service (such as merchandize, wounds, or disabilities). Compared with its long held reluctance to raise the governor's salary, the General Court's and especially its Lower House's willingness to come to the aid of many distraught middle-class petitioners for decades was quite impressive.

On November 16, 1716, the House of Representatives received a "Petition of Hugh Pike, Creepled by a Wound that he received in the Service formerly, against the Indian Enemy, and his Wound still open, whereby he is disabled from Labour, to Support himself and family. Presented to the House; Praying Relief."[64] A resident of Newbury, Pike had been shot through his thigh at Port Royal, subsequently losing the ability to work. The General Court granted him fifteen pounds for his relief every time he petitioned in 1717, 1718, 1719, 1720, 1723, and 1727.[65] The wounded soldier Pike was one of the earliest cases concerning the relief for war veterans, who could now receive pensions after petitioning for aid directly from government. Wounded veterans Samuel Clark of Ipswich, Eleazer Rogers of Plymouth, Sergeant Daniel Tucker of Milton, and Josiah Johnson of Woburn were granted relief from the General Court, which also decided to pay the fees and expenses of their doctors, surgeons, and caretakers.[66] The General Court seldom granted an annual pension to any wounded veteran upon the initial application; indeed, a one-time pension was the most common form of aid. Long-term relief of up to several years was possible but only if qualified veterans reapplied annually. These cases clearly showed not only the possibility for individuals to apply for provincial aid, but also the procedures of how official relief could be obtained.

---

[64] *Journal of the House of Representatives*, 1: 141.
[65] *Journal of the House of Representatives*, 1: 141, 223; 2: 63, 177, 273; 4: 102; 5: 31, 227, 246; 6: 24, 48, 170, 344, 381; 8: 7. The Court granted to Hugh Pike a relief of ten pounds in June 1723 and another one of five pounds in November the same year.
[66] *Journal of the House of Representatives*, for Samuel Clark, 1: 232; 2: 62-3, 177, 272; for Eleazer Roger, 1: 148, 231; 8: 126; for Daniel Tucker, 1: 21, 147; 2: 88-9, 309; 4: 142; 5: 30-1, 118, 132; for Tucker's doctors, surgeons, and care-takers, 1: 28, 219; 2: 70, 109-10, 187, 281, 284; for Josiah Johnson, 8: 260.

For more than sixty years a large number of petitions came to the General Court, which spent considerable time reviewing each of those claims. Any person's petition to the General Court had to pass both chambers' scrutiny to receive financial compensation directly from the provincial treasury, a practice consistent with the tradition that drawing provincial money required the consent of both houses. Most petitioners began proceedings with the House, although a few sent the claim to the Upper Chamber first. In either situation, a concurrence had to be reached before a petitioner or his agent could draw any money from the public treasury. The provincial government did not enact a set of explicit policies concerning relief. Rather, during the review process, it decided—on a case-by-case basis—whether or not a petitioner qualified to receive cash relief. If the answer was affirmative, the Court would further decide the amount and length of the aid.

Cash relief to veterans, especially wounded soldiers, was a principal recourse to many petitioners who, even not in destitution, would certainly appreciate it to receive some cash in a by and large non-cash economy at the time. Rarely did the General Court deny their pleas as long as their cases proved to be credible and their requests reasonable. Veteran petitioners typically described their service and the circumstances of their wounds, explained how their disabilities had adversely affected their livelihood and families, and requested a certain amount of money for relief. Often advised by a specially appointed three-member review committee, the General Court would then decide how much cash relief should be allowed, usually ranging from five pounds to as high as twenty pounds per annum. Records show that from 1715 to 1734 more than forty wounded and sick or aged soldiers received cash relief from the provincial treasury. In addition to the several veterans previously mentioned, Joseph Bramhall (1716),[67] William Chamberlaine (1722),[68] and William Rutter Jr. received relief. Rutter was wounded twice, once through his right hand and the other through his right side. Incapacitated, he and his family fell

---

[67] *Journal of the House of Representatives*, 1: 86, 88.
[68] *Journal of the House of Representatives*, 6: 248, 249-50.

into hardship. In his petition to the Court, he specified no money amount, but left it for the Court to decide. The House granted £5 for his wounds and a pension of £5 per year in 1723.[69]

Also receiving provincial aid in the same period were Amos Smith (who, under Captain John Flint, contracted "a great sickness" and was unable to obtain "an honest livelihood," so he prayed for relief and received £10), Daniel Conner of Pembroke, John Bickmore of Dorchester, Joseph Dimmock of Barnstable, Captain Samuel Jordan, John Bickmore of Dorchester, Nathaniel Alexander of Northampton (who, as a veteran of King Philip's War, was quite old and his son Thomas had died in spring 1725; Alexander was granted £5), Richard Cutt of Kittery, and two dozen others.[70] After the 1730s, wounded soldiers continued to receive pensions, such as John Green of Brookfield (£15), Caleb Johnson of Shrewsbury, Vincent Shuttleworth, and William Jeffrey, but the total number of petitions declined, perhaps because more and more of those soldiers had passed away.

Aid sometimes lasted several years. For example, William Woodard's musket exploded in his left hand; he was initially granted £12 10s. for life. Later the grant was reduced to £8 and the term limited to "the pleasure of this Court."[71] Robert Gray, a quarter gunner at Castle William, lost his hand in battle. The Council "earnestly recommended" relief by granting a continuous governmental pay. The House concurred, and the case was settled in a week from June 19 to 25, 1723.[72] However, Robert Talbot, who contracted diseases in service, was not allowed any relief. His petition was denied twice in 1723.[73] Meanwhile, Josiah Johnson of Billerica, a wounded soldier under Captain John Lovewell at Pigwacket, was granted £18 per annum for three years from June 1, 1734. Likewise, Noah

---

[69] *Journal of the House of Representatives*, 5: 166, 260.
[70] *Journal of the House of Representatives*, 1: 232; 2: 177, 272; 6: 72, 76, 99-100, 111, 121, 123, 151,133, 146, 149, 158, 240, 241, 274, 314, 321, 322, 325, 326, 327, 328-329, 332, 336, 341, 388, 390, 396, 399-400, 419, 421, 426; 8: 12, 13, 19-20, 36, 41-2, 84, 91, 92, 95, 126, 180, 215, 219. 9: 177, 187, 327; 11: 231, 236, 330-31, 388, 345; 12: 134.
[71] *Journal of the House of Representatives*, 5: 97-98, 100, 167, 281.
[72] *Journal of the House of Representatives*, 5: 39, 60.
[73] *Journal of the House of Representatives*, 5: 97, 230.

Johnson of Dunstable, also wounded at Pigwacket, was granted £15 for three years from June 1, 1734.[74]

In addition to disabled veterans, three groups of people who could receive monetary compensation directly from the provincial government: doctors and nurses who attended wounded soldiers, those who had suffered captivity in enemy hands, and veterans who had grievances about their wages. Civilian doctors, nurses, and caretakers had to present their accounts for any compensation, which was generally allowed after a house committee examined the records. The Court granted £57 5s. for medical expenses, nursing, and attendance for Ephraim Moore who, as a wounded soldier under Captain William Cox in 1724, lost his left arm at Mount Desart.[75] The General Court also allowed numerous payments for the said Sergeant Daniel Tucker, who suffered a broken rib during service.[76] The Court allowed Thomas Hogg of Georgetown £4 10s. for his wife who, certified by Dr. Ebenezer Allen, had nursed and cared for the sick soldier John Pike in 1721.[77] The Court also allowed £15 to soldier Thomas Bradbury for doctor bills incurred during his sickness in 1724.[78] For reasons not clear, the only exception during this period was the General Court's denial of Dr. George Pemberton's account.[79]

Many military men and civilians survived captivity, forming a sizable group that received cash relief. The Court granted £17 for the redemption of James McFadden who, as a soldier, was captured by Indians at St. Georges in 1723 and remained captive for two years.[80] During the first two decades of 1700s, others who received similar compensations included James Nap, Benjamin Healey, Jr., Henry Edgar, Samuel Dickinson, James Corse (for both his effort to redeem his sister and his service to the province), Miriam Matthews of Beverly, and Abraham Johnson.[81] Philip Durrell of Arundel received £10

---

[74] *Journal of the House of Representatives*, 12: 76-7, 78.
[75] *Journal of the House of Representatives*, 6: 108, 123, 139-40.
[76] *Journal of the House of Representatives*, 2: 309; 4: 142; 5: 132.
[77] *Journal of the House of Representatives*, 6: 153-54, 171, 184.
[78] *Journal of the House of Representatives*, 6: 200.
[79] *Journal of the House of Representatives*, 9: 203.
[80] *Journal of the House of Representatives*, 6: 408, 426.
[81] *Journal of the House of Representatives*, 6: 191, 197-98, 284-85, 297-98; 8: 35, 36,

for clothing for his son, who had been captured and brought to Montreal by Indians.[82] Although veterans usually received money relief, land was also sometimes used as compensation, which could be desirable to both parties—the province could save cash expenses by disposing of land for improvement while veterans could gain a homestead for family members and later generations. Therefore, it was likely good news when Jonas Smith, John Tozer, Isaac Harrington, and numerous others learned that the General Court had granted them a total of 500 acres of unappropriated lands in York. All were veterans who had paid ransoms to save a wounded and captured fellow soldier, David Tucker, in 1712.[83]

For a variety of reasons, ranging from omissions in muster rolls to some officers' abuses, a number of soldiers did not receive their pay as promised. They were able to recover their wages if they submitted formal complaints. Generally the sums were not more than a few pounds and oftentimes only a few shillings, yet the amount each soldier was able to recover was perhaps as important as a feeling of vindication at the end of the appeal proceedings. Robert Thompson, for instance, a soldier under Colonel Shadrach Walton, was allowed £4 for his two-month service, which was omitted in the muster roll by mistake.[84] The Indian soldier David Job was allowed £4 8s. 7d. for the wages due him on Captain William Canady's roll in 1725.[85] Other soldiers, who recovered wages or assistance by petitioning the General Court included Michael Gilson of Dunstable,[86] Joseph Cross, and at least three other soldiers Hugh Holman, Thomas Varril, and Thomas Black—all alleging that their commanding officer Colonel Johnson Harrman had taken their wages for his own use. They requested relief, which was granted.[87] Soldier Ephraim Ayres challenged Lieutenant John Lane for his unpaid wages of £8 4s., as did solders James Smith for £10 10s., Nathaniel Chapman for £8 19s., David

---

66, 191, 198; 9: 247.
[82] *Journal of the House of Representatives*, 8: 187.
[83] *Journal of the House of Representatives*, 15: 193.
[84] *Journal of the House of Representatives*, 6: 402, 420.
[85] *Journal of the House of Representatives*, 6: 363, 371.
[86] *Journal of the House of Representatives*, 6: 459.
[87] *Journal of the House of Representatives*, 6: 354-55, 396.

Thomas for £10 2s., and David Tylor for a total of £186 14s.[88] Thomas Clark, also a soldier under Captain William Canady at St. Georges for three months in 1725, was not included on any muster roll. He was allowed £4.[89]

The Court also corrected payment errors, such as that of £6 5s. 11d. for soldier Joseph Peck and £8 14s. 10d. to Daniel Elithrop, who had performed the duties of a sergeant at St. Georges while mistakenly reduced to a sentinel on the roll. At the end of 1725, a House Committee comprising Joseph Wilder, Thomas Cushing, and Captain Edward Goddard recommended granting the petitions made by several soldiers—namely, Phineas Richardson, Abner Harris, Seth Read, Ebenezer Sprague, Ebenezer Harnden, and Thomas Williams—all of whom claimed unpaid wages due them under Colonel Edmund Goffe in 1724. The Court also granted £10 to mariner Nicholas Simons, who was taken by pirates to Rhode Island because he killed three of them. He was reduced to a "Man of low Circumstances, and dare not follow the sea any longer for his support and Livelyhood."[90]

Administrative Remedy

A non-cash method of relief was as valuable as a monetary one in Massachusetts, where the provincial treasury was always tight as few strong industries existed locally. Functioning as the high court superior to all county and local courts, the General Court was able to adopt a series of legal and administrative remedies to alleviate grievances, ranging from matters as serious as land titles to compensations for petty losses. The broad capacities of its decisions highlighted the paternalistic role of the provincial government, which served as the final clearinghouse in all sorts of civil complaints and

---

[88] *Journal of the House of Representatives*, 6: 244, 275, 325, 343, 367, 386, 387.
[89] *Journal of the House of Representatives*, 6: 403, 406. Similar cases included Jabez Bradbury (1724), Joseph Peck (though a deserter, but later returned to service, 1724), James Harper (1724), James Stevenson (1724), and John Sargent (1729). *Journal of the House of Representatives*, 6: 17-8, 38, 73, 111, 141, 184; 8: 405.
[90] *Journal of the House of Representatives*, 6: 111, 229, 271, 337, 387, 407.

grievances.[91] When the colonial population was still small during the first half of the eighteenth century, the Court was willing and able to handle a great number of individual petitions. By modern standards, the values of many cases were very insignificant. Yet the serious time and effort the Court was willing to spend showed a strong commitment to its paternalistic responsibilities. As dissimilar and trivial as they may seem, the following decisions the Court made demonstrate how deeply involved the provincial government had become in many property owners' lives of the lower and middle classes—a phenomenon that gradually faded later in the century.

Consistent with the common law tradition, for example, no person other than the legal title holder of real estate could sell the property unless the person could obtain special permission from the General Court, which had the exclusive authority in the commonwealth to grant such power. Many deceased colonists left sizable debt but little cash, and their surviving family members had to sell the deceased's property to satisfy creditors. Before selling any real estate to which they held no title, they had to obtain legal permission. Such was the case of the widow and administratrix of John Menzies, Esq., of Boston, who applied for permission to sell 300 acres of his land, which the Court granted.[92] The Court could also grant relief directly to a debtor if it so decided. John Cowing, a prisoner in the Plymouth jail for debt, received such relief after petition.[93] John Shaw, a poor prisoner, also petitioned for and was granted relief.[94]

Occasionally, a case was not as straightforward as debtor/creditor. The Court debated whether or not the government should pay for the loss of a lamed horse to two

---

[91] Local courts got their share of cases, especially those involving disputes over the support of elderly family members among siblings. For example, Nathaniel and Sarah (Hayward) Brett of Bridgewater fully supported their ninety-year old widowed mother, Sarah Hayward, for twelve years. They had tried to persuade other children and grandchildren of the widow to do "their proportionable part" toward the maintenance of her. But they "utterly refused so to do." The couple then sued two dozen relatives in a petition to the Plymouth General Sessions in December 1731. David Thomas Konig, ed., *Plymouth Court Records, 1686-1859* (Boston: New England Historic Genealogical Society, CD-ROM, 2002).
[92] *Journal of the House of Representatives*, 9: 67.
[93] *Journal of the House of Representatives*, 9: 167.
[94] *Journal of the House of Representatives*, 9: 143.

contested owners, William Maccarty and John Darrell. Unable to rule in favor of either one, it finally granted £10 to the former and £7 12s. to the latter.[95] After improving some land granted by the province, Daniel Waldo was ejected and his land returned to the province after sixteen years of work. He petitioned and was granted a sum of £20.[96] An impressed soldier claimed that the province store had lost his gun, for which he petitioned for 40s.[97] The wounded soldier William Cummings of Nottingham requested to keep a tavern exempt from excise. The petition was denied, but the Court granted him £10 to help pay the excise.[98] Robert Converse and Josiah Converse, sons of Major James Converse, deceased, petitioned for land in exchange for their father's service during the Indian wars. The Court granted them 400 acres between Lancaster, Rutland, and Wachusett Hill.[99] Prison keeper Joseph Young was allowed £16 16s. for keeping numerous prisoners in York.[100] Sometimes, the Court had to rule on fairness as much as on relief. For example, Captain James Woodside conducted fraud and was found guilty of allowing drunkenness and disorder in his company. The House recommended firing him; only the Council's disagreement saved his position.[101] Yet the House prevailed in the case of overturning the wrongful conviction of Henry Joslin of Attleborough.[102]

Rarely could any local officials or county government act beyond provincial legislation, which specified what they might and might not do in relief. However, as the highest legislative, legal, and administrative authority in the colony, the General Court always had the option of exercising its broad powers to go beyond convention to render relief. When it did, the results could be unexpected. It received, for example, a number of petitions for relief from widows whose husbands

---

[95] *Journal of the House of Representatives*, 9: 264, 276; 10: 20.
[96] *Journal of the House of Representatives*, 8: 41.
[97] *Journal of the House of Representatives*, 6: 264, 274-75, 317.
[98] *Journal of the House of Representatives*, 11: 390; 12: 15, 18.
[99] *Journal of the House of Representatives*, 11: 367, 368; 12: 124.
[100] *Journal of the House of Representatives*, 11: 419.
[101] *Journal of the House of Representatives*, 8: 61-2, 63, 68, 105, 123, 257, 258, 268, 269-70, 274, 276, 423; 9: 163, 172-73; 10: 100-101.
[102] *Journal of the House of Representatives*, 10: 223-24, 230-31, 231, 234-36, 237, 238, 239, 240, 242, 245, 265, 275, 278.

died during King Philip's War. In spite of the existing gender prejudice, the court either allowed tax exemption and cash assistance, or affirmed the widows' control over family property, and thus prevented them from falling into poverty.[103] On another occasion, for a burn suffered during public service, Vincent Shuttleworth of Wrentham was granted an annual allowance of £12 for eight years.[104] This was one of the longest terms of pension ever awarded by the Court, which usually did not grant anyone a pension for more than a year in one proceeding. As a victualler of Castle William for more than two and a half years, John Larrabee received £500—the largest sum of payment the Court ever allowed.[105] Perhaps one of the most intriguing situations surfaced when individuals applied to the General Court, pleading to recover lost provincial paper money or bills of credit. For instance, Grace Potter, the widow of Judah Potter, lived in Concord, Middlesex County. She requested relief because she had lost £20 of provincial notes after her late husband's dwelling caught on fire, destroying the bills. The question before the Court appeared to be whether or not the provincial government should be responsible for replacing those lost notes as a result of an individual's misfortune. Heavy-handed paternalism could be a double-edged sword. In this case the Court answered in the affirmative and granted the widow Potter's petition on August 25, 1731.[106] Hers was far from an isolated incident, and the Court subsequently

---

[103] These were the exact decisions that local and county courts were either unwilling or unable to reach. William F. Ricketson, "To Be Young, Poor, and Alone: The Experience of Widowhood in the Massachusetts Bay Colony, 1675-1676," *New England Quarterly* 64 (1991): 113-27.

[104] *Journal of the House of Representatives*, 11: 300, 317.

[105] *Journal of the House of Representatives*, 11: 323, 333. The General Court also granted £50 to Thomas Rich, the only surviving child of Martha Corey alias Martha Rich, who had suffered great losses in 1692. Robert Orange, a lame and infirm mariner of Boston, appealed to the House after Suffolk County justices denied his retailer license. Thomasin Woodwell, wife of Robert Hill of Salem petitioned the General Court to allow her to trade under *coverture* because her husband was in crazed condition and took no care of her. Adam Cogswell, a farmer of Ipswich, was a prisoner of debt. On a £500 bond, he was allowed to stay at the jail-keeper's house after complaining about the horrid condition of the jail. In 1724 the Boston shipwright Jonathan Carey was allowed a compensation of £6 because soldiers had pulled down his house to use the boards for mending boats in service. *Journal of the House of Representatives*, 1: 94; 2: 83; 5: 71, 77, 111-12; 6: 189, 198.

[106] *Journal of the House of Representatives*, 10: 270.

allowed several similar cases in a decade, including one lost bill eaten by rats.[107]

Although a local and county matter in most instances,[108] licensing could become an option in provincial relief. Granting licenses to keep a tavern or to sell liquors (a measure that would not incur any direct costs to the province) was sometimes used to help needy persons support themselves by conducting business at home.[109] If it found cause, the General Court could also reverse decisions made by county and local authorities and grant permission directly to those individuals who had been denied the opportunity to sell liquors, open a tavern, or keep an inn for self-support. Indeed, no fewer than three dozen petitioners had gained permission not from the local and county authorities, but from the provincial government by the end of the 1740s.[110] Yet when petitioners were neither war veterans nor the needy applying for a business license, the General Court tended to become reserved, and its replies varied significantly regardless of the petitioner's social rank. In 1725 the House

---

[107] The Court also allowed James Jones, Jr. £5 10s. for his predicament similar to that of widow Potter's. William Richardson of Lancaster was allowed £8—the value of a credit bill he had lost in a fire in 1732. By a Court order, Joseph Bradley of Haverhill was able to receive 30s. in credit bill, which he lost while his pocket book was burnt. Jonathan Smith of Sudbury recovered £5 of notes after they had been burned in a house fire in 1741, and so did John Bars of Halifax for £7. A replacement note of 50s. went to William Hines of Marblehead, who lost a 30s. and a 20s. bill eaten by rats, an incident certified by Joshua Orne, Esq. *Journal of the House of Representatives*, 11: 15, 99, 229, 366, 382; 19: 25. Similar incidents happened in Rhode Island, Ellen Hartigan-O'Connor, *The Ties That Buy: Women and Commerce in Revolutionary America* (Philadelphia: University of Pennsylvania Press, 2009), 106-107.

[108] A valuable study is David W. Conroy, *In Public Houses: Drink and the Revolution of Authority in Colonial Massachusetts* (Chapel Hill: University of North Carolina Press, 1995).

[109] Stephen Edward Wiberley, Jr., Four Cities: Public Poor Relief in Urban America, 1700-1775, Ph.D. diss., Yale University, 1975, p. 28.

[110] The Court granted a tavern license to Benjamin Ingersol of Falmouth, John Watson of Arundell, John Sale of Boston, Joseph Moulton of Berwick, John Phinney of Falmouth, Nathaniel Coney of Stoughton, Samuel Lord of Berwick, and Comfort Foster of Dorchester. A retail license to sell strong drink was granted to Benjamin Williams, Henry Farwell, Jr. of Dunstable, John Fowle, Jr., and Noah Chaffe of Rehoboth. John Beighton and Smith Woodward of Dorchester were granted a license to keep an inn. The Court granted James Jarvis a license as an inn-holder, who succeeded Richard Avery of Roxbury. Nathaniel Coney of Stoughton was allowed to continue as an inn-holder, which he maintained many years but missed the renewal with local authority. The General Court heard and ruled in nineteen additional cases involving tavern and liquor licenses around 1730. *Journal of the House of Representatives*, 5: 107-108; 8: 18, 21-2, 42-3, 44, 76-7, 258, 260-61, 270; 9: 48, 52, 72, 132, 166, 300;10: 35, 287, 291, 321, 326; 11: 287, 323.

received a petition from Nathaniel Byfield, Esq., who served as attorney to the children and heirs of John Leverett, Esq., the late president of Harvard College. Because Leverett had overspent several hundred pounds while in office, his family and children were now deep in debt and therefore pleaded for relief. Apparently not finding sufficient cause for government to bail out a mismanaged estate, the House denied the petition.[111] Similarly, several children and grandchildren of James Taylor, Esq., deceased, former Treasurer of Massachusetts, petitioned for allowance for his extraordinary service. Their petition was denied by the House.[112]

As people increasingly looked to the provincial government for relief, the General Court got deeper and deeper into some unusual cases. Joseph Maylem, a resident in Boston, requested relief in 1727. He claimed that he had a judgment against a notorious thief John Taylor, who had broken into his house and stolen £144 of money and gold. Convicted, Taylor was sentenced to pay triple the damages and committed to jail. Yet Taylor escaped because of the poor guard and insufficient security of the Boston jail. Maylem therefore requested recourse. Although his loss was real, the House was not convinced that the provincial government was liable in this case. His petition was dismissed in 1727 and again in 1729.[113] At times the Court was simply unable to ascertain critical details at the local level and, consequently, refused to intervene. Perhaps based on this sort of consideration, the Court denied the petition by Josiah Cook, Joseph Scott, Jacob Barklett, and David Cook, residents of Bellingham who had been arrested by local constables "for want of estate" to pay the town assessment.[114] In another case, although the Court allowed £20 to subsidize Scarborough (Maine) to pay the Reverend Hugh Henry in 1725, it denied his request to force the town to fulfill an earlier promise to support him through local taxation and by drawing subsistence from the community store.[115] Also refused was the

---

[111] *Journal of the House of Representatives*, 6: 389.
[112] *Journal of the House of Representatives*, 8: 312.
[113] *Journal of the House of Representatives*, 8: 92-3; 9: 196-97.
[114] *Journal of the House of Representatives*, 8: 111.
[115] *Journal of the House of Representatives*, 6: 11, 67, 243, 256, 324, 348.

petition of John Malcolm, who described that he had been badly maimed by a barrel of pork falling on his leg while serving as a soldier under Captain Joshua Moodey in 1724.[116] A resident of Wells in Maine, Mr. John Storer claimed that Indians had killed his ox, worth £11, which was allowed by the Court.[117] However, James Denney failed to receive a positive response from the Court when he petitioned to receive wages due to his brother Robert Denney, who had been killed by Indians at Fort George.[118] Thus, a genuine misfortune did not necessarily lead to provincial relief, unless the Court could be persuaded that the provincial government should be responsible for the misery.[119]

Land Grant

In addition to the public treasury and a broad range of legal and administrative powers, one of the most valuable resources upon which the General Court relied was the lands and territories under its jurisdiction. Gained from Native American Indians, those lands would rarely go toward any direct help of the poor. Instead, land grant became a crucial instrument in sending hundreds of needy members of the lower and middle class families to the frontiers. Public relief in this form alleviated distress while expanding settlement into the hinterland, which in turn allowed both the poor and struggling members of the lower and middle class families to move and look for opportunities in those newly opened settlements. During the first two decades of the 1700s, the Court granted

---

[116] *Journal of the House of Representatives*, 6: 405, 420.
[117] *Journal of the House of Representatives*, 8: 208.
[118] *Journal of the House of Representatives*, 6: 406.
[119] When William Hansard, a captive by Indians, applied for relief in 1728, claiming his "necessitous circumstances," his petition was denied, *Journal of the House of Representatives*, 8: 286. Capt. Jonathan Bass of Bridgewater took a stranger Jeremiah Jones and prayed relief for his support. His petition was denied, ibid., 11: 350. The Court denied the petition by Joshua Higgins of Barnstable, claiming that his wife Priscilla did not get the one tenth of inheritance she deserved, ibid., 9: 254. The Court declined Isaac Temple's request to recover the money he won in a legal case, ibid., 9: 249. Nor did the Court grant a strong liquor license to Stephen Kingsley and his wife Elizabeth of Boston, ibid., 8: 259. Similarly, Mehitabel Selby of Boston was denied a permit to expand his Crown Coffee-House into a tavern, ibid., 8: 265.

more than 8,000 acres of land as relief or compensation to some 30 petitioners for their services in the past or present hardships of various degrees, averaging 270 acres a piece.[120] Excluding some large tracts totaling 4,200 acres to five prominent families,[121] another 30 grants were made through the 1730s.[122] For example, in 1735 alone, the General Court gave out another 6,000 acres to no fewer than 30 people from 17 families.[123]

The quickly disappearing public land perhaps alarmed the General Court, and the House summarily rejected 29 petitions for land grants on December 21, 1736.[124] Although authorities might have had some second thoughts about how to deal with the rising number of individual petitions, the push for land grants continued, especially under collective actions. For example, several descendants and employees of Joshua Scottow of Boston proposed a plan for 1,149 acres in addition to a grant of 200 acres. Also raised was another proposal for 500 acres to satisfy a petition by Samuel Hunt and others who had been in Fall Fights on the Connecticut River in 1676. Meanwhile, the children and heirs of the late Captain John Wainwright of Haverhill petitioned for a grant of 1,000 acres.[125] Perhaps under these pressures and organized demands, the General Court began to consider townships as a convenient means for satisfying collective petitioners. In 1736, 23,040 acres east of Deerfield were granted to petitioners led by Captain Ebenezer Hut. Meanwhile, the Court reviewed a grant of 1,500 acres to Thomas Plaisted, while looking into a plan of 6 square miles

---

[120] *Journal of the House of Representatives*, 1: 92-93, 102, 143, 161, 162; 8: 18, 42, 54-5, 111, 187, 206, 207, 215, 216, 254, 322; 9: 37-8, 95, 107, 136, 217, 358; 10: 351; 11: 12-3, 28, 30, 31, 75, 90, 124, 130, 132-33, 136, 181, 197, 239-40, 268, 290-91, 318, 333, 350, 381, 399-400, 408; 12: 10, 47, 59-60, 115, 118.
[121] These grants included the following: Governor Jonathan Belcher received 1,000 acres. In 1734 the Court renewed a 1685 grant of 500 acres to Capt. Stoddard Clark. *Journal of the House of Representatives*, 12: 74, 155. It granted Peter Bulkley of Concord 1,000 acres for his service as agent to England, 500 acres to Benjamin Church, Esq., deceased, and 1,200 acres to the heirs of Col. Edward Tyng of Boston, deceased. *Journal of the House of Representatives*, 12: 113, 192; 14: 37.
[122] *Journal of the House of Representatives*, 12: 113.
[123] *Journal of the House of Representatives*, 13: 38-40, 53, 135, 144, 180, 181, 188, 223, 226, 234, 272, 274, 285-86.
[124] *Journal of the House of Representatives*, 14: 167.
[125] *Journal of the House of Representatives*, 14: 62, 77, 132.

(about 22,000 acres) of a township for a petition submitted by Samuel Gallop and company.[126]

Against this backdrop, the province's preference of granting townships over individual tracts had far-reaching implications. A township was usually set at six square miles, and grantors had a minimum of five years to improve the land, including building a church and a public school. One of the earliest townships was granted to soldiers under Captain Robert Lovell, whose company marched in the Narragansett War against Indians in southern Massachusetts and Rhode Island. Located on the banks of the Merrimack River, the township, called Penny-Cook, was granted in 1728 to thirteen of the sixty-two men who had marched with Captain Lovell in 1691.[127] Unlike individual petitions, gaining a township could take a long time. John Goss and fifty-seven others, many of whom were veteran soldiers, petitioned for a six-square-mile township west of Lunenburg in 1728. Their petition was not granted until ten years later.[128] Colonel Joshua Lamb and others petitioned for a township for many years, which was not granted until 1731/2.[129] Not all grantors settled in the new townships. Some were too old and feeble to move, while others had either passed the right to their relations or sold the lot to those who were willing to move to the new communities. In either case, granting new townships—although an early effort to satisfy collective petitioners—pushed settlement into the frontiers and stimulated geographic expansion, population mobility, and agricultural improvement in remote territories.

Moreover, the provincial government's land grants and various relief actions had quietly cultivated a novel awareness among the citizens, who gradually began to see the General Court as the last public office that could save them from distress—an important new development not found in the mother country. Now that Massachusetts allowed both individual and collaborative petitioners to seek recourse at the provincial level, many—especially those who had served for

---

[126] *Journal of the House of Representatives*, 14: 60, 78, 118.
[127] *Journal of the House of Representatives*, 8: 254, 266.
[128] *Journal of the House of Representatives*, 8: 312.
[129] *Journal of the House of Representatives*, 10: 360-61.

the commonwealth—fully expected to receive a reasonable reply from the General Court, which indeed had the power to reverse lower courts' rulings, mend official mistakes, and grant cash compensation, licenses, permits, land, and even townships to those groups of petitioners for relief.

In summary, the transplantation of the English poor law system into the colony underwent a process of mixing and adaptation. Unlike England, where large crowds of the poor swamped urban centers (particularly London), the poor in Massachusetts did not congregate in Boston, but scattered across the colony. Many became permanently poor not because of some single cause of economic or social degradation, but because of a large variety of reasons and conditions, such as old age, declining health, wounds, injuries, and other disabilities. Acting under the long-established principles of paternalism and local responsibilities, villages and towns closely followed the English tradition to maintain the needy, including those Native Indians, African Americans, and women who were indeed legal inhabitants of a community while excluding those white men, women, and children who were not. Thus, insofar as public relief was concerned, the configuration of the impotent poor of those days had a crucial but latent definition that later generations sometimes overlooked: The importance of a person's legal residence superseded the kind of racial and gender classifications frequently highlighted in modern consciousness. For example, a community had both the moral and legal obligations to support a local poor widow or an aged African American, but not a white male stranger. The configuration of the deserving poor and the eligibility of public assistance could thus shift decidedly not because of one's gender or race, but because of the person's lawful settlement and community membership, which were the decisive qualifications for local relief.

Limited to basic necessities and often struggling for funds, the minimum support most colonial communities provided was never enough to eradicate poverty. Yet the variety of assistance eased the pains the poor and many members of the lower and middle classes were suffering. Local relief prevented some of the most vulnerable from becoming homeless, such as widows, widowers, orphans, the lame, the blind, and the sick. Even educating the children of the poor in the almshouse was a normal expenditure in Boston. The willingness of the provincial government to review both individual and group petitions added a new dimension of colonial relief. As the highest legislative, legal, and administrative authority, the General Court combined its strengths and provided a new venue for assistance—a noteworthy departure from the English poor law practice. Dispensing relief through a small pension, a business license, or a land grant, the provincial government became a place where middle class families and especially grieved citizens, government employees, and veteran soldiers could seek their recourse.

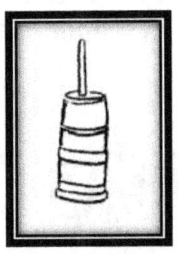

Chapter Two

Financing Relief

Recent scholarship has significantly extended the studies of diverse categories of the poor, whose varied conditions contributed to the floating characteristics of eighteenth-century poverty. Some such characteristics appeared as regional, religious, and cultural variations, whereas others showed in separate race, gender, or age groups.[1] Nonetheless, a missing angle is that historians have often studied colonial poverty as a social and economic problem,[2] but seldom as a financial one. This omission has obscured a fundamental problem that troubled not only the poor, but also the middle classes, who were the main sponsors of charity and relief. Thus, finding a way to improve colonial business and

---

[1] See the wide range of essays and topics in Carla Gardina Pestana and Sharon V. Salinger, eds., *Inequality in Early America* (Hanover, N.H.: University Press of New England, 1999), and in Billy G. Smith, ed., *Down and Out in Early America* (University Park, Penn.: Pennsylvania State University Press, 2004).
[2] See the works cited in the introduction by Gary B. Nash, Carl Bridenbaugh, James A. Henretta, Jesse Lemisch, Stephen Foster, Allan Kulikoff, Douglas Lamar Jones, and Alfred F. Young.

finance would benefit a broad spectrum of people, from lower to middle classes. This chapter uses Boston as a case in point to demonstrate what new information a financial perspective can

Design of Massachusetts paper currency, a bill of six pence. *Acts and Resolves*, 1737, Chapter 11, passed 2 July 1737.

provide for understanding the trans-economic, trans-class, and trans-urban nature of colonial poverty. After an assessment of private charity and public relief, it reexamines and reinterprets those events leading to the establishment of the Boston Linen Manufactory in the 1750s.[3]

---

[3] William R. Bagnall told the stories of the linen manufactory in *Textile Industries of the United States* (1893; New York, 1971), 1:13-19, 28-50. Recent and more extensive studies include Gary B. Nash, "The Failure of Female Factory Labor in Colonial Boston," *Labor History* 20(1970):165-88 (see also his *Urban Crucible*, 189-197); Eric G. Nellis, "Misreading the Signs: Industrial Imitation, Poverty, and the Social Order in Colonial Boston," *New England Quarterly* 59 (1986):486-507; and Laurel Thatcher Ulrich, "Sheep in the Parlor, Wheels on the Common: Pastoralism and Poverty in Eighteenth-Century Boston," in *Inequality in Early America*, 182-200. For comments on Nash's interpretation see the introduction. Focusing on "the intersection of class, gender, and textiles" (193), Ulrich noted that the manufactory might have had a chance to succeed if the economic benefit to the employees had been greater, but she tried not to disagree with Nash directly. See also another account in her book *The Age of Homespun: Objects and Stories in the Creation of an American Myth* (New York: Alfred A. Knopf, 2001), 155-66. Nellis realistically pointed out that as the first centralized and integrated factory of textiles, the Boston linen manufactory had only a "token success" in poor relief and a "modest achievement" in production. The manufactory ultimately failed for its subscribers gravely underestimated the difficulties to carry out their grand design, which was to imitate the successful textile productions in Ireland and Scotland. Unable to compete either with the imported textiles at the high end or with the local homespun products at the low end, the linen manufacture folded in 1759. Not speculating on the sociopolitical motives of those supporting the scheme as Nash did, Nellis saw over-enthusiasm, underestimation in planning, and numerous problems in production as the main causes for the failed enterprise.

Private Charity

By the mid 1700s, about fifteen churches—from Congregationalist and Episcopalian to Baptist and Society of Friends—ministered to Boston's faithful, averaging about one church for every thousand souls.[4] They constituted the town's single largest private source for charity. The churches acquired their funding through pew assessments and contributions made at weekly services. The funds would pay for the salary of a pastor, regular church upkeep (pew cleaning, washing surplice and linen), and the purchase of bread and wine. Whatever money remained after the deduction of these basic costs supported charitable activity.[5]

The amount of money churches needed to collect each week depended upon regular expenses and the pastor's salary, which varied considerably from congregation to congregation. King's Chapel, for example, had to collect £12 to £13 each week,[6] or a yearly equivalent of about £650, to maintain its

---

[4] Boston Record Commissioners, *Report of the Record Commissioners of the City of Boston* (Boston, 1876-1894), 1:4, 6. Cited hereafter as *RRC* in this chapter.
[5] In Boston, unlike elsewhere in Massachusetts, the established churches received no tax revenue.
[6] Unless otherwise indicated, all value amounts are cited in colonial money. Those values can only be understood in relative terms for the exchange rate between Massachusetts currency and the British sterling fluctuated widely throughout the colonial period, especially prior to 1750. See John J. McCusker, *Money and Exchange in Europe and America, 1600-1775: A Handbook* (Chapel Hill, N.C., 1978), especially chapter 3. Massachusetts currency changed from public bills of credit (later referred to as "Old Tenor") to "Lawful Money" in 1750, when the ratio was set at £7.50 Old Tenor to £1.00 Lawful Money, as many continued to keep accounts in Old Tenor. Additionally, pre-1750 issues of paper bills of credit also included New Tenor and Middle Tenor, redeemed at a ratio of £4 Old Tenor to £1 New or Middle Tenor. When the paper currency was first issued in 1690, the exchange ratio was set at £128.33 Massachusetts bills of credit to £100 sterling. About sixty years later in 1749, the ratio reached as high as £1,050 to £100 sterling. When the Lawful Money appeared on March 31, 1750, the new ratio was about £125 Lawful Money (or about £937.50 Old Tenor) to £100 sterling. This ratio then fluctuated within the range of £129 to £135 Lawful Money to £100 sterling until the eve of the American Revolution. McCusker, *Money and Exchange*, 133, 146-50.

pastor and basic church services.[7] Members of most congregations made their contributions in very small amounts that included coppers and wood pence. If they failed to meet their weekly obligations, the church might be unable to pay its pastor and its accounts would immediately fall into arrears. Savings from past profitable years might be used to cover a current deficit, but unless a congregation could secure large sums in donations, it lived at the financial edge and depended on weekly contributions for survival.[8]

Each denomination followed established practices for collecting and distributing charitable funds. Congregational First Church obtained money for poor relief along with regular weekly collections but dispensed it only several times annually. According to the extant records for the early 1700s, the yearly expenditures for charity ranged from £30 in 1717 to £64 in 1723. There were as many as twenty or thirty names on the church's poor list in any given year, with each person receiving between £1.10s. and £1.15s. annually. The widow Bumstead, for example, remained on the list for over fifteen years, from 1715 to 1731.[9] The amount of money she and others received may seem modest, but given that most churches in Boston of this period contained only 150 to 200 families, one cannot help but be impressed that First Church assisted so many people for so long a period of time.

---

[7] King's Chapel records, 1686-1931, box 1, Massachusetts Historical Society (hereafter MHS in this chapter); King's Chapel Records, Financial Records, 1724-1899, box 1, folders 1, 3, 7, 9, 10, 13, 14, 15, 16, 26, 31; box 2, folder 1; box 2, ledger; oversize box 1, MHS.

[8] For example, the Old South (Third) Church collected £67. 18s. 1d. in 1710, but spent £83. 8s. 8d. in the same year. Only savings from previous years maintained the balance of the church accounts. See Joseph Ballard, *Account of the Poor Fund and Other Charities Held in Trust by the Old South Society in Boston* (Boston, 1868), 162-63.

[9] Account book, 1696-1737, Poor relief records of the First Church of Boston, 1696-1737, MHS.

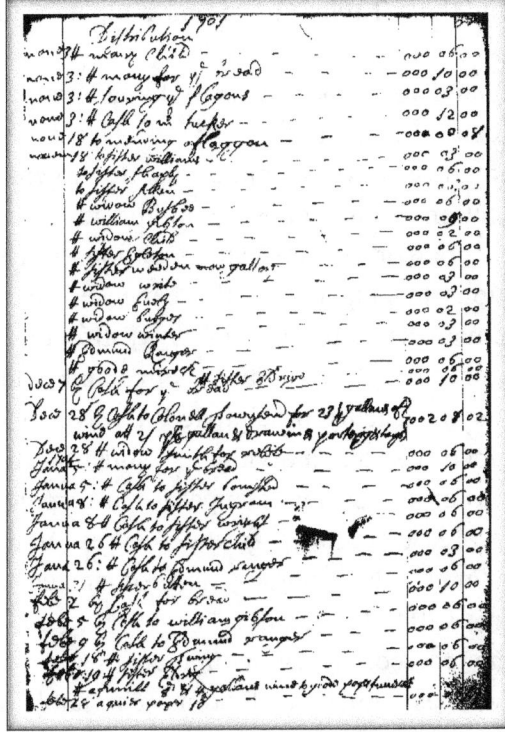

Dispensation of charity to the poor, November 3, 1701, to February 28, 1701/2, The First Church (Old North) in Boston. Religious institutions were a primary source of private charity. (Massachusetts Historical Society)

In line with Anglican tradition, King's Chapel needed a large regular poor collection not only because it supported thirty to forty people but because it dispensed assistance on a weekly basis. On average, the church's weekly cash payments to the poor ranged from £1.7s. to £2.5s., making the demand for charitable donations about £90 to £100 a year. Church records show that many people, such as John Lucas, Sarah Morrison, Elizabeth Hall, Ann Hays, and Lazarus Hubbard, received support on a regular basis for at least several years while others (Christopher Proctor, Elizabeth Gray, John Jarvis, Mrs.

Wainwright, and Jane Taylor) remained recipients for no less than a decade.[10]

Weekly and yearly payments to the indigent constituted only one—albeit the largest—portion of church charity; unexpected circumstances sometimes led to urgent calls for additional collections. Funeral costs could be a heavy burden to many a family, poor or not, and congregations often initiated special collections to help defray the expenses. A variety of natural and human disasters, then as now, also created need, which the churches sought to address. Fires and epidemics, in and around Boston, usually precipitated a wave of charitable need, and sometimes an individual's situation proved so unfortunate as to arouse special sympathy. In response to poor "Mrs. Lasinby breast cut off," as the records of the Brattle Street Church note, the congregation organized a special collection to give £20 to her family.[11]

As time passed, a few congregations expanded the variety of resources aimed at funding charitable activities. Parishioners sometimes made separate cash donations or left real estate legacies, while others created funds for their churches with the accumulated interest earmarked for poor relief. Between 1711 and 1773, Old South Church received twenty-four sizeable charities, including bequests by Captain John Armitage, Deacon Daniel Henchman, Reverend Ebenezer Pemberton, Mary Ireland, Dr. Joseph Sewall, and Thomas

---

[10] King's Chapel records, Financial Records, 1724-1899, box 1, folders 15, 26, MHS. Casting private charity in Boston in a harsh light, one recent examination of poor relief during the First Great Awakening found that "Boston's revival of piety did not loosen their purse strings significantly." Yet the affluent Brattle Street Church dispensed poor offerings averaging £26 per month in 1740 and 1741, making it the city's most generous private institution. That average increased 30 percent to £34 per month in 1743, or over £400 a year—an astonishing level of giving. See J. Richard Olivas, "'God Helps Those Who Help Themselves': Religious Explanations of Poverty in Colonial Massachusetts, 1630-1776," in *Down and Out in Early America*, 276. Olivas's calculations were based on Brattle Street Church's Treasurer Records now in the Department of Rare Books and Manuscripts, Boston Public Library.

[11] Ellis Loring Motte et al., eds., *The Manifest Church: Records of the Church in Brattle Square, Boston, 1699-1872* (Boston, 1902), 25.

Bromfield. Several of their wills specified that all income produced by their invested legacies be distributed to the poor.[12] For example, widow Mary Ireland, a church member from 1703 to 1763, left £133. 6s. 8d. in her will for the poor in addition to the proceeds from selling her estates after the death of her sister Ann Staats, who was to inherit the properties first. Daniel Henchman, an enterprising bookseller at Cornhill near King Street and a long-time overseer of the poor in Boston, gave £65. 13s. 4d. to the poor at his death.[13]

Neither Boston nor any other town offered unbounded charity for the poor. Recipients of assistance not only had to be members in good standing of a church, they also had to suffer unusual circumstances. Poverty alone did not make them eligible for support. The able-bodied poor, especially if "idle," were largely denied any benefits. The Boston Episcopal Charitable Society's charter declared that "All Vagrants Idle and dissolute Persons, of Notorious evil fame are excepted or excluded as unworthy this Charity."[14] Other private charitable organizations had similar provisions. The Scots' Charitable Society, founded in 1657, and the Charitable Irish Society, founded in 1737, clearly stated in their charters, using strikingly similar language, that the charitable contributions of the membership would never be disbursed to "vagrants," "idle persons," or "people of evil repute."[15]

Building renovation and reconstruction, however, placed far more severe limitations on religious charity. During the first half of the eighteenth century several Boston churches replaced or refurbished their meetinghouses, constructed

---

[12] See Ballard, *Account of the Poor Fund*, 10-19.
[13] Mrs. Margaret Blackadore bequeathed more than £66 to the poor of Boston in 1760. *Boston Post-Boy*, August 18, 1760.
[14] Charters (1724, 1741, 1758), Boston Episcopal Charitable Society records, 1724-1905, MHS.
[15] Rules and Orders Agreed upon by the Irish Society in New England for the Management of their Charity, Irish Charitable Society records, 1737-1939, MHS; Scots' Charitable Society, *Rules and Regulations of the Scots' Charitable Society* (Boston, 1800).

decades earlier. New church construction in particular absorbed significant amounts of a congregation's financial resources, making greater distribution of poor relief unlikely. Ten days after a fire destroyed its old wooden meetinghouse in 1711, First Church decided to replace it with a brick building. A grand three-story edifice (later known as the "Old Brick"), the new construction cost £3,849, not counting a new parsonage at £354.[16] Trinity Church borrowed £10,431 for a new structure, including the cost of manufacturing and shipping an organ, and had to repay the loan between 1730 and 1740.[17] King's Chapel, in 1747, topped all rebuilding efforts with an estimated cost of £35,000, not including the £5,000 for a proposed new school plus other accessories.[18]

Since these projects and other new construction created enormous costs, they placed great pressures on church collections. After Old South Church began a collection for its new meetinghouse in 1728, the total amount of its charity given to the poor dropped sharply. The congregation had been dispensing £30 or more a year for many years, but in 1729 it dropped to £9. The church acknowledged that although special subscriptions had defrayed the costs of building the meetinghouse and repairing the parsonage, it remained "so cramped for money in July, 1747, that they were obliged to borrow of the 'church-fund for the poor' £192. 0s. 7d. to pay

---

[16] The new First Church building measured 72 feet long, 44 wide, and 34 high; in 1739, repair of the building cost £131. See *Records of the First Church of Boston, 1630-1868*, vol. 41 of *Publications of the Colonial Society of Massachusetts* (Boston, 1961), 125, 126, 127, 128, 186-87. George E. Ellis indicated that the building was 54 feet wide in his *History of the First Church in Boston, 1630-1880* (Boston, 1881), 170-73. When parishioners came for the Sabbath for the first time on May 3, 1713, Reverend Benjamin Wadsworth gave a sermon entitled "The Glory of This Latter House Shall Be Greater Than the Former." Ellis, *History of the First Church*.

[17] *The Records of Trinity Church, Boston, 1728-1830*, vol. 55 of *Publications of the Colonial Society of Massachusetts* (Boston, 1980-1982), 469-70.

[18] Those figures did not include the additional cost for a church organ at £762 and the cost for furnishing the altar at £67. 8s. sterling. Various financial records, 1747-1764, King's Chapel records, box 1, folders 7, 9, 10, 13, 14, and 15; box 2, folder 1, MHS. See also Henry Wilder Foote, *The Annals of King's Chapel from the Puritan Age of New England to the Present Day* (Boston, 1882-1896, 1940), 1:88-90, 2:42-127.

off 'the deficiency of our ministers.'"[19] However much a congregation felt obliged to offer poor relief, such efforts would always be limited—and sometimes crippled—by the institution's other competing demands and obligations.

Public Relief

Unlike private institutions, which could choose to limit the scope of their charitable offerings, Boston's civil authorities faced broader and more complex obligations of public relief. The town could not ignore provincial laws mandating that it care for the indigent and dispose of the idle or able-bodied poor. Both the almshouse for the former and the workhouse for the latter came under the supervision of the overseers of the poor, who received funds from the town treasury.[20] Yet this simple Elizabethan division, or what the nineteenth century would label the "deserving" and "undeserving" poor, did not accurately reflect colonial realities, nor could the two traditional categories address the problems posed by transients in Boston.[21]

Although not all transients were poor, many proved needy (details in chapter three). Attracted to Boston as the largest seaport and urban center in New England, transients arrived as overseas immigrants, regional migrants, or refugees displaced by war and other natural and human disasters. At first glance, such cases might not seem to pose a serious problem to civil authorities who were under no obligation to

---

[19] Ballard, *Account of the Poor Fund*, 160-76.
[20] For more extensive treatment of the almshouse, the workhouse, and the overseers of the poor in Boston, see Eric Nellis's introduction to *Eighteenth-Century Records of the Boston Overseers of the Poor* (Boston: Colonial Society of Massachusetts, 2007), 17-102.
[21] Eric Nellis also draws the attention to the "working poor," who were mostly the unskilled day laborers. See "The Working Poor of Pre-Revolutionary Boston," *Historical Journal of Massachusetts* 37(1989):137-59. This important category deserves serious further investigation.

assist individuals not recognized as lawful inhabitants of the town. According to provincial law, a person would have to live

Boston overseers of the poor inspected the wards on Wednesday, September 26, 1711. In Ward No. 8, they found Ruth Willey's "frequent resort of men" in the evening, Jersey Jane and daughter making punch early in the morning, several dirty and ragged children who could hardly read, and still some who were of "bad character" and "very defective as to attendance of the public worship." (New England Historic Genealogical Society)

in a community for twelve months before he or she could claim relief.[22] The town could demand a surety of £100 from each new adult migrant and £50 for a child or an elderly person. The money served as an indemnity against the person later becoming a public charge. Anyone unable to afford the surety or find someone willing to post a bond on his or her behalf would be expelled.[23] Like other New England towns, Boston also maintained a "warning out" system, primarily designed to expel poor people who unexpectedly arrived in town. Those who appeared likely to become a financial burden received a

---

[22] For most of the seventeenth century, the law required only three months of residency before becoming an inhabitant. See Nathaniel B. Shurtleff, ed., *Records of the Governor and Company of the Massachusetts Bay in New England* (Boston, 1853-1854), vol. 4, pt.1, p. 365; and *Acts and Resolves, Public and Private, of the Province of the Massachusetts Bay* (Boston, 1869-1922), 1:67. An Act Directing the Admission of Town Inhabitants in 1691 extended that required period to twelve months, which was reaffirmed in 1723. See *Acts and Resolves*, 1:451-53, 2:244-45.

[23] *RRC*, 10:81, 15:242-43, 17:27, 45, 80, 87, 19:70-71.

warning notice subjecting them to a legal removal from the town.[24]

For a variety of reasons, few of these governmental restrictions worked as intended. Boston residents occasionally encouraged some indigents to stay, such as when a Bostonian invited a friend or relative who needed help to remain or when a master tried to retain cheap labor or a servant. Citizens who failed to report transients to the authorities, or even deliberately hid them, became such a headache that in 1743 a town meeting appointed Deacon William Larrabee (tailor) as a searcher with authorization to inspect every household and report the arrival of any strangers.[25]

Official British imperial policies—aimed at the French—and the chaos of the frontier created additional frustration for Boston's civil leaders. In 1703, for example, the provincial government placed Priscilla Smart, a helpless girl who had been driven from Black Point on the Maine border, under the care of the Boston overseers of the poor. The cost of £4. 8s. per year for Smart's care would appear to be an insignificant part of the overseers' expenditures, except that her support lasted for the next ten years.[26] The refugee crisis built up through the first half of the century and culminated at the end of the King George's War (1744-1748), and it reached epidemic proportions through the years of the French and Indian War. In 1707 alone, Boston had to raise an emergency fund of £1,300 to handle the escalating cost of refugee assistance. Throughout the 1740s and 1750s, the almshouse routinely received, on order of the provincial government, wounded soldiers and war prisoners as well as women and

---

[24] *RRC*, 10:55, 13:76, 127, 128, 17:49, 56, 87, 19:38, 39, 40, 42, 44, 46, 49, 56, 59, 132.
[25] *RRC*, 17:44. Several years later, the town also appointed Thomas Williston (cordwainer) and Captain Isaac Dupee (merchant/mariner) as searchers. *RRC*, 19:48-49, 115-16.
[26] *Acts and Resolves . . . of the Province of Massachusetts Bay*, 8:43, 9:298. The province did reimburse the cost of buying shoes and coats for Miss Smart, but not the cost for her regular maintenance of food and shelter.

children displaced by war. Sometimes as many as forty or sixty people would be sent at once, the equivalent of half of the number of the almshouse's regular inmates.[27] On December 26, 1755, a thousand Acadian refugees landed in Boston, part of the nearly seven thousand "French Neutrals" expelled by British authorities from Nova Scotia. Arriving in winter "without the means of support," many of refugees were "aged and broken down in health and spirits." "Even by the laws of war," one local historian recorded, "we do not see how the subsequent treatment of the Acadians could be justified."[28] The contest over who would be responsible to support the refugees (and for how long) became a political ball game. Royal governors, such as Francis Bernard, insisted that local and provincial governments should pay while the latter thought it the responsibility of the crown and his treasury. Claiming they had neither authority nor policy to deal with the foreign poor, Boston overseers of the poor demanded answers from town selectmen, who in turn pressed shipmasters for the regular £100 indemnity for each passenger in misery.[29]

Paying the increasing demands of poor relief proved burdensome. For the first half of the eighteenth century, poor relief constituted one third to one half of the town's yearly assessments,[30] which rose more than ten times from £1,200 in

---

[27] *RRC*, 17:80, 81, 84, 19:50, 57. For more details, see Nellis, introduction to *Eighteenth-Century Records of the Boston Overseers of the Poor*, 113-269.

[28] John G. Metcalf, comp., *Annals of the Town of Mendon from 1659 to 1880* (Providence, R.I., 1880), 275. The most recent account of this tragedy is John Mack Faragher, *A Great and Noble Scheme: The Tragic Story of the Expulsion of the French Acadians from Their American Homeland* (New York, 2005).

[29] Massachusetts General Court and House of Representatives, *Journals of the House of Representatives of Massachusetts*, ed. Worthington Chauncey Ford et al. (Boston, 1919-1990), vol. 32, pt. 2, pp. 285, 317-19, vol. 39:107-08; *RRC*, 19:38, 43, 47, 88, 110, 117-19, 138, 142, 146, 185-87, 193-94, 196, 213-14, 224-26, 239-41, 259, 261-63, 271, 285, 295.

[30] Public relief in Boston, as Nellis pointed out, came in two forms: "outdoor relief" (to private homes) and "indoor relief" (in a public facility such as the almshouse). See his introduction, *Eighteenth-Century Records of the Boston Overseers of the Poor*, 18, 66-68. The yearly expenditures for indoor and outdoor relief from 1738 to 1768 were summarized in Stephen Edward Wiberley, Jr., Four Cities: Public Poor Relief in Urban America, 1700-

1714-1715 to £15,000 in 1745; the latter figure almost doubled to £27,000 three years later.[31] Collecting these assessments on schedule was rare while demands for relief never stopped rising; town officials, therefore, often spent more than they took in. Compounding the situation, provincial taxes also sharply increased through the 1740s:

1743-1744	£3,600
1744-1745	£4,500
1745-1746	£5,400
1746-1747	£5,129
1747-1748	£7,050
1748-1749	£16,380[32]

Tax collection proved especially difficult during this same period when Boston suffered a prolonged population decline and economic downturn, reducing the number of taxpayers by as much as 20 percent, from 3,395 in 1738 to 2,660 in 1745.[33]

The collection also became more difficult, because the scarcity of currency, always a chronic problem in the colonial era, impeded tax payments. Tax collectors, rather than individual payers, who bore prime responsibility for returning tax money to the town treasury, seldom completed their yearly assignments and frequently petitioned for extensions.[34] One person, it seems, understood the problems better than any Bostonian:

1775, Ph.D. diss., Yale University, 1975, p. 76. Nellis analyzed his figures in his introduction to *Eighteenth-Century Records of the Boston Overseers of the Poor*, 68n.

[31] See specific assessment figures in *RRC*, 8:111 (1714-1715), 176 (1723), 221 (1728), 12:110 (1735), 173 (1737), 14:75 (1745), 151 (1748).

[32] *Acts and Resolves . . . of the Province of Massachusetts Bay*, 3:88, 158, 225, 281, 347, 391.

[33] Quoted in Nash, "Failure of Female Factory Labor," 167, and his *Urban Crucible*, 407.

[34] Attempts by town officials to increase revenue collection rates showed mixed results. *RRC*, 8:113, 149, 12:251, 14:89.

The Petition of Mr. John Staniford one of the Collectors of Taxes for this Town, setting forth that many People in his list have dyed beyond sea, . . . and many men have died at home so poor that nothing could be obtained Praying that the Assessors may be Impowered at the time of their making up the Taxes for the year 1745, to make such Abatements as in their Judgment they shall see meet.[35]

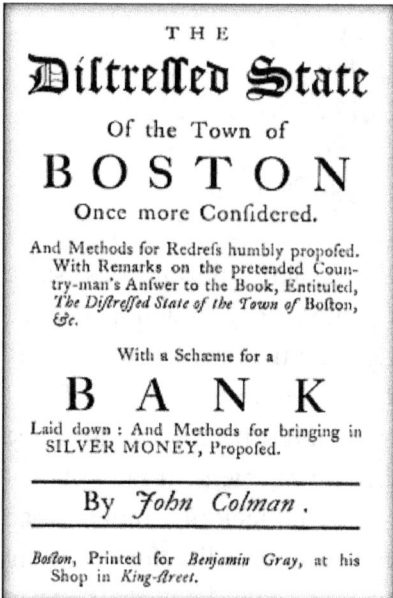

Title page of John Colman's *Distressed State of the Town of Boston* [1720]. An early proponent of liberal policies, he wrote that "if the Government will not come in a project of a Private Bank, I can think of nothing better, then [original] to go on some great & Expensive Work, & Emit Bills to carry it on, as Fortifyng our exposed Settlements, that would Encourage People to sit down, & till the Earth, and raise Hemp and Flax, and so bring down the Prices of Linen and Canvas, as well as Provisions, that we may be able to Export Provisions as in former times to the Islands, whereas we are now beholding to our Neighbours to supply us, this would help to Ballance our Foreign Trade, and consequently in time be a means to bring Silver among us."

Caught between the rising need for tax revenues and the uncertainties of collection, Boston authorities remonstrated before the General Court against the unusually high rate of provincial taxes. They warned that unless conditions changed, it "will Finally be the utter ruine of the Town."[36] They also argued for reductions in expenditures, advice that an auditing

---

[35] *RRC*, 14:88-89.
[36] *RRC*, 19:52. See also 12:177-78 and 14:238.

committee of the town took seriously to assert more control over the almshouse to reduce costs. Eliminating doctors' visits to the institution and replacing them with "a Box of Medicines," they suggested, would be a measure "necessary for reducing the Expences of the Town in Supporting the Almshouse." The committee further proposed that "considering the great Charges the town is at, the Committee humbly move that it be Recommended to all who have the disposal of the Town's money to be as frugal as the nature of the respective Services, and the Interest of the whole will admit."[37] No one, apparently, questioned the impact of such measures on the poor.

    Overseers of the poor could indeed play an important role in reducing expenses. When town funds were not available, for example, they could use their own money rather than seeking credit for official purchases, which permitted them to obtain lower prices for goods and services. Town authorities allowed the practice, since reimbursing overseers, even with interest, proved more economical than using credit.[38] The total cost of maintaining the almshouse and workhouse represented the most expensive items on the overseers' accounts. Records show that for the first nineteen months after the establishment of the workhouse in 1739, the town spent £2,451 for its operations.[39] In 1748, for example, a few individual bills submitted by the master of the workhouse alone amounted to as much as £700. Suspecting that more than the demands of the poor caused the high expenses, the overseers made a personnel change. At a meeting in 1751, they unanimously voted to hire Joseph Lasinbee as the new master. The choice appears to have been an astute one. Surviving accounts of Lasinbee's charges show yearly bills no greater than £30, a drastic turnaround.

---

[37] *RRC*, 14:198-99.
[38] *RRC*, 16:6-7.
[39] Wiberley, "Four Cities," 95-96. Nellis, introduction to *Eighteenth-Century Records of the Boston Overseers of the Poor*, 105-06.

Obviously impressed by Lasinbee's cost reductions, the overseers for the first time in their history voted to reward the master of the workhouse by adding £20 to his annual salary.[40]

An Alternative

A beleaguered Boston found a new remedy to cope with poverty when the linen manufactory opened its doors in 1751.[41] Neither a form of private charity nor one of public relief, the manufacturing enterprise chose what modern economists would call a "job creation" approach to the problem of poverty.[42] Facing ever-dwindling sources of money for both public and private charitable purposes, promoters of the new manufacturing venture offered a unique option: employ needy women and children in spinning and weaving. An ambitious and publicly subscribed industrial scheme, the linen manufactory offered the possibility of simultaneously employing the indigent and promoting the growth of flax in the colony, thereby reducing dependence upon imported textiles, lowering the burden of poor relief on the town, and offering profit-sharing for investors. Subscribers to the plan believed that

---

[40] Workhouse records, 1751-1755, Boston Overseers of the Poor records, 1733-1925, MHS. These items are also available in the microfilm, reel 12, folder 13.

[41] For similar efforts to promote spinning and linen production, such as early interest aroused by the arrival of some weavers from Northern Ireland toward the end of the 1710s, the first spinning school in the 1720s, and the lingering attempt to revitalize the textile business after the 1750s, see Bagnall, *Textile Industries of the United States*, 1:16-19, 28-50; Nash, "The Failure of Female Factory Labor,"165-88 (see also his *Urban Crucible*, 189-97); Nellis, "Misreading the Signs," 486-507; and Ulrich, "Sheep in the Parlor,"182-200.

[42] Nellis has pointed out this mixed nature of the enterprise. See his "Misreading the Signs," 489-90. Differing from Nash's characterization that the manufactory was an exclusively upper-class scheme, he wrote that "one of its novel features was that it was to be funded by broad voluntary individual subscription and not by a narrow alliance of business interests. It was the first nongovernment but public association in America founded for the development of an industry tied both to productive employment of the poor and to commercial enterprise."

Temporary Methods of Relief are very commendable, till something better can be established; but these are of the Nature of Palliatives only; it must be a lasting and permanent Scheme, that may be expected to reach the Root of this Malady. The Linen Manufacture, when thoroughly understood, will appear to be such a Scheme, and under proper Cultivation will, it is apprehended, enlarge it self into a noble Design, so as not only to yield present Relief to great Numbers of poor People, but by gradually extending it Self to all Parts of the Province, seems to promise a perpetual Establishment.[43]

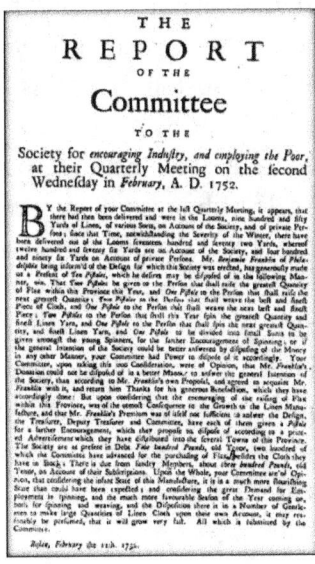

Report of the Committee to the Society for Encouraging Industry and Employing the Poor, February 1752, Boston. It records that Mr. Benjamin Franklin of Philadelphia donated ten pistoles (Spanish gold coins worth 12 to 15s. each) to the endeavors in Boston, his birthplace. (Massachusetts Historical Society)

Although public interest in textile production as a means to deal with poverty had come up in the past,[44] two recent factors

---

[43] Society for Encouraging Industry and Employing the Poor, *Rules of Incorporation for the Society for Encouraging Industry and Employing the Poor* (Boston, 1754), 2-3.
[44] Bay Colony authorities knew the importance of spinning and weaving from the beginning of settlement, and early encouragement to grow hemp and flax stretched back to the 1600s

made the proposal more enticing. The first of these, a serious economic contraction after King George's War, closed many Boston businesses. At the end of the 1740s, for instance, thirty butchers made a living in town; by 1752, all but two or three had closed their shops. The output of cod fishing was cut almost in half. Similar declines took place in the tanning, currying, and shoemaking trades, while "the great decay," as Bostonians called it, also "wreacked havoc" in shipbuilding (plus its 30 affiliated crafts) and distilling, the area's two principal industries.[45] Owners abandoned six local still houses, and those that remained operated at reduced capacities, unable to compete with those expanding shops in Rhode Island, New York, Philadelphia, and elsewhere in the colony. Likewise, when many shipbuilding jobs left Boston for Newburyport or Marblehead and even for Rhode Island, fear gripped the population, moving many to view Boston as "this Once flourishing but now sinking Town."[46]

The precipitous drop in work, as steep as three-quarters of regular business, destroyed the livelihoods of hundreds of shipwrights, naval stores suppliers, blacksmiths, ship joiners, riggers, rope-, stay-, and sail-makers, and other day laborers. The devastation also deprived the poor of one of the few employment opportunities available in the area: shipyards traditionally hired the poor to caulk seams and pick oakum.[47] As the town's economic conditions were deteriorating and the numbers of needy increasing, Boston had to find an alternative

---

when most settlers ignored the colonial government's premiums awarding those who could grow high quality hemp and flax. The arrival of a number of weavers from Northern Ireland in 1718 stirred up local interest in establishing a spinning school. A second move to advocate spinning schools took place in 1735. Bagnall, *Textile Industries of the United States*, 1:1-8; *RRC*, 8:147, 148, 153, 162, 163, 13:76.

[45] William Douglass, *A Summary, Historical and Political, of the First Planting, Progressive Improvements, and Present State of the British Settlements in North-America* (London, 1755), 1: 531, 540.

[46] *RRC*, 14:240.

[47] Nellis, introduction to *Eighteenth-Century Records of the Boston Overseers of the Poor*, 109-10.

solution to the almshouse and the workhouse, both of which depended on public financing. The proposed new textile industry seemed ideal, offering work to the poor and new economic opportunities for the community.

Second, a series of publications on textiles, printed in the British Isles, appeared in Boston, such as the *Extracts from the Essays of the Dublin Society Relating to the Culture and Manufacture of Flax* (1748) and Thomas Prior's *Essay to Encourage and Extend the Linen-Manufacture in Ireland by Premiums and Other Means* (1749).[48] They must have struck a chord in Boston readers who were facing questions of how to find new ways to expand employment and how to deal with the increasing pressure of poor relief. The extensive information and practical advice about flax culture in those pamphlets were particularly appealing, and some glorious predictions of the great benefit of this industry could not have been more tantalizing. One author stipulated that 8,000 acres would produce 1,600 tons of flax, which would in turn employ as many as 48,000 people a year![49] No less enthusiastic was Jared Eliot, a Connecticut minister and physician. In 1748, after thirty years of travel and observation, he published *Essay upon Field-Husbandry* to present his argument that hemp and hemp trade could become the staple to New England that tobacco was to Virginia, rice to Carolina, and sugar to the West Indies.[50]

---

[48] That promotional literature would also include Charles Foreman's *Letter to the Right Honourable Sir Robert Walpole, for Re-establishing the Woollen Manufacturies of Great Britain upon their Ancient Footing, by Encouraging the Linen Manufactures of Ireland* (London, 1732), the Dublin Society's *Essays and Observations* (Dublin; London, 1740), and the anonymous *Remarks on the Present State of the Linnen-Manufacture of this Kingdom and Queries Relating to the Further Improvement Thereof* (Dublin, 1745). The Massachusetts Historical Society has copies of each. The suggestion that the dissemination of Richard Cox's letter of 1750 in Boston (see below) had a singular importance during this period seems to have exaggerated reality. See Nash, "Failure of Female Factory Labor," 174-75, and his *Urban Crucible*, 190-91.
[49] *Remarks on the Present State of the Linnen-Manufacture*, 6.
[50] Jared Eliot, *Essays upon Field Husbandry in New England and Other Papers, 1748-1762* (New York, 1967), 3, 15-16.

The huge potential of flax cultivation and linen manufacture seemed like a panacea. By 1750, when Richard Cox issued his rejoinder to Prior's essay,[51] a subscription drive, undertaken in 1748, for establishing a linen manufactory in Boston had already obtained thirty-five people's signatures (a dozen of them being overseers of the poor), promising £2,250 in support.[52] In the end, the manufacture scheme gathered just under £10,000 in total support. It included, in addition to the sum from the 1748-1750 drive, £1,824 advanced by Thomas Gunter (a Roxbury merchant), £1,500 from the proposed provincial tax income in 1753, £1,291 in donations from neighboring communities,[53] and £200 a year (starting in 1754) from the membership dues of the Society for Encouraging Industry and Employing the Poor, an organization composed of concerned citizens from Boston and the surrounding region. In the end, all efforts of this period raised less than £15,000.

This figure was pale, to say the least, compared with that of the British Linen Company, founded in 1745, which had a capital investment of £70,600 sterling by 1751, in addition to a circulation of promissory notes of £96,000.[54] Starting from only a fraction of the total investment that the British competitor had, the Boston manufacture mounted one of the largest capital drives in the colony up to that time. Undaunted

---

[51] Richard Cox, *A Letter from Sir Richard Cox, Bart. to Thomas Prior, Esq; Shewing, from Experience, a sure Method to establish the LINNEN-MANUFACTURE, and the Beneficial Effects it will immediately produce* (Boston, 1750).
[52] Edward Winslow, "The Early Charitable Organizations of Boston," *New England Historic and Genealogical Register* 44(1890):100-103. The subscribers who served as overseers of the poor included John Barrett, Joseph Sherburne, John Franklin, Daniel Henchman, Jacob Wendell, Ezekiel Lewis, Edward Bromfield, Joshua Cheever, Thomas Hubbard, Ebenezer Storer, James Pitts, Thomas Flucker, William Phillips, and Andrew Oliver.
[53] Wiberley, "Four Cities," 100.
[54] See Alastair J. Durie, ed., *The British Linen Company, 1745-1775* (Edinburgh, 1996), 7-8. Reports from London, Dublin, and Sligo in Ireland informed Boston readers of the broad support the manufacturers received there. *Boston Weekly News-Letter*, May 30, 1754; July 26, 1759. *Boston Evening-Post*, November 24, 1755. No Massachusetts enterprise in the textile industry reached that level of capitalization until the 1810s. Caroline F. Ware, *The Early New England Cotton Manufacture: A Study in Industrial Beginnings* (New York: Russell and Russell, 1966), 301.

by the lack of greater financial backing and the shortage of textile expertise and management experience, Bostonians went on with the linen manufactory scheme in 1751. For a decade or so, the manufactory produced over 17,000 yards of cloth even though a smallpox outbreak halted the entire production for almost six months in 1752.[55] It also stimulated household production—taken on by individuals willing to make or dye cloth not at the factory but at home—which produced at least another 35,000 yards of cloth during the same period. The combined effects of all the economic activities—direct output of the manufactory, spinning and weaving at private households, and payment to regional farmers who grew and processed flax—reached a total yearly value of as much as £10,000.

Failure or Success?

Both to contemporary observers and to historians who have studied the details since, the short life of the linen manufactory (from 1751 to 1759) appeared to end in failure. A closer examination of its records in the context of colonial finance, however, may lead us to a different conclusion. An anonymous record book will further reveal the scope of the manufactory's operations, which were much more extensive than previously imagined. The full value of the experiment is not clear unless one looks at it in two lights: as a charitable effort and as a business venture. Compared with existing relief measures dependent upon the uncertainties of private donations and difficult-to-gather town taxes, the linen manufactory's goal

---

[55] "The REPORT of the Committee of the Society for *encouraging Industry and employing the Poor*, at their Quarter Meeting, February 14th, 1753," *Boston Post-Boy*, February 19, 1753. "The present State of the Linen Manufacture in Boston . . . ," *Boston Evening-Post*, February 26, 1753.

of maintaining the poor through employment actually achieved remarkable success.

The Manufactory House (1754-1808) from William H. Clark, comp., *The Story of Massachusetts*, 3v (New York: The American Historical Society, Inc., 1938), III: 167. Thomas Pemberton wrote, in *Topographical and Historical Description of Boston* (1794), that "The Manufactory House in Long Acre Street is a handsome brick building on the east side of the street. At the west end, fronting Long Acre, was portrayed on the wall a female figure, holding a distaff in her hand, emblematical of industry." Quoted in William R. Bagnall, *The Textile Industries of the United States*, 86. A symbol of local enterprise, the building is also the place where skirmishes took place between defiant Bostonians and the British soldiers and royal authorities in 1768.

Several big investors and subscribers did lose money. Roxbury merchant Thomas Gunter advanced more than £1,800 to erect the linen manufactory's new facility near the Common. Even though the provincial government reimbursed his construction expenses, it failed to pay him the interest due. Other subscribers helped to acquire the land and building for the linen manufactory, including Andrew Oliver (councilor, later secretary of the province and lieutenant governor),

Thomas Greene (brazier), Thomas Hubbard (merchant who willed a charity of £50 to the poor of Old South Church), Middlecott Cooke (gentleman and town selectman), William Clarke (gentleman and physician), Sylvester Gardiner (physician and apothecary), Isaac Winslow (merchant), and William Bowdoin (gentleman and merchant). They never received the full payment of £1,500, which a provincial act granted from collecting a tax on coaches and carriages.[56]

While the manufactory's principal sponsors may have suffered financially, the poor women and needy children the scheme intended to benefit gained a much-welcomed period of stability in their lives. If only for eight years, many families who otherwise would have suffered great privation earned income critical to their survival. Closely tied to a household's domestic economy, early textile production depended upon the labor of families—women and children often performed textile processing for hire at home—and experienced high turn-over rates. In the first half of the nineteenth century, for instance, female workers averaged only twenty-one months in the textile factories and males only twenty-six months.[57] Colonial turn-over rates were probably as high, which could result in three to four times the number of employment opportunities for the poor. Nonetheless, anyone who worked for seven or eight years

---

[56] From 1757 to 1766, Andrew Oliver and others repeatedly petitioned the General Court for the £1,500. They were only able to collect £738. 19s. from 1753 to 1757. See Petition for Province Assistance and other documents relating to the linen manufactory, SC1/series 45X, Massachusetts Archives Collection, 59:381-83, 384, 385, 386-90, 391-94, 427-28, 430-31, 452-54, 456-57, 494-97, 498-99, 509-10.

[57] Thomas Dublin, *Women at Work: The Transformation of Work and Community in Lowell, Massachusetts, 1826-1860* (New York, 1979), 24-25, 70, 184-85. One reason for the high turn-over rate among nineteenth-century female workers was because young girls, whom the employers preferred, would leave and get married after a few years. Rarely would a teenage girl remain at a textile factory for a decade. A similar situation must be true in colonial Boston, even though hardly any data about the linen manufactory's employees survived. According to Jonathan Prude's estimate, the first generation of Samuel Slater's mill operatives were twice as mobile as other local inhabitants in rural Massachusetts, and as much as one half or more of his labor force chose to leave annually from 1814 for two decades. The second generation between 1736 and 1859 experienced an even higher rate of turnover. *The Coming of Industrial Order: Town and Factory Life in Rural Massachusetts, 1810-1860* (Cambridge, Eng., 1983), 144-50, 227-29, 270.

at the linen manufactory enjoyed a continuous level of stability unavailable elsewhere, offering time for poor children to grow up and avoid starvation in the streets.

A full-time spinner at the linen manufactory earned 7s. a week,[58] hardly a munificent wage, but much higher than what the needy received from charity or what an inmate might gain from time in the workhouse. By comparison, none of those who received charitable contributions from Boston's churches received more than 24s. per month between 1750 and 1775—most received far less.[59] Thus, a spinner at the linen manufactory could earn about £17 a year. The manufactory could employ up to sixty full-time spinners and an additional two to three hundred half-time workers (who labored at home) to feed yarn to its twenty-one looms. Total earnings for both full-time and part-time workers could amount to at least £2,000, a figure far exceeding the total amount of religious charity or public relief available elsewhere in Boston.[60] Ironically, the company's records also show that most of its working poor actually enjoyed higher pay than Irish hacklers and spinners.

---

[58] See Nash, *Urban Crucible*, 196. Some male English weavers earned from 7s. to 9s. sterling a week in the late 1700s, while women and girls would earn only 1s. to 2s. by spinning and winding. See Frederic Morton Eden, *The State of the Poor* (1929; New York, 1971), 3:163, 335-37.

[59] Only one needy person received outdoor relief of 24s. a month from the overseers of the poor, while the other thirty-eight persons received from 2s. to 20s. See Wiberley, "Four Cities," 142.

[60] According to Laurel Thatcher Ulrich, in regions of the Old World accustomed to textile production, 8 to 10 spinners were needed to keep one weaver supplied with thread. "Wheels, Looms, and the Gender Division of Labor in Eighteenth-Century New England," *William and Mary Quarterly*, 3d ser., 55(1998):9. Based on this account, the twenty-one looms in the Boston linen manufactory needed 168 to 210 spinners. Assuming only a fraction of them (60) were employed full-time to use the manufactory's sixty spinning wheels, the manufactory had to employ at least the equivalent of 200 to 300 half-time people to make up the remaining 100 to 150 spinners. Assuming that spinners were paid at 7s. a week, and that the part-time spinners at half the amount, the total yearly payment for forty-eight weeks was between £1,915 (if the number 168 is used) and £2,268 (for 210). The total yearly payment for fifty weeks was between £1,995 and £2,362. By comparison, the total public expenditures for indoor and outdoor relief in Boston throughout the 1750s averaged £1,361 a year, the highest being £1,555 in 1757. See Wiberley, "Four Cities," 76.

This practice increased the economic welfare of the workers but decreased the manufactory's competitiveness.[61]

The economic benefits of the linen manufactory would not reach its total until the full process of production, including the output from all three locales of work, had been completed. The long process of linen production was never an exclusively urban enterprise, but involved many steps from flax cultivation and processing to spinning, weaving, bleaching, and dyeing, which were often handled not under one roof in Boston but at numerous individual households in small towns and rural villages. The company's financial records indicate that the new experiment impacted Boston and the colony in three areas: first, on the manufactory premises, for those who needed to work with company tools and under supervision; second, at individual households, for those who could and preferred to work at home with their own tools and at their own pace; and third, in the countryside, for those flax growers and farming families who processed the flax.

Except for a few hired weavers and supervisors, people who had to work on the manufactory premises were most likely Boston's poorer residents, who did not possess the tools necessary for work at home. Their labor contributed to the 17,221 yards of cloth made from the 23,757 hundred weight of flax purchased during the 1750s. Under a general assumption of textile productivity of this era, one hundred weight of flax should produce one yard of cloth. Therefore, the 23,757

---

[61] An extensive record about the history of the Boston linen manufactory, the Ezekial Price Papers at the MHS also contain information concerning the second promotion of textile production in the 1760s. Valuable financial information concerning the earlier endeavors of the 1750s can be found in charts and tables under these headings in the Price papers: "A Table to regulate the Spinners," "Price of Spinning here," "The Cost of Flax, Spinning & Weaving settled June 1756," "Prices of selling Linnin in the Orkneys ß a Letter from Mr. Lindsays 1755," "The Cost of 25 yds Linnin in Scotland accordg to Mr. Trails Scheme at 12/ for 1/ sterling," "Cost of 25 yds Coating & 26 yds Tuken," "Price Weaving in Dublin ß advice from thence in Irish Sterg," "Mr. James Trails Scheme for working Linnin Cloth of March 1755." Because the items in this collection have been assigned page numbers in a table of contents, further citations will make use of page numbers for reference. The charts and tables listed above appear on pages 359, 360, 361, 362.

hundred weight of flax should have produced the same yardage of cloth, not 17,221 yards, which was a clear sign of the manufacture's inefficiency. The establishment of the linen manufactory, however, greatly stimulated flax production in the region, which in turn made spinning and weaving a convenient way of making money for those who had tools and skills to work at home. These individuals produced an additional 35,441 yards of cloth, which had to consume about the same hundred weight of flax, if not more.[62]

Heightened textile producing activities in Boston, either on the premises of the linen manufactory or at private households, benefited flax growers and farmers in the country. Payments for flax alone could produce substantial income for rural families. At 3s. 9d. per hundred weight, the total flax consumed in Boston during this period should have produced up to £11,099 for flax growers: £4,454 for the 23,757 hundred weight of flax purchased by the linen manufactory, plus £6,645 for the 35,441 hundred weight of flax used by individual households. Therefore, even as the company's financial difficulties had gravely worsened by 1758, supporters still boasted that "since the Institution of this Society [the manufactory], much larger Quantities of Flax have been raised in the Province than ever before."[63]

Furthermore, for works of hackling, spinning, dyeing, and bleaching, the linen manufactory paid £19,848; for weaving, £4,560. For work completed at individual households—hackling, spinning, dyeing, and bleaching—35,441 hundred weight of flax would cost £3,5171; for weaving, £9,391. Thus, the total value of transactions for producing the 52,662 yards of

---

[62] Ezekiel Price Papers, 318.
[63] To many people, exporting flax seed proved a more convenient way to increase income than processing and selling flax. "One Gentleman having this Year bought 500 Hogsheads raised within this Province, amounting to £600 Sterling," see the appendix to Thomas Barnard, *Sermon Preached in Boston, New-England, Before the Society for Encouraging Industry and Employing the Poor* (Boston, 1758).

cloth (from a total of 59,198 hundred weight of flax) by the manufactory and by those who worked at home during the period 1751 to 1759 reached £80,069.[64] This impressive sum demonstrates the significant economic impact the linen manufactory had on Boston and the colony. In fact, the estimated value of £10,000 of economic activity generated each year by this new experiment through the 1750s far exceeded the total annual expenditures for public relief in Boston for three decades from 1738 to 1768.[65] The linen manufactory undeniably improved employment opportunities and economic welfare for both urban and rural populations.

The linen manufactory's operations and economic impact went far beyond its premises in Boston, an achievement that has received little recognition so far.[66] A thirty-six page memorandum book kept by an anonymous agent for the manufactory documents the numerous tasks completed by a

---

[64] Prices of flax and costs of hackling, spinning, dying, bleaching, and weaving are calculated according to unit price and other figures and estimates provided in Ezekiel Price Papers, 321.

[65] See Table 3.2 in Wiberley, "Four Cities," 76. Only two years (1748 and 1749) in the table reached £10,000 (Old Tenor) a year, the annual equivalent of just under £1,500 Lawful Money.

[66] Several early documents gave clues to this situation. For example, when the General Court passed legislation in 1753 to grant £1,500 for supporting the new enterprise through taxation on carriages, it specifically wrote into the law that each town in the province would be entitled to send one or more persons to the linen manufactory to learn various crafts without charge. See An Act for Granting the Sum of Fifteen Hundred Pounds to Encourage the Manufacture of Linnen, SC1/series 45X, Massachusetts Archives Collection, 59:386-389. Founded in about 1750, the Society for the Encouraging Industry and Employing of the Poor gained support from communities in and outside Boston. Its membership expanded from three dozen to two hundred, and twenty-six of those new members came from thirteen towns in the province, including Charlestown, Cambridge, Roxbury, Braintree, Germantown, Medford, Situate, Salem, Haverhill, Chelsea, and Nantucket. The widespread interest and participation suggested that those members certainly foresaw that the linen manufactory would benefit not only Boston but also their own communities as well. See Society for Encouraging Industry and Employing the Poor, *Rules for Incorporation for the Society for Encouraging Industry and Employing the Poor*, 1-12. Long after the closing of the linen manufactory, two former operators—Elisha Brown and John Brown—in a petition to the General Court on March 29, 1770, recalled that they for eight years "with cheerfulness instructed any person in the best method of making linen cloths, as several hundreds of persons can testify, and have continually employed numbers of poor persons, belonging to this and the neighbouring towns, in this manufacture." Bagnall, *Textile Industries in the United States*, 46.

large number of piece-workers in small communities in the colony—not regular employees at the manufactory or householders in Boston. In other words, the memorandum book recorded an extensive putting-out system that employed individuals who earned additional income for their families by working at home in rural Massachusetts.[67]

A page from the "anonymous account book" (1755-1759), where the phrase "Manufacturie Bag weighed 3½ " was written toward the end. A record of the piece work by more than 400 individuals, the account book clearly indicates that the Linen Manufactory in Boston provided employment opportunities not only to urban dwellers, but also to several hundred households in rural communities. (Massachusetts Historical Society)

---

[67] Anonymous textile merchant's account book, 1755-1759, Ms. S-304, MHS. Also available on the MHS microfilm set Pre-Revolutionary Diaries at the Massachusetts Historical Society, 1635-1774, reel 1:11. The account book contradicts one of Nash's major claims that the manufactory forced unlucky poor women and children out of their homes and into an institutionalized factory labor system. See Nash, "Failure of Female Factory Labor," 180-87.

How extensive a system? The record book indicates that about four hundred individuals worked for this manufactory agent in some capacity during the four-year period from 1755 to 1759, performing such tasks as "tear black flax," "tear white flax," "spin yarn," "bleach yarn," "dye blue," "dye brown," or "dye black." Perhaps contradicting expectations, only 20 percent of those listed in the account book were female (sixteen were widows). Even more astonishing, the overwhelming number of those the manufactory agent hired to do piece-work in this putting-out system were male property owners, not the poor. About fifty of those men had titles, including one esquire, seven deacons, thirteen captains, two lieutenants, three doctors, and twenty-six masters. One can speculate that even though the document recorded male names, the tasks may have been performed by wives and daughters at home. Yet the author of the memorandum book did differentiate gender in many cases. For example, several entries refer not to a man alone but rather to "Capt. Ames's daughters," "Wife of Joseph Morse," "Benjamin Morse's wife," and "Mrs. Bullard." These carefully registered distinctions indicate that most people named in this book, male or female, did contract with the manufactory agent to work for themselves and expected to receive their pay directly from the agent.[68]

Why several hundred people who were not indigent chose to work for the linen manufactory is unclear. Genealogical records and local histories suggest that economic burdens or uncertainties and family hardship might have propelled many to seek extra work. Abner Ellis, for instance, had recently married when he contracted for work and, perhaps, needed additional income for a new family. When James Penniman agreed to take on work, he was still recovering from

---

[68] An interesting reference to the interplays between family members and textile employment is William M. Reddy, "Family and Factory: French Linen Weavers in the Belle Epoque," *Journal of Social History* 8 (1975), 102-12.

losses, suffered from fires in 1749, that destroyed his house and £75 in bills of credit. Isaac Leland, who suffered much worse luck, contracted several jobs from the manufactory. Born in Holliston in 1730, Leland had lost his father when he was three years old. His mother remarried and moved away, leaving Leland in nearby Medway, where he later married a Mary Smith. Toward the end of 1758, their first son died less than two months after his birth. Giden Albee, from Mendon, Worcester County, married Hiphsebath Clark of Medfield in 1746 and by 1755 had six children when he began taking on jobs with the manufactory. Similarly, Ephraim Chenery, who contracted work seven times from the manufactory, married Hannah Smith when he was twenty-three and had ten children by 1755. A church deacon and prominent resident of Medfield but an unlucky husband, Ephraim Wheelock had lost three wives by the mid 1750s, during which time he sought work from the manufactory agent at least a dozen times.[69]

Kinship and neighborhood proximity may have helped some to obtain work. Cousins Simon Plimpton and Amos Plimpton of Medfield, who labored for the manufactory, came from a textile background. Although Simon was a housewright, his great-grandfather John Plimpton, who came over to New England with John Winthrop in the Great Migration, had been a tailor; several more tailors and dyers remained in the family for most of its history.[70] Still others who came from a cluster of villages in a region about twenty to thirty miles southwest of Boston might have gained work with the manufactory through

---

[69] For Abner Ellis, see *The Record of Births, Marriages and Deaths, and Intentions of Marriages, in the Town of Dedham, 1635-1845* (Dedham, 1886), 1:86, 89, 118. For James Penniman, see William S. Tilden, ed., *History of the Town of Medfield, Massachusetts, 1650-1886* (Boston, 1887), 453. For Isaac Leland, see *Vital Records of Holliston, Massachusetts, to the Year 1850* (Boston, 1908). For Giden Albee, see *Vital Records of Mendon, Massachusetts, to the Year 1850* (Boston, 1920). For Ephraim Chenery and Ephraim Wheelock, see Tilden, *History of the Town of Medfield*, 339, 508-09.

[70] As many as nine Plimptons contracted work with the Boston linen manufactory. For John Plimpton, Simon Plimpton, Amos Plimpton, and other Plimptons, see Tilden, *History of the Town of Medfield*, 462, 460, 456-68.

neighborhood contacts and family connections. Some part-time workers lived in offshoot communities of Dedham, such as Medway, Holliston, Harding, Sherborn, and Wrentham, which lay only about eight to ten miles from each other.[71] Others named in the memorandum book were closely related by marriage, such as the Allens, Boydens, Clarks, Cheneries, Dwights, Hardings, Hinsdells, Lovells, Partridges, Plimptons, and Wights.[72] Medfield enjoyed an especially close relationship with the Boston venture—forty names from that community appeared in the memorandum book.[73] Medfield families headed by Selectman Ezekiel Adams, Selectman and Representative Henry Adams, Selectman Seth Clark, and Representative Joseph Morse may have used their knowledge about Boston to help gain work for themselves and their relatives. Whatever the motivations or connections, the record clearly indicates that many small-town families and individuals benefited from the work opportunities that Boston linen manufactory provided.[74]

---

[71] *Record of Births, Marriages and Deaths, and Intentions of Marriages, in the Town of Dedham*; Metcalf, *Annals of the Town of Mendon*; Tilden, *History of the Town of Medfield*; George Kuhn Clarke, *History of Needham, Massachusetts, 1711-1911* (Cambridge, Mass., 1912); Francis D. Donovan, *The New Grant: A History of Medway* (Medway, Mass., 1976).
[72] *Vital Records of Mendon*; *Vital Records of Holliston*; *Vital Records of Medfield, Massachusetts, to the Year 1850* (Boston, 1903); *Vital Records of Medway, Massachusetts, to the Year 1850* (Boston, 1905); *Vital Records of Uxbridge, Massachusetts, to the Year 1850* (Boston, 1916).
[73] Genealogies in Tilden, *History of the Town of Medfield*.
[74] For example, a number of those families who lived near Medfield's Dwight Bridge sent a petition to the General Court in 1743 complaining that their properties were "under water almost the year round" due to the construction of a nearby provincial causeway. See Medfield Petition by Ezekiel Adams and thirty others, SC1/series 45X, Massachusetts Archives Collection, 1:163. Several of the thirty-one signatures on the petition are no longer legible, but sixteen of those who can be identified had worked with the linen manufactory. They were Ezekiel Adams, Jonathan Adams, Elisa Bowers, Joseph Cheany, Edward Clark, Seth Clark, James Ellice, John Ellice, Moses Ellice, David Lovill, Edward Partridge, Joseph Richardson, Joseph Plimpton, Simon Plimpton, William Plimpton, and Ephraim Wheelock. Much to their regret, the flooding persisted for a decade. See Samuel Watts and Joseph Richards, deposition, July 25, 1752, Miscellaneous Bound Manuscripts Collection, MHS. This document is a copy prepared by Middlecott Cooke, clerk of the Suffolk County Inferior Court of Common Pleas, who also happened to be a subscriber of the linen manufactory scheme.

Aftermath

Religious institutions were the most important source of private charitable relief in Boston, but their ability to fill this role largely depended on the weekly collections—which were uncertain at best. When available, such assistance certainly helped a congregation's sick, disabled, widowed, elderly, or unlucky members, but it offered nothing for nonmembers or the able-bodied working poor. The town's treasury assisted certain categories of the poor, but it hardly covered all who needed help. Even those who could legitimately make a claim for relief might go unaided as colonial Boston experienced declining tax collections and rising numbers of the needy and poor. The linen manufactory experiment not only filled a yawning gap in private and public assistance, it also likely kept many families in and around Boston off the relief rolls by providing incomes that might get them through an especially difficult period in the aftermath of King George's War.

The linen manufactory experiment, rather than an exercise in social control as some modern historians have believed, came about after years of frustration exacerbated by the increasing numbers of needy poor, the limitations of private charity, and the town's inability to collect sufficient tax revenue. The scheme represented a refreshing and compelling alternative to traditional forms of public and private poor relief. Indeed, the company's records and the previously under-utilized memorandum book show that the financial benefits the linen manufactory generated far exceeded the amounts of poor relief that churches and town authorities could pay. Equally important, the linen manufactory offered new economic opportunities for struggling middle-class families, many of whom lived well beyond Boston. It boosted flax cultivation in the countryside, stimulating the economies in those regions. The relief effort of the linen manufactory was as successful as it was far-reaching.

As a business venture, however, several serious limitations proved fatal to the experiment. First, the manufactory lacked a strong and sustained source of capital.[75] Second, the Boston linen manufactory recognized that it could not match the lower production costs of Irish and Scottish linen, because it had to pay a higher unit price in many categories of work to employees.[76] Third, the Boston area had few skilled weavers, a shortage seriously affecting productivity and competitiveness in the textile business.[77] Fourth, even though flax supply did not seem to be a problem,[78] Massachusetts farmers, as well as Boston inhabitants, had not yet developed the kind of skills in linen productions ready to compete on the

---

[75] A lack of funding plagued the Linen Manufactory from start. Subscriptions were not forthcoming despite repeated pleas. Nor were revenues from the carriage tax in spite of several public notices. *Boston Evening-Post*, February 26, 1753; June 11, 1753. *Boston Gazette*, April 23, 1754.

[76] "The Cost of Flax, Spinning & Weaving settled June 1756," Ezekiel Price Papers, 360, clearly indicates that the linen manufactory had lower costs in only three of eleven categories compared to Irish linen producers.

[77] By the company's estimation, a good weaver should be able to "make 12 or 16 yd of cloth/a day of ¾ wide; or 10 or 12 yd/ a day of 7/8 wide; or 8 to 10 yd of cloth/a day of 9/8 wide; or 6 yd/a day of 10/8 wide, using yarn of 6 to 10 hundred & no higher." See Ezekiel Price Papers, 361. The fact that the company could only turn 72 percent of the flax (17,221 yards of cloth from 23,757 hundred weight of flax) it received into cloth may indicate that it could not pay competitive wages to hire good weavers, since private citizens produced much more cloth at home during the same period. In either case, a shortage of skilled weavers severely limited output and endangered financial solvency. No matter how much flax the poor hackled and spun, the inability to produce finished cloth decreased revenue and, thus, jeopardized the entire experiment. Surviving company documents list Elisha Brown as the only full-time weaver and operator; the manufactory paid an annual wage of £212 to him. Ezekiel Price Papers, 314, 316. According to Annie Haven Thwing's research, thirty-nine weavers resided in Boston between 1630 and 1790, but two-thirds of them had died before 1700. Thwing, *Inhabitants and Estates of the Town of Boston, 1630-1800* (Boston, 2001), CD-ROM. The CD makes available the computerized version of the Thwing Index Card File at the MHS. The shortage of skilled weavers remained even a decade later when, in December 1767, James Forrest proposed to bring ten weavers from Northern Ireland to Boston for an estimated cost of £160.10s. Ezekiel Price Papers, 363, 367.

[78] If exports of flaxseeds can be an indicator of flax production, Massachusetts was still far behind Pennsylvania and New York in cultivating flax. In 1771, Boston exported 5,900 bushels of flaxseeds while Philadelphia exported seven times that number and New York seventeen times. By comparison, Boston exported more hops (at least 9,000 pounds in that same period) than any other port. Samuel Eliot Morison, "The Commerce of Boston on the Eve of the Revolution," *Proceedings of the American Antiquarian Society* (1923), 32: 32. Simpler and more direct than linen manufactures, the lucrative business of brewing and distilling attracted not only large imports of molasses but also many farmers' attention to grow hops instead of flax or hemp.

open market. After all, the quality of the cloth depended as much on spinners and weavers in Boston as on those who needed to process the flax before it was shipped to the manufactory. Flax growers or specialized farmers commonly handled the critical steps of deseeding, drying, sorting, retting, breaking, scutching, cleaning, dressing, and packing. Performing these tasks well required years of experience that few local farmers possessed.[79]

Thus, writing to the *Boston Gazette*, a reader from Salem commented, "Altho' these colonies or most of them, began the cultivation of flax very early after settlement, and for many years past have rais'd some hemp, yet we suspect that the most suitable soils, and the best methods of preparing them, with skilful management of the produce, for the manufacturer, are not generally so well understood as they might and ought to be." Convinced that supporting the poor was everyone's duty and that "the most extensive act of charity" was knowledge, the reader heartily recommended all those "who may well understand the European, and especially the Flanders' husbandry, and their methods of cultivating both hemp and flax, even from the choice and dressing the several soils to the finishing act of its preparation for the spinning wheel; that they would honestly and unreservedly communicate what they know to the publick thro' the channel of the weekly papers."[80]

John Adams apparently understood this need as well. Under the penname "Humphrey Ploughjogger," he wrote to the *Boston Evening Post* in 1763 and strongly implored the paper to print any information about "how to raise Hemp, how to fitt our land and feed, how and when to sow it, how to gather the crop

---

[79] For useful details of flax culture and the Irish, Scottish, English, and European linen business and techniques, see Alastair J. Durie, *The Scottish Linen Industry in the Eighteenth Century* (Edinburgh, 1979); Bert Dewilde, *Flax in Flanders through the Centuries* (Tielt, Belgium, 1999); John Horner, *The Linen Trade of Europe* (Belfast, 1920); and Alex. J. Warden, *The Linen Trade* (1864; New York, 1968).
[80] *Boston Gazette*, October 22, 1764.

and when, and how to dress it, and suck like would do a thousand pounds worth of good." Deliberately applying illiterate spelling and rustic dialect, he scolded empty talks about politics and bookish learning: "Good Mr. Elliot did rite sumthing once about farming, but not enuff about Hemp." Indeed, many farmers were told that they could raise good hemp to pay the rates or to send it to London to buy fine cloths, "but no body amongst us knows how to raise it." Adams insisted that informed people "could make every body love um if they would rite about farming, and teech country folks how to pay their rates by raising hemp and such like."[81] Recent studies confirm that few New England farmers specialized in flax cultivation in this period. Toward the end of the eighteenth century, many were still experimenting to acquire rudimentary techniques in processing flax.[82] Thus, it seems highly likely that the linen manufactory failed not only because the region lacked skilled weavers, but also because the company was unable to collect well-treaded flax or hemp at competitive prices from local farmers.

Nevertheless, the new experiment stimulated an estimated £80,000 worth of economic activity in the region during the 1750s, an impressive accomplishment by any measure. By combining private enterprise with community relief, the new textile enterprise extended economic benefits to the working poor in Boston and to hundreds of country farmers and small town families. After all, the linen manufactory's closing did not represent a failure in poor relief. It pointed up the overwhelming difficulties colonists faced trying to establish a new local industry within an imperial system that protected established economic activities elsewhere in the empire.

---

[81] Robert Taylor et al., eds., *Papers of John Adams* (Cambridge, Mass., 1977), 1: 63-66. *Boston Evening-Post*, June 20, 1763. Using the pseudonym of "U," Adams soon wrote another letter to the *Boston Gazette* to address how to raise hemp and the importance of understanding the science of husbandry. *Boston Gazette*, July18, 1763. *Papers of John Adams*, 1: 66-72.

[82] Laurel Thatcher Ulrich, *The Age of Homespun: Objects and Stories in the Creation of an American Myth* (New York, 2001), 281-85.

Chapter Three

Local Exodus

Although no one can deny the importance of the transatlantic migration from the Old World to the New as Bernard Bailyn has masterfully demonstrated in *Voyagers to the West*, local and regional migrations also played a significant role in the Bay Colony, especially from the 1750s to the 1770s.[1] Colonial migrants, or the "strolling poor" as

---

[1] Neither Boston nor Massachusetts was a focus in Bernard Bailyn's wide-ranging study of British emigration to America on the eve of the Revolution. Of the 9,364 emigrants he examined, only 77 (or 0.8%) had gone to the North. "They largely ignored New England," he wrote. The overwhelming majority (or 80%) of them went to five middle and southern colonies—Maryland (25%), New York (21%), Pennsylvania (15%), Virginia (8%), and North Carolina (11%), while the rest went to Canada (8%), South Carolina (1%), Georgia (3%), the Caribbean (5%), and the Floridas (0.04%). *Voyagers to the West: A Passage in the Peopling of America on the Eve of the Revolution* (New York: Vintage Books, 1988), esp. 204-39. Yet Bailyn did point out the evolutions from domestic/local/regional migrations to global/transatlantic migrations, *The Peopling of British North American: An Introduction* (New York: Vintage Books, 1988), 12-15, 20-43. Barry Levy, *Town Born: The Political Economy of New England from Its Founding to the Revolution* (Philadelphia: University of Pennsylvania Press, 2009), 6-8. Similar distribution patterns also took place in the transplantations of convicts and bond servants. Compared with other British North

Douglas L. Jones aptly characterized them in 1975, personified some of the most visible aspects of floating poverty of the past. In recent years, Ruth Wallis Herndon's *Unwelcome Americans* and Cornelia H. Dayton and Sharon V. Salinger's *Warning Out* (forthcoming) have greatly enriched that understanding.

What is less visible, however, is the fact that as the poor in general had many shades, groups, and subgroups, the transient population in Massachusetts was not a monolithic whole but comprised of several discernable segments. Not even counting the numbers of the middle and professional class families who were frequently on the move, that mobile population involved more members of the lower or lower-middle class than those of the poor and needy migrants. Separated by a critical but thin line, they often appeared mixed in modern studies, giving the impression that there was indeed a large group of the strolling poor roaming the province. Meanwhile, because of its long practice in New England, the warning-out system also impressed modern readers as an inhuman tool against the poor, which was only half true. Massachusetts law did require local authority to register and report the names of strangers, and the practice was a mechanism primarily to protect local residents from tax burdens of relief. If the warning-out system did help the middle-class taxpayers by limiting local expenses for relief, it never

---

American colonies, New England were the principal destinations for neither group in the 1700s, David W. Galenson, *White Servitude in Colonial America: An Economic Analysis* (New York: Cambridge University Press, 1981), 219-27, Don Jordon and Michael Walsh, *White Cargo: The Forgotten Story of Britain's White Slaves in America* (New York: New York University Press, 2008), Abbot Emerson Smith, *Colonists in Bondage: White Servitude and Convict Labor in America, 1607-1776* (New York: W.W. Norton & Co., 1971). Douglas Lamar Jones analyzed the trend of domestic migration in *Village and Seaport: Migration and Society in Eighteenth-Century Massachusetts* (Hanover, N.H.: University Press of New England, 1981), 22-39. Large numbers of foreign emigrants did not come to Massachusetts until the last decade of the century see "state paupers" in chapter six below and Oscar Handlin, *Boston's Immigrants, 1790-1880* (Cambridge, Mass.: Harvard University Press, 1991). By comparison, no fewer than 70,000 Scottish, Irish, and German emigrants arrived in Pennsylvania between 1715 and 1775. Sharon V. Salinger, *"To Serve Well and Faithfully": Labor and Indentured Servants in Pennsylvania, 1682-1800* (Cambridge, UK: Cambridge University Press, 1987), 52-57.

succeeded in limiting the movement and resettlement of most migrants, poor or otherwise—or at least, not to the degree that has been thus far assumed.

In either case, given the paucity of surviving evidence, few events can serve as a better yardstick for assessing the actions taken by the poor than a mapping of their movements, which were documented in many warning out records. Hoping for a better life in a new environment, the poor and lower class in particular had more reasons to move than those well-established middle-class families whose estate holdings and deeply rooted local connections gave them less incentive to leave.[2] Yet where did those transients and migrants come from? Who were they? What patterns and challenges did they face in their moves?[3] Finally, what could happen in the end when they attempted to settle down in a community? Based on a larger body of data than previously assembled, this chapter seeks to answer these questions, providing concrete details to the mobile, transient, and multifaceted contours of colonial poverty.

Domestic Migration

To say that most of those on the road under examination were domestic migrants, not foreign immigrants, is an understatement.[4] Numerous warning-out records in

---

[2] See Douglas Lamar Jones's pioneer work, "The Strolling Poor: Transiency in Eighteenth-Century Massachusetts," *Journal of Social History* 8 (1975): 28-54, and "Poverty and Vagabondage: The Progress of Survival in Eighteenth-Century Massachusetts," *New England Historical and Genealogical Register* 133 (1979): 243-54. His *Village and Seaport: Migration and Society in Eighteenth-Century Massachusetts* (Hanover, N.H.: University Press of New England, 1981) used computer programs to analyze the moves of inhabitants, newcomers, in-migrants, and out-migrants at Beverly and Wenham, Essex County.

[3] Olwen Hufton asked similar questions and analyzed various types of the wandering poor and itinerant poverty, "Begging, Vagrancy, Vagabondage and the Law: An Aspect of the Problem of Poverty in Eighteenth-Century France," *European History Quarterly* 2 (1972), 97-123.

[4] In addition to Jones's work, useful references include Richard Le Baron Bowen, *Early Rehoboth* (Rehoboth, 1945-50), 2: 139n. Several scholars studied the issue in regional,

Massachusetts have survived, covering the entire eighteenth century. All of them show that an overwhelming majority of those who had received warnings did not come from overseas, but from local communities and neighboring colonies. In Boston, as many as 9,000 people were warned from 1745 to 1792. Less than a quarter of them were from foreign countries.[5] Purposely assigned by Boston selectmen to warn strangers, Robert Love (retailer) recorded more than 420 cases from January 1765 to August 1766 and 98 cases from May to August 1772.[6] Less than 10 percent of them involved newcomers from foreign lands.[7] From 1701 to 1789, more than 3,400 people in Plymouth County were warned; fewer than 200 (5.5 percent) of them were from Great Britain, France, Ireland, or Holland.[8] Over half a century, approximately 7,500 were warned in Worcester County; only a handful was identified as being from foreign countries.[9]

Moreover, the same statistics indicate that no more than 10 percent of the warnings went to those from other colonies. Only Boston received a larger share (approximately 20 percent) of migrants from numerous seaports, including New York,

---

community, and family structure contexts, Kenneth A. Lockridge, *A New England Town, The First Hundred Years: Dedham, Massachusetts, 1636-1736* (New York: W. W. Norton, 1970), 98; Robert Gross, *The Minutemen and Their World* (New York: Hill and Wang, 1976), 89-94; John W. Adams and Alice Bee Kasakoff, "Migration and the Family in Colonial New England: The View from Genealogies," *Journal of Family History* 9 (1984): 24-43.

[5] Eric Nellis and Anne Decker Cecere, eds., *The Eighteenth-Century Records of the Boston Overseers of the Poor* (Boston: Colonial Society of Massachusetts, 2007), 97-98.

[6] Also appointed, in January 1765, for the same duties were Mr. John Sweetser (peruke maker) and Mr. Cornelius Thayer (leather dresser), who replaced the negligent Mr. Abijah Adams (rope maker). Selectmen agreed to pay them £53 6s. a year for their services. The sum shall be divided in proportion to the number of persons each warned. *Report of the Record Commissioners of the City of Boston* (Boston, 1876-1894), 20:129-31, 139.

[7] Robert Love, Record Book, 1765-1766, Massachusetts Historical Society; List of Warnings Out (May 1 to August 28, 1772), Rare Books and Manuscripts Department, Boston Public Library.

[8] Ruth Wilder Sherman et al., eds., *An Index to Plymouth County, Massachusetts Warning Out from The Plymouth Court Records, 1686-1859* (Plymouth, Mass.: General Society of Mayflower Descendants, 2003).

[9] Francis E. Blake, *Worcester County, Massachusetts Warnings, 1737-1788* (1992; Worcester, Mass.: Franklin P. Rice, 1899).

Philadelphia, Portsmouth, Newport, Annapolis, and Charleston.[10] In Plymouth County, the figure was less than 2 percent; in Worcester County, it was less than 0.4 percent (or some 30 cases). Thus, the overwhelming numbers of those on the road were people roaming from community to community within Massachusetts. A similar pattern of distribution also occurred at Wrentham, formerly Suffolk now Norfolk County. A township of 2,000 souls, it was about 25 miles south by southwest of Boston and 20 miles north of Providence. From 1732 to 1792, town authorities warned about 1,000 people. Only seven cases involved foreigners while some seventy others (7 percent) were from other colonies and fifty were from Cumberland in Rhode Island, which was the town's westerly neighbor.[11] Clearly, the decided majority who came through Wrentham for sixty years was neither from overseas nor from far away colonies, but from within the commonwealth itself.

In fact, most people moved little more than ten to twenty miles each time, not travelling far from where they previously lived.[12] Boston, a principal seaport, attracted people from as many as 150 places in the British Empire, ranging from Nova Scotia to Jamaica. Yet small and close-by communities such as Braintree, Brookline, Cambridge, Charlestown, Chelsea, Dedham, Dorchester, Hingham, Medford, Milton, and Woburn contributed to the provincial capital as many newcomers as big urban centers did, such as New York and Philadelphia.[13] Similarly, outsiders from forty different communities came to Wrentham; the most frequently identified places were Attleborough (28 times), Bellingham (23), Dedham (16), Mansfield (19), Medfield (6), Medway (10), Mendon (16),

---

[10] Robert Love, Record Book, 1765-1766, Massachusetts Historical Society.
[11] Esther L. Friend, "Notifications and Warnings Out: Strangers Taken Into Wrentham, Massachusetts, Between 1732 and 1812," *New England Historical and Genealogical Register* 141 (1987): 179-202, 330-57; 142 (1988): 56-84.
[12] Douglas Lamar Jones, "The Strolling Poor: Transiency in Eighteenth-Century Massachusetts." *Journal of Social History* 8 (1975), 39.
[13] Robert Love, Record Book, 1765-1766.

Needham (6), Norton (45), Rehoboth (14), Stoughtonham (11), and Walpole (25). All these towns (except Rehoboth) were within a radius of ten to fifteen miles from Wrentham. Founded in 1649 and lying across the Mystic River, the town of Malden in Middlesex County was a few miles north by northeast of Boston. Town records showed only two incoming families from far away: one from Halifax, Nova Scotia, and the other from Truro on the Cape. Yet the town warned more than 700 strangers from 1678 to 1794, most of whom came from neighboring communities, such as Boston, Stoneham, Reading, Lynn, Chelsea, Charlestown, Roxbury, Medford, and Salem.[14]

Although Plymouth County warned a considerable number of families from Rhode Island, Connecticut, and Nova Scotia, it sent far more notices to warn those within Massachusetts. Furthermore, only a fraction of the notices warned individuals from Boston, while most warned those from such small towns as Wareham, Rochester, Middleboro, Marshfield, Kingston, Plympton, Duxbury, Halifax, Dartmouth, and Abington. Worcester County witnessed much the same. Less than 20 miles west of Worcester, Brookfield processed 100 cases of warnings to people coming from 46 places in 15 years (from 1750 to 1765). However, 40 percent of those cases involved 19 towns in the county, such as Spencer, Sturbridge, Oxford, Western, Charlton, Oakham, Dudley, Rutland, Leicester, and Upton. Most were within twenty miles of Brookfield. Located in the northeast and bordering Middlesex County, the small town Harvard in Worcester County warned more than 300 people in 150 cases from 1749 to 1785. Although those cases involved 42 different communities, nearly half were from 6 towns within a 10- to 15-mile radius across the Worcester and Middlesex borders—namely, Bolton,

---

[14] George Walter Chamberlain, "Warnings-Out in Malden, Mass., 1678-1794," *New England Historical and Genealogical Register* 92 (1938): 46-60.

Lancaster, Stow, Littleton, Groton, and Shirley.[15] At Weston, Middlesex County, half of its 160 cases of warnings from 1757 to 1803 went to those who had come from the 6 neighboring communities of Newton, Waltham, Lincoln, Needham, Sudbury, and East Sudbury; all of them were located not more than 10 miles away from Weston.[16]

While evidence clearly shows a sturdy movement of migration involving primarily clusters of communities located relatively close to one another, it also indicates an acceleration of that movement, which first started in the 1750s and continued through the next two to three decades. Compared with the late 1740s, the number of strangers in Boston increased by 45 percent during the first half of the 1750s. That number continued to rise until a total of 5,000 strangers had arrived by the end of the 1760s—a figure equal to one third of Boston's own population.[17]

Several counties experience a comparable trend.[18] According to Douglas Jones's study, the rate of transiency in Essex County more than doubled during the first half of the 1760s while in Hampshire County it increased more than 200 percent during the same period.[19] Although the warning-out cases in Plymouth County increased steadily from a few dozen in the 1710s to 157 cases and 300 people in the 1740s, the 1750s saw a 100 percent increase over the previous decade, as

---

[15] Francis E. Blake, *Worcester County, Massachusetts Warnings, 1737-1788* (1992; Worcester, Mass.: Franklin P. Rice, 1899), 8-12, 20-26.
[16] Ann S. Lainhart, comp., "Weston Cautions 1757 to 1803," *New England Historical and Genealogical Register* 144 (1990): 215-24.
[17] Steven Edward Wiberley, Jr., Four Cities: Public Relief in Urban America, 1700-1775, Ph.D. diss., Yale University, 1775, p. 47. See also Allan Kulikoff, "The Progress of Inequality in Revolutionary Boston," *William and Mary Quarterly*, 3rd ser., 28 (1971): 400.
[18] So did the number of bound out orphans in Boston, where authorities made 1,123 indentures from 1720 to1820 and where those cases rose sharply during two particular periods of 1766-74 and 1791-96. Ruth Wallis Herndon, "Proper" Magistrates and Masters: Binding Out Poor Children in Southern New England, 1720-1820," in Herndon and John E. Murray, eds., *Children Bound to Labor: The Pauper Apprentice System in Early America* (Ithaca, N.Y.: Cornell University Press, 2009), 39-51, 217.
[19] Jones, "The Strolling Poor: Transiency in Eighteenth-Century Massachusetts," *Journal of Social History* 8 (1975), 32-33.

did the 1760s over the 1750s. That is to say, nearly 60 percent of all warning-out cases—more precisely, 1,983 people (in 862 cases) out of a total of 3,453 people (in 1,426 cases)—occurred in the 1750s and 1760s, marking the highest numbers of warnings in the county's eighteenth-century history.[20]

Individual communities saw similar if not more dramatic increases. At Malden, in 1745 town authorities warned 15 people to depart—the highest number of strangers in any single year since 1693. However, during the subsequent decade, the town warned 60 people from 1757 to 1759. The town warned as many as 237 people in the 1760s, marking a new high in local history. The record was not matched until another peak occurred between 1772 and 1775, when 88 people were warned.[21] Similarly, Weston warned 300 people from 1757 to 1803; 170 of them were warned during the first 20 years, from 1757 to 1776.[22] In Worcester County, surviving records of 20 townships show that—except for Northborough and Northbridge—80 to 90 percent of all warning-out notices were issued between 1750 and 1776.[23] In other words, of all the 7,500 people who received warnings, more than 6,000 (or 80 percent) were warned during that 26-year period. Lancaster, Leicester, Mendon, and Rutland show similar statistics. The records indicate that for two decades starting in 1750, Lancaster warned 366 of all 386 people who had received warning notices

---

[20] Ruth Wilder Sherman et al., eds., *An Index to Plymouth County, Massachusetts Warning Out from The Plymouth Court Records, 1686-1859* (Plymouth, Mass.: General Society of Mayflower Descendants, 2003).
[21] George Walter Chamberlain, "Warnings-Out in Malden, Mass., 1678-1794," *New England Historical and Genealogical Register* 92 (1938): 46-60.
[22] Ann S. Lainhart, comp., "Weston Cautions 1757 to 1803," *New England Historical and Genealogical Register* 144 (1990): 215-24.
[23] Francis E. Blake, *Worcester County, Massachusetts Warnings, 1737-1788* (1992; Worcester, Mass.: Franklin P. Rice, 1899). Those eighteen townships were Barre, Bolton, Brookfield, Charlton, Douglas, Dudley, Fitchburg, Grafton, Hardwick, Harvard, Holden, Lancaster, Leicester, Leominster, Lunenburg, Mendon, New Braintree, Oakham, Oxford, Paxton, Petersham, Princeton, Rutland, Rutland District, Shrewsbury, Southborough, Spencer, Sturbridge, Sutton, Templeton, Upton, Uxbridge, Warren, Westborough, Western, Westminster, Winchendon, and Worcester.

to date, accounting for 95 percent of the town's history. In Leicester, the ratio was 161 (92 percent) of 174; in Mendon, 298 (83 percent) of 360; and in Rutland, 315 (73 percent) of 428.

Intensification

At least two interrelated reasons may explain the intensified mid-century local migration. The first could be structural. The fixed sizes of an average township, once reaching its full capacity of settlement, tended to generate a self-propelled movement of migration. Carefully laid-out townships of six square miles, the norm since the 1730s, were reasonable plans for initial settlement as towns could not ensure the safety of settlers if spread over too large a territory on the frontiers. Building a closely knit and defensible settlement in a limited geographical area appeared to be a sound strategy to start a nascent plantation. Nevertheless, as a community gradually grew, the standard size of some 23,000 acres (a quarter of them usually occupied by woodlands) would no longer be that accommodating. Generally speaking, a township of that size could only support between 150 family farms (100 acres each) and 300 farms (50 acres each) that were productive enough to support their households. Some townships, where tough terrains or huge woodlands and water surfaces abounded, had a hard time supporting even 100 good farms. After numerous separations, old communities, such as Salem, Concord, and Dedham, were much smaller than six square miles, making them even less feasible for setting up new farms. By the end of the 1740s, 108 townships had been founded.

Only 13 of them had more than 20,000 acres,[24] while more than 30 others had less than 10,000 acres.[25] This means that, as each township matured toward reaching the maximum number of homesteads, those who had not yet established a farm or business were enticed to move elsewhere. It is no accident that this intensified internal migration of the 1750s and 1760s, which coincided with the rapid expansion of new townships during the same period. Both trends reflected the same pressing need for tillable lands beyond established communities.

The second reason for active migration was demographic. The fixed size of a township put special pressure on those who had been born in the 1730s and 1740s, when health conditions improved, birth rates rose, longevity extended, and the population boomed.[26] As Kenneth A. Lockridge has persuasively demonstrated, population increases impacted community growth in the seventeenth century;[27] the situation in the eighteenth century was even more serious. Whereas the population of the colony remained under 100,000 in 1700, it quickly reached 120,000 in the early 1730s, 200,000 in the early 1750s, and 245,000 by 1765.[28] The need for new land was no more acute than among those born in the first half of the century. Too many young people were approaching their majority at the same time, while many of the existing family lots could no longer be further divided and still support the fast-growing number of new generations.

---

[24] They were Gloucester, Andover, Northampton, Westfield, Deerfield, Worcester, Sutton, Brimfield, Sheffield, Sturbridge, Holden, Blandford, and Douglas.
[25] They were Boston, Charlestown, Salem, Watertown, Cambridge, Weymouth, Lynn, Braintree, Woburn, Wenham, Reading, Hull, Manchester, Medfield, Topsfield, Milton, Beverly, Hatfield, Bradford, Medford, Newton, Brookline, Needham, Lexington, Sunderland, Stoneham, Stoughton, Bedford, Wilington, Waltham, Chelsea, and Hardwick.
[26] Richard Holms's study of Bedford and Lincoln clearly shows those characteristics, Communities in *Transition: Bedford and Lincoln, Massachusetts, 1729-1850* (Ann Arbor, Michigan: University Microfilm International [UMI] Research Press, 1978).
[27] Kenneth A. Lockridge, *A New England Town, The First Hundred Years: Dedham, Massachusetts, 1636-1736* (New York, W. W. Norton & Company, 1970).
[28] *Columbian Centinel of Boston*, August 17, 1822. Josiah Henry Benton, *Early Census Making in Massachusetts, 1643-1765* (1905; Charleston, S.C.: Bibliolife, 2010).

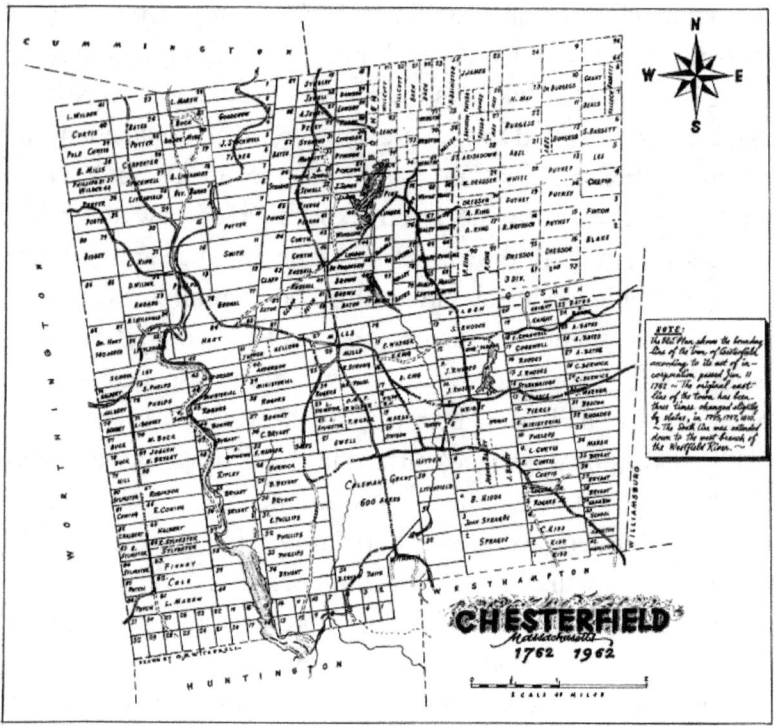

Map of Chesterfield (Hampshire County), 1762-1962. The town would quickly settle as soon as some 300 homesteads were divided, leaving little room for newcomers. Source: *History and Genealogy of the Families of Chesterfield, Massachusetts, 1762-1962* (Northampton, Mass.: Gazette Printing Co., [ca. 1963]).

Several years into a settlement, even a large township of 23,000 acres could yield, by law, only 63 dividable sections of 160 acres each, totaling 10,080 acres; this became the upper limit for cultivation. A section of 160 acres per family, later called a "quarter section," was the standard for meeting the common demand of the day. Based on the condition of soil in most places in Massachusetts, the general expectation in colonial time was that a farmer could not make a decent living and maintain his family on less than 100 acres, which contained a house lot, a meadow, farmland, and woodland. For example, seventeenth-century settlers in Dedham could expect an division averaging 150 acres, 126 acres in Watertown, 150 acres in Medfield, 150 acres in Sudbury, 150 acres or more in Milford, 115 acres in Billerica, 250 acres in Concord, and 100 acres upward in Andover.[29] While the allotment of this sort was beneficial for early settlers, few young sons of the first-generation landowners (called proprietors or original grantees) had any good prospects for inheriting any sizable land in the same community unless their forefathers had significantly increased their land holdings during their lifetimes. The prospect of their grandsons was bleaker still, let alone their great-grandchildren—all of whom would be reaching or passing majority within a few decades. Hence a tantalizing temptation to those younger generations was to move into newly opened areas where land might still be available.

Many family histories illustrated this trend. The Munroes of Lexington, for example, stayed, lived, and died there for three generations, almost without exception, for most of the seventeenth century. Although this big clan produced several patriotic minutemen who fought at the first battle of Lexington, such as Ebenezer (b. 1752), Nathan (b. 1747), William (b. 1742), and John (b. 1748), the fourth generation moved more actively than their predecessors. They left Lexington and were often found living in two dozen towns in Massachusetts and across New England, including Concord, Carlisle, Lincoln, Reading, Harvard, Ashburnham, Wakefield, Westminster, Roxbury, Northboro, Woburn, Lynnfield, Bedford, Billerica, Shrewsbury, Plainfield, Spencer, and Groton as well as Surry, Keene, and Hillsborough in New Hampshire,

---

[29] Kenneth Lockridge, "Land, Population and the Evolution of New England Society 1630-1790," *Past and Present* 39 (1968), 62-80.

Canterbury and Willmington in Connecticut, Pawlet, Poultney, and Grafton in Vermont, and Livermore in Maine.[30]

Born in Yorkshire, England, John Boynton came to Massachusetts with his older brother William in 1638. The two arrived at Rowley in the northeastern part of Essex County. Although Rowley's original grant was more than 20,000 acres, at least one tenth of the area was marshy field good for cutting hay but little else. The size of Rowley also shrunk when, within the next few decades, the northwestern part of the town separated from Rowley and renamed itself Bradford, taking with it 4,500 acres; Georgetown, also in the northwest, separated, taking another 5,000 acres. Thus, Rowley was reduced to approximately 10,000 acres of assessable land, including 2,700 acres of woodland. A versatile and prosperous farmer, William Boynton (who was also a tailor, weaver, planter, and schoolmaster) was able to purchase and add numerous lots to his estate. When he died, he bequeathed a farm to each of his four children. Also a tailor, John Boynton only had an acre and a half next to his brother's. All of his seven children were born in Rowley. His four sons produced thirty-two grandchildren—all born in Rowley.

Yet the consistency began to shake as successive generations came into the world. John's fifteen grandsons had eighty-four children; their birthplaces included Rowley, Bradford, and Groton. John Boynton's fourth generation numbered 155 born from the 1720s through the 1750s at more than a dozen places within some 60 miles from Rowley, including Bradford, Georgetown, Gloucester, Haverhill, Westford, Waltham, Pepperell, Townsend, Lancaster, Lunenburg, Sterling, Milford, and Hollis. The fifth generation (the great-great-great grandchild of John), born after the 1760s, ultimately reached a grand total of 305 born at as many as some

---

[30] Richard S. Munroe, comp., *History and Genealogy of the Lexington, Massachusetts Munroes* (2nd ed.; Florence, Mass., 1986), 1-96.

40 different places not only in Massachusetts, but also in New Hampshire, Maine, Vermont, Connecticut, New York, Canada, Virginia, and Wisconsin.[31] Clearly, if early generations of the Boyntons in the seventeenth century were able to stay in one or two places, it became increasingly difficult for later ones to do so. Pressed both by the growing number of household members and by the limits of the family estate, those who matured by the mid eighteenth century had to be willing to move—a dozen miles at first and then hundreds of miles later—into areas where they might have good prospects for establishing their own freehold.

The gradually enlarged and ripple-shaped dispersion of the Boynton family was by no means unique. Similar spiral movements and migratory expansions occurred repeatedly among many families elsewhere. Most of the early settlers to Rutland, Worcester County, for instance, came from Sudbury, Concord, Marlborough, Lexington, Leicester, and Paxton, all of which were less than thirty-five miles away.[32] Most of those who lived in Amherst, Hampshire County, originally came from Granby, Hadley, Leverett, Shutesbury, Belchertown, Springfield, Montague, Brookfield, Westborough, Pelham, Petersham, and Hardwick, most of which were within a twenty-mile radius.[33]

The yeoman farmer Edward Babbitt (or Bobet in old records) of Taunton was the progenitor of the Babbitt family in Massachusetts. His name first appeared in a government record of 1643, when he was identified as one of the men who was between sixteen and sixty years old and thus able to bear arms. He became one of the proprietors of the "Bloomerie," or the

---

[31] John Farnham Boynton and Caroline Harriman Boynton, comps., *The Boynton Family* (1897; Boston: Goodspeed's Book Shop, 1971), 1-2, 44-194.
[32] Jonas Reed, *A History of Rutland, Worcester County, Massachusetts* (Worcester, Mass.: Mirick & Bartlett, Printers, 1836), 105-162. Timothy C. Murphy, *History of Rutland in Massachusetts, 1713-1968* (Worcester, Mass.: The Heffernan Press, 1970), 35-40.
[33] James Avery Smith, comp., Families of Amherst, Massachusetts (Amherst, Mass., 1984), 4v, his carbon copies at the New England Historic Genealogical Society.

ancient Iron Works of Taunton on Two Mile River in 1652. Apparently, he was doing well and had saved enough money to partner with John Hathaway and Timothy Holloway. Together they purchased 400 acres in Taunton in 1658. He married Sarah Tarne, the daughter of Myles Tarne (a leather dresser of Boston) on July 7, 1654. They had nine children, all of whom were born and lived in Taunton, Dighton, and Berkley, which were within ten miles of each other. Born around the turn of the seventeenth and eighteenth centuries, their fifty-one grandchildren began to live at seven or eight places in Plymouth and Bristol Counties. Except for Dartmouth, which was about twenty miles south of Taunton, all of those communities were within some ten to fifteen miles of each other, such as Middleboro, Freetown, Marshfield, Easton, and Norton.

The picture of the next generation of Babbitt's seventy great-grandchildren presents a dramatic change, however, as they were no longer born and lived in the close proximities of early generations. At least four additional counties and five provinces accounted for their birthplaces, including Bridgewater (Plymouth); Mansfield (Bristol); Swansea (Bristol); Rehoboth (Bristol); Holliston (Middlesex); Leicester, Dana, Barre, Petersham, Brookfield, Oxford, Spencer, and Sturbridge (all in Worcester); Greenwich and Brimfield (Hampshire); New Ashford, Lanesboro, Pittsfield, and Peru (Berkshire); Gloucester, Rhode Island; Hanover, New Hampshire; Richmond and Barnard, Vermont; Colchester, Western, and Killingly, Connecticut; Eastern, New York; and Mendham, New Jersey.[34]

Both the Boyntons and the Babbitts showed a pattern of three gradually extending circles of domestic migration—from the first 10- to 20-mile radius (within a county) to the next 20- to 60-mile radius (crossing county lines) and finally 100 miles

---

[34] William Bradford Browne, *The Babbitt Family History, 1643-1900* (Taunton, Mass.: Old Colonial Society of Taunton, 1912), 13-92.

or more (across provinces). Although most family members seemed to prefer to stay at places close to one another, many of them—especially the poor and the marginal—had to move away to survive. Collectively, the grand expansions in the middle of the century must have consisted of hundreds if not thousands of similar step-by-step moves of individual families. The sharp increase of warning out notices reflects this trend, which was part and parcel of a massive confluence of activities taken by hundreds of individuals and their families, whose migratory moves began with a few dozen miles each time. In other words, the limited sizes of townships constantly forced an ever-growing local population to venture out to seek new lives regionally when possible, or elsewhere when necessary. The intense migratory movements of this period, therefore, did not come from overseas, but originated from the internal and domestic tensions within Massachusetts.[35]

Status

Ultimately, who were those on the move? Although a precise classification of the transients is impossible, some efforts to identify their status can help further understand the mixed natures of colonial poverty and mobility. As James T. Lemon pointed out in *The Best Poor Man's Country*, the less wealthy tended to move more frequently than their more affluent neighbors. Yet if one can trust the accuracy of the warnings-out records and the descriptive skills of those who recorded them, one may see a world of many colors and shades, of which the poor accounted for just one. Indeed, the world of

---

[35] See the experiences of the Tolmans of Dorchester and those of the Stones of Cambridge for examples. Gerald Lee Tolman, comp., *The Descendants of Thomas Tolman (1608)* (Yorba Linda, Calif.: Shumway Family History Services, 1996), 1-71. J. Gardner Bartlett, comp., *Gregory Stone Genealogy: Ancestry and Descendants of Dea. Gregory Stone of Cambridge, Mass., 1320-1917* (Boston: The Stone Family Association, 1918), 41-149.

the transients was neither an exact mirror of the larger society nor a bottomless abyss exclusively for the miserable. Many transients did belong to the competent poor, who were in dire need of help and support, while others came from comfortable families of the middle class with good educations, professional training, and various degrees of experiences in business, medicine, and military service. A close reading of the records shows that the vast majority of those on the road were not the dejected poor; nor were they from a homogeneous body of people. Rather, they consisted of a wide spectrum of different social strata ranging from masters, servants, maids, tradesmen, professionals, and substantial families to the sick, the lame, and the destitute.

Of the 430 cases he warned between 1765 and 1766, Robert Love unequivocally identified one beggar, one old vagrant, one transient without settlement, and 8 poor persons. The strongest words he used to describe the low status of a person were one "in total rags" and another "almost naked." He also identified four persons from the almshouse or workhouse, five blind or lame people, six crazy men (including two refusing to declare their names), and a dozen veteran soldiers. He identified a joiner, a mason, a silversmith, a baker, a painter, two shoemakers, and several servants and maids traveling with their masters. However, he remained silent about the status of the vast majority of those whom he warned, including Indians, free Africans, mulattoes, widows, and foreigners. The lack of description was not due to a lack of space for he never forgot to write down that he "warned [them] in His Majesty's name to depart this town of Boston in 14 days." Most of the 670 names in his record could have been people of low circumstances. Yet nearly all of them were able to find lodging and few were found in the streets.[36]

---

[36] Robert Love, Record Book, 1765-1766, Massachusetts Historical Society.

Most warning-out records in Massachusetts corroborate the scenarios that Love reported. In Worcester County, of the 263 people warned in Bolton from 1742 to 1767, authorities identified one poor girl Sarah Butler from Westborough, a poor family (John McBride, his wife Jane, and their children William, Mary, and Abigail), a poor person named Partick Quiltis, a poor boy Daniel Twitchell from Sherborn, and a poor person Margaret Williams. At Harvard, of the 315 people warned in 150 cases from 1749 to 1785, 9 children, 3 families, one widow, and one old man were identified as definitively poor. In Lancaster, the family of Amariah Roberts, his wife Lucy, and their children Lucy, Amariah, and Ebenezer from Shrewsbury were the only ones described as "very poor" among the 386 individuals warned from 1744 to 1767. In Mendon, 360 people were warned between 1739 and 1783; 26 were registered as poor while the family of John Vickery, his wife Lydia, their children Sarah and Lydia, and a mulatto servant Mary were recorded as "very poor." In Southborough, 186 people were warned from 1737 to 1767; 20 were recorded as poor while Benjamin Garfield, his wife Susanna, and Margaret Bellows were registered as "very poor."[37]

In Wrentham, local inhabitants who reported newcomers did not possess any standard tools for gauging anyone's status, yet they had developed a series of vocabularies to describe what they believed to be the most fitting category of a newcomer's circumstance, ranging from "a good and comfortable estate," "a small estate," "no or little estate," and "low or poor circumstances," to "very low circumstances." They clearly sensed that not all newcomers came from the same social and economic background. Whenever they were unable to determine a case, they frankly reported that the circumstances of a person's estate were unclear. This caution,

---

[37] Francis E. Blake, *Worcester County, Massachusetts Warnings, 1737-1788* (1992; Worcester, Mass.: Franklin P. Rice, 1899), 5-8, 20-26, 28-33, 38-43, 63-66.

which occurred quite frequently in the records, made their unofficial assessment creditable as they did not feel compelled to draw any definitive conclusion immediately after meeting a stranger. Furthermore, people in Wrentham were occasionally sensitive enough to add some personal observations beyond an individual's status. Thomas George said of Benjamin Butler, on February 16, 1769, that he was "about ten years old upon trial as an apprentice to learn my trade . . . a well lively active boy." On November 7, 1759, Robert Blake said of Dorothy Dorr, "a poor child," that she "is pretty healthy and middling industrious." "William Wathebe a youth of seventeen years of age and hath nothing but his hands," Captain Benjamin Shepard reported on February 1, 1770. These local records and personal observations give the impression that, until the 1760s, nearly 60 percent of newcomers had some possessions, while both those of "good and comfortable" and those of "very poor" circumstances accounted for the small minority.[38]

It should be kept in mind that not even the poorest outsiders were homeless beggars or complete strangers. Many moved into a new place where they had acquaintances, relatives, or kinship ties. In Hanover, Benjamin White took in Thomas White, John Rogers took in Wing Rogers and his family, and Samuel Wethrell took in the widow Unis Wethrell.[39] In Weston, Benjamin Peirce took in Heph Peirce of Woburn and Hephzibeth Peirce of Hopkinton, Joseph Whitney took in Daniel Whitney of Sudbury, and Samuel Child took in a newcomer also named Samuel Child of Newton.[40] In Malden, Joseph Sprague took in Jonathan Sprague, his wife Tabitha, and

---

[38] Esther L. Friend, "Notifications and Warnings Out: Strangers Taken Into Wrentham, Massachusetts Between 1732 and 1812," *New England Historical and Genealogical Register* 141 (1987): 179-202, 330-57; 142 (1988): 56-84.
[39] David Thomas Konig, ed., *Plymouth Court Records, 1686-1859* (Boston: New England Historic Genealogical Society, CD-ROM, 2002).
[40] Ann S. Lainhart, comp., "Weston Cautions 1757 to 1803," *New England Historical and Genealogical Register* 144 (1990): 215-24.

their seven children from Medford.[41] In Wrentham, Rueben Pond took in Sarah Adams from Walpole, who was the daughter of George Adams, a resident of Wrentham. George Haws reported to town authorities with confidence that he had taken in Samuel Allen as an apprentice to live with him. "Son of Mr. Abijah Allen of Franklin," he added, "he is eighteen years of age" and "a likely young man." David Pond took in Samuel Pond from Uxbridge, James Bacon took in James Bacon, wife Abigail, and their four children from New Braintree, James Gillmore took in William Gillmore, wife Mary, and their two children from Rehoboth, Benjamin Clark took in Samuel Clark from Rutland, James Blake took in Benjamin Blake from Rehoboth, Josiah Ware took in Mehitable Ware from Needham, James Metcalf took in Lois Metcalf and her two children from Keene, Joseph Streeter took in Chloe Streeter from Middleborough, and Elisha Ware took in Asa and Elisha Ware from Needham.[42]

A significant portion (an estimated 10 to 30 percent) of all transients moved with their families, suggesting that they hoped to keep their family intact while relocating. For example, Brookfield, Worcester County, sent 106 warnings between 1746 and 1767. Half of them involved husbands and wives with their children in addition to a large number of widows, single women, and underage children.[43] In Malden, authorities issued 300 warnings from 1693 to 1794. One third of them involved husbands and wives, with or without children.[44] In Sudbury, almost all of the fifty-four warning-out cases from October

---

[41] Constable Micah Waitt quickly warned the new family to depart. George Walter Chamberlain, "Warnings-Out in Malden, Mass., 1678-1794," *New England Historical and Genealogical Register* 92 (1938): 56.

[42] Esther L. Friend, "Notifications and Warnings Out: Strangers Taken Into Wrentham, Massachusetts, Between 1732 and 1812," *New England Historical and Genealogical Register* 141 (1987): 192, 193, 335, 337, 339, 341, 350; 142 (1988): 65.

[43] Francis E. Blake, *Worcester County, Massachusetts Warnings, 1737-1788* (1992; Worcester, Mass.: Franklin P. Rice, 1899), 8-12.

[44] George Walter Chamberlain, "Warnings-Out in Malden, Mass., 1678-1794," *New England Historical and Genealogical Register* 92 (1938): 46-60.

1756 to October 1766 involved married couples and their children.[45] The same was true in the sixty cases of warnings issued by Sharon, now in Norfolk County, from 1765 to 1809.[46] In Weston, approximately 300 people received warnings between 1757 and 1803; 58 of them were single persons, 138 were underage children, and 51 were husbands, wives, and their children.[47]

Seeking a new future on the road of migration, these uprooted people tried to keep their families together no matter how big they might be. Given the average size of colonial families, most transient parents tended to have two to four children. It is not uncommon to find that some had as many as five to six dependents—a sure sign of potential burdens to town authorities. Some also had grandchildren with them, such as Robert Patrick and his wife Margaret from Rutland in 1763.[48] The number of dependents in some transient families reached as high as seven, eight, or nine children. Malden, for example, warned Ebenezer Knights, wife Mary, and their eight children Alice, Amaziah, Mary, Ebenezer, Ruth, Matthew, Sarah, and Anna to depart in 1735/6. In 1759, the same town warned Jacob Barrett, wife Rebecca, and their eight children Jacob, John, Jonathan, Joseph, Joshua, Nathan, Rebecca, and Mary to leave.[49] The selectmen of Foxborough warned Nelson Miller, wife Sarah, and their eight children Sarah, John, Nelson, Allen, Rebeckah, Patience, Batney, and Polly from Warren in Rhode

---

[45] Winifred Lovering Holman, "Sudbury Warnings," *New England Historical and genealogical Register* 111(1957): 320-21.
[46] Winifred Lovering Holman, "Warnings Out in Sharon, Mass.," *New England Historical and genealogical Register* 105 (1951): 75-76.
[47] Ann S. Lainhart, comp., "Weston Cautions 1757 to 1803," *New England Historical and Genealogical Register* 144 (1990): 215-24.
[48] Francis E. Blake, *Worcester County, Massachusetts Warnings, 1737-1788* (1992; Worcester, Mass.: Franklin P. Rice, 1899), 57.
[49] George Walter Chamberlain, "Warnings-Out in Malden, Mass., 1678-1794," *New England Historical and Genealogical Register* 92 (1938): 48, 49.

Island in 1791.⁵⁰ Wrentham warned Daniel Trask, wife Rachel, and their seven children Hannah, Mary, Daniel, Rachel, Anna, Rhoda, and Luke in 1782 as well as Thomas Wood, his wife Mary, and their nine children Simeon, Reuben, Ama, Comfort, Lavina, Tillson, Joseph, Lusina, and Olney in 1786.⁵¹ The record number of dependents occurred in Plymouth County, where Wareham authorities warned Daniel Hunt, his wife, and their eleven children in 1773.⁵²

Meanwhile, at the opposite end of the spectrum, well-off people and professionals sometimes showed up in the processions of relocation as well. Pembroke Constable James Randall informed the Plymouth County Court in the summer of 1742 that, based on a warrant from selectmen Jonathan Magoune, Joseph Stockridge, and Ichabod Bonney, he had warned Josiah Cushing, Esq., and his wife Mary. The Cushings had come from the neighboring Duxbury, less than ten miles away, and had resided in his town for about sixty days.⁵³ On September 20, 1758, when John Colman notified the selectmen of Malden that he had taken into his house Sarah Eaton and her three children, he also added that they were planning to go to Pepperell in the fall and that Sarah was "worth £200 besides household stuff."⁵⁴ The most famous child in the warning-out records was Joanna Hutchinson, the niece of Lieutenant Governor Thomas Hutchinson. Her nurse Martha Parkhurst

---

⁵⁰ Robert W. Carpenter, comp., "Foxborough, Mass., Warnings, etc." *New England Historical and Genealogical Register* 65 (1911): 42.
⁵¹ Esther L. Friend, "Notifications and Warnings Out: Strangers Taken Into Wrentham, Massachusetts, Between 1732 and 1812," *New England Historical and Genealogical Register* 141 (1987): 348, 354.
⁵² Ruth Wilder Sherman et al. eds., *Index to Plymouth County, Massachusetts Warnings Out* (Plymouth, Mass.: General Society of Mayflower Descendants, 2003), 32.
⁵³ David Thomas Konig, ed., Plymouth Court Records (Boston: New England Historic Genealogical Society, 2002), 2: 229.
⁵⁴ George Walter Chamberlain, "Warnings-Out in Malden, Mass., 1678-1794," *New England Historical and Genealogical Register* 92 (1938): 50.

took her to Cambridge in 1759.[55] Similarly, on April 15, 1770, Wrentham authorities warned Jonathan Hunt, wife Abiel, and their five children, recording that they were "to all appearances in comfortable circumstances." David Man in the same town informed authorities that he had taken into his house Mary Freeman, "a young woman born and brought up in Attleborough . . . a notable person."[56] Abraham Bigelow informed Weston that he had taken into his house Joshua Underwood, who had come from Lexington "in good Circumstances." Samuel Savage told the same town that he had taken in Mary Meresservie. Although she was "in needy Circumstances," he said she was a nurse to Charlotte Tyler, the daughter of late Thomas Tyler, Esq., of Boston. He assured town authorities that the child was "in Comfortable Circumstances," implying that Mary's stay should not become a public expense for Weston.[57] Insisting that they had not yet had the consent of the town to stay, Lancaster summarily warned seven esquires or gentlemen and their families to depart in fifteen days in a single warrant in 1791.[58]

Not everyone on the move was necessarily looking for land, although most were looking for a new beginning of some sort (see Benjamin Rogers's biography below). Constable John Gould of Malden, for example, warned Deacon Benjamin Brintall to leave and return to Chelsea, from which he had come.[59] Perhaps hoping to find a place to establish their practices, a number of doctors migrated, including Thomas

---

[55] Ann S. Lainhart, comp., "Weston Cautions 1757 to 1803," *New England Historical and Genealogical Register* 144 (1990): 216. Joanna Hutchinson was one of the eight daughters of Foster Hutchinson, Esq. in Boston, brother of Thomas Hutchinson.
[56] Esther L. Friend, "Notifications and Warnings Out: Strangers Taken Into Wrentham, Massachusetts, Between 1732 and 1812," *New England Historical and Genealogical Register* 141 (1987): 331; 142 (1988): 81.
[57] Lainhart, "Weston Cautions 1757 to 1803," *New England Historical and Genealogical Register* 144 (1990): 216, 218.
[58] Josiah Henry Benton, *Warning Out in New England, 1656-1817* (1911; Bowie, Md.: Heritage Books, 1992), 2-3.
[59] George Walter Chamberlain, "Warnings-Out in Malden, Mass., 1678-1794," *New England Historical and Genealogical Register* 92 (1938): 58.

Young, the country doctor from New York who turned radical in Boston.[60] More than a few others also received warnings as they traveled. Wrentham did not have a resident physician until 1721 because it drove the first doctor James Stewart (Stuerd) and his family out of town as soon as they had arrived some twenty years earlier. Demanding security, selectmen admonished Eleazer Gay who had received them, indicating that a community of forty-two robust householders would hardly need a medical man.[61] Bolton warned Dr. Daniel Greenleaf, Jr., wife Nancy, and daughter Silence from Harvard in 1766. Hardwick warned Dr. Shubal Winslow in 1766. Uxbridge warned physician Samuel Willard from Worcester in 1773.[62] Malden warned out Doctor Elisha Story, wife Ruth, and their five children from Boston in 1775.[63] After studying medicine with Dr. Francis Kittredge of Tewksbury, Joseph Munroe, who had come from a long line of Munroes in Lexington, moved to Hillsborough, New Hampshire, around 1784. The second physician in the area, he worked hard to survive, making frequent house calls and often going without rest for several days. Exhausted, he died there in 1798 at the young age of 44.[64] Weston warned Dr. Taft Joseph from Braintree in 1789.[65] Cambridge warned physician Samuel Blodget and his wife Jane from Woburn in 1791.[66]

---

[60] Pauline Maier, *The Old Revolutionaries: Political Lives in the Age of Samuel Adams* (New York: Vintage Book, 1982), 101-38.
[61] Samuel Warner, "Historical Sketch of Wrentham," in *History and Directory of Wrentham, Massachusetts* (Boston: Press of Brown Bros., 1890), 37, 51. Thanks to his connections to the Wares, one of the earliest settlers, the first doctor Benjamin Ware began his practice at Wrentham in 1721.
[62] Francis E. Blake, *Worcester County, Massachusetts Warnings, 1737-1788* (1992; Worcester, Mass.: Franklin P. Rice, 1899), 6, 20, 80.
[63] George Walter Chamberlain, "Warnings-Out in Malden, Mass., 1678-1794," *New England Historical and Genealogical Register* 92 (1938): 57.
[64] Richard S. Munroe, comp., *History and Genealogy of the Lexington, Massachusetts Munroes* (2nd ed.; Florence, Mass., 1986), 86-87.
[65] Ann S. Lainhart, comp., "Weston Cautions 1757 to 1803," *New England Historical and Genealogical Register* 144 (1990): 224.
[66] Ann Smith Lainhart, comp. "Cambridge, Massachusetts Notifications and Warnings Out (1788-1797)," *New England Historical and Genealogical Register* 146 (1992): 89.

On his descriptive list of 1772, Robert Love noted—alongside beggars and lamed soldiers—that "Robert Stutson his wife Leady children Hannah Rachel and a servant boy Benjamin Lamaine last from Wellfleet" had arrived as had "James Price a quarter master in the 64 regt for Old England."[67] Indeed, not only wandering soldiers were conspicuous on many warning lists; occasionally officers appeared as well. For example, in Worcester County, Brookfield authorities warned Captain John Dodge, his wife Ruth, and their servant Mary Harcess in 1759. Bolton warned Captain Abijah Moore, his wife, and eight children from Princeton in 1766. Rutland warned Colonel William Arbuthnot, his wife Betty, and his servants Olive Graves and Henry Grover in 1764. After the revolution, authorities continued to warn not only poor and wounded veteran soldiers, but also veteran officers and their families. In June 1782, Rutland warned Colonel Rufus Putnam, wife Persis, and their nine children from Brookfield, perhaps helping explain why the colonel soon became deeply interested in promoting settlement in the Ohio Valley.[68] In 1783, Captain Joseph Pratt was warned at Malden. On March 5, 1784, Malden authorities warned Captain Baxter Downs, his wife Huldah, and their four children Huldah, Isaac, Baxter, and James.[69]

Finally, understanding who received outsiders and took them into their households can shed light on one hidden aspect of migration that has thus far received little attention—namely, the delicate relations between residents and transients. The fact that few transients were unable to find a place to stay in most

---

[67] List of Warnings Out (May 1 to August 28, 1772), Rare Books and Manuscripts Department, Boston Public Library.
[68] Francis E. Blake, *Worcester County, Massachusetts Warnings, 1737-1788* (1992; Worcester, Mass.: Franklin P. Rice, 1899), 7, 9, 53, 57.
[69] George Walter Chamberlain, "Warnings-Out in Malden, Mass., 1678-1794," *New England Historical and Genealogical Register* 92 (1938): 58, 59. According to local history, the ancestors of both a nineteenth-century Massachusetts governor and a Lexington militia captain on the 19th of April 1775 received warnings in the past. D. Hamilton Hurd, comp., *History of Middlesex* County (Philadelphia: J. W. Lewis & Co., 1890), 1: 611.

communities suggested some benefit of entertaining them. Although it should not be denied that many did receive strangers into their households for charitable purposes, several records indicated that strangers—although poor—could become lodgers and tenants for those who had rooms to let. Some also became servants, maids, apprentices, and hired hands for local families. In other words, some residents wanted strangers for help as much as the latter needed the former for room and board. It is not infrequent to find that town authorities had to warn strangers as much as local residents. Thus, after Ebenezer Upham, a constable of Walden, warned Margret Calvin to take her child and leave town, he warned townsman Thomas Knower "not to entertain her any longer." At a town meeting, the townsfolk of Walden voted "not to allow Isaac Wilkenson anything for keeping his sister Bethiah."[70] In Plymouth County, people in Hanover, Halifax, Kingston, Plympton, and Bridgewater received so many outsiders in the late 1750s that authorities felt compelled to warn more than a dozen local households not to entertain strangers any longer, including the families of a minister and an ensign.[71]

A small town of 700 to 800 souls, Weston warned out 300 people in 50 years. Approximately ninety native inhabitants received those strangers, averaging two strangers per family. Nevertheless, 13 families took in more than 30 percent of all the incoming strangers: John Allen, Abraham Bigelow, John Brown, Samuel Child, Joseph Gierfield, Elisha Harrington, Daniel Livermore, and James Stimson (all took strangers 3 times); Samuel Baldwin, Benjamin Pierce, Joseph Roberts, and Thaddeus Spring (5 or 6 times); and Isaac Jones (8

---

[70] George Walter Chamberlain, "Warnings-Out in Malden, Mass., 1678-1794," *New England Historical and Genealogical Register* 92 (1938): 47. Bridgewater authorities forewarned numerous local residents (including a minister) not to keep strangers, on July 29, 1744, August 5, 1748, January 16, 1764, October 10, 1765, David Thomas Konig, ed., *Plymouth Court Records, 1686-1859* (Boston: New England Historic Genealogical Society, CD-ROM, 2002).

[71] David Thomas Konig, ed., *Plymouth Court Records, 1686-1859.*

times). Many were the heads of substantial families, whose wealth and income were consistently valued at the top of local valuations year after year. Among them, Abraham Bigelow, Esq., was perhaps the richest. His personal properties were valued at £96 14s. and real estate at £150 in 1757—the highest in town. Many of those receiving strangers were also active participants in community affairs. Born in 1739, Thaddeus Spring was a young man in this group. Yet both his personal properties and real estate tripled their values in less than a decade in the 1760s. He was later elected as a selectman thirteen times during a fifteen-year period from 1780 to 1795. Isaac Jones, who took in strangers most frequently in Weston, owned the famous Golden Ball Tavern since 1752. He was a selectman ten times between 1772 and 1793 and was elected representative six times between 1784 and 1790.[72]

Twice the size of Weston and three times in population, Wrentham witnessed a similar situation. Fewer than 150 individuals received more than 1,300 outsiders from 1732 to 1812. This fact suggests that receiving strangers involved not only one's willingness, but also one's ability to accommodate them. One of the most active receivers was David Man, an innkeeper. Conveniently located in the center of Wrentham, his business was right at a crossroads, where the post-road between Boston and Providence met the trail between Taunton and Worcester. Not surprisingly, he took in as many as twenty-eight transient persons over half a century, including ten young girls. Several of them were "smart and healthy," according to his descriptions. One of them later married a mail coach driver, and the new couple set up an inn in town. On the list of local inhabitants who took in strangers, 10 names appeared

---

[72] Town of Weston, *The Tax Lists, 1757-1827* (Boston: Alfred Mudge & Son,1897), *passim*. Town of Weston, *Records of the First Precinct, 1746-1754 and of the Town, 1754-1803* (Boston: Alfred Mudge & Son, 1893), *passim*. Daniel S. Lamson, *History of the Town of Weston, Massachusetts, 17630-1890* (Boston: Geo. H. Ellis Co., 1913), *passim*.

repeatedly—Blake, Ware, Fisher, Shepard, Whiting, Pond, Cook, Man, Day, and Haws—taking in 40 percent of all the newcomers over the years. Most of them were established and influential families in Wrentham. The Fishers gave no fewer than 500 births during the century since the town's founding, whereas the Wares and the Blakes had 400 listed under each of their family names.[73] Clearly not considering the warning-out regulations as a strict prohibition, the prominent local residents who took in strangers included three deacons, four physicians, ten captains, one major, and one colonel. Several of them did so routinely, such as Captain Benjamin Shepard (who took in outsiders ten times), Doctor Timothy Stevens (five times), and Doctor Jenks Norton (six times). Occasionally, taking in strangers seemed all but a family tradition. John Whiting took in strangers three times while his son did twice; David Fisher took in stranger four times, and David, Jr., did so eight times. It seems all too obvious that Wrentham's leading families were also leading the way in receiving strangers. This low regard for warning-out regulations further manifested itself in the following case, which showed how easily strangers and residents could switch their roles. Barely ten months after Wrentham had warned William Puffer, his wife Mary, and their six children from Norton in 1768, Puffer not only managed to stay but also took in the stranger Ebenezer Gilbert, his wife Lydia, and their six children from Norton. As required by warning-out regulations, Puffer then duly reported to town authorities what he had done. Yet he suffered no penalty, just like many of his neighbors who received strangers into their households.[74]

---

[73] *Vital Records of Wrentham, Massachusetts to the Year 1850* (Boston, Mass.: New England Historic Genealogical Society, 1910), 2v.
[74] Esther L. Friend, "Notifications and Warnings Out: Strangers Taken Into Wrentham, Massachusetts, Between 1732 and 1812," *New England Historical and Genealogical Register* 141 (1987): 179-202, 330-57; 142 (1988): 56-84.

Removal

Even though the early impulse in Massachusetts to ward off strangers was strong and long lasting, removal was anything but an immediately decided and well calculated policy. The first generation of residents at Dedham pledged, in their Covenant of 1636, that "we shall by all means labor to keep off from us all such as are contrary minded, and receive only such unto us as may be probably of one heart with us."[75] Apparently, this explicit pledge divulged more a desire of keeping a spiritual uniformity among the local residents than any secular consideration. Only gradually did such a special concern give away to a large one relating to the cost of public aid as settled members at many communities frequently confronted with an influx of outsiders. After receiving complaints from numerous townships about the great charges arising from strangers who pressed in without the consent of local inhabitants, the General Court ordered, in 1655, that all towns shall have liberty to prevent strangers from coming in. No town shall be chargeable for those who did not receive the consent of town inhabitants before their stay. Whoever caused their coming in shall relieve and maintain those who later became needy. Town selectmen were empowered to require security from those who may fall into needy condition, or to forbid the entertainment of them.[76] Clearly, communal membership—the officially recognized legal right to reside at a local community—was not an opportunity open for every newcomer, but a privilege to be obtained only after the careful scrutiny and public approval of the existing local inhabitants and officials.

---

[75] Frank Smith, *A History of Dedham, Massachusetts* (Dedham, Mass.: Transcript Press, 1936), 7.
[76] Nathaniel B. Shurtleff, ed. *Records of the Province of the Massachusetts Bay Colony* (Boston: William White, 1854), III: 376-77.

From then on and for the next hundred and forty years, both the General Court and town authorities doubtlessly remained vigilant about that community membership based on a strict classification separating residents from strangers, thereby protecting the interests of those legal inhabitants. Neither of them, however, was able to find out a straight path of how to achieve that goal. Interestingly, the first settlement law of 1659 did not dwell on the issue of removal at all, but focus on the time limit of three months by which local authorities must deliver a legal warrant demanding a stranger to leave, or else the stranger could become eligible for relief.[77] Not until the three-month rule was reaffirmed in 1692 did the law briefly announce the principle of removal in case of a stranger who refused to leave.[78] Although the General Court several years later extended the time limit to twelve month, which was again reiterated in 1722, it did not clarify or elaborate on the removal proceedings until 1767.[79] By then several contested court cases relating to removal had not only confounded local communities, but also intrigued some of the young, bright, and energetic legal professionals in the commonwealth, such as John Adams.

Concerned with the expenses that any support of the poor strangers might incur, town authorities sometimes tried to rid of them as far as the law—however incomplete it may be—allowed. It is now impossible to ascertain why authorities would remain reluctant in pursuing some cases while unrelenting in others. It is clear, however, that local authorities did have some alternative strategies for reducing potential town charges before going to court. A simple method was to require friends and relatives of the newcomers to provide surety,

---

[77] Nathaniel B. Shurtleff, ed., *Records of the Province of the Massachusetts Bay Colony* (Boston: William White,1854), IV, Pt. 1: 365.
[78] *Acts and Resolves, Public and Private, of the Province of the Massachusetts Bay* (Boston: Wright & Potter, 1869), 1: 68. The original wording was "be sent and conveyed."
[79] *Acts and Resolves*, 1: 451-53; 2: 244-45; 4: 911-12. Simply staying for a year without warning was no longer enough; the 1767 law demanded formal approval by the town meeting for any stranger to gain residency at a local community.

require them to put up a bond, or provide direct support for the needy.[80] When none of these solutions worked, authorities might have resorted to physical removal, which proved to be neither inexpensive nor easy.

In an era when no retirement benefits or social welfare existed, local government on occasion found itself caught in the middle of a family feud. "Whereas," Malden records of 1786 show, "Widow Phebe Green complains that her children have not afforded her the support she needs, the Selectmen agree that her daughter Widow Buckman shall care for her and that her children John Green and Jacob Green will pay the costs of said support and to afford her a 'decent' burial at death, John Green to pay $6 a year for the use of the widow's land." Finding no other options available, Malden directed Constable John Sprague to carry John Polle "to the town of Medford whence he came." It also instructed Constable Nathan Wayte to order Daniel Knower, who had taken a child from Boston, "to carry the child out of town."[81] As settlement laws had several provisions that denied a person's residency, town authorities were willing to try different tactics. Thus, after the death of William Pell, Malden saw a chance to rid itself of his widow Rebecca as her husband was originally from Lynn, where he had lived until 1765, when he married Rebecca Howard.[82] They then came to Malden to stay until the husband's death in 1771. To prevent the widow and her two children from becoming residents of Malden, in July 1772 town authorities ordered Constable Ebenezer Shute to warn Rebecca and her children Rebecca and Susanna to depart.[83]

---

[80] George Walter Chamberlain, "Warnings-Out in Malden, Mass., 1678-1794," *New England Historical and Genealogical Register* 92 (1938): 59.
[81] Ibid., 48, 51, 59.
[82] Deloraine P. Corey, comp., *Births, Marriages and Deaths in the Town of Malden, Massachusetts, 1649-1850* (Cambridge, Mass.: Printed at the University Press for the City of Malden, 1903), 66, 165, 279.
[83] George Walter Chamberlain, "Warnings-Out in Malden, Mass., 1678-1794," *New England Historical and Genealogical Register* 92 (1938): 55.

Any decision to remove a stranger was not as easy as it sounds.[84] Compared with Rhode Island and compared with the extensive records of local and county warning-out notices, the scant evidence of removal cases suggests that only a very few of those warnings ever proceeded to a physical eviction of the poor in Massachusetts. Such discrepancies indicate that perhaps no more than one or two out of every thousand who received warning-out notices ever faced an actual threat of removal.

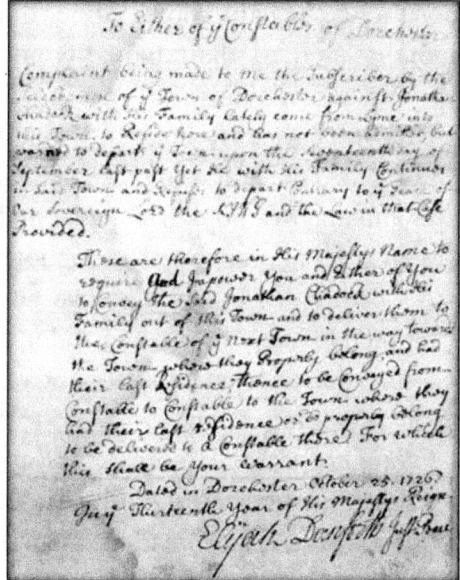

Removal warrant by Elijah Danforth, Justice of the Peace for Suffolk County, to constables of Dorchester to remove Jonathan Chadock and his family back to Lyme (Connecticut), where they most recently came from. Dorchester October 25, 1726. (New England Historic Genealogical Society)

If any township intended to proceed to the removal stage, the town government had to complete several necessary legal procedures: Local selectmen had to authorize constables to warn strangers within twelve months of their arrival as the laws dictated, the warning notice had to be properly recorded at

---

[84] A good comparative reference of the warning-out and removal proceedings is Ruth Wallis Herndon, *Unwelcome Americans: Living on the Margin in Early New England* (Philadelphia: University of Pennsylvania Press, 2001), 4-10.

the County Court of General Sessions of the Peace, and a justice of the peace of the quorum had to issue a warrant to authorize the removal. Any negligence of these steps or the failure to prove their legality and accuracy in court could result in default in a possible lawsuit. Paying for these steps was a small cost compared with the action of removal, which would oblige the town to pay all the expenses on the road for both the constable and the removed. Although the town council of Providence determined, in May 1771, that the single woman Sarah Magee belonged to Boston, the actual removal of her did not commence until three months later. As the removal would cross provincial lines and several counties, all necessary documents had to be properly prepared. Rehoboth, Bristol County, was the first to be informed. Thereafter, town sergeants, constables, or justices in Wrentham, Walpole, Dedham, and Roxbury had to be notified to ensure the proper and continuous relay of Sarah Magee back to Boston.[85] Perhaps because any removal often meant more cost than leaving the strangers alone, town authorities rarely took this drastic step unless removal somehow appeared to be the only option to them.

In addition, many strangers came from far away. Sending all of them back to where they had come from was not only cumbersome, but also downright impossible.[86] Foreigners

---

[85] Warrant[s] of the Removal of Sarah Magee, Rare Books and Manuscripts Department, Boston Public Library. Apparently, Sarah Magee was pregnant at the time of the removal. She was admitted to the Almshouse in Boston at provincial charge on October 1, 1771, and two weeks later she gave birth to a baby boy. Eric Nellis and Anne Decker Cecere, ed., *The Eighteenth-Century Records of the Boston Overseers of the Poor*, Publications of the Colonial Society of Massachusetts, 69 (Boston: The Colonial Society of Massachusetts, 2007), 220, 630.

[86] Records show that colonial authorities, Boston and the provincial government in particular, occasionally did send poor individuals from other colonies or overseas back to where they had come from, such as in the cases of Moses McConnell (February 1760), Mr. Lesly or Lesley (May 1761), John Bennet (July 1761), William Manning (March 1762), Thomas McDaniel (May 1762), Jacob Skweller (June 1767), James Conner (March 1771), a soldier's widow and two children (May 1771), a Hayley the sick chandler from Maryland (April 1772), Michael Larry (May 1772), a woman and four children at the Almshouse (January 1773), and an Ewins bond for Philadelphia (October 1773), *A Report of the*

aside, nobody, including local authorities, knew every stranger's exact birthplace and last abode. For all its efforts to define settlement by birth, marriage, and residency, provincial law was never a sure guide for detecting every newcomer's precise settlement. The hundreds of transients seemed to have infinite ambiguities in addressing these basic questions—when and where they were born, married, widowed, remarried, moved, removed, hired out, bound out, orphaned, or deceased. The uncertainties dissipated only when a town government became absolutely convinced of another town's responsibility to support the transient poor. A lawsuit could thus ensue to force that township to pay for its obligations with the anticipation that, whatever legal expenses were incurred, some other community would ultimately pay them.

Boston authorities learned from experience that a wrong step in the removal proceedings could cost more than the removal itself. In the case of *Chelsea v. Boston* (1769), John Adams successfully argued for the plaintiff Chelsea before the court. The case concerned the proper residence of the poor person William Dix, who was in the almshouse of Boston. Believing that he belonged to Chelsea, Boston authorities secured a warrant from John Hill, a justice of the peace, to send him back to Chelsea. Chelsea selectmen retained John Adams, who wrote a petition on behalf of the town to the Court of General Sessions of the Peace for Suffolk County. He argued that no legal document had proved nor any court decision adjudged Dix to be an inhabitant of Chelsea, which had incurred great expenses for maintaining him who was "poor, lame, and utterly unable to support himself." Moreover, a resident who was rated for poor taxes in Boston, John Hill, Esq., should not be the justice to issue the removal warrant, which could have been tainted for his potential bias in the case. After

---

Record Commissioners of the City of Boston (Boston: Rockwell and Churchill, 1876-1894), 19: 115, 148, 154, 184, 195; 20: 256, 258; 23: 78, 87, 122, 127, 159, 201.

hearing the case, the court was "unanimously of opinion that Justice Hill who granted the warrant had mentioned in said Petition, being at that time an inhabitant of said town of Boston had no legal power so to do and therefore that the prayer of the Petition be granted." Lost in the case, Boston was ordered to take Dix back and pay Chelsea's bill of £20 7s. 4d. for his support in addition to court costs of £5 18s. 2d.[87]

In fact, a number of removal cases became highly contested during the 1760s, when frequent migratory moves alerted local authorities about the need to control the expenses related to strangers. Wrentham selectmen, for instance, brought a case against Attleborough in 1767, claiming that the latter wrongfully sent a poor man named Ebenezer Smith—an inhabitant of Attleborough—to Wrentham. Thus, Attleborough—not Wrentham—was obliged by law to relieve and maintain him "at their own charge." "His removal to Wrentham was irregular and illegal," the selectmen insisted.[88] In Middlesex County, Wilmington complained against Reading for removing the single woman Mary Gilbert into its community. Wilmington selectmen and overseers pointed out a crucial technical detail: Although Reading had warned her in 1763, they had failed to record that warning at the county court as the law required. Gilbert had resided in Reading for two years since and, therefore, had become a legal resident of Reading, which should be responsible for her maintenance. The court agreed, and Reading had to take her back and reimburse the costs and charges Wilmington had incurred in this case.[89]

---

[87] L. Kinvin Wroth and Hiller B. Zobel, eds., *Legal Papers of John Adams* (Cambridge, Mass.: Harvard University Press, 1965), 1: 297-99. Found in the Boston Almshouse as early as August 1765, William Dix was sent back to Boston in January 1770. Eric Nellis and Anne Decker Cecere, eds., *The Eighteenth-Century Records of the Boston Overseers of the Poor* (Boston: Colonial Society of Massachusetts, 2007), 165. *A Report of the Record Commissioners of the City of Boston* (Boston: Rockwell & Churchill, 1893), 23: 16, 17, 54-55.

[88] Wrentham Petition to the Suffolk County Court of General Sessions of the Peace, July 14, 1767, Miscellaneous Bonds, Massachusetts Historical Society.

[89] Middlesex County General Sessions, September 9 to 13, 1766.

The selectmen of Woburn were not as lucky. When they complained against Lexington about a similar situation concerning a woman Mary Powers, the court denied their assertion that Lexington was her legal settlement. Woburn selectmen believed that Lexington had failed to warn her some years ago when she was nine years old. Lexington insisted that they had warned her along with her mother, the husband John McWain (or Mucklewain), and the rest of the family. The court sided with Lexington and concluded that a warning of a family was a proper warning of every individual included in that warning. Woburn then had to pay Lexington the court costs in addition to the expenses for the support of Powers. As many as thirty-one justices attended the Middlesex County Court, which heard and decided two additional cases concerning removals of the poor in *Natick v. Newton* and *Natick v. Medway* during the same session in March 1768.[90]

An aspiring young lawyer in his early thirties, John Adams took note of several such litigations. For example, he commented in his diary about the "sly, artfull, cunning" manner Judge John Cushing had demonstrated in handling the settlement and removal case of "Dumb Tom the Pauper" in 1767.[91] Adams himself worked on at least five cases directly involving the removal proceedings in the 1760s. He was counsel for Lexington and Medway in the previously mentioned cases. The legal disputes between different townships showed the extent to which a community was willing to go to defend its interests, even if this could mean a great deal of time, energy, and money being spent at the court house, not on relief. One of the earliest cases in which Adams was involved was *Roxbury v. Boston*. The case concerned a poor person, Rebecca Choate, whom Roxbury had removed and sent

---

[90] Middlesex County General Sessions, March 15 to 26, 1768.
[91] L. H. Butterfield, ed., *Diary and Autobiography of John Adams* (Cambridge, Mass.: Harvard University Press, 1961), 1: 335-37.

to Boston in 1763. Boston selectmen petitioned the Suffolk County Court and insisted on sending her back to Roxbury, which the court granted in July 1766. Roxbury then appealed to the Superior Court and retained Adams and Jeremy Gridley as counsel. However, their efforts failed because Boston successfully argued that provincial poor law did not grant this kind of appeal in the removal proceedings. The judges agreed, and the appeal was dismissed.[92]

During the same period, Adams also represented Middleboro, which removed Josiah Marshall, who had migrated several times in twenty years. Marshall lived in Plympton from 1747 to 1753, then left for Middleboro to become master of the grammar school. He returned to Plympton in 1758 for a short period before moving again to Pembroke to teach for two years in the early 1760s. He perhaps went from there to Middleboro, which removed him back to Plympton. His exact legal settlement, therefore, was too messy for anyone to ascertain. Finally, the Plymouth County Court ruled the case on a technicality in 1766, deciding that Plympton had to take him back because the town had failed to warn him to depart within the twelve-month limit.[93]

Adams also served as counsel to Brookline in another removal case of 1768, in which he reemphasized the principle that a justice should not be allowed to issue a removal warrant for a town in which he was a resident. In an elaborate courtroom strategy, Adams enumerated that, in the removal proceedings, the person warned and the person removed must be the same person, that authorities must not only notify the constable of the town removing the person, but also the constable of the town receiving the removed, that the town initiating the removal must show evidence establishing the legal

---

[92] L. Kinvin Wroth and Hiller B. Zobel, eds., *Legal Papers of John Adams* (Cambridge, Mass.: Harvard University Press, 1965), 1: 289-93.
[93] Ibid., 1: 294-97.

settlement of the removed, that all names should be specified in the removal warrant if it intended to remove more than one person, and that the court must be clear as to whether the removal of a person would automatically empower authorities to remove the person's goods. Adams's long list of demands and arguments indicated that the removal practices were anything but a well-trodden path in the late 1760s.

Although an English statute, 16 Geo. 2, c. 18.1 (1743), allowed a resident justice to issue a removal warrant for the town, it seemed to be a highly contested principle in the colony. The case of *Brookline v. Roxbury* involved the removal of John Chaddock, his wife, and three children. Roxbury had warned them in 1760 and proceeded to remove them and their possessions to Brookline in January 1767, which led Adams to question whether or not Chaddock had become a legal resident after six years of living in Roxbury. After the Suffolk General Sessions ruled for Brookline, Samuel Fitch, the attorney for Roxbury, sought several legal maneuvers, first by asking for a writ of certiorari and second by filing an assignment of errors. Both maneuvers failed, and the Superior Court upheld the Sessions' ruling that Roxbury should take the Chaddock family back and pay Brookline's account of £67 16s. 4¾ d. as well as court costs of £9 13s. 3d.

The denial of a resident justice to issue any removal warrant seemed to be most detrimental to Boston, where fewer justices were qualified to issue such warrants while the numbers of transients continued to rise. Deeply disturbed, Boston went on to petition the General Court, hoping that a legislative action would reverse the court decision. Signed by selectmen Joseph Jackson, John Hancock, Samuel Pemberton, Henderson Inches, Jonathan Mason, and Ebenezer Storer, the petition protested that the recent court decisions went against the provincial law of 1767, which had allowed residential justices to issue removal warrants for the towns in which they were living. The court decisions deprived the powers of local justices and put a number of towns—especially Boston—at "too much inconvenience and charge." The selectmen warned that Boston's predicament would be the province's too. "The expence of the province is likely to be greatly encreased [originals]" if Boston's justices were no longer allowed to issue warrants for the removal of strangers, many of whom would be charged to the provincial treasury. Facing such pressure, the General Court passed a new law in July 1772, declaring that "the removal of any person, by a warrant obtained from one of his majesty's justices of the peace residing in the town from whence the person is to be sent or conveyed, to any other town, either in or out of the province, shall to all intents and purposes, be deemed as legal a removal as if the warrant had issued from a justice of the peace living in any other town."[94]

In retrospect, although removal was a perfectly legal option for any township, the few surviving cases show more problems than promises in actual removal proceedings during the 1760s, when the local exodus and internal migration reached new highs. The never-ending challenge to identify a transient's exact settlement, the high cost of removal, the manpower and time involved, the unpredictable legal entanglements, and the potential of a prolonged and expensive court battle discouraged local governments from resorting to removal procedures. Migrations and transiency had become such a frequent occurrence that many communities preferred not to take transients too seriously as long as the public treasury could be protected. Migrants and their families provided labor, rent, and services for local residents. Householders, employers, landlords, relatives, and friends always had a way to keep newcomers, who nevertheless had yet to fight for their own legitimate acceptance into a new community. The stern

---

[94] *Act and Resolves*, 5: 198, 260-61. L. Kinvin Wroth and Hiller B. Zobel, eds., *Legal Papers of John Adams* (Cambridge, Mass.: Harvard University Press, 1965), 1: 303-08.

warning-out notices banned them from receiving public aid, but little else.

The intensified mid-century migration created an environment in which moving around relatively unrestrained became a way of life for the strolling migrants. They were not a homogeneous body of the abject poor, but rather a diverse population ranging from officers, veterans, physicians, gentlemen, laborers, and apprentices to servants as well as from married couples and their families to single women, widows, and underage children. Behind the broad spectrum of their dissimilar social and economic situations, many migrants and transients did come from the struggling members of their respective ranks, either high or low in their previous communities. Compared with those families and neighbors who had the luxury of not moving, hardships and uncertainties forced them to leave. In the mix of all the dissimilar family backgrounds, personal experiences, and collective vulnerabilities, they also shared a common desire and spirit as most of those on the move did not look back to the past, but took to the road seeking fresh beginnings.

Resettlement

Sometimes nasty but mostly latent and inconspicuous, the long-lasting tug of war between local inhabitants' attempt to ward off strangers on the one hand and many regional migrants' persistence on moving into a neighboring community on the other provides a useful and yet malleable indicator to gauge the elastic gap between poverty and mobility. Alas, despite an increasing scholarly interest in transiency, few researchers have discovered a tangible method to measure the multiple impacts of warnings-out on domestic migration. By definition, migration was the transient midway between uprootedness and resettlement. For those who frequently moved, a continuous journey from place to place did happen, but was hardly the ultimate goal; finding a suitable home to resettle was. This resettlement could end the migratory move associated with a long search for a new home. It could also mean acceptance of membership into a new community, where the newcomer would finally begin to exchange the role of a stranger for that of a resident. These evolving stages of migration and rotating experiences of the migrants appropriately reflected the transitory natures of eighteenth-century poverty, which constantly influenced the back-and-forth movements between migration and resettlement.

As previously discussed, domestic migration within Massachusetts was not a monolithic whole, but rather a mixture of the poor with many aspiring members of the lower and middles classes. Their different goals and circumstances separated the migrant population into five segments (and their approximate proportions): homeless vagrants (10%), strolling poor (30%), lower class families of limited means (50%), middle and professional class people (5%), and various temporary travelers, visitors, and sojourners (5%). At the low end of the spectrum, some transients took to the road as a way of life, ultimately becoming drifters. Depending on begging and alms for survival, they either were incompetent and too poor to keep a homestead or seldom planned to settle down anywhere anytime soon. Whereas many of them typically came from the dejected poor, including the blind, the crippled, the orphaned, and the widowed, a certain number of run-away law breakers, dislocated refugees, and con men could also fall into this category.[95] Documenting their experiences and whereabouts can be highly difficult, but occasional descriptions in public records do reveal their existence. For example, some newspaper

---

[95] *Acts and Resolves*, 1: 378-81; 5: 46. *Acts and Laws*, 1787: 623-26.

men in Boston felt compelled either to warn locals against traveling quack doctors and impostors or to advise residents to take their linen, clothing, and valuable articles in the yard back to the house after sunset as, according to their estimation, "this is the Season of the Year when Numbers of *Passengers* arrive from a Neighbouring *Land*, whose Summer's Earnings not being sufficient to support them thro' the Winter, introduce themselves here to live upon the honest Industry of the good People of this Place." [96] Several local authorities, such as Brookfield, Oxford, and Worcester in Worcester County, not only warned some newcomers to their communities to leave, but also emphatically characterized them as "transients," giving the impression that the word "stranger" or "poor" was no longer adequate to describe their true status.[97]

The next group, the able-bodied or strolling poor, ventured out to see opportunities in nearby communities, having few resources other than their own family and labor. Unless they knew some relatives and friends, many perhaps did not have a clear plan as to where they really wanted to resettle. Yet they were mentally and physically strong enough to try. Although the warning-out system never completely stopped their movement, it did to a large extent dash their hopes to resettle at a place of their initial choice. Plymouth County records of the 1760s show that only a small fraction of them would succeed in staying in any new community to which they first came. For example, Bridgewater warned Ebenezer Hill, wife Abigail, and five children from Abington, but they managed to stay. Hanover warned Elijah Garnet, wife, and two children to depart, but they disobeyed. Marshfield warned the couple Jeremiah and Elizabeth Hatch, who did not comply but

---

[96] *Boston Post-Boy*, May 25, 1767. *Boston Evening-Post*, November 30, 1767; May 7, 1770.
[97] Francis E. Blake, comp. *Worcester County (Mass.) Warnings, 1737-1788* (Worcester, Mass.: F. P. Rice, 1899), 11, 49, 89.

stayed.[98] Thus, when persevered, a few poor people and families were indeed able to discard the warnings and succeeded in moving into a new place that demanded they leave, thereby becoming *de facto* residents as time went by. However, even if migratory relocation could happen under sheer will, other changes had to wait. No longer transients and strangers, these families would still remain poor long after resettlement, and none of them were able to accumulate enough property to be assessed by their new communities anytime soon.

Meanwhile, many more of those poor being warned had to face two disappointing options: to remove once again further away to somewhere else or to go back to the last place from which they had come. In Plymouth County, where good farmland was limited, evidence shows that of those domestic migrants whose names never appeared on provincial tax rolls, few chose to remove to another community after receiving a warning-out notice. Instead, many felt compelled to take the second option and return to where they first started their journey. Thus, after Rochester authorities warned Jacob Benson from Freetown of Bristol County in 1764, he returned; so did Henry Dillingham and his family, who decided to return to Hanover after they found out that they were not welcome at Scituate, which was less than ten miles away in the same county. Similarly, Peter Jucket returned to Freetown from Rochester, Joseph Hanks returned to Pembroke from Middleborough, Timothy Hatch returned to Chilmark of Dukes County from Rochester, and Elijah Crooker and his family returned to Pembroke from Hanover. The legal barrier of limiting the movements of the poor was not lifted until after independence when, in 1794, the warning-out system finally ended.

---

[98] All individual cases in this segment are based on information from the warning out records, local vital statistics, the provincial valuation of 1771, and the military service and government pension files concerning Massachusetts soldiers during the Revolutionary War.

Supplied with at least some savings and possessions, members of the lower class families on the road of migration had a far better chance than the poor in deciding where to resettle. Records show that nearly all migrants of any modest means were able to choose to resettle within a few years inside or across county lines. For example, more than a dozen townships in Plymouth County warned out 169 men and their families during the 1760s;[99] one in every five of these men's names subsequently appeared on the provincial tax rolls of 1771, indicating that they and their families became accepted residents at various communities, including many of those that had previously ordered their departures. Except for a few cases,[100] nearly all of them were small to modest property owners who paid poll taxes and possessed ratable assets ranging from a few shillings to a few pounds. For example, Bridgewater warned Jonathan Randal's family from Braintree in 1764; they stayed and showed on Bridgewater's tax roll of 1771 for their property valued at £1. Bridgewater also warned Nathaniel Lowden from Pembroke in 1764; he stayed and showed on the same tax roll for a property of £7. Plymouth warned Ebenezer Tinkham from Nova Scotia; he stayed and showed on the tax roll for a property of £2. Plymouth warned Josiah Bradford from Middleborough; he stayed and owned a property of £2 in Plymouth. Scituate warned Henry Richmond and family from Middleborough in 1765; they moved to Plymouth, where they owned £2 of assessable property.

---

[99] It is particularly difficult to trace many single and poor women on the road of eighteen-century migration. Frequently warned by all local authorities, they seldom showed up on tax rolls or other documents. Finding evidential proof to reconstruct their migratory experiences in this period remains a challenge.

[100] Those on the 1771 tax roll without assessable estate included Abraham Howland and his family moving from Pembroke to Plymouth, David Ripley from Hanover to Plimpton, James Bradley from Abington to Bridgewater, Ephraim Eddy from Bridgewater to Norton, Azariah Thrasher and family from Middleborough to Plymouth, Nathaniel Covel from Middleborough to Plymouth, Nehemiah Bryant and family from Middleborough to Plymouth, David Gorham from Nova Scotia to Plymouth, Edward Toten and family from Nova Scotia to Plymouth, and Ephraim Darling from New York to Plymouth.

Scituate also warned Ephraim Cole and family from Middleborough in 1765; they moved to Plympton, where they had a property of £1. Bridgewater warned Levi French from Soughton in 1765; he stayed, owned a property of £6, and had a yearly grain production of 30 bushels. Duxborough warned Ephraim Kempton and his child from Plymouth; they moved to Dartmouth, where he reported a property of £6 and a yearly grain production of 33 bushels. Hanover warned Joshua Pratt and family from Pembroke in 1769; they moved to Bridgewater, where the family owned a property of £20 and had a yearly grain production of 72 bushels.[101]

In the newer Worcester County, where land was still available, seven townships warned out 340 families in the 1760s. About one in every three of them showed on the provincial tax rolls of 1771, indicating an impressive rate of resettlement among the lower class. The distributions of those numbers are as follows:

	Families received warnings	Families stayed where warned	Families became taxpayers in any community
Lancaster	112	21	40 [102]

---

[101] Similar cases are Joseph Mitchell from Nova Scotia, Abraham Howland from Pembroke, Cornelius Smith from Taunton, Samuel Barrow from Plimpton, Ebenezer Hayden Sr. from Pembroke, Micah Allen Middleborough, Josiah Marshall from Plimpton, Jonathan Porter from Bridgewater, Abel Russell warned by Duxborough, Joseph Pettingale warned by Abington, Thomas Fling from Abington, Mark Fo(o)rd from Abington, Isaac Lewis from Middletown, James Colman from Scituate, Thomas Palmer warned by Marshfield, Elijah Leach Sr. from Bridgewater, John Jacobs and Samuel Eddy Sr. warned by Middleborough, Jeremiah Bacon warned by Wareham, Lemuel Delano from Duxborough, Joseph Bartlett Sr. and Jr. from Nova Scotia, and Thomas Toten from Nova Scotia.

[102] Headed by Jonathan Brooks (Charlestown), John Brooks, William Brown (Stow), Thomas Cleland (Colchester in Connecticut), Caleb Church (Harvard), Thomas Grant (New Hampshire), David Goodnow (Marlborough), Stephen Gates (Rowley in Canada), William Judawine (Lunenburg), Joshua Johnson (Stow), Russell Knight (Sudbury), John Loring (Lexington), Thomas Mears (Bolton), Ebenezer Pike, Jr. (Shrewsbury), Jonas Powers (Lunenburg), Moses Russell (Littleton), Benjamin Shed (Lunenburg), Job Spafford (Leominster), Peter Thurston (Pepperell), Jacob Winn (Tewksbury), and Josiah Winn (Bolton), twenty-one families managed to stay at Lancaster. Nineteen others moved again: John Davis (Rutland) to Oxford, Jonathan Fletcher (a minor from Groton) to Rutland District/Barre, Benjamin Goodnow (Shrewsbury) to Petersham, Nathan Goodall (Westborough) to Rutland, Josiah Hosmer (Concord) to Concord, Joseph Houghton (Leominster) to Harvard, Mathew Knight (Leominster) to Winchendon, Gardiner Maynard

Mendon	41	9	13 [103]
New Braintree	18	0	0
Oakham	12	3	5 [104]
Oxford	19	5	7 [105]
Rutland	94	6	40 [106]
Worcester	44	10	19 [107]
Total:	340	54 (15%)	124 (36%)

(Templeton) to Sherburn, Samuel Mason (Lexington) to Winchendon, Hugh Moor (Shirley) to Palmer, Abel Mosman (Princeton) to Princeton, Joseph North (Boston) to Princeton, Reuben Parminter (Rutland) to Princeton, Sylvanus Sawyer (Bolton) to Templeton, John Stearns (Middleton) to Worcester, Nathaniel Sever (Westminster) to Petersham, David Stone (Groton) to Petersham, William Tuffs (Medford?) to New Braintree, and William Withington (Stow) to Stow.

[103] Headed by Benjamin Blake, James Battle(s) (Holliston), Abraham Joslin (Smithfield in Rhode Island), Micah Maddin (Holliston), Joseph Marsh (Douglas), Benjamin Read (Uxbridge), John Wilson, Elias Whitney, Sr. (Framingham), and Elias Whitney, Jr., nine families managed to stay at Mendon. Four others moved again: Read Benjamin (Smithfield) to Rutland, Micah Thayer (Bellingham) to Ware, Peter Thompson (Bellingham) to Charlmont, and Ezra Whitney (Wrentham) to Montague.

[104] Headed by Sheers Berry, Daniel Henderson, and John Stevenson (all from Rutland), three families stayed at Oakham. Two others moved again: Daniel Felton (Marblehead and Rutland) to Petersham and Silas Rice to Rutland.

[105] Headed by Jedediah Blanney, James Brown, John Fessenden, John Morris Jewell (Dudley), and Adams Streeter (Douglas), five families managed to stay at Oxford. Two others moved again: Moses Gage (Andover) to Mendon and Jonathan Rugg to Lancaster.

[106] Headed by George Clark (Worcester), Caleb Harrington, Luke Moore (Sudbury), John Parker, Joseph Wight, and James Williams (Marlborough), six families managed to stay at Rutland. Thirty-four others moved again: Isaac Amsden (Southborough?) to Conway, Olive Graves (Sudbury) to Whatley, Kimball Amsden (Rutland District) to Petersham, Jeremiah Beath (Worcester) to Boothway, Robert Converse (Leicester) to Woburn, Robert Clark to Rutland District, Samuel Duncan (Worcester) to Worcester, Nathan Eager (Leicester) to Lancaster, Aaron Ellis (Dedham) to Winchendon, William English (Spencer) to Greenwich, Daniel Felton (Marblehead and Oakham) to Petersham, Gideon Fisher (Princeton) to Winchendon, James Fuller (Newton) to Lancaster, Samuel Gould (Shrewsbury) to Shirley, John Goodale (Marlborough and) to Conway, Peter Harvey (Holden) to New Salem, Ephraim Heyden (Sudbury) to Sudbury, William Hartwell to Charlmont, Samuel Jones (Brookfield) to Mendon, Joseph Nurse (a minor from Hopkinton) to Hopkinton, Ezekiel Newton, Sr. to Southborough, Ezekiel Newton, Jr. to Southborough, Timothy Newton (Shrewsbury) to Marlborough, David Newton (Paxton) to Southborough, Robert Patrick to Rutland District, Benjamin Pierce (Charlestown) to Weston, Benjamin Parker (Newton) to Southborough, Ephraim Rice (Sudbury) to Petersham, Josiah Rice (Sudbury) to Sudbury, Nathaniel Rice (Sudbury) to Sudbury, William Smith (Western) to Rutland District, David Sprague (a servant from Smithfield in Rhode Island) to Sunderland, James White (Southborough) to Rutland District, and John Winch (Holden) to Framingham.

[107] Headed by Joseph Belknap (Holden), Jonathan Fiske, Samuel Fitts (Sutton), Samuel Griggs (Dedham), Daniel Haven (Dedham), Azael Knight (Stow), Thomas Nichols (Sutton), Joseph Perry (Boston), Moses Redman (Lancaster), and John Wait (Framingham), ten families managed to stay at Worcester. Nine others moved again: James Butler (Charlton) to Lancaster, John Barret (Rutland) to Rutland District, Aaron Farnsworth (Groton) to Groton, Isaac Gleason to Petersham, John Hayden (Boston) to Boston, Isaac Miller (Shrewsbury) to Westborough, John Newton (Marlborough) to Southborough, John Stockwell (Sutton) to Athol, and Peter White (Shrewsbury) to Rutland.

Clearly, except for the situation at New Braintree, a sizable portion of the migrants of modest means were able to resettle and reestablish their homestead in a new community within a few years. Thus, a key difference between this group and the strolling poor was that the lower-class migrants were not easily discouraged after the initial rejection; some 15% of these Worcester County families were able to stay where they had been warned—a small but clear improvement compared with what the poor families experienced. Moreover, many did not return to the old places from which they initially came as the poor did, but instead continued to push on in their journey of migration until they could finally find a new place to settle. Buttressed by their small possessions but attracted to a big future, the lower class demonstrated considerable aggressive, indefatigable, and resilient energies that characteristically distinguished them from the poorer folk on the same road of migration.

As far as the middle class and professional families went, their resettlement was usually not a problem of material qualification, but a matter of time. In addition, although they sometimes did receive warning notices from local authorities as they traveled, many of them were perhaps visitors, sojourners, and passers-by to begin with—namely, they never at all intended to remove into the place they were visiting. Thus, although Pembroke warned Pool Spear from Boston in 1765, he was perhaps not a bit concerned for he owned a property of £13 in Boston. Similarly, when Scituate warned William Gray, also from Boston, in 1766, he did not worry either, because he was a property owner of £33 in that city. Yet the long-time practice of warnings-out could have some psychological impact on the middle class and professional people. Although less concerned with economic and financial matters while migrating or traveling, they sometimes felt compelled to show deference to the local customs that empathically separated strangers from natives. Apparently aware of this sharp divide and highly conscious of his outsider status, a cautious physician gave this public announcement:

> Doctor Sharp of London, being arrived at Boston in his return from Jamaica for England, gives Notice, that he is to be advised with at the Widow Leblonds in Treamount Street, he intending to stay but a few Weeks in this Country: If any are troubled with Cancered Breasts, or other Cancerous, or Scrophulous Tumours, whether in the Throat, or any part of the Body, the King's Evil, Leprosie, Scurvy, Rheumatisms, or Stinking, Rotten Ulcers, proceeding from what Cause Soever. And because he is a Stranger and to prevent the Calumny of designing Men, the Doctor promises where he miscarries of Curing (if Such a thing Should happen) that he will take no Money.[108]

In the end, the good visiting doctor did not even forget to add, "N.B. He gives his advice to the poor Gratis." Apparently, being a stranger could make a highly trained professional from the home country feel very humble indeed in the colony.

※

In summary, during the long history of domestic migration, the warning out system played a dual role of defending relief and managing migration—each with varying effects. In the first role as a convenient tool for defending local relief, it largely succeeded. Tirelessly separating outsiders from natives, the system fostered widespread warnings against any strangers, vigorously protected the local residents' entitlement

---

[108] *Boston Gazette*, October 17, 31, 1720. *Boston News-Letter*, October 17, 1720.

to relief, and thus effectively reduced most newcomers' potential to share that benefit. The system consistently identified, registered, and warned against strangers and transients (especially if they were suspected to be needy), thereby playing a crucial role in protecting community membership from expanding too fast—a common concern of the middle class, who often dreaded extra tax burdens for the maintenance of the poor. It openly helped create two classes of citizens whose distinctions were based not on race, ethnicity, gender, or age, but on the officially accepted legal right of local residency,[109] which was absolutely essential to any community relief.

However, as to the second role it was designed to play in controlling the human flows of migration, the warning-out system was too weak and too unsophisticated to be effective at all. The system never developed into a comprehensive bureaucratic machine powerful enough to impede the vastly active migratory movements within the province. It never led to the practice of, as one critic described the situation in England as late as the mid-1800s, "a most extensive, almost a universal, and nearly indiscriminating liability to 'removal.'" [110] Minimally staffed and financed,[111] the system never received

---

[109] This emphasis on residency may later explain the two-step procedures for foreigners to achieve naturalization in the United States—residency first and then citizenship. However, this subtle but distinctive requirement and local experience has not been fully explored in conjunction with the study of immigration and naturalization policies. Aristide R. Zolberg, *A Nation by Design: Immigration Policy in the Fashioning of America* (Cambridge, Mass.: Harvard University Press, 2006).

[110] George Coode, *On the Law of Settlement and Removal of the Poor* ([London] 1851), 4, 38, 39, 48, 71, 90, 143-45, 184. He estimated that 30,000 cases of removal and more than 15,000 grievances may take place each year because of the existing settlement and removal laws, costing the nation at least 3 to 4 million pounds annually. A sampling of those removal cases and grievances is John Tidd Pratt, *The Laws relating to the Poor* (London: Saunders and Benning, 1833), 121-311.

[111] Little evidence suggests that authorities in Massachusetts even spent as much time to interrogate strangers as their counterparts did in Rhode Island, where many detailed descriptions about the transient population can be found. Ruth Wallis Herndon, *Unwelcome Americans: Living on the Margin in Early New England* (Philadelphia: University of Pennsylvania Press, 2001).

any full-hearted support in most local communities. Middle-class residents including officials, ministers, farmers, and businessmen frequently disregarded the law. Not eager to exclude all strangers at all costs, many local families received these strangers for self-interests by dealing with them as hired hands, helpers, laborers, apprentices, maids, servants, nurses, patrons, clients, boarders, lodgers, renters, employees, craftsmen, partners, and so on. Without any full-fledged local support, the system rarely went so far as to apply the final steps to remove any stranger suspected of low circumstances. Obtaining the new status of local residency was therefore possible for most people on the road of migration, although the strolling poor may have had to fight longer and harder to do so. Aspiring, energetic, and venturesome migrants from the lower and middle classes had realistic potential to achieve local acceptance by moving into the communities they hoped to resettle.

Chapter Four

Meiosis

One of the most highly debated areas in American historiography is whether or not a second revolution took place at home in the era of the Revolution. For example, did poverty play any role in the interval years between the end of the Seven Years' War (1763) and the Battle at Lexington and Concord (1775) in propelling the colonists to rebel? Whig interpretations tend to avoid the question by focusing on political ideology, thereby downplaying the factor of other domestic tensions; meanwhile, revisionist historians' responded in the affirmative largely by overestimating an economic and social conflict between the rich and the poor from within.[1] While recognizing the long existence of degradation throughout the century, the notion of floating poverty nonetheless modified the same question with a key qualifier—namely, in what sense and to what extent poverty played a role in that pivotal decade of epic meiosis.

---

[1] See introduction, notes 4, 5.

Rejecting the fixed pattern of a "yes" or "no" answer to a complex process of historical transformation, the concept of floating poverty helped discern five interlocking facets in that momentous process: (1) The magnitude of poverty was not serious enough to become the root cause of the American Revolution; in other words, the total number of the poor (once again, not those lower and middle class members who were feeling the pains of economic or financial distress) was low, and the scope of penury did not expand to the degree that could lead to a direct and massive internal struggle between the rich and the poor. (2) However, the terror and specter of poverty affecting society in general and, in particular, the middle class's worst fears of falling back into poverty did play a significant role. Compared with the poor who were no strangers to poverty, even if those alarming fears might have been more allegorical and jeremiad than absolutely justifiable or positively quantifiable, the fears themselves were no less important in shaping the perceptional, ideological, and political outlooks of other members in the community—especially its middle classes—who were under that spell. (In this context, Gary Nash's and other similar works need to be taken very seriously and new research needs to be conducted to explore that dimension even further.) (3) Although economic deprivation alone was not the sole villain, it was compounded with other natural calamities and manmade hardships and, hence, could add a great deal of volatility, generated by an unprecedented level of emotional stress and psychological anxiety, to the political chaos and confusions at the time. (4) Large measures of public relief to economically deprived families and victims of diseases, fires, and other misfortunes (such as those of the Boston Massacre and of the Boston Port Bill) not only significantly eased the pains of the native poor and the unfortunate families, but also mobilized the local population, built the alliance between the poor and the middle class, galvanized their energies, aroused their solidarity and patriotism, and thus prepared them for the impending revolution. (5) Corresponding to this social and political realignment, a noticeably new type of rhetoric in many newspaper publications began to proliferate which not only promoted internal unity and Americanism, but also downplayed the link between poverty and individual foibles while attacking external oppression as the root cause for domestic miseries. Property and personal wealth were never the target of this attack; injustice and arbitrary rule from overseas were.

Apparently, a single and undiluted duo of tensions based on social stratification between the haves and the have-nots is inadequate to explain these complexities, many of which were either beyond the control of humans or cross-economic class and trans-social status in nature. Not to deny the power of an ideological or economic interpretation, the notion of floating poverty introduces a different perspective that allows a multi-dimensional approach to the period under examination. Similar to the cell division process of meiosis in which multi-paired chromosomes as well as their different separations and combinations are involved, the pre-revolutionary years showed far more tensions and unconventional realignments than a single focus or a linear interpretation could explain. Yet the growing strengths of all those previously mentioned multiple forces, divisions, combinations, crossovers, and re-combinations ultimately unleashed the energies to fight for independence.

Double-Edged Calamities

If poverty and the fear it engenders never happen in a vacuum, then the threat of poverty and severe anxiety surely do not either, just as momentous turmoil in society is often indicative of a substantial accumulation of forces that have long demanded change. The decade following the end of the Seven Years' War was such a period in history, when the Stamp Act controversy in 1765 turned into a deepening political crisis which ultimately led to the outbreak of war between the thirteen colonies and the mother country. Further compounding these stormy events was the series of domestic challenges from natural calamities and population increases to economic uncertainties that also accelerated during the same period. Rarely did the Bay Colony face so many grave crises affecting both the poor and the middle classes all at once. No matter how much their social ranks and economic circumstances may differ, many experienced widespread anxieties over the threat of stalled economy and witnessed mounting concerns over protection from deadly fires, diseases, and other catastrophes.

Of those threats that were most lethal to human life and of those catastrophes that could destroy the livelihood of all members in society, few were more devastating than fires and epidemics, which repeatedly hit Boston in the 1760s and 1770s. Meanwhile, few events made a community stronger and better organized than the challenges those calamities posted. Mobilizing local resources and manpower to conduct large-scale relief work, such as surveillance, quarantines, inspections, and rescues, required the kind of high-level coordination efforts, organizational skills, and administrative disciplines that only a life-threatening emergency would command.

A town full of wooden structures, Boston was notoriously vulnerable to big and small fires. In 1759 alone, seven fires broke out in Boston. The one on November 14 at Oliver's Dock, according to eyewitness accounts, reduced many to want and poverty. This terrible disaster propelled town authorities and private institutions to join hands in collaborative actions. In a move to seek broad support, Boston selectmen quickly decided to send a letter to neighborhood churches, requesting a collection for relief on the next Lord's day.[2] The following year once again saw seven major fires. On March 20, a strong wind carried an accidental blaze from Cornhill to the waterfront, engulfing four hundred structures in a short time. Estimated damages ranged from £100,000 to £300,000 sterling. Several fine mansions of the well-to-do families were completely destroyed while 214 residents reduced to abject poverty. The destruction was so appalling that sympathetic London merchants collected £3,000 to assist victims. In the end, 439 sufferers received aid in the amount of £13,317 11s. 9d.— an extraordinary charity contributed by good-hearted people across the colonies and from overseas.[3] Although only four fires took place in 1761, the one on the night of January 13 consumed Faneuil Hall, where town selectmen had held their meetings in a special chamber for seventeen years. Within the next five years, from 1765 to 1769, Boston experienced as many as 38 fires, making this period the worst time for fire disasters in colonial history.[4]

Psychologically more frightful than fire were malignant distempers (such as yellow fever, measles, smallpox, and various sorts of influenza) killing four to five hundred people

---

[2] *Report of the Record Commissioners of the City of Boston* (Boston: Rockwell and Churchill, 1876-1894), 19: 102, 103, 105, 107, 111.

[3] News of the fire and victims' names can be found in *Boston Post-Boy* 24 March 1760. *Report of the Record Commissioners of the City of Boston*, 19: 113, 116, 119, 128, 129, 130. Carl Bridenbaugh, *Cities in Revolt: Urban Life in America, 1743-1776* (New York: Alfred A. Knopf, 1965), 102. The General Court quickly passed two acts, on March 29 and June 20, to regulate how to rebuild the destroyed sections in Boston, *Acts and Resolves*, 4: 320-21, 378-80. William Pencak, "The Social Structure of Revolutionary Boston: Evidence from the Great Fire of 1760," *Journal of Interdisciplinary History* 10 (1979): 267-78.

[4] Fire occurred in each year as follows—5 times in 1762, *Report of the Record Commissioners of the City of Boston*, 19: 187, 192, 199, 200, 205; 6 times in 1763, ibid., 9: 244, 258, 260, 273, 282; 4 times in 1764, ibid., 20: 53, 55, 56, 73, 103; 7 times in 1765, ibid., 125, 128, 129, 148, 153, 163, 187; 9 times in 1766, ibid., 20: 195, 206, 217, 218, 219, 239; 6 times in 1767, ibid., 20: 244, 249, 256, 269, 276, 278; 5 times in 1768, ibid., 20: 284, 286, 291, 300; 10 times in 1769, ibid., 23: 3, 4, 12, 18, 21, 35, 36, 43, 51, 52; 2 times in 1770, ibid., 23: 56, 69; 5 times in 1771, ibid., 23: 75, 97, 99; 5 times in 1772, ibid., 108, 113, 118, 137; 7 times in 1773, ibid., 23: 159, 161, 168, 169, 182, 205, 207; 3 times in 1774, ibid., 23: 216, 230, 239; 2 times in 1775, ibid., 23: 243, 247.

every year.⁵ Many remembered that the 1760 influenza epidemic took away the life of Chief Justice Stephen Sewall, whose vacant office then enticed a bitter factional conflict.⁶ Yet people especially feared smallpox, which could break out at anytime without warning. If unchecked, it could quickly spread throughout town, endangering every human life without discrimination.⁷ An influx of transients from land and sea often proved to be the sources of such diseases. In Essex County Marblehead had such a bad experience that a "pox war" took place and deeply divided the maritime community, which split into two factions disagreeing on how to deal with the disease.⁸ Always nervous that some inconspicuous newcomer might bring one of the contagious diseases, Boston tried to keep a watchful eye on strangers and incoming ships from other colonies, foreign countries, and overseas territories such as the West Indies, Bahamas, and Halifax. Preventing a disastrous outbreak through early detection was of the utmost importance for town officials.

Not a single year went by when people did not fear the deadly diseases, but 1764 was one of the worst in memory. Within the first three weeks of January, more than a dozen townsfolk caught smallpox. The news terrified the public, and the threat of contagion was so imminent that the General Court removed itself to Cambridge on January 19.⁹ Boston selectmen shifted into high gear and decided to request permission from the General Court to inoculate if the number of cases

---

⁵ See the death toll from 1701 to 1772 in *Boston News-Letter* 7 January 1773.
⁶ Carol Berkin, *Jonathan Sewall: Odyssey of an American Loyalist* (New York: Columbia University Press, 1974), 24-44.
⁷ Carl Bridenbaugh, *Cities in the Wilderness: The First Century of Urban Life in America, 1625-1742* (New York: Alfred A. Knopf, 1964), 231-47. *Cities in Revolt: Urban Life in America, 1743-1776* (New York: Alfred A. Knopf, 1965), 129.
⁸ George Athan Billias, *General John Glover and His Marblehead Mariners* (New York: Hold, Rinehart and Winston, 1960), 35-48.
⁹ *Report of the Record Commissioners of the City of Boston* (Boston: Rockwell and Churchill, 1889), 20: 15.

approached twenty.[10] They met almost daily and sometimes twice a day and even on the Sabbath to deal with the crisis. The provincial government also issued a general order and demanded ship masters to report any incoming ships carrying infected goods or passengers.[11] Any vessel so determined was quarantined at Castle Island until all patients were cured and all cargo properly cleansed and smoked. No ship or patient could leave until town selectmen were convinced that the ship and its crews and passengers would no longer post a health threat.

Boston selectmen John Scollay and Nathaniel Appleton certified that Eabenezor Stimpson had been so smoked and cleansed as to pass into the country without danger of communicating smallpox to anyone. Boston, August 13, 1776.

As fear and terror spread, many pressed town authorities to begin a general inoculation, even though this early medical practice was far from a pleasant experience. John Adams recorded the following:

> In the Winter of 1764 the Small Pox prevailing in Boston, I went with my Brother into Town and was inoculated under the Direction of Dr. Nathaniel Perkins and Dr. Joseph Warren. This Distemper was

---

[10] The request was granted on January 20, and a town meeting in April finally voted for inoculation. *Report of the Record Commissioners of the City of Boston* (Boston: Rockwell and Churchill, 1889), 20: 14, 15, 16, 18, 57.

[11] Carl Bridenbaugh, *Cities in the Wilderness: The First Century of Urban Life in America, 1625-1742* (New York: Alfred A. Knopf, 1964), 86.

very terrible even by Inocculation at that time. My Physicians dreaded it, and prepared me, by a milk Diet and a Course of Mercurial Preparations, till they reduced me very low before they performed the operation. They continued to feed me with Milk and Mercury through the whole Course of it, and salivated me to such a degree, that every tooth in my head became so loose that I believed I could have pulled them all with my Thumb and finger. By such means they conquered the Small Pox, which I had very lightly. . . .[12]

Surviving that ordeal, Adams was a lucky one. More than a few people died of inoculation, not of the smallpox, during the terrorizing scourge.

By the end of June, smallpox had spread to nearly 700 people in more than 200 families, taking 124 (17 percent) lives—the largest death toll in a single natural disaster to date. Terror settled on the city, as the *Boston Post Boy* wrote. As many as 1,537 people fled and "removed [themselves] into the Country." [13] Among the 5,000 people—one third of the population in town—who had been inoculated, another 46 (fewer than 1 percent) died thanks to the great efforts by twenty-one doctors. In addition, 1,025 of the city's poor were inoculated and treated; more than half received the treatment free of charge. This crisis cost the public treasury several hundred pounds for inoculation, bed, board, nursing, and other medical needs—apart from the damages and losses to business.[14]

---

[12] The Autobiography of John Adams, part one, through 1776, sheet 9 of 53 (1764-1765), The Adams Family Papers: An Electronic Archive, Massachusetts Historical Society, at http://www.masshist.org/digitaladams/aea/browse/autobio1.html.
[13] *Report of the Record Commissioners of the City of Boston* (Boston: Rockwell and Churchill, 1889), 20: 57, 80, 170.
[14] Carl Bridenbaugh, *Cities in Revolt: Urban Life in America, 1743-1776* (New York:

The threat of disease seemed to die down for the next few years, during which time only a handful of cases were found.[15] However, early in 1769, the menace returned. Rumors had it that smallpox had broken out in a regimental hospital at the bottom of the Common, established for 1,500 royal soldiers from Halifax and Ireland. Selectmen went out to inquire and explicitly told the commanding officer General Alexander Mackay that all soldiers with smallpox must be removed to the Provincial Hospital at the West End.[16] The year ended with more than 30 cases of smallpox reported at soldiers' barracks, civilian homes, and municipal hospitals.[17] Although on January 4, 1775, Boston declared that the town "is now entirely free from the Infection of the Small Pox," a week later a lad contracted smallpox at North End. Within the next few months—until the eve of the Lexington alarm of April 19—some fifteen cases of smallpox were reported to Boston selectmen. For anyone who survived those frightful days in early 1764, the resemblance was eerily striking and the situation looked nothing short of another deadly contagion all over again.[18]

Alfred A. Knopf, 1965), 327.

[15] *Report of the Record Commissioners of the City of Boston* (Boston: Rockwell and Churchill, 1889), 20: 154, 156, 157, 190, 274, 284, 296, 300, 308, 316.

[16] *Report of the Record Commissioners of the City of Boston* (Boston: Rockwell and Churchill, 1893), 23: 19.

[17] *Report of the Record Commissioners of the City of Boston* (Boston: Rockwell and Churchill, 1893), 23: 13, 15, 20, 22, 24, 25, 28, 30, 31, 32, 35, 41, 42, 43, 44, 47, 49.

[18] *Boston Post-Boy*, December 26, 1774, p. 3. *Report of the Record Commissioners of the City of Boston* (Boston: Rockwell and Churchill, 1893), 23: 240, 241, 242, 243, 246, 247, 248, 249. For smallpox in the coming months and years see David McCullough, *John Adams* (New York: Simon & Schuster, 2001), 25, 27, 56, 82, 91, 141-42, 143-44, and his *1776* (New York: Simon & Schuster, 2005), 42, 47. What Bostonians feared was only the tip of an iceberg. The scourge continued, ending with an estimated death toll of 130,658. Elizabeth A. Penn, *Pox Americana: The Great Smallpox Epidemic of 1775-82* (New York: Hill and Wang, 2001). See also her essay, "Biological Warfare in Eighteenth-Century North America: Beyond Jeffery Amherst," *Journal of American History* 86 (2000): 1552-80, and Ann M. Becker, "Smallpox in Washington's Army: Strategic Implications of the Disease during the American Revolutionary War," *Journal of Military History* 68 (2004): 381-430.

Hardship and Resilience

Frequent calamities incurred high expenditures as town authorities had to spend large sums to repair damages and care for victims. Not counting the thousands of pounds for inoculation, Boston spent £500 in less than five months to pay for doctors, nurses, hospital keepers, watchers, and grave diggers during the smallpox outbreak of 1764. Rising costs of relief drained public funding, which had long been sinking in the colony's stagnated economy. Heavily dependent on a variety of manufactured products from overseas for local consumption, Massachusetts saw a continuous outflow of hard money to pay for the increasing amount of foreign merchandise colonists desired. Pressed by the need for revenues in several colonial wars, the provincial government increasingly taxed the native population, who had yet to find a major business of local production profitable enough to pay for all the foreign creditors, domestic taxes, and public expenditures.

Except for the 1730s, provincial taxes increased steadily every decade from the beginning of the century. Whereas the population grew by about 25 percent from 1750 to 1765, average taxation rose by as much as 80 percent during those same years.[19] A succession of military expeditions often led to heavy taxation, such as the campaigns against Louisbourg, Cape Breton, and Canada between 1744 and

---

[19] The provincial taxation is as follows by decade—1700 to 1709, £9,400 per year, *Acts and Resolves*, 1: 438-41, 483-86, 494-98,520-25, 533-34, 548-51, 566-70, 589-93, 607-11, 624-28; 1710 to 1719, £10,800 per year (an increase of 14% over previous decade), *Acts and Resolves*, 1: 658-62, 691-95, 711-15, 743-48, 2: 17-22, 52-57, 80-85, 112-18; 1720 to 1729, £21,000 per year (94%), *Acts and Resolves*, 2: 143-48, 174-80, 189-94, 211-17, 2: 251-57, 293-99, 324-30, 352-58, 370-75, 388-95, 440-49, 470-77, 508-15; 1730 to 1739, £20,900 per year (-0.4%), *Acts and Resolves*, 2: 533-41, 565-73, 604-12, 645-54, 679-86, 726-35, 771-80, 802-13, 893-904, 952-64; 1740 to 1749, £31,500 per year (50%), *Acts and Resolves*, 2: 1024-1035, 3: 50-63, 86-100, 156-69, 223-36, 279-90, 345-57, 389-403, 491-92; 1750 to 1759, £35,000 per year (11%), *Acts and Resolves*, 3: 582-94, 684-96, 764-77, 848-60, 875-79, 967-78, 4: 6-17, 145-56; 1760 to 1769, £63,400 per year (81%), *Acts and Resolves*, 4: 247-63, 381-98, 472-85, 583-98, 645-60, 706-19, 818-32, 883-99, 959-73, 5: 5-20.

1748[20] and the expeditions against Kennebeck and Crown Point from 1754 to 1757,[21] while the French and Indian War from 1754 to 1763 cost the colony more than one million pounds.[22] Against this backdrop, the mother country made a bad situation worse as both the Sugar Act of 1764 and the Stamp Act of 1765 demanded payment of new taxes in hard coin.[23] Massachusetts quickly remonstrated with several other colonies, complaining to Parliament that "Money is already become very scarce in these Colonies, and is still decreasing by the necessary Exportation of Specie from the Continent, for the discharge of Debts to British Merchants."[24]

Although soaring public expenses, rising importation and foreign debt, and mounting tax burdens would not disappear anytime soon, colonial productivity was not expanding. Being three million pounds in debt to British merchants, "the trade of this colony was declining fast," said a former colonial agent to London.[25] Determined to find out a solution to escape that economic and financial dependency, the House of Representatives urged the public that "they give all possible Encouragement to the Manufactures of America."[26] Reminiscent of the successes of the 1750s, a group of Bostonians thought of reviving the linen manufactory scheme. Appointed at a town meeting on October 28, 1767, a committee soon reported positively:

---

[20] *Acts and Resolves*, 3: 249, 292, 302, 310, 322, 357, 4: 281.
[21] *Acts and Resolves*, 3: 757, 800, 812, 883, 930, 979, 1022.
[22] *Acts and Resolves*, 4: 160, 199, 215, 268, 270, 335, 370, 375, 421, 427, 460, 490, 491, 538, 578, 602, 623, 665, 680.
[23] Edmund S. Morgan, ed., *Prologue to Revolution: Sources and Documents on the Stamp Act Crisis, 1764-1766* (Chapel Hill: University of North Carolina Press, 1959), 4-8, 35-43.
[24] "The Petition to the House of Commons," in Edmund S. Morgan, ed., *Prologue to Revolution: Sources and Documents on the Stamp Act Crisis, 1764-1766* (Chapel Hill: University of North Carolina Press, 1959), 68.
[25] *Boston News-Letter*, May 23, 1765, Supplement 2.
[26] *Journal of the House of Representatives*, 50: 289, 290.

That it was their opinion this Province had all the natural Advantages for carrying on the Linen Manufacture, and that a sufficient quantity of Flax, may be raised for that purpose, if the Government would give encouragement. . . . They then acquainted the Inhabitants, that they had been informed by good Judges, that Duck or Sail Cloth, has been made in this Province of a superior quality to any commonly imported from Russia.[27]

Subscription for the manufacture of duck and sail cloth, March 15, 1768. Pressed by the need to employ a great number of poor women and children, Boston initiated the new subscription drive less than ten years after the closing of the Linen Manufactory. Overseers of the Poor John Barrett and Henderson Inches (also Edward Payne who became an overseer in the future) led the undertaking as they did for another similar effort in 1764. John Hancock and William Phillips headed this list of subscribers. (Massachusetts Historical Society)

---

[27] *Boston News-Letter*, December 31, 1767.

Thus encouraged, a town meeting in January 1768 unanimously voted to establish a manufacturing of duck or sail cloth. It also decided to start a subscription drive supervised by a committee of six men, most of whom had had experiences in poor relief: John Barrett (an overseer of the poor for twenty-six years), Edward Payne (a future overseer of the poor), Middlecot Cook, Melatiah Bourn (whose brother Nathaniel was a long-time overseer of the poor), Jonathan Williams (an overseer of the poor), and Ezekiel Goldthwait (the town clerk for more than twenty years). As Stephen Edward Wiberley, Jr. has found out that comparing with Philadelphia, New York, and Charles Town, "The overseers of the poor in Boston were the busiest relief officials in the four cities and during their careers had more direct contact with the poor than officials elsewhere."[28] Approximately 200 people pledged support, including 13 of the original 35 subscribers of a similar drive in 1748.[29] Some were prominent men who would become widely known in public life in the coming decade, such as John Hancock, Samuel Quincy, Josiah Quincy, Jr., Joseph Warren, William Bowdoin, Thomas Cushing, Nathanial Appleton (physician), and James Lowell.[30] Other subscribers included at least fifteen past and present overseers of the poor: John Bradford, Samuel Bradford, Ebenezer Storer, John Hunt, John Williams, John Tudor, William Greenleaf, Benjamin Dolbear, William Taylor, Ezekiel Lewis, John Mason, William Phillips (who sent Paul Revere off

---

[28] Stephen Edward Wiberley, Jr., Four Cities: Public Poor Relief in Urban America, 1700-1775, Ph.D. diss., Yale University, 1975, p. 166. Their dedication can hardly be doubted, he further points out, especially among those who served in that office for many years when they often had to pay for relief out their own pocket and only received reimbursement later from government. Ibid., p.177-86.

[29] Those who signed both subscription of 1748 and 1768 were Samuel Grant, John Barrett, Thomas Cushing, Joseph Green, Benjamin Hallowell, Ezekiel Goldthwait, Ezekiel Lewis, Thomas Hubbard, Ebenezer Storer, Thomas Green, William Bowdoin, Josiah Quincy, and William Phillips. Barrett, Hubbard, Storer, and Phillips each served as overseers of the poor for more than twenty years.

[30] Ezekiel Price Papers, Massachusetts Historical Society, 193-96, 333-34.

for the famous alarm in April 1775), John Leverett, Daniel Waldo, and Joseph Waldo.

Also in this group was the Irishman William Molineux, a champion for the working poor and their relief,[31] to whom the town provided loans and advances up to £13,500 over the next few years to employ poor women and children in spinning and processing wool.[32] He worked with several subscribers, including John Rowe, William Dannie, and Jeremiah Lee, all of whom (except for Rowe) later became members of the Tea Party. Fellow Bostonians praised Molineux, who "had for some time been recognized as an impetuous, fearless citizen, whose influence was especially exerted among the working-people."[33] Many believed that Molineux, along with Samuel Adams and Dr. Thomas Young, was one of the radical ring leaders of street action in Boston or, in John Rowe's words, as the "first Leader of Dirty Matters."[34] Whereas his "vigilance and industry" were an inspiration to his associates,[35] Lieutenant Governor Thomas Hutchinson wrote of him in 1770 that "[t]he infamous Molyneux and Young, with Cooper, Adams, and two or three more, still influence the mob, who threaten all who import."[36]

A member of the North Caucus and the Committee of Correspondence, the active Whig Molineux was also "nonimportation chieftain" as the historian Pauline Maier

---

[31] His uncle was the famed "Ingenious [William] Molyneux" (1656-1698), an early proponent of Irish independence. Nellie Zada Rice Molyneux, comp., *History Genealogical and Biographical of the Molyneux Families* (Syracuse, N. Y.: C. W. Bardeen, Publisher, 1904), 134-35, 149, 152-53. Gary Nash, *Urban Crucible*, 333-36. Stephen Edward Wiberley, Jr., Four Cities: Public Poor Relief in Urban America, 1700-1775, Ph.D. diss., Yale University, 1975, pp. 101-09.
[32] *Boston News-Letter*, March 19, 1772.
[33] William V. Wells, *The Life and Public Services of Samuel Adams* (1969; Freeport, New York: 1865-1888), 2: 152.
[34] Anne Rowe Cunningham, ed., *Letters and Diary of John Rowe* (Boston: W. B. Clarke Co., 1903), 286. His reputation reached Salem where some folk named him "General Molineux." *The Essex Gazette*, August 14, 1770.
[35] See John Pitts to Samuel Adams, October 16, 1774, quoted in William V. Wells, *The Life and Public Services of Samuel Adams* (1969; Freeport, New York: 1865-1888), 2: 240.
[36] Quoted in William V. Wells, *The Life and Public Services of Samuel Adams* (1969; Freeport, New York: 1865-1888), 1: 366.

described.[37] Four days after the Boston Massacre, on behalf of town selectmen, he contacted Robert Treat Paine to retain his legal service as counsel for the relatives of the deceased.[38] Along with Samuel Adams, Dr. Joseph Warren, Dr. Young, and others, he was also assigned by the Sons of Liberty to deliver the message warning consignees in Boston not to import tea from Great Britain. As chairman of the committee, he read them the paper and demanded them to sign.[39] He and Dr. Young were the leading members of the radical party that both instigated and participated in the destruction of the tea. In the last public role a month before his sudden death on October 22, 1774, Molineux served on the Committee of Donations, which the town had set up to receive and dispense charities donated from many communities within Massachusetts and from across the colonies for the relief of the poor sufferers after the Boston Port Bill.[40] He committed his last days to the colonial cause, local manufactures, and poor relief.[41]

Similar characteristics spoke well about most of the twenty-six members on the Committee of Donations. Their long efforts to promote colonial interests had earned them the public trust to serve for a common purpose. They included at least five overseers of the poor (William Phillips, Henderson Inches, Edward Proctor, Jonathan Mason, and Henry Hill,

---

[37] David Hackett Fischer, *Paul Revere's Ride* (New York: Oxford University Press, 1994), 301-07. Pauline Maier detailed Molineux's complex relations with the crowd, *From Resistance to Revolution: Colonial Radicals and the Development of American Opposition to Britain, 1765-1776* (New York: W. W. Norton, 1991), 125-31.

[38] William Molineux to Robert Treat Paine, March 9, 1770, Stephen T. Riley and Edward W. Hanson, eds., *The Papers of Robert Treat Paine* (Boston: Massachusetts Historical Society, 1992), 1: xxv-xxvi; 2: 463-64.

[39] William V. Wells, *The Life and Public Services of Samuel Adams* (1969; Freeport, New York: 1865-1888), 2: 104. Anne Rowe Cunningham, ed., *Letters and Diary of John Rowe* (Boston: W. B. Clarke Co., 1903), 252-53.

[40] *Essex Journal*, July 20, 1774. *Essex Gazette*, January 31, 1775. *Massachusetts Gazette*, March 2, 1775. *Journal of the House of Representatives*, 50: 289-90. Arthur M. Schlesinger, *The Colonial Merchants and the American Revolution, 1763-1776* (New York: Longmans, Green & Co., 1918), 315.

[41] Nathaniel Hawthorne turned Molineux's name and career upside down in his short story "My Kinsman, Major Molineux" (1832).

whose collective service in that office totaled more than a hundred years)[42] and several leading Whigs (Samuel Adams, Josiah Quincy, Jr., Thomas Cushing, John Adams, John Brown, and William Molineux, all of whom had been blacklisted by Tories).[43] Still more also became known as earnest supporters for reviving the Boston textile manufactures, such as John Rowe, Thomas Boylston, William Phillips, Josiah Quincy, Jr., Joseph Warren, Thomas Cushing, Nathaniel Appleton, Henderson Inches, Benjamin Austin, Fortesque Vernon, Samuel Patridge, Jonathan Mason, and James Richardson as well as Molineux and John Brown.[44] About one of every five subscribers to the manufacturing schemes of the 1760s became an active Whig in the 1770s. Furthermore, among the 250 publicly known patriotic activists in Boston, one in 10 strongly supported the town's attempt to advance local manufactures, while another 10 would later serve on the Committee of Correspondence in 1774.[45] Clearly, a shared concern over poverty and the poor, an extensive experience in public relief, and a strong commitment to revitalizing Boston economy began to produce a new breed of community organizers whose

---

[42] William Phillips and Henry Hill's father Thomas Hill were among the 35 people who subscribed to the first plan to set up a linen manufactory in Boston in 1748.

[43] A London list of enemies in 1775 identified nine of the committee members—Samuel Adams, William Phillips, Joseph Warren, Fortesque Vernon, Edward Proctor, Samuel Patridge, Benjamin Austin, Jonathan Mason, and John Brown. David Hackett Fischer, *Paul Revere's Ride* (New York: Oxford University Press, 1994), 301-07.

[44] Other committee members were David Jeffries (the town treasurer for 32 years), Thomas Crafts (a Son of Liberty and an active patriot), Gibbins Sharpe (served in the Continental Army), Thomas Greenough (a founder and deacon of the New Brick Church and a firm patriot), Capt. William Mackay (a member of the Committee of Correspondence and president of the Irish Charitable Society), and Mr. John White. *Boston Gazette*, September 26, 1774; December 12, 1774; January 16, 1775; January 23, 1775. *New Hampshire Gazette*, January 13, 1775. Ezekiel Price papers, 75-81, 93-94, 194-96, 333-34, Massachusetts Historical Society. See also Lawrence A. Peskin, *Manufacturing Revolution: The Intellectual Origins of Early American Industry* (Baltimore: Johns Hopkins University Press, 2003), 35, 36, 39, 48.

[45] The estimate was reached by comparing the names in Ezekiel Price papers, 75-81, 93-94, 194-96, 333-34, Massachusetts Historical Society, with those in David Hackett Fischer, *Paul Revere's Ride* (New York: Oxford University Press, 1994), 301-07.

collaboration and leadership skills were crucial in the impending struggles for independence.[46]

Pressures on Expansion

Intense as they were, no commotion had synchronized and no anxiety had streamlined every public act in a single direction during this period. Whereas repeated natural calamities, financial hardships, and economic uncertainties badly hit urban areas along the coast, the number of communities in western rural Massachusetts greatly expanded in the fifteen years from 1760 to 1775. The colony had founded some 80 towns and villages during its first 100 years of settlement. Meanwhile, starting in 1760, in less than two decades the General Court granted permission to establish another eighty-plus towns and plantations, bringing the total number of incorporated communities to half of all the townships existing in Massachusetts today.[47] Such an explosive geographical expansion underscored the unprecedented volatility of the time, affecting the poor and the middle classes alike.[48]

Individually analyzed, communities of rural Massachusetts often appeared peaceable and static. Even if changes did occur, many viewed them as internally driven and significant only to their peculiar local situations.[49] Yet

---

[46] For William Molineux and many of his associates' involvement in illicit trade see John W. Tyler, *Smugglers and Patriots: Boston Merchants and the Advent of the American Revolution* (Boston: Northeastern University Press, 1986).

[47] Growth Chart in Mass., n. d., n. signed, Massachusetts Collection, box 2, folder 8, American Antiquarian Society.

[48] John W. Adams and Alice Bee Kasakoff suggested that as high as 70 to 80 percent of the families they have studied began to move, starting in the 1760s, "Migration and the Family in Colonial New England: The View from Genealogies," *Journal of Family History* 9 (1984), 28.

[49] See Michael Zuckerman, *Peaceable Kingdoms: New England Towns in the Eighteenth Century* (New York: Alfred A. Knopf, 1970) and Robert A. Gross. *The Minutemen and*

underneath the quiet surface and especially considering the colony as a whole, a potent change was gathering momentum. Like any violent eruption in nature, the great expansions of those fifteen years garnered their momentous power through accumulation. These powerful expansions visibly transformed the landscape of the colony only after four kinds of latent social tensions and gradual geographical moves had quietly been making headway for years.

The first quickening came from population increases. Although the population in Boston stagnated, that of the commonwealth increased by more than 30 percent each decade, growing from 164,000 in 1751 to 216,000 in 1760 and 300,000 in 1776.[50] Much of this increase came from the rural and western inlands. For example, incorporated as a township in 1761, Great Barrington in Berkshire County grew from 550 people in 1765 to 961 (an increase of 74 percent) in 1776. Similarly, New Braintree in Worcester County grew from 594 in 1765 to 798 (34 percent) in 1776. Small towns such as New Salem of Hampshire County, Oakham, Petersham, Templeton, and Paxton of Worcester County, and Otis and Patridgefield (later Peru) of Berkshire County all experienced more than 100 percent population increases.[51]

Massachusetts's rocky terrain and barren soil conditions put additional pressure on the constant need to explore new sites of settlements farther and farther away from old ones. Of the eighty townships established during this period, only ten were located in the five eastern counties of Barnstable, Bristol, Essex, Norfolk, and Middlesex,[52] while the rest were located in

---

Their World (New York: Hill and Wang, 1976).
[50] Evarts B. Greene and Virginia D. Harrington, *American Population before the Federal Census of 1790* (1993; New York: Columbia University Press, 1932), 12-19.
[51] All population figures and increases were based on the statistics in the vital records of those named communities respectively.
[52] They are Wellfleet (1775) of Barnstable; Mansfield (1775) of Bristol; Danvers (1775) and Newburyport (1764) of Essex; Ashby (1767), Natick (1762), Pepperell (1775), and Shirley (1775) of Middlesex; Cohasset (1775) and Sharon (1775) of Norfolk.

newer counties such as Hampshire (1662), Worcester (1731), and Berkshire (1761). In Berkshire, more than half of today's thirty-two communities were established during this period.[53] As many as thirty-two townships were set up in Hampshire County, seventeen of which were located in areas west of the Connecticut River.[54] In Worcester, 18 new towns were founded, accounting for 30 percent of all modern-day communities.[55]

A third stimulus for expansion came from a redirected focus of the General Court. The Court had all but ceased to grant land to individuals by mid century, which encouraged a new trend of group petitions for large tracts to start building new plantations. Of all the grants to collective petitioners, the Narragansett Townships and Canada Townships to veteran soldiers and their families deserve further attention. Totaling no fewer than thirty-five in number, these townships constituted a fourth factor that strongly boosted expansions of settlements not only in Massachusetts, but also in neighboring regions—especially Maine and New Hampshire.[56] In an early grant to

---

[53] Seventeen new townships were established during this period in Berkshire County: Alford (1773), Becket (1765), Egremont (1775), Great Barrington (1761), Lanesborough (1765), Lenox (1775), Loudon (1773), New Marlborough (1775), Otis (1773), Pittsfield (1761), Patridgefield (1771, later Peru), Richmond (1765), Sandsfield (1762), Tyringham (1762), West Stockbridge (1774/5), Williamstown (1765), and Windsor (1771).

[54] The thirty-two new towns were established in Hampshire County: Chester (1765), Granville (1775), Ludlow (1774/5), Monson (1775), Palmer (1775), Southwick (1775), Wales (1775), West Springfield (1774), Wilbraham (1763), Amherst (1775), Ashfield (1765), Belchertown (1761), Bernardston (1762), Charlemont (1765), Chesterfield (1762), Colrain (1761), Conway (1775), Granby (1768), Greenfield (1775), Huntington ((1775), Leverett (1774), Montague (1775), New Salem (1775), Norwich (1773), Shelburne (1775), Shutesbury (1761), South Hadley (1775), Southampton (1775), South Brimfield (1762), Ware (1775), Warwick (1763), and Whatley (1771).

[55] The eighteen new townships in Worcester County were Ashburnham (1765), Athol (1762), Barre (1774), Charlton (1775), Douglas (1775), Fitchburg (1764), Hubbardston (1775), New Braintree (1775), Northborough (1775), Northbridge (1775), Oakham (1775), Paxton (1775), Princeton (1771), Royalston (1765), Spencer (1775), Templeton (1762), Westminster (1770), and Winchendon (1764).

[56] George Madison Bodge, *Soldiers in King Philip's War* (Boston: Printed for the Author, 1906), 406-46, and *Year-Book of the Society of Colonial Wars in the Commonwealth of Massachusetts for 1898* (Boston: Rockwell & Churchill, 1898), 139-212. The thirty-five townships have four groups. The first group includes eight Narragansett Townships to those veterans in King Philip's War in 1676—No. 1, lying between the Saco and Pesumpscot Rivers, (now) Buxton, Maine; No. 2, at Wachuset, (now) Westminster; No. 3, Souhegan West, (now) Amherst, New Hampshire; No. 4, Quabbi, west of Hatfield, (now) Greenwich;

Narragansett Townships, a House Committee set these conditions for settlement:

> That each Grantee build a dwelling House of eighteen feet square and seven feet stud at the least on their respective Home Lots, and fence in and break up for ploughing, or clear and stock with English Grass five acres of Land within three years next after their admittance, and cause their respective Lots to be inhabited, and that the Grantees do with the space of three years from the time of their being admitted, build and finish a convenient Meeting House for the publick Worship of GOD, and settle a learned orthodox Minister. . . . And if a sufficient number of Petitioners that have had no Grant within Seven years as aforesaid, viz. Sixty to each Township do not appear, others may be admitted, provided they have fulfilled the Conditions of their former Grant, the Committee to take care that there be sixty three House Lots laid out in as regular compact and defensible manner as the Land will allow of, one of which Lots

---

No. 5, Souhegan East, (now) Bedford; No. 6, (now) Templeton; No. 7, east of No. 1, adjoining Falmouth and Presumpscot Rivers, (now) Gorham, Maine; and No. 8, (now) Voluntown, Connecticut (granted to Connecticut volunteers). The second group has fourteen Canada Townships to those veterans in the expedition against Canada in 1690—1. Dorchester Canada, Ashburnham, Mass.; 2. Ipswich Canada, Winchendon, Mass.; 3. Roxbury or Gardner's Canada, Warwick, Mass.; 4. Sylvester Canada, Richmond, N.H.; 5. Haywood or Rand's Canada, Peterborough, N.H.; 6. Salem Canada, Lyndeborough, N.H.; 7. Cambridge Canada, Lanestown, or New Boston, N. H.; 8. Beverly Canada, Halestown, Weare, N.H.; 9. Rowley Canada, Rindge, N.H.; 10. Gorham Canada, Dumbarton, N.H.; 11. Whitman or Marlborough Canada, Todstown, Henniker, N.H.; 12. Gallup's Canada, Guilford, Vt.; 13. Newbury Canada, Bakerstown, Stevenstown, Salisbury, N.H.; and 14. Newton Canada, Alstead, N.H. The third group gives six grants associated with the Canada Townships, i.e., the equivalent township in Massachusetts for No. 12 was Savoy while the other five equivalent townships were established in Maine—Turner (No. 4), Raymond (No. 8), Bridgton (No. 9), Otisfield (No. 10), and Waterford (No. 11). Lastly, a group of seven townships are named for the old communities where the soldiers had been recruited—Phips Canada (Jay and Canton, Maine), Sudbury Canada (Bethel, Maine), Hingham Canada (Andrewstown, New Hingham, and Chesterfield, Hampshire County, Massachusetts), and Weymouth Canada (Huntstown and Ashfield, Hampshire County, Massachusetts), as well as Fryeburg, Livermore, and Rumford in York County, Maine.

shall be the first settled Minister, one for the second Minister, and one for the School, to each of which an equal proportion of Land shall accrue in all future divisions.[57]

Thus, veteran soldiers' persistent efforts to obtain grants for townships showed to the rest of the population how they might also succeed in their collective endeavors to grow out of the existing communities—a welcome development particularly beneficial to those who had been facing pressure to look for a new home and farmland.

Home Industry and Self-Reliance

Whereas the attempt to promote local business and industry could be traced back to the days of early settlement, the desire became ever stronger as the colony grew. By mid-century, the mother country had engaged the colony in several wars against her rivals. The warfare, though fulfilling her ambitions, plunged Massachusetts into a direct confrontation with European powers, which seriously exposed the colony's financial, economic, and military weaknesses. Although the colony vigorously assisted the mother country, painful memories of a feeble economy fighting against superior powers in some disastrous and costly expeditions did not fade quickly. In the wake of that reality, informed observers and commentators began to explore the potential of how to improve the domestic economy both for a greater contribution to the empire and for a better self-preservation of the colony. Far from control on a reclining scale, the continuous and tightened restraint on the colony after the British victory over the French

---

[57] *Journal of the House of Representatives*, 13: 251.

at the end of the Seven Years' War, however, dashed the middle-class's hope for a speedy revitalization of native economy. The promotion of home industries thus became a defining issue in the public discourse, which took a noticeable turn in its rhetoric.

Gradually but surely the old-fashioned attacks on the idleness of the poor as the bane of society began to fade, while collective poverty as a grave matter of community concern loomed large. Many seemed to have realized that personal foibles, no matter how objectionable they may be, were responsible only for the misfortunes of those individuals. The root cause of the stagnated colonial economy as well as the broad ramifications of poverty that associated with it must lie deeper. In the search for different diagnoses and remedies, several strategies developed and one thought was to take on an offensive against the idleness of the poor and the extravagance of the middle classes in the same breath, hoping industry would rise while waste reduced. "It is very evident," an observer wrote in a Boston newspaper, "that the Encouragement of Manufactures here, by adding a suitable Boundy for encouraging the Industrious, that excel in their respective Performances, would in some degree reform the Idle." "By rendering their Service more necessary," he continued, "the Increase of Business of that kind would enable the Undertakers to pay them greater Wages. Could this be effected, Extravagance would soon be reformed in most of us; for Men employed about that which is profitable, seldom leave Room in their Minds for such Thoughts as tend to subvert their Business."[58]

Other contemporaries, however, sought for broader, if not nobler, answers. "*Patriotism*, or the *Love of our Country*," one wrote, "may be look'd upon as one of the noblest Virtues

---

[58] *Boston Weekly News-Letter*, December 31, 1741.

that ever inhabited the human Breast." "The *public Good* was then the Aim of every Man." And there was never a time that called for "more loudly for the Exercise of this public Spirit" than the present. "God has given us a pleasant Land and a fruitful one." "Nature," he said, "has done enough for us; it is our Business to improve her Gifts." As he suggested for that purpose, "Let us increase our Industry and abate our Extravagance, and the Cry of Poverty will soon cease. I say, let us establish Industry and Frugality, and Prosperity will soon follow them. By these have the *weakest* States been raised to Wealth and Power, while the opposite Vices of Sloth and Luxury have sunk the most *opulent* ones into Poverty and Ruin."[59]

Yet the burdens of raising taxes and supporting provincial expeditions in the latest war were exhausting.[60] While some people celebrated the war by singing "The glorious renovation dawns o'er earth,"[61] others were seriously thinking how to reposition the colony on a more competitive footing. Newspapers frequently published plans calling for innovations and improvements as diverse as projects or proposals on native plants and local husbandry to internal trade. As Boston was contemplating its renewal of the textile manufactory, a small town gentleman donated one hundred dollars in 1768 to be used as premiums for the encouragement of raising the mulberry trees that would feed silk-worms to produce raw silk. The scheme had some initial success. Many families planted several thousand mulberry trees in several communities, and several came to claim the premiums for the extraordinary sizes of their trees, including Mr. Loammi Baldwin of Woburn, the Rev. Jason Haven of Dedham, and Mr. George Sprigs of Boston. Quoting from Dr. Eliot's *Essays upon Field Husbandry*,

---

[59] *Boston Evening-Post*, June 11, 1753.
[60] *Boston Weekly Adviser*, June 5, 1758.
[61] *Boston News-Letter*, September 2, 1762.

observers seemed optimistic that not only good for silk-worms, the mulberry trees were also of quick growth and as durable as red cedar suitable for ship timber and other household carpentry.[62]

After careful inquiries, one thoughtful individual proposed for Massachusetts farmers to improve their way of planting wheat. A farmer once told him that he planted in one year some wheat, which only turned into rye in the end. The predicament, he believed, could lie in the possibility that the farmer may have failed to prepare the field thoroughly, and that he may have sowed a mixture of wheat and rye. The wheat was a more delicate plant than the sturdy rye which, like the weed, could take away all the nourishment the wheat needed if the field was not properly prepared. From a new manual of practical husbandry acquired in London, he suggested that a farmer "must *plow* and *harrow* his Ground 3 or 4 times, to make it as fine as a Garden; then throw it into *Ridges* Six Feet asunder, and a foot high." It was "on the Top of those *Ridges*" that the farmer should plant two or three rows of wheat. If he could properly attend the rows and keep plowing several times until harvest, the farmer would gain a profit twice as much as he might by planting Indian corn in the same field. "Our *Farmers* are in general," he commented, "a Set of honest, industrious, laborious People, who literally get their Bread in the Sweat of their Brow." But they lacked some alternative method of "the true art" of cultivation. He suggested that excerpts from the English manual be printed in inexpensive booklets for the distribution to farmers. He also proposed to have some good English husbandmen to come and demonstrate their techniques for emulation. "This has long been the *Practice* in *England, Scotland,* and *Ireland,* and never fails of Success." "This Method will be easily understood, and will in all Regards,

---

[62] *Essex Gazette*, April 21, 1772. *Massachusetts Spy*, April 9, 1772.

prove the most profitable and beneficial to the *Farmers*," said he, who also predicted that the market in Boston would never be in short supply of naïve-grown wheat if local farmers could execute the plan.[63]

Even though promotions of manufactures and farming dominated most newspaper headlines, commerce was no less enthusiastically recommended as another remedy for self-improvement. Under the title of "The Great Advantage of Trade and Commerce to a Province Considered," one proponent pointed out that "Trade is the Foundation of the Industry of the People." This "appears by Instances too numerous to be mention'd here, as in *England, Holland, Venice, Genoa, Hamburg*, and many other populous States, and Cities in *Europe*," where "an extensive Commerce" was the fabric of society. Take the Dutch, for example, "who from a Set of Fishermen, Soldiers, and Cheesemongers, compell'd to seek an Asylum amongst Hogs and Morasses, have acquir'd the Appellation of the High and Mighty States." The key to that dramatic transformation was a spirit of industry and an active participation in foreign and domestic trade, which now employed "not less than Fifty Thousand Men." If this positive model was not persuasive enough, "compare then this Hive of industrious Bees with the Drones of the *Spanish* Dominions, where you will find their inland Towns, notwithstanding their *Peruvian* Treasures thinly inhabited; the People wretched, dispirited, and unemploy'd; and all owing to the want of an active foreign Commerce." Clearly, "as Trade has dwindled away, the most potent Cities and Towns have been depopulated: Witness the famous Cities of *Tyre, Corlith*, Suez, Alexandria, &c. and . . . *Antwerp* in the *Low Countries, Dunkirk* in

---

[63] *Boston Evening-Post*, October 15, 1759.

Flemings, and even *Southampton*, *Ipswich*, and *Winchelsea*, in *England*."[64]

The proponent was certainly aware that a mutual prejudice existed between the landed and trading interests. While others saw the two as "separate and incompatible," he believed that to be a fallacy which produced "severe Obloquy and Contempt" against trade. Commerce was a great ally to the landed interest, he insisted, because a flourishing commerce would provide full employment, which in turn would "greatly increase the number of inhabitants." Only a full employment and growing population would "raise the Prices of Commodities, and consequently the Rents and value of Land," which would benefit the land owners to the extent that no other businesses could. Trading was also highly valuable to common laborers, including the poor. He explained that "in countries where Trade is most effectually extended, and has the greatest Influence, there the Poor live best and their Wages are highest; where Wages are highest, the Consumption of Provisions is most increased, the Rate of Provisions is highest; and where Provisions are dearest, the Rents and lands are advanced most." Therefore, no one should fear about advancing trade, which would bring prosperity to merchants, land owners, farmers, field helpers, and daily laborers alike. "In short," he concluded, "it is commerce alone which can constitute the Wealth, Power, and Grandeur of a Nation, by promoting the Spirit of Industry amongst its People."[65]

Poverty under Oppression

In so far as the focus of this book is concerned, perhaps the most impressive shift of rhetoric in public discourse was the

---

[64] *Boston News-Letter*, September 2, 1762.
[65] *Boston News-Letter*, September 2, 1762.

changing perspective through which middle-class writers would rethink poverty and its causes. No longer considering poverty either a purely personal matter stemming from individual misfortunes or a limited internal matter to be dealt with on a community basis as convention had always dictated, an increasing number of middle class observers began to look for a broader connection between local poverty and a sinister source from overseas. They unequivocally concluded that external oppression caused domestic deprivation.

More than a few attributed the local sagging economy to the greed of big import-export houses, wholesale merchants, London bankers, and Scottish factors whose tightened loans and credit led to widespread colonial poverty and suffering. Modern scholars confirmed this transatlantic connection. Several big swings, detailed by Marc Egnal and Joseph A. Ernst, propelled the British trade expansion that benefited the colonies starting in the 1740s. Yet at each of the low ebbs, particularly the one after the Seven Years' War, the colonies acutely felt those drowning effects, which they characterized as "our emergency from the present alarming Scarcity of Money, and consequent Stagnation of Trade; and from the almost universal increasing Complaints of Debt and Poverty." [66]

In this time of "stringency," "economic grievances," "bitterness of depression," "debt contraction," and "financial panic," Egnal and Ernst found a broadening involvement of the lower and middle classes, who joined with leading colonial merchants in protest and remonstration. [67] Applying graphic descriptions as disturbing as any ideological ones, some charged the British government that its "people were sinking under poverty and oppression." [68] Others blamed external

---

[66] *Boston Gazette*, September 2, 1767. *Boston Post-Boy*, October 26, 1767.
[67] Marc Egnal and Joseph A. Ernst, "An Economic Interpretation of the American Revolution," *William and Mary Quarterly*, 3d ser. 29 (1972), 3-32.
[68] *Boston Post-Boy*, March 12, 1770.

abuses that "evidently tend to oppress and enslave us."[69] Feeling "the galling yoke of oppression and slavery," still others used incendiary terms ranging from "baleful designs," "odious views," and "impending Evil" to "servile Subjection."[70] Convinced that "whenever the Americans dissolve their union with Britain, in consequence of her oppression, she will thereby receive a fatal wound to her commerce," some went so far as to insist that America's "total slavery is the object of the British ministry."[71] Even William Pitt the Elder, Earl of Chatham, described the situation in Boston after the Port Bill as being "reduced to beggary and famine [of] 30,000 inhabitants."[72]

Traumatized by the economic and financial devastation more directly than poorer members of society, local merchants and members of the middle class were badly shaken in the roller-coaster moves in an increasingly unpredictable but definitively restrictive environment. Quickly organized into the Society for encouraging Trade and Commerce within the Province of Massachusetts Bay in 1763,[73] they complained about the damning effects of Parliament's revenue acts on several major Massachusetts economic activities, such as fishery, lumber, shipbuilding, and the carrying trade of rum and sugar. For example, in the shipbuilding industry, plummeting trade and falling demand reduced the business by at least two thirds, and "the tradesmen formerly employ'd in this branch of business now obliged to procure a livelihood in some manufacture, or starve."[74] Several of their most active participants, such as Thomas Brattle, Isaac Smith, William Phillips (Standing Committee), John Barrett (Standing

---

[69] *Boston Evening-Post*, August 30, 1773.
[70] *Boston Evening-Post*, August 30, 1773. *Essex Journal*, July 20, 1774.
[71] *Essex Journal*, July 20, 1774.
[72] *New-England Chronicle*, October 26, 1775.
[73] Arthur M. Schlesinger, *The Colonial Merchants and the American Revolution, 1763-1776* (New York: Longmans, Green & Co., 1918), 59-60.
[74] *Observations on Several Acts of Parliament* ([Boston] Edes & Gill, 1769), 4.

Committee), William Molineux, Edward Payne, Melatiah Bourne, and Ezekiel Goldthwait, had become quite familiar with issues of poverty in the past because they either served as overseers of the poor or were long committed to the cause of relief. It is interesting to observe that, throughout this period of increasing economic and financial hardships, these members and their Society raised no plan to dodge their paternalistic roles by reducing public aid, which had always made up a sizable portion of local expenses in the past.[75] Instead, they seemed to feel that the most alarming threats to their tax burdens came not from within, but from without.

The first threat was the cost of conducting business. As trade restrictions tightened, the required bonds, certificates, and cockets became increasingly complicated.[76] Local businessmen suffered losses of both time and money because of these cumbersome proceedings, which were, it is believed, a direct consequence of the new trade regulations passed by Parliament as well as the ministry's ambition of reorganizing the customs service in the colonies.[77] The second threat was the loss of income. The Sugar Act of 1764, the Stamp Act of 1765, and the Revenue Act of 1767 imposed new duties, thereby threatening to undercut the profits of ship owners and merchants. For example, Boston imported approximately a million and a

---

[75] The overseers' drafts also increased from about £2,000 each year in the early 1760s to an average of more than £3,000 in the early 1770s. Stephen Edward Wiberley, Jr., Four Cities: Public Poor Relief in Urban America, 1700-1775, Ph.D. diss., Yale University, 1975, pp. 76, 178.

[76] When a local vessel was carrying any enumerated goods, the master must give bond with a surety that the ship should be landed in some British colony or in Great Britain. Before sailing, he secured a certificate from the customs office, stating that a bond was given and the cocket completed. Documenting every article on board a ship, a cocket stated that all regulations had complied with and all duties paid. A passenger or crew member's possession of any article not entered upon the cocket would subject the vessel and its cargo to seizure and even condemnation. Edward Channing, "The American Board of Commissioners of the Customs," *Proceedings of the Massachusetts Historical Society* (1910), 43: 478, 482-83, 485.

[77] *Observations on Several Acts of Parliament* ([Boston] Edes & Gill, 1769), 9-12.

quarter gallons of molasses each year.[78] "The duty on molasses," the Society remonstrated, "tho' reduced to one penny per gallon, which at first sight may appear but small, yet it is one tenth part of the value (when brought to market) is really large, and will be a discouragement to a trade which has insinuated itself into, and is a great spring to every branch of business among us."[79] The third threat came from the abusive behavior of the customs officials and naval officers, who often bullied the locals. In the name of enforcing trade regulations, they sometimes exacted high fees, zealously searched vessels, and not infrequently subjected them to seizure—all of which could generate extra money and prizes, supplementing their fixed salaries.[80]

Furthermore, one of the most damning threats as well as one of the most costly was the fast expansion of an unprecedented imperial bureaucracy in the colony,[81] in which

---

[78] Samuel Eliot Morison, "The Commerce of Boston on the Eve of the Revolution," *Proceedings of the American Antiquarian Society* (1923), 32: 41.

[79] *Observations on Several Acts of Parliament* ([Boston] Edes & Gill, 1769), 5.

[80] For complaints of high fees, see Joseph R. Frese, "Some Observations on the American Board of Customs Commissioners," *Proceedings of the Massachusetts Historical Society* (1969), 81: 11-25. Official deputations authorized naval officers to command revenue vessels and to make seizures. The organization the American Board of Commissioners of the Customs in 1767 greatly increased the use of these vessels. The regular pay for a lieutenant on a small vessel was 4s. per diem, making a seizure and its prize money very attractive. Edward Channing, "The American Board of Commissioners of the Customs," *Proceedings of the Massachusetts Historical Society* (1910), 43: 485. The British laws of this period allowed one half of the value of seized goods and penalties to the seizer in case of seizures at sea, and one third to the seizer in case on land. Dora Mae Clark, "The American Board of Customs, 1767-1783," *American Historical Review* (1940), 45: 799-800.

[81] The American Board of Customs had five commissioners, whose jurisdiction included 42 ports and 9 centers across all the British North American colonies, Newfoundland, Quebec, Halifax, St. Augustine, Pensacola, Mobile, Bahamas, and Bermuda. Various offices of the customs comprised of a cashier and paymaster, a comptroller general, an inspector of imports and exports and register of shipping, a solicitor, a secretary to the board, and four clerks for the secretary's office. To which should add these officials and employees working inside or outside of the customs houses—collectors, comptrollers, surveyors, searchers, preventive officers, land waiters, tide waiters, tide surveyors, boatmen, and watermen. *Boston Post-Boy*, October 26, 1767. *Boston Evening Post*, November 23, 1767. Dora Mae Clark, "The American Board of Customs, 1767-1783," *American Historical Review* (1940), 45: 781-82, 784, 791, 792, 793. Edward Channing, "The American Board of Commissioners of the Customs," *Proceedings of the Massachusetts Historical Society* (1910), 43: 479-81, 484. For the offices and enforcement of customs and trade regulations prior to 1767 see Charles M. Andrews, *The Colonial Period of American History* (New Haven, Conn.: Yale University Press, 1938), 4: 144-221.

the number of public institutions was minimum while the key local officials—such as the selectmen and overseers of the poor—remained unpaid offices for decades. As part of Charles Townsend's ambitious plan, the Commissioners of Customs Act of 1767 authorized the establishment of the American Board of Customs Commissioners (headquarters in Boston), which—in conjunction with the Vice-Admiralty Courts—would enforce trade regulations. Thus,

> Besides the vast charge for troops, men of war, and cutters stationed here to prevent any clandestine trade and to support any officers of the customs in putting these acts (which have regularly been submitted to) in execution. The courts of vice-admiralty are constituted, with a salary of £600 a year to each of the judges, a board of commissioners with a salary of £2500 per annum, also an additional number of Custom House officers appointed by that board, amounting in the whole to near 200, some of whom have salaries from £30 to £50 per annum.[82]

Obviously, supporting such a large imperial machine would fall primarily on the shoulders of the middle class, whose merchants, businesspeople, tradesmen, and property owners comprised the majority of taxpayers and provided the locals with most of the employment, business, and trade opportunities. Even if relief had been a principal public expense in the past, it never rose to the same threatening level as the amount of money now demanded to support the royal bureaucracy. It is estimated that the above mentioned new offices alone would

---

[82] Charles M. Andrews, "The Boston Merchants and the Non-Importation Movement," *Publications of the Colonial Society of Massachusetts* (Cambridge, Mass.: University Press, 1917), 19: 178.

add well over £10,000 a year to the costs paid for by the business and middle class community.

The loathsome prospect must have seemed very depressing indeed to townships such as Boston, Salem, Marblehead, Gloucester, Newburyport, and Nantucket, all of which heavily depended on maritime commerce. "Robbers not content with plundering a rich individual now and then," one man writing to the *Boston Evening Post* warned, "as he may fall their way, but endeavouring to establish a plan to deprive the whole community of their *all* that is valuable in life."[83] Surely, despite strong local protest and resistance, paying the salaries of various customs officials and employees ultimately cost the colonists £20,000 a year while the total annual expenditures for managing the customs system amounted to more than £32,000. Even after these deductions, the American Board of Customs was able to send £8,000 to £9,000 back to the English exchequer each year from 1767 to 1776.[84] The customs duties collected in Boston far exceeded any other major port in the North American colonies, including New York, Philadelphia, Newport, and Charleston. Boston also gained the dubious distinction of having more royal officials on its payroll than "all the other continental colonies put together."[85] Not counting their salaries, the Boston collectors' fees for a year and three months were valued at £1,291.[86] Worse still, custom officials and naval officers harassed people and forced frequent seizures, costing great losses and many legal fees to local businessmen and merchants. Even in times of non-importation, a substitute collector at Salem took up as much as £443 sterling in fees

---

[83] *Boston Evening Post*, February 5, 1770.
[84] Dora Mae Clark, "The American Board of Customs, 1767-1783," *American Historical Review* (1940), 45: 803. Edward Channing, "The American Board of Commissioners of the Customs," *Proceedings of the Massachusetts Historical Society* (1910), 43: 484.
[85] Samuel Eliot Morison, "The Commerce of Boston on the Eve of the Revolution," *Proceedings of the American Antiquarian Society* (1923), 32: 50.
[86] Dora Mae Clark, "The American Board of Customs, 1767-1783," *American Historical Review* (1940), 45: 797.

alone for a six-month period during 1768-69. In the absence of an explicit instruction from the home government, Henry Hulton, one of the five Customs Commissioners, collected a "hospital tax" of £18,265 from 1767 to 1777, averaging £2,000 a year. He took a total of £1,596 (or 10% after a share to a local collector) as his commission, which was a handsome addition to his annual salary of £500.[87] "But these duties," as John Adams concluded, "though more had been collected in this province than in any other" merely "put some plunder, under the name of thirds of seizures, into the pockets of the governors."[88]

Facing these severe difficulties and abuses, the middle class resorted to several strategies—none of which called for a reduction of public relief, which would impact the poor immediately. Instead, they initiated and led an arduous movement of protest against British policies. As James Otis put it, "The TAX! the TAX! is undoubtedly at present the apparent matter of Grievance."[89] Domestically, they promoted non-consumption and non-importation, which relied heavily on the principles of industry, economy, self-denial, and self-restraint. However, unlike in the past, when much of the promotional literature on work ethic targeted the idle and the able-bodied poor, this renewed emphasis on industry and frugality was mostly aimed at middle class families, urging them to work harder, save more, reduce luxuries, curtail extravagance, and—if ever possible—avoid excessive ornaments and superfluities completely.[90] Few newspaper publications failed to carry some

---

[87] A mandate of 6d. deduction from all British mariners' monthly wages supported the royal hospital for disabled seamen at Greenwich. Although the tax could be extended to the colonies, it was never seriously collected for forty years. Joseph R. Frese, "Some Observations on the American Board of Commissioners," *Proceedings of the Massachusetts Historical Society* (1969), 81: 5, 25-29.

[88] John Adams, *Novanglus; Or, A History Of The Dispute With America From Its Origin, In 1754, To The Present Time* (1775), No. 4.

[89] *Boston Evening-Post*, November 30, 1767. *Boston Post-Boy*, November 30, 1767.

[90] Arthur M. Schlesinger, *The Colonial Merchants and the American Revolution, 1763-1776* (New York: Longmans, Green & Co., 1918), 63-64, 107-08.

announcement concerning this sort of persuasion throughout this period. The rhetorical shift was such that "a true Patriot" (a.k.a. a Tory) retorted that much of the so-called domestic productivity and manufacturing existed only "in newspapers."[91]

As a public campaign was clearly underway, the *Boston Gazette* happily reported, on September 2, 1767, "It is with Pleasure we can inform our Readers, That within the last Year, Thirty Thousand Yards of Cloth were Manufactured in one small Country Town in this Province." "We are confidently told," it went on to say, "that in the Town of Lynn upwards of Forty Thousand Pair of Women's Shoes have been made in one Year, equal in Goodness to any imported from Abroad." The report concluded that, "It is judged that the Spirit of Frugality and Œconomy prevails in our Country Towns, as the Demand for European Superfluities is of late very greatly diminished."

According to the *Massachusetts Gazette*, Middleton in Essex County—a small town of 500 residents—produced 20,522 yards of cloth in one year from January 1769 to January 1770, averaging some 40 yards per person.[92] In Bristol, according to the *Boston Post-Boy*, some gentlemen were considering "the Manufacture of Window Glass and other kind of Glass Ware." They went to London, met several principal merchants from this province, and endeavored to get the duty on glass removed. To their dismay, they discovered an opposite outcome: "further Duties upon many Sorts of Goods exported to America."[93] News from other towns was more encouraging. Referring to a paper mill in Milton, an announcement called upon "All Persons that incline to promote our PAPER MANUFACTURE" to save rags, cotton, and linen and send

---

[91] *Boston Evening-Post*, November 23, 1767.
[92] Middleton had 90 houses and between 70 and 80 looms. *Massachusetts Gazette*, March 12, 1770.
[93] *Boston Post-Boy*, March 7, 1768, supplement.

them to an agency in Salem.[94] Although the mill began operation as early as 1730, the proprietors changed its name to Liberty Paper Mill in 1770.[95] The Boston merchant John Gore, Jr. apparently knew the value of attracting customers by advertising merchandize by "North-American Manufactures, viz. Blue, black, claret coloured and mix'd Cloths," as well as "fine Hatfield Thread" and "Lynn Shoes."[96] When colonial businessman Peter Etter and his sons advertised their worsted, thread, and cotton stockings, they deliberately made it clear that their products were "Manufactured in Braintree." They were willing to give a 10% discount to anyone who would appreciate the local products, while declaring their intention to pay cash to any families in the countryside that produced raw silk. Such seriousness about promoting local business and merchandise did not go unnoticed. In an explicitly reciprocal manner, a group of the Sons of Liberty publicly showed their support by announcing that they "now have an Opportunity of manifesting their Regard for the Encouragement of our Manufactures, by calling at the above Store, and buying some of the above mentioned Articles."[97]

In reality, the non-consumption and non-importation movement was not a complete success by any means, as it generated as much confusion and discord as consensus[98]—as did the scheme of promoting domestic productions. Nevertheless, the public's response was widespread and the local population's enthusiasm infectious. "The Subscription

---

[94] *Essex Gazette*, March 20, 1770. *Boston Gazette*, May 27, 1776.

[95] It was the forerunner of Crane & Co., Inc. today. Among others, the company continues to produce high-quality currency and security paper.

[96] Arthur M. Schlesinger, *The Colonial Merchants and the American Revolution, 1763-1776* (New York: Longmans, Green & Co., 1918), 65, 123. *Boston Gazette*, May 8, 1769; June 4, 1770, supplement.

[97] *Boston Evening-Post*, November 23, 1767; November 30, 1767.

[98] Charles M. Andrews, "The Boston Merchants and the Non-Importation Movement," *Publications of the Colonial Society of Massachusetts* (Cambridge, Mass.: University Press, 1917), 19: 224-36, 251-59. Arthur M. Schlesinger, *The Colonial Merchants and the American Revolution, 1763-1776* (New York: Longmans, Green & Co., 1918), 156-80.

Rolls," Boston's initial proposal clearly stated, were "for encouraging Œconomy, Industry, our won Manufactures, and the disuse of foreign Superfluities." In unambiguous terms, its selectmen "strongly recommend that this Measure to Persons of all Ranks, as the most honorable and effectual way of giving a public Testimony of their Love to their Country, and of endeavouring to save it from ruin."[99] From Newburyport in the north to Plymouth in the south, people responded. Charlestown and Dedham unanimously decided to support the ideas of economy and manufacturers, and the subscriptions rolls were "filling up fast."[100] Not counting the ripple effect in other colonies,[101] similar events happened both at several communities adjacent to Boston, such as Cambridge and Roxbury, and at many others far away from the metropolis, such as Watertown, Waltham, Billerica, Grafton, Bridgewater, Littleton, Westford, Leicester, Acton, and Lexington.[102] Most townsfolk highly approved "the truly patriotic Spirit" of Boston, insisting on industry and frugality not simply as the cures for reforming personal weaknesses, but also more importantly as the country's "grand Sources of Wealth and Independence."[103]

Things have come full circle, or so it seems. When Boston first began to experiment with a linen manufactory in the 1750s, most people were preoccupied with the question of

---

[99] *Boston Post-Boy*, October 26, 1767; November 30, 1767.
[100] *Boston Evening-Post*, November 23, 1767; March 5, 1770.
[101] Examples of Connecticut and New York, *Boston Gazette*, January 15, 1770. *Essex Gazette*, March 20, 1770. *Boston Evening Post*, June 18, 1770.
[102] *Essex Gazette*, March 20, 1770. *Boston Evening-Post*, February 5, 1770. Charles M. Andrews, "The Boston Merchants and the Non-Importation Movement," *Publications of the Colonial Society of Massachusetts* (Cambridge, Mass.: University Press, 1917), 19: 191-93, 213. In the province twenty four towns supported Boston's initiative of non-consumption. Arthur M. Schlesinger, *The Colonial Merchants and the American Revolution, 1763-1776* (New York: Longmans, Green & Co., 1918), 110.
[103] *Essex Gazette*, March 20, 1770. *Boston Gazette*, January 15, 1770.

how to reduce domestic poverty and employ the local poor. Few anticipated such an endeavor would have any larger implication than a temporal relief. Perhaps a handful thought otherwise. Charles Chauncy disagreed with those who declared that "the *Linen Manufacture* is *too great* an Undertaking for so poor and small a People." He confidently insisted that "the *Linen Manufacture* has proved a noble Source of Wealth to other People. And why may not we reap the like Benefit from it? Our natural Advantages to carry it on are well adapted to the Purpose. We are in these Respects, exceeded by no People on the Earth."[104] Building on such an experience and inspired by a similar idealism a decade later, Boston renewed its efforts to promote domestic productions. Quickly spreading across New England, the model soon transpired a practical step to combat external oppression into a symbolic act of patriotism.

For "every *Cato* of yours, we shall be able to shew you a *Cornelia*," a female writer declared to the public in a long letter. She observed that a "noble flame of patriotism" has begun to "diffuse itself thro' all ranks of people." "Let me inform you," she stressed, "we have a good deal of publick spirit." When women had to choose in matters concerning the future, she went on, "I can assure you that we Matrons, who are mothers and mistresses of families, and know that our husbands and sons must prosper or decline, with our flourishing or sinking country, will not hesitate a moment about resigning everything inconsistent with the general welfare." "I would consider æconomy with a view to the public good," she said, "and in that light I wou'd give the preference to every suitable article manufactured among ourselves." As to the reasons she continued, "It must doubtless give a sensible pleasure to every virtuous woman, to think that any part of her dress has

---

[104] Charles Chauncy, The *Idle-Poor* Secluded from the *Bread of Charity* by the *Christian Law* (Boston: Thomas Fleet, 1752), 5-22.

employed the poor of her own country, provided food for the Orphan, or made the widow's heart to leap for joy."[105]

"There is certainly a very considerable revulsion in the body-politic here," observed Jared Ingersoll from the neighboring Connecticut. Middle class men and merchants in Boston "turned their thoughts, seemingly in earnest, from navigation to the encouragement of our own manufactures, urging the absolute necessity of it. [. . .]They have actually entered into associations, advanced monies, and set numbers of hands to spinning."[106] Meanwhile, "Wear none but your own country Linnen," one wrote to the *Boston Post-Boy*, to "encourage our own Manufactory." Homespun products thus became a proud testimony of Americanism among many men, women, children, and even Harvard graduates[107]—so much so that some royal officials reported to London that "when the riots and disorders here were at their height on the occasion of the stamp act, these manufacturers were greatly boasted of, and the quantity then made greatly magnified by those who were desirous of distinguishing themselves as American patriots, and would wear nothing else."[108] The renewed interest in the home industry and its popular symbolism inspired much enthusiasm. In Massachusetts and across New England, no fewer than 1,800 women in big and small communities took part in various

---

[105] *Boston Evening-Post*, February 4, 1765. Reprint of a lady Sophia Thrift to the Society for the Promotion of Arts, Agriculture, and Œconomy in the *New-York Gazette*.
[106] From J. I. to T. W. Esq., New Haven, 6 July 1764, *Boston Evening-Post*, November 3, 1766.
[107] *Boston Post-Boy*, November 16, 1767. Linda K. Kerber, *Women of the Republic: Intellect and Ideology in Revolutionary America* (Chapel Hill: University of North Carolina Press, 1980), 38-42. Mary Beth Norton, *Liberty's Daughters: The Revolutionary Experience of American Women, 1750-1800* (Boston: Little, Brown and Company, 1980), 166-69. Alfred F. Young, *Liberty Tree: Ordinary People and the American Revolution* (New York: New York University Press, 2006), 116-17, 124-26. Charles M. Andrews, "The Boston Merchants and the Non-Importation Movement," *Publications of the Colonial Society of Massachusetts* (Cambridge, Mass.: University Press, 1917), 19: 193-95. Arthur M. Schlesinger, *The Colonial Merchants and the American Revolution, 1763-1776* (New York: Longmans, Green & Co., 1918), 110.
[108] Victor S. Clark, *History of Manufactures in the United States* (New York: McGraw-Hill Book Company, 1929), 1: 210.

spinning matches or demonstrations, and several dozen local newspaper articles reported on these activities in 1769 alone.[109] Putting relief and domestic manufacturing on a broad community base, these collective local activities underscored a nascent but fervent belief in building the productive strengths for "our Country" and a "rich and flourishing People."[110] Remarkably, rising external pressures produced a deep sense of internal crisis, while an active search for solutions led to an increasing awareness of the importance of domestic unity, self-determination, self-exertion, self-reliance, and—ultimately—self-government.

---

[109] *Boston News-Letter* June 22, 1769; July 6, 1769; September 28, 1769, Supplement 2. *Boston Evening-Post*, June 5, 1769; July 3, 1769; September 4, 1769. Laurel Thatcher Ulrich, *The Age of Homespun: Objects and Stories in the Creation of an American Myth* (New York: Alfred A. Knopf, 2001), 178. Mary Beth Norton, *Liberty's Daughters: The Revolutionary Experience of American Women, 1750-1800* (Boston: Little, Brown and Company, 1980), 166.

[110] A small pamphlet recommending Industry, Frugality and the Linen Manufacture, *Boston Evening-Post*, June 11, 1753.

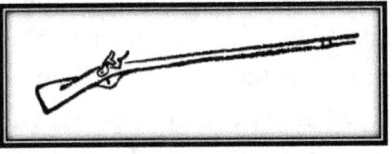

Chapter Five

Soldiering

If America was the poor men's best country, it was because they fought to create it. The American Revolution might have never succeeded without strong support from the poor, who actively participated in the War for Independence. The call for independence galvanized the poor and the lower-middle classes, whose joint efforts and combined sacrifices propelled the American Revolution to success. Although scholars agree with the general assumption that poor people played an important role in this period, few have seriously studied the specific situations in Massachusetts, which contributed more than 20 percent of the continental troops during the war. This chapter fills this void by examining the roles the poor played during those pivotal years that established the nation.[1]

---

[1] All information concerning individual soldiers, sailors, veterans, and their careers in this chapter comes from local history, vital statistics, military records, and pension files. Multiple sources of evidence have been used to ensure the accuracy of each case.

Reliance

That poor members of society often supplied most soldiers in the past is hardly new in history.[2] Yet, while some may not deny the role the poor played in the struggle for independence, to what extent society relied on the poor to conduct the war is not as clear. In fact, few townships in Massachusetts could meet their draft quotas without counting on the able-bodied poor as an important source to fill the ranks. Although not qualified to vote and sometimes not even a legal inhabitant of the community in which they resided, some poor volunteered in the local militia and many more went on to join the Massachusetts regiments and the Continental Army. Newcomers or those who had received warning-out notices made up about 4 to 5 percent of the regular troops (90 to 100 men per company) and 7 to 8 percent of the local militia (40 to 50 men per company). The impoverished—both native and incoming—counted for as much as one half of all enlisted militia men and soldiers. If these assumptions hold, at least 10,000 to 15,000 poor men in Massachusetts fought during the war.[3]

Boston, the hotbed of patriotic fervor, recruited more than 3,000 men on its behalf to fight the war. Only about 7 percent of them were the property owners whose names appeared in the tax valuation of 1771, a crucial document for reviewing the economic status of typical Massachusetts

---

[2] The Bay Colony had a history of impressing marginal men (such as those of low socio-economic status, with no deep roots in local communities, but occasionally of criminal records or debt) into the militia. Kyle F. Zelner, *A Rabble in Arms: Massachusetts Towns and Militiamen during King Philip's War* (New York: New York University Press, 2009).

[3] Recent discussions about the social/economic status of Massachusetts militiamen and soldiers are Charles Neimeyer, "'Town Born, Turn Out': Town Militias, Tories, and the Struggles for Control of the Massachusetts Backcountry," and Walter Sargent, "The Massachusetts Rank and File of 1777," in John Resech and Walter Sargent, eds., *War and Society in the American Revolution: Mobilization and Home Fronts* (DeKalb, Ill.: Northern Illinois University Press, 2007), 23-41, 42-69.

residents shortly before the war. Whereas nearly all of the officers from ensigns and lieutenants to captains and majors were property owners and taxpayers, the overwhelming numbers of privates were not. Of those soldiers who were ratable residents, more than half had a rental value of less than £10 a year.[4] A close look also shows that, the longer term of service, the more likely small property owners and the poor were to be enlisted. Dividing all enlistment terms into five groups according to the number of months served results in the following distribution of average property values of army recruits representing Boston:[5]

£15 for service from 1 to 9 months[6]
£12 for service from 10 to 19 months[7]
£14 for service from 20 to 29 months[8]

---

[4] Philip Swain, "Who Fought? Boston Soldiers in the Revolutionary War" (Honor Thesis in American History, Tufts University, 1981), 60, 62.

[5] All computations below were based on the information of Boston soldiers and officers in Philip Swain, "Who Fought? Boston Soldiers in the Revolutionary War" (Honor Thesis in American History, Tufts University, 1981), 115-242. Yet some discrepancies were found between his numbers and the data in Bettye Hobbs Pruitt, ed., *The Massachusetts Tax Valuation of 1771*(1978; Camden, Me.: Picton Press, 1998). The categorizations here were, therefore, more illustrative than definitive.

[6] The first group included 42 servicemen (and their taxable rental value in parentheses)—David Adams (£5), William Adams (£7), James Addams (£5), Adam Airs (£2), James Allen (£10), Benjamin Andrews (£10), John Bacon (£3), John Barber (£18), John Barnes (£16), John Barrett (£7), William Bennet (£9), William Bowes ((£40), Edward Burbeck (£5), John Cades (£5), Lewis Channy (£4), Joseph Clough (£14), Gilbert Colesworth (£10), Edmund Dolbeare (£8), Nathaniel Dunn (£7), Thomas Emmons (£22), John Gardner (£10), Moses Grant (£23), John Hancock (£60), William Hart (£70), Eleazer Jackson (£33), Henry Johnson (£12), John Joy (£26), Joseph Loring (£17), Thomas Loring (£8), Thomas Lloyd (£16), John Mill (£5), Anderson Philips (£8), Samuel Pierce (£7), Henry Prentiss (£13), Edward Prevear (£10), John Richardson (£6), Edward Rumney (£8), William Smith (£33), John Sumner (£20), James Thompson (£9), William Torrey (£8), and Joseph Watts (£4).

[7] The second group included 19 servicemen—Nathaniel Barker (£36), William Barker (£4), John Barry (£6), William Cooper (£26), William Dawes (£21), William Farmer (£4), John Gill (£46), Samuel Greenleaf (£5), Robert McClary (£12), John New (£5), Thomas Perkins (£4), Charles Perrill (£10), William Perry (£13), Thomas Reed (£9), Levi Stutson (£13), Richard Walker (£10), Thomas Webb (£4), John Williams (£5), and Stephen Winter (£5).

[8] The third group included 18 servicemen—Francis Booth (£7), Gawen Brown (£33), William Cromic (£20), Patrick Daily (£3), Michael Edwards (£17), Benjamin Hall (£17), John Hardey (£3), William Hickling (£13), John Holland, Sr. (£10), Thomas Holland (£8), John Langdon (£46), James Marston (£5), James Otis (£42), Aaron Perbeck (£6), John Sheppard (£9), Zebulon Sylvester (£5), William Taylor (£13), and William Thompson (£11).

£12 for service from 30 to 39 months[9]
£11 for service from 40 months or more[10]

All told, only a fraction of the taxpayers and property owners engaged in military service, which stood at four percent—200 commissioned officers and enlisted men from assessed households out of 5,500 Bostonians on the 1771 tax rolls. The vast majority of Boston soldiers came from the marginal and transient segments in society including large numbers of newly arrived migrants and poor strangers, whose ratio of participation was at least three to four times as high as that of the long-time local proprietors and householders. In the short period of three years between 1771 and 1773 Robert Love, the town searcher for nearly a decade, warned out 1,126 outsiders coming to Boston, including 450 adult men, 360 women, and 300 children. About 15 percent or 71 of those adult men, married or single, later became soldiers, and 22 (30%) of them were enlisted for three and more years in the war.[11] In fact,

---

[9] The fourth group included 23 servicemen—William Adcock (£7), John P. Barnard (£20), William Candell (£11), James Crawford (£8), Temple DeCosta (£16), Benjamin Eustus (£20), Ebenezer Freeman (£17), Andrew Gardner (£8), John Hill (£16), Joseph Ingraham (£10), Ebenezer Jackson (£4), Henry Little (£26), Thomas Mitchel (£11), William Moore (£7), William Page (£10), John Pierce (£2), Samuel Pierce (£5), William Pitts (£9), John Popkin (£10), John Townsend Preston (£26), Joseph Ransford (£3), Thomas Rice (£6), and Richard Salter (£26).

[10] The last group included 41 servicemen—Ebenezer Ballard (£3), Samuel Bass (£26), William Bell (£13), Jonathan Brown (£18), Thomas Brown (£26), John Callender (£4), Robert Campbell (£4), Thomas Cartwright (£11), Nathaniel Cushing (£9), Thomas Daken (£8), Joseph Dyer (£10), Thomas Fitch (£8), Francis Green (£46), Jabez Hatch (£20), Abraham Hunt (£3), Edward Hunt (£13), Henry Jackson (lodger), John Madden (£13), John McClary (£2), Christopher Minot (£10), John Mitchel (£8), Benjamin Mourfort (£3), John Nowell (£20), George Oglesvie (£6), Simeon Osborn (£7), Elias Parkman (£10), William Perkins (£10), Paul Revere (£20), James Shepherd (£10), Holmes Simpson (£7), John Simpson (£5), John Snelling (£6), William Spooner (£20), Abraham Tuckerman (£3), Benjamin Waldo (£10), John Welch (£4), Jacob Wendall (£13), John White (£36), Robert William (£5), William Williams (£20), and John Wright (£10).

[11] The 71 men representing Boston and other towns (in brackets) in service (3 years or more with *) were—John Berry, Rufus Bent, Matthew Bird (Dorchester), Benjamin Bussey, Anthony Castikin, Samuel Champney, *Michael Crosby (Newburyport), Thomas Cummings, Moses Draper (Dedham), Isaac Greenleaf (Medford), Prince George, James Gorden (Scituate), Enoch Hayden (Braintree), Oliver Hunt (Milton), *Peter Jackson, James Ives, Ignatius Jordan (Stoughton), Peter Larken (Westford), Jonathan Nash (Braintree), *Joseph Niles (Braintree), Jonathan Nurse (Barre), Hugh O'Brine (Roxbury), *Daniel

Boston enlisted a total of more than seven hundred common soldiers for the term of three years or during war, but few of them were registered local property owners or taxpayers.

Similarly, from 1769 to 1789, 14 townships in Plymouth County warned 357 adult men and their families to depart; more than 100 of them served in the Revolutionary War.[12] Of the same data, 119 adult males were warned in the first 5 years (1769-1774); 46 of them enlisted in the war while 28 of the enlisted men served for those communities that had originally warned them to leave.[13] Records from Wrentham,

---

Parker (Malden), Thomas Pratt (Abington), Charles Perrin (died at Valley Forge), *Silas Phillips (Easton), Samuel Richards (Dedham), *Charles Richey, John Swain, Laban Sprague (Scituate), Nathaniel Seaver (Brookline), Ezra Tilden (Stoughton), Elijah Tuttle (Cambridge), Spencer Vose, Ezra Wait (Lynn), John Wentworth (Stoughton), *Enoch Wentworth (Stoughton), Elijah Withington (Dorchester), Josiah Brown (Waltham), William Champney, *Benjamin Clark (Framingham), Joshua Davis, Jr., Jason Fairbanks, Daniel Fowler (Swansey), *Thomas Harris, *John Handley, *John Hamilton, *John Hayward, *Daniel Haley, Thomas Hadley (Stoneham), James Hughes, *Benjamin Hunt, Joseph Ingolls, *Gershom Joy (Stoughton), *John Lewis, James Lovell, Patrick Lyon (Sturbridge), *John Mitchell, Richard Nash, *Jacob Reed, John Ruthford, *Richard Rowen, *James Shepard, *John Spear, *Benjamin Smith, Thomas Studley (Scituate), William Studley (Scituate), Benjamin Studley (Scituate), William Waters (Abington), John Walker (Rehoboth), and Thomas Williams (Dorchester). Warning out book from 1771 to 1773, Boston Overseers of the Poor Records, 1733-1925, roll 1, folder 4, Massachusetts Historical Society. Unfortunately for modern historians, Boston did not keep warning records from 1774 to 1790; or it did but the records did not survive. A similar trend took place during the French Revolution as Alan Forrest, after examining 2,832 volunteer soldiers, pointed out that "it was not the sons of the professional classes who were dashing to fight for France." Most of the soldiers were tradesmen, manual workers, and immigrants; some of them were "frequently living in conditions of the utmost misery and degradation." "The Condition of the Poor in Revolutionary Bordeaux," *Past and Present* 59 (1973), 161-163.

[12] Data collected from David Thomas Konig, ed., *Plymouth Court Records, 1686-1859* (Boston: New England Historic Genealogical Society, CD-ROM, 2002), Ruth Wilder Sherman, Robert M. Sherman, and Robert S. Wakefield, comp., *An Index to Plymouth County, Massachusetts, Warnings Out from the Plymouth Court Records, 1686-1859* (Plymouth, Mass.: General Society of Mayflower Descendants, 2003), and *Massachusetts Soldiers and Sailors of the Revolutionary War*, 17 vols. (Boston: New England Historic Genealogical Society, CD-ROM, 2006).

[13] The 28 men were Ebenezer Andrews Jr. from Taunton for Hanover, Lemuel Bates from Pembroke for Hanover, Elnathan Benson from Wareham for Plympton, Jeptha Benson from Middleborough for Plymton, Job Caswell from Pembroke for Hanover, Job Caswell Jr. from Pembroke for Hanover, Robert Corthell from Hingham for Hanover, Calvin Curtis from Scituate for Hanover, Joseph Darling from Plympton for Duxbury, Samuel Darling from Hingham for Duxbury, Samuel Darling Jr. from Plympton for Duxbury, Henry Darling (no settlement, b. Hanover, warned by Scituate and Hanover) for Hanover, Daniel Darling from Scituate, warned by Abington and Pembroke, for Pembroke, Daniel Darling Jr. b. Abington, warned by Pembroke, for Pembroke and Roxbury, William Green from Taunton for Plymouth, Samuel Hollis (no settlement, b. Weymouth, m. Plymouth), warned

Weston, and Lancaster also suggested a broad participation of the poor. Led by Captain Oliver Pond, Captain Benjamin Hawes, and Captain Lemuel Kollock, three Wrentham companies marched on the alarm of April 19, 1775. Their muster rolls listed a total of 116 men, including all officers and soldiers. Only 54 of them were rated in 1771—37 for property tax and 17 for a poll tax only.[14] The other 62 men might not have been rated for several reasons, including (1) they were too poor to be rated, (2) they were under age in 1771, and/or (3) they were newcomers after 1771.[15] Whatever the reason for their omissions, it is not to exaggerate to say that more than half of those volunteer militiamen were from small estates or of no

---

by Kingston, served for Kingston, also Plymouth and Hanover, Nathaniel King from Plymouth for Kingston, Reuben Muxam (b. Rochester, m. Middleborough), warned by Wareham, served for Wareham, Daniel Pratt from Plymouth for Plympton, John Rickard from Plymouth for Plympton, Isaac Robinson from place unknown for Kingston, John Robinson Jr. from place unknown for Kingston, Richard Smith from Raynham, warned by Pembroke from Hanover, served for Pembroke, William Thorn from place unknown for Wareham, Benjamin Tubbs from Pembroke, warned by Plympton, served for Middleborough and Plympton, Joshua Waterman from Plymouth for Kingston, Josiah Waterman from Plymouth for Kingston, and Josiah Waterman Jr. from Plymouth for Kingston.

[14] The 37 men rated for property tax were Capts. Oliver Pond, Benjamin Hawes, Lemuel Kollock, Lts. Timothy Guild, Joseph Everett, Sergeants Elias Bacon, David Ray, Abijah Blake, William Puffer, Jesse Everett, Corporal Elijah Farrington, and Privates John Blake, Benjamin Day, Benjamin Rockwood, Stephen Blake, James Blake, David Man, Samuel Brastow, Daniel Holbrook, David Holbrook, Turil Gilmore, Samuel Pettee, Joseph Ware, Jeremiah Day, Ichabod Turner, Daniel Messinger, Isaac Fisher, Obediah Man, Ebenezer Blake, Benjamin Shepard, John Bates, John Dale (money lent), Ephraim Hunt, James Blake, Jonathan Shepard, Ebenezer Fisher, Jr., and Joseph Hancock. The 17 men rated for poll tax were Lts. Wigglesworth Messinger, Hezekiah Ware, Noah Pratt, Sergeant John Whiting, Drummer Hezekiah Hall, and Privates John Druce, Jonathan Felt, Joseph Field, George Man, John Porter, Oliver Rouse, Jr., Jacob Blake, Oliver Ware, Samuel Baker, Stephen Pettee, Elisha Turner, and David Ware.

[15] The 62 militiamen were Sergeants Nathan Blake, Daniel Guild, Corporals Nathan Hancock, Beriah Braston, Aguilla Robbins, Timothy Pond, Drummer Jason Blake, Fifers Christopher Burlingame, Daniel Cobb, and Privates William Wetherbee, Isaac Clewly, Asa Day, Jonathan Everett, Samuel Frost, John Fisher, Timothy Hancock, David Everett, Jeremiah Hartshorn, Theodore Kingsbury, Ebenezer Kollock, Benjamin McLane, James Newhall, Abijah Pond, Jacob Mann, Peter Raysey, Benjamin Ray, Deodat Fisdale, Daniel Ware, — Ware, John Needham, Moses Craig, William Green, Jason Richardson, Ephraim Knowlton, Jacob Daggett, Oliver Harris, Samuel Wood, Ebenezer Field, John Kingsbury, Jeremiah Cobb, Henry Holbrook, Jacob Holbrook, Samuel Richardson, Jr., Nathan Kingsbury, John Hawes, Ebenezer Gilbert, Daniel Mumm, Stephen Harding, Aaron Hall, Lm. Messinger, Isaac Richardson, Daniel Gould, Joseph Hawes, Jr., Joseph Cook, Jr., Nicholas Barton, Ralph Freeman, Samuel Bolkom, Jeremiah Pond, Benjamin Guild, 2d., Ebenezer Allen, Nathan Moses, and Jesse Ballou.

ratable property at all. Judging by the traditional standard that those paying no property tax were considered poor, the Wrentham militia can be characterized as the poor men's army as the composition of this local militia—from its captains to its privates—was evidently closer to the middle- and lower-ranks in society. A heavy dependence on those lesser and poorer members of the community to raise the local militia began long before the battle at Lexington and Concord started.[16]

Although a smaller town, Weston rated the productivity of its inhabitants higher than that in Wrentham. Yet its militiamen showed the same characteristics. The Weston valuation of 1771 indicated that 44 of the 177 rated households were able to produce 100 or more bushels of grain annually. Only 12 of those 44 household heads joined the local militia.[17] The muster roll of Captain Samuel Lamson's company listed 103 men who had marched on the Lexington alarm. In addition to the 12 men who were valued at 100 bushels a year or higher, 11 others were rated with a household output from 20 to 80 bushels a year.[18] Another 17 men were rated for poll tax only.[19] The rest of the volunteer militiamen, or 60 percent of Captain Lamson's soldiers, were not rated at all,[20] although all his

---

[16] A comparable case is John Shy, "Hearts and Minds in the American Revolution: The Case of 'Long Bill' Scott and Peterborough, New Hampshire," in his *A People Numerous and Armed: Reflections on the Military Struggles for American Independence* (New York: Oxford University Press, 1976), 163-79.

[17] The 12 men were Capt. Samuel Lamson, Lt. Jonathan Fisk, and Privates Jonathan Stratton, Benjamin Peirce, Increase Leadbetter, Isaac Hobbs, Joseph Whitney, Joseph Steadman, Jonas Pierce, John Lamson, Thaddeus Fuller, and Joseph Peirce.

[18] The 11 men were Lt. Mather Hobbs, Corporals Abijah Steadman and Simeon Smith, and Privates John Walker, Jr., Thomas Rand, Samuel Child, Jonas Harrington 3d, John Bemis, William Whitney, Samuel Train, Jr., and Joel Smith.

[19] The 17 men were Sergeants Josiah Steadman, Josiah Seaverns, John Wright, Abraham Hews, Drummer Samuel Nutting, and Privates Isaiah Bullard, John Warren, Jr., Micah Warren, Isaac Flagg, Isaac Cory, William Bigelow, Nathaniel Parkhurst, Samuel Fisk, Ebenezer Steaman, William Bond, Moses Peirce, and Daniel Stratton.

[20] The 63 unrated privates were Nathan Hager, John Allen, Jr., Jonathan Warren, William Hobart, John Frost, Abijah Warren, Isaac Walker, James Jones, Amos Jones, David Sanderson, Abraham Harrington, Samuel Underwood, Eben Brackett, Oliver Curtis, Josiah Corey, Reuben Hobbs, Thomas Rand, Jr., Benjamin Rand, David Fuller, David Livermore, Jacob Parmenter, Thomas Corey, Roger Bigelow, Elijah Kingsberry, Jonas Underwood, Convers Bigelow, John Stimpson, Thomas Williams, Elisha Stratton, Benjamin Bancroft,

officers and staff were. This suggests that, like Wrentham, 80 of the 103 militiamen in Weston were either from poor families or from families of very limited grain-producing capacities.[21]

Lancaster had 474 taxpayers in 1771. Although 144 of them had had a yearly output of 100 or more bushels of grain, only 54 men from this group served as soldiers in the war.[22] According to the 1771 valuation list, Lancaster's 188 soldiers showed the following distribution in regard to their farm income:

47 had no house, land, or grain output[23]
18 had a house but no grain output[24]
18 had a house and a grain production of 40 bushels or less[25]
19 had a house and a grain production of 45 to 50 bushels[26]

Samuel Twitchell, William Bond, Jr., John Flint, John Norcross, William Cary, Daniel Lawrence, Jedediah Bemis, Lemuel Stimpson, Benjamin Dudley, William Lawrence, Elias Bigelow, Abraham Anderson, Josiah Allen, Jr., Daniel Benjamin, Nathaniel Boynton, Eben Phillips, Jedediah Wheeler, Benjamin Peirce, John Peirce, William Jones, John Gould, Solomon Jones, Phineas Hager, Paul Coolidge, Samuel Taylor, Jos. Lovewell, Peter Cary, Samuel Woodward, Elijah Allen, Hezekiah Wyman, Joseph Jennison, Daniel Bemis, and Amos Parkhurst. N. B. Several of these men's fathers were rated, such as John Allen, Sr., Thomas Rand, Sr., and Benjamin Bancroft, Sr.

[21] For the militia personnel of Weston see Daniel S. Lamson, *History of the Town of Weston, Massachusetts, 1630-1890* (Boston: Press of Geo. H. Ellis Co., 1913), 79-80. For the valuation data of Weston see Bettye Hobbs Pruitt, ed., *The Massachusetts Tax Valuation List of 1771* (1978; Camden, Me.: Picton Press, 1998), 288-93.

[22] Henry S. Nourse, *The Military Annals of Lancaster, Massachusetts, 1740-1865* (Clinton, Mass.: W. J. Coulter, 1889), 385-89.

[23] The 47 men were Jonas Powers, Joseph Wheelock, Israel Cook, Samuel Sawyer, Jr., Asa Smith, Joshua Sawyer, John Sergeant, Abel Wyman, Josiah Wilder, James Pratt, Joshua Johnson, Moses Osgood, John White, Jr., Andrew Haskel, Jacob Zwear, Joseph Beaman, Adam Fleeman, Joseph Nichols, Jotham Woods, Titus Wilder, Salmon Goodfry, James Fuller, Asaph Wilder, John Priest, Abel Wright, Ethan Kendal, Mathew Wyman, Benjamin Houghton, Jr., Samuel Churchel, Ephraim Powers, Joseph Fairbanks, John May, John Dunsmoor, Thomas Kendall, John Kindrick, John Wheeler, Obediah Gross, William Ball, Samuel Wilder, Ebenezer Brooks, Jacob Kilburn, Joseph House, Aaron Geary, Joseph Bayley, Oliver Atherton, Samuel Flood, and Abiel Abbott.

[24] The 18 men (of no grain production) were Stanton Carter, Jeremiah Haskel, John Stuart, David Hosly, Robert Phelps, Jonas Wyman, Thomas Cleland, James Clark, Thomas Mears, John Willard, Jonathan Knight, Peter Thurston, Aaron Dressor, Hezekiah Whitcomb, John Moors, Enoch Dole, Thomas Grant, and Isaac Evelith.

[25] The 18 men (with a yearly grain output of 40 bushels or less) were Elijah Wood, Jonathan Whitcomb, John Wheelock, Jr., Ephraim Whitcomb, Samuel Herring, Aaron Willard, Jr., Jonathan Sawyer, Daniel Goss, Thomas Brooks, Jonathan Moors, Micah Harthan, Nathan Gary, Benjamin Priest, Moses Burpee, Benjamin Houghton, George Hibroth, Jabez Brook, and Nathaniel Sawyer.

15 had a house and a grain production of 60 to 75 bushels[27]
17 had a house and a grain production of 80 to 90 bushels[28]
24 had a house and a grain production of 100 to 110 bushels[29]
14 had a house and a grain production of 120 to 130 bushels[30]
9 had a house and a grain production of 140 to 160 bushels[31]
5 had a house and a grain production of 200 to 220 bushels
2 had a house and a grain production of 300 bushels or more.[32]

Thus, of the 188 soldiers, 65 had no farm income and 37 had less than 50 bushels a year. This indicates that more than half of Lancaster soldiers came from day laborers, poor families, or households of subsistence. Moreover, about 500 additional names of soldiers did not appear on the 1771 tax rolls at all, suggesting that Lancaster must have recruited more poor persons, newcomers, emerging young householders, and traveling strangers into the ranks.

As the war dragged on after the siege of Boston ended in March 1776, finding and engaging poor persons in long-term enlistment (for six months or more) became increasingly

---

[26] The 19 men were Abner Haskel, Aaron Willard, Jonathan Wheelock, Nathaniel Beaman, Cyrus Fairbanks, Nathaniel Wright, John Hewitt, John Hawks, James Houghton, John Loring, John Nichols, John Bennett, Timothy Haywood, John Snow, Nathaniel Jones, Samuel Snow, John Warner, William Jewett, and Stephen Wilder.

[27] The 15 men were Abijah Philips, John Brooks, James Goodwin, Ephraim Wilder, Thomas May, Joseph Sever, John Parson, Abijah Houghton, Caleb Whitney, Shubael Bailey, Samuel Prentice, John Wheelock, Jabez Fairbanks, Josiah Fairbanks, and Samuel Carter.

[28] The 17 men were Joseph Sawyer, Asa Wilder, John Carter, Peter Willard, Roger Bartlet, Moses Sawyer, Daniel Robbins, Thomas Ross, Phinihas Wilder, William Greenleaf, Fortunates Eager, Joel Osgood, Samuel Thurston, William Phelps, Nathaniel White, Gersham Flagg, and Josiah Winn.

[29] The 24 men were John Wilder, Elisha White, Samuel Joslyn, Joshua House, Joshua Phelps, Samuel Sawyer, Jonathan Prescott, Jonathan Whitney, Nathaniel Houghton, Joseph Bennitt, James Richardson, Samuel Bailey, Seth Haywood, Solomon Holman, Nathan Burpee, Solomon Stuart, Henry Haskel, Oliver Moors, Ephraim Richardson, Ephraim Willard, Jonathan Wilder, Jr., Amos Rugg, Paul Sawyer, and Jacob Bennitt.

[30] The 14 men were David Willard, Asael Phelps, Ephraim Sawyer, David Osgood, Thomas Sawyer, Manasah Sawyer, William Richardson, Elisha Sawyer, Amo Knight, James Wilder, William Dunsmoor, Teley Richardson, Joshua Fletcher, and Joseph White.

[31] The 9 men were Ebenezer Buss, Thomas Bennitt, Joel Houghton, Daniel Rugg, Daniel Willard, Joshua Fairbanks, Jonathan Fairbanks, Peter Ayres, and Ephraim Boynton.

[32] The 5 men were Jonathan Wilder, David Wilder, John White, Aaron Sawyer, and John Prescott. The last two were Asa Whitcomb and Ebenezer Allen.

critical as the interest and willingness to serve of those of substance and status dwindled. Such a divergent trend became so apparent at Concord where the earliest armed resistance began that "the very character and social meaning of the war were transformed," as the historian Robert A. Gross has pointed out, "from a voluntary struggle to a battle by conscript and eventually from a community-wide effort to a poor man's fight." Slipping away from the widespread voluntary participation at the beginning of the war, the portion of voluntary soldiers at Concord dropped to as low as a quarter of the total enlisted men in 1778; two years later "only eight of the sixteen men who signed up for three-years terms had any known connection to the town."[33]

Consistent with what Gross found out about Concord, the rate of enlistment and participation from poor people and their families at many communities in Massachusetts never declined. Instead, it not only sustained but also increased throughout the war. Records show that Wrentham warned out four poor men and their families—Jonathan Felt in 1769, William Puffer in 1768, Eleazer Fisher in 1767, and William Wetherbee in 1770[34]—who subsequently enlisted and fought in the war on behalf of Wrentham.[35] Although not poor, Jesse Ballou was born in the area of Wrentham, which later became Cumberland, Rhode Island. He was warned in 1762, but enlisted for both Massachusetts and Rhode Island during the war. Felt, Puffer, and Ballou marched with the Wrentham militia responding to the alarm of Lexington on April 19, 1775. Felt continued to serve thereafter and was promoted to captain in 1780. Puffer's son George also enlisted and served in 1778

---

[33] Robert A. Gross, *The Minutemen and Their World* (New York: Hill and Wang, 1976), 146-52.

[34] Esther L. Friend, "Notifications and Warnings Out: Strangers Taken into Wrentham, Massachusetts, Between 1732 and 1812," *New England Historical and Genealogical Register* 141 (1987): 191, 199, 330, 351; 142 (1988): 82, 84.

[35] Unless otherwise indicated in this chapter, summary information of individual soldiers' lives and careers can be found in the section of biographies below.

and 1780. Fisher continued his service during the siege of Boston and again in 1777 and 1780.

At least three poor strangers to Weston became patriotic soldiers, and all of them responded to the first shot at Lexington. Born in Medford, Samuel Nutting and his parents received warnings from several townships when he was young. Weston warned him, his wife, and family in 1772. He marched with the Weston militia responding to the alarm of April 19, 1775. Two years later he served in the company under Captain Jonathan Fisk, the same person who had warned him to depart from Weston a few years earlier. Weston authorities also warned Nathan Boynton (whose father Jacob was the great-grandson of John Boynton of Rowley), his mother Mary, and several siblings numerous times. At 14, Boynton became an apprentice to Isaac Cory of Weston in 1771. He marched on the alarm of April 19, 1775, and served again later the same year. Born in 1757, Peter Cary's parentage was not clear. Weston warned him in 1773, when Isaiah Bullard took him as an apprentice. Serving in Captain Samuel Lamson's company of militia, both he and his master responded to the Lexington alarm. Whereas Bullard resumed his civilian life soon afterward, Cary continued to serve during the siege of Boston and enlisted again and again throughout the war in 1778, 1779, 1782, and 1783.

Lancaster authorities warned out four men who later represented the town in service during the war. Born in 1747, Thomas Cleland came from Colchester, Connecticut, and was warned in 1765. He served as a private shortly after the battle at Lexington. He enlisted for more than two years from 1777 to 1779, and continued to serve until March 1781, when he was reported to have deserted. Lemuel Gates was from Rowley, Canada. Lancaster warned him, his parents, and siblings in 1763. He was a fifer in 1775, served as gunner in the Continental Army for three years, and became a sergeant in 1780. His brother Samuel also enlisted for Lancaster. He too was a gunner in the same company as Lemuel and served in the Continental Army for three years, beginning in 1777. Born in Holden, Elijah Ball came to Lancaster from Shrewsbury, some 12 miles to the south. He enlisted as a private and marched in response to the alarm of April 19, 1775. He was a sergeant and served for three months in 1777. His older brother Daniel fought in the war for Shrewsbury. As a private, he marched to Cambridge on the alarm of April 19, 1775. He later served for three months, from August to October 1775.

If any town's effort to entice the poor into service was due to a shortage of manpower, townsfolk's willingness to serve side by side with the poor in the revolutionary forces could be more than a matter of expediency. The traditional sense of social hierarchy separated people according to their distinct status. Yet the same stratification also necessitated a mutual dependency, which only deepened during war. Whereas the middling sort and the able-bodied poor had a history of interaction in civilian life, the continuous war activity soon made it clear that they now relied on each other's support to survive. More than either the top or the bottom tiers of society, the middle to the lower-middle classes and the able-bodied poor took most of the direct responsibilities in fighting the war. In fact, those who did participate in military services tended not to be members of the richest families, whose wealth could free them from enlistment. In Wrentham, 15 taxpayers had the ability to produce 100 or more bushels of grain in 1771. Only four joined the local militia.[36] Meanwhile, no fewer than 140 merchants, professionals, and substantial Bostonians paid a fine of 10 pounds each to avoid enlistment in the Continental Army in 1776, when authorities drafted 258 men from the 12 wards in

---

[36] The 15 family heads were Simon Slocomb, Daniel Thurston, Asa Whiting, Nathan Aldis, John Clark, Asa Fairbank (a captain), Nathaniel Hawes, Benjamin Shepard, Elisha Ware (a sergeant), Stephen Turner, Jr., William Hewes, Abijah Blake (a private), James Boyden, David Fales, and John Smith (a colonel).

town.³⁷ Hampered by their decayed mental and physical condition, the impotent and wretched poor at the other end of the spectrum were less likely to qualify to serve. Nevertheless, if they were able and willing to join the army, the fact that they had received public aid in the past would not disqualify them from enlistment. John McCl(e)ary, a frequent recipient of town relief, engaged in war activity on behalf of Boston. A legal resident and rated householder, he was not an abject poor, but one who had received outdoor relief as many times as he was entitled to.³⁸

John McCleary asked the overseer of the poor Samuel Abbott for wood, March 11, 1771, one of his many requests over the years. (Baker Library, Harvard Business School)

---

³⁷ They included such notable individuals as Nathanial Appleton, Samuel Austin, George Bethune, Caleb Blanchard, James Bowdoin, Thomas Boylston, Dr. Thomas Bulfinch, Ezekiel Goldthwait, Henderson Inches, William Mackay, John Pitts, Ebenezer Storer, Benjamin Waldo, and Samuel Wentworth. *Report of the Record Commissioners* (Boston, 1894), 25: 19-23. Annie Haven Thwing, *Inhabitants and Estates of the Town of Boston, 1630-1800* (Boston: New England Historic Genealogical Society, CD-ROM, 2001).
³⁸ John McClary in Ward No. 2 received wood from town on April 17, 1769, February 19, 1770, and June 5, 1770, as well as 3s. of cash on June 1, 1770. He paid a single poll tax as a householder in 1771, owned a tan house, and was rated to have a real property of £3 in an estimated annual rental income. The records of his first enlistment dated at Cambridge on May 13, 1775. A matross or a bombardier, he served a short term of less than two months in that year. He later enlisted again at Boston for the town. The Continental Army paid him from January 1, 1777 to December 24, 1779, when Lt. Osgood Carleton certified that the said McClary, a sergeant in his company and formerly in Capt. Benjamin Wallcut's company, Col. Thomas Marshall's regiment, "being unfit for military duty on account of lameness contracted while in service, was accordingly discharged." Eric Nellis and Anne Decker Cecere, eds., *The Eighteenth-Century Records of the Boston Overseers of the Poor* (Boston: Colonial Society of Massachusetts, 2007), 889, 899, 902. Bettye Hobbs Pruitt, ed., *The Massachusetts Tax Valuation List of 1771* (1978; Camden, Me.: Picton Press, 1998), 12. *Massachusetts Soldiers and Sailors of the Revolutionary War* (Boston: Wright & Potter, 1896-1908), 10: 430, 432. Records in these titles further suggest that public aid recipients John Hobbs, Samuel Chandler, Thomas Rice, James Flood, John Morrison, and Thomas Welch in Boston might have also enlisted in the American Revolution. But evidence is still needed to establish the definitive connections between these needy individuals and their roles in military service.

A militia company was a diminutive hierarchy that had captains, lieutenants, and ensigns at its top and sergeants, corporals, and privates below them. Yet a militia company was not an exact copy of civilian society, transplanting every element proportionally into its new system. A significantly reorganized institution, the militia company consisted of a large number from the lower strata of a general community. As the records from Wrentham, Weston, and Lancaster indicate, although the recruitment of the militia depended on a steady supply of the poor, rarely did they have the chance to enter the force as officers unless through subsequent promotions.[39] An overwhelming majority of them served as common soldiers while their substantial neighbors held various offices.

Divide

Whether the American Revolution truly was the poor men's war can be responded by considering their enemy: the loyalists. Curiously, although not a few historians were seriously committed to finding social stratification and class antagonism between the haves and have-nots, seldom did they look into the material status of the loyalists. Gary Nash's massive data of the century, for example, stopped in 1775 and did not mention nearly a thousand loyalists who went on board with General William Howe and sailed for Halifax at the end of the Siege of Boston in March 1776. Doubling their number

---

[39] Almost every captain of the Wrentham militia came from modest families. Except for Capt. Thomas Bacon and Capt. Benjamin Hawes whose estates were valued at 90 and 70 bushels per annum respectively, many were rated for no more than 50 bushels a year, such as Capt. Lemuel Kollock 50, Capt. Samuel Cowell 40, Capt. Samuel Fisher 25, Capt. John Boyd 16, and Capt. Oliver Pond 15. For the militia personnel see Samuel Warner, "Historical Sketch of Wrentham," in *History and Directory of Wrentham, Massachusetts* (Boston: Press of Brown Brothers, 1890), 59-61. For valuation data of Wrentham see Bettye Hobbs Pruitt, ed., *The Massachusetts Tax Valuation List of 1771* (1978; Camden, Me.: Picton Press, 1998), 530-41.

within the next few years, these loyalist refugees included, among others, the royal governor, thirteen members of his council, twelve representatives, eighteen clergymen, two hundred customs officials, and many eminent families, whose wealth and possessions surpassed even the richest Americans.[40] A deep social and economic gap separated the rich from the middle and lower classes, let alone the poor, during this period—that is, a clear class division existed between the rich loyalists and meager patriots.[41]

Records show that many of those who had steadfastly defended the king were substantial property owners, big merchants, royal appointees, and imperial officers.[42] At least 600 of them left information concerning their family wealth in their pension files and in the Massachusetts tax rolls for 1771.[43]

---

[40] David Hackett Fischer, *Washington's Crossing* (New York: Oxford University Press, 2004), 9. Richard Frothingham, *History of the Siege of Boston* (Boston: Little, Brown, and Co., 1903), 311-12. James H. Stark, *The Loyalists of Massachusetts and the Other Side of the American Revolution* (Boston: Printed by the Author, 1910), 133-36. Samuel Eliot Morison, "The Commerce of Boston on the Eve of the Revolution," *Proceedings of the American Antiquarian Society* (1923), 32: 51. Arthur M. Schlesinger, *The Colonial Merchants and the American Revolution, 1763-1776* (New York: Longmans, Green & Co., 1918), 602. Lorenzo Sabine estimated that the total number of loyalist refugees from various parts of Massachusetts may have reached two thousand, *Biographical Sketches of Loyalists of the American Revolution* (Boston: Little, Brown and Co., 1864), 1: 25-26.

[41] If Boston instead of Massachusetts is the sole focus of analysis, the picture can look different. John W. Tyler, *Smugglers and Patriots: Boston Merchants and the Advent of the American Revolution* (Boston: Northeastern University Press, 1986); "Persistence and Change within the Boston Business Community," in Conrad E. Wright and Katheryn P. Viens, eds. *Entrepreneurs: The Boston Business Community, 1700-1850* (Boston: Massachusetts Historical Society, 1997), 95-119. However wealth and possessions are highlighted here in this segment, religious affiliations, personal animosities, kinship ties, varied perceptions of and commitment to law and order, differences of temperament, regional history, neighborhood networks and affinities also influenced people's attitudes toward the opposing camps. Joseph S. Tiedemann, Eugene R. Fingerhut, and Robert W. Venables, eds., *The Other Loyalists: Ordinary People, Royalism, and the Revolution in the Middle Colonies, 1763-1787* (Albany, N.Y.: State University of New York Press, 2009).

[42] Bernard Bailyn examined the rise and fall of those "colonial member[s] of the British ruling class" in *The New England Merchants in the Seventeenth Century* (Cambridge, Mass.: Harvard University Press, 1955) and *The Ordeal of Thomas Hutchinson* (Cambridge, Mass.: Harvard University Press, 1974).

[43] James H. Stark, *The Loyalists of Massachusetts and the Other Side of the American Revolution* (Boston: Privately Printed for the Author, 1910). E. Alfred Jones, *The Loyalists of Massachusetts: Their Memorials, Petitions, and Claims* (London: The Saint Catherine Press, 1930). Peter Wilson Coldham, *American Loyalists Claims* (Washington, D.C.: National Genealogical Society, 1980), v. 1. David E. Maas, ed., *Divided Hearts,*

Meanwhile, a comparative review of the two belligerent camps indicates that most leading patriots were men of modest fortunes who had either less than £40 of rental value in town or less than 100 bushels of annual grain output in the country.[44] A handful of them were wealthier, such as John Hancock, James Bowdoin, James Otis, James Warren, William Phillips, Joseph Hawley, and William Molineux. According to the *Massachusetts Tax Valuation List of 1771*, Hancock had real estate at a yearly rental value of £60, 3 warehouses, 22,672 feet of wharf surface, 2 slaves, 594 tons of vessels, £7,000 of merchandise, £11,000 in lending money, and 5 horses. Bowdoin had 1 house, real estate valued at £100 per annum, 2 slaves, £5,120 in lending money, and 2 horses. Otis had 1 house, real estate valued at £40 per annum, 1 slave, and 1 horse. Warren, of Plymouth, had 3 houses, 1 warehouse, real estate valued at £80 per annum, 75 tons of vessels, £700 of merchandise, 3 horses, 10 oxen, 13 cattle, 5 swine, 240 acres of pasture good for 40 cows, and 23 acres of tillage with a yearly production of 350 bushels. Phillips had 1 house, real estate valued at £93 per annum, £2,076 of merchandise, £3,630 in lending money, and 2 horses. Hawley, of Northampton, had 1 house, 1 barn, real estate valued at £22 per annum, £200 in lending money, 1 horse, 3 cattle, 2 swine, 5.5 acres of pasture for 4 cows, and 18.5 acres of tillage with a grain production of 148 bushels a year. Molineux had 1 house, 1 warehouse, real estate valued at £46 per annum, £3,630 in lending money, and 2 horses.[45]

Massachusetts Loyalists, 1765-1790: A Biographical Directory (Boston: The New England Historic Genealogical Society, 1980). Bettye Hobbs Pruitt, ed., *The Massachusetts Tax Valuation List of 1771* (Boston: G. K. Hall & Co., 1978).

[44] This group includes Samuel Adams, John Adams, Joseph Warren, John Gill, Josiah Quincy, Paul Revere, Isaiah Thomas, Moses Gill, Samuel Barrett, Edward Davis, William Greenleaf, Moses Grant, and Fortesque Vernon. Other than a house and some rental value, few of them had warehouses, wharf surface, money for lending, horses, or tillage. See Pruitt, *The Massachusetts Tax Valuation List of 1771*.

[45] See also Robert E. Brown, *Middle-Class Democracy and the Revolution in Massachusetts, 1691-1780* (Ithaca, N. Y.: Cornell University Press, 1955), 18.

Yet few of these middle-class rebel leaders could match the enormous wealth and financial power their political foes possessed. Approximately 160 loyalists appeared on the same tax list of 1771. Of them, 49 had a shop (or barn, still house, tan house, warehouse, and/or mill) in addition to 1 dwelling house for each of the taxpayers, 40 had 1 or more slaves, 26 had real estate worth £40 to £49 in yearly rental, 16 had real estate valued at more than £50, 14 had merchandise valued at £1,000 or more, 4 had wharf surface of more than 1,000 feet, 7 had lending money of £1,000 and upwards, 3 had yearly commissions of £300 and above, 3 had vessels of more than 100 tons, and 18 had enough improved land capable of producing more than 100 bushels of grain annually.[46]

Meanwhile, merchants and importers of British merchandise had staggering stocks, devoted loyalists held lucrative offices, and the Episcopal ministry was exempt from taxation. Indeed, the loyalists possessed overwhelming wealth and privilege in as many material categories as any contemporary could imagine.[47] Henry Barnes of Marlborough,

---

[46] William Vassall, Esq., of Boston, for example, had 1 house, and a real estate worth £80 per annum, 3 slaves, 4 horses, and 1 cattle. Nathaniel Ray Thomas, Esq., of Marshfield, had 1 house, a real estate worth £99, 2 horse, 11 oxen, 11 cattle, 35 goats, 8 swine, 220 acres of pasture good for 55 cows, 25 acres of tillage with a yearly grain production of 375 bushels. Isaac Royall, Esq., of Medford, had a real estate worth £120, 5 slaves, £119 of lending money, 7 horses, 4 oxen, 8 cattle, 4 swine, 55 ½ acres of pasture good for 26 cows, 7 acres of tillage with a yearly grain production of 155 bushels. Benjamin Pickman, Esq., of Salem, had 1 house, ¾ of a still house, 4 warehouses, 1,300 feet of wharf surface, a real estate worth £147, 2 slaves, 563 tons of vessels, £4,100 worth of merchandise, 1 horse, 4 acres of tillage with a yearly grain production of 80 bushels. Josiah Edson and his son of Bridgewater had 1 house, a real estate valued at £27, 2 horses, 3 oxen, 8 cattle, 60 acres of pasture good for 12 cows, and 15 acres of tillage with a grain production of 130 bushels a year. The owner of a large estate worth £7,500 sterling, Abijah Willard of Lancaster had 1 house, a real estate valued at £24 per annum, 6 horses, 4 oxen, 6 cattle, 26 goats, 1 swine, 40 acres of pasture good for 18 cows, 12 acres of tillage with a grain production of 180 bushels a year. Nathaniel Dickinson of Deerfield had 2 houses, a real estate valued at £54, 5 horse, 2 oxen, 15 cattle, 13 goats, 6 swine, 46 acres of pasture good for 20 cows, 50 acres of tillage with a grain production of 350 bushels a year. See Bettye Hobbs Pruitt, ed., *The Massachusetts Tax Valuation List of 1771* (1978; Camden, Me.: Picton Press, 1998), and E. Alfred Jones, *The Loyalists of Massachusetts: Their Memorials, Petitions, and Claims* (London: The Saint Catherine Press, 1930), 48-50, 69-74, 114-18.

[47] Dr. John Calef of Ipswich had a ship of 300 tons, with cargo, valued at £4,200 sterling. Nicholas Ward Boylston held wealth in bonds and personal securities worth £3,000 to

an importer of British goods, had a pearl ash works and distillery in Boston. He exported large quantities of pearl ash and held as many as 8,000 acres of land in the countryside. Describing himself as a gentleman of fortune in Boston, John Lindall Borland held land valued between £6,000 and £7,000. His father, John Borland, Esq., had an estate valued at £2,000 sterling per annum from his vast holdings in Massachusetts and Rhode Island. In Salem, William Browne's property was worth £33,000. John Chandler of Worcester had an income of £1,300 a year. He claimed a loss of property valued at £11,067 during the war and was granted £7,221 by the English government.[48] Known as "King Hooper," the merchant and manufacturer of cordage, Joseph Hooper of Marblehead possessed huge wealth. His son Robert Hooper was a Mandamus Councillor. The family claimed a loss of property in the amount of £9,160. Eliakim Hutchinson, Judge of the Court of Common Pleas, the grandson of a Councillor, and a Councillor himself,[49] was certainly a man of eminence and luxury, who owned "Shirley

---

£4,000 or more. His uncle Nicholas Boylston also left him £3,000 worth of property. The merchant Gilbert Deblois of Boston was an importer of goods valued at £200,000. He had an annual profit of £1,200 sterling. His relation Lewis Deblois, also a merchant in Boston, had a business valued at £31,027 by 1774. Benjamin Lynde, Esq., of Salem, had £2,900 to lend, and John Worthington, Esq., of Springfield, had £3,500. The Rev. John Troutbeck was assistant chaplain, with the Rev. Henry Caner (who also claimed a loss of property at £3,900), of King's Chapel. The estimate of his estate in 1772 included three dwelling houses in Boston and one in the country, a library worth £266, a chariot valued at £133 in London, two chaises of £30 each, and lands in New York, Connecticut, New Hampshire, and Massachusetts, as well as debts of £2,000 due to his wife Sarah as the sole executrix of her father, making the estate totaling £30, 293 currency, equal to at least £22,719 sterling. After Troutbeck's death, the widow Sarah Troutbeck claimed a loss of £3,043 to the British government, and was allowed £769. She received a pension of £80 until her death in 1816. E. Alfred Jones, *The Loyalists of Massachusetts: Their Memorials, Petitions, and Claims* (London: The Saint Catherine Press, 1930), 48-50, 69-74, 114-18.

[48] A statistical study is Wallace Brown, *The King's Friend's: The Composition and Motives of the American Loyalist Claimants* (Providence, R.I.: Brown University Press, 1965), 19-42, 294-98. For the process of claiming and recovering those losses see Mary Beth Norton, *The British-Americans: The Loyalist Exiles in England, 1774-1789* (Boston: Little, Brown and Co., 1972), 42-61, 185-222. Carol Berkin, *Jonathan Sewall: Odyssey of an American Loyalist* (New York: Columbia University Press, 1974), 144-153. Sheila L. Skemp, *William Franklin: Son of a Patriot, Servant of a King* (New York: Oxford University Press, 1990), 267-76.

[49] Nian-Sheng Huang, "The Impeachment of Justice Hall." *Massachusetts Historical Review* (2010), 12: 109-10.

Place," valued at £12,000. It was the finest estate in Roxbury that he purchased from his father-in-law Governor Shirley, who built "Shirley Hall," the palatial mansion on the eighty-acre estate, with all material, wood frames, and bricks imported from England. The son-in-law's confiscated property in Suffolk County alone totaled £21,400.[50] Thomas Hutchinson, the eldest son of and personal attorney to Governor Hutchinson, claimed a property loss of £14,148, for which he was allowed £6,025 in addition to a pension of £40 per annum for his loss of income as a royal official.[51] A representative to the General Court for thirty years, a justice of the peace for Worcester County, a judge of the Court of the Common Pleas, and a Mandamus Councillor, John Murray (of Rutland) was one of richest men in Massachusetts. The rental income for his great estate amounted to £26,000, and his fortune was four times bigger than that of either of his two fellow councillors—Nathaniel Hatch of Dorchester and Richard Lechmere of Taunton. He claimed to have lost £21,832, for which he was granted £9,774.[52]

---

[50] E. Alfred Jones, *The Loyalists of Massachusetts: Their Memorials, Petitions, and Claims* (London: The Saint Catherine Press, 1930), 41-42, 58-61, 76, 81-83, 165-66, 169, 279-80. James H. Stark, *The Loyalists of Massachusetts and the Other Side of the American Revolution* (Boston: Printed for the Author, 1910), 178-80.

[51] In the heat of the Stamp Act crisis, an angry Boston crowd attacked the mansion of Thomas Hutchinson, chief justice and lieutenant governor of Massachusetts, on the night of August 26, 1765. In addition to the wanton destruction and physical damage, the mob carried away £900 sterling in cash. The total loss of property was estimated at £2,218 sterling, based upon an exhaustive list of household possessions Hutchinson provided to the home government, which was as long as ten printed pages. In spite of these substantial setbacks, he continued heavy investment in the lucrative tea trade, averaging £1,000 a year for the remainder of the 1760s. Through the early years of the next decade until the ensuing tea party crisis, "his liquid capital—nearly £4000—was invested in East India Company stock, and in addition his crown salary of £1500 sterling per annum was drawn from the income of the tea duty in America." Bernard Bailyn, *The Ordeal of Thomas Hutchinson* (Cambridge, Mass.: Harvard University Press, 1974), 35-36, 154, 259, 273. James Kendall Hosmer, *The Life of Thomas Hutchinson: Royal Governor of the Province of Massachusetts Bay* (Cambridge, Mass.: The Riverside Press, 1896), 351-61. Hutchinson sailed for England on June 1, 1774 after the arrival of the new governor Thomas Gage in May.

[52] E. Alfred Jones, *The Loyalists of Massachusetts: Their Memorials, Petitions, and Claims*, 173-74, 216-17. Still, those loyalists whose claims for lost properties exceeded £3,000 included at least the following—John Joy of Hingham, Richard Lechmere, Daniel Leonard, Henry Lloyd of Boston, Widow Mary Loring of Roxbury, the Chief Justice Peter Oliver and his second son Peter Oliver, Lt. Governor Thomas Oliver, Adino Paddock, Sir William Pepperall, William Lee Perkins of Boston, Capt. David Phipps, James Putnam of Worcester,

Individually speaking, the possessions of a John Hancock, a James Bowdoin, or an Elbridge Gerry might rival those of a wealthy loyalist. [53] Collectively, however, the loyalists were clearly the elite class whose power and wealth, buttressed by their political privileges and close commercial ties to the mother country, overshadowed the patriots from the middling to lower ranks as completely as anyone could see. Yet the gap between the upper class of the loyalists and the patriots of modest means was but one side of the dichotomy. What further separated the two camps was a total disconnect between the rich loyalists and the poorest members in Massachusetts. Perhaps because of their enormous wealth, which allowed them to hire ample help and service, rarely did the 600 loyalists ever take in any distressed stranger or wandering person. Meanwhile, of the several hundred recorded names of those who had taken in strangers in Boston, Weston, Wrentham, Cambridge, Dedham, and Malden, almost none became a loyalist, although not all necessarily turned into ardent patriots. Records show that some of the most well-known loyalists were Colonel Elisha Jones, of Weston, and his eleven sons, who all stood for the

---

Brigadier General Timothy Ruggles of Hardwick, the merchant and ironmaster Esq. Joseph Scott of Boston, the Attorney-General Jonathan Sewall, the Brookline lawyer Samuel Sewall (1745-1811), Jonathan Simpson, the Younger (b. 1752), John Vassall of Boston, Francis Waldo of Falmouth, and Samuel Waterhouse, the officer at the Custom House in Boston. E. Alfred Jones, *The Loyalists of Massachusetts: Their Memorials, Petitions, and Claims* (London: The Saint Catherine Press, 1930), 185-86, 189-91, 191-94, 196, 198-99, 224-25, 225-26, 226-27, 232-33, 233-34, 235, 240-41, 251-53, 256, 258-59, 259-60, 262, 283-85, 285-86, 290-91. Adding to these wealthy people were a legion of surveyors, searchers, tidesmen, boatmen, comptrollers, deputies, commissioners of custom houses, pilots, mariners, officers, justices, judges, councilors, barristers, attorneys, and doctors who could draw an annual pension of the British government from £10 and £20 to as high as £300 or more. E. Alfred Jones, *The Loyalists of Massachusetts: Their Memorials, Petitions, and Claims*, 119, 120, 121, 125, 130-33, 139, 140-42, 144-45, 159-60, 163, 166, 167, 179-81, 189-91, 212-13, 218, 236-37, 239, 266-69, 278-79, 290-91, 292-93, 293-94, 295, 298-300, 301, 303.

[53] Although not recorded on *The Massachusetts Tax Valuation List of 1771*, the Gerry family estate at Marblehead was valued at £7,919 in 1775. Hancock's estate was assessed at £60 on the same list, but he claimed a "loss of £100 sterling for a year's rent on his house as a result of the Boston siege." Robert E. Brown, *Middle-Class Democracy and the Revolution in Massachusetts, 1691-1780* (Ithaca, N. Y.: Cornell University Press, 1955), 18, 34, 95.

king.⁵⁴ The wealthiest family in the community, the Jones took in only one Mathew Blake, aged 24, from Ireland, while their less affluent neighbors received 300 wanderers over five decades. This suggests that, despite the settlement regulations and the warning-out system, struggling vagrants and traveling families were most likely to find boarding, shelter, help, and some degree of compassion not at the great estates of the local and provincial elite, but in the humble households of the middle- to lower-class families, who indeed opened their doors to accept the poor.⁵⁵

The repeated acceptance of the poor strangers through the colonial era never resolved the problem of poverty. The interaction nonetheless helped cement a local bond. When in later years the patriots of every community badly needed manpower to conduct the war, they turned to the poor for support. Rich Tories had not only alienated the middle class, but had also lost an opportunity to extend a helping hand to most of the poor, who would contribute mightily to the loyalist downfall during the revolution.

Participation

Gresham Flagg Lane, the son of John "Ters" and Martha (Flagg) Lane, was born in Bedford, Middlesex County, on July 30, 1753. When he was nineteen years old, he went to Weston but was warned to leave. He went back to Bedford, where he became a sergeant serving in the Revolutionary War. He married Lydia Sally Thomas in 1775. The couple had

---

[54] E. Alfred Jones, *The Loyalists of Massachusetts: Their Memorials, Petitions, and Claims* (London: The Saint Catherine Press, 1930), 182-85.
[55] Robert Love's record book (January 29, 1765 to August 27, 1766), Massachusetts Historical Society; List of warnings out (May 1 to August 28, 1772), Rare Book and Manuscripts Department of the Boston Public Library. *New England Historical and Genealogical Register* 92 (1938): 46-60 (Malden); 142 (1988): 56-84 (Wrentham); 144 (1990): 215-24 (Weston).

thirteen children, naming one son George Washington Lane and another Freeman Lane. Many others went through a similar experience, moving from a person of low circumstances to a common soldier serving the patriotic cause.

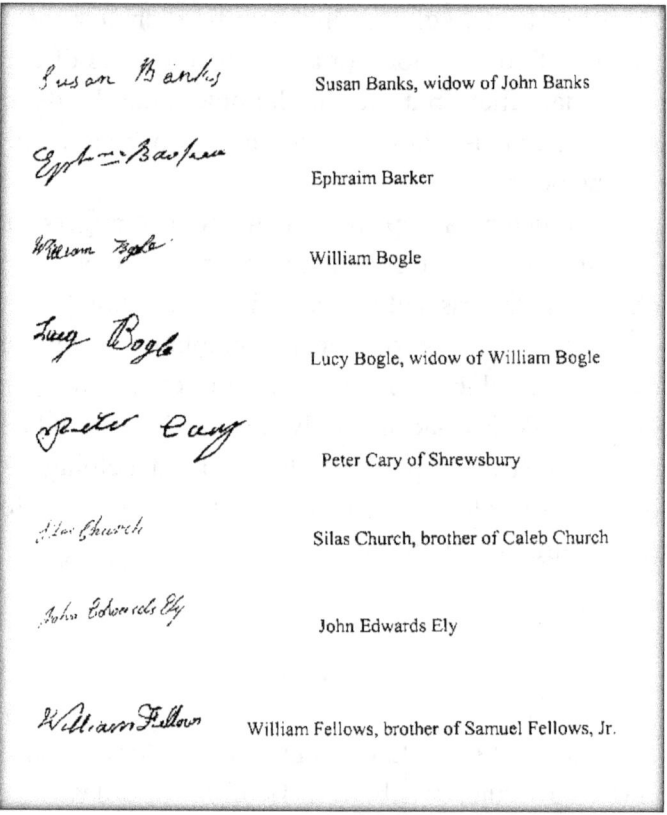

Signatures by veterans of the Revolutionary War and their widows who applied for federal pensions. (National Archives)

Longing for self-rule and identity, former bound-out orphans were an active group of participants in the war. Their willingness to join the fight for independence became even stronger if they were also looking for freedom from bondage. The strong urge to achieve liberation was perhaps deeply personal to those bound-out orphans whose terms would end on the eve of the revolution. Between 1734 and 1776, Boston overseers of the poor bound out some 700 orphans who had been born at or brought to the almshouse. A large percentage of the boys whose indentures ended in the early 1770s joined the military service for various townships to which they had been sent. Records show that about fifty-three bound-out apprentices reached the age of twenty-one from 1770 to 1775. More than a quarter of them enlisted during the revolution, including Thomas Lillie (bound out to Marblehead), Thomas Craige (Worcester), Bartholemew Lynch (Marblehead), John Davis (Hadley), John Banks (Grafton and later Alstead, New Hampshire) and his younger brother Thomas Banks (Hatfield), Thomas Caryl [Cariel] (Southborough), Encoh Jarvis (Marblehead), Francis Akley (Holden), Benjamin Champney (Boston), William Bright (Salem), Matthew Hopkins (Boston), Joseph Maxfield (Springfield), Mark Noble (Hadley), and William Shirley (Marblehead). [56] Thus, despite their sad childhood, these bound-out orphans actively responded to the calls for military service; the rate of their participation was as impressive as anyone else's, if not more. In addition to their relative health and young age, which made them suitable candidates, one hidden aspect of their active participation lay in the fact that not one of their masters—who might have persuaded their bound boys to substitute for their obligations to enlist—had served. Joseph Maxfield's terms, for instance, would not end until 1778. He enlisted in 1776 and served again from 1779 to 1782 for three years. It is therefore reasonable to

---

[56] W. Graham Millar, "The Poor Apprentices of Boston Indentures of Poor Children Bound Out Apprentices by the Overseers of the Poor of Boston, 1734-1776" (M. A. Thesis, College of William and Mary, 1958). Millar's work laid the foundation for Lawrence W. Towner's article, "The Indentures of Boston's Poor Apprentices, 1734-1805," *Publications of the Colonial Society of Massachusetts* 43 (Boston, 1966): 417-68. Ruth Wallis Herndon, "Children and Masters: Tracking Eighteenth-Century New Englanders through Indentures," *New England Ancestors* 4 (2003): 22-24.

assume that his master must have allowed his early release once his apprentice had agreed to go into service.

If everything else being equal while poor households happened to have a large number of children, they seemed to have sent more family members to the war than others, which was one of the most significant sacrifices they made to the revolution. Caleb Church, whose family received warnings five or six times from several townships in Worcester County, participated in the battle in April 1775.

Property schedule of veteran Caleb Church of Ashfield, Franklin County, August 20, 1823. (National Archives)

After responding to the Lexington alarm, his younger brother Silas later served during the siege of Boston and again in 1777. Both Elijah Ball and his brother Daniel marched on the Lexington alarm, one for Lancaster and the other Shrewsbury. Warned several times by Weston authorities, three members of the Elisha Cox family fought for independence while one of them, Ensign Elisha Cox, died for the cause. His superior

Colonel William Bond called him "a good officer."[57] Coming from Boxford, Essex County, Daniel and Sarah Symonds Black and their five children were warned at Holden, Worcester County. All three of their sons—Jacob, Daniel, and John—served during the revolution. After being warned by Bridgewater, Ebenezer Hill, wife Abigail Hill, and their five children (from Abington) refused to leave. All three of their sons—Daniel, Solomon, and John—enlisted in the war for Bridgewater. Although not utterly destitute, of those who had received warning notices at one township or another, many joined the revolution with their siblings and relations nonetheless—Jonathan Barrett and his brother Samuel; Thomas Burnham and his brother John; William Bogle and his brother Thomas; Lemuel Gates and his brother Samuel; Luther Graves and his brother Calvin; Thomas Harris, Jr. and his brothers Daniel and Samuel; Samuel Fellows, Jr. and his four brothers John, Solomon, William, and Willis; Jonathan Johnson and his brother Job; Edward Payson and his brother David; William Puffer and his son George; Zenas Gibbs and his two brothers Frederick and Jonas; and Asa Haven and his two brothers Ebenezer and Daniel.

Compared with people of better circumstances, families of the lower classes not only sent more members, they generally enlisted more times and served for longer durations. As late as three years into the war until early 1778, both officers and militiamen generally served for a short term, ranging from several days to several months; most tried not to serve more than six months a year. Those who enlisted for one, two, or three years or for the duration of the war were often from families of little estate. By the same token, it rarely

---

[57] For the Cox family's experiences before the war see Douglas Lamar Jones, "The Transformation of the Law of Poverty in Eighteenth-Century Massachusetts," in Daniel R. Coquillette, ed., *Law in Colonial Massachusetts, 1630-1800* (Boston: The Colonial Society of Massachusetts, 1984), 181-83.

happened that a poor person served only one term of enlistment. Most joined and rejoined the service, and many enlisted up to three years or for the duration of the war—the longest term of service in the revolution. If possible, few people from substantial backgrounds chose this option of long service. Based on a study of a random collection of some seventy poor men, this book can positively confirm that eighteen of them enlisted for three or more years, which showed a high rate (one out of four) of prolonged service among those of low circumstances.[58]

Yet their experiences were not out of the ordinary. The case of Lancaster provides further illustration. By several orders of the General Court (on December 5, 1776, January 27, 1777, and February 3, 1778) and subsequently by Congressional Resolve of December 2, 1780, Massachusetts towns were required to send one seventh of all males sixteen years old or older to form twenty regiments of the Continental Army in Massachusetts. Under these orders, Lancaster had to procure a quota of 138 men. Of those whose names have survived, 29 also appeared on the 1771 valuation list. Thus, those who signed up for a term of three years appeared to have come from the following groups:

2 from those whose yearly output of grain was 100 bushels[59]
3 from those whose yearly output of grain was from 80 to 90 bushels[60]
4 from those whose yearly output of grain was from 60 to 75 bushels[61]

---

[58] They include these soldiers—Abraham Aldrich enlisted for three years but deserted after several months. John Atkinson three years. Ephraim Barker served for six years. Jonathan Barrett three years. Ichabod Bozworth served for three years. Luke Chapin three years. Thomas Cleland served for the duration of the war. John Fellows served for three years. Jonathan Felt served several years. Both Lemuel Gates and his brother Samuel for three years. Zenas Gibbs three years. Joseph Langley served for more than three years. John Doyle Legg enlisted at least five times. Thomas Lillie enlisted for three years but was disabled soon after enlistment. Joseph Ransford served for almost six years. Jabez Steven served for three years. Levi Vinten for the duration of the war.
[59] They were Joseph Bennitt and Henry Haskel.
[60] They were Roger Bartlet, Gersham Flagg, and Peter Willard.
[61] They were Shubael Bailey, Abijah Philips, John Wheelock, and Caleb Whitney.

2 from those whose yearly output of grain was from 45 to 50 bushels[62]
3 from those whose yearly output of grain was 40 bushels or less[63]
3 from those who had a house but no yearly output of grains[64]
10 from those who had no house, no land, or grain output[65]

Clearly, unlike early in the war—from the Lexington alarm to the end of the Boston siege—when the call of service meant a few days to a few months, no resident whose yearly grain production exceeded 100 bushels was now willing to serve for a three-year term while those households of 50 bushels or less a year continued to contribute the bulk of the new quota Lancaster badly needed to fill. As a single group, these landless laborers contributed the highest percentage of the long-term soldiers. While other groups' participation had declined as the duration of enlistment extended, people of small fortunes or no property at all played more significant roles in the army than what they had contributed to the short-term services when the war first started.

The heavy demand for soldiers was a difficult task for any township that suffered a chronic shortage of labor. The congressional resolves and the General Court's orders of 1778 added more pressure, forcing many communities into a frantic search for new solutions. One such solution was to divide a local community into the same number of "classes" (or "squadrons") as the assigned quota a township had received. Each "class" was in turn responsible for furnishing the allocated soldiers. All households in each class were rated for any supplies, bounty money, or taxes for the support of the soldier and his family. Constables were authorized to take the body of anyone who failed to pay the assessed rate. If no person in the class volunteered to serve for the sum the class had

---

[62] They were John Hewitt and Aaron Willard.
[63] They were Jabez Brook, Samuel Herring, and Jonathan Sawyer.
[64] They were Thomas Cleland, Isaac Evelith, and Thomas Grant.
[65] They were Joseph Bailey, Andrew Haskel, Joseph House, Joshua Johnson, Jacob Kilburn, James Pratt, John Priest, John Wheeler, Joseph Wheelock, and Jotham Woods.

agreed to offer, a lottery ensued to determine which household in the class would provide the soldier. Whomever the lot hit had to enter the army for as long as the term would require or find a substitute.[66]

Because many people were reluctant to enlist for three years, finding a substitute for hire became a common practice soon after the passing of 1777-78 resolves. Indeed, townships gladly accepted anyone willing to enlist, and it was not infrequent that two communities would compete with each other for the same soldier to fulfill their quota. Thus, Lancaster submitted to the army, in addition to its residents who had volunteered to serve, quite a few servants, "bounty-jumpers," "hired slaves," "hired strollers," or "hired foreigners." They included, according to the town's own descriptions, "Perley Rogers, a negro," "Charles Stuart, a mulatto," "Jonas Carter, a hired Lunenburg man," "Peter Franklin, a negro," "Ephraim Fuller, aged sixteen," "Job Lewis, a negro," "Abel Moor, claimed by Bolton," "Robert Skinner, a hired stroller, claimed by Bolton," "Cornelius Tigh, a substitute, claimed by Bolton," "Asa Wyman, aged seventeen," "John Wyman, aged seventeen," "Edom London, a negro slave, claimed by Winchendon," "Reuben Kendall, a negro," "Matthew Wyman, credited to Lunenburg," "Elisha Houghton, claimed by Harvard," and "Cain Lewis, a negro."[67] Meanwhile, enlistee William Deputin openly acknowledged to have accepted fifty-four pounds (Lawful Money) to substitute for a certain class in town. The army deemed Lancaster's three other recruits "unfit for service": "Clark Gibbs, 60 years old. Rheumatic and decrepid with age,"

---

[66] Bedford had a typical situation of this sort in 1780. Abram English Brown, *History of the Town of Bedford, Middlesex County, Massachusetts, from Its Earliest Settlement to the Year of Our Lord 1891* (Bedford: Published by the Author, 1891), 26-27.
[67] "Among the black soldiers in the Continental Army were former slaves who served longer than most white soldiers for less pay." Charles Royster, *A Revolutionary People at War: The Continental Army and American Character, 1775-1783* (Chapel Hill: University of North Carolina Press, 1979), 241-42.

"Lemuel Shed, infirm," and "Jotham Wood, 41, bodily deformed."[68]

In these gloomy years Lancaster was by no means the only town scrambling for soldiers. Hired or not, voluntary or substituting, native or transient alike, the warm bodies of the poor now became a hot commodity whose impoverishment was far less of a concern under the grave pressure of war. Every community was willing to pay a price to recruit them for enlistment. A widespread campaign was underway across the commonwealth to include the poor in the ranks of a fighting force. Local residents of Billerica in Middlesex County, for example, were highly active in supporting the American cause from the start. A total of 104 townsmen from all social ranks joined the militia, which participated in various actions in 1775, including the march to the Lexington alarm. Colonel William Tompson, one of the three highest taxpayers in town, paying £6 a year, was a participant as were 67 other men who had paid a tax ranging from 10s. and £1 to £5 a year. Another 36 men were non-taxpayers or non-residents, accounting for approximately 30 percent of the militia force. As the war continued, however, poor individuals and outsiders became the main source for recruitment. Of the thirty-six men who enlisted in 1777 for three years, only fifteen of them were taxpayers. Eight men paid ten shillings a year. John Needham paid the highest at £2 6s. 7d. a year. Clearly, far fewer substantial taxpayers volunteered for the long-term enlistment in 1777 than they had done for the short-term service two years earlier. As a result, the town had little choice but to recruit more than half of the enlisted men from non-taxpayers, non-residents, or strangers.[69]

---

[68] Henry S. Hourse, *The Military Annals of Lancaster, Massachusetts, 1740-1865* (Clinton, Mass.: W. J. Coulter, 1889), 178-94.
[69] Henry A. Hazen, *History of Billerica, Massachusetts* (Boston: A. Williams and Co., 1883), 234-51.

In late 1779, people from the small town of Wilbraham in Hampshire County keenly felt the mounting pressure of recruitment. "The difficulties which hindered the raising of men continued to accumulate," as they recalled. "The demand was imperative, the work well-nigh impossible. A desperate rally was made in October, and £400 were raised for the soldiers' bounty and mileage money, and subscriptions were opened that the money might be promptly obtained." A month later the town voted to raise £2,860 for those soldiers who would serve for nine months.[70] No sooner had a town meeting at Westborough, Worcester County, voted in July 1776 that "every man should pay his just proportion in supporting the war from April ye 19, 1775, and so forward" than their resolve was tested. In addition to horses, shoes, stockings, and shirts for the troops, Westborough, like every other town, was ordered to provide supplies such as beef, cattle, sheep, butter, cheese, rye, and Indian meal for the relief of the besieged Boston. The town had to borrow a loan of £400,000 for its share. In 1775, the town paid £4 for each man who responded to the Lexington alarm. In 1780, the town had to pay £17,780 for 14 men who had agreed to enlist for the reinforcement of the Continental Army, averaging £1,270 per soldier.[71]

These staggering sums and prices reflected the horrendous currency depreciation during the war years. Dropping as much as 400 percent, the precipitate decline of the credit bills made recruitment efforts extra difficult. In Middlesex County, Sudbury voted a bounty of £20 in bills of credit to a soldier in 1777, but granted a bounty of £15 in specie or £600 in bills in 1781. The town paid £4,929 to a full muster roll of 113 soldiers and officers in 1778. Two years later, it had

---

[70] Chauncey E. Peck, *The History of Wilbrahm, Massachusetts* (Wilbraham, 1913), 128, 129.
[71] Heman Packard DeForest, *The History of Westborough, Massachusetts* (Westborough, 1891), 165, 166, 169, 171.

to raise £10,000 to pay off as few as 14 men in exchange for their promise to enlist.[72] For all the face value of credit bills, the enlisted men gained little. Soldiers generally received their bounties in state bills and town notes, and their pay in Continental money, which at the end of their term of service could neither meet the expenses of their outfit nor pay the taxes they had owed to the government.[73] Facing these obstacles, some communities improvised. New Bedford, Bristol County, gave out £1,356 9s. 1d. in cash bounties to those who would engage in the continental service.[74] Sunderland, Hampshire County, decided to lower the ongoing rate from one silver dollar for forty Continental dollars to one for seventy-five. Knowing how desirable merchandise could be, the town also voted to add a pair of shoes as a bounty to each of its enlisted men.[75] Costing 7s. a pair in the late 1770s, good shoes for men could be worth as much as £14 in the early 1780s, when commodities were often preferred over money.[76] Townsfolk in Royalston, Worcester County, decided to raise as much as £1,000 Spanish milled dollars to hire soldiers. They also promised that any resident who was willing to serve for the term of three years could receive "ten cows, heifers three years old with calf or with calves by their sides." The strategy seemed to have worked. In the end, twenty-four soldiers came from other places to serve for Royalston, becoming lawful residents

---

[72] Alfred Sereno Hudson, *The History of Sudbury, Massachusetts, 1638-1889* (Sudbury, 1889), 401, 403-05, 413.
[73] James M. Crafts, *History of the Town of Whately, Mass.* (Whately, 1899), 227.
[74] Leonard Bolles Ellis, *History of New Bedford and Its Vicinity, 1602-1892* (Syracuse, N.Y.: D. Mason & Co., 1892).
[75] John Montague Smith, *History of the Town of Sunderland, Massachusetts* (Greenfield, Mass.: E. A. Hall & Co., 1899), 140, 141.
[76] See the price list of Westborough, Heman Packard DeForest, *The History of Westborough, Massachusetts* (Westborough, 1891), 167. A legend of this era said that a constable was about to pay the town treasurer for buying a pair of oxen, which would cost £40. After inquiring how much a mug of cider would sell, he settled the account by paying three and one-third mugs of the drink. Rufus P. Stebbins, *An Historical Address* (Boston: George C. Rand, 1864), 245.

after the war. They accounted for one fifth of all the revolutionary veterans living in Royalston at the time.[77]

It is clear that despite their low circumstances, the able-bodied poor, people of meager means, laborers, non-residents, outsiders, strangers, wanderers, transients, and non-whites became an indispensable force in the revolution. Especially as the war dragged on, no township could afford to exclude them. On the contrary, recruiting the willing poor to serve was a top priority for every community, which understood in unmistaken terms that a regular supply of them for the patriotic army was a critical condition for achieving independence.

Vicissitudes

One out of every four to five enlisted men in any maritime community in Massachusetts could be a seaman. As such, the vicissitudes of a typical life in military service would involve work on land as much as that at sea, which will be discussed first.

On April 26, 1775, a week after the Battle at Lexington and Concord, the Provincial Congress ordered Captain John Derby and his schooner *Quero*, one of the earliest patriot ships, to set sail for Dublin, Ireland, and therewith to reach Benjamin Franklin in London. A year later, no sooner had the Siege of Boston ended than Massachusetts began to pay increasing attention to the naval operations that George Washington and Congress decided to engage. From then on the active

---

[77] They were Maj. John Bacheller, William Brown, John Eillis, Joseph Emerson, Ammi Falkner, Caleb Felch, Nathan Felch, Samuel Felch, Samuel Felch, Jr., Benjamin Leathe, from Reading, Nathan Bliss, David Cook, Lt. John Davis from Rehoboth, Samuel W. Bowker from Rutland District, Benjamin Clark from Abington, Silas Foster, Jonathan Wellington, and Capt. Enoch Whitmore from Acton, Lt. Micah French, — Perham, Josiah Waite from Athol, Lt. Edward Holman from Sutton, Col. Ebenezer Newell from Brookfield, and Nathan B. Newton from Southborough. Lilley B. Caswell, *The History of the Town of Royalston, Massachusetts* (Published by the Town of Royalston, 1917), 403, 411-12.

participation of hundreds of Massachusetts sailors and marines in the Revolutionary War made several ship captains (both native and foreign born) legendary figures in naval history, including John Paul Jones, John Manley, John Haraden, and Luther Little. Yet unlike these naval officers, who the rank and file were and what concrete experiences they had on the ships have remained murky since the publication of Jesse Lemisch's provocative article "Jack Tar in the Streets" more than forty-years ago. Not until recently did Paul A. Gilje's *Liberty on the Waterfront* (2004) and Daniel Vickers's *Young Men and the Sea* (2005) filled some of the gaps by their extensive studies of marine culture and sailors' life in the age of the revolution and the early republic. Furthermore, an analysis of a sample of a thousand marines and seamen of this period indicates that few people were more diverse and more elusive to any simple classification than those who manned the 500-600 state ships/vessels/privateers that Massachusetts authorized to build or commissioned to launch into action.[78]

Massachusetts's long maritime tradition would not necessarily paint a positive portrait of its seamen, nor would its numerous coastal communities automatically explain why some men were willing to venture out for the sea while others were not.[79] Contemporary descriptions and modern investigations often give a mixed account concerning the virtues and vices of the sailors. Some likened them to the closest proletariat early America ever had, while others frowned upon their highly erratic life style and temperamental behavior, which frequently

---

[78] Ralph D. Paine, *The Ships and Sailors of Old Salem* (Chicago: A. C. McClurg & Co., 1912), 159-61. Jesse Lemisch, "Jack Tar in the Streets: Merchant Seamen in the Politics of Revolutionary America," *William and Mary Quarterly*, 3d Ser., 25 (1968), 371-407. Paul A. Gilje's *Liberty on the Waterfront* (Philadelphia: University of Pennsylvania Press, 2004). Gardner Weld Allen, *Massachusetts Privateers of the Revolution* (Boston: Massachusetts Historical Society, 1927). William M. Fowler, Jr., *Rebels under Sail: The American Navy during the Revolution* (New York: Charles Scribner's Sons, 1976). Jack Coggins, *Ships and Seamen of the American Revolution* ([New York] Promontory Press, 1969), 74.

[79] Francis D. Cogliano, *American Maritime Prisoners in the Revolutionary War: The Captivity of William Russell* (Annapolis, M.D.: Naval Institute Press, 2001), 1-3.

shifted from swearing, fighting, and violence to heavy drinking, gambling, and whoring. Two ship captains clearly understood these conflicting traits, and each began to recruit his men by adopting a strategy that he believed would work the best. The famed John Paul Jones stressed gentlemanly qualities and the glorious cause in his advertisement. Betting on a down-to-earth approach, Elisha Hinman—an equally committed commodore of the day—unabashedly used strong liquor as the lure in his recruitment campaign.[80] Either way, the result was a crew "of all ages, kinds and descriptions" and not a few "in the various stages of intoxication." If many were passionate believers in the patriot cause, those who were attracted to money, freedom, adventure, and rebellion (or all of the above) could be equal in number. Some were no doubt experienced sailors, others had never worked on any ship such as landsmen and boys (so-termed regardless of their age), and still more were "lads of twelve and thirteen," such as those taken as officers' servants, cabin-boys, and powder-boys. For example, when William Cotton enlisted to serve on a ship in 1778, he was only ten years old and three feet eight inches tall. In fact, so many under-age boys got on board to serve that Mill Prison in Plymouth, England, where more than a thousand captured New England privateersmen were imprisoned, had a school run by William Russell (the 31-year-old Boston schoolteacher turned a crew member who had no prior seafaring experience) to keep those youngsters out of trouble.[81]

---

[80] Jones's advertisement was quoted in almost every book about him. Ralph D. Paine, *The Ships and Sailors of Old Salem* (Chicago: A. C. McClurg & Co., 1912), 70-71. Samuel Eliot Morison, *John Paul Jones: A Sailor's Biography* (Annapolis, Md.: Naval Institute Press, 1999), 140. Hinman's advertisement is less known, *Independent Ledger* (Boston), December 4, 1780. A lively illustration of the relationships between a captain and his crew is Even Thomas, *John Paul Jones: Sailor, Hero, Father of the American Navy* (New York: Simon & Schuster, 2003), 165-67.

[81] Ralph D. Paine, *The Ships and Sailors of Old Salem* (Chicago: A. C. McClurg & Co., 1912), 70, 128, 146. Francis D. Cogliano, *American Maritime Prisoners in the Revolutionary War: The Captivity of William Russell* (Annapolis, M.D.: Naval Institute Press, 2001), 71-72.

Depending on its size, a small vessel (such as a snow or a sloop) needed a dozen men to operate, while a large one (such as a schooner, a frigate, or a brigantine) required several dozen to several hundred. Once on board, a private could expect to receive 6 2/3 dollars (or £2) for his service per calendar month while his captain 32 dollars (or £9 12s.).[82] Under the rules set by the Naval Committee of the United Colonies in 1775, a private's weekly provision would consist of 7 pounds of bread, 4 pounds of beef, 2 pounds of pork, 4 pounds of potatoes (or turnips and pudding), 2 ounces of butter, 8 ounces of cheese, ½ pint of rice, 1 pint of peas, and ½ pint of rum (per day), totaling about 6s. in cost.[83] If the attraction of glory and the allure of prize money could be huge for any patriotic seaman and privateer, so could potential risks and vital costs. At Salem, which sent out 148 privateers during the war, an agreement stipulated that "if any one shall first discover a sail which shall prove to be a Prize, he shall be entitled to Five hundred dollars." A seaman was entitled to one thousand dollars for first boarding any vessel during an engagement, one thousand dollars for losing a joint, two thousand dollars for losing an eye, and four thousand dollars for losing a leg or an arm. All seamen and their officers were entitled to one half of all the captured prizes; the state took the other half. Yet they also forfeited their shares of the prizes if they quit or abandoned their duty, pilfered any money or goods, caused any disturbance on board, refused

---

[82] For more details see Samuel Eliot Morison, *John Paul Jones: A Sailor's Biography* (Annapolis, Md.: Naval Institute Press, 1999), 90-97.

[83] Jack Coggins, *Ships and Seamen of the American Revolution* ([New York] Promontory Press, 1969), 210-11. The sum of 6s. was computed according to the commodity prices set by a committee consisting of representatives from Connecticut, Massachusetts, New Hampshire, and Rhode Island (December 31, 1776), *Independent Chronicle* (Boston), January 23, 1777 (except for white bread 4d. lb. or brown bread 2 ½ d. lb. which were based on the average of Boston assizes). For example, grass-fed beef of the best quality was 3d. lb., pork 4½ d. lb., potatoes 1¼ d. 4 lb., butter 1¼ d. 2 oz., peas 1 ½ d. pint, and New England rum 5 ¾ d. pint. See also *Act and Resolves*, 5: 670-671.

officers' command, behaved with cowardice, got drunk in the time of action, or became mutinous.[84]

In reality, no prize money could be realized until a maritime court was set up and all legal proceedings followed. Generally speaking, the court would not process any single capture each time when a libel was filed, but often group half to a dozen privateer cases together for trial, which could be a long wait for any crew member who was pressed to cash his prize.[85] In addition, whereas officers could receive one third of the net proceeds and a captain could have as many as six or more shares of the prize money, a low-ranking seaman and a landsman usually had only one or half a share, which was unlikely to make him as fabulously rich as some legend claimed. For example, after eighteen months of service ending in 1777, Capt. John Paul Jones received little more than 3,000 dollars for his share of prize money. Hence, a landsman and a low-ranking seaman on his crew could only receive either 250 or 500 dollars each for their shares respectively, averaging 14 to 28 dollars a month.[86]

Thus, going to the sea may have required a stronger sense of commitment than what was commonly credited to those enlisted marines and sailors, who would be facing both an un-predictable future and a temporary deployment. Most privates of marines, ordinary seamen, landsmen, or boys served short terms—from one to several months allowing a ship to sail from Massachusetts to the Carolinas, the West Indies, and return. Cruises to allied countries such as Spain and France may

---

[84] Ralph D. Paine, *The Ships and Sailors of Old Salem* (Chicago: A. C. McClurg & Co., 1912), 65-67, 96. Frank A. Gardner, "State Schooner Diligent," *Massachusetts Magazine* 3 (1910), 40-46.
[85] *Boston Gazette*, June 16, 1777; *Continental Journal*, July 25, 1776. *Independent Chronicle*, September 26, 1776, August 21, 1777, April 29, 1779. Gardner Weld Allen, *Massachusetts Privateers of the Revolution* (Boston: Massachusetts Historical Society, 1927), 53-55. Richard Buel, Jr., *In Irons: Britain's Naval Supremacy and the American Revolutionary Economy* (New Haven, Conn.: Yale University Press, 1998), 116-18.
[86] Samuel Eliot Morison, *John Paul Jones: A Sailor's Biography* (Annapolis, Md.: Naval Institute Press, 1999), 94.

take as long as six months, but rarely any longer unless extended for damages and delays in some bad engagement with the enemy. The turnover rate could also be high as a result of those serious losses of manpower from the sickness, deteriorating health, wounds, injuries, captivity, and deaths as well as desertion that many crews frequently suffered.[87] Sometimes, even experienced seamen and captains could be unemployed. Thus, Capt. John Allen Hallet petitioned in August 1780 that, as "he had served the State satisfactorily in previous commands & had been kept on shore & out of employ for a long space of time & had refused private offers," he asked the Board of War to fulfill its earlier promise and allow him to command a new vessel purchased by the state.[88] If Capt. Hallet, who commanded eight vessels for numerous cruises between 1776 and 1782 (a feat rarely attempted by most seamen),[89] still felt the need for employment, other sailors and marines must have felt the same, no matter how many prizes they had seized.

Unlike the state troops and the Continental army, which regularly had hundreds of common soldiers enlisted for one, two, three, and even more years, most Massachusetts sailors and seamen got on board for only a very brief period and then disappeared, making their lives and service extremely difficult to trace. In light of this situation, a statement (the geographical names in it have been modernized) by Samuel Webb (b. 1754,

---

[87] Officers were by no means exempted from those sufferings. Three grape-shots hit Capt. Luther Little's face in a battle and permanently disfigured him—he was fortunate to survive at all. Ralph D. Paine, *The Ships and Sailors of Old Salem* (Chicago: A. C. McClurg & Co., 1912), 98-116.
As daring and popularly known as John Paul Jones in those days, Capt. John Manley "received several wounds and blows, particularly in his left leg and left shoulder (by which he was lanced), the leg being thereby rendered lame, and the toes of his left foot contracted; the heavy blow on the shoulder depriving him of the free use of his left arm." National Archives, United States Revolutionary War Pension: John Manley incomplete file. See also James L. Nelson, *George Washington's Secret Navy: How the American Revolution Went to Sea* (New York: McGraw Hill, 2008), 168-69, 235-36, 307-11, 318.
[88] Frank A. Gardner, "State Ship Tartar," *Massachusetts Magazine* 4 (1911), 43-48.
[89] Gardner Weld Allen, *Massachusetts Privateers of the Revolution* (Boston: Massachusetts Historical Society, 1927), 45, 66, 71, 137, 152, 222, 236, 289-30.

Scituate) is quoted below in full to compensate somewhat for the lack of any records evidencing a serviceman's life at sea.

> In the year 1777 and in the month of March of that year, I enlisted as a marine on board of a Letter of Marque brig called the *Ranger*, which brig was commanded by Capt. Israel Turner of Pembroke, and was a Government Vessel. We sailed from Boston about the month of March 1777 bound to Bilbao in Spain for military stores for the army, but was taken by a British ship, called *Peace and Plenty* mounting twelve guns off Cape Finisterre about twenty days after leaving Boston and was carried into Lisbon & from thence to Belfast in Ireland & there remained two months, from thence I was taken on board a British Ship and sent to Spit Head in England and there put on board a British Man of War called the *Diligence* and there confined six months, & from thence against my will was taken on board a British frigate called the *Hazard* and carried out the Straits to the Island of Majorca and from there to Lisbon, being on board six months & then came from there in a Dutch ship bound to Madeira, but was taken again and carried to the West of Ireland and detained seventeen months and from thence went to Lisbon & from there to Cádiz, and attempted to come home in a ship bound to Plymouth in Massachusetts, commanded by John Howland Ricket, but when we were within thirty hours sail of Plymouth, we were taken by two twenty-gun ships and carried back to Kinsale in Ireland and from thence to Spit Head in England & from thence to Plymouth and confined in Prison thirteen months until I was exchanged for one of Cornwallis' men, that was taken in Virginia—and thus finally after absence of

nearly five years—I came Home—Capt. Nath.^{al.} Spooner, John Washburn, & a Mr. Morton of Plymouth, were in Prison with me & were exchanged with me, who are to the last of my knowledge and belief dead.[90]

A spirited fighter and true survivor, Samuel Webb finally returned home after an ordeal of five years in captivity, during which time he was carried by no fewer than a half dozen enemy ships and confined in seven cities in four countries.

Foot soldiers generally served longer terms than seamen and sailors, which provided them almost twice the number of opportunities to receive small or big promotions in a diversified military organization. Based on an analysis of the service careers of 3,000 soldiers and 1,000 seamen, about five in every hundred men serving in the navy had a chance to receive promotions, while the number in the army was ten. Performance on board of a ship depended on diligence and courage as well as a long accumulation of experience, which perhaps explains the low rate (3%) of promotion from the inexperienced low-rank boys/landsmen to seamen among the 1,000 crew members studied in the data. Although experience did matter, military service on land was wide open for recognition accorded with a broad range of competence, skills, hard work, endurance, and bravery. Of those 1,020 enlisted men who entered the army at the lowest rank of private in the above data, about 15% got promoted. Many were small promotions, such as from a private to a matross, a bombardier, or a gunner. Some also appeared more like lateral changes of positions or reassignments than anything else, such as from a drummer to a fifer or the other way around. However, some did

---

[90] National Archives, United States Revolutionary War Pension: R11246.

mean real promotions and pay increases, such as from a drummer to a drum major or from a fifer to a fifer major.[91]

Moreover, several dozen privates rose to corporals and no fewer than fifty privates or corporals were promoted to sergeants, which indicated a clear advancement in ranks. Yet could these soldiers further their careers by entering the ranks of officers? The answer is "yes." Records show that 15 sergeants broke through the top ranking of soldiers and became officers. Among them, Asa Copeland and John Eayers became conductors; William Dawes, William Richards, Christopher Wallcut, Benjamin Brown, Ebenezer Floyd, and Andrew Garritt were promoted to ensign; Luke Howell, Joseph Ford, and James Leary were promoted to second lieutenant; Richard Skilling was promoted to first lieutenant; George Reab and Etham Moore were promoted to lieutenant; and Sergeant Daniel McKlain was not only promoted to ensign, but also rose from second lieutenant and first lieutenant to the rank of captain.

In fact, of the forty-five captains of the troops recruited from Boston, many had prior experience serving at a lower rank before receiving their appointment, and no fewer than two dozen were promoted from lieutenants and adjutants. Although Sergeant McKlain's rise was exceptional and not every captain began his career as a foot soldier, several individual advancements in the army did show the potential of an upward mobility, which sometimes did relate the story of a soldier becoming an officer. For example, William Price was a gunner and later rose to become second lieutenant, first lieutenant, and lieutenant. Similarly, Richard McClure, a bombardier, was first promoted to gunner, then to sergeant, and finally to second lieutenant. John Meacham was a corporal, then a sergeant, and finally a lieutenant. Andrew McIntire rose from a corporal to a sergeant and finally a lieutenant. Benjamin Callander, John

---

[91] Such as from drummer to drum major—Jonathan Kinney, Daniel Reed, Richard Ryan, Robert Steel, and from fifer to fifer major—William Owen.

Coats, and Michael Combler entered the service as privates, but all three soldiers later rose to become lieutenants.

Nevertheless, a less glowing aspect of the lives of the enlisted men was the proverbial problem of desertion, which often troubled recruiters, muster masters, and field officers alike, as well as many towns and villages that paid bounties to those soldiers for entering the service in the first place.[92] A total of 220 desertion cases were found among 4,000 soldiers and sailors recruited in Boston, resulting in a ratio of 5.5% with the following characteristics:

1. Only a handful of desertions (3 cases or less than 2%) took place during the early stages of the war in 1775-76, when most local militiamen served short-terms, from several days to a few months.[93]
2. An overwhelming number of desertions (170 cases or 77%) happened between 1777 and 1780, when the long-term service of three years or for the duration of the war was implemented and when an increasing number of non-residents were hired as substitutes to fill a community's quota.[94]
3. Nearly two-thirds of all cases (142) occurred under the terms of serving for three years or the duration of the war.[95]

---

[92] Newspapers published rewards for returning deserters during the war almost as frequently as those for runaways in colonial days. *Boston Gazette*, June 16, 1777. *Continental Journal*, July 25, 1776. *Independent Chronicle*, September 26, 1776, August 21, 1777, April 29, 1779. In a single publication, Col. Henry Jackson announced that 58 soldier deserted his Massachusetts battalion, *Providence Gazette*, June 19, 1779.
[93] The three soldiers were John Green, John Jones, and Philip Marchant.
[94] Such as Peter Le Beauf (for Boston; 1778), Peter Milzard (Braintree; 1779), John Mitchel Jr. (Boston; 1778), William Mooney (Boston; 1779), Charles More (Boston; 1778), John Howland (Boston; 1778), Gregory O'Bryan (Boston; 1778), Michael Orgue (Danvers; 1779), John Potts (Weymouth; 1778), George Sorry (Boston; 1778), William Tector (Boston; 1778), and Edward Thompson (Upton; 1779).
[95] See William Dodge (for Braintree), Robert Ford (Hingham), Samuel Fry (Blandford), James Granger (Boston), John Green (Boston), John Hamilton (Boston), John Hayward (Holliston), Barnabas Henley (Boston), Pitman Howard (Ipswich), and Stephen Hunt (Boston).

4. One-third of desertions (79 cases) involved those soldiers who were hired as a substitute for an outside community to serve for three or more years.[96]

Although these characteristics revealed some general trends in context, no fixed pattern of behavior or any single reason could explain all desertion. For example, after enlistment, some enlistees never joined (e.g., James Clark, Enoch Green, Peter Hughson, and John Key), while others joined the service but deserted in a few months (e.g., Daniel Fowler, Anthony Gruell, Adam Henry, and Isaac Hufle), a few weeks (e.g., William P. Emmorell, Martin Frederick, Peter Gilson, and Gabriel Wallick), or a few days (e.g., Amos Greene in fifteen days, Simon Darior in fourteen, Alexander Smart in four, and William Teetor in three). Such a spread of choices in timing seems to suggest that for those who never showed up at the musters and for those who left the service shortly afterward, they perhaps never intended to serve but planned their leaving from early on. Yet the idea of desertion may only come to other soldiers gradually as they began to experience the real harshness and brutality of war.

Not an easy thought in good conscience, desertion could have been a painful decision for many enlisted men, who must have some compelling personal reasons for reaching this critical point. Before he quit, the Irish soldier James Salmon served continuously for almost four years from the beginning of the war in 1776. Corporal William Kelly deserted in 1780; he had been sick since 1778. Archibald Hunter enlisted for Weymouth for the term of three years. He deserted shortly

---

[96] See the cases of John Bennett (for Waltham), John Bowles (Cohasset), Amos Brown (Abington), John Butler (Brookline), Robert Campbell (Roxbury), Thomas Carr 2d (Bridgewater), James Casey (Weymouth), Joseph Cough (Bellingham), John Crosby (Cambridge), and John Davis (Hingham).

before the expiration perhaps because his had some family difficulties. Similarly, Private John Conneley was serving for Middleton; he left the troops—perhaps for his wife, who was coming to Boston. A good soldier, Roger Taylor was promoted from corporal to sergeant. He was never absent from duty for three years starting in 1777; however, for reasons unclear, he deserted in 1780. Born in England, Richard Ryan was a loyal soldier who enlisted in 1777 for the duration of war. Although he deserted in 1780, he returned to service the next year, later suffered a rupture, and was pensioned in 1783 and 1787. Still more perplexing is Private James Shepard's story. Shepard also enlisted in 1777 for three years or the duration of the war; he abandoned the service twice (March and December 1778) but came back and continued to serve each time in August 1778 and May 1779. Not until several months later in September 1779 did he desert again and never reappear. Private John Ryan, a transient from Nova Scotia, enlisted for Bridgewater for three years or the duration of the war. He deserted after a year but returned to service; he was present at Valley Forge in the winter of 1777-78.

In fact, almost 40 deserters (18%) did not leave for good, but ultimately returned to service, which clearly showed the conflicting concerns and mixed interests soldiers were facing during this extremely volatile and trying period. Wavering perhaps was not necessarily a sign of weakness, but a realistic reflection of the long, arduous, and unpredictable path that many common soldiers were treading. For example, born in Cork, Ireland, John Madden was a private serving for Stoughton as early as 1775. He deserted after almost seven years of service. Still he returned and received an honorable discharge by General George Washington in 1783. His sense of pride was perhaps no less than that of three exemplary soldiers: Adam Myer, Anthony Shappo, and Joshua Gray. Myer was a German farmer who received one service stripe when discharged in 1782 after serving in the army for Boxford for three years. Shappo was a laborer who also received one service stripe when discharged in 1782 after serving a full term of three years. Gray—a Boston native serving since 1776 for the duration of the war—received two service stripes (a rare honor and recognition indeed) when discharged by the commander-in-chief in 1783.

The last note about wartime soldiers concerns a reversal of sorts. After the victory at Yorktown and in the days and months that followed, desertion dropped by as much as 90%, down to eighteen cases in four years from 1781 to 1784, indicating a precipitous decline of tension as peace and normality finally begin to return. However, military recruitment continued, especially for the need of defending Castle and Governor's Islands in Boston Harbor. Representing more of a source of regular wages, stable income, and good security than any imminent danger, enlistment for those posts became increasingly attractive and not a few viewed them as employment opportunities rather than military sacrifices. Interestingly, although most long-term obligations (from six months to one year and up) were discontinued while a short three-month commitment became the standard, many enlistees then volunteered to extend their terms once, twice, thrice, and even more. Quite a few went on and on, serving for a series of consecutive terms and stretching their stay in the service from months to years. Thus, as Captain Lieutenant William Burbeck's company (from 1779 to 1781) and especially Captain Thomas Cushing's company (from 1781 to 1787) alternated guarding Castle and Governor's Islands, about fifty-eight of their soldiers routinely served for three, six, twelve, fifteen, and eighteen months; some of them served as many as thirty-three months, or eleven successive three-month terms.

What is still more striking is that the majority of those soldiers guarding these islands shared but a few family names, such as Canterbury (2), Dyer (2), Hollis (2), Joy (2), Shaw (2), Webb (2), and Turrell (2); more than half of all the soldiers bore one of six surnames: Howard (3), Kimball (3), Trufant (3), Torrey (3), French (6), and Thayer (15),[97] suggesting that they might belong to some close-knit circles of friends and relatives who encouraged and supported one another to enlist for those enviable if not lucrative positions. For instance, soldier Sylvanus French, whose grandmother was Ether Thayer, married Hannah Thayer, who was the younger sister of Abraham Thayer—a private and quarter gunner on Castle and Governor's Islands. Both men served in Captain Cushing's company with two other privates—Ephraim Capen and James Faxon. All four men (French, Thayer, Capen, and Faxon) were born and raised in Braintree. Capen had thirteen siblings; his mother was Ruth Thayer, and he was likely named for her father Ephraim Thayer. Faxon's elder sister Dorcas married Nathaniel Thayer in 1776. The couple gave birth to Sylvanus Thayer (1785-1872) who, at age nine, stayed with the Faxons in New Hampshire. Later known as the "Father of West Point," Colonel Sylvanus Thayer also supervised the construction of Fort Independence on Castle Island in the nineteenth century.

Indeed, among the last groups of enlistees, Private Zebah Thayer's career illustrates an unexpected turnaround toward the end of this prolonged war. Born in 1764 at Braintree, which was home to several Thayers, he was the youngest boy of Zachariah and Lydia (Pray) Thayer's fourteen children. Moving to Boston and enlisting at the age of seventeen, he repeatedly extended his terms again and again and served on

---

[97] They included Jacob Canterbury, John Canterbury; Joseph Dyer, Nathaniel Dyer; Isaac Hollis, Jesse Hollis; Benjamin Joy, Turner Joy; Jesse Shaw, Josiah Shaw; John Webb, Joseph Webb; Abraham Howard; Ebenezer Howard, Zebulon Howard; Colson Trufant, Jonathan Trufant, Joshua Trufant; Elias Torrey, Jacob Torrey, Abner Torrey; Ahaz French, Nathaniel French, Samuel French, Stephen French, Sylvanus French; Abner Thayer, Abraham Thayer, Alexander Thayer, Benjamin Thayer, Demetrius Thayer, Ebenezer Thayer, John Thayer, Jonathan Thayer, Moses Thayer, Oliver Thayer, Peter Thayer, Robert Thayer, Solomon Thayer, Titus Thayer, and Zebah Thayer.

Castle and Governor's Islands non-stop until 1787. Although a common laborer by profession, he apparently saved enough money, married Elizabeth Freeman the year after his discharge, and started to buy and sell land and houses in Boston during the next decade.[98]

Veterans

The revolution that succeeded in winning independence for the thirteen colonies did not end poverty, which continued to haunt hundreds of those common soldiers who fought in the war. Through individual valor or various opportunities, some soldiers did achieve distinction and moved up on the social ladder. Yet many were wounded, disabled, captured, imprisoned, missing, or lost at sea while others were killed or died of cold, sickness, diseases, and countless other miseries. Still more remained where they had been before the war, returning to the same needy circumstances of impoverishment, penury, and distress.

Soldiers from wealthier backgrounds had a better chance of readjusting to civilian life. A sizable homestead, an established business, and a dependable financial chest blessed a veteran wishing to return to his home of peace and stability. As previously mentioned, Isaiah Bullard of Weston took in Peter Cary as his apprentice in 1773. Although both had served as privates in Captain Samuel Lamson's company and had marched on the Lexington alarm, Bullard quickly returned as a civilian. The value of his property rose steadily and he served several town offices during the next ten years. In 1778 he paid a

---

[98] Deceased in 1830, Zebah Thayer is 57462 in Thwing Index. Similar to his case, others may include Titus Thayer (Thwing 57456), John Thayer (clerk; Thwing 57435), and Moses Thayer (stay-maker/tailor; Thwing 2421); all of them could have been the same above named soldiers stationed on Castle and Governor's Islands through the 1780s while thereafter buying and selling land and houses in Boston in the 1790s.

town tax of £122. Meanwhile, Cary continued to serve until the end of the war in 1783. Weston paid various wages for his service, but Cary never held enough property to be rated afterward.

Susanna Fisher, widow of Eleazer Fisher

Samuel Gates, brother of Lemuel Gates

Thaddeus Gibson

Judith Harris, widow of Daniel Harris (son of Thomas Harris)

Clarissa Howard, widow of Andrew Howard

John [Doyle] Legg

Lucretia Oak, widow of Calvin Oak

Signatures by veterans of the Revolutionary War and their widows who applied for federal pensions. (National Archives)

Moses Dickinson was born in Sunderland, Hampshire County, but moved to Amherst, where many Dickinsons resided. From a small farm of nine acres he managed to build a substantial estate. A respectable citizen in the community, he was elected town meeting moderator several times during the

1760s and selectmen no less than a dozen times. He was a representative to the General Court in 1775 and 1777, when he acquired the title of esquire. Four of his sons served in the war—Moses, Jr., Aaron, Medad, and Elijah. Moses Jr. died in 1778. Aaron practiced a trade while expanding his farm from 20 acres in 1780 to 30 acres 5 years later. Medad had a trade, a farm of 8 acres, $600 in cash, and $900 in goods in 1780. He was elected selectman numerous times in the late 1790s and early 1800s before serving as a representative to the General Court in 1810 and 1811. Elijah rose from a soldier to a militia ensign, captain, and colonel in the service. He was also elected selectman numerous times through the 1790s and early 1800s, when his estate included a 50-acre farm plus 200 acres of unimproved land. He owned a carriage and came to be called a gentleman.

Of the other veterans who were not long-time residents of a local community but served in the war, perhaps no more than 15 percent managed to stay where they had first enlisted. Within this group, those soldiers who had deeper roots and stronger connections fared better than those who did not. Moses Sr.'s cousin Waitstill Dickinson, for example, did well. He served in the war several times in 1775, 1776, and 1778, yet he was also able to double his estate from 20 acres in 1780 to a 40-acre farm and 140 acres of land in 1790. So did Giles Church, who was born and raised in Amherst. He was an enlisted man and a participant in Shays's Rebellion. A carpenter and farmer, he had 13 acres of crops by 1780 and was an active miller after 1800. He married Lois Billing of Amherst, and the couple had 11 children. He died in Amherst in 1807. Joel Moody was the son of John and Sarah (Dickinson) Moody. He was born in 1743 in Granby, just south of Amherst. He was a sergeant during the war and returned to Amherst afterward. He was a selectman in 1784 and owned a 20-acre farm and 50 acres of undeveloped land. After serving the war and even after his participation in Shays's Rebellion, Joseph Stratton Temple returned to Shrewsbury, where he had been born. He married Susanna Hemenway in Shrewsbury in 1786 and had four children by 1790. Born in Plymouth, Plymouth County, Caleb Stutson moved to Plympton in the same county, where his mother had been born. He enlisted there during the revolution and returned afterward. He and his wife had raised a family of five children there by 1790. Isaac Gould was from Sudbury but moved to Weston. He enlisted for Sudbury but settled at Weston, where he had a household of five members in 1790. He became a taxpayer in 1793 and died there three years later.

As previously mentioned, Jesse Ballou, the son of an established local farmer, was warned by Wrentham authorities not because of his circumstances, but because of the fact that the part of town in which he was born subsequently separated from Wrentham to form part of Cumberland, Rhode Island. Consequently, Ballou served for both Wrentham and Cumberland during the war and maintained close contact with his hometown. In 1782, he took in Daniel Trask, wife Rachel, and their seven children, whom Wrentham authority soon warned. The act did not stop him from receiving more strangers. Four years later, he took in Thomas Wood of Swansea, wife Mary, and their nine children. Although Wrentham warned them, Ballou seemed untroubled to have hired the family to work on his farm there.[99] Similarly, a war veteran whom Wrentham had warned in the 1760s, William Puffer took in Lidea Wetherel from Norton in 1781.[100] Another fellow soldier who had a warning-out record but did better than most was

---

[99] Esther L. Friend, "Notifications and Warnings Out: Strangers Taken into Wrentham, Massachusetts, Between 1732 and 1812," *New England Historical and Genealogical Registry* 141 (1987): 348, 354.

[100] As early as 1769 William Puffer took in Ebenezer Gilbert, wife Lydea, and their six children Nathaniel, Amy, Bathsheba, Ebenezer, Zilpah, and Abigail. Both Ebenezer, Sr. and Jr. enlisted as soldiers for Wrentham during the war. Esther L. Friend, "Notifications and Warnings Out: Strangers Taken into Wrentham, Massachusetts, Between 1732 and 1812," *New England Historical and Genealogical Registry* 141 (1987): 201, 347.

Jonathan Felt. He rose from a private on the march to Lexington to a captain five years later. He married Eunice Brastow of Wrentham in 1784. She was the younger sister of Samuel Brastow, who was also a private on the same march to Lexington. Once established, Felt reported to town authorities in 1796 that he had taken in a stranger named Isaiah Morse from Foxborough.[101]

Born in Dorchester, Thomas Harris went with his parents and siblings to Fitchburg, Worcester County, where authorities warned them. They managed to stay. Thomas and his two brothers Daniel and Samuel enlisted for Fitchburg. Daniel married Judith Goodall in Fitchburg in 1780. They had 12 children. He died in Fitchburg in 1820. Edward Payson was born in Rowley, Essex County, in 1757. After serving in the war, he married Eunice Nicols in Winchendon, Worcester County, but returned to Rowley, where the family grew into six members by 1790. Jesse Mason was a yeoman at Lanesboro, Berkshire. He participated in the revolution and Shays's Rebellion. He stayed at Lanesboro and had a household of eight members by 1790. An orphan at the almshouse in Boston, Thomas Lillie was bound out to Joseph Sellman, the shoreman of Marblehead, Essex County. Lillie enlisted for three years for Marblehead during the war. Disabled in 1777, he became an invalid but continued lived in Marblehead until 1794. Similarly, William Shirley also enlisted for Marblehead during the war. He returned, married Annis Mayley of Marblehead, raised a large family of eight children, and finally died there in 1807. Like Lillie, he too had been a bound-out orphan from the almshouse in Boston.

Not having a legal settlement or a good prospect of gaining one, many veterans opted for some hopeful future

---

[101] Esther L. Friend, "Notifications and Warnings Out: Strangers Taken into Wrentham, Massachusetts, Between 1732 and 1812," *New England Historical and Genealogical Registry* 142 (1988): 64.

elsewhere. Perhaps as many as 40 to 50 percent of the poor veterans moved again after the war away from the communities in which they had enlisted during the revolution. Their action strongly resembled the pre-war migration patterns of moving through three gradually expanded circles—first within a county, then crossing county lines, and finally across state lines. Only this time, a large number of veteran families did not seem content to stay within the commonwealth; they were willing and prepared to move to other states altogether. As peace returned after the war, many communities showed little more inclusive promise to many veterans than they had before the war.

If that was the case, neighboring communities and nearby counties often became the first place veteran soldiers would choose to go where they might be better treated. Thus, Caleb Church, who served for Oakham in Worcester County during the war, moved to and died in Ashfield, Hampshire (later Franklin) County. Ensign Elisha Cox enlisted for Waltham, Middlesex County, and died during the war. His son, also named Elisha, moved to Marlborough in the same county. A veteran and a participant in Shays's Rebellion, Humphrey Bigelow left Shrewsbury, where he had been born, and married and settled in Grafton, Worcester County. Soldier Ichabod Bozworth was from Cumberland, Rhode Island. He enlisted for Wrentham, but moved to Bellingham, Norfolk County, after the war. He died in Franklin of the same county in 1820. His widow Ruth (Bradley) Bozworth moved to Upton, Worcester County, but died in Grafton in the same county in 1850.

John Atkinson moved numerous times in life. Born in East Haddam, Hartford (later Middlesex) County, Connecticut, he moved with his parents to Massachusetts, where several town authorities in five counties warned them, including Harvard, Worcester County, and Boston in Suffolk County, Sudbury and Cambridge in Middlesex County, Bridgewater in

Plymouth County, and Pelham in Hampshire County. He enlisted for Pelham during the war, but moved to Prescott in Hampshire County after the war. Born in Shirley, Middlesex County, Jonathan Barrett went to Lunenburg, Worcester County, where he served during the revolution. He moved to Lancaster after the war. Luke Chapin enlisted for Brimfield, Hampshire County, during the war, but moved to Palmer in the same county afterward. Oliver Chickering enlisted for Sherborn, Middlesex County, during the war, but moved to Rutland, Worcester County, where he died in 1831. William Bogle was born in Oxford, Worcester County, where he enlisted during the war. He moved to and settled in Weston, Middlesex County, where he married Lucy Tilton of Weston in 1786. Born in Leominster and moving several times with his parents, Luther Graves enlisted for Lancaster during the revolution but moved back to Leominster after the war. He and his wife Phoebe Jewett raised a large family of five girls and three boys before he died in Leominster in 1790.

At least three townships in Middlesex County—Watertown, Charlestown, and Weston—warned the Nutting family whenever it showed up in their communities. Samuel, a young man in the family, managed to stay in Weston during the 1770s, when he enlisted for the town during the revolution. Although his son, also named Samuel, married Mary Peirce of Weston and settled there, veteran Samuel removed to Watertown after the war and died in Newton in 1808. William Puffer enlisted for Wrentham during the revolution and returned there for a while. However, he died in Monson, Hampden County, in 1809. Coming from Bristol, Bristol County, Rhode Island, Timothy Munro moved to and enlisted for Rutland during the war. He married Lucretia Gates in 1781 and had a family of three children by 1790. He died in Princeton, Worcester County.

Still others not only moved, but also left Massachusetts for good. This group accounted for about 20 to 30 percent of the poor veterans—a significantly larger proportion than those domestic migrants during the pre-war years. Available land in the newly independent United Stated certainly attracted these veterans, whose wartime experience had perhaps made them more accustomed to moving across long distances than many civilians. Artemas Cox, the son of Elisha Cox in Weston, enlisted during the war but moved to Sagadahoc County in Maine after the war. A laborer from Connecticut, Ephraim Baker enlisted for Sudbury, Middlesex County. He participated in Shays's Rebellion and took an oath of allegiance in 1787. He moved to Buffalo, Niagara County, in New York, where he applied for a federal pension in 1818. He died in Concord, Erie County, in New York in 1826. Born in Boxford, Essex County, Jacob Black enlisted for Holden, Worcester County, during the war. Afterward he moved to Marshfield, Washington County, Vermont. An orphan at the Boston almshouse, John Banks was bound out to Andrew Adams, a local housewright in Grafton. Banks served the local militia for three months in 1775 and moved to Alstead, Cheshire County, New Hampshire, where he raised a family of eleven children. Thomas Craige was also an orphan at the Boston almshouse. He had been bound out to Worcester, but after his master's death during the French and Indian War, he moved to Northampton, where he enlisted. In 1802, he again moved to Windsor County, Vermont, where he applied for a federal pension in 1833 when he was 79 years old. Twin brothers Willis and William Fellows enlisted for Shelburne, Hampshire County. After the war, Willis moved to Bloomfield, Greene County, but died in Crawford County, Indiana. William moved to Watertown, Jefferson County, New York. Enlisted in Hampshire County during the war, Andrew Howard subsequently moved several times from Westfield and Palmer to Belchertown, where he applied for a federal pension in 1818. He died, however, in Oakfield in Fond du Lac County, Wisconsin, in 1849 at the age of 85.

Jonathan Hunter was born in Marlborough, Middlesex County. During the revolution he had lived in Roxbury, but first enlisted at Petersham, where he returned after the war. He and his wife had seven children by 1790. He then moved to Chelsea, Vermont, in 1806. He moved again to Plattsburg, New York, in 1812. When he applied for a federal pension in 1832, he was living in Clinton County, New York. Coming from Canada with his parents to Worcester County, Lemuel Gates enlisted for Lancaster in 1775. He served, along with his brother Samuel, for three years in the Continental Army from 1777. He married Lydia Whittemore of Lancaster, but died in Pennsylvania in 1806. Born in Stow, Middlesex County, Thaddeus Gibson moved several times in the 1760s and finally enlisted for Bellingham, Suffolk (later Norfolk) County, during the revolution. He moved to Milford, Worcester County, for four years after he left the service. He moved again to Henniker, Hillsborough (later Merrimack) County, New Hampshire in the early 1780s, where he died in 1834. The son of Clark and Hannah Gibbs of Rutland, Worcester County, Zenas Gibbs received a warning from Holden authorities in 1765. He enlisted for Rutland during the revolution, but afterward moved to Branford, Connecticut, for six years. He then moved to New Hartford in Oneida County, New York, where he died in 1840. Gersham Flagg Lane was born in Bedford, Middlesex County. Weston warned him in 1772. He went back to Bedford, where he enlisted during the revolution. He married Lydia Sally Thomas in 1775 and had thirteen children, most of whom were born in Weatherfield, Windsor County, Vermont. The couple died in Springville, Susquehanna County, Pennsylvania—he in 1838, and she in 1841.

Calvin Oaks's parentage and birthplace were unclear. He served in the 10th Worcester County regiment during the war, but moved to Windham County, Vermont, afterward. At least three Massachusetts soldiers—Christopher Stocker, Cato Freeman, and Mark Noble (an orphan from the almshouse in Boston)—left for Rhode Island after serving in the war.[102] Joseph Maxfield was also an orphan in Boston. He served in the Massachusetts Line during the revolution, but moved to Colchester, New London County (formerly in Massachusetts), Connecticut. He later moved again to Windham County, also in Connecticut. Levi Vinten was born in Braintree, Suffolk County, but moved to New Braintree, Worcester County, where he enlisted during the revolution. He later moved first to Genesee County and then to Harland in Niagara County, New York, where he died in 1820. Born in Attleborough, Bristol County, John Slack moved to Wrentham, Norfolk County, where he enlisted. He moved to New London, New Hampshire, after the war. He moved again at least twice within New Hampshire. Born in Waltham, Middlesex County, Jabez Stevens served for Fitchburg, Worcester County, during the revolution. After the war, Weston and Cambridge authorities warned him. He then moved back to Fitchburg, but passed away in Ohio in 1849 or 1850. Ebenezer Cooley was born in Brimfield, Hampshire County, where he served in the revolution. He participated in Shays's Rebellion and died in Lebanon, New York, in 1817. Asahel Stearns was born in Brookfield, Worcester County. He enlisted for the town during the revolution. He married Captivity (family name not known) in 1784 and had a family of four children at Williamstown, Berkshire County, in 1790. From that northwest corner of the state they moved north to Rutland County in Vermont, where he died in 1815. The widow stayed until 1840, when she removed to Onondaga County, New York, to live with her son. Born in Boston, Joseph Ransford enlisted in 1776 when he was

---

[102] Ruth Wallis Herndon, *Unwelcome Americans: Living on the Margin in Early New England* (Philadelphia: University of Pennsylvania Press, 2001), 71-75, 100-03, 103-06.

not yet 14 years old. He served in the continental forces on land and at sea for six years, but left Massachusetts after the war. He married Rachel Holman in Kentucky, and the couple moved numerous times across several counties in Kentucky, Ohio, and Indiana. They finally settled in Fairbanks, Sullivan County, Indiana, where both passed away between 1849 and 1852.

Moving alone did enable people to escape poverty. As many as 33,300 veterans and their families in Massachusetts applied for federal pensions, suggesting that a significant portion of them still faced difficulties in life long after the war ended. Veterans in good circumstances tended not to apply for assistance. They perhaps accounted for 10 to 15 percent of the veteran population. Another 10 to 15 percent applied for pensions more as a benefit than as an absolute need. William Bogle, a transient from Oxford, Worcester County, to Weston, Middlesex County, was among the lucky few who settled relatively well in his adopted community. After he returned at the end of war, he married Lucy Tilton of Weston in 1786. When he appeared on the town tax rolls several years later, he owned one dwelling house, four acres of improved land, twenty acres of pasture, fifty acres of unimproved land, one horse, six oxen, seven cows, and two swine.[103] He did receive a federal pension of $80 a year in 1832. At the time of his death in 1839, his properties were valued at $4,653, including his homestead with several building structures and 196 acres of land valued at $4,000. However, his personal debts and funeral expenses amounted to $635.16. His widow received a pension of $65.21 per annum in 1844. When she died two years later, she left an estate of $1015.75 and a total debt (including her funeral costs) of $1186.45.[104]

---

[103] *Town of Weston: The Tax Lists, 1757-1827* (Boston: Alfred Mudge & Son, 1897), 181.
[104] Middlesex Probate Records: 2125.

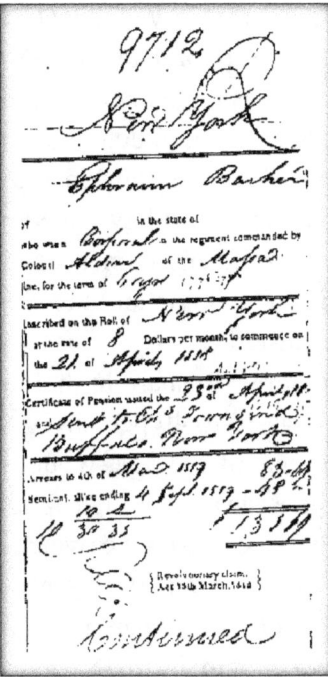

Ephraim Barker's pension card, which allowed him $8 per month to commence on April 21, 1818, when he resettled in New York after the revolution. (National Archives)

William's brother Thomas Bogle, however, was not as prosperous. Serving in the Massachusetts Line for six years, he received a federal pension of $80 a year in 1818, when he was living in Wardsboro in Windham County, Vermont. In 1820, he had 100 acres of land worth $500 and a personal estate valued at $78.50. Three years later, except for clothing and bedding, his real and personal properties amounted to $47.59. They included one cow, one calf, one heifer, three sheep, one old kettle, one iron pot, one old desk, six old kitchen chairs, one old armchair, one old pine table, four knives and forks, one old cutter, some old farm tools, and crockery ware. He sold the 100 acres for cash to pay for his mortgage and debt totaling more than $900. Many of his farm tools and much of his furniture were worn out, and he had no regular income but a few dollars here and there. "And I do also swear," he declared in his pension application of 1823, "that my occupation is that a common labourer, my health is poor and unable to perform hard labor.—My wife Elizabeth is 64 years of age, of a slender Constitution, and unable to perform much labor.—I have 8 children living, but they are all of age and left me except one son—who is 33 years old—and whom I have lived with." After serving his country and supporting his numerous children and several grandchildren, the veteran Bogle and his wife Elizabeth seemed indeed poor and exhausted.

Some had no better stories to share in their applications than Bogle. Perhaps as many as 30 to 40 percent of the veterans were in serious distress because of old age, wounds, declining health, personal debt, and the large size of their families. For all the gratuity and relief he received, the veteran Ichabod Bozworth was not doing well. He obtained a bounty land of 100 acres in 1793. Credited for a total of 7 years in service, he was granted a pension of $8 per month in 1818, when he was a resident of Bellingham, Norfolk County. He wrote in his petition that "I am in reduced circumstances in life & have need of assistance from the Country I served." He held no real property in 1820, and his personal estate totaled $16.10, including one chest and one chest of drawers, two tables, seven chairs, a brass kettle, some glassware, earthenware, and cooking ware. He died in Franklin, Norfolk County, on November 16, 1820. His widow Ruth moved to Upton, Worcester County, and received a pension in the same amount of $96 per annum from 1848 to 1850, when she died at Grafton, Worcester County. Veteran Peter Cary had been a captive in the war. He settled in Shrewsbury, Worcester County, where he applied for and received a federal pension in 1818. An inventory showed that assessed at $108.22, his properties included no more than an old house, a barn, a cow, two tables, seven chairs, and numerous household items. He had a family to support, and his wife was "in very low state of health." He died in 1832.

Property schedule of veteran Peter Cary of Shrewsbury, Worcester County, July 10, 1820. (National Archives)

The returning soldier Caleb Church bought 30 acres of land in Oakham in 1777. He also bought land in Ashfield in 1785 and appeared in the census there in 1790. Although his son Seth built a house in Ashfield and served as a selectman and representative for the town, he was not on the tax roll for

1793. Claiming poor health and the inability to support himself, he applied for and was granted a federal pension of $8 a month in 1818. His personal properties, valued at $16.60 in 1823, included such items as 1 pig, 1 old cart, 1 plow, 1 ax, 1 hoe, 1 pot, 1 old kettle, 3 old chests, 1 cupboard, 1 table, 6 chairs, 2 pails, 1 poor saddle and bridle, and 2 spinning wheels. He could not sign his name. After serving in the war for six years, Ephraim Barker moved several times. At the age of 59, he applied for a federal government pension on April 21, 1818 from Buffalo, Niagara County, New York. He was granted a pension at the rate of $8 per month. Two years later, he petitioned again. He listed his belongings valued at $112, including a mare and a colt, two hogs and two pigs, one old wagon, one old sleigh, one plow, one kettle, one pot, and some knives and forks. However, he stated that he was "indebted to individuals in about the sum of three hundred and twenty dollars," and that a weak shoulder and pain in the heart prevented him from working in the fields. He was thus unable to support himself.

After his service, Thaddeus Gibson moved to New Hampshire, ultimately settling on a 300-acre farm in Henniker in the early 1780s. He received a pension of $8 per month in 1818. In 1820, his properties included a horse, a wagon and harness, a cow, a hog, ten sheep, ten lambs, one plough, one sleigh, one chest with drawers, one old desk, ten chairs, one kettle, three axes, and numerous other household articles, totaling $120.50. His personal debt, however, amounted to $147. Veteran Andrew Howard's finances were only slightly better. At 54, he applied for a federal pension on May 12, 1818, at Belchertown in Hampshire County. He was granted $8 per month. In 1820 the value of his properties was $123.75 while that of his debt $91.

Property schedule of veteran Thaddeus Gibson of Henniker, Hillsborough (later Merrimack) County, New Hampshire, July 11, 1818. (National Archives)

After the war, the orphan John Doyle Legg moved to Oswegatchie in St. Lawrence County, New York, where he applied for a federal pension in 1818. No longer under dire circumstances, he owned 80 acres worth $200 and some personal possessions, including 1 old horse, 2 cows, 1 calf, 2 hogs, 2 pigs, 26 sheep, 1 plough, 1 pot, 1 tea kettle, 5 spoons, 6 knives, 6 forks, 6 bowls, 2 pictures, 1 tea pot, 1 tea cup and 2 saucers, 6 chairs, 1 table, 2 platters, 3 plates, 1 cupboard, 1 lantern, 1 coffee pot, 1 wooden bottle, and 1 jug. Yet on his application he stated that "he is by occupation a farmer but is old and his constitution so much enfeebled as to be unable to labour hard, that his wife is also very infirm being in her sixty eighth year and is entirely unable to labour." The couple had no children living with them. The children were all of age, had separate households, and were in no condition to offer any assistance. He also had an orphaned grandchild to support. John Legg was granted a pension of $8 a month.

Just as old age was a natural problem everyone had to face, a large family was a common burden to many of the veterans. John Banks moved from Grafton, Worcester County, to Alstead, Cheshire County, New Hampshire. He served in both Massachusetts and New Hampshire Lines during the revolutionary war. In 1776, he married Susan Prentiss, the eldest daughter of his employer Nathaniel Sartell (or Sartle) Prentiss and had had eleven children in Alstead by 1800. Leaving the family to settle at Waltham, Massachusetts, his eldest son Nathaniel was the father of Nathaniel Sartell Prentiss Banks, a politician, Civil War general, and local hero in the nineteenth century. John Banks passed away in 1824, and his widow applied for and received a federal pension in the amount of $219.66 in 1837. After serving almost six years, Joseph Ransford (a soldier from Boston) was only 21 years old at the war's end in 1783. He married in ten years and had eight children by 1813 while moving with his wife Rachel and family in three states—Kentucky, Ohio, and Indiana. As previously indicated, Jesse Ballou of Wrentham/Cumberland was not exactly poor. Yet he had eight children from three marriages and had adopted three more from his relatives. After he died in 1800, his third wife and widow Elizabeth (Pitts) Ballou applied for a federal pension in 1831 when she was eighty-three years old. She was granted a pension of $20 a year until her death ten years later.

The end of the war hardly brought any immediate prosperity for those veterans who had come from the lower ranks of society. The small percentage of them who managed to stay where they had been enlisted suggested insecurity while the large numbers of those who moved or who applied for pensions further indicated that life had not become any easier for them after the war. To most of those poor soldiers and needy veterans, the American Revolution was a great experience, but little else. No splendid honor or adulation would glorify their extended military services and uncommon contributions any time soon, nor would they receive much deferential treatment in places where they had not established legal residency by the time of enlistment. Life conditions and family circumstances were as disappointing as ever, and many were willing to take to the road again and again, looking for change and improvement. Their achievements lied not in how many were better off right after the revolution, but in the monumental sacrifices they had made during the war. The fact that they survived the ordeals of those tumultuous years at all was testimonial to the enduring faith, determination, and fighting spirit they possessed. What the poor soldiers in the American Revolution achieved was not a drastic turnaround of their own livelihood, but a fresh beginning for subsequent generations. Their children and children's children were now able to start life anew from a more stable family background and a freer environment than they had ever experienced in the past.

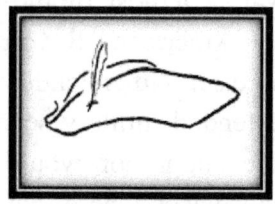

Chapter Six

"As Much Sorrow As Joy"

The end of the Revolutionary War opened a new chapter of poverty. Economic recovery after independence was slow, whereas the increases of the needy rose fast and spread wide. Lingering wartime rummage and chaos unleashed more volatile, insidious, potent, and disturbing forces in society than ever before. Poverty not only did not disappear, but it also worsened and grew in size and tenacity. People took to the road again, starting a new surge of domestic migration involving civilians, refugees, veterans, laborers, single women, displaced tradesmen, and widows of deceased soldiers. Shays's Rebellion, although brutally suppressed, revealed the danger of ignoring the just claims of those in serious distress. The need for relief persisted not only in Charlestown, Cambridge, Salem, and Boston, but also in many rural areas where big and small communities continued to observe old poor law practices and only occasionally debated alternative strategies to accommodate the growing number of the poor. Various private charity organizations and benevolent societies did increase fast in the post-war years, when the state government finally ended the century-old warning out system but instigated few innovations in public aid.

Exacerbation

The condition of the poor deteriorated as the economy slumped during the war. The long struggle for independence consumed a great deal of resources and demanded much manpower from local communities. Taking care of the deserving poor, soldiers' families, and war refugees during this time of deprivation and high inflation was particularly hard for local authorities. No sooner had the British siege of Boston started (specially after the battle of Breed's Hill and Bunker Hill) than Boston and Charlestown authorities began to feel the need to transport many of their local poor and sickly to other communities—first to Watertown, Chelsea, Salem, and Newburyport, and then to numerous communities further in the hinterland such as Shirley, Wilmington, Attleboro, Andover, Leominster, Lunenburg, Littleton, and Groton.[1] Overwhelmed, Salem overseers of the poor complained to the General Court that "many Poor who entered there since the Commencement of the present Troubles, are now in the Continental Army, and have left Families that are supported at the Expence of that Town; praying Direction of the Court."[2] At a town meeting assembled at Faneuil Hall in Boston on April 11, 1781, the

---

[1] *Journal of the House of Representatives*, 51, Pt. 1: 45, 91, 158, 164, 177-78, 227-28, 234; 51, Pt. 2: 230, 227, 287; 51, Pt. 3: 111, 177.
[2] *Journal of the House of Representatives*, 51, Pt. 1, 8-9, 10-11, 26, 56, 234. The General Court later compensated various communities for their care of the Boston and Charlestown poor, who were sent back after the siege. *Journal of the House of Representatives*, 51, Pt. 1: 91, 177-78; 51, Pt. 3: 177, 179,183.

overseers of the poor "presented in a most affecting manner the present suffering and almost perishing condition of the Poor in the Almshouse." They pleaded for emergency funding or, as they warned, the almshouse would close. They made it clear that, unless townspeople were willing to provide the funding, they would soon see the poor roaming around, knocking on doors, and begging. Alarmed, the town meeting quickly voted for a special subscription of £2,000.[3]

Smaller communities faced a similar predicament. In Middleborough, a community of 800 people in Plymouth County, town selectmen paid more than £2,300 to care for its poor over four months from January to April 1781.[4] The charge of the poor counted for at least one third of the annual expenses in Braintree, which spent £90 of its £245 budget on the poor in 1770. However, a few years into the war, in 1778, the town had to raise £4,000 to pay for its debt. Just one year later, the number rose to £6,000.[5] Worthington, Hampshire County, raised £120 in 1778 to meet soldiers' needs. The next year, the residents voted to raise £600 to pay for 12 blankets and bounties for their soldiers. In 1780, the town raised £2,130 to clothe the soldiers and £5,000 for beef to feed the troops. The neighboring town of Murrayfield (now Chester) did the same when it raised £5,000 for 3,840 pounds of beef in 1780. Less than a year later, it had to raise another £8,000 to buy beef. About the same time, a town meeting in Mendon voted to raise £1,344 in silver money to pay for those soldiers enlisted for three years. On September 10 the same year, townspeople again voted "to raise £520, silver money, to discharge old debts the

---

[3] Townsfolk also agreed to allow those subscribers to deduct the amount they subscribed to the emergency fund from their shares in the town's next round of taxation. Almshouse Subscription Ward 4, April 11, 1781, New England Historic Genealogical Society.

[4] Middleborough (Mass.) Overseers of the Poor Record, 1780-1795, n. p., New England Historic Genealogical Society.

[5] The yearly expenses were £150 in 1740 and £450 Old Tenor (£150 New Tenor) in 1747. Samuel A. Bates, ed., *Records of the Town of Braintree, 1640-1793* (Randolph, Mass.: Daniel H. Huxford, Printer, 1886), 232, 281, 428, 493.

town owed, £40 for the support of the poor the present year and £54 for the support of the soldiers' families, being £614 in the whole, all in silver or gold."[6]

The end of the war did little to end the heavy debt and deep misery into which many had sunk. Massachusetts had a wartime debt of more than £3,000,000, including obligations to the federal government and back pay to veterans.[7] The inhabitants of Mendon wrote to the General Court on May 24, 1784:

> That notwithstanding the good people of this Commonwealth have (by the hand of a kind Providence) been preserved through a long distressing war, which is now happily terminated, and the Blessings of Peace restored to our borders. Although partaking of diverse other Blessings, both public & private, yet there are certain matters of grievances which we labor under and look up to this Honorable Court for a redress of some, among which we beg leave to mention the following viz.:
>
> 1. The granting of an Impost to Congress for their sole use and improvement, and paying the same into their hands, we conceive to be unconstitutional and dangerous.
>
> 2. We conceive the half pay or commutation to the officers of the Continental army, to be a public grievance, and pray that the Honorable Court will take

---

[6] John G. Metcalf, comp., *Annals of the Town of Mendon, from 1659 to 1880* (Providence, R. I.: E. L. Freeman & Co., 1880), 402, 403.

[7] James M. Crafts, *History of the Town of Whately, Massachusetts Including a Narrative of Leading Events from the First Settlement of Hatfield: 1661-1899* (Orange, Mass.: D. L. Grandall, 1899), 235. Another estimated was as high as £17,000,000, see Lilley B. Caswell, *The History of the Town of Royalston, Massachusetts* (Printed by the Town of Royalston, 1917), 413.

every constitutional measure to prevent the payment of the same.[8]

3. The burden of large sums of Continental Currency, lying on the hands of good people of this Commonwealth in general & the neglect of other States to redeem their proportion of the same we regarded as a grievance and pray that this Court will still continue their exertions to have it taken off our hands, and, if further neglected, to stop a sufficiency of appropriation to Congress for the redemption of the same.

4. The good people of this Commonwealth are greatly distressed for want of a circulating medium, by means of which a part of the community become a prey to the avarice and extortion of others; we therefore pray that every possible means may be used to increase the quantity of circulating medium to prevent the mischief that will otherwise come.[9]

Mendon's petition spoke what many individuals had on their mind, even those who might not be poor in the first place. Unfortunately, the General Court was slow to respond to these complaints and more than a few—veterans and civilians alike—suffered as a result. In Hampshire, the County Court of

---

[8] Knowing that retired British officers could receive half pay for life after service, officers of the Continental Army hoped for the same. Congress reluctantly agreed in 1779, but four years later opted to commutate half pay for life to five years' full pay. Louis Clinton Hatch, *The Administration of the American Revolutionary Army* (New York: Longmans, Green, and Co., 1904), 71-85, 176-78. See also House of Representatives, *Resolutions, Laws, and Ordinances Relating to the Pay, Half Pay, Commutation of Half Pay, Bounty Lands, and Other Promises Made by Congress to the Officers and Soldiers of the Revolution; to the Settlement of the Accounts between the United States and the Several States; and to Funding the Revolutionary Debt* (1838; Baltimore, M.D.: Genealogical Publishing Co., 1998). James M. Crafts, *History of the Town of Whately, Massachusetts Including a Narrative of Leading Events from the First Settlement of Hatfield: 1661-1899* (Orange, Mass.: D. L. Grandall, 1899), 234.
[9] John G. Metcalf, comp., *Annals of the Town of Mendon, from 1659 to 1880* (Providence, R. I.: E. L. Freeman & Co., 1880), 417-18.

Common Pleas prosecuted nearly 3,000 debt cases between 1784 and 1786. In Worcester County, one out of every three people on the polls had fallen into arrears and thus faced court persecutions.[10] For example, an experienced soldier of colonial wars, Captain Reuben Dickinson of Amherst was a selectman and a member of the Committee of Correspondence. Leading his company at Cambridge in 1775, at Ticonderoga in 1776, and at Saratoga in 1777, he had served in the war as long and hard as anyone. Yet he was heavily in debt after the war, and his land was attached to satisfy his creditors, Martin Cooley and Nathaniel Smith of Rutland. Disillusioned with state policies and frustrated by losing his properties, he again recruited several dozen Amherst men to join forces with Captain Daniel Shays, who had been one of Dickinson's earliest recruits shortly after the Lexington alarm. Blacklisted by the state attorney general, he finally sold the remainder of his farm and moved to Vermont.[11] According to Jonathan Smith, who studied this period:

> There was no property exempt from seizure except the clothes on debtor's back. The officer could take the bed upon which the debtor slept, the last potato in his cellar and the only sow and pig in his barn to satisfy the execution. Property at the execution sale brought nothing approaching the real value. There was no homestead exemption. The debtor could only look on while the sheriff sold the house over his head and the last mouthful of his provisions for the winter at a fifth

---

[10] John L. Brooke, "To the Quiet of the People: Revolutionary Settlements and Civil Unrest in Western Massachusetts, 1774-1789," *William and Mary Quarterly*, 3rd ser. 46 (1989): 432.
[11] James Avery Smith, comp., Families of Amherst, Massachusetts (Amherst, Mass.: Property of the Author, 1985), 1: 203. Leonard L. Richards, *Shays's Rebellion: The American Revolution's Final Battle* (Philadelphia: University of Pennsylvania Press, 2002), 95-96.

of their real value, knowing at the end he would be turned into the streets with his family.

A hero at Saratoga, Colonel Timothy Bigelow commanded the 15th Regiment of General John Glover's Brigade,[12] one of the finest units in the Continental Army. However, after the war, Smith wrote, "Timothy Bigelow, one of the Worcester's most distinguished soldiers, spent the last days of his life within the limits of the County Jail for debts in support of his family while he was absent in the war."[13] According to another scholar, for the majority of the Massachusetts corps who returned home from war, "it was a heartbreaking scene that greeted them. The demand of creditor, the loss of homestead, the nightmare of debtor's cell . . . There was no way out; mounting debt, outrunning the returns of a dislocated and sluggish economy, enveloped common men without much discrimination." Worth $400 in cash upon entering the war, Lieutenant Joseph Bascomb of Concord was penniless when he left it. A veteran of Bunker Hill, Major William Ballard of Amesbury owned a good estate at the start of the war, but was reduced to poverty in the first years of peace.[14]

Meanwhile, town officials—from selectmen, assessors, and tax collectors to constables—had to deal with not only a long list of delinquent taxpayers, but also the delicate issue of how to collect taxes on time while disposing of the depreciating money as fast as they could. Abatement was one option local

---

[12] Although the general wrote that he shall "retire home a Beggar," the poverty John Glover and his family suffered after the war was exaggerated. George Athan Billias, *General John Glover and His Marblehead Mariners* (New York: Hold, Rinehart and Winston, 1960), 189-201.
[13] Quoted in Timothy C. Murphy, *History of Rutland in Massachusetts, 1713-1968* (Worcester, Mass.: The Heffernan Press, 1970), 73-74.
[14] Sidney Kaplan, "Veteran Officers and Politics in Massachusetts, 1783-1787," *William and Mary Quarterly*, 3rd ser., 9 (1952), 46-47.

governments often applied for sorely distressed families.[15] Demanding extra carefulness and diligence from constables and tax collectors was another. Not surprisingly, these two offices were the least attractive to fill at this time. Thus, a town meeting in Springfield concluded that "the blood-bought privilege and honors of self-government were not to be put on like a garland of roses." "To meeting [meet] the unpaid State taxes assessed in old Continental money, it was directed that Treasurer William Pynchon, Jr., issue 'his warrants of distress upon the Constables that had the old Continental money committed to them,' and Pynchon was also directed to dispose of both the new money and the old Continental bills in his hands as best he could."[16] To compensate for the devastating devaluation of currency, residents in Middleborough offered to provide veterans and their families with daily necessities in lieu of an exclusive use of government bills of credit. Veteran families had faced a most difficult time while healthy men had gone into service, leaving the old, infirm, women, and children behind to tend the fields. At a town meeting in early 1778, Middleborough selectmen decided to form a committee of seven "to take care of the families of the soldiers." They soon authorized the town treasurer to "hire the sum of $200. for the use of the committee to procure necessaries for the families of the soldiers in the continental service." Two years later at a town meeting on June 14, 1780, they further voted that those 55 men who had promised to enlist for six months in the army could choose to be paid by "farming produce or silver money or lumber or paper currency." They also decided that each soldier

---

[15] Dudley abated William Jorden's tax in 1783, Ebenezer Hebberds's in 1785, and nine persons' in 1790. *Town Record of Dudley, Massachusetts* (Pawtucket, R. I.: Adam Sutcliffe Co., 1893-94), 2: 254, 264, 336. In October 1777 and again in October 1778, Weston abated a dozen people's taxes, including Elisha Cox's. Town of Weston, *Records of the First Precinct, 1746-1754 and of the Town, 1754-1803* (Boston: Alfred Mudge & Son, 1893), 240, 256, 257, 259.

[16] Mason A. Green, *Springfield, 1636-1886: History of Town and City* (Boston: Press of Rockwell and Churchill, 1888), 299, 309.

should receive 200 half-weight of bloomery bar iron per month for their pay or farming produce in proportion to the same value or 400 continental dollars to each 100 weight of iron.[17]

In a similar vein, the town instructed its representatives to the General Court in 1786 to pay close attention to legislative discussions in regard to the ongoing financial crisis. Like many communities opposing the new state policy that tax must be paid in specie, people in Middleborough strongly favored "a Lively Medium of Trade" and a paper money as "a Legal Tender in all Payments Throughout this State." Their instructions stated:

> That there have been Divers poor familys that have had but one Cow that has ben [original] taken for Rates where by the Poor wido and others have been Put to Extrem Poverty and wholly Depedent on the neighbours &c. that you shod use your Influence that Something may be Done to Releive Such Porpous that the Constables and Collectors for there tax Shod not be obligd Suddenly to Drive to Extramity for Gathering the [same].[18]

Against this backdrop they expected all legal execution of debt cases to be suspended until a medium of trade could be instituted. They insisted that "a medium of trade is necessary in a Common Wealth as blood in the vean of the Hemain body." They therefore recommended that a duty on all superfluities and a bank of paper money be established. They also suggested that "a Small tax to be paid in flaxseed & [unclear and torn] in the country towns and in fish and oil in the Seaport towns

---

[17] Thomas Weston, *History of the Town of Middleboro,* Massachusetts (Boston: Houghton, Mifflin and Co., 1906), 142-43.
[18] The General Court passed the Tender Act of July 1782, which made neat cattle and other articles a legal tender.

Might answer Sum valuable purpus in the lew of hard money." Finally, they thought that "the Constitution might be amended" and that "the minds of the Common Wealth might be known and if the two thirds agrea upon an amendment we might be in a way to accomplish it."[19]

Seeking solutions, no fewer than two dozen convention meetings or adjournments took place in Worcester, Hampshire, and Berkshire Counties.[20] Thirty-two towns sent delegates to attend one in Leicester on May 15, 1786. The meeting listed the following grievances:

> 1. The sitting of the Gen. Court in Boston. 2. The want of a circulating medium. 3. The exhorbitance of the layers' fee table. 4. The present mode of administration by the Court of Common Pleas. 5. The appropriation of the impost and excise to the payment of the interest of the State debt. 6. The grants made by the Gen. Court to the Attorney General & others. 7. Too many office-holders and their salaries too large. 8. The State furnishing money to Congress while our account with Congress remained unsettles.[21]

Under pressure, the General Court slowly softened its stance on tax payment in hard coin, especially after Shays's Rebellion. Governor James Bowdoin, who had led the effort to suppress the uprising, lost his gubernatorial reelection to John Hancock by a preponderant margin in summer 1787. Later that year, the

---

[19] Thomas Weston, *History of the Town of Middleboro,* Massachusetts (Boston: Houghton, Mifflin and Co., 1906), 577-79.
[20] John L. Brooke, "To the Quiet of the People: Revolutionary Settlements and Civil Unrest in Western Massachusetts, 1774-1789," *William and Mary Quarterly,* 3rd ser. 46 (1989): 430, 447.
[21] John G. Metcalf, comp., *Annals of the Town of Mendon, from 1659 to 1880* (Providence, R. I.: E. L. Freeman & Co., 1880), 428-29.

Return of eleven prisoners in Northampton gaol after the failure of Shays's Rebellion. April 9, 1787. Samuel Anderson, Jr. (twenty-five years old, from Blandford, Hampshire County) was committed for sedition and treason. James Perry (forty-two years old, a former justice of the peace from Easton, Bristol County), Alpheus Colton (twenty-one years old, a captain under Shays, from Longmeadow, Hampshire County), John Brow, Jr. (from Whately, Hampshire County), Thomas Killam (or Kilham, thirty-five years old, from Westfield, Hampshire County), and Samuel Noble (thirty-three years old, from Westfield) were committed on state warrants. Five others were imprisoned for theft or an inability to pay legal costs and taxes. (Massachusetts Historical Society)

government finally passed an Act for the Relief of Poor Prisoners, which allowed the discharge of those imprisoned debtors after they had sworn to the fact that they had no sufficient estate, real or personal, to pay for their debt.[22] Coming out of imprisonment temporarily alleviated the debtor, but the expediency did not lessen the enormous financial burden many families and the state were still facing. A substantive step toward reducing the heavy debt did not occur

---

[22] 1787 Ch. 29, *Acts and Resolves* (Boston, 1893), 590-93.

until several years later in 1792 when, under Treasury Secretary Alexander Hamilton's insistence, the federal government decided to assume the debt the several states had incurred during the war.

Migration

The population of Massachusetts increased some 20 percent (by 70,000) from 1775 to 1790.[23] During the same period, the General Court issued no land grants to any individuals.[24] In an attempt to raise £163,200 through a lottery for the state treasury, the only exception was the sale, allowed on November 9, 1786, of 50 townships in Lincoln County, Maine.[25] From 1760 to 1775, the General Court granted an average of four townships each year; this figure dropped to two a year during the last quarter of the century. Moreover, half of those newly incorporated areas were either too small and close to urban centers or too remote and rugged to encourage any expansion of agriculture. The number of farms, therefore, remained well below 100 in those two dozen communities until the second half of the nineteenth century.[26] Those who were

---

[23] Evarts B. Greene and Virginia D. Harrington, *American Population before the Federal Census of 1790* (1993; New York: Columbia University Press, 1932), 12-19. Bureau of the Census, Department of Commerce and Labor, *A Century of Population Growth: From the First Census of the United States to the Twelfth, 1790-1900* (Washington: Government Printing Office, 1909), 10.
[24] *Journals of the House of Representatives of Massachusetts*, 52-55 (1776-1779), *passim*.
[25] *Acts and Resolves 1786-87*, 97-102. *American Herald and the Worcester Recorder* 18 June 1788. *Essex Journal* 2 July 1788. *Independent Chronicle* 29 January 1789. *Cumberland Gazette* 24 July 1788. Mabel Cook Coolidge, *The History of Petersham* (The Petersham Historical Society, 1948), 158.
[26] They include Hamilton, Lynnfield (all in Essex County), Quincy, Randolph, Canton, Dover, Foxborough (all in Norfolk County), Boxborough, Tyngsborough (all in Middlesex county), Ward (now Auburn), Gerry (now Phillipston), Gardner (all in Worcester County), Goshen, Montgomery, Leyden, Holland, Russell, Plainfield (all in Hampshire County), Hancock, Washington, Dalton, Clarksburgh, Mount Washington, and New Ashford (all in Berkshire County). Elias Nason, *A Gazetteer of the State of Massachusetts* (Boston: B. B. Russell, 1890), *passim*.

still looking for a homestead realized that land was becoming harder and harder to find inside the commonwealth, where most of the desirable tracts for farming had already been taken after more than 150 years of settlement, reducing many family farms to a pitiful acre or two.[27]

A newcomer of small property with limited financial resources had a particularly difficult time eking out a living in an established township. Continuously moving around became the only option for those who would not give up any opportunity. Hardly any struggling individual or family remained still in one place during the last decades of the century, resulting in a new era of active migration. Alan Taylor detailed that migration, particularly to Maine and New York, in two lucid scholarly monographs—*Liberty Men and Great Proprietors* (1990) and *William Cooper's Town* (1995). Other studies have revealed several personal stories. The parents of Deborah Gannett Sampson, the wartime heroine, "led a rather transient and unsettled life." Born in Plympton, Plymouth County in 1760, she became a bound-out servant at age ten in Middleborough in the same county. Some eight years later she left, wandered through Taunton, Rochester, New Bedford, and Boston, but finally arrived at Bellingham (Norfolk Co.), where she enlisted for the neighboring Uxbridge in Worcester County. She moved again after the war and settled at Sharon, also in Norfolk County.[28] Martha Ballard, an indefatigable midwife in Maine, moved several times before her family finally settled in Augusta, Kennebec County, then under Massachusetts jurisdiction.[29] At the age of six, Mark Noble, an orphan at the Boston almshouse, was bound out to Hadley. He later moved to

---

[27] Barry Levy, *Town Born: The Political Economy of New England from Its Founding to the Revolution* (Philadelphia: University of Pennsylvania Press, 2009), 2.
[28] Alfred F. Young, *Masquerade: The Life and Times of Deborah Sampson, Continental Soldier* (New York: Alfred A. Knopf, 2004), 24-27, 85-86. Class No. 2 of Uxbridge paid her a bounty of £60 to serve in the Continental Army for the term of 3 years.
[29] Laurel Thatcher Ulrich, *A Midwife's Tale: The Life of Martha Ballard, Based on Her Diary, 1785-1812* (New York: Vintage Books, 1991).

Brookfield and Pittsfield and enlisted during the war for both towns. After his desertion in 1780, he showed up in Rhode Island and enlisted for Cranston. However, he was sent back to Massachusetts and served there for the rest of the war. He moved back to Providence, worked as a laborer, and fell into deep financial trouble in the 1790s.[30] The end of the war only brought "as much sorrow as joy" according to the veteran sergeant Joseph Plumb Martin, whose recounts of his wartime experiences have become a classic since their first publication in 1830. Born on Thanksgiving Day in Berkshire in 1760, he went to live with his grandparents in Connecticut, where he enlisted. Penniless, he moved to and settled in Maine after the war. Never able to accumulate any wealth for the next sixty-six years, he once wished that "I shall one day find land enough to lay my bones in."[31]

Some soldiers of African descent bucked the trend of moving away from where they had come, perhaps because they had few options and acquaintances elsewhere. Agippa Hull went back to Stockbridge in Berkshire, where he had enlisted. So did Peter, the former slave boy from Lincoln. After a three-year enlistment, he returned and died there in the winter of 1791-92.[32] Still some drifting veterans became involved with criminal activity, which reached a new high in the post-war years. Several notorious property offenses of burglary and

---

[30] Ruth Wallis Herndon, *Unwelcome Americans: Living on the Margin in Early New England* (Philadelphia: University of Pennsylvania Press, 2001), 103-06, 213-14. Eric Nellis and Anne Decker Cecere, eds., *The Eighteenth-Century Records of the Boston Overseers of the Poor* (Boston: Colonial Society of Massachusetts, 2007), 648.
[31] James Kirby Martin, ed., *Ordinary Courage: The Revolutionary War Adventures of Joseph Plumb Martin* (3rd ed.; Malden, Mass.: Blackwell Publishing, 2008), 177, 180. For Martin's and many others' hope to obtain land in a long fight with several big proprietors (one of them was General Henry Knox) see Alan Taylor, *Liberty Man and Great Proprietors: The Revolutionary Settlement on the Maine Frontiers, 1760-1820* (Chapel Hill: University of North Carolina Press, 1990).
[32] Gary B. Nash and Graham R. G. Hodges, *Friends of Liberty: Thomas Jefferson, Tadeusz Kościuszko, and Agrippa Hull* (New York: Basic Books, 2008). Joyce Lee Malcolm, *Peter's War: A New England Slave Boy and the American Revolution* (New Haven, Conn.: Yale University Press, 2009).

robbery led to the executions of William Huggins (alias), Dirick Grout, and Johnson Green; all three had served for the patriotic cause during the war.[33]

Bridgewater selectmen Ephraim Cary, Eleazer Cary, and Daniel Keith issued a warrant to town constables to warn Ebenezer Scott, James Shaw, his wife Sarah Shaw, and their two children Sarah and John, from Milton, Suffolk County, to depart town or give sufficient security to avoid town charges. Bridgewater, July 7, 1777, the second year of Independence. Many poor law practices seem to have continued without interruption after the declaration of independence. (New England Historic Genealogical Society)

Collective experience reaffirmed these individual cases. Weston warned out thirty people in 1789, signaling the sharpest rise of incoming migrants the community had seen in thirty years.[34] Ware, a township of 700 people in Hampshire County,

---

[33] Daniel A. Cohen, "A Fellowship of Thieves: Property Criminals in Eighteenth-Century Massachusetts," *Journal of Social History* 22 (1988), 72-73, 85. See also his *Pillar of Salt, Monument of Grace: New England Crime Literature and the Origins of American Popular Culture, 1674-1860* (New York: Oxford University Press, 1993), 117-42.

[34] Ann S. Lainhart, "Weston Cautions 1757 to 1803," *New England Historical and Genealogical Register* 144 (1990), 223-24.

warned out 51 strangers in 1790 alone.[35] Goshen, a community of no more than 600 residents in the same county, warned out more than 100 people in 1791,[36] while Northampton, a bigger town of 1,600, warned out "well over 200 people."[37] Easton in Bristol County had a population of 1,000, but warned out 100 families and some 150 persons in the first two months in 1790.[38] At Foxborough, selectmen Ebenezer Warren, Nathaniel Clerk, and George Straton issued a warrant on December 26, 1791, directing constables to warn out 15 families from 13 communities in 5 counties and 3 states, totaling 125 people.[39] Chelmsford selectmen warned out 112 persons in one warrant issued on January 20, 1794.[40]

Not only had migrants increased in large numbers, but they were increasingly identified as laborers, single women, spinsters, widows, low-skill workers (such as butchers), and foreigners. Of those 75 people Malden warned out in 1790, the majority were laborers, or foreigner laborers, and cordwainers.[41] On a single day in May 1791, Cambridge warned 24 families and 127 persons from 36 towns in 6 counties within the state; of them, 24 were laborers, 3 foreigners, 4 single women, 14 spinsters, 7 widows, and 3 butchers.[42] Dedham warned out 101 people in 1790, including 6

---

[35] Arthur Chase, *History of Ware, Massachusetts* (Cambridge, Mass.: Harvard University Press, 1911), 125.
[36] Hiram Barrus, *History of the Town of Goshen, Hampshire County, Massachusetts,, from Its First Settlement in 1761 to 1881 with Family Sketches* (Boston: Published by the Author, 1881), 23-24.
[37] Christopher Clark, *The Roots of Rural Capitalism: Western Massachusetts, 1780-1860* (Ithaca, N.Y.: Cornell University Press, 1990), 56.
[38] *Easton Town Records* (1789-1816), 2: 32-33, 34-35, 35-37, 45, 46, 70-71, 92-93, 105-06, see Barbara Tourtillott's transcripts at htt://www.tourtillot.org/easton/index.html.
[39] "Foxborough, Mass., Warnings, etc.," *New England Historical and Genealogical Register* 65 (1911): 41-42.
[40] "Warning-Out in Chelmsford, Mass., 1790, 1794," *New England Historical and Genealogical Register* 83 (1929): 116-68.
[41] "Warnings-Out in Malden, Mass., 1678-1794," *New England Historical and Genealogical Register* 92 (1938): 59-60.
[42] Ann Smith Lainhart, "Cambridge, Massachusetts Notifications and Warnings Out (1788-1797)," *New England Historical and Genealogical Register* 146 (1992): 87-90.

laborers, 34 single women, and 6 widows.[43] On November 3, 1793, Northborough warned out 56 persons, including 5 families, 7 laborers, 9 minors, 2 single women, and 4 spinsters.[44] Salem warned out 261 people in 1791, most of whom had come from 46 towns in Massachusetts, Maine, New Hampshire, Connecticut, New York, Virginia, and Newfoundland. As a seaport, Salem attracted a high number of mariners (62) and fishermen (12) both domestically and from England, Ireland, Scotland, Germany, Italy, Spain, and France. Meanwhile, common laborers (41) accounted for the second largest group of all those incoming strangers with a trade. Lastly, Salem warned at least 13 widows and several veteran soldiers of the Revolutionary War, including Thaddeus Willington, the butcher of Waltham; William Chandler, the tailor of Rowley; George Bruce, the butcher of Woburn; Jonas D. Bosson of Roxbury; Joseph Chandler, the laborer of Andover; John Bishop, the laborer of Marblehead; and John Brown, the carpenter of Lynn.[45]

Compared with the situations before the war in the early 1770s (see chapter 5), three new characteristics noticeably changed the patterns of incoming migration to Boston. The first was a significant expansion of that influx of migrants. Whereas incoming strangers numbered less than 400 a year between 1771 and 1773, that number more than tripled to 1,355 a year between 1791 and 1792. The second was a sharp increase of single females who were warned out by Boston authorities. Whereas they accounted for 30 percent of the pre-war migrants to the city, they now comprised more than 40 percent of the post-war cohort. The third was a growing number of oversea

---

[43] Robert Brand Hanson, ed., *Vital Records of Dedham, Massachusetts, 1635-1845* (Camden, Me.: Picton Press, 1997), 489-567.
[44] Francis E. Blake, *Worcester County, Massachusetts, Warnings, 1737-1788* (1899; Camden, Me.: Picton Press, 1992), 45-46.
[45] "Salem Warnings, 1791," *Essex Institute Historical Collections* 43 (1907): 345-352. Douglas Lamar Jones, "The Strolling Poor: Transiency in Eighteenth-Century Massachusetts," *Journal of Social History* 8 (1975): 40.

immigrants, whose presence had remained small until the eve of the Revolution. The post-war years witnessed a significant shift and one-fifth of the 2700 outsiders who came to Boston in 1791-92 were not from within the commonwealth but from foreign lands. England, Ireland, Africa, Scotland, France, Germany, and the West Indies surpassed many local communities and neighboring states in providing some of the largest groups of newcomers to Boston.[46]

These trends indicate that Massachusetts's labor market was again undergoing a major change, instigated by a renewed surge of migratory movements by those individuals and families looking for new places to live. As in the past, many local residents were willing to take the migrants in and at some communities such as Dedham, half of the newcomers managed to stay.[47] John Foxcroft wrote to Cambridge selectmen on April 24, 1789:

> Sir, This is to inform you that on Thursday the sixteenth instant, I admitted into my Farm house Mr. Benjamin Pratt his wife & four children, viz. Sally, Hannah, Esther, Benjamin, from Chelsea together with a young man by the name of William Banks of whose character & Circumstances, I have such an

---

[46] The top ten local communities where many domestic migrants (in brackets) came from included Charlestown (171), Salem (111), Cambridge (95), Hingham (86), Lynn (76), Braintree (75), Marblehead (62), Malden (56), Newton (45), and Roxbury (43) while some foreign places were equally impressive—England (168), Ireland (141), Africa (93), Scotland (46), France (41), Germany (40), and the West Indies (16). Warning out book from 1791 to 1792, Boston Overseers of the Poor Records, 1733-1925, roll 1, folder 4, Massachusetts Historical Society. See also Daniel Scott Smith, "Female Householding in Late Eighteenth-Century America and the Problem of Poverty," *Journal of Social History* 28 (1994): 83-107; Jacqueline Barbara Carr, "A Change 'As Remarkable as the Revolution Itself': Boston's Demographics, 1780-1800," *New England Quarterly* 73 (2000): 583-602; Carr, *After the Siege: A Social History of Boston, 1775-1800* (Boston: Northeastern University Press, 2005), 101-02.

[47] Barry, Levy, *Town Born: The Political Economy of New England from Its Founding to the Revolution* (Philadelphia: University of Pennsylvania Press, 2009), 286-88.

opinion, that I have entrusted them with the care of my farm.[48]

Likewise, Jonas Wyeth wrote to selectmen of the same town,

> Gentlemen, this may certify that on August 24th 1789, I hired into my family one Jenny Wire aged thirty years, of Scotch descent, was born in her passage to New England, her mother was received into the house of one David Thomson of Woburn, and dying there, left the aforesaid Jenny, who soon after adopted the name of Thomson, after the family in which she lived. Now going by the name of Jenny Thomson. At the age of fifteen she the aforesaid Jenny went from David Thomson's aforesaid to dwell with Mr Joseph Wright of Woburn, from whence she came to my house. Cambridge Nov^r: 12th 1789[49]

The need for help went both ways, and townsfolk—including some local officials—were forthcoming about how many strangers they had taken and why they had taken them in. William Jancks of Wrentham received into his house the family of Thomas Woos, his wife Molly, and their nine children Simon, Reuben, Comfort, Tillson, Joseph, Olney, Amy, Levina, and Lucina from Franklin. Benjamin Hawes informed Wrentham authority that he had taken into his house Lucinda Thayer. She was an eleven-year old, "very poor but a well harty girl well grown," whose mother and siblings lived in Medway. Townsman Benjamin Shepard took in John Bradburn (formerly from Europe) of Newton, as a servant. Amos Walton took in

---

[48] Ann Smith Lainhart, "Cambridge, Massachusetts Notifications and Warnings Out (1788-1797)," *New England Historical and Genealogical Register* 146 (1992): 79-80.
[49] Ibid., 77.

Marquis Metcalf from Franklin as his apprentice. David Fisher, Jr., hired Levi Lane from Foxborough to work at nailing and Hannah Lewis, "a black woman" from Rhode Island as "a hired servant." He informed Wrentham selectmen that "her occupation is housework, spinning &c."[50] William Ward wrote on March 7, 1789, "I took on my Place, lying on the Northerly part of Weston about the first of April 1788 as a Tennant one Joseph Bacon and his wife Martha who came immediately from Lincoln." Thaddeus Spring also informed Weston selectmen that he took in Lemuel Brackett, a cordwainer from Needham, his wife, and their seven children Lemuel, Samuel, Curtis, Sukey, Ebenezer, Joseph, and Polly. In fact, a selectman himself and reelected more than a dozen times in the post-war period, Spring took numerous people into his house, including in the soldier Nathan Boynton and his wife from Waltham as tenants in April 1781, Continental soldier John Shepard and his wife and children from Newton in December of the same year. He took in four more families and some fifteen people between 1788 and 1789, including Samuel Cobb, his wife, and one child, David Stearns and his family, Stephen Harrington and family from Princeton, William Gill, a Briton, his wife, and five children from Needham, and Dr. Joseph Taft of Braintree.[51]

Convinced that the never-lessening migration was a problem, the General Court passed its Act Providing for the Support of the Poor in 1789, which aimed to penalize not so much strangers as those who entertained them. Any resident of any town who received, admitted, or entertained any non-inhabitant of the same town for more than ninety days without a written notification to the town authority would forfeit five pounds. In order to prevent "the importation of poor, vicious,

---

[50] Esther L. Friend, "Notifications and Warnings Out: Strangers Taken into Wrentham, Massachusetts, Between 1732 and 1812," *New England Historical Genealogical Register* 141 (1987): 357; 142 (1988): 59-64.
[51] Ann S. Lainhart, "Weston Cautions 1757 to 1803," *New England Historical Genealogical Register* 144 (1990): 222-24.

and infirm persons who may prove chargeable to the Commonwealth," the law further stated that any ship master must report the names of all passengers on board his vessel, including "their Nation, Age, Character & Condition." Anyone who neglected this rule would be fined fifty pounds. Any ship master who knowingly brought in a convict or a person of "a dissolute, infamous & abandoned Life & Character" would also be fined fifty pounds.[52]

Meanwhile, the new state constitution of 1780 redefined franchise to depend on both property and residency. No one could be elected governor unless he was a resident for 7 years and a freeholder of 1,000 pounds. Each senator must be an inhabitant of the commonwealth for 5 years and have a freehold of 300 pounds or a personal estate of 600 pounds. Males who were at least twenty-one years old were eligible to vote only if they held a freehold with an annual income of three pounds or a personal estate of sixty pounds. All voters were required to be a resident for at least one year.[53] An act concerning the Settlement of a Citizen in 1789 reiterated how property and residency continued to define a Massachusetts citizen. It stated that:

> every person being a citizen of this Commonwealth,[54] who shall be seized of an estate of freehold, in any particular town or district of the clear annual income of *three pounds*, & shall reside thereon, or within the same town or district occupying & improving the same, in person, for the space of two whole years, or who after the age of twenty-one years successively, or shall reside in such town or district for the space of

---

[52] *Acts and Resolves 1788-89*, 98-102.
[53] *Acts and Resolves 1780-81*, [3]-[30].
[54] A citizen of the commonwealth was defined as anyone residing in any part of the state who was not warned to depart in 1767. *Acts and Resolves 1788-89*, 408.

two years successively without being warning to depart the same in manners hereafter provided, shall be deemed and taken to be an inhabitant of the same town or district.[55]

Clearly, receiving a warning-out notice remained a serious hindrance to a person's residency, which could in turn deprive his franchise. The law did allow settlement to be granted to individuals according to where they had been born and where women had married their husbands. However, it denied settlement to sojourns who came to a community for reasons such as nursing, education, imprisonment, and stranded sickness. Most importantly, the law gave the local community the final say over a person's residency. Thus, a person who could obtain the vote of any town at a regular town meeting would "be deemed and taken to be an inhabitant of the same."[56]

Tracking down all the places individuals lived was seldom easy, especially for those who moved frequently. Deciding one's legal settlement could be just as perplexing. Past provincial statute had never successfully resolved many convoluted situations in real life; the new state constitution, which still sanctioned warning, fared no better. Originally designed to prevent paying relief to outsiders, the practice of warnings-out had only been partially useful in controlling public expenses. Yet the continued use of the warnings to define one's residency was as cumbersome as it was ineffective. Moreover, the 1789 act seriously underestimated those who had an interest in receiving, boarding, hiring, entertaining, and keeping strangers. Restricting their movements by law did not seem to discourage those who needed outsiders as boarders, lodgers, tenants, maids, nurses, servants, apprentices, laborers,

---

[55] *Acts and Resolves 1788-89*, 408-10.
[56] *Acts and Resolves 1788-89*, 409.

helps, and field hands as much as strangers needed them for employment and shelter.

Five years later, the Act Providing for the Relief and Support, Employment and Removal of the Poor superseded the 1789 act and other laws relative to "warning out, or removal of the poor." Passed on February 26, 1794, the new act attempted to overhaul the poor relief system.[57] It repealed all previous laws concerning warnings and removals, thereby ending the warning-out system. Nevertheless, the practice of sending warning notices lingered, although actual removal of the poor—a procedure never widely adopted in the past—did come to an end. Apprehensive about the burden of relief charges, more than a few communities resisted the blanket acceptance of newcomers, and some continued to take note of strangers well into the early 1800s. Wrentham, for instance, reported a few dozen people in the 1810s and registered the last case of incoming strangers in 1826.[58]

Modification

The persistence of poverty led some to reconsider institutional responses of a different sort. Whereas most towns and villages managed to get along without either a poorhouse or a separate office of the overseers of the poor (distinct from that of the selectmen) through the colonial era, many began to feel the need to have them as the century drew to an end. Change

---

[57] Ch. 59, 1793, *Acts and Resolves 1792-93*, 479-93.
[58] Esther L. Friend, "Notifications and Warnings Out: Strangers Taken into Wrentham, Massachusetts, Between 1732 and 1812," *New England Historical Genealogical Register* 142 (1988): 62-78. Looking back to the 1830s, Sir George Nicholls still called the English settlement laws and regulations "wicked," "stupid," and "a vicious anachronism." "No greater tyranny," he went on to say, "could well be conceived than the prevention of the poor man from going to the place where his labour is in demand at good wages, and his confinement in the place where his labour is not required." *A History of the English Poor Law* (New York: Augustus M. Kelley, 1967), 3: 342.

was in the air as communities began to update old methods of supporting the poor. Rarely coordinated under any central plan and none radical in nature, three new trends in poor relief at the local level gradually took shape.

First, an increasing number of communities began to establish the office of the overseers of the poor. Although permitted by law under the royal charter of 1691, only a handful of colonial towns (e.g., Boxford, Needham, and Abington) had such an office separate from that of the selectmen.[59] Major population centers like Boston and Salem did have the overseers, yet most small communities let their selectmen handle matters involving the poor. However, over time, several townships felt the pressure of ever-growing local businesses, including how to support a growing number of the poor. The office of the overseers was therefore adopted in the hope that the distinct office might lead to an effectual management of the poor. Records show, for example, that Westborough chose George Andrews, Timothy Warren, and Abijah Gale as the first overseers of the poor in 1770.[60] Weston elected its overseers in 1773 but ceased to elect them in 1792.[61] Braintree established the office in 1774, Bellingham in 1775, Bernardston in 1790 (when it had a population of 691), Lee in 1791, Haverhill in 1808, Bedford in 1834, and Berlin from 1842 to 1851.[62]

---

[59] Boxford elected Deacon Timothy Foster to be the first overseer in 1732. Sidney Perley, *The History of Boxford, Essex County, Massachusetts* (Boxford: Published by the Author, 1878), 175. Needham had overseers in 1751. George Kuhn Clarke, *History of Needham, Massachusetts, 1711-1911* (Cambridge, Mass.: Privately Printed at the University Press, 1912), 674. Abington had them in 1761. David Thomas Konig, ed., *Plymouth Court Records, 1686-1859* (New England Historic Genealogical Society, CD-ROM, 2002).
[60] Heman Packard DeForest and Edward Craig Bates, *The History of Westborough, Massachusetts* (Westborough, [Mass.]: Published by the Town, 1891), 145.
[61] Town of Weston, *Records of the First Precinct, 1746-1754 and of the Town, 1754-1803* (Boston: Alfred Mudge & Son, 1893), 188, 420, 428.
[62] Samuel A. Bates, ed., *Records of the Town of Braintree, 1640-1793* (Randolph, Mass.: Daniel H. Huxford, 1886), 443-444. George F. Partridge, *History of the Town of Bellingham, Massachusetts, 1719-1919* (Bellingham: Published by the Town, 1919), 137. The Historical Records Survey, Division of Community Service Programs, Work Projects Administration, Inventory of City and Town Archives of Massachusetts, No. 6 Franklin

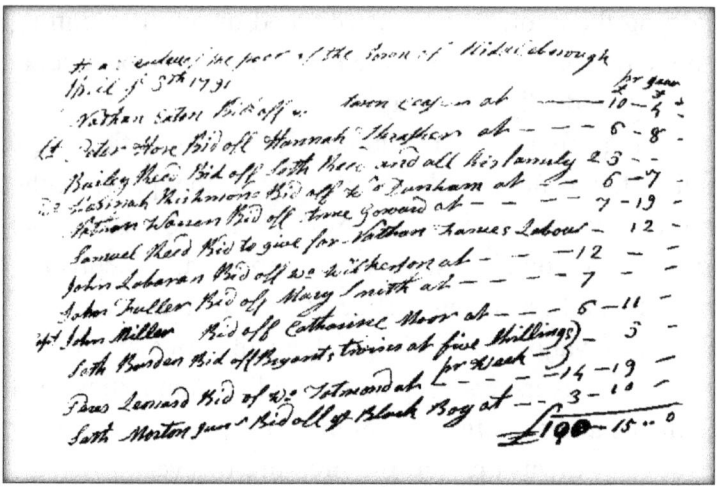

Public vendue of the poor at Middleborough, April 5, 1791. An increasingly common practice at many communities toward the end of the century. (New England Historic Genealogical Society)

Second, cost was always a concern for any township faced with the task of maintaining the impotent poor, widows, the blind, and the lame. Keeping expenses down became a key focus toward the end of the century, when various townships adopted public vendues, or the sale of the poor to the lowest bidder. For much of the colonial period, local authorities frequently sent the impotent poor to the households of those individuals who had agreed to maintain them. The cost of maintenance was not always a predetermined sum. Instead,

---

County, Vol. 2 Bernardston (Boston: The Historical Records Survey, 1941), 21, 56.
Records of the Town of Lee from Its Incorporation to A. D. 1801 (Lee, Mass.: Press of the Valley Gleaner, 1900), 66, 87, 100. (But Lee seemed to have given up the office of the overseers and went back to that of the selectmen's in late 1790s.) George W. Chase, *The History of Haverhill, Massachusetts, from Its First Settlement in 1640 to the Year 1860* (Haverhill: Published by the Author, 1861), 481.
Louis K. Brown, *Wilderness Town: The Story of Bedford, Massachusetts* (1968), 154-55.The Historical Records Survey, Division of Community Service Programs, Work Projects Administration, Inventory of City and Town Archives of Massachusetts, No. 14 Worcester County, Vol. 5 Berlin (Boston: The Historical Records Survey, 1941), 63.

town officials would only need to reimburse the caretaker's account in the end, while special medical care and funeral costs were often additional.[63] Thus, towns had to raise the needed funds after they had already been spent.[64] This sort of informal arrangement worked when the poor numbered relatively few early in the century.[65] Yet local communities increasingly shifted to public vendues for their attempts to curb rising costs as the number of poor gradually rose. On October 4, 1790, a town meeting in Lee voted "to Vendue the keeping of Ebenezer Handy a poor child for six Months to come, on the following Conditions—viz the Child to be victualed, Cloathed & Schooled as much as he can attend during the Said term of six Months, The Child to be sufficiently cloathed for Winter, and returned with his cloaths in as good repair as they now are— The Town to pay the Schooling viz The teaching over and above What he is vendued at."[66] Public vendues were by no

---

[63] Topsfield allowed John Houey for keeping the wife of William Auriel 16s. at a town meeting on September 18, 1719, allowed the widow Hannah Herrick £2 16s. 4d. lawful money for taking care of Samuel Tutoos ten weeks in his last sickness at a town meeting on September 18, 1750, and paid for digging Tutoos's grave and coffin at 10s. 8d. at another town meeting a month later. *Town Records of Topsfield, Massachusetts* (Topsfield, Mass.: The Topsfield Historical Society, 1917), 1: 210; 2: 82. A Westborough town meeting on October 31, 1763 granted Jonas Bond £1 7s. 9d. for boarding Ruth Buck and her child nine weeks and two days. Another one on November 12, 1764 voted to grant £6 for the support of widow Mary Woods. Westborough, Town Records, 1718-1777, Film Collection, Family History Library, Salt Lake City, 158, 172. The town of Weston paid doctors' charges and the cost to maintain several widows as the accounts of the town treasurer showed many times. Town of Weston, *Records of the First Precinct, 1746-1754 and of the Town, 1754-1803* (Boston: Alfred Mudge & Son, 1893), 115, 123, 130-31, 191.

[64] Braintree records show that a town meeting on September 2, 1700 voted that the town would be at the cost and charge for carrying widow Woodland to Mendon to her son Tompson who had agreed to receive and keep her. Another town meeting on March 3, 1701 voted that Doctor John Bailey of Roxbury should have £8 for keeping Abigail Neale, "provided he take up therewith & give the town no farther trouble." On March 4, 1706, a town meeting voted that "Josiah Owen should have Forty Shillings paid him yearly for ten years together for keeping Mary Owen." In 1700 Braintree already had a deficit for its revenues amounted to £236 9s. 8d. while its expenses £245 11s. 1½ d. The support of the poor was £90 (or 36%) of all the town charges. Samuel A. Bates, ed., *Records of the Town of Braintree, 1640-1793* (Randolph, Mass.: Daniel H. Huxford, 1886), 44, 48, 50, 63, 428.

[65] *Watertown Records* (Watertown, Mass.: Press of Fred G. Barker, 1894-1904), 2: 189-90.

[66] *Records of the Town of Lee from Its Incorporation to A. D. 1801* (Lee, Mass.: Press of the Valley Gleaner, 1900), 60, 66. A year later the town decided to bind out Ebenezer Handy to a tailor. A town meeting on December 19, 1791 voted "to give John Green twelve pounds on condition of his taking Ebenezer Handy a poor child and keeping him till he shall be 21

means a proven remedy, as townsfolk of Amherst found out when Daniel Kellogg, a prosperous local farmer, cheated the town through false claims of providing for his insane, "wretched and distressed" brother.[67] Yet the method all but became a regional hallmark in poor relief, continuing into the next century.[68]

A third trend also focused on cost savings. Rather than send the poor to private households for care and support, they were kept at a central location (a poor farm or a poorhouse) under the supervision of a keeper appointed by the local government. Boston and Salem had had an almshouse for a long time, Ipswich had a house of correction in 1656, and Northampton had a poorhouse in 1705 and a house of correction in 1706/7.[69] Except for places such as Harvard, Hatfield, and Westborough,[70] most small communities did not

---

years of age, and learn him the Taylors trade, also reading writing and arithmetick—Said sum to be paid at three payments—viz 4 pounds a year till the whole be paid."

[67] Christopher Clark, *The Roots of Rural Capitalism: Western Massachusetts, 1780-1860* (Ithaca, N.Y.: Cornell University Press, 1990), 57-58.

[68] Benjamin J. Klebaner, "Pauper Auctions: The 'New England Method' of Public Poor Relief," *Essex Institute Historical Collections* (Essex, Mass., 1955), 91: 195-210. Auburn let its poor go to the lowest bidder as late as 1857. The Historical Records Survey, Division of Professional and Service Projects, Work Projects Administration, Inventory of City and Town Archives of Massachusetts, No. 14 Worcester County, Vol. 3 Auburn (Boston: The Historical Records Survey, 1940), 17.

[69] Joseph B. Felt, *History of Ipswich, Essex, and Hamilton* (Cambridge, [Mass.]: C. Folsom, 1834), 113. James Russell Trumbull, *History of Northampton, Massachusetts, from Its Settlement in 1654* (Northampton, [Mass.]: Press of Gazette Printing Co., 1898), 1: 473.

[70] Harvard had an almshouse in 1749 to support Joseph Blood and family to 1778. Henry S. Nourse, *History of the Town of Harvard, Massachusetts, 1732-1893* (Harvard: W. Hapgood, 1894), 126. Different from the almshouse for all the impotent poor of a whole community, Harvard's individually assigned almshouse for one needy family was not unique. Hatfield considered building a poor house for keeping Thomas Bracy, but later decided to buy a little house for the same purpose at 20s. in the 1690s. Daniel White Wells and Reuben Field Wells, *A History of Hatfield, Massachusetts, 1660-1910* (Springfield, Mass.: F. C. H. Gibbons, 1910), 124-125. Similarly, the small workhouse at Westborough was perhaps meant not to accommodate more than one or two families. Erected on the land owned by Timothy Warren, it was a one-story building of thirty feet and sixteen, costing the town £26 13s. 4d. in 1767. Heman Packard DeForest and Edward Craig Bates, *The History of Westborough, Massachusetts* (Westborough, [Mass.]: Published by the Town, 1891), 145.

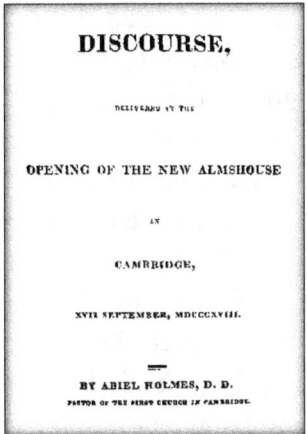

Reverend Abiel Holmes's discourse at the opening of a new almshouse at Cambridge, September 17, 1818. (New England Historic Genealogical Society)

have any institution for the poor until late in the century. Weston had a workhouse in 1772 while Malden had one in 1773, Douglas had one in 1775, and Harvard had one in 1785. Springfield built a poorhouse in 1802.[71] After arranging the local poor at a price ranging from three to five cents a day (10 to 15 dollars a year) for support at private homes in the early 1800s, Athol purchased a farm for $1,856 in 1827 and converting it into a poorhouse.[72] Haverhill began to consider a workhouse in 1789 and had a poorhouse in 1817 and a workhouse in 1835. Lunenburg brought its first poor farm from

---

[71] Town of Weston, *Records of the First Precinct, 1746-1754 and of the Town, 1754-1803* (Boston: Alfred Mudge & Son, 1893), 190, 202. Deloraine P. Corey, *The History of Malden, Massachusetts, 1633-1785* (Malden: Published by the Author, 1899), 408. "Warnings-Out in Malden, Mass., 1678-1794," *New England Historical and Genealogical Register* 92 (1938): 56. William A. Emerson, *History of the Town of Douglas, from the Earliest Period to the Close of 1878* (Boston: F. W. Bird, 1879), 55. Henry S. Nourse, *History of the Town of Harvard, Massachusetts, 1732-1893* (Harvard: W. Hapgood, 1894), 126, 127. Mason A. Green, *Springfield, 1636-1886: History of Town and City* (Boston, Press of Rockwell and Churchill, 1888), 367, 394.

[72] The Historical Records Survey, Division of Community Service Programs Work Projects Administration, Inventory of City and Town Archives of Massachusetts, No. 14 Worcester County, Vol. II Athol (Boston, Mass.: The Historical Records Survey, 1941), 28, 29.

Jonathan Parker for $3,424 in 1828. Braintree had a poor farm and almshouse by 1828. Bedford purchased a farm for the poor in 1833. Millbury appointed a committee "to inquire into the cause of pauperism" and accepted the committee's suggestion to purchase a farm for the poor for under $6,000 in 1834. The following year, the same town chose three overseers of the poor to "take under their care the paupers of the town" and to manage the poor farm. New Bedford spent $17,000 to build a new almshouse, which opened in January 1847.[73] Clearly, serious efforts to set up local institutions for public poor relief became a new trend around the turn of the century.

A designated building for the poor was a major undertaking for many small communities. It was not unusual for decades to pass before some of them could reach any consensus. Proponents who championed institutional relief soon discovered that a poor institution might not be any less inexpensive than keeping the poor at individual houses, nor would the idea of building one be an easy sell to local residents. Braintree, for example, began to consider a poorhouse as early as 1747. Numerous committees were formed, reports made, proposals presented, and town meetings called to deliberate time and again, yet no poorhouse was purchased or built until four decades later.[74] A warrant at Westborough announced that

---

[73] George W. Chase, *The History of Haverhill, Massachusetts, from Its First Settlement in 1640 to the Year 1860* (Haverhill: Published by the Author, 1861), 441, 481, 493-94, 506. Anon., *Lunenburg, The Heritage of Turkey Hills* (n. p., 1977), 286. H. Hobart Holly, ed., *Braintree Massachusetts Its History* (Braintree, Mass.: Braintree Historical Society, 1985), 79. Abram English Brown, *History of the Town of Bedford, Middlesex County, Massachusetts, from Its Earliest Settlement to the Year of Our Lord 1891* (Bedford: Published by the Author, 1891), 32-33. Louis K. Brown, *Wilderness Town: The Story of Bedford, Massachusetts* (1968), 154-55. Simeon Waters, Simon Farnsworth, and Samuel D. Torrey were chosen as a Board of Overseers of the Poor Farm and Town Poor. *Centennial History of the Town of Millbury, Massachusetts* (Millbury: Published by the Town, 1915), 120-24. Leonard B. Ellis, *History of New Bedford and Its Vicinity, 1602-1892* (Syracuse, N.Y.: D. Mason & Co., 1892), 303.

[74] In 1755, Braintree received a proposal from neighboring Milton about building a workhouse jointly. Samuel A. Bates, ed., *Records of the Town of Braintree, 1640-1793* (Randolph, Mass.: Daniel H. Huxford, 1886), 281-82, 283, 286, 329, 340, 341, 344, 388, 399, 422, 425, 443-44, 495, 498, 531, 553, 555, 569, 556, 558, 560, 562, 576. See also

inhabitants needed to vote at a town meeting on October 31, 1763, on whether or not the town should build a workhouse. Three years later, townspeople still had not decided the matter.[75] Amherst began to consider building a poorhouse in 1778; fifty years later townspeople were still debating whether they should build or hire a house for that purpose. It was not until the end of the 1830s that a series of town meetings finally agreed on the idea of a town farm by allotting $1,200 to selectmen for implementation.[76] Mendon began a similar process as early as 1763, seeking to choose between building a workhouse and renting one. It voted the following year to raise £20 to hire a house, provide stock, and buy tools and materials "to set the Poor to work." Half a century later, town meetings revisited the same issue by appointing a committee to consider and report on the subject of a possible house for the poor. In 1827, the town seriously considered buying Anson Aldrich's farm to convert it to a poor farm. However, a town meeting did not vote to purchase a farm to support the poor until 1830.[77]

Regardless of how much time and effort local officials and residents spent, the cost of maintaining the needy did not decline, and some basic expenditures seemed unavoidable. At a Lee town meeting on May 31, 1790, it was voted that

---

William S. Pattee, *A History of Old Braintree and Qunicy* (Quincy, Mass.: Green & Prescott, 1878), 90.

[75] Westborough, Town Records, 1718-1777, Film Collection, Family History Library, Salt Lake City, 157, 178, 179, 183.

[76] Carpenter and Morehouse, comp., *The History of the Town of Amherst, Massachusetts, 1731-1896* (Amherst, Mass.: Press of Carpenter & Morehouse, 1896), 79, 80, 207, 225-226, 227, 228.

[77] The meeting further voted to accept the report of the selectmen recommending the purchase of Caleb Mowry's farm for a poor farm. It also authorized the overseers of the poor, Obadiah Wood, Johnson Legg, and Rufus Paine, to furnish the farm with all necessary stock, farming tools, household furniture, and utensils for the maintenance and support of the poor thereon. New rules and by-laws were formulated to regulate the new institution, which began to surpass the public schools and road maintenance as the most costly item on the town budget. Whereas the schools often took half of all town charges in the past, the support of the poor and incidental expenses in 1846 reached $1,600, which was more than the funding for schools and highway repairs combined. John G. Metcalf, *Annals of the Town of Mendon, from 1659 to 1880* (Providence, R.I.: E. L. Freeman & Co., 1880), 294, 295, 500, 501, 502, 517, 526, 527, 528, 539, 542-43, 598.

"Ebenezer Jenkens Esq. be and hereby is directed to apply to the Select Men or overseers of the poor for the town of Stoughton—and inform them that there is one of their poor in this Town whom they are desired to provide for: and that in case of their Neglect, the said Jenkens is hereby directed to prosecute the matter to final judgment." [78] Simply put, if Stoughton would not care for its poor, townsfolk at Lee—tired of bearing the expenses for their neighbors—would resort to legal actions in court.

Boston

Few communities felt the brunt of poverty more acutely than large population centers, such as Charlestown, Cambridge, Salem, Newburyport, and of course Boston—the largest of them all. Within several decades after independence, Cambridge had built a new almshouse, and Charlestown had established the Mclean Asylum for the Insane. Local citizens organized benevolent societies in Dorchester and Newburyport. The latter, where a workhouse existed as early as its incorporation in 1764, decided to build a new one in 1793. Within thirty years, townsfolk again felt the need to enlarge the workhouse by building a three-story brick addition forty feet long and thirty-four feet wide.[79] Meanwhile, a female charitable society was formed in Salem, where the town government spent between $15,000 and $16,000—about 60 percent of its annual budget—on the poor.[80] Yet it was in Boston that a wide array of activity was taking place during this period. The gradual

---

[78] *Records of the Town of Lee from Its Incorporation to A. D. 1801* (Lee, Mass.: Press of the Valley Gleaner, 1900), 59.
[79] John J. Currier, *The History of Newburyport, Massachusetts, 1764-1905* (1906; Somersworth, N.H.: New Hampshire Publishing Company, 1977), 1: 142-45.
[80] *Expenses of the Town of Salem for the Year Ending March, 1818, Expenses of the Town of Salem for the Year Ending March, 1819*, and *Overseers' Report, March 1, 1819*.

transformation to rebuild the city, detailed by the historian Jacqueline Barbara Carr, strongly affected the lives of the middle and lower sorts of Bostonians, including poor city dwellers, newcomers, transients, women, and African Americans. Some of their families began to move from neighborhood to neighborhood and from job to job in search of a better life, creating a new micro- and inner-migration in the city.[81]

Both public and private sectors responded to the general atmosphere of change. In the public arena, relief institutions first faced challenges. In 1790 a committee reported to the town meeting about the appalling conditions of the almshouse. Constructed at the northwest corner of the Common a century earlier, it was foul, disease-ridden, and over-crowded. According to the report, the building "is too near the Center of the Town, and not sufficiently Large to accommodate the Number of the poor at present in the House—previous to the War—the number did not exceed 150 or 180 in the Winter season, nor 100 or 120 in Summer—There are in the present month of August between 270 & 280 in the ensuing Winter it is Probable that there will be between 300 and 400." Echoing this gloomy depiction, the Reverend John Clarke went so far as to declare a few years later that the almshouse "is wholly inadequate to the purpose."[82] Rebuilt in 1801, the much larger almshouse doubled its capacity and could now hold up to 500 inmates.[83] However, it was replaced again twenty years later by a newly constructed House of Industry, which combined the functions of both the old almshouse and the workhouse.

---

[81] Jacqueline Barbara Carr, *After the Siege: A Social History of Boston, 1775-1800* (Boston: Northeastern University Press, 2005).
[82] John Clarke, *A Discourse Delivered before the Humane Society of the Commonwealth of Massachusetts* (Boston: Belknap and Hall, 1793), 25. Rev. Clarke was the first recording secretary of the society.
[83] *Miscellaneous Remarks on the Police of Boston* (Boston: Buckingham and Hilliard, 1814), 5.

Ironically, the rebuilding and expansion of the almshouse and workhouse in Boston only led to a diminishing role of Boston's overseers of the poor, who had lost authority to city managers over the administration of poor relief.[84] Strongly advocated by Mayor John Quincy, a new set of reformist ideas redefined the poor according to their abilities to work. Breaking away from the traditional binary of the impotent and able-bodied poor, the new concept divided them into four categories:, "1st, the poor by reason of age; 2nd, the poor by reason of misfortune; 3rd, the poor by reason of infancy; 4th, the poor by reason of vice."[85] On the surface, the new idea only expanded the notion of the impotent poor into three sub-categories (age, misfortune, and infancy). Yet this revised classification signaled a new direction facing the poor. Treated as paupers, all of them now had to work at the new institution. As far as the new breed of municipal managers could tell, the task of reducing public expenses for relief directly related to an effort to increase the poor's participation in work. This doctrine of control and centralization prevailed, and the two-century old division between the almshouse (for the impotent poor) and the workhouse (for the able-bodied poor) became obsolete. John Quincy and a special committee he chaired insisted that "the most economical" mode of maintaining the poor was to combine the two old-fashioned institutions into one. On May 7, 1821, a Boston town meeting voted to accept the committee's recommendation of erecting a House of Industry, which would cost $19,612 to build in South Boston.[86]

---

[84] Eric Nellis and Anne Decker Cecere, eds., *The Eighteenth-Century Records of the Boston Overseers of the Poor* (Boston: The Colonial Society of Massachusetts, 2007), 13-14.
[85] Boston Town Records, 1814 to 1822 (Boston: 1906), 37: 187. See also Josiah Quincy, *Report of the Committee on the Subject of Pauperism and a House of Industry in the Town of Boston* (Boston, 1812).
[86] *Boston Town Records, 1814 to 1822* (Boston: 1906), 37: 273. Justin Winsor, *The Memorial History of Boston* (Boston: Ticknor and Company, 1881), 3: 230.

As public relief programs were undergoing revisions,[87] the private sector and voluntary associations also developed new forms of charities. A host of philanthropic societies sprang up around the turn of the century, marking a new milestone in the American charity movement.[88] Often addressing a particular social problem, these charitable societies went beyond the tradition of helping the impotent or the able-bodied poor by moving into a series of targeted domains. They broadened the scope of conventional charity and greatly expanded benevolent activities by specializing in work for children, women, the lunatic, the sick of various sorts, the unfortunate, the needy of ethnic origins, widows of deceased ministers, or the intemperate. No fewer than a dozen institutions were founded during this period, including the Humane Society of the Commonwealth of Massachusetts (1785), the Massachusetts Charitable Society (1786), the Congregational Charitable Society (1795), the Boston Dispensary (1796),[89] the Massachusetts Charitable Fire Society (1799), the Boston Female Asylum (1800), the Massachusetts General Hospital (1811), the Howard Benevolent Society (1812), the Boston Asylum for Indigent Boys (1814), the Boston Society for the Moral and Religious Instruction of the Poor (1817), the Penitent Females' Refuge (1822), the Society for the Employment of the Female Poor (1827), the Massachusetts Charitable Eye and Ear Infirmary (1827), and the Boston Lying-In Hospital (1832).

---

[87] Eric Nellis and Anne Decker Cecere, eds., *The Eighteenth-Century Records of the Boston Overseers of the Poor* (Boston: The Colonial Society of Massachusetts, 2007), 69-80.
[88] Conrad E. Wright, *The Transformation of Charity in Postrevolutionary New England* (Boston: Northeastern University Press, 1992).
[89] Unlike a hospital which was a business, the Boston Dispensary was a charity, which would send a physician and medicine to a sick poor person. *Miscellaneous Remarks on the Police of Boston* (Boston: Buckingham and Hilliard, 1814), 17. Daniel L. Marsh, ed., *The Story of Massachusetts* (New York: The American Historical Society, Inc., 1938), 3: 243. Recognizing the charitable nature of the Dispensary the Boston Female Asylum ruled that sick children at her institution would receive medicine from the Dispensary. *The Institute of the Boston Female Asylum, Organized Sept. 26, 1800* (Boston: Russell and Cutler, 1801), 8. *An Account of the Rise, Progress, and Present State of the Boston Female Asylum* (Boston: Russell and Cutler, 1803), 15.

Supported by the Episcopal Church, large-scale humanitarian reforms in England sometimes adopted a central strategy, such as the charity school movement. Little uniformity characterized the philanthropic renaissance in Massachusetts, where most charitable activity remained local in scale and diverse in purposes. However, at least four reoccurring topics and themes tended to draw the public's attention. The first was temperance. Advancing one step from the colonial belief that idleness was the bane of all evils, charity advocates were now convinced that drunkenness was the root of idleness as much as temperance was its cure. "Intemperance is not the least cause of poverty," said the Reverend Abiel Holmes. Pastor of Congregational Church in Cambridge, he believed that "intemperance, while it enervates the intellectual and moral powers, and incapacitates a person to do the duties of his proper station or profession, is itself a most expensive vice." Deeply disturbed by the scenes of drunkards haunting the taverns, sauntering the streets, and frequenting shops, he asserted that this single vice had incomparably contributed more than any other toward the public's aversion to intemperance.[90]

Insisting that "excessive drinking, gaming, idleness and debauchery" were "to the dishonour of human nature and the great injury of society," the General Court stripped the right to dispose of property from heavy drinkers, obsessive gamblers, or habitual idlers who exposed "himself or herself , or his or her family, or any of them, to want or suffering circumstances." Instead, only authorized local selectmen could dispose of such property, acting as court-appointed legal guardians. The Court further empowered the overseers of the poor to set to work or bind out to service "all such persons." The Court ruled

---

[90] Abiel Holmes, *A Discourse Delivered at the Opening of the New Almshouse in Cambridge, September 17, 1818* (Cambridge: Hilliard and Metcalf, 1818), 10-11.

> [t]hat the Selectmen in each town shall cause to be posted up in the houses and shops of all taverners, innholders, and retailer, as aforesaid, within such towns or districts, a list of the names of all the persons reputed common drunkards, or common tipplers, or common gamesters, misspending their time and estate in such houses. And every keeper of such house or shop, after notice given him as aforesaid, that shall be convicted before one or more Justices of the Peace, of entertaining or suffering any of the persons in such list, to drink, or tippler, or game, in his or her house, or any of the dependencies thereof, or of selling them spirituous liquor, as aforesaid, shall forfeit and pay the sum of *Thirty Shillings*.[91]

These rulings strongly encouraged local authorities to combat intemperance—so much so that town officials considered it one of their most important duties to stop "excessive drinking, gaming, idleness, or profligacy of any kind." Eager to save their towns from great expenses for relief, local officials believed that they had the power not only to control individual behavior, but also to prevent taverns, inns, and retail shops—designed for "public convenience and usefulness"—from corrupting into "haunts of vice, destructive of health, the peace of families, and good order of society."[92]

Second, a spiritual approach considered any absence from public worship and any ignorance of religious knowledge to be as appalling as any form of material paucity. Some

---

[91] Ch. 68, 1786: An Act for the Due Regulation of Licensed Houses, *Laws and Resolves 1786-7* (1889), 214.

[92] Ch. 68, 1786: An Act for the Due Regulation of Licensed Houses, *Laws and Resolves 1786-7* (1889), 206-16. Ch. 30, 1788: An Act for Erecting Work House for the Reception and Employment of the Idle and Indigent, *Laws and Resolves 1788-89* (Boston: 1894), 42-48. "The Selectmen and Overseers of the Poor of the Town Cambridge to Their Fellow Citizens," in Abiel Holmes, *A Discourse Delivered at the Opening of the New Almshouse in Cambridge, September 17, 1818* (Cambridge: Hilliard and Metcalf, 1818), 29-40.

estimated that 18,000 people (about half of the population in Boston) routinely failed to attend church service and that hundreds of poor children never saw a copy of the Holy Scripture at home. Organized as the Society for the Moral and Religious Instruction of the Poor, this new charity used a significant portion of its funding to print and distribute thousands of copies of religious literature. It also set out to provide basic religious instructions to poor children by establishing Sunday schools. Admitting as many as 500 boys and girls from poor families, the first two Sunday schools shared space with the public schools on Mason and School Streets. They taught young students how to read the Bible, recite religious verses, and respond to catechisms. Sponsors of the Sunday schools stressed that the morally and religiously improved mindset of the poor children would lead to an inner strength of rectitude, the best asset for combating poverty. They further believed to have seen a glimpse of hope after learning that those who attended Sunday schools for a year were able to memorize numerous hymns, catechisms, and hundreds of passages from Scripture.[93] Of course, this sort of optimism was often balanced with a stern warning to the youngsters that the fear of God would always be a precondition of one's true piety. As one director of the society, Josiah Vinton, Jr., warned, God is not all mercy. He said that the wickedness of a rebellious heart and a continuous obsession not with work, but with sports, plays, dress, fashion, self-love, and various vanities of this world could soon exhaust His patience.[94]

    Third, some private institutions began to perform certain relief functions that previously fell under the public domain. For example, named in honor of the English

---

[93] *Report of the Boston Society for the Moral and Religious Instruction of the Poor* (Boston, 1817); *Second Annual Report of the Boston Society for the Moral and Religious Instruction of the Poor* (Boston, 1818).
[94] [Josiah Vinton, Jr.], *An Address Delivered to the Children of Sunday School in Boston on the Last Sabbath in December, 1818* (Boston, 1819).

philanthropist John Howard, the Howard Benevolent Society attempted "to furnish employment for the honest poor."[95] In addition, the Boston Asylum for Indigent Boys was incorporated "for the charitable purpose of relieving, instructing and employing indigent Boys belonging to the town of Boston." Its 800 subscribers included such prominent Bostonians as John Hancock, William Phillips, Paul Revere, and Josiah Quincy. This organization ran its asylum in a similar manner that overseers of the poor had run the workhouse. Elected by its membership, a board of nine managers administered the business of the asylum. The board selected a master or matron to supervise the day-to-day affairs of the asylum. Only the board of the managers could authorize any boy to be admitted into or discharged from the asylum. Preferring those born in Boston, the board allowed boys who were three to twelve years old to remain at the asylum until disposed of. Just as the city overseers could dispose orphans,[96] the managers had power to send the institutionalized boys to foster families. All parents and guardians of the boys were required to surrender the right to the boys by signing a promise not to interfere with the institution's decisions over the boys' futures or to visit them at the asylum without the consent of a manager. Parents and guardians received no compensation from the boys' work at the asylum and were not allowed to induce any child to leave the institution. Two years after the asylum's incorporation, thirty boys had learned to read, write, and cipher while they performed tasks such as knitting socks and folding books for sale.[97]

---

[95] *Howard Benevolent Society, Organized in Boston, June 1, 1812* (Boston: Ezra Lincoln, 1819).
[96] For details see Sharon Braslaw Sundue, "Class Stratification and Children's Work in Post-Revolutionary Urban America," in Simon Middleton and Billy G. Smith, eds., *Class Matters: Early North America and the Atlantic World* (Philadelphia: University of Pennsylvania Press, 2008), 198-204.
[97] Boston Asylum for Indigent Boys, *An Account of the Boston Asylum for Indigent Boys* (Boston: Nathaniel Willis, 1816).

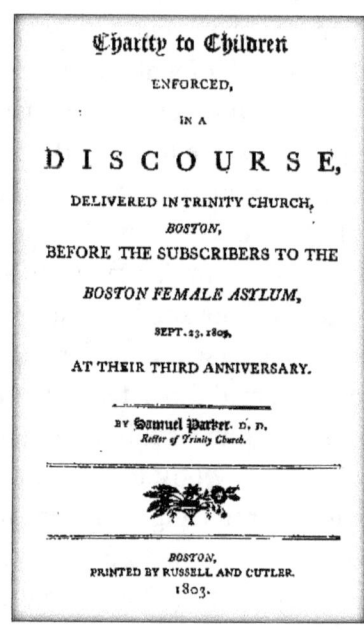

Title page of Samuel Parker's discourse *Charity to Children Enforced* delivered in Trinity Church before the subscribers of the Boston Female Asylum. Boston, 1803. Organized on September 26, 1800, the goal of this charitable institution was to raise funds for the benefit of female orphan children from three to ten years of age. Its 300 members included Mrs. John Adams and Mrs. John Hancock. (American Antiquarian Society)

In fact, gender-specific relief had taken place several years earlier when the Boston Female Asylum, imitating a model in Baltimore, had been organized in 1800. Aimed at helping female orphans, the society attracted 300 to 400 subscribers, including Abigail Adams, Mrs. Samuel Adams, Elizabeth Bowdoin (widow of Governor Bowdoin), Mrs. John Hancock, and Mrs. William Phillips. Governed by a board of fourteen ladies, the society housed female orphans from three to ten years old. Similar to city overseers, it was also responsible for choosing suitable families in which to place the girls when they reached a proper age. It selected a governess whose ability and virtue, the society hoped, could ensure the proper care and instruction of these female orphans. The society's rules dictated that the orphans "shall be dressed alike in a plain and simple attire," and "shall be arranged in classes, according to their age, capacity, or improvement" to learn to read, write, sew, and do all kinds of domestic duties "until old enough to be placed in virtuous families." In 1801, the society received twelve orphans. When it was incorporated two years later, the number increased to twenty-five.[98]

Finally, as the loss of parentage is one of the most tragic human sufferings, a large body of literature on the topic of charitable giving often addressed the public's varied attitudes from understanding and sympathy to insensitivity and apathy. Speaking on behalf of the Female Asylum in 1803, Samuel Parker, Rector of Trinity Church, reminded his audience that "we were born not solely for our own good, but for the good of others, may we be led to the exercise of Charity and Benevolence, toward all our fellow-creatures, and consider ourselves as indispensably obliged to contribute all in our power to their happiness."[99] Running the charity cost the asylum at least $1,400 annually, while its membership subscription fluctuated between $1,200 and $1,300. Counting its building fund, stock, interest from money lending, and sales of sermons and other literature, the society could barely balance its accounts every year,[100] which seriously threatened the survival of the society if no new funding was forthcoming. According to Reverend Parker, female orphans were "the most helpless of our species." He further stated,

> We are assembled to provide those whose fathers and whose mothers are gone down to the silent grave; who have no father but God, who has put it into the hearts of the Members of this Institution, to rescue these

---

[98] *The Institute of the Boston Female Asylum, Organized Sept. 26, 1800* (Boston: Russell and Cutler, 1801); *An Account of the Rise, Progress, and Present State of the Boston Female Asylum* (Boston: Russell and Cutler, 1803).
[99] Samuel Parker, *Charity to Children Enforced* (Boston: Russell and Cutler, 1803), 6.
[100] Statement of Expenses and Subscriptions to the Boston Female Asylum (on the end page) in Thomas Baldwin, *A Discourse Delivered before the Members of the Boston Female Asylum, September 26, 1806* (Boston: Russell and Cutler, 1806).

> Orphans from a state of abject poverty; to preserve them from the devious paths of sin, by instilling into their tender minds the principles of virtue and religion, and to instruct them to be useful members of society.[101]

He went on to explain that riches are gifts of God "intended for our good, for the exercise of virtue, to furnish liberality, to make us the instrument of his mercy." Because the poor shall always be with us, he told his listeners that "it is by means of their poverty, that we may make our riches, blessings indeed; as we have thereby an opportunity of employing them to the best purpose." He concluded by encouraging his listeners to "embrace the happy occasion of being Charitable, with a certainty of being useful."[102]

From a pragmatist point of view, suffering provided opportunities alongside challenges. When Reverend Thomas Baldwin, the minister of the Second Baptist Church in Boston, spoke before an audience of 1,500 people in 1806, he drew their attention to the positive side of giving. Acknowledging that life consisted of both joy and sorrow, pleasure and pain, gratification and disappointment, he pointed out that happiness lies largely in "our social connections." Among all charities and in the most liberal hearts of all the philanthropists, he insisted, "none has a higher claim to public patronage, than the Boston Female Asylum."[103] Down-to-earth and unequivocal, some secular discourse went a step further. Cheerful care for the poor was tantamount to happiness, according to Mary Robson Hughs. A self-appointed authority on moralism, she rarely missed a chance to put a good spin on the traditional virtue of donations.

---

[101] Samuel Parker, *Charity to Children Enforced* (Boston: Russell and Cutler, 1803), 10.
[102] Ibid., 14, 27.
[103] Thomas Baldwin, *A Discourse Delivered before the Members of the Boston Female Asylum, September 26, 1806* (Boston: Russell and Cutler, 1806), 5, 6, 11, 21, 27.

Instead of considering charity a burden, she suggested the pleasure and delightfulness of loving fellow creatures. "Do you wish to be happy?" she asked. If so, consider life as a school where pious Christians would volunteer to help the poor, one of God's commands. Because no one could be happy against the will of the Almighty, she pointed out that "a truly pious and virtuous life" was a sure way to secure "a peaceful death and a joyful resurrection."[104] Indeed, a growing number of urban miseries tested local citizens' conscience, social values, and moral sensitivities. The close of the century did not leave poverty behind, but rather brought more challenges to the old city's attitudes toward the poor, abilities to control poverty, and inventiveness in voluntary charity and institutional relief.

State Paupers

Despite all the evolving situations at the local level, no municipal or county government was willing to pay for the support of a new category of needy people—the state paupers,[105] whose numbers had significantly grown after independence. Aware that the discontinuation of the warning-out policy in 1794 would not ban people from drifting, Massachusetts passed an act concerning what constituted a person's legal settlement, which was a prerequisite for public relief. Detailing a variety of scenarios, the law enumerated twelve conditions under which a person could gain legal settlement, such as by adopting the settlement of one's parents, through marriage, by working at the place as a hired apprentice,

---

[104] [Mary Robson Hughs], *An Affectionate Address to the Poor* (Boston: Munroe and Francis, 1815).
[105] First used by the English and continental countries, an increasing adoption of the word "paupers" indicated a new trend of the late eighteenth and early nineteenth centuries. Gertrude Himmelfarb, "The New Poor Law: Pauper versus Poor," *The Idea of Poverty: England in the Early Industrial Age* (New York: Alfred A. Knopf, 1984), 8, 147-76.

or by serving a local office for one year. In principle, the law allowed one to obtain legal settlement if the person was 21 years old and had a yearly rent or profit of $3 for 3 years, or was assessed to have an estate of £60 or a yearly income of £3 12s. for 5 consecutive years. Gaining a settlement qualified an individual for local relief should the person become poor and stand in need of support.[106] Replacing the old requirement of not being warned in a year, the requirements of a legal settlement were meant to be the new precondition of public relief.[107]

Comprehensive as they might be, these prerequisites left room to disallow a legal settlement for some of the most vulnerable people in society, such as many drifting people of the propertyless, infirm, or lonesome elderly. A new category of poor thus emerged from this complication. Known as the state paupers, although living in Massachusetts, they had no legal settlement for any town that would support them and had to rely on state relief for survival. In 1795, the state treasury paid the sum of $5,776—5 times the figure from the previous decade —to 48 towns and numerous individuals for their support of the state poor.[108] The number continued to rise in subsequent years, with the state paying $14,110 in 1797, $18,097 in 1798, $17,128 in 1800, and $19,799 in 1802.[109] In other words, supporting the state poor at various local communities accounted for 65 percent—and sometimes as high as up to 80 percent—of the commonwealth's annual expenditures, more than all the remaining state expenses combined, including the maintenance of the state militia, prisons, sheriffs, and printers.

---

[106] Ch. 34, 1793, *Acts and Resolves, 1792-93* (1895), 439-42.
[107] The settlement laws were amended numerous times during the nineteenth and twentieth centuries, but were not completely abandoned until 1974. *Acts and Resolves* 1974, ch. 260, sec. 17, 141.
[108] *Acts and Resolves 1786-87*, 407-408. *Acts and Resolves 1794-95*, 501-03.
[109] *Acts and Resolves 1794-95*, 586-93; *Acts and Resolves 1796-97*, 601-609; *Acts and Resolves 1798-99*, 608-18; *Acts and Resolves 1800-01*, 548-61.

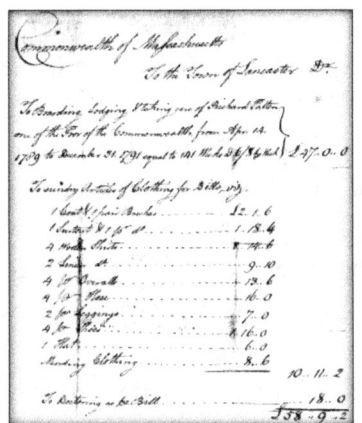

Lancaster bill to the commonwealth for maintenance of the state poor Richard Patton for 141 weeks from 14 April 1789 to 31 December 1791 at 6/8 per week. Patton was a foreigner who was discharged in 1783 after serving in the Continental Army. (Massachusetts Archives)

This escalating cost of relief by the state treasury revealed an invisible population of the poor, whose names seldom appeared on town records, local tax rolls, county court files, or city directories. In almost every town across the commonwealth, their obscure circumstances were as varied as their sufferings. William Barton was a prisoner of war after the defeat of General John Burgoyne in 1777. Densa Tooly was the illegitimate child of Elizabeth Tooly, who had died without legal settlement. Coming from Ireland, James Thompson had no settlement. The transient Rebecca Gardner was an invalid who became a charge to Easthampton. Claiming that they had no idea of whether the transient John Lee belonged to any town in the United States, Swansea selectmen paid for his maintenance while he was sick and buried him after his death. A man named Philip Royle from Ireland simply left his wife and four children at Warwick, where the local residents had to take care of them. George De Silva was an insane Portuguese who ended up at the Roxbury almshouse. Born in Ireland in 1732, Richard Patten enlisted in the American Revolution for Leominster and Stow. He was a private who served in the

Continental Army for a three-year term from 1777. An invalid toward the end of the war, he became a charge to Lancaster, where he died on April 8, 1797, at the age of 65 as one of the state's poor.[110]

The selectmen of York reported to the Committee on Accounts of the General Court that "one Hannah Downs, a poor widow, formerly of a place called Star Island at the Isles of Shoals, in the State of New Hampshire, sled from thence for fear of the Enemy at the beginning of the late War with Great Britain, and took up her residence in the said town of York, from that time to the time of her death." In her escape, she froze her feet and needed constant medical care and nursing. The town spent £12 18s. 6d. for her maintenance in 1792.[111]

Seth Copeland's charge to selectmen of Chelsea for providing milk, potatoes, butter, and beef to old Mr. John Goodwin, a state poor. Chelsea, January 24, 1792. (Massachusetts Archives)

---

[110] Committee on Accounts, series 9, roll 21, nos. 7, 9, 10, 11, 15, 16, 19, 22, 24, 25, 27, 29, 43, and 66, Massachusetts State Archives.
[111] Committee on Accounts, series 9, roll 21, no. 62, Massachusetts State Archives.

As unfortunate as widow Downs's experience might have been, many a poor person had a more perplexing past. For example, no one knew for certain where John Woodin had been born—perhaps at Middleton or Salem or somewhere near. His mother ran from Boston to pursue a man who had left her pregnant, yet neither the father nor the mother had legal settlement in the commonwealth. Their son remained in Boston until he, at age twenty, went to Connecticut, where he drifted again for several years. He repeated the same pattern of wandering after he moved to New York. In 1757 or 1758, he went into service in Rhode Island and was later wounded and crippled at Ticonderoga. He received a pension from Rhode Island, but moved to Connecticut in 1766. Two years later, he moved to Uxbridge, Worcester County, where he was warned. He then moved through Mendon, Douglas, and Sutton before returning to Connecticut. Therefore, when selectmen of Danvers, Essex County, attempted to recount their encounters with him in 1798, they simply summarized that "he was always strolling from town to town & never became an inhabitant of any Town nor ever paid a Tax in any Town during his life."[112]

Similarly, when the selectmen and overseers of the poor of Belchertown tried to trace the past of one Joseph King, they concluded that "on the best evidence, [. . .] the said Joseph King has not gained a Settlement in any Town or District within this Commonwealth." In fact, he had lived in Windsor in Vermont between 1769 and 1770. The next year he was in Charlestown in New Hampshire, where he stayed until 1785, when he drifted to Worcester. He remained there until August 1798, when he moved to Belchertown.[113]

---

[112] Committee on Accounts, series 9, roll 38, no. 27, Massachusetts State Archives.
[113] Committee on Accounts, series 9, roll 42, no. 40, Massachusetts State Archives.

Timothy Arnold, Jeremiah Lawrence, and Norman Sloan, selectmen and overseers of the poor for the town of Washington, Berkshire County, certified to the commonwealth the status of Phebe Clark. Born in New London, Connecticut, she was "totally blind and unable to do anything toward her support." She was sixty-eight years old and her husband died in 1778 while serving in the Continental Army. She had no legal settlement and was considered a state poor. January 20, 1800. (Massachusetts Archives)

The selectmen of Washington, Berkshire County, also faced no easy task in providing a precise account of Phebe Clark, who—after two marriages and relocations from four states and at least seven towns—had become a state poor in their community. In their best effort, they wrote:

> We the Selectmen and overseers of the Poor in the Town of Washington in the County of Berkshire & Commonwealth of Massachusetts—Do hereby certify, that Phebe Clark now living in said Washington, has become poor and incapable of supporting herself, the said Phebe came into the said town of Washington, from Lenox in said county, in the month of September 1798. She came into this Commonwealth from Bennington in the State of Vermont in the month of April 1796. She resided not in any Town in this Commonwealth long at a time, but travelled from one town to another as a transient person after she came to said Washington, without gaining [in]habitancy in any town—and we certify that she has not gained a Settlement in any town or district within the Commonwealth in any of the ways pointed out in an act passed February eleventh in the year of our Lord 1794 specifying what shall constitute a legal Settlement—and we further certify that she has no kindred within the Commonwealth by law obliged to support her—The said Phebe Clark is now sixty eight years old, was born in New London in the State of Connecticut in the year 1732. She moved from there to Elizabeth Town in the State of New Jersey and resided there ten years and was married there—from thence moved to Branford in said State of Connecticut and lived there a short time—then she moved to North Carolina and lived there seven years where her husband died—Then she moved to Killingsworth in said State of Connecticut, from thence she moved to Bennington in the State of Vermont aforesaid, where

she married again, her husband went into the Continental Army and died there in the year 1778. he was from said Bennington & left no property whereby she could be supported—Since that time she has remained a single woman & has travelled from one part of the Country to another without property until she came to said Washington—The said Phebe Clerk is totally blind and unable to do anything towards her support—She has been provided for and supported by said town of Washington from the Third day of November in the year 1798—We do further certify that the foregoing Statement is made on the best evidence we can obtain, and with all the dilligence we were capable of—

Washington January 20th, 1800

Timothy Arnold	Selectmen & Overseers
Jeremiah Lawrence	of the Poor for the Town
Norman Sloan	of Washington—[114]

Because the state would always promise to pay, the maintenance of the state poor could mean opportunities for those who provided service. Doctors often charged regular fees for visits to the sick. Northampton employed the physician David Phelps for the care of John Magee, who was a Hessian soldier with rapture in the abdomen, and his wife, who was bedridden and extremely sick. Traveling 5.5 miles each time, Phelps made as many as 80 visits during a five-month period from May to October in 1791, charging £39 1s. 11d. at the rate of 5s. 6d. per visit.[115] Various suppliers also charged for a long list of merchandise, such as wood, beef, corn, potatoes, milk,

---

[114] Committee on Accounts, series 9, roll 42, no. 111, Massachusetts State Archives.
[115] Committee on Accounts, series 9, roll 21, no. 56, Massachusetts State Archives.

butter, molasses, tea, pork, rice, bacon, mutton, peas, shoes, stockings, hosen, shirts, linen, handkerchiefs, jackets, hats, and leggings.[116] When the homeless state paupers died, townships usually paid for the funeral expenses, which could be a considerable sum—particularly in urban communities. Salem and Newburyport, for example, often charged the state more than £1,000 for the care of the state poor.[117] Sometimes charging the state as high as more than £3,000, Boston cared for 123 paupers belonging to the state in 1794 and 150 in 1798, excluding 22 burials.[118]

The large number of state paupers went hand in hand with a growing ethnic diversity that Massachusetts had not previously experienced. Salem and Newburyport selectmen frequently reported that they received Frenchmen, Irishmen, Dutchmen, and a host of other foreigners who badly needed relief.[119] Boston saw a long list of the needy who had come from as many as some three dozen places, including not only Halifax, Portsmouth, Cumberland, Isles of Shoals, New London, New York, Philadelphia, Connecticut, Rhode Island, Carolina, Georgia, Virginia, and New Jersey, but also London, Liverpool, Bristol, Amsterdam, and Scotland, Ireland, Spain, Germany, France, Malta, the West Indies, Africa, Hispaniola, and Poland. Toward the end of the century, poor immigrants from Ireland began to outnumber those from Scotland and England. In 1798, 20 percent of the state paupers in Boston were of Irish origin, compared to only 13 percent English, 7 percent German, and less than 5 percent Scottish.[120]

---

[116] Committee on Accounts, series 9, roll 21, nos. 12, 19, 21, 66; roll 30, *passim*, Massachusetts State Archives.
[117] Committee on Accounts, series 9, roll 33, roll 38, roll 46, Massachusetts State Archives.
[118] Committee on Accounts, series 9, roll 30, roll 38, Massachusetts State Archives.
[119] Committee on Accounts, series 9, roll 38, nos. 63, 89, Massachusetts State Archives.
[120] Committee on Accounts, series 9, roll 38, no. 10, Massachusetts State Archives. Jacqueline Barbara Carr, *After the Siege: A Social History of Boston, 1775-1800* (Boston: Northeastern University Press, 2005), 105.

The foreignness of the poor did not go unnoticed, nor did the soaring cost to maintain them. In a statement submitted to the state auditors, Petersham selectmen complained that David Rice and Zebediah Freeman were foreigners and "real paupers" who were "unable to pay any expenses" toward their own support. Groton felt that it had been stuck with John Claffin Wright, a deserter of the British Army, along with his wife and three children, as well as William Benetrate, also from the British Army, along with his wife and one child. Beverly was obliged to support Jane McComb from Ireland, while Colrain maintained several strangers including two Europeans Daniel McDougall and William Wilson.[121] Jane Wood cost Billerica as much as $4 a week to support for she was "very infirm, being afflicted with a paralytic disorder." A servant from Scotland, she came to America with one Daniel McNeal, who had paid for her passage. Both were warned to depart by Billerica authorities in April 1741 when they first arrived. Wood died in 1797, when she was eighty years old.[122] Four selectmen of Hardwick—David Allen, Job Dexter, Elisah Warner, and Prince Nye—wrote to the General Court in unequivocal terms:

> that John Veal a Native of England, came into this town in the capacity of a Common labourer, with his wife, and has been back & forward tranciently [original] for twenty years past; he was warned out of this town according to the law, & has never gained a legal inhabitancy in this town or in any other town within the state, that we can find out, his wife has long been sick & has been supported by the assistance & charity of the neighbours, together with what labour

---

[121] Committee on Accounts, series 9, roll 38, nos. 12, 18, 37, 73, Massachusetts State Archives.
[122] Committee on Accounts, series 9, roll 38, no. 8, Massachusetts State Archives.

he was able to perform. They are now upwards of seventy years of age & he is infirm & unable to do any kind of labour & the town of Hardwick has been obliged to support them the year past.[123]

Veal and his wife were among the many immigrant transients who constantly kept on the move. Born in Great Britain, John Alstat came to Edgertown, Dukes County, at the age of seventeen. In 1777 he moved to Conway, Hampshire County, where he stayed about eight years. He then removed to New York State, where he stayed for two or three years. He returned to and lived in Conway until 1793, when he moved to Deerfield. After a year and half, he again "returned to the town of Conway and in the summer of 1795 threw himself upon the town for support," according to town selectmen. They affirmed that "he never had an Interest or any Property in Conway sufficient to entitle him to Inhabitancy therein." They further stated that, "We have the fullest evidence that he has no Legal Settlement in any town in this Commonwealth and no kindred obliged by Law to support him or contribute in any way toward his maintenance." Finally, they declared that "Upward of seventy years of ago, [he was] infirm and almost blind."[124]

Facing an ever-rising number of state poor and suspecting excess charges by local providers, Massachusetts authorities struggled to find a method to curb expenses. They passed laws—first in 1796 and then in 1799—to require local authorities to submit detailed accounts to certify the status of the state poor and justify their requested reimbursement that the state treasurer should pay for relief.[125] They allowed salaries to overworked members on the Committee on Accounts, who would now have the time and incentive to examine the

---

[123] Committee on Accounts, series 9, roll 30, no. 27, Massachusetts State Archives.
[124] Committee on Accounts, series 9, roll 38, no. 15, Massachusetts State Archives.
[125] *Acts and Resolves 1794-95*, ch. 122, 582-83. *Acts and Resolves 1798-99*, ch. 67, 89-90.

incoming bills and certificates, submitted by local communities, more closely than before. Yet none of the measures seemed to work. The cost of state relief rose to the astonishing number of nearly half a million dollars in the 1850s. The state finally decided to build three almshouses to house the state paupers in 1851. Officially opened three years later, each of these facilities at Bridgewater, Tewksbury, and Monson had a capacity of housing 500 inmates. Thus began the new era of state-directed intervention in institutional relief.[126]

---

[126] *Acts and Resolves 1852*, ch. 275, An Act in relation to Paupers Having No Settlement in This Commonwealth, 190-93. Report of the Joint Committee Appointed to Investigate the Whole System of the Public Charity Institutions of the Commonwealth of Massachusetts (Boston: William White, 1859), *passim*, especially 3-86, 127-53. See also Justin Winsor, ed., *The Memorial History of Boston* (Boston: Ticknor and Company, 1880-81), 2: 256. Daniel L. Marsh, ed., *The Story of Massachusetts* (New York: The American Historical Society, Inc., 1938), 3: 223.

Conclusion

Rarely was Massachusetts ever free from poverty throughout the eighteenth century, nor did that poverty always remain undivided, monolithic, static, or one dimensional. It showed a series of floating characteristics for at least three reasons. First, the poor in the Bay Colony did not come from a single group of homogeneous people; instead, they consisted of a wide range of dissimilar groups and categories, such as orphans, servants, the lame, the blind, the crippled, the elderly, widows, transients, laborers, apprentices, wounded soldiers, veterans, the unemployed, and dislocated families. Second, no single cause, but rather a great variety of situations produced poverty, including old age, diseases, war, natural disasters, economic crises, financial distress, population spikes, and marital and domestic problems. Third, moving in various directions and shifting through different phases, the fluid nature of poverty did not lead to any universal ending, but generated many localized and individualized consequences, as the ample evidence provided in this book shows. Charity and relief programs alleviated miseries. A weak colonial economy and frequent natural disasters exacerbated anxieties and pains, while waves of land expansions and population upsurges during the middle of the century propelled struggling families to move from community to community. Coming from diverse backgrounds, few poor people pursued an identical path in a singly predictable fashion throughout their lifetime. Sometimes close to despair and damnation, sometimes close to change and improvement, their careers seldom showed any unison but oscillated between these two opposite poles more frequently and more drastically than those of the affluent.

Furthermore, different poor people received differential treatment in early Massachusetts. Working in a decentralized manner, local communities, churches, benevolent institutions, and mutual-help organizations took primary care of the impotent poor, which was consistent with the reformed notions of charity and relief. Alleged to be responsible for many social problems, idleness was punishable as much as a sin as a crime under provincial laws, which compelled the able-bodied poor to work. Colonial policies and public institutions were less effective in dealing with the transient poor, whose numbers rose sharply from the 1750s to the 1770s. Yet these were not the desperate poor, who were looking for the first instance to attack the rich, although drastic street actions did occur from time to time.[1] Most able-bodied poor in the colony belonged to a transitory class consisting of bound-out children, indentured servants, apprentices, day laborers, refugees, non-residents, seamen, migrants, and newly arrived immigrants of low circumstances. Difficult and unstable, their lives went through a floating status for days, months, and even years, such as displaced laborers looking for the next opportunity of employment, newcomers gaining legal settlement, or bound servants finishing their terms. Yet few of them ever stuck to a synchronized situation as most poor people and families had to deal with varied circumstances at different times and places—a

---

[1] Pauline Maier, *From Resistance to Revolution: Colonial Radicals and the Development of American Opposition to Britain, 1765-1776* (New York: Random House, 1973). Dirk Hoerder, *Crowd Action in Revolutionary Massachusetts, 1765-1780* (New York: Academic Press, 1977). William Pencak, "Ebenezer Mackintosh," in Lawrence Block, ed., *Gangsters, Swindlers, Killers, and Thieves: The Lives and Crimes of Fifty American Villains* (New York: Oxford University Press, 2004), 141-45. Additional food riots (1710, 1713, 1737) and anti-impressment riots (1741, 1747) can be found in Jack Tager, *Boston Riots: Three Centuries of Social Violence* (Boston: Northeastern University Press, 2001).

Conclusion

condition least conducive to a shared experience or a common ideology.[2] Many warning-out records registered a pattern of local and regional migratory volatilities. The commotions and movements during this transitional stage suggested both the social predicaments those domestic migrants were facing on the one hand and the personal struggles they were encountering on the other. Not entirely free from individual frustration and discontent, they as a group also had an acute need and strong desire for change. What kept them on the move was not how to stay at the same place as they had been in the past, but how to seek new opportunities to improve their lives elsewhere in the future.

Poverty was never predestined to mean failure nor mobility success. Despite the fact that the minimum cost of living was attainable for most single working adults, the despondent subsistence and insecurity forced the lower social strata to improve their lot, even though industry and frugality did not always bring about wealth and prosperity. What most poor people experienced during this period was neither a doomed failure nor a promised success, but a strenuous and prolonged fight between poverty and mobility. Driven by despair, striving for hope, and frequently shifting between the two ends, their constant exertions mixed poverty with mobility. Such a mixing of life and death struggles resonated in the larger society where other groups could face similar situations. It was not eternal damnation in a hell of perpetual destitution or miraculous salvation under the spell of glorious fortune, but periodic swings between ever-present poverty and ever-tempting mobility that opened the possible reciprocity through which the poor and the middle classes were able to join forces.

---

[2] For a similar situation in a vastly changed modern environment see Stanley Aronowitz's extensive studies based on his personal experience and insight, *False Promises: The Shaping of American Working Class Consciousness* (Durham, N. C.: Duke University Press, 1992).

Conclusion

The American Revolution clearly involved such a powerful reciprocity, galvanizing both the poor and the middle classes whose collective efforts propelled the struggle for independence to success, although their class distinctions evidently existed and never disappeared before or since.

The alignment and realignment that the poor chose greatly influenced the outcome of the American Revolution and beyond. Alternately stereotyped as lazy, vile, or violent, most of the poor were nevertheless neither helpless victims of low circumstances nor passive recipients of charity and relief. The floating nature of poverty also shaped a new society in which the lower sorts were as ambitious about upward mobility as many others in the community, which gradually learned to accept the populous actions as a common form of protest. Poverty did widen and deepen as the eighteenth century came to a close, yet Massachusetts did not experience a class war—perhaps not because the gap was negligible, but because those frequent undulating moves between poverty and mobility outran potential extremities.[3] In other words, the middle class, rising against those who had mistreated them, was frequently in need of help from those below them while members of the lower classes and the poor, striving for a better future, were as willing and determined as anyone to transform their destinies into one of those above them.

---

[3] A classical pattern of class war stresses the uncompromising divide between two extremities which often take the form of two classes between the haves and the have-nots, or between the rich and the poor. Peter Novick recounted Marxist influences on American historiography in *That Noble Dream: The "Objectivity Question" and the American Historical Profession* (Cambridge, UK: Cambridge University Press, 1988), 415-68. For recent discussions about class in early America see Greg Nobles, "Class," in Daniel Vickers, ed., *A Companion to Colonial America* (Malden, Mass.: Blackwell Publishers, 2003), 259-87; The special issue on "Class and Early America," *William and Mary Quarterly*, 3d ser., 63 (2006), *passim*; Michael A. McDonnell, *The Politics of War: Race, Class, and Conflict in Revolutionary Virginia* (Chapel Hill: University of North Carolina Press, 2007); Simon Middleton and Billy G. Smith, eds., *Class Matters: Early North America and the Atlantic World* (Philadelphia: University of Pennsylvania Press, 2008).

Biographies

Abraham Aldrich
Born in 1743, Abraham Aldrich was the son of Noah and Sarah (Fletcher) Aldrich of Uxbridge, Worcester County. Sarah died in 1751, and Noah married Rachel Thayer of Mendon in 1753. Ten years later, Noah Aldrich, wife Rachel, and children Abraham, Jesse, and Noah moved from Uxbridge to Mendon, where the town authority warned them.

Abraham Aldrich married Levina Taft of Uxbridge at Mendon in 1768. He enlisted for Mendon during the revolution. He was a private in Captain Andrew Peter's company, Colonel Joseph Read's regiment, serving more than three months in 1775. He joined the Continental Army from the first company of Mendon for the term of three years until 1780. He was reported deceased in August or September 1777.

John Atkinson
The son of John and Mary Atkinson, John Atkinson was born at East Haddam, Hartford (later Middlesex) County, Connecticut, in 1765. The family soon came to Massachusetts, and town authorities of Harvard, Worcester County, warned the parents and their children John and Mary in 1767.

Several years later, they moved to Boston, where Robert Love, in May 1772, warned John Atkinson, wife Mary, and children John, Rebeckah, Seth, and Joseph from Sudbury, Middlesex County. The authority of Bridgewater, Plymouth

County, also warned the family twice in early 1775. The family subsequently moved to Cambridge for a few months, as the son John later recalled, and then moved to Pelham, Hampshire County. At the age of sixteen, he joined the Continental Army as a resident of Pelham for three years in 1781. He was described as a farmer who was five feet tall and of light complexion and light hair. A few years after the war, he moved to the part of New Salem that later became Prescott, Hampshire County. He applied for and received a federal pension in 1832.

Jacob Baker
Born in 1744, Jacob Baker was the son of Jacob and Grace Baker of Concord, Middlesex County. He lived in Lincoln and married Hannah Ball in 1770. They had a son, also named Jacob, in February 1771. The family moved to Weston and stayed at Elizabeth Hager's house, but was warned by town authorities in April 1771.

Jacob became a private in Captain William Smith's company, Colonel Abijah Pierce's regiment, which marched on the alarm of April 19, 1775. He served for four days.

Elijah Ball
The son of Phenias and Martha Ball, Elijah Ball was born at Holden, Worcester County, in 1748. Lancaster authorities warned him, indicating that he traveled from Shrewsbury, about 12 miles south of Lancaster.

Enlisted for Lancaster, he was a private in Captain Benjamin Houghton's company, Colonel John Whitcomb's regiment, which marched on the alarm of April 19, 1775, to Cambridge, serving 9½ days. He again served as a sergeant for three months from September to November 1777.

His older brother Daniel (b. 1742) fought in the war for Shrewsbury. He was a private in Captain Robert Andrew's company, which marched on the alarm of April 19, 1775, from

Shrewsbury to Cambridge, serving nine days. He also served in Captain Job Cushing's company, Colonel Jonathan Ward's regiment, for three months from August to October 1775.

Both Elijah and Daniel received veteran pensions. Daniel died in 1830 and Elijah in 1834.

John Banks

An orphan at the Almshouse in Boston, John Banks was born in 1745. He was bound out to Andrew Adams, the housewright of Grafton, Worcester County, in 1759. He was to receive two suits and £13 6s. 8d. at the end of his terms in 1766 when he reached twenty-one years of age. He went with his new employer Nathaniel Sartell (or Sartle) Prentiss, in late 1774 or early 1775, to Alstead, Cheshire County, New Hampshire, where he became a resident.

Hearing of the battle at Lexington on April 19, 1775, he went down to Cambridge and enlisted in the same month. He was a private in Captain Luke Drury's company, Colonel Jonathan Ward's regiment, serving for eight months. In 1777 he served for more than a month in Captain Webb's company at Ticonderoga. He also served as a private for more than nine months in the New Hampshire Line.

He married Susan (in her pension application but otherwise also Susanna or Susannah) Prentiss, the eldest daughter of Nathaniel Prentiss, at Alstead on July 25, 1776. They raised a large family of eleven children. His eldest son Nathaniel Prentiss Banks (b. 1783) was the father of General Nathaniel Sartell Prentiss Banks of Waltham, Massachusetts, who was a local hero in the nineteenth century. John Banks died at Alstead on February 2, 1824. His widow applied for a federal pension in 1837 when she was seventy-six years old. It was granted at the rate of $31.38 per year for seven years from 1831 to September 4, 1837; she received a sum of $219.66.

Ephraim Barker

Ephraim Barker was born on February 28, 1759, in Pomfret, Connecticut, to Ephraim and Hannah (Crow) Barker.

A laborer by occupation, he joined the revolution as a private from Sudbury, Middlesex County and marched in Captain Joseph Smith's company, Colonel James Barrett's regiment, on the Lexington and Concord alarm of April 19, 1775. Beginning in 1776, he served as a corporal in the Continental Army for six years in the Revolutionary War. Five feet eight inches tall, he had light complexion and dark hair. He was honorably discharged by General George Washington on June 10, 1783.

He participated in Shays's Rebellion, took an oath of allegiance in 1787, and marked an "x" under his name.

He later moved several times. At the age of 59, he applied for a federal government pension on April 21, 1818, from Buffalo, Niagara County, New York. He was able to sign the petition this time and was granted a pension at the rate of $8 per month. Two years later, he petitioned again. He listed his belongings valued at $112, including a mare and a colt, two hogs and two pigs, one old wagon, one old sleigh, one plow, one kettle, one pot, and some knives and forks. He stated, however, that he was "indebted to individuals in about the sum of three hundred and twenty dollars," and that a weak shoulder and pain in the heart prevented him from working in the fields. He was thus unable to support himself.

On September 5 or 6, 1817, he married Rebecca Lush by common law in Boston, Niagara County (later Erie County), New York. She brought three children Ezra, Daniel, and Phebe from a previous marriage to live with him. He died at Concord in Erie County, New York on November 1, 1826. Widow Rebecca applied for a pension in McHenry County, Illinois, on July 27, 1855, when she was eighty-four years old. Her application was granted at the rate of $96 a year.

Biographies

Jonathan Barrett

Born in Shirley, Middlesex County, on November 13, 1757, Jonathan Barrett was the youngest son of Samuel and Rebeckeh Barrett's six children. Moving to Lunenburg, Worcester County, the family was warned by town authorities first in May 1760 and again in May 1763.

Serving for Lunenburg, Jonathan Barrett enlisted in the Continental Army in Captain Joseph Bellow's company, 8th Worcester County regiment, in 1778 for the term of three years. He also served as a private in Captain Sylvanus Smith's company, Colonel Timothy Bigelow's regiment, for three years, beginning in January 1780.

A resident of Leominster, his brother Samuel (b. 1752) enlisted for six months to reinforce the Continental Army in 1780. He was described as being five feet seven inches tall and of ruddy complexion.

Jonathan married Phoebe Warner and moved to Lancaster, Worcester County. In 1818, he applied for and received a federal pension at the rate of $80 a year. He died in 1849, at the age of 92. His descendants were recognized by the Daughters of the American Revolution.

Benjamin Barton

Born in 1761, Benjamin Barton was the son of Timothy and Hepzibath Barton of Charlton, Worcester County. His mother died in 1766, and he went to Leicester, where the town authority warned him in 1767.

He enlisted for Leicester during the revolution as a private in Captain March Chase's company, Colonel Nathan Sparhawk's regiment, for more than two months in 1778.

Phineas Barton

Born in 1752, Phineas Barton was the son of John Barton and Abigail (Dana) Barton of Oxford, Worcester County.

He married Elizabeth Hasey of Leicester in 1772. They moved from Charlton to Leicester, where the town authority warned them and their son Elijah in 1773. Phineas enlisted for Leicester as a private in Captain Thomas Newhall's company, which marched to Cambridge on the alarm of April 19, 1775. He served 9½ days.

He died at Leicester in 1827. His descendants were recognized by the Daughters of the American Revolution.

Humphrey Biglow

Humphrey Biglow was born in 1761, the only son of Samuel and Phebe Biglow of Shrewsbury, Worcester County.

He first joined the fight for independence in December 1776 and then enlisted five more times. He was a private in Captain Moses Harrington's company, Colonel Nicholas Dike's regiment, serving for two months and twenty-eight days in 1777. He served again in June 1777 for one month, in September 1777 for three months, in October 1779 for three months, in August 1780 for three months, and in September 1781 for three months.

He participated in Shays's Rebellion and signed an oath of allegiance in 1787.

He married Hannah Whipple, also of Shrewsbury, in Grafton on October 26, 1791. He applied for a federal pension in 1832, which was granted at $53.33 a year. He died on October 2, 1842.

Jacob Black

Born in December 1752, Jacob Black was the youngest son of Daniel and Sarah (Symonds) Black of Boxford, Essex County. In May 1763, almost a year after the family moved to Holden, Worcester County, the parents and their five children John, Lydia, Daniel, Jacob, and Abigail were warned by town authorities.

All three sons participated in the American Revolution, serving for Holden. Jacob was a private in Captain James Davis's company, Colonel Ephraim Doolittle's regiment, which marched on the alarm of April 19, 1775. He was a corporal, serving eight months in Captain John Jones's company of the same regiment later that year during the siege of Boston.

Daniel (bap. 1750) was a private in Major Paul Raymond's company, 1st Worcester Co. regiment, which marched on the alarm of April 19, 1775, to Cambridge. He served briefly, for only 3½ days.

John (bap. 1743), the oldest brother, was a corporal in Captain James Davis's company, Colonel Benjamin Flagg's regiment, which marched to Hadley on August 19, 1777, on an alarm, serving five days. He served again in 1779 and 1782.

Jacob lived at Holden until 1789, when he moved to Berlin, Washington County, Vermont. He lived there until 1823, when he moved to Marshfield in the same county. He applied for and received a federal pension of $29.33 a year in 1832.

William Bogle
Born on March 30, 1757, William Bogle was the younger of two sons of John and Mary (Hunkins) Bogle of Oxford, Worcester County.

In 1772, Weston authorities warned John Bogle, wife, and three children Thomas, William, and Hannah from Oxford, whose economic circumstances were described as unknown.

William served for Oxford as a private in Captain John Town's company, which marched on the alarm of April 19, 1775, to Roxbury. He enlisted again in Captain William Campbell's company, Colonel Ebenezer Learned's regiment, later that year for more than three months. He also served for Newton with a group of men enlisted from Middlesex County, in Captain Joseph Fuller's company, Colonel Samuel Thatcher's regiment, for the term of nine months from the time of their arrival at Fishkill on June 20, 1778. At that time he was described as twenty-one years old and five feet eight inches tall.

His older brother Thomas Bogle (b. 1755), Oxford (also given Newton), was a private in Captain William Campbell's company, Colonel Ebenezer Learned's regiment, serving for three months and one week in 1775. He again served briefly in 1776, 1780, and then for two years from 1781 to 1782, when he was promoted to corporal. He married Elizabeth Fuller of Newton on September 15, 1778, and they had eight children. He and his family settled at Wardsboro, Windham County, Vermont, where he applied for and received a pension of $8 per month in 1818. He died on August 16, 1826. His widow continued to receive the pension and died on August 22, 1839.

William Bogle settled at Weston after the war. He married Lucy Tilton at Weston on September 1, 1786. He received a federal pension of $80 a year in 1832. At the time of his death on October 17, 1839, his properties were valued at $4,653, including his homestead with the buildings and 196 acres of land at $4,000. His personal debts and funeral expenses amounted to $635.16. The widow received a pension of $65.21 per annum from 1844. When she died two years later, she left an estate of $1,015.75 and a total debt (including her funeral costs) of $1186.45.

Nathan Boynton

Nathan Boynton was born on October 16, 1757. His father was Jacob Boynton, of Waltham, and his mother was Mary, whose family name was not known, although she owned the church covenant of Waltham in October 1755. After the couple had four children Elizabeth (b. 1756), Nathan, Molly (b. 1762), and Jacob (b. 1765), the father died and his widow married Samuel Hager of Watertown in 1768.

When Nathan was two years old, Weston selectmen warned him, his mother Mary, and his older sister Elizabeth.

They were poor and townsman Braddyll Smith took them into his house.

A few years later, Elisha Hobbs of Weston took into his house Nathan Boynton of Watertown under low circumstances on July 9, 1765. This was about three months before his father's death. Nathan was eight years old.

After his mother remarried Samuel Hager, Nathan again showed on Weston's warning-out records, which stated that Isaac Hager took him into his house on April 1, 1771. Nathan was from Waltham, serving as Isaac Cory's apprentice. He was fourteen years old.

The outbreak of the fight at Lexington and Concord drew the young Nathan, then eighteen, into action. He was a private in Captain Samuel Lamson's company, which marched on the alarm of April 19, 1775. He served two days. He also served during the siege of Boston in Captain Abijah Child's company, Lieutenant Colonel William Bond's (later Gardner's) regiment at Prospect Hill later in the same year.

Nathan Boynton married Beulah Eaton of Sudbury, Middlesex County, on December 31, 1778. The couple had two sons Nathan (b. c1779) and Perkins (b. 1782).

Like his great-great-grandfather John of Rowley, Nathan Boynton was by trade a tailor. He died before 1801. His descendants were recognized by the Daughters of the American Revolution.

Ichabod Bozworth
The son of Ichabod and Joanna (Cushman) Bozworth, Ichabod Bozworth was born in Cumberland, Rhode Island, on February 17, 1749. Coming from Bellingham, Norfolk County, he, his (first) wife Chloe (Cook), and son Joseph were warned by Wrentham authorities in 1771.

He served as a private during the Revolutionary War, first in Captain Andrew Peters's company, Colonel Joseph

Read's regiment, in 1775, serving three months. In 1778 he enlisted in the Continental Army and joined Captain Japhet Daniels's company, Colonel Thomas Nixon's regiment, for three years. He was described as five feet eight inches tall, of ruddy complexion, with brown hair and light eyes. He was discharged on January 1, 1784, and received an $80 gratuity for serving during the war.

He married his second wife, Ruth Bradley (b. 1758) of Rehoboth, in 1785 and had seven children. He received a bounty land of 100 acres in 1793. Credited for a total of seven years in service, he was granted a pension of $8 per month in 1818, when he was a resident of Bellingham. He wrote in his petition that "I am in reduced circumstances in life & have need of assistance from the Country I served." He held no real property in 1820 and his personal estate totaled $16.10, including one chest and one chest of drawers, two tables, seven chairs, a brass kettle, some glass ware, earth ware, and cooking ware. He died in Franklin, Norfolk County, on November 16, 1820. His widow moved to Upton, Worcester County, and received a pension in the same amount or $96 per annum from 1848 to 1850, when she died in Grafton, Worcester County, on September 2.

Caleb Bridges

A father of three children, Caleb Bridges was from Spencer, Worcester County. He joined the American Revolution and marched as a private in Captain John Woolcott's company of rangers, responding to the alarm at Lexington and Concord on April 19, 1775. He served again in November 1775 and in 1777.

He participated in Shays's Rebellion and took an oath of allegiance in 1787, when he marked an "x" under his name. He died in Spencer in 1812.

Biographies

Thomas Burnham
Thomas Burnham was the son of Nathaniel and Elizabeth Burnham. The date and place of his birth were unclear. His family was twice warned in Worcester County. In 1766 Lunenburg warned his father Nathaniel, mother Elizabeth, him, and his siblings Ruth, John, and Job. A year later Bolton warned the family again; this time a new sibling was included on the list—Francis.

Both Thomas and his brother John served for Bolton in the war. Enlisting on April 28, 1775, Thomas was in Captain Robert Longley's company, Colonel Asa Whitcomb's regiment, for three months. Struck ill by a fever in July 1775, he was taken home in August and discharged in November. His father Nathaniel Burnham petitioned from Bolton, on March 10, 1776, asking that he be paid for expenses incurred during his son's sickness. Thomas went back into service in Captain Joseph Sargent's company, first in Colonel Josiah Whitney's regiment and then in Colonel Abijah Stearns's, in 1777, serving 67 days.

John was a private in Captain Joshua Brown's company, Colonel Timothy Bigelow's regiment, and served from May 1777 to the end of 1779. He continued to serve in the same regiment from January 1780 to May 1780, when he was described as twenty years old, five feet teen inches tall, and of light complexion. After serving in the Continental Army for another four months and twenty-seven days, he was discharged on December 8, 1780.

Peter Cary of Shrewsbury
Born in 1760, Peter Cary's parentage was not clear.

A private in Captain Moses Ashley's company, Colonel and later Brigadier General John Paterson's regiment, in December 1775, he participated in the expedition to Canada. In a failed deployment in 1776, he was captured and kept as a prisoner for two months. He was then sent to Montreal and

Halifax, where he was put on a ship that arrived at Boston on July 4, 1777. He was finally released through an exchange of captives. He was in the militia at the taking of Burgoyne and in the artillery before being taken as a prisoner at Bennington.

Suffering long after his enlistment expired, he was not formerly discharged nor was he called again to join the Continental Army. Only Captain Ashley paid him off.

He married Beulah Pratt (b. 1763) of Shrewsbury, Worcester County, where he settled. He applied for and received a federal pension in 1818. An inventory of 1820 showed that his property, valued at $108.22, included a poor old house, a barn, a cow, two tables, seven chairs, and other household items. He had a family to support and his wife was "in very low state of health." He died in 1832. His descendants were recognized by the Daughters of the American Revolution.

Peter Cary of Weston
Peter Cary was born in 1757. His parentage was not clear. Weston warned him from Natick in 1773 when Isaiah Bullard, a fence viewer, took him as an apprentice. Enlisting for Weston, Peter was a private in Captain Samuel Lamson's company, which marched on the alarm of April 19, 1775, serving two days. His master Bullard was also a private in the same company, serving three days. Peter was encamped at Prospect Hill during the siege of Boston in late 1775. Enlisting for Weston again in 1778, he served nine months from the time of his arrival at Fishkill, New York, in Captain William Weston's company, Colonel Eleazer Brooks's regiment. He was described as twenty-one years old and five feet six inches tall. The town paid him £12 for his enlistment in March and April 1778, £140 in 1779, £12 in 1782, and £13. 15s. 1d. in 1783.

Both of Isaiah Bullard's parents were from Weston. Born in 1750, he married Mary Peirce in 1771, when he began to pay a poll tax. For the next several years, he served several town offices while his properties increased. He paid a tax of more than £122 in 1778. Peter Cary was never rated.

Luke Chapin

The son of Luke and Elizabeth (Ferry) Chapin, Luke Chapin was baptized on July 18, 1762, at the First Church in Brimfield, Hampshire County.

Both father and son joined the patriotic forces during the revolution. The father was a sergeant and died at Ticonderoga on October 3, 1776. Luke Chapin served for Brimfield in the Continental Army for a term of three years in the war.

He participated in Shays's Rebellion. He signed an oath of allegiance in 1787 and identified himself as a husbandman at Palmer, Hampshire County.

Both his mother Elizabeth and aunt Abigail (Munn) were revolutionary pensioners, the latter for her deceased husband Captain Jonathan Chapin, who was the uncle of Luke Chapin.

Oliver Chickering

Born in 1753, Oliver Chickering was one of John (of Dedham) and Mary (Dewing) Chickering's seven children. He married Tabitha Hooker in 1772, perhaps at Medfield, Norfolk County. They moved to Sherborn, Middlesex County, where Oliver enlisted during the revolution.

He joined the Continental Army in 1779, when he was described as a resident of Sherborn who was twenty-six years old, five feet ten inches tall, and of light complexion (although described as having a dark complexion in another description in 1780). After serving nine months, he enlisted for six months in 1780 and was discharged at the end of the year.

Two years later, he and his family moved from Sherborn to Rutland, where the town authority warned him, wife Tabitha, and their children Oliver, Nathan, Calvin, and Betsy.

He began to draw a federal pension of $8 per month in 1818. He died at Rutland on February 21, 1831, and his wife Tabitha in 1840. Their descendants were recognized by the Daughters of the American Revolution.

Caleb Church

Born on June 3, 1746, Caleb Church was the son of Joshua and Alice (or Annis, Alles, Anna Johnson) Church, one of their eleven children. Although many of his siblings were born in Harvard, his birthplace was unclear.

Records show that the Churches were warned numerous times at various places in Worcester County from 1764 to 1766:

At Templeton, on May 8, 1764, Joshua Church, his wife Alice, children Joshua, Silas, and Huldah from Harvard since May 1, 1764, were warned. On the same day at Templeton, Caleb Church, from Harvard since May 1, 1764, was warned.

At Templeton, on May 21, 1765, Caleb Church's wife Elizabeth Church, from Bolton since April 29, 1765, was warned.

At Lancaster, on January 7, 1766, Caleb Church from Harvard, his wife Elizabeth, from Bolton, their child Hannah from Templeton, were warned.

At Bolton, on May 11, 1766, Caleb Church, wife Elizabeth since April 7, 1766, and child Hannah, from Lancaster since May 1765, were warned.

At Harvard, on August 19, 1766, Caleb Church, wife Elizabeth, and daughter Hannah from Bolton since June, 1766, were warned.

During the American Revolution, Caleb Church, a resident of Oakham, Worcester County, enlisted as a militia man in April 1775 and again in the spring of 1776 for five months. Records also show that he served in the Continental

Army for nine months before he enlisted for another nine months from his arrival at Fishkill on June 7, 1778, in Captain John Crawford's company, Colonel James Convers's regiment. He was described as being thirty-two years old, five feet ten inches tall, and of light complexion.

His younger brother Silas Church, born in Bolton, Worcester County, in 1751, also participated in the revolution. A resident of Templeton, he served, as a private in Captain Ezekiel Knowlton's company, Colonel Nathan Sparhawk's regiment, which marched on the alarm of April 19, 1775, to Cambridge. He also enlisted during the siege of Boston and was stationed at Winter Hill. He enlisted again in 1777, marched on an alarm of Bennington, and was present at Saratoga. Silas Church married Mary Osgood of Templeton on November 25, 1771, in Lancaster. They had three daughters and seven sons at Templeton, where both parents died—she in 1817, at 66, and he in 1845, at 94.

Caleb Church married three times. His first wife was Tamar Warner; they were married on May 11, 1762, in Harvard. The seventeen-year-old Tamar died four days after her infant died in February 1763. He then married Elizabeth Walker of Bolton on July 11, 1764, in Bolton. They had three daughters and five sons. His last marriage was with Hannah Pool, who died in March 1837 at the age of 93.

Caleb Church bought 30 acres of land in Oakham in 1777. He bought land in Ashfield, Hampshire (later Franklin) County, in 1785 and was counted in the census there in 1790. His son Seth built a house in Ashfield and served as a selectman and representative for the town.

Caleb Church was not on the tax roll for 1793. He applied for a pension in 1818, claiming poor health and the inability of self-support. His personal properties were valued at $16.60 in 1823. He could not sign his name.

Biographies

Caleb Church died in Ashfield in June 1827 at the age of eighty-one.

Giles Church

Born in Amherst in 1754, Giles Church was the son of Samuel and Margaret (Smith) Church.

During the Revolutionary War, Giles Church enlisted as a private in Captain Reuben Dickinson's company, Colonel Benjamin Ruggles Woodbridge's regiment, on May 8, 1775. He served for three months. He rejoined Captain Reuben Dickinson's company, Colonel Elisha Porter's regiment, in July 1777. He marched to Moses Creek and served thirty-eight days. The last time he served again in the same company and regiment was in 1778.

He participated in Shays's Rebellion and signed an oath of allegiance in 1787.

A carpenter and farmer, he had thirteen acres of crops by 1780 and was an active miller after 1800. He married Lois Billing of Amherst, and the couple had eleven children. He died in Amherst in 1807.

Thomas Cleland

Thomas Cleland was born in 1747; his parentage is not clear. He was warned by Lancaster authorities in 1765, indicating that he was from Colchester, Connecticut.

Enlisting for Lancaster in April 1775, he was a private in Captain Ephraim Richardson's company, Colonel Asa Whitcomb's regiment. He was a corporal, serving for twenty-nine months from April 1777 until the end of 1779, when he was described as a resident of Cochesett who was thirty-two years old, five feet four inches tall, of dark complexion with black hair and black eyes. He enlisted as a sergeant to serve for the duration of the war, starting in December 1779. He received pay until March 1781, but was reported to have deserted on March 29.

Ebenezer Cooley
The son of Ebenezer and Mary (Barnes) Cooley, Ebenezer Cooley was born on March 3, 1737, in Brimfield, Hampshire County. He joined the Revolutionary War as a private and marched to Bennington in Captain John Kirkland's company, Colonel John Dicenson's regiment, on the alarm of August 16, 1777, serving eight days. He also served briefly in Captain Abraham Salisbury's company, which went to Pittsford, Vermont, in October 1777.

He participated in Shays's Rebellion and signed an oath of allegiance in 1787.

He married Lydia Russell in Greenwich, Hampshire County, on January 9, 1760. He died in Lebanon, Madison County, New York, on April 1, 1817. His descendants were recognized by the Daughters of the American Revolution.

James Cowan, Jr.
Born in 1761, James Cowan, Jr., was the youngest son of James and Margaret (Hunter) Cowan of Pelham, Hampshire County.

At sixteen, he was a private in David Cowen's company, 4th Hampshire regiment, which marched on an alarm in Bennington on August 17, 1777. He served six days, including travel home.

He participated in Shays's Rebellion and signed an oath of allegiance in 1787.

Elisha Cox
Born in Dorchester in 1721/22, Elisha Cox was a servant of Ebenezer Hobbs in Weston before he came of age. He married Anna Warren, daughter of Jonathan and Sarah Warren of Watertown, in 1741. The couple owned the covenant of the

church in Waltham and gave birth to nine children: Anne (b. 1741), Esther (b. 1743), Sybil (b. 1745), Elisha (b. 1748), Ezekiel (b. 1750), Eli (b. 1753), Jonathan (b. 1755), Sarah (b. 1759), and Artemas (b. 1762).

In 1752, the couple and their five children moved from Waltham to Weston, but officials there warned them out and removed them back to Waltham. Furthermore, a boundary dispute between the two communities led to a highly charged contest, which caught the Cox family in the mix. In 1761, Waltham selectmen warned the couple and their eight children. Both Waltham and Weston authorities insisted that the other community was the legal abode of the Cox family and hence responsible for any relief of its support. The Cox family was hopelessly entangled, and the case finally went up to the Middlesex County Court, which ruled that—although some thought that the Cox family was living on the Waltham border of Weston—they were in fact living on the Weston border of Waltham. They were, therefore, legal residents of Weston.

The legal trouble did not dampen the Cox family's patriotism. Three of its members fought for American independence, and one of them died for the cause.

Enlisting for Waltham, the eldest son Elisha Cox was a sergeant in Captain Abraham Peirce's (Waltham) company, which was called out by Colonel Thomas Gardner on the alarm of April 19, 1775, to march to Lexington and Concord. He served for three days while his company served as guards until Saturday, the fourth day after the fight at Concord. Described as six feet tall, he was sergeant in Captain Abijah Childs's company, Colonel Thomas Gardner's regiment, from August until the end of December 1775, serving ninety-eight days during the siege of Boston.

He was an ensign in Colonel Gardner's (37th) regiment the following year. He died of smallpox on Isle Aux Noix during the expedition against Canada. In a letter dated "Crown

Point, July 11, 1776," Colonel William Bond wrote, "Ensign Cox, a good officer, died June 25."

Elisha's brother Ezekiel Cox enlisted for Harvard. He was a private in Captain Jonathan Davis's company, Colonel John Whitcomb's regiment, which marched on the alarm of April 19, 1775, to Cambridge. He left the place of rendezvous on April 26, serving seven days and being reported as having deserted.

Enlisting for Harvard again, Ezekiel Cox was a private in Captain Benjamin Brown's company, Colonel Michael Jackson's regiment. The Continental Army pay accounts indicated that he served from April 1, 1777, to December 1779. His residence was Harvard, and his service was credited to the town. After his enlistment of three years, he continued to serve in Captain Thomas Hartshorn's company, Colonel Jackson's regiment from January 1 to 28, 1780.

At the age of 16, Artemas, Elisha's youngest brother, enlisted on April 1, 1778, for three months. He was a guard in Cambridge in Captain Daniel Harrington's company, Colonel Jonathan Reed's regiment (also given as on a list of men under Major Samuel Lamson, of Weston, detached from Colonel Eleazer Brooks's regiment to relieve the guards in Cambridge). Thereafter, he enlisted three more times: first, from October 3 to December 3, 1778, for service in Rhode Island; second, in Captain Samuel Heald's company, Colonel John Jacobs' regiment, from September 30 to November 30, 1779; and finally, in Captain Abraham Anderson's company and Colonel Cyprain How's Middlesex regiment, from July 27 to October 30, 1780.

Father Elisha Cox died in 1788. Most of his children either married or left Weston. Artemas Cox moved to Wawkeeg, a part of Bowdoin in Sagadahoc County, Maine, but promised to provide support, clothing, and maintenance for his mother Anna Cox, who still lived in Weston. On October 29, 1800, he

Biographies

signed a bond of $800 to Weston to indemnify the town from any public expense in the support of his mother for life.

Ensign Cox married Sarah Bemis in 1768 and had a son named Elisha, who later became a resident of Marlborough. He married Molly Bruce in 1791. They named their first son Elisha. Ensign Elisha Cox's descendants have been recognized by the Daughters of the American Revolution.

Thomas Craige
Born on February 14, 1754, Thomas Craige was an orphan at the Almshouse in Boston. At five years of age, he was bound out to Samuel Birdy, who was to provide two suits at the end of his terms in 1771 when Thomas turned twenty-one. The master, a peruke maker of Worcester, was killed during the French and Indian War. Craige then moved to live in Northampton, where he later enlisted during the Revolutionary War. He first served in Captain Jonathan Wales's company of militia for five months starting in June 1776. He also volunteered in Captain Jonathan Stearns's company, Colonel John Dickinson's regiment, from July to August 1777, marching with his company on an alarm at Ticonderoga. He responded to the order issued by Sheriff Elisha Porter to join Captain Hezekiah Russell's (second) company of volunteers, Second Hampshire County regiment, which went against the insurgents at Springfield, Hadley, and Northampton in 1782.

He lived in Northampton until 1783, when he moved to Westminster. He moved again to Windsor County, Vermont, in 1802. He applied for a federal pension in 1833 when he was seventy-nine years old. Credited as a sergeant serving for seven months during the war, he received a yearly pension of $35.

Moses Dickinson
Born on January 22, 1718, Moses Dickinson was the son of Nathaniel and Hannah (Luke) Dickinson of Sunderland,

Hampshire County. Moses married Thankful Smith of Sunderland and moved to Amherst by 1745, settling on a small farm of nine acres. His estate grew steadily and reached 40 acres on the eve of the revolution. A respectable citizen in the community, he was elected town meeting moderator several times during the 1760s and selectmen no less than a dozen times. He was a representative to the General Court in 1775 and 1777, when he acquired the title of esquire.

He and his wife had ten children, three of whom served in the revolution. Born in 1749, their son Moses, Jr., had a small farm of thirteen acres and two oxen in 1773. He served as a sergeant in a detachment of Captain Thomas W. Foster's company of matrosses commanded by Lieutenant James Hendrick in Colonel Ruggles Woodbridge's regiment, which marched to Cambridge on April 20, 1775, in response to the Lexington alarm of the day earlier. He served again in 1775 and 1778. He died probably in 1778, and his widow Mary Boltwood subsequently married Daniel Cooley, a lawyer, in 1782.

Son Aaron (b. 1753) was in Captain James Hendrick's company at Charlestown in January 1776. He was also a corporal in Captain Reuben Dickinson's company, Colonel Elisha Porter's regiment, in 1778.

Son Medad (b. 1755) was also a private in Captain Thomas W. Foster's company of matrosses, Colonel Ruggles Woodbridge's regiment, which marched on April 20, 1775, in response to the Lexington alarm a day earlier. Joining Captain Thomas Waite Foster's train of artillery, Colonel Woodbridge's regiment, Medad served again in late April the same year. He also enlisted in Captain Reuben Dickinson's company, Colonel Elisha Porter's regiment, in 1778.

Son Elijah (b. 1760) was a private in Captain John Thompson's company, Colonel Leonard's regiment, from May to July 1777. His company marched to reinforce the Northern Army. He soon went back to serve in August the same year as a private in a company commanded by Lieutenant Noah Dickinson, Colonel Elisha Porter's regiment, which marched to New Providence on an alarm. Enlisting in Captain Reuben Dickinson's company, Colonel Elisha Porter's regiment in late 1777, he marched to Stillwater on an alarm. He brought his military experience back to town after he retired from active service. He became a militia ensign in 1790, a captain in 1795, a major in 1796, and a colonel by 1800.

For his part of involvement, father Moses was credited for civil and patriotic service during the war. He (as well as son Medad) was active in Shays's Rebellion and took an oath of allegiance in 1787. Yet after supporting a large family for many years, he grew older and his property declined from the height of 45 acres of developed and 240 acres of undeveloped land in 1780 to a 30-acre farm and 35 acres of undeveloped land in 1795. He died on April 9, 1803. His descendants as well as those of son Elijah's were recognized by the Daughters of the American Revolution.

Waitstill Dickinson

Son of John and Esther Dickinson, Waitstill Dickinson was born in Amherst in 1750.

He became a private in Captain Reuben Dickinson's company of Minutemen, Colonel Benjamin Ruggles Woodbridge's regiment, which marched on the Lexington and Concord alarm of April 19, 1775. He served again in 1776 and 1778.

He participated in Shays's Rebellion and signed an oath of allegiance in 1787. A respectable citizen in the community, he doubled his estate from 20 acres in 1780 to a 40-acre farm and 140 acres of undeveloped land in 1790. He married Lucretia Montague probably in 1780 and they had five children. He died in 1792 at Amherst.

Biographies

Jacob Edson

Born in 1765, Jacob Edson was one of the eight children of Jacob and Betty (Packard) Edson of Bridgewater, Plymouth County.

Jacob was a private in Captain Josiah Hayden's company, Colonel Balley's regiment, which marched on the Lexington and Concord alarm of April 19, 1775. He also served several days in early 1776.

He participated in Shays's Rebellion and signed an oath of allegiance in 1787.

John Edwards Ely

The son of Caleb and Mary Ely, John Edwards Ely was born in 1745 at West Springfield. He was a private in Captain Enoch Chapin's company of Minutemen, who marched on April 20, 1775, in response to the Lexington and Concord alarm the day earlier. He enlisted on April 28 the same year and served for more than three months. He joined the Continental Army from January 1 to December 31, 1780. His finally served one more time in June 1782.

He participated in Shays's Rebellion and signed an oath of allegiance in 1787.

He applied for a federal government pension on April 17, 1818, at West Springfield, Hamden County, and was granted one of $8 per month.

Samuel Fellows, Jr.

Samuel Fellows, Jr., was born in Harvard, Worcester County, on February 13, 1739. He was the eldest son of Samuel and Eunice (Heald) Fellows's eleven children.

The family moved to Shelburne, where the father became first deacon of the Congregational Church in 1770. A representative to the General Court, he performed patriotic service, which was later recognized by the Daughters of the

Biographies

American Revolution. Five of his children served during the revolution, all enlisting for Shelburne.

Samuel Fellows, Jr., enlisted on May 10, 1775, and served for two months as a private in Captain Agripps Wells's company, Colonel Asa Whitcomb's regiment. He enlisted again in February, July, and September 1777. He was five feet five inches tall and had a light complexion. His last enlistment was in July 1780, at the age of 42.

His younger brother John (b. 1751) was a private in Captain Oliver Avery's company of Minutemen, who marched on April 21, 1775, in response to the alarm two days earlier. Enlisting again later that year, he also served almost half a year in three separate tours in 1777. Some twenty years younger than his brother Samuel, Solomon, at nineteen, enlisted to serve for three months in 1780. He had a light complexion and was five feet four inches tall.

Twin brothers William and Willis (b. 1758) served as privates in Captain Samuel Taylor's company, Colonel Nicholas Dike's regiment, in September 1776. Both were stationed at Dorchester Heights during the siege of Boston. Both participated in the battle at Ticonderoga. Both also enlisted in the Continental Army for a term of three years from March 1778 to 1781.

The boys' father died in 1781, and their mother died in 1795 at the age of seventy-eight.

Samuel Fellows, Jr., participated in Shays's Rebellion and took an oath of allegiance in 1787, when he marked an "x" under his name. He married Mary Blodgett in Shelburne in 1763. He fell down the cellar stairs and died on December 15, 1823.

John was a carpenter, acquired the title of gentleman, and served as a representative to the General Court. He married Mary (Molly) Pool in 1778. Solomon also became a deacon and served as a selectman and assessor. He died in 1816.

Three brothers, William, Willis, and Thomas, owned saw and grist mills in Shelburne. In 1805, Willis sold 111 acres of land and a saw mill. He moved to Bloomfield, Greene County, Indiana, in 1825, while his twin brother William was in Watertown, Jefferson County, New York. William married Aliff Peck in 1783. Willis married Sarah Hart in 1781. He died at the age of eighty-two in Crawford County, Illinois, in 1840.

Descendants of Samuel, John, and Willis were recognized by the Daughters of the American Revolution.

Jonathan Felt
Born in 1747, Jonathan Felt was the eldest son of Jonathan and Lovel or Lovewell (Welds) Felt of Dedham. The father was born in Rumney Marsh (later Chelsea), but the couple was from Attleborough, Bristol County, where they married in 1746. Dedham warned them when they came to lodge at Ebenezer Everett's house shortly after their son was born. They gave birth to nine more children at Dedham, but Lovel died suddenly in childbed in 1764, at about thirty-six years of age. The father married again the following year, and the son left for Wrentham, where the authority warned him in 1769.

Becoming a resident of Wrentham, Jonathan Felt was a private in Captain Oliver Pond's company of Minutemen, who marched on the alarm of April 19, 1775, serving eight days. Rising gradually through the ranks, he was a corporal in Colonel Joseph Read's regiment from May to November 1775; a first lieutenant in Colonel William Shepard's regiment from January 1777; and a captain lieutenant and then a captain in 1780. In May 1782 he was transferred to Lieutenant Colonel John Brook's regiment, where he served until June 1783.

He married Eunice Brastow of Wrentham in 1784, and they had four children. He reported to town authority that he took in a stranger in 1796. He died at Wrentham in 1800. His descendants were recognized by the Daughters of the American Revolution.

Eleazer Fisher

Born on July 5, 1759, Eleazer Fisher was the son of Eleazer and Mary (Maccany) Fisher. The family was warned by Wrentham authorities in 1767.

Eleazer, Jr., was a matross in Captain Perez Cushing's company for several months during the siege of Boston in 1776 and in the 9th company, Colonel Edward Crafts's artillery regiment, for more than six months from November 1776 to May 1777. He enlisted again as a private in Captain Asa Fairbanks's company, Colonel Benjamin Hawes's regiment, in October 1777 and in Captain John Metcalf's company, 4th Suffolk County regiment, which marched to Rhode Island to respond to an alarm on July 28, 1780.

He married Susanna Bowditch at Wrentham on February 17, 1789, and died at Franklin, Norfolk County, on June 3, 1818. His widow, a resident of Franklin, received a federal pension of $34.57 per annum in 1848.

Timothy Flagg

Born in Waltham, Middlesex County, on March 10, 1740, Timothy Flagg was the younger son of Bezaleel and Susannah Flagg. In less than a decade, both parents died, one in 1745 and the other four years later. Timothy Flagg married Elizabeth Pierce in 1761, and the couple moved to Weston the next year when they were warned by town authorities.

He was a private in Captain Abraham Peirce's (Waltham) company, called out by Colonel Thomas Gardner on the alarm of April 19, 1775, to march to Lexington and Concord. He served three days. At five feet seven inches tall, he served again later that year at Prospect Hill during the siege of Boston. His company marched at the taking of Dorchester

Heights in 1776. He also enlisted from December 1776 to March 1777.

He died in or about 1790 and his descendants were recognized by the Daughters of the American Revolution.

Lemuel Gates

Lemuel Gates was born on April 29, 1758. In May 1763, the town of Lancaster, Worcester County, warned the father Stephen Gates, mother Dinah, and children Lemuel, Samuel, and Dinah. They were described as coming from Rowley, Canada.

Enlisting for Lancaster, Lemuel Gates was a fifer in Captain Abijah Wyman's company, Colonel William Prescott's regiment, in 1775. He later served in the Continental Army in 1777 for three years as a gunner. In 1780, he was a sergeant in Captain David Cook's company, 3rd Artillery regiment. He was described as five feet ten inches tall and of fair complexion.

His brother Samuel (b. 1757) also enlisted for Lancaster during the war. Described as being of fair complexion and serving as a fifer and sometimes a gunner in the same company as Lemuel, he enlisted in the Continental Army for three years in March 1777.

Lemuel Gates married Lydia Whittemore; he died on September 30, 1806, in Pennsylvania. His descendants were recognized by the Daughters of the American Revolution.

Zenas Gibbs

Born on May 3, 1757, Zenas Gibbs was the son of Clark and Hannah Gibbs of Rutland. He was warned at Holden, Worcester County, in 1765.

Enlisting for Rutland, he was a private in Captain Adam Wheeler's company, Colonel Ephraim Doolittle's regiment, during the siege of Boston at Winter Hill in 1775. He served again in 1776 and 1777. Enlisting for a term of three years, he joined Captain Wheeler's company, Colonel Thomas Nixon's regiment. He deserted twice but finally reported to duty. He was discharged on April 29, 1781.

His younger brother Frederick joined the Continental Army in 1781 for Rutland for three years. He was described as a farmer who was seventeen years old, of dark complexion, and five feet ten inches tall.

His older brother Jonas (b. 1754) served as a private in Captain David Bent's company, Colonel Nathan Sparhawk's regiment, in August 1777, and marched from Rutland to Bennington on an alarm.

After the war, Zenas Gibbs moved to Branford, Middlesex County, Connecticut, for six years, then moved to New Hartford in Oneida County, New York, where he applied for a federal pension in 1832. At about the same time Frederick Gibbs also lived in Oneida County. Zenas Gibbs died on August 14, 1840. His descendants were recognized by the Daughters of the American Revolution.

Thaddeus Gibson

The second child of Jonathan and Mary (Forristall) Gibson, Thaddeus Gibson was born at Stow, Middlesex County, in June 1753. His father died the next year, leaving no will. Thaddeus went to Holliston, Middlesex County, where his mother was from, and continued to Wrentham, Norfolk County. Authorities there warned him in 1768, and he moved ten miles west to Bellingham.

Soon after the battle at Lexington in May 1775, he enlisted for Bellingham in Captain Samuel Cobb's company, Colonel Joseph Read's regiment, and served for three months. He was a sergeant in Captain Samuel Warren's company, Colonel Joseph Read's regiment, from January 1776 to February 1777. As he recalled, "immediately after the British left Boston, [he] marched to Providence, R.I., thence to New

London, Conn., thence by water to the City of New York, thence to Fort Washington, thence to White Plains, was in the battle there; after the battle, crossed the River Hudson, marched to Trenton NJ was in the battle there; after the battle, marched to Morrisontown NJ and was there honorably dismissed, serving 6 wks after the expiration of the year."

After his discharge, Gibson lived in Milford, Worcester County, for four years. He then moved to New Hampshire and finally settled on a 300-acre farm in Henniker, Hillsborough (later Merrimack) County, in the early 1780s. He received a pension of $8 per month in 1818. In 1820 his properties included a horse, a wagon and harness, a cow, a hog, ten sheep, ten lambs, one plough, one sleigh, one chest with drawers, one old desk, ten chairs, one kettle, three axes, and sundry other household articles, totaling $120.50. His debt amounted to $147. He married twice: first to Elizabeth Summer (b. 1754), of Mendon, in Bellingham on February 2, 1778, and second to Lydia Kemp of Henniker on March 30, 1831. All nine of his children were from the first marriage. He died in Henniker on February 23, 1834. His descendants were recognized by the Daughters of the American Revolution.

Isaac Gould

In June 1773 the town of Weston, Middlesex County, warned Isaac Gould and his wife Sarah Hoar from Sudbury, where they married three months earlier. Their circumstances were not clear to Weston authorities.

Enlisting for Sudbury, Middlesex County, Isaac Gould was a private in Captain Joseph Smith's company, Colonel James Barrett's regiment, which marched on the alarm of April 19, 1775; he served three days. He also served as a gunner during the siege of Boston and as a bombardier for three months in 1777.

Biographies

He was born perhaps in 1750 and died in 1796. His descendants were recognized by the Daughters of the American Revolution.

Luther Graves
Born in Leominster on April 20, 1749, Luther Graves was one of Peter and Lydia (Heald) Graves's twelve children.

The family moved several times. In 1760, they were in Bolton, which warned the mother Lydia Graves and her four children Luther, Calvin, Elizabeth, and Lydia. Four years later, Lancaster warned Luther, who traveled from Stow, Middlesex County.

Luther settled in Lancaster, Worcester County, where he married Phoebe Jewett of Lancaster in 1772. He was a sergeant in Captain Samuel Sawyer's company of Minutemen, Colonel John Whitcomb's regiment, which marched on the alarm of April 19, 1775. He served more than three months during the siege of Boston in Captain Ephraim Richardson's company, Colonel Asa Whitcomb's regiment, in late 1775.

Enlisting for Leominster, his younger brother Calvin (b. 1754) was a private in Captain Able Wilder's company, Colonel Ephraim Doolittle's regiment, in 1775. He later served more than five months in 1776.

Luther Graves and his wife moved to Leominster, where eight of their children were born. He died of nervous fever there on August 13, 1790. His descendants were recognized by the Daughters of the American Revolution.

Daniel Harris
Born in Dorchester in July 1752, Daniel Harris was the son of Thomas and Lucy (Peirce) Harris from Watertown. Fitchburg authority warned the father, the mother, and their children Hannah, Josiah, Daniel, and Lucy in 1766.

All enlisting for Fitchburg, three of Thomas's sons fought in the American Revolution. Born in Dorchester on July 2, 1746, the eldest son Thomas, Jr., was a private in Captain Ebenezer Woods's company of Minutemen, Colonel Asa Whitcomb's regiment, which marched on the alarm of April 19, 1775, serving six days. He soon enlisted again and served for more than three months in 1775.

Daniel Harris was a private in Captain Ebenezer Bridge's company of Minutemen, Colonel John Whetcomb's regiment, which marched to Cambridge on the alarm of April 19, 1775. He served six days. He again enlisted and served three months during the siege of Boston at Prospect Hill later that year. He served for five months in 1776 and was promoted to sergeant.

As brother Thomas, Samuel Harris (b. 1749) was a private in Captain Ebenezer Wood's company of Minutemen, Colonel Asa Whitcomb's regiment, which marched on the alarm of April 19, 1775. He served five days.

Mother Lucy Harris died on January 19, 1798, at Fitchburg, where Samuel still lived in 1837. Little is known about what happened to his brother Thomas. Daniel Harris married Judith Goodall (or Goodale) in Fitchburg on June 15, 1780. They had eight daughters and four sons. He died in Fitchburg on December 16, 1820, and she died, at seventy-six, in Cambridge on May 4, 1837. Daniel Harris's descendants were recognized by the Daughters of the American Revolution.

Asa Haven

The son of Daniel and Mehetable Haven, Asa Haven was born in Framingham in Middlesex County on May 27, 1742.

Warned by the selectmen of Brookfield, Worcester County, to depart town on May 21, 1765, Asa removed to Blandford, Hampshire County, where he stayed and served in the Revolutionary War in 1777, 1777-78, and 1779-80. A private in the Continental Army, he joined Captain Lebbeus Ball's company in Colonel William Shepard's regiment. He also served in the 12th company, 3rd Hampshire County regiment, as attested by Lieutenant Samuel Sloper (as the captain) on April 6, 1779. His term of service expired in April 1780.

He participated in Shays's Rebellion and took an oath of allegiance in 1787, when he marked an "x" under his name.

His two older brothers also left Framingham. Coming to Oxford, Worcester County, in August 1758, Ebenezer Haven, his wife, and family were warned to depart on May 9, 1759. Another brother Daniel married Betty Ellis of Dedham on January 13, 1762, but Dedham authorities did not allow them to stay unless they could give security. Warned to depart on February 18, 1765, the couple and their child went to Worcester, where they were warned again a year after their arrival on May 11, 1766. Daniel served as a private for Worcester in Captain Timothy Bigelow's company of Minutemen that marched on the alarm of April 19, 1775. He was also serving in Captain Jonas Hubbard's company, Colonel Jonathan Ward's regiment, later that year when he died.

Andrew Howard
Andrew Howard was born on August 21, 1764, in Sturbridge, Worcester County, to Thomas and Mary (Pemer) Howard.

At the age of seventeen, he was enlisted in Hampshire County to join the Continental Army on May 15, 1781. A farmer, he was five feet two inches tall and had a light complexion and light hair. He enlisted to serve the town of West Springfield for three years.

He was a participant in Shays's Rebellion and took an oath of allegiance in 1787, when he marked an "x" under his name.

He married Clarissa Clark on September 28, 1797, at East Hampton. Moving several times from Westfield and Palmer to Belchertown, the couple had children Clarissa, Irene, Solomon B. (b. 1803), Theodosia (b. 1805), and Lucy (b. 1810).

When he was fifty-four, he applied for a federal government pension on May 12, 1818, in Belchertown in Hampshire County. He was granted for $8 per month. In 1820, his properties were valued at $123.75, and his personal debt at $91.

He died on September 14, 1849 at the age of eighty-five in Oakfield, Fond du Lac County, Wisconsin. Widow Clarissa also applied for a government pension at Oakfield on April 23, 1850, when she was seventy-nine years old.

Jonathan Hunter

Born on January 24, 1754 in Marlborough, Middlesex County, Jonathan Hunter was the youngest child of Edward and Tabitha Hunter.

He was a private in Captain Daniel Haws's company, Colonel Samuel Holden Parsons's (10th) regiment. He enlisted in Worcester County in December 1775 and in August 1777, serving two short terms.

He participated in Shays's Rebellion and signed an oath of allegiance in 1787.

Although he lived at Roxbury, he first enlisted at Petersham, to which he returned after the revolution. He then moved to Chelsea, Orange County, Vermont, in 1806. He moved again to Plattsburg, Clinton County, New York, in 1812. He applied for a pension on August 2, 1832, when he still lived in Clinton County, New York. He died on March 21, 1834. His wife was Hannah Walkup (year of marriage unclear), and his descendants were recognized by the Daughters of the American Revolution.

Jonathan Johnson

Jonathan Johnson was one of John and Zerviah Johnson's six children. The exact date and place of his birth are not certain. He was born probably in Marlborough, Middlesex County, in 1744. The First Church at Marlborough recorded his and his siblings' baptisms, but never their mother's name.

In 1757 the family went to Bolton, Worcester County, where the town authority warned both the parents and their children David, Jonathan, Noah, Daniel, Job, and Lydia. In 1765 Jonathan, his wife, and their children went from Woodstock to Sturbridge, Worcester County, where they were also warned.

Enlisting for Sturbridge, both Jonathan and his brother Job fought in the revolution. Jonathan was a private in Captain Adam Martin's company, Colonel Ebenezer Learned's regiment. He enlisted in May 1775 for three months and was discharged in September that same year.

Job Johnson (b. 1750) was a private in Captain Timothy Parker's company of Minutemen, Colonel Jonathan Warner's regiment, which marched on the alarm of April 19, 1775. He served fourteen days.

Gersham Flagg Lain (or Lane)

Son of John "Ters" and Martha (Flagg) Lain, Gersham Flagg Lain was born in Bedford, Middlesex County, on July 30, 1753.

After Weston authorities warned him in 1772, he went back to Bedford, where he became a sergeant serving in the Revolutionary War. In 1778 he served one month, fifteen days, including five days to travel 100 miles home, in Captain Joseph Bradley Varnum's company, Colonel William McIntosh's regiment, on an expedition to Rhode Island.

He married Lydia Sally Thomas in 1775. The couple had thirteen children. Most of them were born in Weatherfield, Windsor County, Vermont; one was named George Washington

Lain and another Freeman Lain. Both Lain and his wife died in Springville, Susquehanna County, Pennsylvania—he in 1738 and she in 1841. His descendants were recognized by the Daughters of the American Revolution.

Joseph Langley
Joseph Langley was born in Dorchester in about 1728. His parentage was not clear. He married Sarah Merow (or Meroth), also of Dorchester, in 1754. Robert Love recorded on April 1 or 2, 1765, that "Joseph Langly last from Dorchester to town yesterday his wife named Sarah his children Names is [original] Lucey Sarah Joseph Jean & Samuell Lives in a house of Captn. Joseph Hinckee att the South End Warned in his magistys Name to Depart this town of Boston in 14 days." Enlisting for Dorchester, he joined as a private in Captain Samuel Curtis's company, Colonel Ebenezer Learned's regiment, in 1775. Two years later he enlisted in the Continental Army for three years. He was at camp near Valley Forge and died in early 1778. A year later Dorchester selectmen certified that his widow Sarah Langley was the proper person to receive the wages or gratuity due him.

James Lealand
Born in 1745 in Grafton, Worcester County, James Lealand was the eldest son of James Lealand of Sherborn and Lucy (Warren) Lealand of Grafton.

Enlisting for Sherborn, Middlesex County, on June 20, 1775, he was a private in Captain Jacob Miller's company, Colonel Ephraim Doolittle's (24th) regiment. He first served for one month and fourteen days, then again in October of the same year.

He participated in Shays's Rebellion and signed an oath of allegiance in 1787.

John Doyle Legg

Born in 1755, John Doyle Legg was an orphan at the Almshouse in Boston. At the age of six, he was bound out to George Hodge, the tailor of Northampton, Hampshire County. He was to receive two suits at the end of his terms in 1776 when he reached twenty-one.

As a private, he marched in Captain Jonathan Allen's company of Minutemen, General Pomeroy's regiment, on April 20, 1775, in response to the alarm a day earlier. He served eight days. Enlisting again a week later, he served for a year during the siege of Boston. He also enlisted for several months in 1777, marched to Ticonderoga, and joined the expedition to Stillwater and Saratoga. He enlisted and served in the Continental Army for nine months in 1778, nine months in 1779, and six months in 1780, when he was described as engaging for Northampton, being twenty-five years old, five feet three inches tall, and of light complexion. He was discharges on April 28, 1781.

The last record of his service said that he was a private in Captain Ebenezer Strong's company of volunteers, 2nd Hampshire County regiment, which was raised against the insurgents at Northampton by order of Elisha Porter, County Sheriff, in June 1782. His company marched to support the government at Springfield, Northampton, and Hadley.

After the war, he moved to Oswegatchie in St. Lawrence County, New York, where he applied for a federal pension in 1818. At the time, he owned eighty acres of land worth $200 and some personal possessions, including one old horse, two cows, one calf, two hogs, two pigs, twenty-six sheep, one plough, one pot, one tea kettle, five spoons, six knives, six forks, six bowls, two pictures, one tea pot, one tea cup and two saucers, six chairs, one table, two platters, three plates, one cupboard, one lantern, one coffee pot, one wooden bottle, and one jug. He was granted a pension of $8 a month.

Biographies

Thomas Lillie

Born in 1755, Thomas Lillie was an orphan at the Almshouse in Boston. He was bound out to Joseph Sellman, the shoreman of Marblehead, Essex County, in 1760. He was to receive two suits at the end of his term in 1776, when he would turn twenty-one. Enlisting for Marblehead in 1777, he was to serve as a private for three years in the Continental Army from Colonel John Glover's (5th) Essex County regiment. He was disabled in September the same year. In 1792 the commonwealth included his name on a list of applicants for invalid pension submitted to Congress. He still lived at Marblehead in 1794.

Jesse Mason

Jesse Mason was the second son and one of the thirteen children of Nathan and Lillis (Hale) Mason of Swansea, Bristol County. He was a carpenter by trade and married Lois Mason on February 23, 1739/40. The couple had eight children in Swansea before they moved to Lanesborough, Berkshire County, in 1770 or shortly after. They had four more children. Four additional children died young, and Lois Mason passed away on September 1, 1788. Jesse Mason became a yeoman at Lanesborough.

During the Revolutionary War, he was a private in Captain Daniel Brown's company, which marched from Lanesborough to Meloomscuyck near Bennington in August 1777, serving six days. He again served in the same company, Colonel Benjamin Simonds's regiment, for three days on the alarm at Berkshire on October 20, 1780. On both occasions, his sons David (b. 1761) and Nathan (b. 1762) marched in the same company with him. Nathan was also a private in Captain Samuel Low's company, Colonel Benjamin Simonds's regiment, which went to St. Croix in July 1777, serving fifteen days.

Jesse Mason participated in Shays's Rebellion and signed an oath of allegiance in 1787. The federal census of 1790 showed that his household consisted of three males and five females at Lanesborough. He died on October 17, 1823.

Joseph Maxfield

Joseph Maxfield was an orphan in the Almshouse of Boston. Born in 1758 he was bound out, at the age of eight, to Abraham Burbank, a yeoman of Springfield, Hampshire County. The terms were to serve for thirteen years until December 15, 1778, when he, at twenty-one years of age, would receive two suits and £13. 6s. 8d.

The revolution came before those terms ended. He began to serve in Massachusetts Line in January 1776 and through most of the year. He was a private in the Continental Army for three years, from 1779 through 1782. He was furloughed in December 1782 and was on a list of men entitled to $80 gratuity allowed by the Congressional Act of May 15, 1778.

He married Hannah (b. 1760) and moved to Colchester, New London County (formerly in Massachusetts), Connecticut, where he applied and received a pension for $8 per month in 1818. He removed to Windham County, Connecticut, and finally received a bounty land, allowed by Congress to veteran soldiers, in 1830.

Joel Moody

Joel Moody was the son of John and Sarah (Dickinson) Moody. He was born in 1743, probably in Granby, Hampshire County, just south of Amherst.

A farmer, he owned ten acres of land, a horse, and nine sheep in Amherst by 1770. He was a corporal in Lieutenant Noah Dickenson's company of militia, which marched to Cambridge on the Lexington and Concord alarm of April 19,

1775. He also served as a sergeant through the war in 1776, 1777, and 1778. A selectman in 1784, he owned a twenty-acre farm and fifty acres of undeveloped land in 1785.

He participated in Shays's Rebellion and signed an oath of allegiance in 1787.

Timothy Munro
Born in Bristol, Bristol County, Rhode Island, on February 6, 1747, Timothy Munro was the son of Nathaniel and Mary Munro.

After moving to Rutland, Worcester County, he enlisted as a private in Captain David Bent's (Rutland) company of militia, Colonel Nathaniel Sparhawk's regiment, which marched to Cambridge on April 20, 1775, in response to the Lexington alarm of the day earlier. He served in the same company and marched from Rutland to Bennington in August 1777 on an alarm. A sergeant in Captain William Henry's company, Colonel Josiah Whitney's regiment during the summer of the same year, he engaged in another march responding to an alarm in Rhode Island.

He participated in Shays's Rebellion and signed an oath of allegiance in 1787.

He married Lucretia Gates on April 12, 1781, in Rutland, where the couple raised three sons and two daughters by 1794. After receiving a federal pension of $26.63 a year in 1831, he died at Princeton, Worcester County, on February 7, 1836. His descendants were recognized by the Daughters of the American Revolution.

Samuel Nutting
Born in 1728, Samuel Nutting was the son of the brick-maker Samuel and his wife Jane (Hunnewell) Nutting of Medford.

In 1740, the father went from Cambridge to Watertown and was warned out by the selectmen. Several years later he gained a residence there. After 1752, he moved to Sherburn, where he died. His widow Jane Nutting was in Needham in 1762 and was warned to leave Watertown in the same year. She was warned out of Charlestown two years later. She spent her last days in Newton. Son Samuel had three marriages. He first married Lydia Stratton in Weston in 1751. After her death in 1764, he married Olive Ames of Groton.

In 1759, he went from Waltham to Lincoln, where he was warned. In 1770 Westford warned out his daughter Azubah (b. 1761), and in 1771 his son Samuel (b. 1752) and daughter Lydia (b.1757) were warned by Weston officials. Several months later their records again showed that "Jonathan Fisk took into his house Samuel Nutting, Olive his wife & one child named Olive, from Waltham, June 1, 1772, in low circumstances." Olive died shortly after and the widower married Sarah Learned of Watertown in the same year.

During the revolution, father Samuel Nutting was a drummer in Captain Samuel Lamson's company of militia, which marched on the alarm of April 19, 1775, serving three days. He was also on the list of men comprising one-sixth part of the militia of Weston as being returned by Captain Jonathan Fisk, who warned Nutting several years earlier, dated Weston, August 18, 1777.

His son Samuel settled in Weston and married Mary Peirce there in 1774. The couple owned a covenant in 1775 and had their daughter Polly in 1776. Father Samuel lived in Watertown (Weston used to be the western section of Watertown) until 1787. He died in Newton on July 11, 1808, aged eighty. Local people called him "captain."

Calvin Oak (or Oaks)
Calvin Oak was born in 1759; his birthplace is unclear.

After joining the Continental Army in July 1779, he served first in Captain Timothy Boutelle's company, Colonel

John Rand's regiment, and then in Captain William Warner's company of the 10th Massachusetts regiment. Discharged in April 1780, he was five feet six inches tall and had a light complexion.

He participated in Shays's Rebellion and signed an oath of allegiance in 1787.

He married Lucretia Fuller of Leominster on March 20, 1782. He died at the age of fifty-six on November 8 or 10, 1815. The widow applied for a federal government pension at Athens in Windham County, Vermont, on August 29, 1838, when she was about seventy-five years old. The application was granted for $56.66 a year.

Edward Payson

The eldest son of James and Elizabeth Payson, Edward Payson was born at Rowley, Essex County, in 1757. He responded to the Lexington and Concord alarm of April 19, 1775, serving for four days. He again served many more months during the Revolutionary War in 1775, 1778, and 1779. He was discharged in February 1779. His younger brother David also enlisted during the war and served at one time under the command of Captain Daniel Shays in 1780.

Edward Payson participated in Shays's Rebellion and signed an oath of allegiance in 1787.

He married Eunice Nichols in Winchendon, Worcester County, on September 2, 1781. They had four children named David (b. 1783), Elizabeth (b. 1788), Harriet (b. 1794), and Mary (b. 1797).

Edward died in 1802. His widow Eunice died in Keene, New Hampshire, on June 9, 1841. At the age of 64, his daughter Elizabeth P. Clark applied for a federal government pension in Franklin County, New York, on December 4, 1852.

Biographies

William Puffer

Born on April 24, 1734, William Puffer was the eldest son of William and Rebecca (Ware) Puffer of Wrentham. He married Mary Wetherell of Norton on February 27, 1753. The couple had at least five children in Norton by the early 1760s. When they moved back to Wrentham in 1768, the town authority warned them and their children Molly, William, Timothy, George, Phoebe, and Tisdal.

William Puffer enlisted for Wrentham as a sergeant in Captain Lemuel Pollock's company, Colonel John Smith's regiment, which marched on the alarm of April 19, 1775. He served four days.

His son George (b. 1761) also served for Wrentham as a private in Captain Jacob Haskins's company, Colonel John Jacobs's regiment. He enlisted in July 1778 and served six months. He joined Captain John Bacon's company, Colonel Ebenezer Thayer's regiment, in 1780 for three months.

William Puffer died in Monson, Hampden County, on January 15, 1809. His descendants were recognized by the Daughters of the American Revolution.

Joseph Ransford

The son of Joseph and Elizabeth (Collins) Ransford (or Rainsford), Joseph Ransford, Jr., was born in Boston on October 21, 1762. His father paid no property tax in the poll in 1771 and was taken into the Almshouse twice in 1773 and 1783 for his lameness.

Not yet fourteen years old, the son enlisted for Cambridge in January 1776 and served as a fifer in Captain Edward Crafts's company, Colonel Henry Knox's artillery regiment. A year later he re-enlisted in Boston in the spring of 1777. This time he engaged for Dedham for three years, serving as a private in Colonel John Crane's regiment of Continental Artillery. He was at the Battle of Monmouth, New Jersey, in

1778, and was described to be five feet three inches tall and of light complexion. Before his discharge at West Point in the spring of 1780, Captain Thomas Wells signed a paper certifying that Joseph Ransford, of his company in Colonel Crane's regiment, had not been absent from camp since August 1777 and that he "was thereby entitled to gratuity."

He soon reenlisted and served four more terms, of three months each, until the end of January 1781, going on duties with his company to stations in Boston and Rhode Island. Later that year in Boston, he entered as a fifer on board the ship *Alliance*, which would carry Marquis de Lafayette back home. The thirty-four-gun frigate was under the command of Captain John Barry (the later famed commodore), who led the last naval battles in the war. After the mission was completed, Ransford went on a second tour from New London, Connecticut, to France again. He was in two engagements with British vessels on the two cruises. He finally came back on *Alliance* by way of the West Indies, landed at Providence, Rhode Island, in late March 1783, and was discharged after serving for twenty-two months.

Growing up with the war and still a young man at its end, Joseph Ransford removed from Massachusetts. On April 16, 1793, he married Rachel Holman (b. 1774, Vigo County, Indiana) in Woodford County, Kentucky. The couple had eight children: Edward (b. 1794), Joseph (b. 1796), Henry Collins (b. 1799), Samuel (b. 1800), Sarah (b. 1803), Elizabeth (b. 1806), Thomas (b. 1810), and William (b. 1813). They moved numerous times across Kentucky, Ohio, and Indiana, where they finally settled down.

They owned a house, twenty acres of land (eight of them improved), a cow, a few hogs and sheep, and no other property. He applied for and was granted a federal pension of $8 per month beginning in 1820, when he and his family resided in Sullivan County, Indiana. He died there at the age of eighty-seven in Fairbanks Township on October 4, 1849. His widow Rachel Ransford applied for and continued to receive a federal pension from 1851. She passed away at seventy-eight, also in Sullivan County, Indiana, on July 9, 1852. Their descendants were recognized by the Daughters of the American Revolution.

Jonathan Raymond

Born in Beverly, Essex County on December 12, 1734, Jonathan Raymond was the son of Jonathan and Hephzibah (Leech) Raymond of Salem.

He married Susannah White in Beverly on October 4, 1756. The family moved to Lexington, from where they continued to Westminster in Worcester County. Six months after their arrival, town authorities warned them to depart in August 1762.

Jonathan Raymond gained residency in Westminster and was a private from that town in Captain Elisha Jackson's company in 1777. He also served in the Continental Army for a term of nine months. He served another term of nine months in 1778.

A participant in Shays's Rebellion, he took an oath of allegiance in 1787 and marked an "x" under his name.

Benjamin Richardson

Benjamin Richardson was an orphan at the Almshouse in Boston. Born in 1733, he was bound out, at fourteen, to David Bell, a bricklayer of Boston. He was to serve for seven years as an apprentice and should receive two suits at the end of his terms in 1754, when he reached twenty-one years of age. He did become a bricklayer and set up a household in Boston. He married Ann, whose last name was not known. They had two children, Benjamin and Ann. In 1771 his annual income was estimated at £16. Although he was able to acquire properties and was indeed buying land in Boston, his assets did not qualify him for any poll or real estate taxes. His household was rated to have two non-taxable polls in 1771.

Benjamin Rogers
Born on July 11, 1714, in Leominster, Worcester County, Benjamin Rogers was the second son of John and Susanna (Marston or Marson) Rogers.

Although family tradition hinted that the Rogers might be related to the martyr John Rogers, who was burned in Smithfield, England, in 1554, John Rogers' parents Jeremiah and Dorcas Rogers were humble people, who in their old age depended on town charity. Their son John Rogers was a Harvard graduate of 1705. Four years later he became the first settled minister of Boxford, Essex County. He married Susanna Marston in Leominster in 1709, and they had ten children. Their sons John Jr. (b. 1712), Benjamin, and Nathaniel (b. 1718) attended Harvard College, but Benjamin left college in 1734 and thus became a non-graduate of 1736.

A man of ability and considerable learning as well as a man of blunt, plain, and direct speech, Reverend John Rogers also held liberal views of religion, which worried his parishioners. In 1743 they finally dismissed him, but he refused to give the parsonage back to the parish which, he insisted, owed him a large sum of back salaries. The battle continued until 1749, when he left for Leominster, where his son John was the minister. However, he left Benjamin to stay and hold onto the parsonage. He finally died in 1755 without settling the dispute. His widow continued the fight until her death in 1757. The dispute finally ended in 1759 when his sons John and Nathaniel Rogers agreed to settle the matter for £210. Benjamin also transferred the parsonage to Reverend Elizur Holyoke, the incoming minister to settle over the congregation.

Caught in this bitter feud, Benjamin Rogers apparently tried to seek refuge in the neighboring Topsfield. Nevertheless, Topsfield selectmen issued a warrant against him, wife Alice (Perly) Rogers, and their children, who were warned to depart town. Denying their residence, town authorities entered the return of the warrant into the General Sessions of the Peace, Essex County, on August 1, 1749.

The town did give them some temporary relief. On March 6, 1750, the selectmen voted and "allowed to Mr. Benjamin Rogers for house room for children at school" for 5s. The town still called him "Mr." because he was not exactly poor. He was simply out of place. It is interesting to note that although the town did not grant them residency, it did allow some relief for their children. This unusual gesture of kindness may have to do with the fact that the town hired Benjamin's brother Nathaniel as a school teacher in 1742, 1744, and 1748.

Benjamin Rogers married Alice Perley in 1734 and the couple had nine children. After his wife died in about 1751, he married Lois Pierce of Lancaster. They had two children. He died ten years later at Boxford in his father's second, not first, parish.

William Shirley
Born in 1751, William Shirley was an orphan at the Almshouse in Boston. He was bound out to Joseph Striker, the sailmaker of Marblehead, Essex County, in 1760. He was to receive two suits at the end of his terms in 1772, when he should be twenty-one years old.

Enlisting for Marblehead, he was a private in Captain John Merrett's (7th) company, Colonel John Glover's (21st) regiment. His company marched and camped at Cambridge for several months during the siege of Boston in 1775. He also served as a sailmaker aboard the brigantine *Massachusetts*, commanded by Captain John Fisk. He was on the same vessel under the same commander for about five months in 1777.

He married Annis Mayley of Marblehead in early 1777; they had eight children. He died in Marblehead on April 4, 1807. His descendants were recognized by the Daughters of the American Revolution.

John Slack

John Slack was born in Attleborough, Bristol County, on April 28, 1756. His parentage was not clear; perhaps he was the son of William and Sarah (Goff or Goos) Slack and a grandson of John and Bethiah (Woodcock) Slack of Attleborough.

He was warned by authorities of Wrentham in 1768. He was a private for Wrentham in Captain Oliver Pond's company, Colonel Joseph Read's (20th) regiment, in 1775, serving three months and seven days. He recalled that he remained at Roxbury until the night before the battle of Bunker Hill, when he was stationed as a guard on Dorchester Point. Later he returned to his company at Roxbury until night, and marched to Cambridge with the regiment on the same evening of the Bunker Hill battle. The next day he marched to Winter Hill and was assigned to throwing up fortifications on Winter Hill as the British cannons fired at them. From September to October 1777, he was also enlisted in Captain Samuel Cowell's company, Colonel Benjamin Hawes's regiment, for a secret expedition to Rhode Island.

He resided in Wrentham until the end of the war. He then moved to New London, New Hampshire. About twelve or thirteen years later he moved again to Andover, New Hampshire where he stayed until 1831. He then moved to Clarksville, New Hampshire, adjoining Stewartstown in Coos County. There he applied for a pension in January 1833 and was granted $36.66 a year.

Asahel Stearns

Asahel Stearns was born on September 23, 1759, in Brookfield, Worcester County, the son of Reuben and Mary (Peters) Stearns.

Engaged for Brookfield, he first participated in the Revolutionary War in February 1776, then again in 1779, 1780, 1781, and 1783. At five feet ten inches tall and of light complexion, he was a private in various companies under Colonel Thomas Nixon's Massachusetts regiment and under Lieutenant Colonel Calvin Smith's regiment.

He participated in Shays's Rebellion and took an oath of allegiance in 1787, when he marked an "x" under his name.

He married Captivity, whose family name was not known, on January 1, 1784. They had a son (name unknown) and a daughter Lucy, who married John Wakeley of Wells in Rutland County, Vermont.

He died on May 27, 1815. His widow applied for a federal government pension from Rutland County on October 3, 1839, when she was seventy-five years old. Her pension was granted at $80 a year. The next year she moved to Onondaga County, New York, to live with her son.

Jabez Stevens

Jabez Stevens was born in Waltham, Middlesex County, on February 13, 1758. His parentage is unclear.

He served for Fitchburg, Worcester County, as a private in the Continental Army from 1777 for three years. He was at Valley Forge and was discharged in 1780.

He married first Esther Bemis in June 1784 and later Sarah Ellis. Weston authorities warned him as a laborer and his wife Esther in 1785. Cambridge authorities warned them as well in 1791, when his household had four members in the federal census. In 1793 a town meeting at Fitchburg voted to abate his tax of £2. 6s. 10d. ¾. He passed away in Ohio in

Biographies

about 1849 or 1850. His descendants were recognized by the Daughters of the American Revolution.

Caleb Stutson
Son of Caleb and Abigail Stutson, Caleb Stutson was born in Plymouth on August 12, 1755. His mother was the daughter of Lieutenant Samuel Bradford of Plympton. He joined the Revolutionary War as a private for Plympton in Captain John Bradford's company, Colonel Theophilus Cotton's regiment, in October 1775. Later he also served in the Continental Army from June 1777 until the end of 1779 and again from January to October 1780.

After participating in Shays's Rebellion, he took an oath of allegiance in 1787 and marked an "x" under his name.

He married Jane Bryant of Plympton, where they settled. The couple had one son and four daughters by 1792. He applied for a federal pension in 1818 and again in 1823. Four years later they both passed away within less than three months of each other. He died first on August 10 when he fell from a load of hay and broke his neck.

Joseph Stratton Temple
Born on June 27, 1762, Joseph Stratton Temple was the son of Joseph and Mary Temple of Shrewsbury, Worcester County.

Enlisting on August 30, 1781, Joseph St. Temple was a private in Captain Daniel Bowker's company, Lieutenant Colonel Joseph Webb's regiment, which was raised to reinforce the Continental Army. He served three and a half months.

He participated in Shays's Rebellion and signed an oath of allegiance in 1787.

He married twice, first to Susanna Hemenway at Shrewsbury in September 1786; the couple had five daughters and three sons. He later married the widow Submit Goodenow of Grafton in May 1817. He applied for and was granted a federal pension of $26.68 a year in 1837.

Daniel Tucker

Born on November 9, 1756, Daniel Tucker was the son of Jedediah and Joanna Tucker of Shrewsbury, Worcester County. As a drummer, he marched to Cambridge on the Lexington and Concord alarm of April 19, 1775 in Captain Job Cushing's company of militia, Colonel Artemas Ward's regiment, serving nine days. He again served in the Revolutionary War for three months in 1775 as well as in 1776 and 1777.

He participated in Shays's Rebellion and signed an oath of allegiance in 1787.

In December 1776, he married Rachel Noyes in Shrewsbury, where they had three sons and two daughters by 1793. His descendants were recognized by the Daughters of the American Revolution.

Levi Vinten (or Vinton)

Born on June 5, 1760, Levi Vinten was the youngest son of the eleven children of Nathaniel Vinten of Braintree, Norfolk County, and Ann (Green) Vinten. On August 18 the same year, he was baptized at Weymouth, where his parents were married and lived.

The Vintens moved to New Braintree, Worcester County, and then to Chesterfield, Hampshire County, in about 1777. Enlisting for New Braintree, Levi Vinten was a private in Captain John Hastings's company, Colonel Henry Jackson's regiment, serving a term of three years. Immediately after his term ended on December 31, 1779, he enlisted for another term from January 1 to September 1, 1780, as a regiment return certified at camp near Morristown showed on April 30, 1780.

He participated in Shays's Rebellion, took an oath of allegiance in 1787, and marked an "x" under his name.

Biographies

He married Jerusha Fenton of Williamsburgh, Hampshire County, on May 15, 1787. They had ten children. To prevent them from gaining a settlement, Goshen, a small town set off from Chesterfield in 1781, warned the three Vinten brothers Nathaniel, Abiathar, and Levi in 1790. However, they stayed. The Vinten family had a homestead in the southeast corner of the town close to Hyde Hill Road. Levi became a taxpayer and a member of the Baptist Society in 1814, but his family moved out to New York State three years later.

Levi Vinten applied for a federal pension from Genesee County, New York on May 22, 1818. It was granted for $8 a month. He soon became a resident of the new township of Hartland (from 1812) in Niagara County, New York, where he died on September 20, 1820. His descendants joined the Daughters of the American Revolution.

No fewer than seven of Levi Vinten's relations were Revolutionary veterans: brother Abiathar (b. 1758); brother Nathanial (b. 1755); brother Samuel (bap. 1757); brother-in-law Asa Shaw, who married Levi's sister Hannah (b. 1743/4); brother-in-law Ezekiel White, Jr., who married his sister Sarah (b. 1747); Sarah Levi's father-in-law Ezekiel White, Sr., a soldier; and brother-in-law Daniel Corthell, who married Levi's sister Anne (b. 1753). The descendants of the White family were recognized by the Daughters of the American Revolution.

Chronology

1629

May 28

The Massachusetts Bay Company proposes to erect a house of correction for the better governing and ordering of the people.

1630

August 23

The first Court of Assistants orders that the governor and deputy governor, for the time being, shall always be justices of the peace and that four assistants (Sir Richard Saltonstall, Mr. Isaac Johnson, Mr. John Endicott, and Mr. Roger Ludlow) shall be justices of the peace for the present time. They shall have the same powers as the justices of the peace have in England for reforming abuses and punishing offenders. Any justice shall have power to imprison an offender, but shall not inflict any corporal punishment without the presence and consent of one of the assistants.

1631

May 18

The General Court orders that no man shall be admitted to the freedom of this body politic (i.e., to become a freeman) except members from one of the churches within the commonwealth.

1634

September 3

Against the great, superfluous, and unnecessary expenses occasioned by "some new & immodest fashions," the General Court orders that no person, either man or woman, shall hereafter make or buy any apparel, either woolen, silk, or linen, with any lace on it, silver, gold, silk, or thread, under the penalty of forfeiting such clothes. Nor shall any man and woman make or buy any slashed clothes (other than one slash in each sleeve, and another in the back), cutworks, embroidered or needle work caps and bands, gold and silver girdles, hatbands, belts, ruffs, or beaver hats under the same penalty.

The General Court also orders that no servant shall receive land in any plantation until he has proved his faithfulness to his master during the time of his service.

1636

August 15

The Covenant of Dedham first signs and ultimately acquires the endorsement of 125 people who pledge, among others, that "we shall by all means labor to keep off from us all such as are contrary minded, and receive only such unto us as may be probably of one heart with us."

1637

May 17

The General Court orders that no town or person shall receive any stranger with intent to reside in this jurisdiction nor allow any lot or habitation to anyone or entertain any such a person for more than three weeks, except for the one who had allowance under the hand of one of the Council or of two magistrates. A forfeiture of £100 applies to each violation if the violator is a town and £40 applies if the violator is a person.

1637

July 20

John Oldham is found dead; the Pequot War continues until 1638.

1638

September 6

After considering that both freemen and church members pay voluntary contributions while some inhabitants, who are neither freemen nor church members, may receive relief but do not voluntarily contribute, the General Court orders that every inhabitant in any town is liable to contribute to all charges, both in church and commonwealth, whereof he does or may receive benefit.

1639

June 6

The General Court rules that a county court, or two magistrates out of court, shall have power to determine all differences arising from a lawful settling and providing for poor persons. They shall also have the power to dispose of any unsettled persons into any town as they shall judge to be the easiest of the country and most appropriate for the maintenance of such persons and families.

1639

October

The Court of Assistants of Plymouth Colony rules that no one shall be admitted as an inhabitant into the plantation of Sandwich without the approbation of the church and any of the assistants that the plantation shall choose.

1640

May 13

The General Court orders that the two-penny loaf bread must weigh at least twelve ounces. Whosoever sells lighter weight shall forfeit his bread.

1641

The Massachusetts Body of Liberties is enacted, offering nearly one hundred provisions, including the liberties of women, children, servants, foreigners, and strangers.

1645
May 14

The General Court chooses a committee to consider a law for disposing inmates and settling impotent aged persons or vagrants.

1646
November 4

The General Court orders that every township shall present to the Quarterly Court all idle and unprofitable persons, including all children who are not diligently employed by their parents. The Court shall have power to dispose of them for their own welfare and the improvement of the common good. This law is reaffirmed on 4 November 1649.

1647
May 20

The General Court allows freemen to choose inhabitants who, although non-freemen, have taken the oath of fidelity, to have their vote in town affairs, such as the elections of selectmen and the assessment of rates. No non-freeman shall have his vote unless he is twenty-four years old and has no evil carriage against the government and church.

1647
October 27

The General Court enacts a law regulating tax rates and valuation for public charges, updating a major ruling of taxation passed on November 4, 1646. The law sets a poll tax of 2s. 6d. per head for every male person from sixteen years old and upward and a rate of one penny for every pound of estate, real or personal.

1648
May 26

To clarify the law of May 20, 1647, the General Court decides that all Englishmen who are settled inhabitants and householders who are at least twenty-four years old and of honest and good conversation, being rated at twenty pounds estate in a single country rate, may vote in town affairs, participate in local elections and assessments of rates, or serve as jurymen and constables.

1652
May 26

The General Court orders that all settled inhabitants and all strangers who have stayed for more than two months are required to take the oath of fidelity before a county court or a magistrate out of court or forfeit £5 a week for any refusal.

1655
May 23

After hearing complaints from various townships about great charges arising from strangers pressing in without the consent of local inhabitants, the General Court orders that all towns shall have the liberty to prevent strangers from coming in. No town shall be chargeable for any people who did not receive the consent of town inhabitants before their stay. Whoever caused their coming in shall relieve and maintain those who later become needy. Town selectmen are empowered to require security from those who may become needy or to forbid the entertainment of them.

1655
May 23
The General Court orders that a house of correction be erected in each county at the county's charge.

1656
May 14
The General Court orders that a county court shall have the power to decide to use a county prison as a house of correction until the latter is constructed. It also lays out the rules and responsibilities for town selectmen to regulate the institution and for a master of the house to govern its inmates.

1657
The Scots' Charitable Society is formed.

1659
May 11
The General Court passes the first extensive settlement law. It states that no person shall reside in any town for more than three months if a notice of warning is served by a constable or a selectman. If such a person continues to stay and if the town fails to petition the county court to prosecute the case, the inhabitants of the said town shall provide for relief to said person in case of need. Each county court shall hear and determine all complaints and settle all poor persons in any town, which shall entertain and provide for them at a town charge. A town may appeal to the Court of Assistants if it shall grieve at the disposal of the county court that may settle, at the county's

charge, anyone whose legal residency cannot be defined by the current law in any town of the county.

1661
May 22
The General Court expands a law of 1658 to prevent the intrusions of Quakers. It states that vagabond and wandering Quakers shall be stripped, tied to a cart, whipped through town, and conveyed to the constables of the next town, where they shall suffer the same until reaching the outward-most towns of this jurisdiction. Vagabond and wandering Quakers thus thrice convicted shall be sent to a county house of correction, severely whipped, branded with the letter "R" on the left shoulder, and sent to the outward-most towns of the jurisdiction. For those thus punished who shall return again, they shall be prosecuted as incorrigible rogues and enemies to the common peace, be apprehended and committed to the country jail, and be proceeded against at the next Court of Assistants according to the law of October 19, 1658, for their banishment on pain of death.

1661
November 27
The General Court suspends executing the laws against Quakers.

1662
May 7
To prevent increasing profaneness and irreligiousness caused by vagrants and vagabond life, the General Court orders constables to apprehend any inhabitants or foreigners who, leaving their families, relations, and dwelling places, wander from town to town. Magistrates have authority to examine them to identify rogues and vagabonds. Those so determined shall

receive corporal punishment. They shall either be sent back to their abode if known or, if not, be sent to a house of correction to wait for further decisions by a county court.

1662
October 8
The General Court reinstates the 1661 law against Quakers, provided that their whipping shall be through but three towns. Those magistrates or commissioners signing such a warrant shall specify the names of the towns and the number of the stripes given at each town.

1662
Prompted by a £100 bequest from Henry Webb, Robert Keayne's £120 legacy, and other subscriptions, Boston's first Almshouse opens. A wooden structure on Beacon Street, it houses only a few poor persons and is burned down in about a year.

1664
August 3
The General Court orders that church membership is no longer required in the admission of freemen. All Englishmen (of orthodox religion, in full communion with some church, of freeholders of ratable estate, with the value of ten shillings in valuation, of twenty-four years old, of householders, and settled inhabitants in this jurisdiction) may present themselves and their desire to the General Court for the admittance to the freedom of this commonwealth. A majority of vote at the General Court shall grant them the freedom of the body public.

1668
October 14

The General Court rules that those who greatly neglect their callings or misspend what they earn, whereby their families are in much want and in need of relief from others, shall be considered under the law as idle persons, who could be sent to a house of correction.

1672
October 8
The General Court orders that all strangers coming into this country shall have liberty to sue one another in any courts of the colony and that any inhabitant may be sued by any stranger who is engaged in maritime or merchant navigation.

1675
Metacom's (King Philip's) War until 1676.

1682
October 11
Finding many idle persons in sundry towns, especially in Boston, the General Court decides to regulate them. Tithingmen in each town inspect all families and report to selectmen the names of idlers, who are defined as those who either greatly neglect their particular callings and do not follow any lawful employment or misspend their time. The selectmen forward the names to magistrates, who are empowered to issue warrants to constables, demanding the idle persons to work. Those who refuse to work are sent to a house of correction to work. Their earnings at the house of correction are used for their necessities and relief. Any person or persons who think they were wrongly treated may complain to a county court for redress.

1682
Boston votes to rebuild the Almshouse destroyed by fire.

1684
June 18
Massachusetts loses its 1629 charter by a judgment of the high court of chancery of England.

1686
A new brick Almshouse is built at the northwest corner of the Common in Boston.

1689
In April, the ouster of Sir Edmund Andros effectually ends the Dominion of New England since 1686.

1691
October 7
Massachusetts becomes a royal colony under a new chapter granted by William and Mary.

1692
Salem witchcraft hysteria begins in January/February and trials last until May 1693.

1692
October 12
An Act for the Better Observation and Keeping of the Lord's Day disallows any work, labor, business, game, sport, play, recreation, and travel on the Sabbath.

1692
November 16
An *Act for Regulating of Townships, Choice of Town Officers, and Setting Forth Their Power* rules that the freeholders and other inhabitants of each town, ratable at twenty pounds estate, to one single rate besides the poll, are to meet annually and

choose town selectmen and overseers of the poor. Town selectmen are empowered to assess the inhabitants and other residents within such town for all county and town charges for the maintenance and support of the ministry, schools, and the poor. Town selectmen or overseers of the poor are empowered to take effectual care that all children, youth, and other persons of able body do not live idly or misspend their time loitering. One or more justices of the peace have the power to send anyone who is fit and able to work but who refuses to work to a house of correction, where he or she can be whipped up to ten lashes and be kept to hard labor until discharge. With the consent of two justices, the selectmen or overseers of the poor have the power to bind any poor children to be apprentices until the age of twenty-one for a boy and eighteen for a girl. After residing in a town for three months without receiving a warning notice, a person can gain settlement of the town and be eligible for relief, with the town bearing the charges for such relief unless the needy person has able-bodied family members and close relatives. Constables or other persons appointed by the selectmen can warn a person out by serving a warrant, which includes the names of such persons, the time of their stay, and the date of when the warning is issued. Those warnings are returned to and recorded at the court of quarter sessions. If a person is properly warned but refuses to depart in fourteen days, a constable may remove the person by a warrant of a justice of the peace.

1693
June 8
An *Act for the Restraining the Taking Excessive Usury* disallows any interest of more than 6% or a rate of six pounds in the hundred for a year.

1693/4

February 24

An *Act for the Relief of Ideots and Distracted Persons* rules that selectmen or overseers of the poor have the power to take effectual care and make necessary provision for the relief, support, and safety of those impotent or distracted persons who are naturally in want of understanding and thus incapable to provide for themselves. Also under their care are those who, by the providence of God, fall into distraction, becoming *non compos mentis* while no family relations can provide for them.

1694

June 18

An *Act for Granting unto Their Majesties a Tax of Twelvepence a Poll, and One Penny on the Pound for Estates* specifies who qualifies as assessors and how assessment and valuation are to be conducted. In a community of fewer than 40 families, an assessor must have an asset of £40; an assessor in a community of more than 40 families must have an asset of £100; a Boston assessor must have an asset of £300. Assessment applies to all males, eighteen years or older, except for elders, ministers, schoolmasters, and Harvard president, fellows, and students. Also exempted are the old aged, the infirm, and those under extreme poverty, at the discretion of the assessor. A true list of all male persons is made to show a true estimate of all estates, both real and personal, according to the method herewith mentioned.

Valuation of the poll: For all male persons eighteen years or older; all Negroes, mulattos, and Indian servants; and all females sixteen years or older, the rate is twelve pence per poll.

Valuation of all real estate: For houses, warehouses, mills, cranes, wharfs, tan-yards, arable, pasture and meadow ground, all other lands enclosed or under improvement, the rate is one penny on the pound for the value thereof.

Valuation of houses to be let: For houses, warehouses, tanyards, mills, cranes, wharfs, the rate is fourteen years' rent or income, without any allowance or seduction for repairs.

Valuation of all lands for renting: The rate is twenty years' rent or income.

Valuation of farmers and tenants: The farmer or occupier of any house or lands (being assessed for the same in his occupation and reimbursed one-half of what he shall so pay toward said assessment, by the landlord or lessor) is allowed to discount the same out of his rent.

Valuation of goods: For all goods, wares, merchandise (except those that have paid impost), trading stock, money at interest, and all boats and small vessels, the rate is one penny on the pound.

Valuation of income: For every handicraft-man, the rate is one penny on the pound for his income.

Valuation of farm animals: For every ox and horse exceeding four years of age, the rate is 40s.; for every cow exceeding three years, 30s.; all sheep above one year old, £4 per score; and all swine above one year old, £6 per score.

1694/5

March 12

An *Act to Prevent the Deserting of the Frontiers* states that, in the present war (King William's War), inhabitants of Wells, York, Kittery, Aimsbury, Haverhill, Dunstable, Chelmsford, Groton, Lancaster, Marlborough, and Deerfield shall forfeit all their estates should they desert those frontier settlements. Every person fit for service but removed from the frontier is to forfeit his estate. No male person of sixteen years and older who has no lands or tenements in the frontier plantations and towns can move into them on pain of forfeiting £10. On March 23, 1699/1700, Brookfield, Mendon, Woodstock, Salisbury,

Andover, Billerica, Hatfield, Hadley, Westfield, and Northampton are added to the list.

1694/5
March 14
An *Act for Preventing of Men's Sons or Servants Absenting Themselves from Their Parent's or Master's Service without Leave* states that inhabitants have sustained great damage by their sons and servants deserting their service without consent of their parents or masters and entering themselves on board private man-of-war or merchants' ships. Therefore, no commander of any private man-of-war or master of any merchant ship or vessel shall receive, harbor, entertain, conceal, or secure on board such ship and vessel any such son and servant on pain of £5 per week. Any escaped servant or servant so found is required to extend his service for up to one year.

1696
December 3
An *Act for the Due Assize of Bread* specifies grain prices and the weight of penny white loaf, wheaten bread, and household bread. For inspection, clerks of the market in each town are empowered to enter any place, once a week if not more often, where bread is baked for sale. All bread found violating the assize is seized. The selectmen in each town have the power to inquire, state, and record the middle price of wheat once a month or more often as they see cause. The local assize of bread is to be made known by posting it in public places.

1699
June 26
In an *Act for the Suppressing and Punishing of Rogues, Vagabonds, Common Beggars, and Other Lewd, Idle and Disorderly Persons and Also for Setting the Poor to Work*, the

General Court orders that a house of correction be built in every county, at the county's charge, for the purposes of keeping, correcting, and setting to work of rogues, vagabonds, common beggars, and other lewd, idle, and disorderly persons. The county prison could be used for the same purposes until such a house of correction is built in a county. Justices of the peace at the General Sessions may appoint a master of the house of correction. The General Sessions or one justice of the peace out of the court have power to commit to the house of correction all rogues, vagabonds, and idlers going about in any town or county begging. Also included are such persons using any subtle craft, juggling or unlawful games or plays, or presenting themselves to have knowledge in physiognomy, palmistry or pretending they can tell destinies and fortunes or discover where lost or stolen goods may be found, as well as common pipers, fiddlers, runaways, stubborn servants or children, common drunkards, nightwalkers, pilferers, wanton and lascivious persons, either in speech or behavior, common railers, brawlers, and those who neglect their callings, misspend what they earned, and do not provide for themselves or families.

An inmate is to be whipped ten lashes when first committed. The master of the house of correction has the power to set all inmates to work and punish them by putting fetters or shackles on them, by whipping up to ten stripes each time, or by reducing their food.

Justices of each county at their General Sessions are authorized to make necessary rules and regulations for the house of correction. Any town that has committed any person or persons to the house of correction is to provide, at the town's charge, suitable and necessary material to the master of the house for the detention and labor during their commitment. Any parent or master whose children or servants are committed to the house of correction are to provide, at their own cost, suitable and necessary material to the master of the house for the inmates' detention and labor during their commitment.

Inmates may keep eight pence out of every shilling they earn at the house of correction. The master uses the rest of the money for the upkeep of the house. If the inmate is a master or household head, the surplus of his earnings may be used for the support and relief of his family.

If the house of correction has to maintain those inmates who are weak, sick, and unable to work, town selectmen are to reimburse the master of the house for the expenses of keeping those weak and sick persons from their community. If they are servants and minors, their masters and parents are to reimburse the house of correction.

The master may use the earnings by those who are committed to his custody for their relief or to fulfill the deficiencies arising from their maintenance. The master keeps an exact account of all earnings and profits made by the labor of those under his custody. He presents the account to the justices at their General Sessions, who decide his allowance from that account.

Town authorities have the power to decide whether any surplus from the earnings are to be paid to the town or to any parent or master who has inmates at the house of correction.

No master of the house of correction can refuse or neglect to keep such accounts or he will be liable to fines or other punishments set by the General Sessions.

Any town that intends to build a workhouse has the power to grant a tax or assessment for raising a stock of necessary and suitable materials, tools, and implements for the employment and setting the poor to work at such a house.

Town selectmen are to proportion such a tax or assessment on the inhabitants in the most just and equal manner according to the rules for proportioning the province tax.

Town selectmen are to grant warrants for collecting such a tax in the same manners of collecting other town rates or assessments.

Selectmen and those justices of the peace residing in town are empowered to nominate and appoint three or more persons as a master and wardens to inspect and govern all persons employed at the workhouse.

The master and wardens are to manage, use, and employ the stock of necessary and suitable materials, tools, and implements for the employment and setting of the inmates to work at the workhouse.

Two justices of the peace, one of them being of the quorum, have the power to commit to the workhouse all able-bodied persons who receive public alms, live idly or disorderly, misspend their time, or go about begging.

Inmates at the workhouse are to be kept and held strictly to work.

Moderate whipping or setting in the stocks is to be applied to idle and disorderly inmates and those who do not duly perform their tasks.

The master and wardens have the power to demand, sue for, recover, and receive any gifts, bequests, and donations for the use of the poor or for and toward stock for the workhouse. The master and wardens are responsible for making accounts of all money and stock committed to them by any towns that have power to grant their allowances. All stock, profits, and improvements obtained for the workhouse are to be kept entire and applied for maintaining, keeping, and repairing of said house.

1700/1
March 12

In an *Act Directing the Admission of Town Inhabitants*, the General Court rules for the better prevention of persons obtruding themselves on any town in this province.

Every ship master is to deliver a perfect list of the names of all passengers, including their servants and their circumstances as far as he knows, to the receiver of the impost, on pain of forfeiting £5 for every passenger omitted if he is so convicted at the General Sessions. The ship master is liable to carry out any passenger who is impotent, lame, or infirm and who cannot procure sufficient sureties to town government.

The receiver of the impost is required to inform all ship masters about the law, and shall transmit all lists or certificates of passengers to a town clerk, who is required to return such lists or certificates to town selectmen. Upon the complaint made by the selectmen, every justice of the peace is empowered to take sufficient security of a ship master who is to appear before the General Sessions to answer charges of omitting or not reporting passengers.

No one shall be eligible for relief unless the person or persons have continued their residence for twelve months without warning. No one shall be admitted as a lawful inhabitant unless the person makes known his desire to town selectmen and obtains their approbation or the approbation of the town where he desires to live.

If anyone returns to town after he or she was properly warned and removed by warrant from a justice, the person will be proceeded against as a vagabond.

1701
June 19
An *Act to Encourage the Sowing and Well Manufacturing of Hemp within This Province* allows a partnership or company to purchase hemp raised in the province at four pence farthing per pound.

1701
June 30

An *Act Prescribing the Form of a Warrant for Collecting of Town Assessments, &c.* authorizes a tax collector, by virtue of his warrant, to seize the body of any person for want of goods or chattels and to commit him to prison until the person pays the rates or assessments.

1703
July 28

An *Act Relating to Molato and Negro Slaves* states that no mulatto or Negro slaves are to be discharged or granted liberty unless a sum of £50 is given to secure and indemnify the town from all charges.

1703
November 27

In an *Act of Supplement to the Act Referring to the Poor, &c.* the General Court clarifies that it is a misunderstanding to construe that the provision (in the law of November 16, 1692) of binding out poor children apprentices only extends to those whose parents receive alms. Selectmen or overseers of the poor, with the assent of two justices of the peace, have the power to bind out all children whose parents are not assessed for public taxes for province or town charges. Male children are to be bound out until they are twenty-one and females until eighteen or their time of marriage.

Selectmen or overseers of the poor, with the assent of two justices of the peace, have the power to set to work all persons, married or unmarried, of able bodies, who—having no means to maintain themselves—live idly and with no lawful trade or business.

All single persons of either sex under the age of twenty-one must live under orderly family government. No woman of ill fame, married or unmarried, can receive or entertain lodgers in her house, although this act is not to be construed to hinder any single woman of good repute from the exercise of any lawful trade or employment.

Selectmen, constables, and tithingmen are ordered to see the due observation of this act. They can complain and inform against any transgressions to the justices of the peace or to the General Sessions. Justices of the peace and the General Sessions are empowered to convict those who live idly or disorderly and commit such persons to the house of correction or workhouse. Those so committed are to remain and be kept to labor until an order of discharge from the General Sessions or until they can give assurance, to the satisfaction of the General Sessions, that they will reform.

1703/4
February 29
French soldiers and their Native American allies raid Deerfield.

1710
Grain riots occur in Boston, first in early 1710 and again in spring 1713, against Andrew Belcher, Commissioner General during Queen Anne's War.

1711/2
March 19
An *Act against Intemperance, Immortality and Prophaneness, and for Reformation of Manners* lays out rules to regulate inns, taverns, ale-houses, victualers, houses of common entertainment, and retailers of strong liquors out of doors. No singing, fiddling, piping, or any other music, dancing or reveling is allowed in public houses on pain of forfeiting 10s.

Also, those who give evil communication, wicked, profane, impure, filthy, and obscene songs, composures, writings, or prints, libel or mock-sermons, mimicking of preaching can be fined up to £20 or be ordered to stand on the pillory, with an inscription of the crime in capital letters affixed over the head, according to the discretion of the justices at quarter sessions.

1714

Early this year John Colman, Oliver Noyes, Nathaniel Byfield, William Tailer, and Elisha Cooke, Jr., propose to create a private bank secured by land mortgages. Governor Joseph Dudley responds with a proposal for a public bank that issues paper money.

1720

July 23

An *Act to Regulate the Price and Assize of Bread* states that covetous and evil-disposed persons have, for their own gain, deceived and oppressed his Majesty's subjects, more especially the poorer sort. For remedy thereof, the General Court repeals the act of December 3, 1696. The selectmen of each town have the power to set the assize and weight of all sorts of bread for sale, making reasonable allowance to the bakers for their charges, pains, and livelihood. If convicted before a justice of the peace with two witnesses, a baker who fails to observe the assize is to forfeit 20s. A justice of the peace, a selectman, or two clerks of the market have the power to enter into any house or bakery to inspect the weight of the bread. They have the power to confiscate any deficient bread to be given to the poor. Violators are to forfeit £3. The act includes an extensive chart listing price and weight of bread for wheat from 4s. to 15s. per bushel.

1720

December 27

John Colman and five others of a committee recommend to a Boston town meeting to establish a spinning school.

1722

June 27

An *Act for Encouraging the Linnen Manufacture, and the Making of Canvas or Duck Proper for Ships' Sails* states that the raising of flax and hemp for the making of linen cloth and canvas for ships' sails, etc., would be of great service to the trade and business of this province by land and sea. The General Sessions are to pay double price for the finest linen cloth (twenty yards in length and one yard in width) made of flax grown and processed in the province.

1722

June 29

An *Act in Addition to the Act Directing the Admission of Town Inhabitants* (March 12, 1700/1) indicates that ships may arrive at a place where there is no impost office. According to the General Court, wherever no receiver of impost dwells, ship masters are to make a list of all passengers to town selectmen and give sufficient bond to keep the town harmless from all manners of charges caused by the needs of the arriving passengers. Any ship master who neglects or refuses to give bond within five days of his arrival is to forfeit £200. Every ship master is to deliver to the receiver of the impost or selectmen or a town treasurer, within twenty-four hours of arrival, a perfect list of the names and circumstances of all the passengers, so far as he knows, on pain of forfeiting £100. No passengers, strangers, servants, or others are to settle in any town in this province unless they have resided for twelve months in town without warning. Passengers, strangers, servants, and others who travel from town to town will be warned out and sent by authority back to their last abode.

1722
July 3

An *Act to Enable the Overseers of the Poor and Selectmen to Take Care of Idle and Disorderly Persons* states that some idle, dissolute, and vagrant persons, having some estate, and accordingly ratable, take no care of their families, nor improve their estates to the best advantage. Previous laws of November 16, 1692, and June 29, 1699 did not authorize the overseers and selectmen to inspect them. Now, overseers and selectmen are empowered to inspect any such idle, dissolute, and vagrant persons who have ratable estates but take no care of their families, nor improve their estates to the best advantage, misspend their time and money, and live idle, vagrant, and dissolute lives. The overseers and selectmen are to treat them as if they were poor indigent and impotent persons. They have the power to bind out their children to good families, improve their estates to the best advantage, and apply the produce and income toward the support of them and their families. Any such idle person who feels aggrieved may appeal to the General Sessions.

1723
June 24

An *Act in Further Addition to an Act Entitled "An Act Directing the Admission of Town Inhabitants"* (March 12, 1700/1) states that town inhabitants are to forfeit £5 if they receive, admit, and entertain any strangers as inmates, boarders, and tenants for more than forty days without giving a written account to the town clerk or one and more selectmen of the time they first receive, admit, and entertain those strangers, the place where they more recently came from, and their circumstances.

Chronology

1723

A freestanding house of correction (Bridewell) opens near the Almshouse in Boston.

1724
December 8
An *Act to Retrench the Extraordinary Expence at Funeral* states that the giving of scarves at funerals is a great and unnecessary expense to the detriment of the province. No scarves are allowed at funerals on pain of forfeiting £20.

1729
June 15
An *Act for Encouraging the Raising of Flax within This Province* states that 18s. 8d. is to be awarded for every one hundred twelve pounds of water-rotted, well–cured, and clean-dressed flax of this province.

1731
April 2
An *Act for Naturalizing Protestants of Foreign Nations, Inhabiting within This Province* rules that any foreign Protestant who has taken the oaths of allegiance and supremacy and paid a record fee of 5s. is to be naturalized after one year in residence.

1731
April 2
The General Court allows 29s. for every one hundred twelve pounds of water-rotted, well-cured, and clean-dressed hemp of this province.

1735

July 3

In an *Act for Employing and Providing for the Poor in the Town of Boston*, the General Court orders that the annual town meeting of Boston has the power to choose twelve overseers of the poor from the twelve wards in town. Each overseer is to inspect and visit the ward. Overseers are to meet once every month to consider the most appropriate methods of the discharge of their office. Either for the decay of trade or for the ill habits of the idle and slothful, the poor become more numerous. For want of employment and for setting them to work, the General Court also orders that the Boston town meeting has the power to decide to erect a house for the reception and employment of the idle and poor of the town. The overseers of the poor have the power to regulate the workhouse. Boston is authorized to raise £3,000 per annum for the workhouse.

The overseers of the poor have the power to inspect, order, and govern the workhouse. They also have the power to appoint a master and one or more assistants for the immediate care and oversight of the workhouse. The overseers have the power to make orders and bylaws for the workhouse. The town meeting has the power to review, approve, and disapprove the orders and bylaws. One overseer has the power to send any idle and indigent person to the workhouse for twenty-four hours. Two overseers have the power to send anyone to the workhouse until the person is discharged by the majority of the overseers at their monthly meeting. The overseers of the poor have the power to bind out children whose parents are not rated for their personal estates. Although rated for public taxes, some people are unable to provide for or are negligent to the support of their children. To correct this great negligence and great scandal of dangerous consequences, the overseers have the power to bind out those children who are so grossly ignorant that they are unable to distinguish the alphabet at six years old, to good families for a decent and Christian education. In other words, the overseers have the power to bind out ignorant children as much as they do to those children whose parents are poor, infirm, and not rated for public taxes. Each overseer is responsible for a particular ward. The overseers have the power to warn any intruder who is not an inhabitant to depart from town. They have power to direct constables to proceed to remove anyone who refuses to obey or neglects their orders.

1735
July 3
An *Act in Further Addition* to *Explanation of the Act Entitles "An Act for Regulating Townships, Choice of Town Officers, &c."* (November 16, 1692) updates a law of July 4, 1734. It states that no one is qualified to vote in the choice of officials or in any other affairs at any town meeting unless the person has a ratable estate of twenty pounds besides the poll. Real estate is to be valued at what the rents or income of the property for the last six years would amount to, were it to be let at a reasonable rate. Personal estate and faculty are to be assessed according to the rules of valuation.

1737
In early spring a band of Bostonians disguise themselves as clergymen to destroy three market buildings to protest the rising prices.

1737
The Charitable Irish Society is formed.

1738/9

Contiguous to the Almshouse, the first Workhouse, a large brick building of 120 feet long, opens in Boston. The two buildings occupy the whole length of Park Street.

1739

December 5

John Colman and 395 others set forth to the General Court that a considerable number of merchants and traders will support a plan called a land bank. On March 10, 1739/40, the Scheme of the Land Bank (also known as the Manufactory Scheme) is published in broad sheet, announcing that it is beginning to accept subscribers. The scheme to encourage the local economy by emitting the manufactory notes based on land security prompts intense controversy. Friends quickly mobilize for endorsement while foes organize for an attack, including the proposal of a competing Silver Bank Scheme announced in the same month. Disallowed by the royal governor and home government, the Land Bank folds within the year. Governor Jonathan Belcher issues two proclamations in four months strictly forbidding such a scheme. Using his prerogatives, he further undermines it by threatening to remove from office those commissioned justices of the peace and military officers who would support the scheme. The governor also rejects the nominations of Samuel Watts and John Choate for House Speaker; both men have been directors of the Land Bank. The controversy lingers, however, as legal action concerning many outstanding notes persists through the next three decades. Three commissions are appointed—in 1744, 1759, and 1767—with the charge to bring a speedy and complete finishing of the scheme. However, a fire in 1748 destroys many bank records at the courthouse, compounding the matter to no small degree.

1740

Construction of Faneuil Hall begins in Boston. On Thursday, October 9, George Whitefield comes to the Almshouse and enlarges on these words, "the Poor receive the Gospel." He then goes to the Workhouse and prays with and exhorts a great number of people, besides those belonging to the Workhouse, for an hour.

1741
May 12

An affidavit obtained by the government states that 1,000 men will rise in Boston on the nineteenth and 20,000 in the country (involving perhaps Milton, Braintree, Bridgewater, Stoughton, Salem, and Worcester) are to come to Boston. If corn is there and the merchants will not let them have it, they are to throw them into the dock. On May 14, an arrest warrant is issued to preserve the King's peace and dignity.

1741
June 8

Three hundred people gather in an anti-impressment riot in Boston. A similar riot occurs on October 30.

1741
October 14

Act in Further Addition to the Several Acts for the Better Observation and Keeping the Lord's Day identifies idlers and loitering persons as the likely Sabbath breakers, who are subject to 20s. fine for the first offense, 40s. for the second, plus sufficient security for good behavior.

1742

Boston's 1686 Almshouse is expanded.

1742/3

January 15

The General Court reiterates, in its act of 1742-43 Chapter 28, that a qualified voter must have—besides the poll—a ratable estate of twenty pounds, assessed in real estate (such as rents or income for the space of six years) or in personal estate and faculty estimated according to the rules of valuation. This law is renewed and extended six times—in 1747, 1756, 1762, 1767, 1776, and 1779—until it is superseded by the qualification requirements set in the state constitution of June 15, 1780.

1742/3

January 15

In an *Act in Addition to the Several Laws of this Province Relating to the Support of Poor and Indigent Persons*, the General Court establishes the rules for redressing neglect of the indigent by selectmen and overseers of the poor and for settling disputes between towns over their charges for the poor. Justices at General Sessions have the power to settle disputes between towns over their liability of poor charges. They also have the power to fine a delinquent selectman or an overseer of the poor up to 40s. for negligence or refusal to take care of the poor; the fine is to be applied for the support of the poor in his town. Justices at General Sessions have the power to assess inhabitants of a town for its poor charge if such town neglects or refuses to support the poor. The assessment is to be added to the town's county tax and collected and paid to the county treasury. Justices have the power to order the fund to be dispensed for the support of the poor and indigent. Justices have the power to order a refund to anyone who has paid to support the poor because of the neglect of the town selectmen or overseers.

1743

September 17

In an *Act for Erecting of Workhouses for the Reception and Employment of the Idle and Indigent*, the General Court empowers every town to erect a workhouse if needed. A town is to choose five, seven, or nine overseers of the house at its annual meeting in March. The overseers in turn have power to choose a master and any necessary assistants for the immediate care and oversight of the workhouse. The overseers are to meet once a month to make orders and rules for the regulation of the house. The town meeting has the power to prove or revoke such orders and rules. Any number of towns is empowered to erect a workhouse, at the joint charge and for their common benefit, for the employment of indigent or idle persons. These towns have the power to appoint a master and other assistants for the inspection, regulation, and government of such house. If they misbehave, the master and his assistants can be removed from office by overseers, five of whom are selected by each town.

All overseers have quarterly meetings at the workhouse to inspect the management of the house. Duly assembled overseers may choose a moderator to regulate the business of the meeting, who may vote only in the case of a draw. All overseers are sworn to the faithful discharge of their duties. A clerk is chosen annually to record all votes and orders. Overseers have the power to make orders and bylaws for the regulation of the workhouse. Several towns are to pay the yearly stipend or allowance to the master and assistants and pay for the charges of keeping the workhouse in repair. The payments are in proportion to what each town is rated in the province tax. Overseers have the power to commit persons to the workhouse by writing under their hands. The number of persons who can be committed to the workhouse is allotted in proportion to each town, which is not to send more persons than its allotment. All poor and indigent persons who are maintained by or receive alms from the town are liable to be sent to the workhouse. All able-bodied persons who have no estate or means to maintain themselves, who refuse to work, who neglect to do so and live a dissolute or vagrant life, and who have no lawful business or calling to gain an honest living are liable to be sent to the workhouse. All persons who have some ratable estate but not enough to qualify them to vote in town affairs, who neglect the due care and improvement of the estate by consuming their time and money in public houses or by misspending what they earn to the impoverishment of themselves and families, and who are likely to become chargeable to the town are liable to be sent to the workhouse.

No town can send any person to the workhouse unless it has provided its share of the necessary material for the stock of the workhouse. The overseers may require additional material, tools, and implements from any town that has sent a person who may need those additional material, tools, and implements for work. The master of the workhouse is to keep those special material, tools, and implements separate from the common stock provided by other towns. The master is accountable to the overseers of each town for the stock, profits, and earnings generated through the labor of those inmates under his care. The master is to keep a register of the names of those who are committed, the time of their committal and discharge, and the earnings by their labor. The master provides the register to the overseers whenever they need to inspect it. All controversies between the master and the overseers are resolved at the overseers' general meeting. No town is to be charged for the support and relief of any person committed to the workhouse without the permission of the overseers in that town. No person is to be discharged from the workhouse without the permission of the overseers who first committed him or by the permission of the overseers at a general meeting or the justices of the peace at General Sessions. Every person so committed to the workhouse, if fit and able to work, is to be held and kept strictly and diligently employed in labor during his or her confinement. Any inmate's idleness, negligence, refusal to work, or stubborn and disorderly conduct is to be punished according the orders and rules of the house, not repugnant to the laws of the province. One third of the earnings by the inmate is used toward his or her support. Overseers may also order any annual allowance to any inmate from his or her earnings over and above the one-third sum. The overseers have the power to dispose of the prime stock and two thirds of the earnings generated from the labor of the inmates to the master for his service and for the expenses of keeping the inmates at a rate that the overseers and the master have agreed upon. All the rest of the materials or incomes are to be used for the town. Any town or towns may decide to discontinue their workhouse and use it for other purposes.

This law is not to be construed to abridge any of those powers already granted to Boston and its overseers of the poor with regard to a workhouse in the law of July 3, 1735.

1747
November 17
An anti-impressment riot takes place in Boston and continues for several days, involving numerous seamen, servants, and African Americans. Separately, on December 9, a fire destroys the courthouse where the General Court sits.

1748
March 10
Thirty-five townspeople including a dozen overseers of the poor subscribe to a linen manufacture scheme in Boston and decide to hold a meeting to discuss the matter further at the Workhouse on March 16.

1748
May 16
One of ten directors of the Silver Bank Scheme in 1740, Boston merchant Huge Hall, is removed from office as justice of the peace by impeachment proceedings for his misuse of power.

1750/1
February 6
An *Act to Regulate the Importation of Germans and Other Passengers Coming to Settle in This Province* states that too many Germans and other passengers arriving in one ship can cause deaths and bring in contagious distempers. The act limits the number of passengers of an incoming ship, which must allow a space of 6 foot by 1 foot 6 inches for every passenger 14 years old and upwards. Ship captains will forfeit £5 for violation.

1750/1
February 14
An *Act for Preventing and Suppressing of Riots, Routs and Unlawful Assemblies* bars any meeting of twelve persons with clubs or other weapons. Whether armed or not, any assembly of fifty people or more is unlawful. Violators are to forfeit all their lands, tenements, goods, and chattels and be sentenced to jail for one year. Anyone so convicted will also be subject to whipping thirty-nine stripes on the naked back at the public whipping-post before incarceration; the same will be repeated once every three months thereafter until the end of the convict's prison term.

1751
August 21
Two hundred leading citizens of Boston and other towns organize a Society for Encouraging Industry and Employing the

Poor at the Old South Meeting House. Incorporated in 1754, the Society actively promotes flax cultivation in the country and linen manufacturers in Boston.

1751
The Boston Linen Manufactory starts operations, which continue until 1759.

1753
September 15
A lot of 126 feet by 215 feet on the east side of Long Acre Street in Boston is purchased, where the Manufactory House is to be built.

1756
June 8
The General Court rules that a ship master is to be fined £100 for every sick, impotent, or infirm person brought into this province.

1757
April 13
The General Courts passes an *Act for Regulating the Hospital on Rainsford's Island and Further Providing in Case of Sickness*.

1757
April 15
The General Court grants a petition by Joseph Palmer, gentleman of Germantown in Braintree. A lottery of £1,215 is allowed and 10% of the prize money can be used for helping him continue the manufacture of glass, on which foreign Protestants come to depend for their livelihood.

1757

December 1

The General Court lays out rules for quartering and billeting officers and soldiers in defense of North America. Through an act of Parliament, payment for a commissioned officer of foot, under the rank of a captain, is one shilling sterling per diem, fourpence for a foot soldier, and sixpence for an officer's horse.

1759

February 13

The General Court rules on town charges incurred for the care of lewd women at their lying-in with bastard children. With the assent of two justices of the peace, selectmen and overseers of the poor have the power to bind out for up to five years any unmarried woman who has a bastard child and whose support of her lying-in comes from the town. Masters and mistresses are to forfeit £5 if they neglect their duties to educate apprentices and servants. Justices are to hold apprentices and servants responsible for their remaining terms if they desert their services.

1759

October 20

The General Court passes *An Act for the Relief of Poor Prisoners for Debt*. It orders that, if any person imprisoned for debt claims to have no estate sufficient to support him or her in prison, the gaoler will appeal to two justices—one of them being of the quorum—who are to issue a notification to the creditor or creditors of such a prisoner. The notification, which must be given forty days before the caption of the law, signifies the prisoner's desire to take the privilege and benefit allowed by this act. That is to say,

The prisoner is to take an oath, certified by justices of the peace under their hands and seals. The gaoler will set the prisoner at liberty upon receiving such a certificate, unless the creditor, his agent and attorney, executor or administrator give security to the gaoler for the payment of three shillings sixpence per week toward the support of the prisoner. The gaoler will detain the prisoner as long as said sum is paid and will release the prisoner when the payment stops. The gaoler will forfeit and pay the sum of debt the prisoner owed if he refuses to release the prisoner after the certification of his oath is issued. The prisoner will suffer any penalty for willful perjury if anything turns out contrary to the oath. All and every judgment against the any estate of the prisoner is to remain good and effectual in law. To satisfy the debt, the creditor may take out a new execution against the lands, tenements, goods, and chattels of the prisoner, except for his or her wearing apparel, bedding, and tools necessary for his or her trade or occupation. The creditor may add any weekly charges if he has provided for the prisoner's support.

1763
February 17
An *Act Declaring and Regulating the Standard of Wheat Imported into This Province and for Preventing Abuses by Millers* rules that light-colored wheat is to be of fifty-eight pounds each bushel. All other sorts of wheat are to be of sixty pounds each bushel. Millers in Boston, Roxbury, and Charlestown should use suitable mill-stones, fans, and screens.

1763
April 14
The Society for Encouraging Trade and Commerce within the Province of Massachusetts Bay is established in Boston. It has a membership of 146 persons and a Standing Committee of 15.

1765
March 22
The Stamp Act crisis emerges, lasting until March 18, 1766.

1767
March 19
An *Act in Addition to the Several Laws Already Made Relating to the Removal of Poor Persons Out of the Towns Whereof They Are Not Inhabitants* sets the rules for coping with poor persons from other provinces. A justice of the peace has the power to issue a warrant for sending a poor person out of this province, by land or water, based on what as he believes is the most convenient and least costly. The poor person, who neither belongs to this province nor has gained a legal settlement, is to pay for his own removal if he is able to pay for the charge; if not, this province shall pay. Constables of each town are to convey a poor person from county to county and from town to town until the province or colony where the poor person first came as the justice's removal warrant directs. Every constable is to keep of a fair account of the charges for conveying the poor person through his town. The constable is to forward the account to the selectmen, who should apply for reimbursement from the provincial treasury. The reimbursement of the charges for conveying a poor person to his or her settlement within this province is to follow the steps already provided by law. No person is to come, dwell, or gain an inhabitancy within any town of this province unless such a person first makes his or her desire known to the selectmen, who have the power to grant or deny such a request at a general meeting. No town is liable for the charges to maintain anyone who did not receive permission to reside from town selectmen. Upon the application of selectmen, a justice of the peace is empowered to issue a warrant to remove any of those, except for apprentices under local masters, who were not properly admitted as legal

inhabitants, together with their children—whether born before or after their coming to town, in wedlock or otherwise—back to where they properly belong. Every constable is to have his action certified before he delivers the warrant to a constable of the next county.

1767
October 28
The Boston town meeting appoints a seven-member committee to consider several measures for employing the poor "by reviving the Linen Manufacture, and in such other Ways as shall be thought most beneficial." This plan leads to a new subscription drive on March 15, 1768, when some 200 people pledge support, including 13 of the 35 subscribers in 1748.

1768
In the fall, Bostonians resist the quartering of General Thomas Gage's soldiers at the Manufactory House.

1770
March 5
The Boston "Massacre" occurs.

1770
March 29
William Molineux petitions the General Court in a last attempt to make use of the Manufactory House for textile productions.

1770
April 26
In an *Act in Addition to . . . An Act for Suppressing and Punishing of Rogues, Vagabonds and Common Beggars and Other Lewd, Idle and Disorderly Persons and for Setting the Poor to Work* (June 29, 1699), the General Court recognizes

that the old act "is oftentimes rendered very difficult." A main reason is the long distance between the place where such persons are found and the place where the house of correction is located; as a result, those who were thus found and taken according to the law often escape without any punishment. Furthermore, this situation has encouraged many from distant parts to come to this province, where "his majesty's good and industrious subjects here are frequently burthened and imposed by such vagrant, idle and disorderly persons." The court orders that the General Sessions and one or more justices of the peace out of court have the power to commit all such persons to a house of correction or to punish them either by setting in the stocks (not to exceed three hours) or by whipping (not to exceed ten stripes).

1771
July 4
An *Act in Addition to the Several Acts or Laws of This Province, Impowering the Selectmen or Overseers of the Poor of Towns to Bind Poor Children Apprentices* reveals a problem: Selectmen and overseers have the authority to bind out those poor children who or whose parents are inhabitants, but they do not have power to bind out those who or whose parents do not belong to their towns, which are often chargeable for their support. "[I]t often happens that poor children and minors do come, or are brought into, and found dwelling in, towns to which they do not belong, and thereby much charge and expence is occasioned and incurred, either for the removal of such children and minors to the places where they belong (either within or without the province), or for their support in the places where they are found, when, at the same time, they might be placed and bound apprentices in the towns where they found dwelling, as much to their own benefit, and the benefit of the public, as in any other place." The General Court therefore

orders that overseers of the poor, with the assent of two justices, have the power to bind out any poor children and minors who are found in any town or district in the province and who may incur an immediate public expense for their support or removal, provided that: (1) their circumstances are such that even if they do belong to the town they would be bound out as apprentices, according to the law; (2) males are to be bound out until the age of twenty-one and their indentures state that they will be instructed in reading, writing, and ciphering; (3) females are to be bound out until the age of eighteen and their indentures state that they will be instructed in reading and writing, if they are capable; and (4) the towns where the poor children and minors belong, not where they come to dwell or where they serve as apprentices, are still liable for their support and relief in case of need.

1772
April 25
An *Act for Incorporating the Overseers of the Poor of the Town of Boston* states that many charitable persons would like to bequeath "considerable sum of money, and other interest and estate, to the poor of the town of Boston." Yet they are "wholly frustrated" because the overseers of the poor are not incorporated. The General Court orders the incorporation of the overseers of the poor of Boston. Regarding any money, interest, and estate, real or personal, being given, granted, bequeathed or devised to the poor in Boston, the overseers of the poor in Boston "are hereby enabled in the same capacity to receive, manage, lease, let and dispose the same, according to their best discretion, to and for the use and benefit of the poor of the said town."

1772
July 14

An *Act in Addition to and Explanatory of the Several Laws Already Made Relating to the Removal of Poor Persons Out of the Towns Whereof They Are Not Inhabitants* states that several General Sessions and county courts have construed the laws of November 16, 1692, and March 19, 1767, in such a manner that a warrant of removal is considered illegal if it was signed by a justice residing in the same town as where the poor person was found. The General Court orders that a justice of the peace has the power to issue a warrant to remove a poor person found in the town of that justice's residence. The cost of the removal is to be charged to the town of the poor person's last abode or settlement, not where the poor person is found, sent out, and removed from.

1773
December 16
The Boston Tea Party occurs.

1774
Intolerable or coercive acts are passed, including the Boston Port Bill (effective June 1), the Administration of Justice Act (May 20), the Massachusetts Government Act (May 20), the Quartering Act (June 2, which extends to apply to all colonies), and the Quebec Act (May 20, which extends Canada's boundaries to the Ohio River, cutting into territories claimed by Massachusetts, Connecticut, and Virginia).

1774
March 8
An *Act for Employing and Providing for the Poor in the Town of Salem and for the Better Regulating the Workhouse in Said Town* states that Salem has lately found it necessary to erect a workhouse for the employment of the poor. The General Court gives Salem town meeting the power to choose five or more

overseers of the poor, who are to conduct monthly meetings for the discharge of their duties. The overseers have the power to inspect and regulate the workhouse; appoint a master and one or more assistants for the immediate care and oversight of the persons in the workhouse; and make orders and bylaws for the workhouse at their monthly meetings. The overseers are to present the orders and bylaws to the town meeting, which will prove or revoke them. Each overseer has the power to send any idle and indigent person to the workhouse for twenty-four hours. Two overseers have the power to send any idle and indigent person to the workhouse until discharged by the majority of the overseers at a monthly meeting. The overseers have the full power of binding out the children of parents who are unable to or negligent in providing for their children, provided that such parents are not rated for their personal estate or faculty. The overseers have the power to warn all intruders and non-inhabitants to depart the town. The overseers have the same power as selectmen to order removal of strangers, and constables of the town are to comply with the orders.

1775
April 19
The Battle at Lexington and Concord occurs, and the siege of Boston begins, lasting until March 17, 1776.

1777
January 25
The General Court passes an *Act to Prevent Monopoly and Oppression* to regulate labor wages and commodity prices, hoping to combat the avaricious conduct and exorbitant prices that have had fatal and distressful consequences for soldiers and the poorer part of the community.

1780
June 15
Presented for ratification on March 2, *A Constitution or Form of Government for the Commonwealth of Massachusetts* is adopted. The qualifications established for voters: every male inhabitant of twenty-one years of age, residing in a town of this commonwealth for a year, with either a freehold estate in the same town of the annual income of three pounds or any estate of the value of sixty pounds. For representatives: an inhabitant of a town for one year, with a freehold in the same town of the value of one hundred pounds or any ratable estate of two hundred pounds. For senators: an inhabitant of this commonwealth for five years, with a freehold of three hundred pounds or a personal estate of six hundred pounds. For governor and lieutenant governor: an inhabitant of this commonwealth for seven years, of Christian religion, with a freehold of one thousand pounds.

1786
August 15
Delegates from 37 towns hold Worcester County Convention at Leicester until August 17.

1786
August 22
Delegates from 50 towns hold Hampshire County Convention at Hatfield until August 25.

1786
The last week in August, a county convention is held at Lenox, Berkshire.

1786
August 31

Unrest and fighting occur in Shays's Rebellion until February 4, 1787.

1786
October 3
Delegates from 18 towns adjourn the Middlesex County Convention in Concord.

1788
March 26
An Act for Suppressing and Punishing of Rogues, Vagabonds, Common Beggars, and Other Idle, Disorderly and Lewd Persons is the first poor law passed after the revolution. With some minor revisions, it has essentially the same provisions as the laws of November 16, 1692, June 29, 1699, July 3, 1722, September 17, 1743, and April 26, 1770. It reads, in part, that any justice of the peace, as well as the Court of Sessions, may send and commit unto the house of correction to be kept and governed according to the rules and orders thereof, all (1) rogues, vagabonds and idle persons, going about in any town or place in the county, begging; (2) persons using any subtle craft, juggling or unlawful games or plays, or feigning themselves to have knowledge in physiognomy or palmistry or pretending that they can tell destinies or fortunes or discover where lost or stolen goods may be found; (3) common pipers, fiddlers, runaways, stubborn servants or children, common drunkards, common night walkers, pilferers, wanton and lascivious persons, in speech, conduct, or behavior; and (4) common railers or brawlers who neglect their callings or employment, misspend what they earn, and neither provide for themselves nor support their families. A new addition empowers any justice to warn an African to depart if the African has stayed in the commonwealth for more than two months.

1789

June 23

An Act Determining What Transactions Shall Be Necessary to Constitute the Settlement of a Citizen in Any Particular Town or District rules that those who came to live in the province before April 10, 1767 for a year without warning will be inhabitants, as will those who, coming after that date, obtained the approbation of a town meeting for their dwelling in the community. A person may become an inhabitant if the person establishes a freehold, resides therein, improves the same for two years, and has an annual income of three pounds. One may also become an inhabitant if the person lives in town for two years without warning or pays a town tax for five consecutive years after the age of twenty-one. A woman who marries a man of any town will become an inhabitant of the same town. Children born in wedlock in any town will be deemed inhabitants of the same town with their parents. Children born otherwise will be inhabitants of the towns with the mother until they obtain their own settlement. No person can have more than one legal settlement at one time.

1790

Increasing numbers of immigrants from Ireland begin to arrive in Boston.

1794

February 11

The General Court enacts an *Act Ascertaining What Shall Constitute a Legal Settlement of Any Person in Any Town or District within This Commonwealth, So As to Entitle Him to Support Therein in Case He Becomes Poor and Stands in Need of Relief and for Repealing All Laws Heretofore Made Respecting Such Settlement*. As a precondition for relief, a legal settlement may be obtained by means of marriage, birth, property, or service. In other words, (1) a married woman will always follow the settlement of her husband, (2) legitimate children will follow the settlement of their father, (3) illegitimate children will follow the settlement of their mother at the time of their birth, (4) a person who is at least twenty-one years old and who takes rents and profits three years successively from an estate or freehold at three pounds per annum will gain a settlement, (5) a person who is at least twenty-one years old and is assessed at either £60 of estate or a yearly income of £3.12s., paying a town tax for five years, will gain a settlement, and 6) any person who serves one year as a town clerk, treasurer, selectman, overseer of the poor, assessor, constable, or collector of taxes will gain a settlement. (Not until May 28, 1974, is this insistence that relief requires a legal settlement repealed according to St.1974, c. 260, §17.)

1794
February 26
The General Court passes an *Act Providing for the Relief and Support, Employment and Removal of the Poor*. It repeals, in part, previous laws relative to warning out and removal of the poor. However, all those who are chargeable but found in other towns can be removed back to where they have settled. The requirement of a legal settlement for relief stands.

1801
Designed by Charles Bulfinch, a newly constructed Almshouse at Barton's Point doubles the size of the old Almshouse in Boston.

Bibliography

Primary Sources

Printed records.

Acts and Resolves, Public and Private, of the Province of the Massachusetts Bay, 1692-1780; *Acts and Laws of Massachusetts*, 1780-1805. 34 vols. Boston: Wright & Potter, 1869-1922.

Bates, Samuel A., ed. *Records of the Town of Braintree, 1640-1793*. Randolph, Mass.: Daniel H. Huxford, 1886.

Dann, John C., ed. *The Revolution Remembered: Eyewitness Accounts of the War for Independence*. Chicago: University of Chicago Press, 1980.

Dunn, Richard S., James Savage, and Laetitia Yeandle, eds. *The Journal of John Winthrop, 1630-1649*. Cambridge, Mass.: Harvard University Press, 1996.

Harris, Nathaniel. *Records of the Court of Nathaniel Harris*. Watertown, Mass.: Historical Society of Watertown, 1893.

Hill, Don Gleason, ed. *The Early Records of the Town of Dedham, MA, 1659-1673*. Dedham, Mass., 1894.

Journals of the House of Representatives of Massachusetts, 1715-1778. 53 vols. Boston: Massachusetts Historical Society, 1919-1988.

Bibliography

Konig, David Thomas, ed. *Plymouth Court Records, 1686-1859*. Boston: New England Historic Genealogical Society, CD-ROM, 2002.

Martin, James Kirby, ed. *Ordinary Courage: The Revolutionary War Adventures of Joseph Plumb Martin*. Malden, Mass.: Blackwell Publishing, 2008.

Massachusetts Soldiers and Sailors of the Revolutionary War. 17 vols. Boston: Wright & Potter, 1896-1908.

Nellis, Eric, and Anne Decker Cecere, eds. *The Eighteenth-Century Records of the Boston Overseers of the Poor*. Boston: Colonial Society of Massachusetts, 2007.

Pruitt, Bettye Hobbs, ed. *The Massachusetts Tax Valuation List of 1771*. repr., Camden, Me.: Picton Press, 1998.

The Records of the Town of Cambridge (Formerly Newtowne) Massachusetts, 1630-1703. Cambridge, Mass., 1901.

Records of the Town of Lee from Its Incorporation to A. D. 1801. Lee, Mass.: Press of the Valley Gleaner, 1900.

Report of the Record Commissioners of the City of Boston, vols. 1, 2, 5, 7, 8, 9, 10, 12, 13, 14, 15, 17, 19, 20, 23, 25, 27, 29, 33, 37. Boston: Rockwell and Churchill, 1876-1906.

Riley, Stephen T., and Edward W. Hanson, eds. *The Papers of Robert Treat Paine*. 2 vols. Boston: Massachusetts Historical Society, 1992.

Shurtleff, Nathaniel B., ed. *Records of the Province of the Massachusetts Bay Colony*, 6 vols. Boston: William White, 1853-1854.

The Statutes of the Realm. 11 vols. repr., Buffalo, N.Y.: William S. Hein & Co., 1993.

Town of Weston, *Records of the First Precinct, 1746-1754 and of the Town, 1754-1803*. Boston: Alfred Mudge & Son, 1893.

Town of Weston, *The Tax Lists, 1757-1827*. Boston: Alfred Mudge & Son, 1897.

Town Record of Dudley, Massachusetts. 2 vols. Pawtucket, R. I.: Adam Sutcliffe Co., 1893-94.

Watertown Records. 3 vols. Watertown, Mass.: Press of Fred G. Barker, 1894-1904.

Whitemore, William H., comp. *The Colonial Laws of Massachusetts: Reprinted from the Edition of 1672 with the Supplements through 1686.* Boston: Rockwell and Churchill, 1887.

Wroth, L. Kinvin, and Hiller B. Zobel, eds. *Legal Papers of John Adams.* 3 vols. Cambridge, Mass.: Belknap Press, 1965.

Manuscript collections.

At the American Antiquarian Society: Ephraim Abbot Papers. Joseph Allen Papers. Elijah Brigham Papers. Draper-Rice Family Papers. Samuel Flagg Records. Felton Family Papers. Hampshire County (Mass.) Court Records, 1677-1696, 1786-1826. Daniel Henchman Papers. Henshaw Family Papers. William Heywood Account Book, 1760-1794. Heywood Family Papers. Holden (Mass.) First Congregational Church Records. Holliston (Mass.) Papers. Thomas Legate Account Books, 1758-1802. Joseph Lemmon Papers. Massachusetts Collection, 1629-c.1869. Massachusetts Court of Common Pleas (Suffolk County) Record Book, 1783-1790. Beriah Norton Account Book, 1764-1819. Paine Family Papers. Quabbin Towns Records. Benjamin Read Judicial Records, 1786-1800. Daniel Smith Account Book, 1707-1711. Suffolk County (Mass.) Justice of the Peace Notebook, 1731-1763. Ward Family Papers. Ware (Mass.) Record Book, 1814-1832.

At Baker Library, Harvard University: Samuel Abbot Collections.

At the Massachusetts Historical Society: Adams-Morse Papers. Amory Family Papers. (Boston) Charitable Irish Society Records. Boston Episcopal Charitable Society Records. Cushing Family Papers. First Church (Watertown, Mass.)

Records. Charles Henry Frankland Diary, 1755-1813. Henry Gardner Papers. Hugh Hall Papers. Abiel Holmes Papers. Giles Kellogg Papers. King's Chapel Records. Massachusetts Charitable Society Records. May Family Papers. Metcalf Family Papers. Miscellaneous Bond Manuscripts Collection. New Bedford Benevolent Society Records. James Otis II Papers. Police Report of Boston 1814. Poor Relief Records of the First Church of Boston. Ezekiel Price Papers. Quincy Family Papers. Roxbury Almshouse Records. Charles Russell Papers. Salem Overseers of the Poor Annual Report 1818. Savage Family Papers. The Scots' Charitable Society Records. John Soughgate Diaries, 1770-1797. Spooner Family Papers. Stoddard Family Papers. Trustees' Report of the (Boston) Society for the Employment of the Female Poor, 1827-1834. Artemas Ward Diary and Record Book, 1758-1805. Ward-Perry-Dexter Papers. Webb Family Papers.
At the New England Historic Genealogical Society: Middleborough (Mass.) Overseers of the Poor Record, 1780-1795.

Warning-out records.

Blake, Francis E., comp. *Worcester County (Mass.) Warnings, 1737-1788*. Worcester, Mass.: F. P. Rice, 1899.
Easton Town Records. 2 vols. 2 (1789-1816): 32-33, 34-35, 35-37, 45, 46, 70-71, 92-93, 105-106. In Barbara Tourtillott's transcripts at http://www.tourtillot.org/easton/index.
Hanson, Robert Brand, ed. Transients, Strangers, Servants, Sojourners, and Warnings Out. In *Vital Records of Dedham, Massachusetts, 1635-1845*, 489-567. Camden, Me.: Picton Press, 1997.

Love, Robert. Record book, January 29, 1765 to August 27, 1766 (Massachusetts Historical Society). List of warnings out, May 1 to August 28, 1772 (Boston Public Library).

New England Historical and Genealogical Register 57 (1903): 141-143 (Walpole); 65 (1911), 39-43 (Foxborough); 70 (1916): 283 (Northbridge); 83 (1929): 164-168 (Chelmsford); 92 (1938): 46-60 (Malden); 105 (1951): 75-76 (Sharon); 111 (1957): 320-321 (Sudbury); 141 (1987): 179-202, 330-357; 142 (1988): 56-84 (Wrentham); and 144 (1990): 215-224 (Weston).

Sherman, Ruth Wilder, Robert M. Sherman, and Robert S. Wakefield, comps. *An Index to Plymouth County, Massachusetts, Warnings Out from the Plymouth Court Records, 1686-1859*. Plymouth, Mass.: General Society of Mayflower Descendants, 2003.

Warning-out books, 1745-1770, 1771-1773, 1791-1792, in Boston Overseers of the Poor Records, 1733-1925. Microfilms, reel 1, vols. 1, 2 (Massachusetts Historical Society).

Secondary Sources

Adair, Douglass and John A. Schutz, eds. *Peter Oliver's Origin & Progress of the American Revolution: A Tory View*. Stanford, Calif.: Stanford University Press, 1967.

Adams, John W., and Alice Bee Kasakoff. "Migration and the Family in Colonial New England: The View from Genealogies." *Journal of Family History* 9 (1984): 24-43.

Allen, David Grayson. *In English Ways: The Movement of Societies and the Transferal of English Local Law and Custom to Massachusetts Bay in the Seventeenth Century*. New York: W.W. Norton, 1982.

Anderson, Fred. *A People's Army: Massachusetts Soldiers and Society in the Seven Years' War*. Chapel Hill: University of North Carolina Press, 1984.

Andrew, Donna T. *Philanthropy and Police: London Charity in the Eighteenth Century*. Princeton, N.J.: Princeton University Press, 1989.

Andrews, Charles M. "The Boston Merchants and the Non-Importation Movement." *Publications of the Colonial Society of Massachusetts* 19 (Boston, 1918): 159-259.

Arndt, Johann. *True Christianity*, trans. Peter Erb. New York: Paulist Press, 1979.

Aronowitz, Stanley. *False Promises: The Shaping of American Working Class Consciousness*. Durham, N. C.: Duke University Press, 1992.

Bagnall, William R. *The Textile Industries of the United States*. Cambridge, Mass.: Riverside Press, 1893.

Bailyn, Bernard. *Atlantic History: Concept and Contours*. Cambridge, Mass.: Harvard University Press, 2005.

―――. *The Peopling of British North America: An Introduction*. New York: Alfred A. Knopf, 1986.

―――. *Voyagers to the West: A Passage in the Peopling of America on the Eve of the Revolution*. New York: Alfred A. Knopf, 1986.

―――. *The Ideological Origins of the American Revolution*. Cambridge, Mass.: Belknap Press, 1967.

Baker, Jennifer J. *Securing the Commonwealth: Debt, Speculation, and Writing in the Making of Early America*. Baltimore: Johns Hopkins University Press, 2005.

Barrus, Hiram. *History of the Town of Goshen, Hampshire County, Massachusetts from Its First Settlement in 1761 to 1881 with Family Sketches*. Boston: Published by the Author, 1881.

Batinski, Michael C. *Jonathan Belcher, Colonial Governor*. Lexington, Ken.: University Press of Kentucky, 1996.

Beard, Charles Austin. *The Office of Justice of the Peace in England in Its Origin and Development*. New York: Columbia University Press, 1904.

―――. *An Economic Interpretation of the Constitution of the United States*. New York: Macmillan Publishing Co., 1913.

Becker, Carl Lotus. *The History of Political Parties in the Province of New York, 1760-1776*. repr. Madison, Wis.: University of Wisconsin Press, 1960.

Benedict, William A., and Hiram A. Tracy. *History of the Town of Sutton, Massachusetts from 1704 to 1876*. Worcester, Mass.: Sanford & Company, 1878.

Benton, Josiah Henry. *Warning Out in New England, 1656-1817*. Boston: W. B. Clarke Company, 1911.

Billias, George Athan. *General John Glover and His Marblehead Mariners*. New York: Hold, Rinehart and Winston, 1960.

Blackstone, William. *Commentaries on the Laws of England*. 4 vols. repr., Chicago: Chicago University Press, 1979.

Blake, John B. *Public Health in the Town of Boston, 1630-1822*. Cambridge, Mass.: Harvard University Press, 1959.

Bodge, George Madison. *Soldiers in King Philip's War*. Boston: Printed for the Author, 1906.

Boorstin, Daniel J. *The Americans: The Colonial Experience*. New York: Vintage books, 1958.

Breen, T. H. *The Marketplace of Revolution: How Consumer Politics Shaped American Independence*. New York: Oxford University Press, 2004.

Bremer, Francis J. *John Winthrop: America's Forgotten Founding Father*. New York: Oxford University Press, 2003.

Breul, Frank R., and Steven J. Diner, eds. *Compassion and Responsibility: Readings in the History of Social Welfare Policy in the United States*. Chicago: University of Chicago Press, 1980.

Bridenbaugh, Carl. *Cities in the Wilderness: The First Century of Urban Life in America, 1625-1742*. New York: Ronald Press, 1938.

-----. *Cities in Revolt: Urban Life in America, 1743-1776*. New York: Alfred A. Knopf, 1955.

-----. *The Colonial Craftsman*. repr., New York: Dover Publications, 1990.

Brock, Leslie V. *The Currency of the American Colonies 1700-1764: A Study in Colonial Finance and Imperial Relations*. New York: Arno Press, 1975.

Brooke, John L. "To the Quiet of the People: Revolutionary Settlements and Civil Unrest in Western Massachusetts, 1774-1789." *William and Mary Quarterly*, 3rd ser., 46 (1989): 426-462.

-----. *The Heart of the Commonwealth: Society and Political Culture in Worcester County, Massachusetts, 1713-1861*. Amherst, Mass.: University of Massachusetts Press, 1992.

Brown, Abram English. *History of the Town of Bedford, Middlesex County, Massachusetts*. Bedford, Mass.: Published by the Author, 1891.

Brown, Katherine. "The Controversy over the Franchise in Puritan Massachusetts, 1954-1974." *William and Mary Quarterly*, 3rd ser., 33 (1976): 212-241.

Brown, Louis K. *Wilderness Town: The Story of Bedford, Massachusetts*. n.p., 1968.

Brown, Robert E. *Middle-Class Democracy and the Revolution in Massachusetts, 1691-1780*. Ithaca, N. Y.: Cornell University Press, 1955.

Brundage, Anthony. *The English Poor Laws, 1700-1930*. Basingstoke, UK: Palgrave, 2002.

Bushman, Richard L. *From Puritan to Yankee: Character and the Social Order in Connecticut, 1690-1765*. Cambridge, Mass.: Harvard University Press, 1967.

Carp, Benjamin L. *Rebels Rising: Cities and the American Revolution*. New York: Oxford University Press, 2007.

Carpenter, —, and — Morehouse, comps. *The History of the Town of Amherst, Massachusetts, 1731-1896*. Amherst, Mass.: Press of Carpenter & Morehouse, 1896.

Carr, Jacqueline Barbara. "A Change 'As Remarkable as the Revolution Itself': Boston's Demographics, 1780-1800," *New England Quarterly* 73 (2000): 583-602.

—----. *After the Siege: A Social History of Boston, 1775-1800*. Boston: Northeastern University Press, 2005.

Caswell, Lilley B. *The History of the Town of Royalston, Massachusetts*. n.p., Published by the Town of Royalston, 1917.

Chase, Arthur. *History of Ware, Massachusetts*. Cambridge [Mass.] The University Press, 1911.

Chase, George Wingate. *The History of Haverhill, Massachusetts, from Its First Settlement in 1640 to the Year 1860*. Haverhill [Mass.]: Published by the Author, 1861.

Chauncy, Charles. The *Idle-Poor* Secluded from the *Bread of Charity* by the *Christian Law*. A Sermon Preached in Boston, before the Society for *Encouraging Industry* and *Employing the Poor*. Aug. 12. 1752. Boston: Thomas Fleet, 1752.

Clark, Christopher. *The Roots of Rural Capitalism: Western Massachusetts, 1780-1860*. Ithaca, N.Y.: Cornell University Press, 1990.

Clark, Victor S. *History of Manufactures in the United States, 1607-1860*. New York: McGrew-Hill, 1929.

Clarke, George Kuhn. *History of Needham, Massachusetts, 1711-1911*. Cambridge, Mass.: Printed by the Author, 1912.

Cohen, Daniel A. "A Fellowship of Thieves: Property Criminals in Eighteenth-Century Massachusetts." *Journal of Social History* 22 (1988): 65-92.

Colman, Benjamin. *A Sermon for the Reformation of Manners*. Boston: T. Fleet and T. Crump, 1716.

Bibliography

-----. *Righteousness and Compassion; The Duty and Character of Pious Rulers*. Boston: J. Draper, 1736.

-----. *The Merchandise of a People Holiness to the Lord*. Boston: J. Draper, 1736.

-----. *The Unspeakable Gift of God; A Right Charitable and Bountiful Spirit to the Poor and Needy Members of Jesus Christ*. Boston: J. Draper, 1739.

Connington, Helen Webber. *History of Barre: Windows into the Past*. Barre, Mass.: The Barre Historical Commission, 1992.

Conroy, David W. *In Public Houses: Drink and the Revolution of Authority in Colonial Massachusetts*. Chapel Hill: University of North Carolina Press, 1995.

Cook, Edward M. *The Father of the Towns: Leadership and Community Structure in Eighteenth-Century New England*. Baltimore: Johns Hopkins University Press, 1976.

Coolidge, Mabel Cook. *The History of Petersham, Massachusetts*. n.p., For the Petersham Historical Society, 1948.

Copies of Letters from Governor Bernard, &c., to the Earl of Hillsborough. Boston: [Benjamin] Edes and [John] Gill, 1769.

Coquillette, Daniel R., ed. *Law in Colonial Massachusetts, 1630-1800*. Boston: Colonial Society of Massachusetts, 1984.

Corey, Deloraine Pendre. *The History of Malden, Massachusetts, 1633-1785*. Malden [Mass.]: Published by the Author, 1899.

Crafts, James M. *History of the Town of Whately, Massachusetts Including a Narrative of Leading Events from the First Settlement of Hatfield: 1661-1899*. Orange, Mass.: D. L. Grandall, 1899.

Crandall, Ralph J. "New England's Second Great Migration: The First Three Generations of Settlement, 1630-1700." *New England Historical and Genealogical Register*, 129 (1975): 347-360.

Crane, Elain Forman. *Ebb Tide in New England: Women, Seaports, and Social Change, 1630-1800*. Boston: Northeastern University Press, 1998.

Cray, Jr., Robert E. *Paupers and Poor Relief in New York City and Its Rural Environs, 1700-1830*. Philadelphia: Temple University Press, 1988.

Cummings, Abbott Lowell, ed. *Rural Household Inventories Establishing the Names, Uses and Furnishings of Rooms in the Colonial New England Home, 1675-1775*. Boston: Society for the Preservation of New England Antiquities, 1964.

Currier, John J. *The History of Newburyport, Massachusetts, 1764-1905*. repr., Somersworth, N.H.: New Hampshire Publishing Company, 1977.

Dalton, Michael. *The Countrey Justice, Containing the Practise of the Justices of the Peace Out of Their Sessions*. London, Printed for the Societie of Stationers, 1622.

Davis, Andrew McFarland. "Papers Relating to the Land Bank of 1740." *Publications of the Colonial Society of Massachusetts* 4 (Boston, 1910): 1-200.

-----. *Currency and Banking in the Province of the Massachusetts Bay*. 2 vols. repr., New York: Augustus M. Kelley, 1970.

Davis, Natalie Zemon. *Society and Culture in Early Modern France*. Stanford, Calif.: Stanford University Press, 1975.

Dayton, Cornelia Hughes. *Women before the Bar: Gender, Law, and Society in Connecticut, 1639-1789*. Chapel Hill: University of North Carolina Press, 1995.

-----, and Sharon V. Salinger. *Warning Out: Robert Love's Search for Strangers in Pre-Revolutionary Boston*. (Forthcoming)

Defoe, Daniel. *An Essay upon Projects*, ed. Joyce D. Kennedy et al. repr., New York: AMS Press, 1999.

-----. *Giving Alms No Charity and Employing the Poor*. London: Booksellers of London and Westminster, 1704.

DeForest, Heman Packard. *The History of Westborough, Massachusetts*. Westborough [Mass.]: n.p., 1891.

Demos, John. *A Little Commonwealth: Family Life in Plymouth Colony*. New York: Oxford University Press, 1970.

Donovan, Francis D. *The New Grant: A History of Medway*. Medway, Mass.: n.p., 1976.

Douglass, William. *A Summary, Historical and Political, of the First Planting, Progressive Improvements, and Present State of the British Settlements in North-America*. 2 vols. London: Reprinted for R. Baldwin, 1755.

Dowdell, E. G. *A Hundred Years of Quarter Sessions: The Government of Middlesex from 1660 to 1760*. Cambridge, UK: Cambridge University Press, 1932.

Drake, Samuel G. *The History and Antiquities of Boston*. Boston: Luther Stevens, 1856.

Drumm, Nelde K., and Margaret P. Harley. *Lunenburg: The Heritage of Turkey Hills, 1718-1978*. Leominster, Mass.: A. & L. Graphics, 1977.

Dublin, Thomas. *Women at Work: The Transformation of Work and Community in Lowell, Massachusetts, 1826-1860*. New York: Columbia University Press, 1979.

Dufour, Ronald P. *Modernization in Colonial Massachusetts, 1630-1763*. New York: Garland Publishing, 1987.

Dunn, Elizabeth E. "'Grasping at the Shadow': The Massachusetts Currency Debate, 1690-1751." *New England Quarterly* 71 (1998): 54-76.

Eden, Frederic Morton. *The State of the Poor, or, An History of the Labouring Class in England*. 3 vols. repr., Bristol, UK: Thoemmes Press, 2001.

Edes, Henry H. "Memoir of Dr. Thomas Young, 1731-1777." *Publication of the Colonial Society of Massachusetts* 11 (Boston, 1910): 2-54.

Egnal, Marc. *Divergent Paths: How Culture and Institutions Have Shaped North American Growth.* New York: Oxford University Press, 1996.

─────. *New World Economies: The Growth of the Thirteen Colonies and Early Canada.* New York: Oxford University Press, 1998.

─────, and Joseph Ernst, "An Economic Interpretation of the American Revolution." *William and Mary Quarterly*, 3rd ser., 29 (1972): 3-32.

Ellis, Leonard Bolles. *History of New Bedford and Its Vicinity, 1602-1892.* Syracuse, N. Y.: D. Mason & Co., 1892.

Emerson, William A. *History of the Town of Douglas, from the Earliest Period to the Close of 1878.* Boston: F. W. Bird, 1879.

Emery, Samuel Hopkins. *History of Taunton, Massachusetts from Its Settlement to the Present Time.* Syracuse, N.Y.: D. Mason & Co., 1893.

Erb, Peter C. ed. *Pietists: Selected Writings.* New York: Paulist Press, 1983.

Everitt, Alan. "Social Mobility in Early Modern England." *Past and Present* 33 (1966): 56-73.

Faragher, John Mack. *A Great and Noble Scheme: The Tragic Story of the Expulsion of the French Acadians from Their American Homeland.* New York: W.W. Norton, 2006.

Feer, Robert A. *Shays's Rebellion.* New York: Garland Publishing, Inc., 1988.

Fehler, Timothy G. *Poor Relief and Protestantism: The Evolution of Social Welfare in Sixteenth-Century Emden.* Aldershot, UK: Ashgate Publishing, 1999.

Felt, Joseph B. *History of Ipswich, Essex, and Hamilton.* Cambridge, Mass.: Charles Folsom, 1834.

Fischer, David Hackett. *Historians' Fallacies: Toward a Logic of Historical Thought.* New York: Harper & Row, 1970.

─────. *Albion's Seed: Four British Folkways in America.* New York: Oxford University Press, 1989.

―――. *Paul Revere's Ride.* New York: Oxford University Press, 1994.

―――. *Washington's Crossing.* New York: Oxford University Press, 2004.

Foster, Stephen. *Their Solitary Way: The Puritan Social Ethic in the First Century of Settlement in New England.* New Haven, Conn.: Yale University Press, 1971.

Gee, Henry, and William John Hardy, eds. *Documents Illustrative of English Church History.* London: Macmillan and Co., 1910.

Geremek, Bronislaw. *Poverty: A History.* Oxford, UK: Basil Blackwell Ltd., 1994.

Gilje, Paul A. *Rioting in America.* Bloomington, Ind.: Indiana University Press, 1996.

Graham, Millar, W. The Poor Apprentices of Boston Indentures of Poor Children Bound Out Apprentices by the Overseers of the Poor of Boston, 1734-1776. M. A. thesis, College of William and Mary, 1958.

Grassby, Richard. *The Business Community of Seventeenth-Century England.* Cambridge, UK: Cambridge University Press, 1995.

Green, Mason A. *Springfield, 1636-1886: History of Town and City.* Boston: Rockwell and Churchill, 1888.

Greene, Evarts B., and Virginia D. Harrington. *American Population before the Federal Census of 1790.* repr., Baltimore, Md.: Genealogical Publishing Co., 1993.

Greenwood, Isaac J., ed., *The Revolutionary Service of John Greenwood of Boston and New York, 1775-1783.* New York: De Vinne Press, 1922.

Greven, Jr., Philip J. *Four Generations: Population, Land, and Family in Colonial Andover, Massachusetts.* Ithaca, N. Y.: Cornell University Press, 1970.

Gross, Robert A. *The Minutemen and Their World.* New York: Hill and Wang, 1976.

―――, ed., *In Debt to Shays: The Bicentennial of an Agrarian Rebellion*. Charlottesville, Va.: University Press of Virginia, 1993.

Harris, Richard Colebrook. *The Seigneurial System in Early Canada; A Geographical Study*. Kingston, Can.: McGill-Queen's University Press, 1984.

Hatch, Louis Clinton. *The Administration of the American Revolutionary Army*. New York: Longmans, Green, and Co., 1904.

Hartigan-O'Connor, Ellen. *The Ties That Buy: Women and Commerce in Revolutionary America*. Philadelphia: University of Pennsylvania Press, 2009.

Hay, Douglas et al., *Albion's Fatal Tree: Crime and Society in Eighteenth-Century England*. London: Penguin Books, 1975.

Hazen, Henry A. *History of Billerica, Massachusetts*. Boston: A. Williams and Co., 1883.

Henderson, Edith G. *Foundations of English Administration Law: Certiorari and Mandamus in the Seventeenth Century*. Cambridge, Mass.: Harvard University Press, 1963.

Henretta, James A. "Economic Development and Social Structure in Colonial Boston." *William and Mary Quarterly*, 3d ser., 22 (1965): 75-92.

Herndon, Ruth Wallis. *Unwelcome Americans: Living on the Margin in Early New England*. Philadelphia: University of Pennsylvania Press, 2001.

―――. "Children and Masters: Tracking Eighteenth-Century New Englanders through Indentures," *New England Ancestors* 4 (2003): 22-24.

―――. and John E. Murray, eds., *Children Bound to Labor: The Pauper Apprentice System in Early America*. Ithaca, N.Y.: Cornell University Press, 2009.

Hill, Christopher. *The World Turned Upside Down: Radical Ideas during the English Revolution*. New York: Penguin Books, 1991.

―――. *Society and Puritanism in Pre-Revolutionary England.* New York: St. Martin's, 1997.

―――. *Intellectual Origins of the English Revolution Revisited.* Oxford, UK: Clarendon Press, 2001.

Himmelfarb, Gertrude. *The Idea of Poverty: England in the Early Industrial Age.* New York: Alfred A. Knopf, 1984.

Hitchcock, Tim. *Down and Out in Eighteen-Century London.* London: Hambledon and London, 2004.

Hoerder, Dirk *Crowd Action in Revolutionary Massachusetts, 1765-1780.* New York: Academic Press, 1977.

Hoffman, Ronald, and Peter J. Albert, eds. *Women in the Age of the American Revolution.* Charlottesville, Va.: University Press of Virginia, 1989.

Holly, H. Hobart, ed. *Braintree Massachusetts Its History.* Braintree, Mass.: Braintree Historical Society, 1985.

Holton, Woody. *Forced Founders: Indians, Debtors, Slaves, and the Making of the American Revolution in Virginia.* Chapel Hill: University of North Carolina Press, 1999.

Howes, Frederick G. *History of the Town of Ashfield, Franklin County, Massachusetts from Its Settlement in 1742 to 1910.* n.p., Published by the Town, ca.1910.

Huang, Nian-Sheng. "The Impeachment of Justice Hall." *Massachusetts Historical Review* (2010), 12: 101-117.

―――. "Financing Poor Relief in Colonial Boston" *Massachusetts Historical Review* (2006), 8: 73-103.

―――. *Franklin's Father Josiah: Life of a Colonial Boston Tallow Chandler, 1653-1745.* Philadelphia: American Philosophical Society, 2000.

Hudson, Alfred Sereno. *The History of Sudbury, Massachusetts, 1638-1889.* n. p., The Town of Sudbury, 1889.

Hufton, Olwen H. *The Poor of Eighteenth-Century France.* Oxford, UK: Oxford University Press, 1974.

Hunt, Lynn, ed., *The New Cultural History.* Berkeley, Calf.: University of California Press, 1989.

Hutchinson, Thomas. *The History of the Colony and Province of Massachusetts-Bay*, ed. Lawrence Shaw Mayo. 3 vols. Cambridge, Mass.: Harvard University Press, 1936.

Innes, Stephen, ed., *Work and Labor in Early America*. Chapel Hill: University of North Carolina Press, 1988.

Innes, William C. *Social Concern in Calvin's Geneva*. Allison Park, Penn.: Pickwick Publications, 1983.

Jacob, Margaret, and James Jacob, eds. *The Origins of Anglo-American Radicalism*. London: George Allen & Unwin, 1984.

Jones, Douglas Lamar. "The Strolling Poor: Transiency in Eighteenth-Century Massachusetts." *Journal of Social History* 8 (1975): 28-54.

-----. "Poverty and Vagabondage: The Progress of Survival in Eighteenth-Century Massachusetts." *New England Historical and Genealogical Register* 133 (1979): 243-254.

-----. *Village and Seaport: Migration and Society in Eighteenth-Century Massachusetts*. Hanover, N.H.: University Press of New England, 1981.

Jones, E. Alfred. *The Loyalists of Massachusetts: Their Memorials, Petitions, and Claims*. London: The Saint Catherine Press, 1930.

Jordan, W. K. *Philanthropy in England, 1480-1660*. New York: Russell Sage Foundation, 1959.

Judd, Sylvester. *History of Hadley, Including the Early History of Hatfield, South Hadley, Amherst and Granby, Massachusetts*. repr., Camden, Me.: Picton Press, 1991.

Jütte, Robert. *Poverty and Deviance in Early Modern Europe*. Cambridge, UK: Cambridge University Press, 1994.

Kamensky, Jane. *Governing the Tongue: The Politics of Speech in Early New England*. New York: Oxford University Press, 1997.

Kammen, Michael. *People of Paradox: An Inquiry Concerning the Origins of American Civilization*. New York: Vintage Books, 1973.

Kanstroom, Daniel. *Deportation Nation: Outsiders in American History*. Cambridge, Mass.: Harvard University Press, 2007.

Katz, Stanley N., ed., *Colonial America: Essays in Politics and Social Development*. 2d. ed. Boston: Little, Brown and Company, 1976.

Kelso, Robert W. *The History of Public Poor Relief in Massachusetts, 1620-1920*. Boston: Houghton Mifflin Company, 1922.

Kinney, Arthur F., ed., *Rogues, Vagabonds, & Sturdy Beggars: A New Gallery of Tudor and Early Stuart Rogue Literature Exposing the Lives, Times, and Cozening Tricks of the Elizabethan Underworld*. repr., Amherst, Mass.: University of Massachusetts Press, 1990.

Klebaner, Benjamin J. "Pauper Auctions: The 'New England Method' of Public Poor Relief." *Essex Institute Historical Collections* 91 (1955): 195-210.

Kulikoff, Allan. "The Progress of Inequality in Revolutionary Boston." *William and Mary Quarterly*, 3d ser., 28 (1971): 375-412.

-----. *The Agrarian Origins of American Capitalism*. Charlottesville, Va.: University Press of Virginia, 1992.

-----. *From British Peasants to Colonial American Farmers*. Chapel Hill: University of North Carolina Press, 2000.

Kümin, Beat A. *The Shaping of a Community: The Rise and Reformation of the English Parish, c. 1400-1560*. Hants, UK: Scolar Press, 1996.

-----, ed., *Reformations Old and New: Essays on the Socio-Economic Impact of Religious Change, c. 1470-1630*. Aldershot, UK: Scolar Press, 1996.

Lambard, William. *Eirenarcha, or, Of the Office of the Justices of the Peace*. repr., Clark, N. J.: Lawbook Exchange, Ltd., 2003.

Lamson, Daniel S. *History of the Town of Weston, Massachusetts, 17630-1890*. Boston: Press of Geo. H. Ellis Co., 1913.

Landau, Norma. *The Justices of the Peace, 1679-1760*. Berkeley, Calif.: University of California Press, 1984.

-----, ed., *Law, Crime and English Society, 1660-1830*. Cambridge, UK: Cambridge University Press, 2002.

Lee, Charles R. "Public Poor Relief and the Massachusetts Community, 1620-1715." *New England Quarterly* 55 (1982): 564-585.

Lemay, J. A. Leo. *The Life of Benjamin Franklin*. 3 v. Philadelphia: University of Pennsylvania Press, 2006-2009.

Lemisch, Jesse. "Jack Tar in the Street: Merchant Seaman in the Politics of Revolutionary America." *William and Mary Quarterly*, 3d ser., 25 (1968): 371-407.

-----. "The American Revolution Seen from the Bottom Up." In Barton J. Bernstein, ed., *Towards a New Past: Dissenting Essays in American History*, 3-45. New York: Pantheon Books, 1968.

Lemon, James T. *The Best Poor Man's Country: A Geographical Study of Early Southeastern Pennsylvania*. New York: W. W. Norton, 1976.

Leonard, E. M. *The Early History of English Poor Relief*. repr., New York: Barnes & Noble, 1965.

Lepore, Jill. "Historians Who Love Too Much: Reflections on Microhistory and Biography." *Journal of American History* 88 (2001): 129-144.

Levy, Barry. *Town Born: The Political Economy of New England from Its Founding to the Revolution*. Philadelphia: University of Pennsylvania Press, 2009.

Lindberg, Carter. *Beyond Charity: Reformation Initiatives for the Poor*. Minneapolis, Minn.: Augsburg Fortress, 1993.

Lockridge, Kenneth A. "Land, Population and the Evolution of New England Society, 1630-1790." *Past and Present* 39 (1968): 62-80.

-----. *A New England Town, The First Hundred Years: Dedham, Massachusetts, 1636-1736*. New York: W. W. Norton, 1970.

London, Jack. *The People of the Abyss*. repr., London: Pluto Press, 2001.

Loring, James Spear. *The Hundred Boston Orators*. Boston: John P. Jewett and Company, 1855.

Lynch, Katherine A. *Individuals, Families, and Communities in Europe, 1200-1800: The Urban Foundations of Western Society*. Cambridge, UK: Cambridge University Press, 2003.

Maas, David E., ed., *Divided Hearts, Massachusetts Loyalists, 1765-1790: A Biographical Directory*. Boston: New England Historic Genealogical Society, 1980.

Maier, Pauline. *From Resistance to Revolution: Colonial Radicals and the Development of American Opposition to Britain, 1765-1776*. New York: Random House, 1973.

Main, Jackson Turner. *The Social Structure of Revolutionary America*. Princeton, N. J.: Princeton University Press, 1965.

Malcolm, Joyce Lee. *Peter's War: A New England Slave Boy and the American Revolution*. New Haven, Conn.: Yale University Press, 2009.

Mann, Bruce H. *Neighbors and Strangers: Law and Community in Early Connecticut*. Chapel Hill: University of North Carolina Press, 1987.

Martin, John Frederick. *Profits in the Wilderness: Entrepreneurship and the Founding of New England Towns*. Chapel Hill: University of North Carolina Press, 1991.

Mather, Cotton. *Bonifacius: An Essay upon the Good*, ed. David Levin. Cambridge, Mass.: Belknap Press, 1966.

Matson, Cathy, ed. *The Economy of Early America: Historical Perspectives and New Directions*. University Park, Penn.: Pennsylvania State University Press, 2006.

Mayhew, Henry. *London Labour and the London Poor*, ed. Victor Neuburg. London: Penguin Books, 1985.

---- et al. *The London Underworld in the Victorian Period: Authentic First –Person Accounts by Beggars, Thieves, and Prostitutes*. repr., Mineola, N.Y.: Dover Publications, 2005.

McCullough, David. *John Adams*. New York: Simon & Schuster, 2001.

----. *1776*. New York: Simon & Schuster, 2005.

McCusker, John J., and Russell R. Menard. *The Economy of British America, 1607-1789*. Chapel Hill: University of North Carolina Press, 1991.

McDonnell, Michael A. *The Politics of War: Race, Class, and Conflict in Revolutionary Virginia*. Chapel Hill: University of North Carolina Press, 2007.

McGiffert, Michael., ed. *In Search of Early America: The William & Mary Quarterly, 1943-1993*. Richmond, Va.: William Byrd Press, 1993.

McManus, Edgar J. *Law and Liberty in Early New England, Criminal Justice and Due Process, 1620-1692*. Amherst, Mass.: University of Massachusetts Press, 1993.

McWilliams, James E. *Building the Bay Colony: Local Economy and Culture in Early Massachusetts*. Charlottesville, Va.: University of Virginia Press, 2007.

Metcalf, John G., comp. *Annals of the Town of Mendon from 1659 to 1880*. Providence, R.I.: E. L. Freeman & Co., 1880.

Middleton, Simon, and Billy G. Smith, eds. *Class Matters: Early North America and the Atlantic World*. Philadelphia: University of Pennsylvania Press, 2008.

Minot, George Richards. *The History of the Insurrections in Massachusetts*. 2nd ed. Boston: James W. Burditt & Co., 1810.

Mohl, Raymond A. *Poverty in New York, 1783-1825*. New York: Oxford University Press, 1971.
Molyneux, Nellie Zada Rice, comp. *History Genealogical and Biographical of the Molyneux Families*. Syracuse, N. Y.: C. W. Bardeen, Publisher, 1904.
Morgan, Edmund S. *The Puritan Family: Religion and Domestic Relations in Seventeenth-Century New England*. New York: Harper & Row, 1966.
-----. *The Stamp Act Crisis: Prologue to Revolution*. Chapel Hill: University of North Carolina Press, 1995.
-----. *The Puritan Dilemma: The Story of John Winthrop*. Boston: Little, Brown and Company, 1958.
-----, ed. *Prologue to Revolution: Sources and Documents on the Stamp Act Crisis, 1764-1766*. Chapel Hill: University of North Carolina Press, 1959.
-----, ed., *Puritan Political Ideas, 1558-1794*. Indianapolis, Ind.: Bobbs-Merrill Co., 1965.
-----. *American Slavery, American Freedom: The Ordeal of Colonial Virginia*. repr., New York: W. W. Norton, 2003.
Morris, Richard B., ed. *Government and Labor in Early America*. repr., Boston: Northeastern University Press, 1981.
Murphy, Timothy C. *History of Rutland in Massachusetts, 1713-1968*. Worcester, Mass.: Heffernan Press, 1970.
Nash, Gary B. "The Failure of Female Factory Labor in Colonial Boston." *Labor History* 20 (1970): 165-188.
-----. *The Urban Crucible: Social Change, Political Consciousness, and the Origins of the American Revolution*. Cambridge, Mass.: Harvard University Press, 1979.
-----. *Race, Class, and Politics: Essays on American Colonial and Revolutionary Society*. Urbana, Ill.: University of Illinois Press, 1986.
-----. *The Unknown American Revolution: The Unruly Birth of Democracy and the Struggle to Create America*. New York: Viking, 2005.

─────, and Graham R. G. Hodges. *Friends of Liberty: Thomas Jefferson, Tadeusz Kościuszko, and Agrippa Hull*. New York: Basic Books, 2008.

Neimeyer, Charles Patrick. *America Goes to War: A Social History of the Continental Army*. New York: New York University Press, 1996.

Nellis, Eric G. "Misreading the Signs: Industrial Imitation, Poverty, and the Social Order in Colonial Boston." *New England Quarterly* 59 (1986): 486-507.

Nelson, William E. *Americanization of the Common Law: The Impact of Legal Change on Massachusetts Society, 1760-1830*. repr., Athens, Ga.: University of Georgia Press, 1994.

Newell, Margaret Ellen. *From Dependency to Independence: Economic Revolution in Colonial New England*. Ithaca, N.Y.: Cornell University Press, 1998.

Newman, Simon P. *Embodied History: The Lives of the Poor in Early Philadelphia*. Philadelphia: University of Pennsylvania Press, 2003.

Nicholls, George. *A History of the English Poor Law*. 3v. New York: Augustus M. Kelley, 1967.

Nourse, Henry S. *The Military Annals of Lancaster, Massachusetts, 1740-1865*. Clinton, Mass.: W. J. Coulter, 1889.

─────. *History of the Town of Harvard, Massachusetts, 1732-1893*. Harvard [Mass.]: W. Hapgood, 1894.

O'Brien, George. *An Essay on the Economic Effects of the Reformation*. repr., New York: Augustus M. Kelley, Publishers, 1970.

Olasky, Marvin. *The Tragedy of American Compassion*. Washington, D.C.: Regnery Gateway, 1992.

Olson, Jeannine E. *Calvin and Social Welfare: Deacons and the Bourse francaise*. Selinsgrove [Penn.]: Susquehanna University Press, 1989.

Paradise, Scott H., comp. *The Story of Essex County*. 4 vols. New York: American Historical Society, 1935.

Parker, Charles H. *The Reformation of Community: Social Welfare and Calvinist Charity in Holland, 1572-1620.* Cambridge, UK: Cambridge University Press, 1998.

Parkhurst, Eleanor. "Poor Relief in a Massachusetts Village in the Eighteenth Century." *Social Service Review* 11 (1937): 446-464.

Partridge, George F. *History of the Town of Bellingham, Massachusetts, 1719-1919.* Bellingham [Mass.]: Published by the Town, 1919.

Pattee, William S. *A History of Old Braintree and Quincy.* Quincy, Mass.: Green & Prescott, 1878.

Peck, Chauncey E. *The History of Wilbraham, Massachusetts.* n.p., The Town of Wilbraham, 1913.

Penn, Elizabeth A. *Pox Americana: The Great Smallpox Epidemic of 1775-82.* New York: Hill and Wang, 2001.

Perley, Sidney. *The History of Boxford, Essex County, Massachusetts.* Boxford [Mass.]: Published by the Author, 1878.

Perlman, Selig. *A Theory of the Labor Movement.* repr., New York: Augustus M. Kelley, 1949.

Peskin, Lawrence A. *Manufacturing Revolution: The Intellectual Origins of Early American Industry.* Baltimore, Md.: Johns Hopkins University Press, 2003.

Pestana, Carla Gardina, and Sharon V. Salinger, eds., *Inequality in Early America.* Hanover, N.H.: University Press of New England, 1999.

Phillips, James Duncan. *Salem in the Eighteenth Century.* Boston: Houghton Mifflin Company, 1937.

Pound, John. *Poverty and Vagrancy in Tudor England.* London: Longman Group Ltd., 1971.

Powers, Edwin. *Crime and Punishment in Early Massachusetts, 1620-1692: A Documentary History.* Boston: Beacon Press, 1966.

Priest, Claire. "Currency Policies and Legal Development in Colonial New England." *Yale Law Journal* 110 (2001): 1303-1405.

Prude, Jonathan. *The Coming of Industrial Order: Town and Factory Life in Rural Massachusetts, 1810-1860* Cambridge, UK: Cambridge University Press, 1983.

Pullan, Brian S. *Rich and Poor in Renaissance Venice: The Social Institutions of a Catholic State, to 1620*. Oxford, UK: Blackwell Publishers, 1971.

-----. "Catholics, Protestants, and the Poor in Early Modern Europe." *Journal of Interdisciplinary History* 35 (2005): 441-456.

Quincy, II, Josiah. *Reports of Cases Argued and Adjudged in the Superior Court of Judicature of the Province of Massachusetts Bay between 1761 and 1772*. repr., New York: Russell & Russell, 1969.

Quincy, III, Josiah. *Report of the Committee on the Subject of Pauperism and a House of Industry in the Town of Boston*. Boston: n.p.,1812.

Rabushka, Alvin. *Taxation in Colonial America*. Princeton, N.J.: Princeton University Press, 2008.

Reed, Jonas. *A History of Rutland, Worcester County, Massachusetts*. Worcester, Mass.: Mirick & Bartlett, 1836.

Resech, John, and Walter Sargent, eds., *War and Society in the American Revolution: Mobilization and Home Fronts*. DeKalb, Ill.: Northern Illinois University Press, 2007.

Richards, Leonard L. *Shays's Rebellion: The American Revolution's Final Battle*. Philadelphia: University of Pennsylvania Press, 2002.

Ricketson,William F. "To Be Young, Poor, and Alone: The Experience of Widowhood in the Massachusetts Bay Colony, 1675-1676," *New England Quarterly* 64 (1991): 113-127.

Rockman, Seth. "Work in the Cities of Colonial British North America." *Journal of Urban History* 33 (2007): 1021-1032.

―――. *Welfare Reform in the Early Republic.* Boston: Bedford, 2003.

―――. *Scraping By: Wage Labor, Slavery, and Survival in Early Baltimore.* Baltimore: Johns Hopkins University Press, 2009.

Rollins, Alden M. *Vermont Warnings Out.* 2 vols. Camden, Me.: Picton Press, 1993, 1997.

Rosswurm, Steven. *Arms, Country, and Class: The Philadelphia Militia and "Lower Sort" during the American Revolution, 1775-1783.* New Brunswick, N.J.: Rutgers University Press, 1987.

Rothman, David J. *The Discovery of the Asylum: Social Order and Disorder in the New Republic.* Boston: Little, Brown and Company, 1971.

Russell, Howard S. *A Long, Deep Furrow: Three Centuries of Farming in New England.* Hanover, N.H.: University Press of New England, 1976.

Rutman, Darrett B. *Winthrop's Boston: A Portrait of a Puritan Town, 1630-1649.* repr., New York: W. W. Norton, 1972.

Safley, Thomas Max, ed. *The Reformation of Charity: The Secular and the Religious in Early Modern Poor Relief.* Boston: Brill Academic Publishers, 2003.

Salinger, Sharon V. *"To Serve Well and Faithfully": Labor and Indentured Servants in Pennsylvania, 1682-1800.* Cambridge, UK: Cambridge University Press, 1987.

Savage, Edward H. *Police Records and Recollections, or Boston by Daylight and Gaslight for Two Hundred and Forty Years.* repr., Montclair, N.J.: Patterson Smith, 1971.

Schlesinger, Arthur Meier. *The Colonial Merchants and the American Revolution, 1763-1776.* repr., New York: Frederick Ungar Publishing Co., 1957.

Shy, John. "Hearts and Minds in the American Revolution: The Case of 'Long Bill' Scott and Peterborough, New Hampshire," in his *A People Numerous and Armed: Reflections on the*

Military Struggles for American Independence, 163-179. New York: Oxford University Press, 1976.

-----. "A New look at Colonial Militia," *William and Mary Quarterly*, 3rd ser., 20 (1963): 175-185.

Simmons, Richard C. *Studies in the Massachusetts Franchise, 1631-1691*. New York: Garland Publishing, 1989.

Slack, Paul, *Poverty and Policy in Tudor and Stuart England*. London: Longman, 1988.

-----. *The English Poor Law, 1531-1782*. Cambridge, UK: Cambridge University Press, 1995.

-----, ed. *Rebellion, Popular Protest and the Social Order of Early Modern England*. repr., Cambridge, UK: Cambridge University Press, 2008.

Smith, Abbot E. *Colonists in Bondage: White Servitude and Convict Labor in America, 1607-1776*. Chapel Hill: University of North Carolina Press, 1947.

Smith, Adam. *The Wealth of Nations*, ed. Edwin Cannan. New York: Modern Library, 1994.

Smith, Billy G., ed., *Down and Out in Early America*. University Park, Penn.: Pennsylvania State University Press, 2004.

-----. *The "Lower Sort": Philadelphia's Laboring People, 1750-1800*. Ithaca, N.Y.: Cornell University Press, 1990.

Smith, Edward Church, and Philip Mack Smith, *A History of the Town of Middlefield, Massachusetts*. Menasha, Wis.: n. p., 1924.

Smith, John Montague, Henry W. Taft, and Abbie T. Montague, *History of the Town of Sunderland, Massachusetts, 1673-1899*. Greenfield, Mass.: E. A. Hall & Co., 1899.

Smith, Jonathan. "Toryism in Worcester County during the War for Independence." *Proceedings of the Massachusetts Historical Society* 48 (1915): 15-35.

Smith, Joseph H., ed., *Colonial Justice in Western Massachusetts (1639-1702)*. Cambridge, Mass.: Harvard University Press, 1961.
Smith, Preserved. *The Age of Reformation*. New York: Henry Holt and Co., 1920.
Spufford, Margaret, ed. *The World of Rural Dissenters, 1520-1725*. Cambridge, UK: Cambridge University Press, 1995.
Stark, James H. *The Loyalists of Massachusetts and the Other Side of the American Revolution*. Boston: Printed for the Author, 1910.
Stebbins, Rufus P. *An Historical Address Delivered at the Centennial Celebration of the Incorporation of the Town of Wilbraham, June 15, 1863*. Boston: George C. Rand & Avery, 1864.
Stone, Lawrence. "Social Mobility in England, 1500-1700." *Past and Present* 33 (1966): 16-55.
-----. *The Family, Sex and Marriage in England, 1500-1800*. New York: Harper & Row, 1977.
Swain, Philip. Who Fought? Boston Soldiers in the Revolutionary War. Honor Thesis in American History, Tufts University, 1981.
Szatmary, David P. *Shays' Rebellion: The Making of an Agrarian Insurrection*. Amherst, Mass.: University of Massachusetts Press, 1980.
Tager, Jack. *Boston Riots: Three Centuries of Social Violence*. Boston: Northeastern University Press, 2001.
Tawney, R. H. *Religion and the Rise of Capitalism*. repr., New York: Mentor Books, 1963.
Taylor, Alan. *Liberty Men and Great Proprietors: The Revolutionary Settlement on the Maine Frontier, 1760-1820*. Chapel Hill: University of North Carolina Press, 1990.
Taylor, Robert J. *Western Massachusetts in the Revolution*. Providence, R. I.: Brown University Press, 1954.

Temple, Josiah Howard. *History of the Town of Palmer, Massachusetts*. Springfield, Mass.: Published by the Town of Palmer, 1889.

Thompson, E. P. *The Making of the English Working Class*. New York: Vintage Books, 1966.

-----. *Customs in Common*. New York: The New Press, 1993.

Tiedmann, Joseph S. *Reluctant Revolutionaries: New York City and the Road to Independence, 1763-1776*. Ithaca, N.Y.: Cornell University Press, 1997.

Tilden, William S., ed. *History of the Town of Medfield, Massachusetts, 1650-1886*. Boston: n. p., 1887.

Todd, Margo. *Christian Humanism and the Puritan Social Order*. Cambridge, UK: Cambridge University Press, 1987.

Towner, Lawrence W. "The Indentures of Boston's Poor Apprentices: 1734-1805." *Publications of the Colonial Society of Massachusetts* 43 (1966): 417-468.

Tracy, Patricia J. "Re-Considering Migration within Colonial New England." *Journal of Social History* 23 (1989): 93-113.

Trattner, Walter I. *From Poor Law to Welfare State: A History of Social Welfare in America*. New York: Free Press, 1999.

Trumbull, James Russell. *History of Northampton, Massachusetts, from Its Settlement in 1654*. Northampton, Mass.: Gazette Printing Co., 1898.

Tryon, Rolla Milton. *Household Manufactures in the United States, 1640-1860*. repr., New York: Augustus M. Kelley, 1966.

Tyler, John W. *Smugglers and Patriots: Boston Merchants and the Advent of the American Revolution*. Boston: Northeastern University Press, 1986.

Ulrich, Laurel Thatcher. *Good Wives: Image and Reality in the Lives of Women in Northern New England, 1650-1750*. repr., New York: Vintage Books, 1991.

-----. *A Midwife's Tale: The Life of Martha Ballard, Based on Her Diary, 1785-1812*. New York: Vintage Books, 1991.

-----. *The Age of Homespun: Objects and Stories in the Creation of An American Myth*. New York: Alfred A. Knopf, 2001.

Van Tyne, Claude Halstead. *The Loyalists in the American Revolution*. Gloucester, Mass.: Peter Smith, 1959.

Vaughan, Alden T., ed., *The Puritan Tradition in America, 1620-1730*. repr., Hanover, N.H.: University Press of New England, 1997.

Vickers, Daniel. *Farmers and Fishermen: Two Centuries of Work in Essex County, Massachusetts, 1630-1850*. Chapel Hill: University of North Carolina Press, 1994.

-----, with Vince Walsh. *Young Men and the Sea: Yankee Seafarers in the Age of Sail*. New Haven, Conn.: Yale University Press, 2005.

Vives, Juan Luis. *On Assistance to the Poor*, trans. Alice Tobriner. Toronto: University of Toronto Press, 1999.

Walter, John, and Roger Schofield, eds. *Famine, Diseases and the Social Order in Early Modern Society*. New York: Cambridge University Press, 1989.

Ware, Caroline F. *The Early New England Cotton Manufacture: A Study in Industrial Beginnings*. repr., New York: Russell and Russell, 1966.

Washburn, Emory. *Historical Sketches of the Town of Leicester, Massachusetts during the First Century from Its Settlement*. Boston: John Wilson and Son, 1860.

Waters, Jr., John J. "Hingham, Massachusetts, 1631-1661: An East Anglian Oligarchy in New World." *Journal of Social History* 1 (1968): 351-370.

Webb, Sidney and Beatrice. *The Parish and the County*. repr., London: Frank Cass and Co., 1963.

Weber, Max. *The Protestant Ethic and the Spirit of Capitalism*. repr., New York: Charles Scribner's Sons, 1958.

Weeden, William B. *Economic and Social History of New England, 1620-1789*. 2 vols. repr., Williamstown, Mass.: Corner House Publishers, 1978.

Weir, David A. *Early New England: A Covenanted Society*. Grand Rapids, Mich.: William B. Eerdmans Publishing Company, 2005.

Wells, Daniel White, and Reuben Field Wells. *A History of Hatfield, Massachusetts, 1660-1910*. Springfield, Mass.: F. C. H. Gibbons, 1910.

Weston, Thomas. *History of the Town of Middleboro, Massachusetts*. Boston: Houghton, Mifflin and Co., 1906.

Whitefield, George. *A Continuation of the Reverend Mr. Whitefield's Journal from Savannah, June 25, 1740, to His Arrival at Rhode-Island, His Travels in the Other Governments of New-England, to His Departure from Stanford for New-York*. Boston: D. Fowle, 1741.

Wiberley, Jr., Stephen Edward. Four Cities: Public Poor Relief in Urban America, 1700-1775. Ph.D. diss., Yale University, 1975.

Wood, Gordon S. *The Creation of the American Republic, 1776-1787*. New York: W. W. Norton, 1972.

-----. *The Radicalism of the American Revolution*. New York: Vintage Books, 1993.

Wright, Conrad E. *The Transformation of Charity in Postrevolutionary New England*. Boston: Northeastern University Press, 1992.

-----, and Katheryn P. Viens, eds. *Entrepreneurs: The Boston Business Community, 1700-1850*. Boston: Massachusetts Historical Society, 1997.

Year-Book of the Society of Colonial Wars in the Commonwealth of Massachusetts for 1898. Boston: Rockwell & Churchill Press, 1898.

Young, Alfred F., ed. *Beyond the American Revolution: Explorations in the History of American Radicalism*. Dekalb, Ill.: Northern Illinois University Press, 1993.

——. *The Shoemaker and the Tea Party: Memory and the American Revolution*. Boston: Beacon Press, 1999.

——. *Masquerade: The Life and Times of Deborah Sampson, Continental Soldier*. New York: Alfred A. Knopf, 2004.

——. *Liberty Tree: Ordinary People and the American Revolution*. New York: New York University Press, 2006.

Zelner, Kyle F. *A Rabble in Arms: Massachusetts Towns and Militiamen during King Philip's War*. New York: New York University Press, 2009.

Zemsky, Robert. *Merchants, Farmers, and River Gods: An Essay on Eighteenth-Century American Politics*. Boston: Gambit Inc., 1971.

Zuckerman, Michael. *Peaceable Kingdoms: New England Towns in the Eighteenth Century*. New York: Alfred A. Knopf, 1970.

Name Index

[Names in boldface have biographies.]

—, Mary (servant, very poor), 101
—, Peter (African American, patriotic soldier), 249
—, Tom ("Dumb Tom," pauper), 119

Abbot, Samuel (overseer of the poor), 27, 29, 185
Adams, Abigail, 274
Adams, Andrew (housewright), 225
Adams, Ezekiel (selectman, received piece work), 79
Adams, Henry (representative, received piece work), 79
Adams, John (selectman witnessing poverty), xiii-xiv; xxix; (on raising hemp), 82-83; (legal practice in removal cases), 113, 117, 119-121; (inoculation), 140-141; (Whig), 149, 166
Adams, Samuel (of modest fortune, patriot), 147, 148, 149
Adams, Samuel, Mrs., 274
Adams, Sarah (daughter of George Adams, warned), 103
Akley, Francis (orphan, patriotic soldier), 195
Albee, Giden (received piece work), 78
Aldrich, Abraham, 293
Aldrich, Anson (farmer), 265
Alexander, Nathaniel (veteran petitioner), 35
Alexander, Thomas (son of Nathaniel, dead), 35
Allen, David (selectman), 286
Allen, Ebenezer, Dr., 36

Allen, John (of Weston, took strangers), 109
Allen, Samuel (son of Abijah Allen, warned), 103
Alstat, John (state pauper), 287
Ames, —, Capt., (received piece work for his daughter) 77
Anderson, Samuel, Jr. (arrested), 246
Andrews, George (selectman), 259
Appleton, Nathaniel (selectman, subscriber), 140, 146, 149
Arbuthnot, Betty (wife of William, warned), 108
Arbuthnot, William, Col. (warned), 108
Armitage, John, Capt. (donor), 54
Arnold, Timothy (selectman), 282, 284
Atkinson, John, Jr. (son of John and Mary, patriotic soldier), 223, 224, 293
Atkinson, John, Sr. (warned), 223
Atkinson, Mary (wife of John the Elder, warned), 223
Austin, Benjamin (subscriber), 149
Ayres, Ephraim (veteran petitioner), 37

Babbitt (Bobet), Edward (business proprietor), 97-98
Bacon, Abigail (wife of James Bacon, from New Braintree, warned), 103
Bacon, James (from New Braintree, warned), 103
Bacon, James (of Wrentham, took strangers), 103
Bacon, Joseph (warned), 255

Name Index

Bacon, Mary (wife of Joseph, warned), 255
Bagnall, William R. (author), 70
Baker, Ephraim (patriotic soldier), 225
Baker, Jacob, 294
Baldwin, Loammi, Mr. (prize winner for mulberry trees), 156
Baldwin, Samuel (took strangers), 109
Ball, Daniel (Elijah's brother, warned, militia man), 184, 196
Ball, Elijah (warned, militia man), 184, 196, 294
Ballard, Martha (midwife), 248
Ballard, William (Continental major), 242
Ballou, Elizabeth Pitts (married to Jesse), 234
Ballou, Jesse (warned, militia man), 182, 221, 234
Banks, John (orphan, patriotic soldier), 195, 225, 234, 295
Banks, Nathaniel (son of John), 234
Banks, Nathaniel Sartell Prentiss (son of Nathaniel), 234
Banks, Susan Prentiss (wife of John), 194, 234
Banks, Thomas (orphan, patriotic soldier), 195
Banks, William (warned), 253
Barker, Ephraim, Jr. (patriotic soldier), 194, 229, 232, 296
Barklett, Jacob (petition denied), 43
Barnes, Henry (of Marlborough, loyalist), 189-190
Barrett, Jacob (father of eight, warned), 104
Barrett, Jacob, Jr. (son of Jacob and Rebecca, warned), 104
Barrett, John (Boston overseer of the poor, subscriber), 145, 146, 161
Barrett, John (son of Jacob and Rebecca, warned), 104
Barrett, Jonathan (son of Jacob and Rebecca, warned), 104
Barrett, Jonathan (son of Samuel and Rebeckeh, warned, patriotic soldier), 197, 224, 297
Barrett, Joseph (son of Jacob and Rebecca, warned), 104
Barrett, Joshua (son of Jacob and Rebecca, warned), 104

Barrett, Mary (daughter of Jacob and Rebecca, warned), 104
Barrett, Nathan (son of Jacob and Rebecca, warned), 104
Barrett, Rebecca (wife of Jacob Barrett, warned), 104
Barrett, Rebecca, Jr. (daughter of Jacob and Rebecca, warned), 104
Barrett, Samuel, Jr. (son of Samuel and Rebeckeh, patriotic soldier), 197
Barton, Benjamin, 297
Barton, Phineas, 297
Barton, William (state pauper), 279
Bascomb, Joseph (Continental lieutenant), 242
Beers, Jabez (care provider), 30
Bellows, Margaret (very poor, warned), 101
Benetrate, William (state pauper), 286
Benson, Jacob (warned), 126
Bernard, Francis, Gov., 60
Bickmore, John (veteran petitioner), 35
Bigelow, Abraham, Esq. (took strangers), 106, 109, 110
Bigelow, Humphrey (patriotic soldier), 223, 298
Bigelow, Timothy (Continental colonel), 242
Billing, Lois (married to Giles Church), 220
Bishop, John (patriotic soldier, warned), 252
Black, Daniel (warned), 197
Black, Daniel, Jr. (son of Daniel and Sarah, warned, patriotic soldier), 197
Black, Jacob (son of Daniel and Sarah, warned, patriotic soldier), 197, 298
Black, John (son of Daniel and Sarah, warned, patriotic soldier), 197
Black, Sarah Symonds (wife of Daniel, warned), 197
Black, Thomas (veteran petitioner), 37
Blake, Benjamin (warned), 103
Blake, Jacob (militia man), 225
Blake, James (took strangers, militia man), 103
Blake, Mathew (warned), 193

Name Index

Blake, Robert (took strangers), 102
Blodget, Jane (wife of Samuel Blodget, warned), 107
Blodget, Samuel, Dr. (warned), 107
Bogle, Elizabeth (wife of Thomas), 230
Bogle, Lucy (married to William Bogle), 194
Bogle, Thomas (son of John and Mary, warned, patriotic soldier), 197, 229-230
Bogle, William (son of John and Mary, warned, patriotic soldier), 194, 197, 224, 228, 299
Bond, William (Continental colonel), 197
Bonney, Ichabod (selectman), 105
Borland, John, Esq. (father of John Lindall), 190
Borland, John Lindall (of Boston, loyalist), 190
Bosson, Jonas D. (patriotic soldier, warned), 252
Bourn, Melatiah (committee member), 146, 162
Bourn, Nathaniel (overseer of the poor), 146
Bowdoin, Elizabeth, 274
Bowdoin, James, 188, 192, 245
Bowdoin, William (merchant, subscriber), 71, 146
Boylston, Thomas (subscriber), 149
Boynton, Beulah Eaton (wife of Nathan Boynton, warned), 255
Boynton, Jacob (father of Nathan, deceased), 183
Boynton, John (emigrant), 96
Boynton, Nathan (son of Jacob, warned, militia man), 183, 255, 300
Boynton, William (emigrant), 96
Bozworth, Ichabod 2nd (patriotic soldier), 223, 230, 301
Bozworth, Ruth Bradley (wife of Ichabod 2nd), 223, 230
Brackett, — (wife of Lemuel Brackett, warned), 255
Brackett, Curtis (son of Lemuel, warned), 255
Brackett, Ebenezer (son of Lemuel, warned), 255
Brackett, Joseph (son of Lemuel, warned), 255

Brackett, Lemuel (warned), 255
Brackett, Lemuel, Jr. (son of Lemuel, warned), 255
Brackett, Polly (daughter of Lemuel, warned), 255
Brackett, Samuel (son of Lemuel, warned), 255
Brackett, Sukey (daughter of Lemuel, warned), 255
Bradburn, John (warned), 254
Bradbury, Thomas (sick soldier), 36
Bradford, John (overseer of the poor, subscriber), 146
Bradford, Josiah (warned), 127
Bradford, Samuel (overseer of the poor, subscriber), 146
Bramhall, Joseph (wounded soldier), 34
Brastow, Eunice (married to Jonathan Felt 2nd), 222
Brastow, Samuel (militia man), 222
Brattle, Thomas (trade organization member), 161
Bridges, Caleb, 302
Bright, William (orphan, patriotic soldier), 195
Brintall, Benjamin, Dea. (warned), 106
Bromfield, Thomas (donor), 55
Brow, John, Jr. (arrested), 246
Brown, Benjamin (promoted in service), 212
Brown, John (of Boston, weaver), 149
Brown, John (of Lynn, patriotic soldier), 252
Brown, John (of Weston, took strangers), 109
Browne, William (of Salem, loyalist), 190
Bruce, George (patriotic soldier, warned), 252
Buckman, — (widow, daughter of Green Phebe), 114
Bullard, Isaiah (Peter Cary's master, militia man), 183, 218, 219
Bumstead, —, widow (on charity), 52
Burbeck, William, Capt. Lt., 216
Burgoyne, John, 279
Burnham, John (son of Nathaniel and Elizabeth, warned, patriotic soldier), 197

Name Index

Burnham, Thomas (son of Nathaniel and Elizabeth, warned, patriotic soldier), 197, 303
Butler, Benjamin (at ten, warned), 102
Butler, Sarah (poor, warned), 101
Byfield, Nathaniel, Esq. (attorney), 43

Calvin, Margret (warned), 109
Canady, William, Capt., 37, 38
Capen, Ephraim (soldier/guard), 217
Capen, Ruth Thayer (soldier Ephraim Capen's mother), 217
Carter, Jonas (hired soldier), 200
Cary, Eleazer (selectman), 250
Cary, Ephraim (selectman), 250
Cary, Peter (of Shrewsbury, patriotic soldier), 194, 230-231, 303
Cary, Peter (of Weston, warned, militia man), 183, 218, 219, 304
Caryl (or Cariel), Thomas (orphan, patriotic soldier), 195
Chaddock, John (in removal case), 121
Chadock, Jonathan (removed), 115
Chamberlaine, William (wounded soldier), 34
Champney, Benjamin (orphan, patriotic soldier), 195
Chandler, Benjamin (promoted in service), 212
Chandler, John (of Worcester, loyalist), 190
Chandler, Joseph (patriotic soldier, warned), 252
Chandler, William (patriotic soldier, warned), 252
Chapin, Luke 2nd (patriotic soldier), 224, 305
Chapman, Nathaniel (veteran petitioner), 37
Chauncy, Charles, Rev., 170
Chenery, Ephraim (received piece work), 78
Chickering, Oliver (patriotic soldier, warned), 224, 305
Child, Samuel (from Newton, warned), 102
Child, Samuel (of Weston, took strangers, militia man), 102, 109
Choate, Rebecca (poor, removed), 119

Church, Caleb (warned, patriotic soldier), 196, 223, 231-232, 306
Church, Giles (patriotic soldier), 220, 308
Church, Seth (son of Caleb, selectman), 231
Church, Silas (Caleb's brother, warned, patriotic soldier), 194, 196
Clark, Benjamin (took strangers), 103
Clark, Hiphsebath (married to Giden Albee), 78
Clark, James (deserted from service), 214
Clark, Phebe (state pauper), 282-284
Clark, Samuel (from Rutland, warned), 103
Clark, Samuel (wounded soldier), 33
Clark, Seth (selectman, received piece work), 79
Clark, Thomas (veteran petitioner), 38
Clark, William (physician, subscriber), 71
Clark, William H. (compiler), 70
Clarke, John, Rev., 267
Cleland, Thomas (warned, militia man), 183, 308
Clerk, Nathaniel (selectman), 251
Coats, John (promoted in service), 212-213
Cobb, Samuel (warned), 255
Cole, Ephraim (warned), 128
Colman, John (of Boston, land banker), 62
Colman, John (of Malden, took strangers), 105
Colton, Alpheus (arrested), 246
Combler, Michael (promoted in service), 213
Conneley, John (service and desertion), 215
Conner, Daniel (veteran petitioner), 35
Converse, James, Maj. (deceased), 40
Converse, Josiah (son of James), 40
Converse, Robert (son of James), 40
Cook, David (petition denied), 43
Cook, Josiah (petition denied), 43
Cook, Middlecot (subscriber, committee member), 71
Cooke, Middlecott (gentleman, subscriber), 71, 146

Name Index

Cooley, Ebenezer 2nd (patriotic soldier), 227, 309
Cooley, Martin (creditor), 241
Cooper, Samuel (Whig), 147
Copeland, Asa (promoted in service), 212
Copeland, Seth (foodstuff provider), 280
Cornwallis, Charles, 210
Corse, James (service to the province), 36
Cory, Isaac (Nathan Boynton's master, militia man), 183
Cotton, William (at 10, serving on patriotic ship), 206
Cowan, James, Jr., 309
Cowing, John (debtor), 39
Cox, Ann Warren (married Elisha Cox 1st), 196
Cox, Artemas (son of Elisha and Ann, patriotic soldier), 225
Cox, Elisha 1st (married Ann Warren, warned), 196, 309
Cox, Elisha 2nd (son of Elisha 1st and Ann, warned, Continental ensign), 196, 223
Cox, Elisha 3rd (son of Elisha 2nd and Sarah), 223
Cox, Richard (pamphleteer), 68
Cox, William, Capt., 36
Craige, Thomas (orphan, patriotic soldier), 195, 225, 312
Crawford, Mary (in almshouse), 22
Crook, Elijah (warned), 126
Cross, Joseph (veteran petitioner), 37
Cummings, William (veteran petitioner), 40
Cushing, John (judge), 119
Cushing, Josiah, Esq. (warned), 105
Cushing, Thomas (Whig), 146, 149
Cushing, Thomas, Capt., 216, 217
Cushing, Thomas, Mr. (on House committee, subscriber), 38
Cutt, Richard (veteran petitioner), 35

Danforth, Elijah (justice of the peace), 115
Dannie, William (subscriber, Tea Party), 147
Darior, Simon (deserted from service), 214
Darrell, John (horse owner), 40

Davis, John (orphan, patriotic soldier), 195
Dawes, William (promoted in service), 212
Denney, James (brother of Robert, petition denied), 44
Denney, Robert (killed), 44
Deputin, William (substitute soldier), 200
Derby, John, Captain (patriotic ship master), 204
De Silva, George (Portuguese), 279
Dexter, Job (selectman), 286
Dickinson, Aaron (son of Moses the Elder, patriotic soldier), 220
Dickinson, Elijah (son of Moses the Elder, patriotic soldier), 220
Dickinson, Medad (son of Moses the Elder, patriotic solider), 220
Dickinson, Moses, Jr. (son of Moses the Elder, patriotic soldier), 220
Dickinson, Moses, Sr. (selectman), 219-220, 312
Dickinson, Reuben (Continental captain), 241
Dickinson, Samuel (suffered in captivity), 36
Dickinson, Waitstill (patriotic soldier), 220, 314
Dill, George (on relief), 2, 3
Dillingham, Henry (warned), 126
Dimmock, Joseph (veteran petitioner), 35
Dix, William (poor), 117, 118
Dodge, John, Capt. (warned), 108
Dodge, Ruth (wife of John, warned), 108
Dolbear, Benjamin (overseer of the poor, subscriber), 146
Dolbeare, David (province poor), 22
Dorr, Dorothy (poor child, warned), 102
Downing, George (province poor), 22
Downs, Baxter, Capt. (warned), 108
Downs, Baxter, Jr. (son of Baxter and Huldah, warned), 108
Downs, Hannah (state pauper), 280, 281
Downs, Huldah (wife of Baxter, warned), 108
Downs, Huldah, Jr. (daughter of Baxter and Huldah, warned), 108
Downs, Isaac (son of Baxter and

Name Index

Huldah, warned), 108
Downs, James (son of Baxter and Huldah, warned), 108
Durrell, Philip (his son in captivity), 36

Eastwick, Thomas (in almshouse), 22
Eaton, Beulah (married to Nathan Boynton), 255
Eaton, Sarah (warned), 105
Eayers, John (promoted in service), 212
Edgar, Henry (suffered in captivity), 36
Edson, Jacob, 315
Eliot, Jared (essayist), 67, 156; (mentioned by John Adams), 83
Elithrop, Daniel (veteran petitioner), 38
Ellis, Abner (received piece work), 77
Ely, John Edwards (patriotic soldier), 194, 315
Emmorell, William P. (deserted from service), 214
Etter, Peter (businessman), 168

Farmer, Paul (almshouse master), 22
Faxon, Dorca (sister of James, wife of Nathaniel Thayer), 217
Faxon, James (soldier/guard, brother of Dorcas), 217
Fellows, John (Samuel the Elder's son, patriotic soldier), 197
Fellows, Samuel, Jr. (warned, patriotic soldier), 197, 315
Fellows, Solomon (Samuel the Elder's son, patriotic soldier), 197
Fellows, William (Samuel the Elder's son, patriotic soldier), 194, 197, 225
Fellows, Willis (Samuel the Elder's son, patriotic soldier), 197, 225
Felt, Jonathan 1st (warned), 182
Felt, Jonathan 2nd (warned, militia man), 222, 317
Fisher, David (took strangers), 111
Fisher, David, Jr. (took strangers), 111, 255
Fisher, Eleazer 1st (warned), 182
Fisher, Eleazer 2nd (warned, militia man), 219, 318

Fisher, Susanna (widow of Eleazer 2nd), 219
Fisk, Jonathan (militia lieutenant), 183
Fitch, Samuel (attorney), 121
Flagg, Timothy, 318
Flint, John (captain), 35
Floyd, Ebenezer (promoted in service), 212
Ford, Joseph (promoted in service), 212
Fowler, Daniel (deserted from service), 214
Foxcroft, John (took strangers), 253
Franklin, Benjamin, Mr., (donor), 65, 204
Franklin, Peter (African American, hired soldier), 200
Frederick, Martin (deserted from service), 214
Freeman, Apphia (African American, on relief), 2
Freeman, Cato (patriotic soldier), 227
Freeman, Elizabeth (married to Zebath Thayer), 218
Freeman, Mary (warned), 106
Freeman, Zebediah (state pauper), 286
French, Levi (warned), 128
French, Sylvanus (soldier/guard), 217
Fuller, Ephraim (at 16, hired soldier), 200

Gale, Abijah (selectman), 259
Gallop, Samuel (land grant), 46
Gardiner, Sylvester (physician, subscriber), 71
Gardner, Rebecca (state pauper), 279
Garfield, Benjamin (poor, warned), 101
Garfield, Susanna (wife of Benjamin, warned), 101
Garnet, Elijah (warned), 125
Garritt, Andrew (promoted in service), 212
Gates, Lemuel (son of Stephen and Dinah, warned, militia fifer), 183, 184, 197, 219, 226, 319
Gates, Lucretia (married to Timothy Munro), 224
Gates, Samuel (son of Stephen and Dinah, warned, patriotic soldier), 183, 197, 219, 226

Name Index

Gay, Eleazer (took strangers), 107
George, Thomas (took strangers), 102
Gerry, Elbridge (Whig), 192
Gibbs, Clark (of Rutland), 226
Gibbs, Clark (recruit of Lancaster, unfit for service), 200
Gibbs, Frederick (son of Clark and Hannah, patriotic soldier), 197
Gibbs, Hannah (wife of Clark of Rutland), 226
Gibbs, Jonas (son of Clark and Hannah, patriotic soldier), 197
Gibbs, Zenas (son of Clark and Hannah, warned, patriotic soldier), 197, 226, 319
Gibson, Thaddeus (warned, patriotic soldier), 219, 226, 232, 233, 320
Gierfield, Joseph (took strangers), 109
Gilbert, Ebenezer (warned, militia man), 111
Gilbert, Lydia (wife of Ebenezer, warned), 111
Gilbert, Mary (single woman, removed), 118
Gill, William (warned), 255
Gillmore, James (took strangers), 103
Gillmore, Mary (wife of William Gillmore, warned), 103
Gillmore, William (warned), 103
Gilson, Michael (veteran petitioner), 37
Gilson, Peter (deserted from service), 214
Glover, John (Continental general), 242
Goddard, Edward, Capt. (on House committee), 38
Goffe, Edmund, Col., 38
Goldthwait, Ezekiel (town clerk, subscriber), 146, 162
Goodall, Judith (married to Daniel Harris), 222
Goodwin, John, Mr. (state pauper), 280
Gore, John, Jr. (merchant), 168
Goss, John (land grant), 46
Gould, Isaac (warned, patriotic soldier), 221, 321
Gould, John (of Malden, constable), 106
Graves, Calvin (son of Peter and Lydia, warned, patriotic soldier), 197
Graves, Luther (son of Peter and Lydia, warned, patriotic soldier), 197, 224, 322
Graves, Olive (servant of William and Betty Arbuthnot, warned), 108
Gray, Elizabeth (on charity), 53
Gray, Joshua (service honor), 215, 216
Gray, Robert (veteran petitioner), 35
Gray, William (warned), 130
Green, Enoch (deserted from service), 214
Green, Jacob (son of Phebe Green), 114
Green, John (son of Phebe Green), 114
Green, John (veteran petitioner), 35
Green, Johnson (patriotic soldier, crime), 250
Green, Nathaniel (on relief), 2, 30
Green, Phebe (widow, complained about her children), 114
Greene, Amos (deserted from service), 214
Greene, Thomas (brazier, subscriber), 71
Greenleaf, Daniel, Jr., Dr. (warned), 107
Greenleaf, Nancy (wife of Dr. Daniel Greenleaf, Jr., warned), 107
Greenleaf, Silence (daughter of Daniel and Nancy, warned), 107
Greenleaf, William (of Boston, overseer of the poor, subscriber), 146
Greenwood, John (patriotic soldier), xxviii
Gridley, Jeremy (counsel), 120
Grout, Dirick (patriotic soldier, crime), 249-250
Grover, Henry (servant of William and Betty Arbuthnot, warned), 108
Gruell, Anthony (deserted from service), 214
Gunter, Thomas (merchant), 68, 70

Haftings, Thomas (selectman), 30
Hall, Elizabeth (on charity), 53
Hallet, John Allen, Captain, 209
Hamilton, Alexander, 247

Name Index

Hancock, John (selectman, subscriber, later gov.), 121, 145, 146, 188, 192, 245, 273
Hancock, John, Mrs., 274
Handy, Ebenezer (poor child, kept by public vendue), 261
Hanks, Joseph (warned), 126
Haraden, John, Captain, 205
Harcess, Mary (servant of John and Ruth Dodge, warned), 108
Harnden, Ebenezer (veteran petitioner), 38
Harrington, Elisha (took strangers), 109
Harrington, Isaac (veteran petitioner), 37
Harrington, Stephen (warned), 255
Harris, Abner (veteran petitioner), 38
Harris, Daniel (son of Thomas and Lucy, warned, patriotic solider), 197, 219, 222, 322
Harris, Judith (widow of Daniel Harris), 219
Harris, Lucy Peirce (wife of Thomas the Elder, warned), 222
Harris, Samuel (son of Thomas and Lucy, patriotic solider), 197, 222
Harris, Thomas, Jr. (son of Thomas and Lucy, warned, patriotic soldier), 197, 222
Harris, Thomas, Sr. (warned), 222
Harrman, Johnson, Col., 37
Hatch, Elizabeth (wife of Jeremiah, warned), 125
Hatch, Jeremiah (warned), 125
Hatch, Nathaniel (of Dorchester, loyalist), 191
Hatch, Timothy (warned), 126
Hathaway, John (business partner), 98
Haven, Asa (warned, patriotic soldier), 197, 323
Haven, Daniel, Jr. (Asa's brother, warned, patriotic soldier), 197
Haven, Ebenezer (Asa's brother, warned, patriotic soldier), 197
Haven, Jason, Rev. (prize winner for mulberry trees), 156
Hawley, Joseph (Whig), 188
Hawes, Benjamin (of Wrentham, militia captain, took strangers), 178, 254
Haws, George (took strangers), 103

Hays, Ann (on charity), 53
Healey, Benjamin, Jr. (suffered in captivity), 36
Hemenway, Susanna (1st wife of Joseph Stratton Temple), 221
Henchman, Daniel, Dea. (overseers of the poor, donor), 54, 55
Henry, Adam (deserted from service), 214
Henry, Hugh, Rev. (petition denied), 43
Hill, Abigail (wife of Ebenezer, warned), 125, 197
Hill, Daniel (son of Ebenezer and Abigail, warned, patriotic soldier), 197
Hill, Ebenezer (warned), 125, 197
Hill, Henry (overseer of the poor), 148
Hill, John (son of Ebenezer and Abigail, warned, patriotic soldier), 197
Hill, John, Esq. (justice of the peace), 117, 118
Hill, Rebecca (visitor to workhouse), 27
Hill, Solomon (son of Ebenezer and Abigail, warned, patriotic soldier), 197
Hinman, Elisha, Captain, 206
Hogg, Thomas (his wife—a caretaker), 36
Holland, Nathaniel (on relief), 2
Holloway, Timothy (business partner), 98
Holman, Hugh (veteran petitioner), 37
Holman, Rachel (married to Joseph Ransford 2nd), 228
Holms, Abiel, Rev., 263, 270
Hooper, Joseph (of Marblehead, loyalist), 190
Hooper, Robert (son of Joseph, loyalist), 190
Hopkins, Matthew (orphan, patriotic soldier), 195
Houghton, Elisha (hired soldier), 200
Howard, Andrew (patriotic soldier), 219, 225-226, 232, 324
Howard, Clarissa (widow of Andrew Howard), 219
Howard, John (English philanthropist), 273

Name Index

Howe, William (British general), 186
Howell, Luke (promoted in service), 212
Hubbard, Lazarus (on charity), 53
Hubbard, Thomas (overseer of the poor, subscriber), 71
Hufle, Isaac (deserted from service), 214
Huggins, William (alias, patriotic soldier, crime), 249
Hughs, Mary Robson, 276-277
Hughson, Peter (deserted from service), 214
Hull, Agippa (African American, patriotic soldier), 249
Hulton, Henry (Customs Commissioner), 166
Hunt, Abiel (wife of Jonathan Hunt, warned), 106
Hunt, Daniel (father of eleven children, warned), 105
Hunt, John (overseer of the poor, subscriber), 146
Hunt, Jonathan (warned), 106
Hunt, Samuel (land grant), 45
Hunter, Archibald (service and desertion), 214-215
Hunter, Jonathan (patriotic soldier), 226, 325
Hut, Ebenezer (land grant), 45
Hutchinson, Eliakim (loyalist), 190-191
Hutchinson, Joanna (niece of Lt. Gov. Thomas Hutchinson, warned), 105
Hutchinson, Thomas, Lt. Gov., 105, 147, 191
Hutchinson, Thomas, Jr. (son of Lt. Gov. Thomas Hutchinson, loyalist), 191

Inches, Henderson (selectman, overseer of the poor), 121, 145, 148, 149,
Ingersoll, Jared (Connecticut), 171
Ireland, Mary (widow, donor), 54, 55

Jackson, Joseph (selectman), 121
Jancks, William (took strangers), 254
Jane, Jersey (Ward No. 8), 58
Jarvis, Encoh (orphan, patriotic soldier), 195
Jarvis, John (on charity), 53

Jeffrey, William (veteran petitioner), 35
Jenkens, Ebenezer, Esq., 266
Jewett, Phoebe (married to Luther Graves), 224
Job, David (Native Indian, soldier), 37
Johnson, Abraham (suffered in captivity), 36
Johnson, Caleb (veteran petitioner), 35
Johnson, Job (son of John and Zerviah, warned, patriotic soldier), 197
Johnson, Jonathan (son of John and Zerviah, warned, patriotic soldier), 197, 326
Johnson, Josiah (of Billerica, wounded soldier), 35
Johnson, Josiah (of Woburn, wounded soldier), 33
Johnson, Noah (wounded soldier), 36
Jones, Elisha (of Weston, loyalist), 192, 193
Jones, Isaac (took strangers), 109, 110
Jones, John Paul, Captain, 205, 206
Jordon, Samuel, Capt. (petitioner), 35
Joseph, Taft, Dr. (warned), 107
Joslin, Henry (wrongfully convicted), 40
Jucket, Peter (warned), 126

Keith, Daniel (selectman), 250
Kellogg, Daniel (farmer), 262
Kelly, William (service and desertion), 214
Kempton, Ephraim (warned), 128
Kendall, Reuben (African American, hired soldier), 200
Key, John (deserted from service), 214
Killam (or Kilham), Thomas (arrested), 246
King, Joseph (state pauper), 281
Kittredge, Francis, Dr., 107
Knights, Alice (daughter of Ebenezer and Mary, warned), 104
Knights, Amaziah (son of Ebenezer and Mary, warned), 104
Knights, Anna (daughter of Ebenezer and Mary, warned), 104

Name Index

Knights, Ebenezer (father of eight children, warned), 104
Knights, Ebenezer, Jr. (son of Ebenezer and Mary, warned), 104
Knights, Mary (wife of Ebenezer, warned), 104
Knights, Mary, Jr. (daughter of Ebenezer and Mary, warned), 104
Knights, Matthew (son of Ebenezer and Mary, warned), 104
Knights, Ruth (daughter of Ebenezer and Mary, warned), 104
Knights, Sarah (daughter of Ebenezer and Mary, warned), 104
Knower, Daniel (took a child), 114
Knower, Thomas (warned not to entertain strangers), 109
Kollock, Lemuel (militia captain), 178

Lamaine, Benjamin (servant boy of Robert and Leady Stutson, warned), 108
Lamb, Joshua, Col. (land grant), 46
Lamson, Samuel (militia captain), 179, 183, 218
Lane, Freeman (son of Gresham Flagg and Lydia Sally Lane), 194
Lane, George Washington (son of Gresham Flagg and Lydia Sally Lane), 194
Lane (or Lain), Gresham Flagg (warned, patriotic soldier), 193, 226, 326
Lane, John, Lt., 37
Lane, John "Ters" (father of Gresham Flagg), 193
Lane, Levi (warned), 255
Lane, Lydia Sally Thomas (married to Gresham Flagg), 193
Langley, Joseph, 327
Larrabee, John (victualler), 41
Larrabee, William, Dea. (searcher), 59
Lasinbee, Joseph (workhouse master), 63-64
Lasinby, —, Mrs. (surgery), 54
Lawrence, Jeremiah (selectman), 282, 284
Lealand, James, 327
Leary, James (promoted in service), 212

Lechmere, Richard (of Taunton, loyalist), 191
Lee, Jeremiah (subscriber, Tea Party), 147
Lee, John (state pauper), 279
Legg, John Doyle (orphan, patriotic soldier), 219, 233-234, 328
Leland, Isaac (received piece work), 78
Leverett, John (overseer of the poor, subscriber), 147
Leverett, John, Esq. (deceased), 43
Lewis, Cain (African American, hired soldier), 200
Lewis, Ezekiel (overseer of the poor, subscriber), 146
Lewis, Hannah (African American, warned), 255
Lewis, Job (African American, hired soldier), 200
Lillie, Thomas (orphan, patriotic soldier), 195, 222, 329
Little, Luther, Captain, 205
Livermore, Daniel (of Weston, took strangers), 109
London, Edom (African American, hired soldier), 200
Love, Robert (searcher), 87, 100, 101, 108, 176
Lovell, Robert, Capt. (deceased), 46
Lovewell, John, Capt., 35
Lowden, Nathaniel (warned), 127
Lowell, James (subscriber), 146
Lucas, John (on charity), 53
Lynch, Bartholomew (orphan, patriotic soldier), 195

Maccarty, William (horse owner), 40
Madden, John (service and desertion), 215
Magee, — (John Magee's wife), 284
Magee, John (state pauper), 284
Magee, Sarah (single woman, removed), 116
Magoune, Jonathan (selectman), 105
Malcolm, John (petition denied), 44
Man, David (took strangers, militia man), 106, 110
Manley, John, Captain, 205
Marshall, Josiah (school teacher, in removal case), 120
Martin, James (province poor), 22

Name Index

Martin, Joseph Plumb (patriotic soldier), 249
Mason, Jesse (patriotic soldier), 222, 329
Mason, John (overseer of the poor, subscriber), 146
Mason, Jonathan (selectman, overseer of the poor), 121, 148, 149
Matthews, Miriam (suffered in captivity), 36
Maxfield, Joseph (orphan, patriotic soldier), 195, 227, 330
Maylem, Joseph (petitioner), 43
Mayley, Annis (married to William Shirley), 222
McAfee, Aguis (province poor), 22
McBride, Abigail (daughter of John and Jane, warned), 101
McBride, Jane (wife of John, warned), 101
McBride, John (poor, warned), 101
McBride, Mary (daughter of John and Jane, warned), 101
McBride, William (son of John and Jane, warned), 101
McClary (or Mcleary), John (on relief, Patriotic soldier), 185
McClure, Richard (promoted in service), 212
McComb, Jane (state pauper), 286
McDougal, Daniel (state pauper), 286
McFadden, James (suffered in captivity), 36
McIntire, Andrew (promoted in service), 212
McKlain, Daniel (promoted in service), 212
McNeal, Daniel (warned), 286
McWain (or Mucklewain), John (warned), 119
Meacham, John (promoted in service), 212
Menzies, John, Esq. (deceased), 39
Meresservie, Mary (nurse, warned), 106
Metcalf, James (took strangers), 103
Metcalf, Lois (warned), 103
Metcalf, Marquis (warned), 255
Miller, Allen (son of Nelson and Sarah, warned), 104
Miller, Batney [original] (child of Nelson and Sarah, warned), 104
Miller, John (son of Nelson and Sarah, warned), 104
Miller, Nelson (father of eight, warned), 104
Miller, Nelson, Jr. (son of Nelson and Sarah, warned), 104
Miller, Patience (daughter of Nelson and Sarah, warned), 104
Miller, Polly (daughter of Nelson and Sarah, warned), 104
Miller, Rebeckah (daughter of Nelson and Sarah, warned), 104
Miller, Sarah (wife of Nelson, warned), 104
Miller, Sarah, Jr. (daughter of Nelson and Sarah, warned), 104
Molineux, William (Whig), 147-149, 162, 188
Moodey, Joshua, Capt., 44
Moody, Joel (patriotic soldier), 220, 330
Moody, John (father of Joel), 220
Moody, Sarah Dickinson (mother of Joel Moody), 220
Moor, Abel (hired soldier), 200
Moore, Abijah, Capt. (warned), 108
Moore, Ephraim (wounded soldier), 36
Moore, Etham (promoted in service), 212
Morrison, Sarah (on charity), 53
Morse, Benjamin (received piece work for his wife), 77
Morse, Isaiah (warned), 222
Morse, Joseph (representative, received piece work for his wife), 77, 79
Morton, —, Mr. (patriotic serviceman, captive), 211
Munro, Timothy (patriotic soldier), 224, 331
Munroe, Ebenezer (minuteman), 95
Munroe, John (minuteman), 95
Munroe, Joseph, Dr., 107
Munroe, Nathan (minuteman), 95
Munroe, William (minuteman), 95
Murray, John (of Rutland, loyalist), 191
Myer, Adam (service honor), 215

Nap, James (suffered in captivity), 36
Neal, Henry (poor), xx
Needham, John (militia man), 201
Nichols, Eunice (married to Edward

Name Index

Payson), 222
Noble, Mark (orphan, patriotic soldier), 195, 227, 248-249
Noble, Samuel (arrested), 246
Norton, Jenks, Dr. (took strangers), 111
Nutting, Jane Hunnewell (wife of Samuel 1st, warned), 224
Nutting, Samuel, 1st (warned), 183, 224
Nutting, Samuel, 2nd (warned, militia drummer), 183, 224, 331
Nutting, Samuel, 3rd (son of Samuel 2nd, warned), 224
Nye, Prince (selectman), 286

Oak (or Oaks), Calvin (patriotic soldier), 219, 227, 332
Oak, Lucretia (widow of Calvin Oak), 219
Oliver, Andrew (councilor, subscriber), 70
Otis, James (patriot), 166, 188

Paine, Robert Treat (attorney), 148
Parker, Samuel, Rev., 274, 275, 276
Parkhurst, Martha (nurse, warned), 105
Patrick, Margaret (wife of Robert Patrick, warned), 104
Patrick, Robert (warned), 104
Patridge, Samuel (subscriber), 149
Patten, Richard (patriotic soldier, state pauper), 279
Patton, Richard (from Ireland, patriotic soldier, state pauper), 279-280
Payne, Edward (overseer of the poor), 145, 146, 162
Payson, David (Edward's brother, patriotic soldier), 197
Payson, Edward (warned, patriotic soldier), 197, 222, 333
Peacock, Elizabeth Crane (wife of Robert), xiii
Peacock, Robert (poor), xiii
Peck, Joseph (veteran petitioner), 38
Peirce, Benjamin (took strangers, militia man), 102
Peirce, Heph (warned), 102
Peirce, Hephzibeth (warned), 102
Peirce, Mary (of Weston, married to Samuel Nutting 3rd), 224

Pell, Rebecca, Jr. (daughter of William and Rebecca, warned), 114
Pell, Rebecca Howard (widow of William Pell, warned), 114
Pell, Susanna (daughter of William and Rebecca, warned), 114
Pell, William (deceased), 114
Pemberton, Ebenezer, Rev. (donor), 54
Pemberton, George, Dr. (petition denied), 36
Pemberton, Samuel (selectman), 121
Pemberton, Thomas (author), 70
Penniman, James (received piece work), 77
Perkins, Nathaniel, Dr. (inoculation), 140
Perry, James (arrested), 246
Phelps, David, Dr., 284
Phillips, William (overseer of the poor, subscriber), 145, 146, 148, 149, 161, 188, 273
Phillips, William, Mrs., 274
Pierce, Benjamin (took strangers), 109
Pike, Hugh (wounded soldier), 33
Pike, John (sick soldier), 36
Pilsberry, Mary (in almshouse), 22
Pitt, William, the Elder, 161
Plaisted, Thomas (land grant), 45
Plimpton, Amos (received piece work), 78
Plimpton, John (tailor), 78
Plimpton, Simon (received piece work), 78
Polle, John (sent back to Medford), 114
Pond, David (took strangers), 103
Pond, Oliver (militia captain), 178
Pond, Rueben (took strangers), 103
Pond, Samuel (warned), 103
Potter, Grace (widow of Judah, lost provincial bill), 41
Potter, Judah (deceased), 41
Powers, Mary (in removal case), 119
Pratt, — (wife of Benjamin, warned), 253
Pratt, Benjamin (warned), 253
Pratt, Benjamin, Jr. (son of Benjamin, warned), 253
Pratt, Esther (daughter of Benjamin, warned), 253

Name Index

Pratt, Hannah (daughter of Benjamin, warned), 253
Pratt, Joseph, Capt. (warned), 108
Pratt, Joshua (warned), 128
Pratt, Sally (daughter of Benjamin, warned), 253
Prentiss, Nathaniel Sartlell (or Sartle) (father of Susan), 234
Prentiss, Susan (married to John Banks), 234
Price, James (quarter master, warned), 108
Price, William (promoted in service), 212
Prior, Thomas (pamphleteer), 67
Proctor, Christopher (on charity), 53
Proctor, Edward (overseer of the poor), 148
Puffer, George (son of William 2nd and Mary, warned, patriotic soldier), 182, 197
Puffer, Mary (wife of William Puffer, 1st, warned), 111
Puffer, William 1st (warned), 111, 182
Puffer, William 2nd (warned, militia sergeant), 197, 221, 224, 334
Putnam, Persis (wife of Rufus, warned), 108
Putnam, Rufus, Col. (warned), 108
Pynchon, William, Jr. (town treasurer), 243

Quiltis, Patrick (poor, warned), 101
Quincy, John, Mayor, 268
Quincy, Josiah, Jr. (subscriber), 146, 149, 273
Quincy, Samuel (subscriber), 146

Randal, Jonathan (warned), 127
Randall, James (constable), 105
Ransford, Joseph 2nd (patriotic soldier), 227, 234, 334
Ransford, Rachel (wife of Joseph Ransford 2nd), 234
Raymond, Jonathan, 336
Reab, George (promoted in service), 212
Read, Seth (veteran petitioner), 38
Revere, Paul (reprimanded, patriot), 146, 273
Rice, David (state pauper), 286
Richards, William (promoted in service), 212
Richardson, Benjamin, 336
Richardson, James (of Boston, subscriber), 149
Richardson, Phineas (veteran petitioner), 38
Richmond, Henry (warned), 127
Ricket, John Howland, Captain, 210
Roberts, Amariah (poor, warned), 101
Roberts, Amariah, Jr. (son of Amariah and Lucy, warned), 101
Roberts, Ebenezer, (son of Amariah and Lucy, warned), 101
Roberts, Joseph (took strangers), 109
Roberts, Lucy (wife of Amariah, warned), 101
Roberts, Lucy, Jr. (daughter of Amariah and Lucy, warned), 101
Robinson, George (care provider), 2
Rogers, Benjamin, 106, 337
Rogers, Eleazer (wounded soldier), 33
Rogers, John (of Hanover, took strangers), 102
Rogers, Perley (African American, hired soldier), 200
Rogers, Wing (warned), 102
Rowe, John (subscriber), 147, 149
Royle, Philip (from Ireland), 279
Russell, William (patriotic sailor), 206
Rutter, William, Jr. (wounded soldier), 34
Ryan, John (service and desertion), 215
Ryan, Richard (service and desertion), 215

Sampson, Deborah Gannett (patriotic soldier), 248
Sanger, —, (widow, on relief), 2
Savage, Samuel (took strangers), 106
Scollay, John (selectman), 140
Scott, Ebenezer (warned), 250
Scott, Joseph (petition denied), 43
Sellman, Joseph (shoreman), 222
Sewall, Joseph, Dr. (donor), 54
Shappo, Anthony (service honor), 215, 216
Sharp, — (doctor from London), 131
Shaw, James (warned), 250
Shaw, John (debtor), 39

Name Index

Shaw, John (son of James and Sarah 1st), 250
Shaw, Sarah 1st (wife of James, warned), 250
Shaw, Sarah 2nd (daughter of James and Sarah 1st), 250
Shays, Daniel (Continental captain), 241, 246
Shearmen, —, Mrs. (on relief), 2
Shed, Lemuel (recruit of Lancaster, unfit for service), 201
Shepard, Benjamin (of Wrentham, substantial farmer), 254
Shepard, Benjamin, Capt. (took strangers), 102, 111
Shepard, James (service and desertion), 215
Shepard, John (patriotic soldier, warned), 255
Shirley, William (orphan, patriotic soldier), 195, 222, 338
Shirley, William, Gov., 191
Shuttleworth, Vincent (veteran petitioner), 35, 41
Simons, Nicholas (veteran petitioner), 38
Skilling, Richard (promoted in service), 212
Skinner, George (in almshouse), 22
Skinner, Robert (drifter, hired soldier), 200
Slack, John (warned, patriotic soldier), 227, 339
Sloan, Norman (selectman), 282, 284
Smart, Alexander (deserted from service), 214
Smart, Priscilla, (refugee), 59
Smith, Amos (sick soldier), 35
Smith, Ebenezer (poor), 118
Smith, Ephraim (blind, on relief), 2
Smith, Hannah (married to Ephraim Chenery), 78
Smith, Isaac (trade organization member), 161
Smith, James (veteran petitioner), 37
Smith, Jonas (veteran petitioner), 37
Smith, Mary (married to Isaac Leland), 78
Smith, Nathaniel (creditor), 241
Spear, Pool (warned), 130
Speer, Samuel (shoemaker), 30
Spooner, Nathanial, Captain, 211

Sprague, Ebenezer (veteran petitioner), 38
Sprague, John (constable), 114
Sprague, Jonathan (warned), 102
Sprague, Joseph (took strangers), 102
Sprague, Tabitha (wife of Jonathan, warned), 102
Sprigs, George, Mr. (prize winner for mulberry trees), 156
Spring, Thaddeus (took strangers), 109, 110, 255
Staats, Ann (sister of Mary Ireland), 55
Staniford, John, Mr. (tax collector), 62
Stearns, Asahel (patriotic soldier), 227, 340
Stearns, Captivity (wife of Asahel), 227
Stearns, David (warned), 255
Stevens, Jabez (patriotic soldier, warned), 227, 340
Stevens, Timothy, Dr. (took strangers), 111
Stewart (or Stuerd), James, Dr. (warned), 107
Stimpson, Eabenezor (cleansed), 140
Stimson, James (took strangers), 109
Stocker, Christopher (patriotic soldier), 227
Stockridge, Joseph (selectman), 105
Storer, Ebenezer (selectman, overseer of the poor, subscriber), 121, 146
Storer, John (petitioner), 44
Story, Elisha, Dr. (warned), 107
Story, Ruth (wife of Elisha Story, warned), 107
Straton, George (selectman), 251
Streeter, Chloe (warned), 103
Streeter, Joseph (took strangers), 103
Stuart, Charles (mulatto, hired soldier), 200
Stutson, Caleb 2nd (patriotic soldier), 221, 341
Stutson, Hannah (daughter of Robert and Leady, warned), 108
Stutson, Leady (wife of Robert, warned), 108
Stutson, Rachel (daughter of Robert and Leady, warned), 108
Stutson, Robert (warned), 108

Name Index

Taft, Joseph, Dr. (warned), 255
Talbot, Robert (veteran petitioner), 35
Tarne, Myles (leather dresser), 98
Tarne, Sarah (married to Edward Babbitt), 98
Taylor, James, Esq. (deceased), 43
Taylor, Jane (on charity), 54
Taylor, John (thief), 43
Taylor, Roger (service and desertion), 215
Taylor, William (overseer of the poor, subscriber), 146
Teetor, William (deserted from service), 214
Temple, Joseph Stratton (patriotic soldier), 221, 341
Thayer, Abraham (soldier/guard, brother of Hannah), 217
Thayer, Ephraim (father of Ruth Thayer), 217
Thayer, Ether (soldier Sylvanus French's grandmother), 217
Thayer, Hannah (married to Sylvanus French), 217
Thayer, Lucinda (at 11, warned), 254
Thayer, Lydia Pray (wife of Thayer Zachariah), 217
Thayer, Nathaniel (soldier/guard), 217
Thayer, Sylvanus, Col. (son of Nathaniel and Dorcas Faxon Thayer), 217
Thayer, Zachariah (married Lydia Pray), 217
Thayer, Zebath (son of Zachariah and Lydia Pray Thayer, soldier/guard), 217-218
Thomas, David (veteran petitioner), 37-38
Thomas, Lydia Sally (married to Gersham Flagg Lane), 193, 226
Thompson, James (from Ireland, state pauper), 279
Thompson, Robert (veteran petitioner), 37
Thomson, David (of Woburn), 254
Tigh, Cornelius (hired soldier), 200
Tilton, Lucy (married to William Bogle), 224, 228
Timson, Sippeo (African, on relief), 2
Tinkham, Ebenezer (warned), 127

Tompson, William (militia colonel), 201
Tooly, Densa (state pauper), 279
Tooly, Elizabeth (mother of Densa, deceased), 279
Topkin, Hannah (husband left no support), 29
Tozer, John (veteran petitioner), 37
Trask, Anna (daughter of Daniel and Rachel, warned), 105, 221
Trask, Daniel (father of seven children, warned), 105, 221
Trask, Daniel, Jr. (son of Daniel and Rachel, warned), 105, 221
Trask, Hannah (daughter of Daniel and Rachel, warned), 105, 221
Trask, Luke (son of Daniel and Rachel, warned), 105, 221
Trask, Mary (daughter of Daniel and Rachel, warned), 105, 221
Trask, Rachel (wife of Daniel, warned), 105, 221
Trask, Rachel, Jr. (daughter of Daniel and Rachel, warned), 105, 221
Trask, Rhoda (daughter of Daniel and Rachel, warned), 105, 221
Tucker, Daniel (of Milton, wounded sergeant), 33, 36
Tucker, Daniel (of Shrewsbury), 342
Tucker, David (wounded soldier), 37
Tudor, John (overseer of the poor, subscriber), 146
Turner, Israel, Captain, 210
Twitchell, Daniel (poor, warned), 101
Tyler, Charlotte (daughter of Thomas), 106
Tyler, Thomas, Esq. (deceased), 106
Tylor, David (veteran petitioner), 38

Underwood, Joshua (warned), 106
Upham, Ebenezer (constable), 109

Varril, Thomas (veteran petitioner), 37
Veal, John (state pauper), 286-287
Vernon, Fortesque (subscriber, Whig), 149
Vickery, John (poor, warned), 101
Vickery, Lydia, Jr. (daughter of John and Lydia, warned), 101
Vinten (or Vinton), Levi (son of Nathaniel 1st and Ann Green,

Name Index

patriotic soldier, warned), 227, 342
Vinton, Josiah, Jr. (director), 272

Wadsworth, Benjamin, Rev., 11, 13, 14
Wainwright, —, Mrs. (on charity), 54
Wainwright, John, Capt. (deceased), 45
Waldo, Daniel (Boston overseer of the poor, subscriber), 147
Waldo, Daniel (petitioner), 40
Waldo, Joseph (overseer of the poor, subscriber), 147
Wallcut, Christopher (promoted in service), 212
Wallick, Gabriel (deserted from service), 214
Walton, Amos (took strangers), 254
Walton, Shadrach, Col., 37
Ward, William (took strangers), 255
Ware, Asa (warned), 103
Ware, Elisha (of Needham, warned), 103
Ware, Elisha (of Wrentham, took strangers, sergeant), 103
Ware, Josiah (took strangers), 103
Ware, Mehitable (warned), 103
Warner, Elisha (selectman), 286
Warren, Ann (married to Elisha Cox 1st), 196
Warren, Ebenezer (selectman), 251
Warren, James (patriot), 188
Warren, Joseph, Dr. (inoculation, subscriber), 140, 146, 148, 149
Warren, Timothy (selectman), 259
Washburn, John (patriotic serviceman, captive), 211
Washington, George, 204, 215, 216
Wathebe, William (at seventeen, warned), 102
Wayte, Nathan (constable), 114
Webb, Samuel (patriotic sailor, captive), 209-211
Wetherbee, William (warned, militia man), 182
Wetherel, Lidea (warned), 221
Wethrell, Samuel (took strangers), 102
Wethrell, Unis (widow, warned), 102
Wheelock, Ephraim, Dea. (received piece work), 78

White, Benjamin (took strangers), 102
White, Thomas (warned), 102
Whiting, John, Mr. (took strangers, militia sergeant), 111
Whitney, Daniel (warned), 102
Whitney, Joseph (took strangers, militia man), 102
Whittemore, Lydia (married to Lemuel Gates), 226
Wilder, Joseph, Mr. (on House committee), 38
Wilkenson, Bethiah (sister of Isaac), 109
Wilkenson, Isaac (disallowed to keep sister), 109
Willard, Samuel, Dr. (warned), 107
Willey, Ruth (Ward No. 8), 58
Williams, John (of Boston, overseer of the poor, subscriber), 146
Williams, Jonathan (overseer of the poor), 146
Williams, Margaret (poor, warned), 101
Williams, Thomas (veteran petitioner), 38
Willington, Thaddeus (patriotic soldier, warned), 252
Wilson, William (state pauper), 286
Winthrop, John, Gov. 78
Winslow, Isaac (merchant, subscriber), 71
Winslow, Shubal, Dr. (warned), 107
Wire, Jenny (warned, a.k.a. Jenny Thomson), 254
Wood, Ama (daughter of Thomas and Mary, warned), 105, 221
Wood, Comfort (daughter of Thomas and Mary, warned), 105, 221
Wood, Jane (state pauper), 286
Wood, Joseph (son of Thomas and Mary, warned), 105, 221
Wood, Jotham (recruit of Lancaster, unfit for service), 201
Wood, Lavina (daughter of Thomas and Mary, warned), 105, 221
Wood, Lusina (daughter of Thomas and Mary, warned), 105, 221
Wood, Mary (wife of Thomas Wood, warned), 105, 221
Wood, Olney (son of Thomas and Mary, warned), 105, 221
Wood, Reuben (son of Thomas and

Name Index

Mary, warned), 105, 221
Wood, Simeon (son of Thomas and Mary, warned), 105, 221
Wood, Thomas (father of nine children, warned), 105, 221
Wood, Tillson (son of Thomas and Mary, warned), 105, 221
Woodard, William (veteran petitioner), 35
Woodin, John (state pauper), 281
Woodside, James, Capt. (delinquent), 40
Woos, Amy (daughter of Thomas and Molly, warned), 254
Woos, Comfort (daughter of Thomas and Molly, warned), 254
Woos, Joseph (son of Thomas and Molly, warned), 254
Woos, Levina (daughter of Thomas and Molly, warned), 254
Woos, Lucina (daughter of Thomas and Molly, warned), 254
Woos, Molly (wife of Thomas, warned), 254
Woos, Olney (son of Thomas and Molly, warned), 254
Woos, Reuben (son of Thomas and Molly, warned), 254
Woos, Simon (son of Thomas and Molly, warned), 254
Woos, Thomas (warned), 254
Woos, Tillson (son of Thomas and Molly, warned), 254
Wright, John (of Weston, militia sergeant) p. 291, 327
Wright, John Claffin (state pauper), 286
Wright, Joseph, Mr. (of Woburn), 254
Wyeth, Deborah Parker (wife of Nicolas, on relief), 2, 29
Wyeth, Jonas (took strangers), 254
Wyeth, Nicolas (on relief), 2, 28-29
Wyman, Asa (at 17, hired soldier), 200
Wyman, John (at 17, hired soldier), 200
Wyman, Mathew (hired soldier), 200

Young, Joseph (prison keeper), 40
Young, Thomas, Dr. (Whig), 106-107, 147, 148

Place Index

Abington, 89, 125, 197, 259
Acton, 169
Africa, 253, 285
Alexandria, 158
Alstead (Newton Canada), New Hampshire, 195, 225, 234
Amesbury, 242
Amherst, Hampshire Co., 97, 219, 220, 241, 262, 265
Amsterdam, 285
Andover, 95, 237, 252
Annapolis, 87
Antwerp, 158
Arundel, 36
Ashburnham (Dorchester Canada), 95
Ashfield (Weymouth Canada), Hampshire Co. (now Franklin Co.), 196, 223, 231
Athol, 263
Attleborough, Bristol Co., 40, 88, 118, 227, 237
Augusta, Maine, 248

Bahamas, 139
Baltimore, 274
Barnard, Vermont, 98
Barnstable, 35
Barnstable County (1685-), 151
Barre, Worcester Co., 98
Bedford (formerly Souhegan East), 95, 193, 226, 259, 264
Belchertown, 97, 226, 232, 281
Belfast, Ireland, 210
Bellingham, Norfolk Co., 43, 88, 223, 226, 230, 248, 259
Bennington, Vermont, 283
Berkley, 98

Berkshire County (1761-), 98, 151, 152, 222, 227, 245, 249, 282, 283
Berlin, Worcester Co., 259
Bernardston, 259
Beverly, 36, 286
Bilbao, Spain, 210
Billerica, Middlesex Co., 35, 95, 169, 201, 286
Black Point (on the Maine border), 59
Blandford, Hampshire Co., 246
Bloomfield, Indiana, 225
Bolton, Worcester Co., 89, 101, 107, 108,
Boston, xix, xx, xxiv, xxvi, 11, 21, 22, 23, 25, 27, 28, 31, 39, 43, 45, 47, 50-76, 79-83, 87, 88, 89, 90, 98, 100, 106, 107, 108, 114, 116, 117-118, 119-120, 121-122, 130, 135, 137-138, 139-142, 143-150, 151, 155, 156, 161-166, 168, 169, 171, 174-177, 181, 183, 184-185, 186, 188, 190, 192, 195, 196, 199, 200, 202, 204, 206, 210, 212, 213, 215, 216, 217, 218, 222, 223, 225, 227, 228, 234, 236, 237, 248, 252-253, 259, 262, 266-277, 281, 285
Boston Harbor, 216
Boxford, Essex Co., 197, 216, 225, 259
Bradford, 96
Braintree, Suffolk Co., xiii, 88, 107, 127, 168, 217, 227, 255, 259, 264
Branford, Connecticut, 226, 283
Breed's Hill, 237

Place Index

Bridgewater, Plymouth Co., 98, 109, 125, 127, 128, 169, 197, 215, 223, 250, 288
Brimfield, Hampshire Co., 98, 224, 225, 227
Bristol, England, 285
Bristol, Rhode Island, 224
Bristol County (1685-), 98, 116, 126, 151, 203, 227, 246
Bristol County, Rhode Island, 224
British Empire, 88
Brookfield, Worcester Co., 35, 89, 97, 98, 103, 108, 125, 227, 248
Brookline, 88, 120, 121,
Buffalo, Niagara County, New York, 225, 232
Bunker Hill, 237, 242

Cádiz, Spain, 210
Cambridge, Middlesex Co., 2, 88, 106, 107, 139, 169, 184, 192, 223, 227, 236, 241, 251, 253, 254, 263, 266, 270
Canada, 97, 143, 226
Canada Townships, 152-153
Canterbury, Connecticut, 96
Cape Breton, 143
Cape Cod, 89
Cape Finisterre, 210
Carlisle, 95
Carolina, 67, 285
Castle Island, 35, 41, 140, 216, 217, 218
Charleston, South Carolina, 88, 146, 165
Charlestown, Middlesex Co., 28, 88, 89, 169, 224, 236, 237, 266
Charlestown, New Hampshire, 281
Charlton, Worcester Co., 89
Chelmsford, 251
Chelsea (formerly Rumney Marsh), 88, 89, 106, 117-118, 237, 253, 280
Chelsea, Vermont, 226
Cheshire County, New Hampshire, 234
Chester (formerly Murrayfield), Hampshire Co., 238
Chesterfield (Hingham Canada), Hampshire Co., 94
Chilmark, Dukes Co., 126
Clarksburgh, Berkshire Co.
Clinton County, New York, 226

Colchester (formerly in Massachusetts), Connecticut, 98, 183, 227
Colrain, 286
Concord, Erie County, New York, 225
Concord, Middlesex Co., xxvii, 41, 92, 95, 97, 134, 182, 204, 242
Connecticut, 23, 67, 89, 97, 171, 225, 249, 252, 281, 285
Connecticut River, 45, 152
Conway, Hampshire Co., 287
Cork, Ireland, 215
Cranston, Rhode Island, 249
Crawford County, Indiana, 225
Crown Point, 144
Cumberland, Rhode Island, 88, 182, 221, 223, 234, 285

Dana, Worcester Co., 98
Danvers, Essex Co., 281
Dartmouth, Bristol Co., 89, 98, 128,
Dedham, Norfolk Co., 79, 88, 92, 95, 112, 116, 156, 169, 192, 251, 253
Deerfield, Hampshire Co., 45, 287
Dighton, 98
Dorchester, 28, 35, 88, 115, 191, 222, 266
Douglas, 263, 281
Dover, Norfolk Co.
Dublin, Ireland, 67, 204
Dudley, 89
Dukes County (1695-), 287
Dunkirk, 158
Dunstable, 36, 37
Duxbury, Plymouth Co., 89, 105, 128,

East Haddam, Hartford (later Middlesex) Co., Connecticut, 223
East Sudbury, 90
Eastern, New York, 98
Easthampton, 279
Easton, Bristol Co., 98, 246, 251
Edgertown, Dukes Co., 287
Elizabethtown, New Jersey, 283
England, xxv, 14-20, 25, 28, 31, 47, 108, 157, 158, 191, 215, 252, 253, 270, 286
Essex County (1643-), 90, 96, 139, 151, 167, 197, 222, 225

- 443 -

Place Index

Europe, xxv, 7, 12, 15, 18, 82, 154, 158, 254

Fairbanks, Indiana, 228
Fall Fights (on Connecticut River), 45
Faneuil Hall, 138, 237
Fitchburg, Worcester Co., 222, 227
Fond du Lac County, Wisconsin, 226
Fort George, 44
Fort Independence, 217
Foxborough, Norfolk Co., 104, 222, 251, 255
France, 87, 208, 252, 253, 285
Franklin, Norfolk Co., 103, 223, 230, 254, 255
Franklin County (formerly part of Hampshire Co.; 1811-), 45, 97, 196, 225, 286
Freetown, Bristol Co., 98, 126

Genesee County, New York, 227
Genoa, 158
Georgetown, Essex Co., 36, 96
Georgia, 285
Germany, 252, 253, 285
Gibraltar, the Strait of, 210
Gloucester, Essex Co., 96, 165
Gloucester, Rhode Island, 98
Goshen, Hampshire Co., 251
Governor's Island, 216, 217, 218
Grafton, Vermont, 96
Grafton, Worcester Co., 169, 195, 223, 223, 225, 230, 234
Granby, Hampshire Co., 97, 220
Great Barrington, 151
Great Britain, 67, 87, 287
Greene County, Indiana, 225
Greenwich (formerly Quabbi), Hampshire Co., 98
Groton, Middlesex Co., 90, 95, 96, 237, 286

Hadley, 97, 195, 248
Halifax, Nova Scotia, 89, 139, 142, 186, 285
Halifax, Plymouth Co., 89, 109,
Hamburg, 158
Hampden County (formerly part of Hampshire Co.; 1812-), 224
Hampshire County (1662-), 90, 98, 152, 224, 225, 227, 232, 238, 240, 245, 246
Hanover, New Hampshire, 98
Hanover, Plymouth Co., 102, 109, 125, 126, 128,
Harding, 79
Hardwick, 97, 107, 286-287
Harland, New York, 227
Hartford (later Middlesex) County, Connecticut, 223
Harvard, Worcester Co., 89, 95, 101, 107, 223, 262, 263
Hatfield, 168, 195, 262
Haverhill, 45, 96, 259, 263
Henniker, New Hampshire, 226, 232, 233
Hillsborough (later Merrimack) County, New Hampshire, 95, 107, 226, 233
Hingham, 88
Hispaniola, 285
Holden, Worcester Co., 195, 197, 225, 226
Holland, 87, 158,
Hollis, New Hampshire, 96
Holliston, Middlesex Co., 78, 79, 98
Hopkinton, 102

Indiana, 228, 234
Ipswich, 33, 262
Ipswich, England, 159
Ireland, 87, 142, 157, 193, 252, 253, 279, 285, 286
Isles of Shoals, 285
Italy, 252

Jamaica, 88
Jefferson County, New York, 225

Keene, New Hampshire, 95, 103
Kennebeck, 144
Kennebec County, Maine, 248
Kentucky, 227, 234
Killingly, Connecticut, 98
Killingsworth, Connecticut, 283
Kingston, 109,
Kinsale, Ireland, 210
Kittery, Maine, 35

Lancaster, 40, 90, 91, 96, 101 106, 128, 178, 180-181, 183-184, 186, 196, 198-199, 224, 226, 279, 280

- 444 -

Place Index

Lanesboro, Berkshire Co., 98, 222
Lebanon, New York, 225, 227
Lee, Berkshire Co., 259, 261, 265, 266
Leicester, Worcester Co., 89, 91, 92, 97, 98, 169, 245
Lenox, Berkshire Co., 283
Leominster, Worcester Co., 224, 237, 279
Leverett, 97
Lexington, Middlesex Co., xxvii, 95, 97, 106, 107, 119, 134, 142, 169, 179, 182, 183, 196, 199, 204, 218, 222, 241
Lincoln, Middlesex Co., 90, 95, 249, 255
Lincoln County, Maine, 247
Lisbon, 210
Littleton, 90, 169, 237
Livermore, York County, Maine, 96
Liverpool, 285
London, 83, 131, 138, 144, 157, 167, 171, 204, 285
Longmeadow, Hampshire Co., 246
Louisbourg, 143
Low Countries, 158
Lunenburg, Worcester Co., 46, 96, 224, 263
Lyme, Connecticut, 115
Lynn, 89, 114, 168, 252
Lynnfield, Essex Co., 95

Madeira, 210
Maine, 23, 97, 152, 225, 248, 249, 252
Majorca, 210
Malden, Middlesex Co., 89, 91, 102, 103, 104, 105, 106, 107, 108, 109, 114, 192, 251, 263
Malta, 285
Mansfield, Bristol Co., 88, 98
Marblehead, 66, 139, 165, 190,195, 222, 252
Marlborough, Middlesex Co., 97, 189, 223, 226
Marshfield, Plymouth Co., 89, 98, 125,
Marshfield, Washington County, Vermont, 225
Medfield, Norfolk Co., 78, 88, 95,
Medford, Norfolk Co., 88, 89, 103, 183

Medway, 78, 79, 88, 119, 254
Mendham, New Jersey, 98
Mendon, 78, 88, 91, 92, 101, 129, 238, 239-240, 265, 281
Merrimack River, 46
Middleboro, 89, 98, 103, 120, 126, 127, 128, 238, 243, 244, 248, 260
Middlesex County (1643-), 89, 90, 98, 119, 151, 193, 201, 223, 224, 224, 225, 226, 227, 228
Middleton, 167, 215, 281
Milford, Worcester Co., 95, 96, 226
Millbury, 264
Milton, 33, 88, 167, 250
Monson, Hampden Co., 224, 288
Montague, 97
Montreal, 37
Mount Desart, 36
Murrayfield (later Chester), Hampshire Co., 238
Mystic River, 89

Nantucket, 165
Nantucket County (1695-), 165
Narragansett Townships, 152-154
Natick, 119
Needham, 88, 90, 103, 255, 259
New Ashford, Berkshire Co., 98
New Bedford, Bristol Co., 203, 248, 264
New Braintree, Worcester Co., 103, 129,130, 151, 227
New England, 57, 58, 67, 78, 83, 85, 95, 171, 206, 254
New Hampshire, 23, 97, 152, 217, 232, 252
New Hartford, New York, 226
New Jersey, 285
New London, Connecticut, 282, 283, 285
New London, New Hampshire, 227
New Salem, Hampshire Co., 151,
New York (city), 87, 88, 146, 165, 285
New York (province), 97, 106, 229, 248, 252, 281, 287
Newbury, 33
Newburyport, 66, 165, 169, 237, 266, 285
Newfoundland, 252
Newport, Rhode Island, 87, 165

Place Index

Newton, 90, 119, 224, 254, 255
Niagara County, New York, 225, 227
Norfolk County (1793-), 88, 151, 230
North Carolina, 208, 283
North End, Boston, 142
Northampton, 35, 188, 225, 246, 251, 262
Northborough, 91, 95, 252
Northbridge, 91
Norton, Bristol Co., 45, 98, 221
Nottingham, 40
Nova Scotia, 60, 88, 89, 127, 215,

Oakfield, Wisconsin. 226
Oakham, Worcester Co., 89, 129, 151, 223, 231
Ohio, 227, 228, 234
Ohio Valley, 108
Oneida County, New York, 226
Onondaga County, New York, 227
Oswegatchie, New York, 233
Oxford, Worcester Co., 89, 98, 125, 129, 224, 228

Palmer, Hampshire Co., 224, 226
Pawlet, Vermont, 96
Paxton, 97, 151
Pelham, Hampshire Co., 97, 224
Pembroke, Plymouth Co., 35, 105, 126, 127, 128, 130, 210,
Pennsylvania, xviii, 226
Penny-Cook, 46
Pepperell, 96, 105
Peru (formerly Patridgefield), Berkshire Co., 98
Petersham (formerly Nichewoag), Worcester Co., 97, 98, 151, 226, 286
Philadelphia, 65, 87, 88, 146, 165, 285
Pigwacket, 35, 36
Pittsfield, Berkshire Co., 98, 248
Plainfield, Hampshire Co., 95
Plattsburg, New York, 226
Plymouth, 33, 127, 128, 169, 188, 211, 221,
Plymouth, England, 206, 210
Plymouth County (1685-), 39, 87, 88, 89, 90, 98, 98, 105, 109, 120, 125, 126- 128, 177, 221, 224, 238, 248

Plympton, 89, 109, 120, 128, 221, 248
Poland, 285
Portsmouth, 87, 285
Poultney, Vermont, 96
Prescott, Hampshire Co., 224
Princeton, Worcester Co., 108, 224
Providence, Rhode Island, 88, 249

Reading, 89, 95, 118
Rehoboth, Bristol Co., 88, 89, 98, 103, 116
Rhode Island, 38, 46, 66, 89, 104, 115, 182, 190, 227, 249, 255, 281, 285
Richmond, Vermont, 98
Rochester, 89, 126, 248
Rowley, Canada, 183
Rowley, Essex Co., 96, 222, 252
Roxbury, 68, 70, 89, 95, 116, 119- 120, 121, 169, 191, 226, 252, 279
Royalston, Worcester Co., 203-204
Russia, 145
Rutland, Worcester Co., 40, 89, 91, 92, 97, 103, 104, 108, 129, 191, 224, 226, 241
Rutland County, Vermont, 227

Sagadahoc County, Maine, 225
St. Georges, 36, 38
St. Lawrence County, New York, 233
Salem, 28, 31, 89, 92, 165, 168, 190, 195, 236, 237, 252, 259, 262, 266, 281, 285
Saratoga, 241, 242
Scarborough, York County, Maine, 43
Scituate, 126, 127, 128, 130, 210,
Scotland, 157, 252, 253, 285, 286
Sharon, Norfolk Co., 104,
Shelburne, Hampshire Co., 225
Sherborn, Middlesex Co., 79, 101, 224
Shirley, Middlesex Co., 90, 224, 237
Shirley Hall, Roxbury, 191
Shirley Place, Roxbury, 190-191
Shrewsbury, 35, 95, 101, 184, 196, 221, 223, 230, 231,
Shutesbury, 97
South Boston, 268

Place Index

South Carolina, 208
Southampton, England, 159
Southborough, 101, 195
Spain, 208, 252, 285
Spanish Empire, 158
Spencer, Worcester Co., 89, 95, 98
Spit Head, England, 210
Springfield, Hampden Co., 28, 97, 195, 263
Springville, Pennsylvania, 226
Star Island, the Isles of Shoals, New Hampshire, 280
Sterling, Worcester Co., 96
Stockbridge, Berkshire Co., 249
Stoneham, 89
Stoughton, 128, 215, 266
Stoughtonham, 88
Stow, Middlesex Co., 90, 226, 279
Sturbridge, Worcester Co., 89, 98
Sudbury, Middlesex Co., 90, 95, 97, 102, 103, 202, 221, 223, 225
Suez, 158
Suffolk County (1643-), 88, 115, 120, 191, 223, 227, 250
Sullivan County, Indiana, 228
Sunderland, Hampshire Co., 203, 219
Surry, New Hampshire, 95
Susquehanna County, Pennsylvania, 226
Sutton, 281
Swansea, Bristol Co., 98, 221, 279

Taunton, 97, 191, 248
Templeton, 151
Tewksbury, 107, 288
Ticonderoga, 241, 281
Townsend, Middlesex Co., 96
Trenton, xxviii
Truro, 89
Two Mile River, 98
Tyre, 158

Upton, Worcester Co., 89, 223, 230
Uxbridge, Worcester Co., 103, 107, 248, 281

Valley Forge, 215
Venice, 158
Vermont, 97, 241
Virginia, xvii, 67, 97, 210, 252, 285

Wachusett Hill, 40

Wakefield, 95
Walpole, 89, 103, 116,
Waltham, Middlesex Co., 90, 96, 169, 223, 227, 234, 252, 255
Wardsboro, Vermont, 229
Ware, Hampshire Co., 250
Wareham, 89, 105
Warren, Rhode Island, 104
Warwick (Roxbury Canada), 279
Washington, Berkshire Co., 282-284
Watertown, Middlesex Co., 2, 28, 29, 30, 95, 169, 224, 237
Watertown, New York, 225
Weatherfield, Vermont, 226
Wellfleet, 108
Wells, Maine, 44
West End, Boston, 142
West Indies, 67, 139, 208, 253, 285
West Point, 217
Westborough, Worcester Co., 97, 101, 202, 259, 262, 264
Western, 89,
Western, Connecticut, 98
Westfield, 226, 246
Westford, 96, 169
Westminster (formerly Wachuset), 95
Weston, 90, 91, 102, 104, 106, 107, 109-110, 178, 179-180, 183, 186, 192, 193, 196, 218, 219, 221, 224, 225, 226, 227, 228, 255, 259, 263
Weymouth, 214
Whately, 246
Wilbraham, Hampshire Co., 202
Williamstown, Berkshire Co., 227
Willmington, Connecticut, 96
Wilmington, Middlesex Co., 118, 237
Winchelsea, England, 159
Winchendon (Ipswich Canada), Worcester Co., 222
Windham County, Connecticut, 227
Windham County, Vermont, 227, 229
Windsor County, Vermont, 225, 226, 281
Wisconsin, 97
Woburn, 33, 88, 95, 102, 107, 119, 156, 252, 254

Place Index

Worcester, 89, 107, 125, 129, 190, 195, 225
Worcester County (1731-), 87, 88, 89, 91, 98, 101, 103, 108, 125, 128-130, 151, 152, 191, 196, 197, 222, 223, 224, 225, 226, 227, 228, 230, 231, 234, 241, 242, 245, 281
Worthington, Hampshire Co., 238
Wrentham, Norfolk Co., 41, 79, 88, 89, 101, 102, 103, 105, 106, 107, 110-111, 116, 118, 177, 178, 179, 182, 184, 186, 192, 221, 222, 223, 224, 227, 234, 254, 255, 258

York County, Maine, 37, 40, 280
Yorkshire, England, 96
Yorktown, 216

Subject Index

The able-bodied/competent/ undeserving poor, 14, 16-18, 20, 55, 57, 125-126, 184, 268, 290. *See also* migration/migrants

African American soldiers, 249

The aging and elderly: problem of family support of, 21, 114; and surety, 58; in John Quincy's classification, 268; old Mr. John Goodwin, a state poor, 280. *See also* private charity and relief, relief/public aid, veterans

Almshouse/poor house/poor farm, 12, 16, 20, 21-23, 31, 63, 117, 238, 258, 262-266, 267, 268, 288

Binding out, 23-24. *See also* orphans

Bridewell/house of correction: English origins, 16, 17-18; in Massachusetts, 20, 24

Captivity, 36-37, 209-211

Charitable institutions/organizations: Scots' Charitable Society (1657), 55; Charitable Irish Society (1737), 55; Boston Episcopal Charitable Society (1724), 55; booming in post-war Boston, the Humane Society of the Commonwealth of Massachusetts (1785), the Massachusetts Charitable Society (1786), the Congregational Charitable Society (1795), the Boston Dispensary (1796), the Massachusetts Charitable Fire Society (1799), the Boston Female Asylum (1800), the Massachusetts General Hospital (1811), the Howard Benevolent Society (1812), the Boston Asylum for Indigent Boys (1814), the Boston Society for the Moral and Religious Instruction of the Poor (1817), the Penitent Females' Refuge (1822), the Society for the Employment of the Female Poor (1827), the Massachusetts Charitable Eye and Ear Infirmary (1827), and the Boston Lying-In Hospital (1832), 269. *See also* Linen Manufactory, Society for Encouraging and Employing the Poor

Charitable institutions/organizations in England: hospitals, 12, 17; schools, 17; charity school movement, 270

Charity, *see* private charity and relief

Children in poverty: boys, 23-24, 273; girls, 23-24, 119, 274-276;

Subject Index

schooling as outdoor relief, 28, 338; education in prison, 206; of veterans, 45; and surety, 58; textile work, 71; migrants with large families, 103, 104-105, 254, 255; large number in need of relief in Boston, 145; naming, 193-194; serving in the Revolutionary war, 206; of veterans, 221, 222, 223, 224, 226, 227, 231, 233, 234; future generations, 235. *See also* binding out

Churches' charity and other activity (in Boston): Baptist, 51; Brattle Street Church, 54; Congregational, 51, 270; Episcopalian, 51, 270; First Church (Old North), 11, 52, 53, 56; "Old Brick," 56; Old South, 54-55, 56-57; King's Chapel, 51-52, 53-54, 56; Second Baptist, 276; Society of Friends, 51; Trinity Church, 56, 274, 275-276; membership required, 55. *See also* religion/Christianity and poverty

Class, class conflict, class consciousness, class struggle, class war, "second revolution," xv, xx-xxii, xxii-xxiv, 1, 134, 205, 292

Classes/social-economic strata: ambiguity/confusion about them, xix, xx-xxii, xxii-xxiv, 1-2, 8-9. *See also* the poor, the lower class, the middle class, and the rich/upper class

Cost of living: basic/minimum, xxv, 4-7; benchmark, 4-5; significance, 7-8

Cost of relief: in England, 15; Watertown, 29-30; Boston, 59, 60-61; measures to cut cost, 62-64; during the Revolution, 237-239; post-war era, 260-266; Salem, 266; for the commonwealth to maintain state paupers, 278; for local communities to support state poor, 285

Community: its essential role in local relief, 14, 20; its English origins, 14, 16

Community membership/legal residency/settlement: key to public relief, xxiv-xxv, 47, 58, 112, 113; admission to almshouse, 21; required to receive outdoor relief, 28; more important than gender, racial, or ethnic distinctions of modern time, 30-31; required 3 months of stay without warning to gain (1659, 1692), 113, 349; required 12 months of stay without warning to gain (1701, 1722), 113, 360, 365; residency and franchise in the 1780 state constitution, 256; new settlement regulations, 256-258; public relief continued (until 1974) to require legal residency after the warning-out system officially ended by 1794, 258, 389; twelve conditions to determine one's settlement, 277-278

Diet: and minimum cost of living, 4-5; at almshouse, 22-23; on naval ship, 207; to state poor, 280, 284-285

English administrative control over the poor, 15-16, 19

English poor laws, 15 (1495, 1531, 1598), 18 (1552), 19 (1562), 25 (1723), 121 (1743)

English poor law institutions, 15-18

English poor law reforms, 18-20, 132

English precedents critical to Massachusetts: xvii, xxv, xxv, 14-20

Family: a poor one, xiii-xiv; migrants moving with, 103-105; veterans and their, 218-235. *See also* Biographies

Finance and relief: missing from scholarship, 49-50; local

- 450 -

Subject Index

community, xxvi, 29-30, 59, 60-61, 266; provincial, 32-38, 40-44; church collections, 51-55; short of fund at churches, 55-57; pressures on Boston, 60-64, 143; inadequate investment capital, 68-69, 70-71, 81; overseers using personal resources, 63; lack of competitive product and pricing, 72-73; subscription drives, 68 (1748), 145 (1764), 145 (1768); insistence on warning out, 113; in removal disputes with neighboring communities, 114-123; wartime finance, 143-144; demand payment in hard coin, 144, 238, 243, 244, 245; imperial policies and colonial business and finance, 159-166; inflation and recruitment, 202-203; war debt and misery, 238-247; public vendue, 260-262; for the commonwealth to maintain state paupers, 278; for local communities to support state poor, 285; to curb expenses on state poor, 287-288. *See also* cost of relief, the middle class, taxation

Fires, 54, 137-138

Flax/hemp cultivation and public relief, 64-83

Floating poverty: defined, xiv, xxviii-xxix; not static or single dimensional views, xxv, xxix-xxx, 134-136, 290; status in flux, 290; oscillating between poverty and mobility, 291-292; conclusion, 289-292

Foreigners, 116, 251, 253, 254, 279, 284, 285-287

"French Neutrals," *see* refugees

Historians and their works cited:
Bernard Bailyn, 84
Carl Becker, xxii
Jacqueline Barbara Carr, xxi, 267
Cornelia H. Dayton, 85
Marc Egnal, 160
Joseph A. Ernst, 160
David Hackett Fischer, xvii
Stephen Foster, 28
Paul A. Gilje, 205
Robert A. Gross, 182
Ruth Wallis Herndon, xxi, 85
Douglas L. Jones, 85, 90
Jesse Lemisch, 205
James T. Lemon, 99
Carter Lindberg, 11
Pauline Maier, 147-148
Gary B. Nash, xix, 186
J. Richard Olivas, xx
Seth Rockman, xxi
Sharon V. Salinger, 85
Billy G. Smith, xx
Jonathan Smith, 241, 242
Alan Taylor, 248
Daniel Vickers, 205
Stephen E. Wiberley, Jr., 146
Alfred F. Young, xx
Howard Zinn, xxii

House of Industry, 267-268

Idleness/idlers, xv, 13-14, 15, 16-17, 24, 25, 55, 155, 290

Improvement schemes: mulberry trees, 156-157; new method in husbandry, 157-158; commerce, 158-159. *See also* Linen Manufactory, textiles

The incompetent/deserving poor, xxv; its English origins, 14, 16-17; in Massachusetts, 20-21, 28-31, 57; in post-war Boson, 268

Indoor relief, xxv, 20-21

Justice of the peace: in England, 16, 19; in Massachusetts, 31, 115, 116, 117-118, 121-122

Laborer, 7, 215, 216, 230, 251, 252, 286, 287, 290

Land grants, 44-47

Linen Manufactory: experiment by Society for Encouraging and Employing the Poor, xix, xxvi, 64-79, 80-83; to revive the scheme in

Subject Index

1767 and later, 144-147, 149; in national pride/patriotism, 170-172

The lower class: defined, 11; connected but not to be confused with the poor, xxii, 8-9, 85, 135; and the middle class, 85; in migration, 101-103; in resettlement, 124, 127-130; from 1763 to 1775, 135; as soldiers in the Revolutionary war, 174-176, 179-181; the lower the soldier's family circumstances, the more chances he would serve for three years, 198-199; willingness to join forces with the middle class in the Revolution, 292

Massachusetts: influenced by the Old World, xxv, 11-20; departure from English practices, xxv-xxvi, 28, 47-48

Massachusetts laws regulating the poor:
Court order of 1655, 112, 348
Settlement law (1659), 113, 349
Act for Regulating of Townships (1692), 28, 32, 113, 353-354
Additional Act to Admission of Town Inhabitants (1722), 113, 365
Workhouse regulations (1735), 25, 368
Additional Act to the Removal of Poor Persons (1767), 113, 380
Regulation of Licensed Houses (1786), 270-271
Act for the Relief of Poor Prisoners (1787), 246
Act Providing for the Support of the Poor (1789), 255
Settlement of a Citizen (1789), 256-258, 388
Settlement Act (1793), 277-278
Act Providing for the Relief and Support, Employment and Removal of the Poor (1794), 258, 389
Certificates required for proving the status of state paupers (1796, 1799), 287-288

Massachusetts poor law institutions, 20-27. *See also* almshouse, Bridewell

Massachusetts provincial government: as relief agency, xxv, 31-32; processing individual petitions, 33-38, 48; administrative remedies, 38-44; land grant, 44-47; dealing with state paupers, 277-288

Massachusetts provincial/state poor, 32, 277-288

Massachusetts terrain and soil, 151

Medical care: need of, 22; cutting cost of, 62-63; during smallpox outbreak, 141; reimbursement for nursing wounded soldiers and doctor bills, 36

The middle class: defined, 11; mentioned, xv, 8, 10; swayed to pay the poor rate in England, 18-19; widows, 23; in almshouse, 22; as donors, 54-55; in migration and resettlement, 105-107, 130-131; interest in receiving strangers, 108-111, 257-258; from 1763 to 1775, 135; Whigs and Whig activity, 146, 147-149, 161-162, 166; hope to expand domestic industries and exert self-control, 154-172; imperial policies hurting more directly local businesses and the middle class than the poor, 159-166; observers, newspapers commentators, and public discourse, 159-161; comparing wealth with the rich/upper class, 188; as soldiers in the Revolutionary war, 174-176, 179-181; the wealthier the soldier's family background, the less likely he would serve for three years, 198-199; needed help from those below them, 292

Migration/migrants: the Great Migration, 19; attracted to Boston, 57, 88, 267; diverse backgrounds of migrants, 99-108, 123, 124; involving more lower to lower-

Subject Index

middle classes than the abject poor, 85, 100, 101; more domestic than foreign, 86-92; more small towns than large urban centers, 88-90; spikes in the 1750s, 1760s, and 1770s, 90-92, 122, 123, 290; travel in short distances, 88, 89, 90; gradual spread across county and provincial lines, 95-99; poor transients, 99-101, 124-126; the lower classes, 101-103, 127-130; not complete strangers, 102-103; families on the move, 103-105; professionals and middle class in migration, 105-107, 130-131; military personnel, 108; middle-class families, local officials, and professionals receiving migrants, 108-111, 122, 132-133; resettlement, 123-131; post-war era, 247-258. *See also* refugees, warning out

Military life: the army as a new social structure, 184-186; promotion opportunities in service, 211-213; desertion, 213-216; service toward the end of the War, 216-218

Militia, 177-181, 201

Mobility, xv, 10, 292. *See also* migration/migrants, poverty and mobility

Orphan/orphanage: at almshouse, 23-24; bound-out orphans became soldiers, 194-196, 222, 225, 227, 233, 248-249, 330, 338; female asylum, 274-276. *See also* almshouse, binding out, women

Outdoor relief: xxv, 28-31, 185

Overseers of the poor: in England, 16, managing the almshouse, 21; managing the workhouse, 25; not yet separated from the office of selectmen for small communities, 27-28, 258; using personal fund/credit, 63; support the plan to produce duck or sail cloth, 146; on Committee of Donations, 148-149; of Salem, 237; of Boston, 238; established the office after the war, 259; declining role in post-war Boston, 268

Paradigms/interpretative frameworks of poverty: polarized views, xv-xvi; dichotomous models of, such as the rich vs. the poor, xiv, xx-xxi, 134, 136; the haves vs. the have-nots, xiv, xv, 80, 136; "yes" or "no" answers to a "second revolution," 134-135; not quite applicable to Massachusetts, if research based primarily on racial distinctions, xvii-xviii; focused on ethnicity, xviii; focused on gender, xviii, xix-xx; 1-2, 75-79; neglect of the key role community membership played, 30-31, 47; neglect of a financial aspect, 49-63; underestimation of the Boston experiment in the 1750s, 64-83; underestimate wide volatilities from 1763 to 1775, 134-136; not take into account the wealth of the loyalists, 186-193; need to reconsider the multi-dimensional and ever shifting characteristics of poverty, 136, 289-292. *See also* community membership, floating poverty, poverty and mobility, migration/migrants, the poor, the lower class, the middle class

Petition and relief, *see* Massachusetts provincial government

The poor: configuration, 3-10; heterogeneity, xiv, 289; categorization after the Protestant Reformation, 12-13; fighting spirit, tenacity, and desires for mobility, xxviii, xxix, 235, 292; contributions to the Revolution, xxvi-xxvi, 173, 174-186, 234-235; alliance with the lower and middle classes, 135-136, 137, 184, 291-292; possessions of poor veterans, 196, 228, 229, 230-234; classified by John Quincy, 268

Subject Index

The poor who participated in the Revolutionary War, 174-186, 193-204; excepting the impotent and wretched poor, 185. *See also* soldiers/sailors in the American Revolutionary War, veterans

Population: population decline in Boston, 61; population growth, 93 (1730s, 1740s), 151 (1751-1776); and expansion of townships, impact on domestic migration, 93-99; especially in rural western Massachusetts, 150-152

Poverty: causes, xiv-xv, 30, 289; degrees of, 11-14; manifestations, xiii-xiv, xxiv, 1, 10; from poor individuals to collective poverty of Americans, 155; American poverty under British oppression, 159-166

Poverty and mobility, xvi, 123-133, 211-213, 289-290, 291

Private charity and relief: Boston churches and charitable organizations, 51-57, 80, 269; required membership for aid, 55; personal donations, 54-55, 138; important to deserving poor, 290. *See also* charitable institutions/organizations, churches' charity and other activity

The Protestant Reformation and its impacts on notions of poverty and relief and on classification of the poor, xvi, 11-14

Provincial relief/aid, *see* Massachusetts provincial government

Public vendue, 260-262

Punishment of the poor: in England, 17. *See also* idleness/idlers, Bridewell

Refugees: from the frontiers, 59-60; "French Neutrals," 60

Relief/public aid to the poor: Watertown, 2-3; concept and practice from England, 14-20

Relief/public aid to the lower and middle classes, 30, 32, 75-79

Religion/Christianity and poverty: "the poor shall be with you," xxiii; the sinful and the noble poor, 11; holiness of poverty, 12; changing attitudes toward the poor, 12-13; indiscriminate almsgiving, 19; Bible reading, 26; individual ministers, 11, 13-14, 18-19, 170, 267, 270, 274, 275-276; charity school movement, 270; moral and spiritual instruction to the poor, 271-272; self-appointed moralist, 276-277

Removal disputes at court:
Middleboro v. Plympton (1766), 120
Roxbury v. Boston (1766), 119-120
Wilmington v. Reading (1766), 118
Wrentham v. Attleborough (1767), 118
Brookline v. Roxbury (1768), 120-121
Natick v. Medway (1768), 119
Natick v. Newton (1768), 119
Woburn v. Lexington (1768), 119
Chelsea v. Boston (1769), 117-118

The rich/upper class: defined, 11; mentioned, xxi, xxiv; mostly loyalists, their names and wealth, 186-193; compared with the possessions of the middle-class Whigs, 188; tended not to serve in the Revolutionary war, 184-185

Selectmen, 21, 115, 117, 118, 120, 121, 122, 139, 140, 142, 220, 231, 238, 241, 242, 280, 281, 282-284. *See also* overseers of the poor

Subject Index

Self-reliance and home industry (1763-1775), 143-150, 154-159, 167-172

Shays's Rebellion, xxviii, 220, 221, 222, 223, 224, 227, 236, 245, 246

Smallpox, 138-142

Soldiers during the colonial period: wounded soldiers and their petitions, 33-36; payment issues, 37-38

Soldiers/sailors in the American Revolutionary War: estimated numbers of those who were poor, 174, 180-181; the poorer the soldiers, the longer the service terms, 174-177; the longer the war, the more need for recruiting the poor, 181-184, 201; warned in the past but became soldiers—some enlisted for the same communities that had warned them, 177, 182-184; bound-out orphans became soldiers, 194-196; poor households tended to have multiple family members in service, 196-197; soldiers serviced for long terms, 197-198; the meager the soldier's family background, the more chances he would serve for the term of three years or more, 198-199; many poor became substitute/hired soldiers, 199-201; recruited but unfit to serve, 200-201; non-taxpayers, non-residents, and strangers as soldiers,176, 178,181, 201, 204; bounties and enticements in recruitment, 202-204; granting legal settlement to attract recruits, 203-204; sailors, 204-211; promotion opportunities in service, 211-213; desertion, 213-216; service toward the end of the war, 216-218

Stamp act crisis, xxvi, 137, 144, 162

Strangers: needed by locals, 59, 108-111, 122, 257-258. *See also* migration/migrants, surety, warning out

Surety, 58, 113

Taxation and public relief: the establishment of the English poor rate, 18-19; provincial tax increases, 61, 143-144; tax collection, 61-62; after the war, 242-243

Temperance, 270-271

Textiles: production and public relief, 64-83; self-help and patriotism, 167-172. *See also* Linen Manufactory

Town/township: granted to veterans, 46; Canada Townships, 152-153; Narragansett Townships, 152-154; limited size of, population growth, and migration, 46, 92-99; expansion into west rural Massachusetts from 1760 to 1775, 150-152. *See also* community, community membership

Veterans: of the colonial period, 33-38, 46; and expansion of frontier townships, 45-46, 152-154; of the Revolutionary War, 218-235; from comfortable family backgrounds, 218-220; legal residents returning to where they enlisted, 220-221; warned in the past but returned after the war, 221-222; without a legal settlement before the war, moved again after it, 222-224; those moved across state lines, 225-228; applicants for federal pensions, 228-235; possessions of poor veterans, 196, 228, 229, 230-234

Voluntary contributions for charity and relief: European tradition, 18; ending "indiscriminate almsgiving" in England, 19

Wages, 7, 72, 155

Subject Index

Warning out: the system of, xv, 58-59, searchers, 59, 87, 100, 101, 108, 176; removal, 112-123; resettlement, 123-131; impact on cost of public relief, 85, 113, 122-123, 131-132; impact on restraining movement, 85, 123, 132-133; low regard of, 111; warned in the past, some began to receive strangers themselves, 111, 221, 222; warned in the past but became soldiers in the Revolution, 177, 182-184; granting legal settlement to attract recruits, 203-204; in post-war era, 250-252; order residents not to keep poor and dissolute strangers, ship masters not to bring them as passengers, 255-256. *See also* community membership, migration/migrants

Wars and campaigns during the colonial period mentioned: King Philip's War, 41 Narragansett War, 46 campaigns against Louisbourg, Cape Breton, and Canada (1744-1748), 143 King George's War (1744-48), 59, 66, 80

expeditions against Kennebeck and Crown Point (1754-1757), 144 Seven Years' War/French and Indian War, xxvi, 59, 134, 137, 144

Widows, 2, 52, 77, 100, 102, 103, 114, 131, 223, 226, 227-228, 230, 234, 251, 281

Women: individual cases, 24, 27; feminization of poverty, 23; female inmates at workhouse, 26-27; single women, 2, 23, 54, 103, 109, 116, 118, 119, 251, 252, 283; textile work, 71-73, 77; large number in need of relief in Boston, 145; home industry and patriotism, 170-172. *See also* children, binding out, orphan/orphanage

work: at the workhouse, 17-18, 26; calling, 14; at private household, 30; decline in Boston, 66; piece work, 75-79. *See also* Linen Manufactory, self-reliance and home industry, textiles

Workhouse/house of correction, 17, 24-27, 31, 63-64, 262, 263, 265, 266, 268. *See also* Bridewell

About the Author

Nian-Sheng Huang is professor of history at California State University Channel Islands. A former student of Professor Michael Kammen at Cornell University, Huang received his Ph.D. degree in history in 1990. He is the author of *Benjamin Franklin in American Thought and Culture* (1994) and *Franklin's Father Josiah* (2000), both published by the American Philosophical Society. He wrote, designed, and illustrated *Floating Poverty*, and published it in 2012.

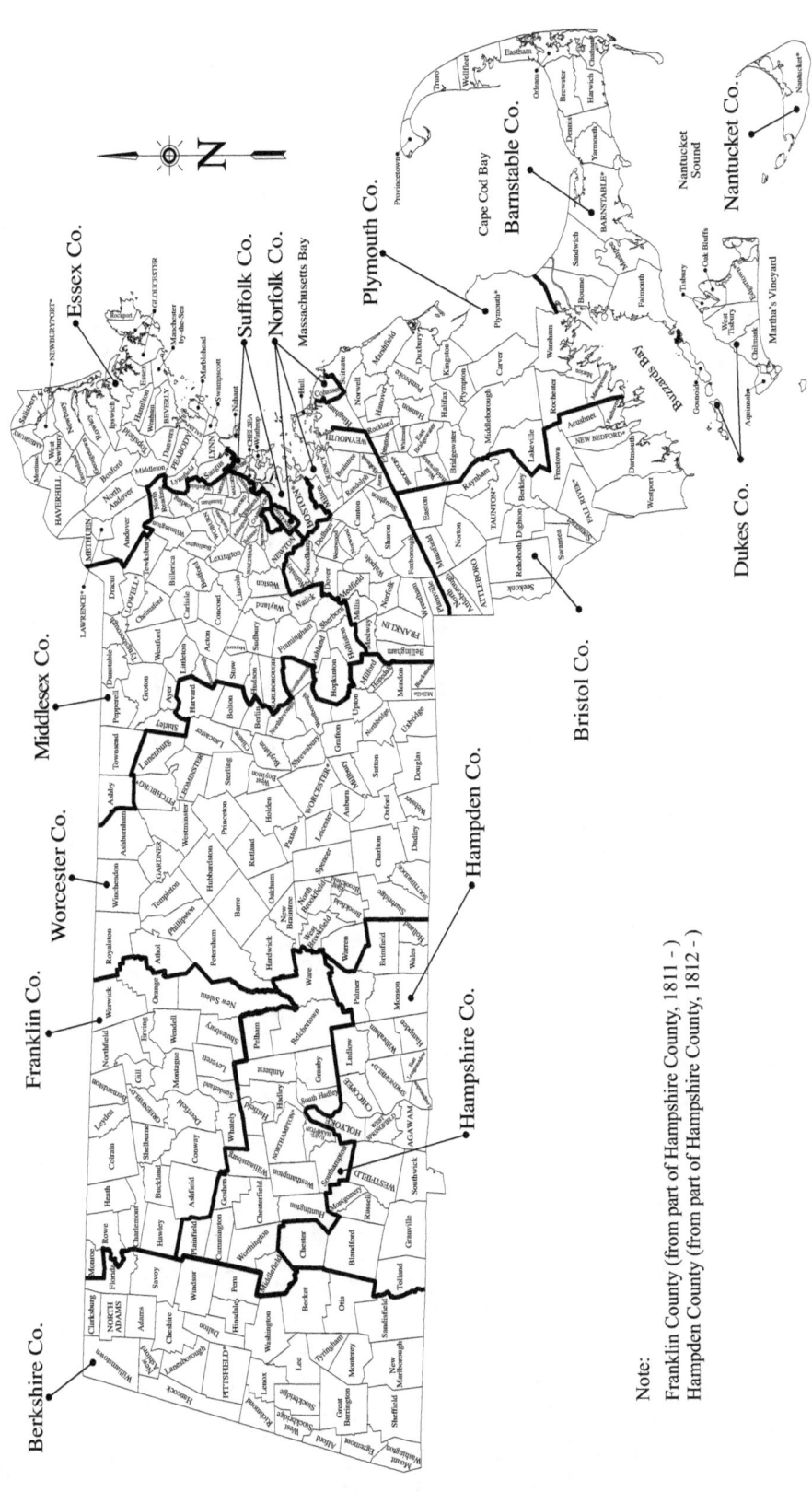

Note:
Franklin County (from part of Hampshire County, 1811 -)
Hampden County (from part of Hampshire County, 1812 -)

www.ingramcontent.com/pod-product-compliance
Lightning Source LLC
Chambersburg PA
CBHW071432300426
44114CB00013B/1404